前世を記憶する子どもたち

イアン・スティーヴンソン
笠原敏雄＝訳

角川文庫
22797

角川文庫海外作品

オー・ヘンリー傑作集1
賢者の贈り物
オー・ヘンリー
越前敏弥＝訳

アメリカ文学史上屈指の短編の名手、オー・ヘンリー。300編近い作品のなかから、もっとも有名な「賢者の贈り物」をはじめ、「警官と賛美歌」「金のかかる恋人」「春の献立表」など名作全16編を収録。

オー・ヘンリー傑作集2
最後のひと葉
オー・ヘンリー
越前敏弥＝訳

アメリカ文学史上屈指の短編の名手、オー・ヘンリー。第2集は、表題作「最後のひと葉」をはじめ、「二十年後」「救われた改心」「水車のある教会」「運命の道」など、珠玉の名作12編を収録。

シャーロック・ホームズ
絹の家
アンソニー・ホロヴィッツ
駒月雅子＝訳

ホームズが捜査を手伝わせたベイカー街別働隊の少年が惨殺された。手がかりは、手首に巻き付けられた絹のリボンと「絹の家」という言葉。ワトソンが残した新たなホームズの活躍と、戦慄の事件の真相とは？

モリアーティ
アンソニー・ホロヴィッツ
駒月雅子＝訳

ホームズとモリアーティが滝壺に姿を消した。現場を訪れたアメリカの探偵とスコットランド・ヤードの刑事は、モリアーティに接触しようとしていたアメリカ裏社会の首領を共に追うことに——。衝撃的ミステリ！

007 逆襲のトリガー
アンソニー・ホロヴィッツ
駒月雅子＝訳

ゴールドフィンガー事件の後、ボンドは任務先でロケット開発に対するソ連の妨害行為を察知。スメルシュと接触する韓国人実業家のシンに目をつけ、米国の記者と名乗る美女・ジェパディと共に調査を開始する。

角川文庫海外作品

運のいい人の法則

リチャード・ワイズマン博士
矢羽野　薫＝訳

英国の心理学者リチャード・ワイズマン博士は、幸運と不運を隔てるものに興味を抱き、調査を開始。十年の歳月と数百人への調査から辿り着いた、「運のいい人」に共通する四つの法則とは――!?

恐るべき子供たち

ジャン・コクトー
東郷青児＝訳

第一次大戦後のパリ。社会から隔絶された「部屋」で暮らす、4人の少年少女。同性愛、近親愛、男女の愛……さまざまな感情が交錯し、やがて悲劇的な結末を迎えるまでの日々を描いた小説詩。

クリスマス・キャロル

ディケンズ
越前敏弥＝訳

文豪ディケンズの名声を不動のものにしたクリスマス・ストーリーの決定版！　冷酷非道な老人が、クリスマス前夜に現れた3人の精霊によって自らの人生を反省し、人間らしい心をとりもどしていく。

アルプスの少女ハイジ

ヨハンナ・シュピリ
松永美穂＝訳

雄大なアルプスの自然を背景に、純真で心やさしい少女ハイジが、人々に奇跡と幸せをもたらしていく物語。『朗読者』の翻訳で毎日出版文化賞を受賞したドイツ文学者・松永美穂氏による、渾身の完訳。

1984

ジョージ・オーウェル
田内志文＝訳

ビッグ・ブラザーが監視する近未来世界。過去の捏造に従事するウィンストンは若いジュリアとの出会いをきっかけに密かに日記を密かに書き始めるが……人間の自由と尊厳を問うディストピア小説の名作。

角川文庫発刊に際して

角川源義

第二次世界大戦の敗北は、軍事力の敗北であった以上に、私たちの若い文化力の敗退であった。私たちの文化が戦争に対して如何に無力であり、単なるあだ花に過ぎなかったかを、私たちは身を以て体験し痛感した。西洋近代文化の摂取にとって、明治以後八十年の歳月は決して短かすぎたとは言えない。にもかかわらず、近代文化の伝統を確立し、自由な批判と柔軟な良識に富む文化層として自らを形成することに私たちは失敗して来た。そしてこれは、各層への文化の普及滲透を任務とする出版人の責任でもあった。

一九四五年以来、私たちは再び振出しに戻り、第一歩から踏み出すことを余儀なくされた。これは大きな不幸ではあるが、反面、これまでの混沌・未熟・歪曲の中にあった我が国の文化に秩序と確たる基礎を齎らすためには絶好の機会でもある。角川書店は、このような祖国の文化的危機にあたり、微力をも顧みず再建の礎石たるべき抱負と決意とをもって出発したが、ここに創立以来の念願を果すべく角川文庫を発刊する。これまで刊行されたあらゆる全集叢書文庫類の長所と短所とを検討し、古今東西の不朽の典籍を、良心的編集のもとに、廉価に、そして書架にふさわしい美本として、多くのひとびとに提供しようとする。しかし私たちは徒らに百科全書的な知識のジレッタントを作ることを目的とせず、あくまで祖国の文化に秩序と再建への道を示し、この文庫を角川書店の栄ある事業として、今後永久に継続発展せしめ、学芸と教養との殿堂として大成せんことを期したい。多くの読書子の愛情ある忠言と支持とによって、この希望と抱負とを完遂せしめられんことを願う。

一九四九年五月三日

前世《ぜんせ》を記憶《きおく》する子《こ》どもたち

イアン・スティーヴンソン　笠原敏雄《かさはらとしお》＝訳

令和３年　８月25日　初版発行
令和６年　11月25日　６版発行

発行者●山下直久

発行●株式会社KADOKAWA
〒102-8177　東京都千代田区富士見2-13-3
電話　0570-002-301（ナビダイヤル）

角川文庫 22797

印刷所●株式会社KADOKAWA
製本所●株式会社KADOKAWA

表紙画●和田三造

●お問い合わせ
https://www.kadokawa.co.jp/（「お問い合わせ」へお進みください）
※内容によっては、お答えできない場合があります。
※サポートは日本国内のみとさせていただきます。
※Japanese text only

ISBN 978-4-04-111417-9　C0198

◆◇◇

本書は、一九九〇年二月に日本教文社より刊行された
単行本を加筆・修正のうえ文庫化したものです。

索引

項目中の（　）は，その語の説明の他に，中の語が含まれる場合と含まれない場合があることを，〔　〕は，前の語と置き換わる場合があることを，「→」は参照項目をそれぞれ示している。

事項

【サ行】

【ナ行】

人　名

当事者名の索引は訳者のウェブサイト「心の研究室」に掲載しています。あわせてご参照ください。
http://www.02.246.ne.jp/~kasahara/

参考文献

1. Aldrich, C. K. 1963. The dying patient's grief. *Journal of the American Medical Association* 184: 329–31.
2. Altus, W. D. 1966. Birth order and its sequelae. *Science* 151: 44–49.
3. Anonymous. 1973. My daughter changed sex. *Good Housekeeping*, May, p. 87.
4. Ayer, A. J. 1963. *The concept of a person and other essays*. London: Macmillan.
5. Bacon, F. 1639. *Sylva Sylvarum or, A naturall historie*. 5th ed. London: William Rawley.
6. ———. 1915. *The advancement of learning*. London: J. M. Dent and Sons. (First published in 1605.)
7. Bagehot, W. 1873. *Physics and politics*. New York: D. Appleton.
8. Baker, H. J., and Stoller, R. J. 1968. Can a biological force contribute to gender identity? *American Journal of Psychiatry* 124: 1653–58.
9. Baker, L. R. 1981. Why computers can't act. *American Philosophical Quarterly* 18: 157–63.
10. Baker, R. A. 1982. The effect of suggestion on past-lives regression. *American Journal of Clinical Hypnosis* 25: 71–76.
11. Balfour, G. W. 1935. A study of the psychological aspects of Mrs. Willett's mediumship. *Proceedings of the Society for Psychical Research* 43: 43–318.
12. Barber, T. X. 1961. Experimental evidence for a theory of hypnotic behavior: II. Experimental controls in hypnotic age-regression. *International Journal of Clinical and Experimental Hypnosis* 9: 181–93.
13. Barker, D. R., and Pasricha, S. 1979. Reincarnation cases in Fatehabad: A systematic survey in North India. *Journal of Asian and African Studies* 14: 231–40.
14. Barrett, W. F. 1926. *Death-bed visions*. London: Methuen.
15. Baudelaire, C. 1967. *Oeuvres complètes*. Lausanne: La Guide du

Livre.
16. Bell, C. 1931. *The religion of Tibet*. London: Oxford University Press.
17. Beloff, J. 1980a. Could there be a physical explanation for psi? *Journal of the Society for Psychical Research* 50: 263–72.
18. ———. 1980b. Is normal memory a "paranormal" phenomenon? *Theoria to Theory* 14: 145–62.
19. Berger, H. 1940. *Psyche*. Jena: Verlag von Gustav Fischer.（ベルガーの体験談の翻訳は次の論文から引用した。Gloor, P. 1969. Hans Berger on the electroencephalogram of man. *Electroencephalography and Clinical Neurophysiology*, supplement no. 28.）
20. Bergson, H. 1913. Presidential address. *Proceedings of the Society for Psychical Research* 26: 462–79.
21. ———. 1957. *L'évolution créatrice*. Paris: Presses Universitaires de France.（First published in 1907. American edition: *Creative Evolution*. Translated by Arthur Mitchel. New York: Random House, 1944.）
22. ———. 1959. *Matière et mémoire: Essai sur la relation du corps à l'esprit*. Paris: Presses Universitaires de France.（First published in 1896.）
23. Bernheim, H. 1947. *Suggestive therapeutics: A treatise on the nature and uses of hypnotism*. Translated from 2nd and revised French edition by Christian A. Herter. New York: London Book.（First published in 1889.）
24. Bernstein, M. 1965. *The search for Bridey Murphy*. New York: Lancer Books.（First published by Doubleday, 1956.）
25. Besterman, T. 1933. An experiment in "clairvoyance" with M. Stefan Ossowiecki. *Proceedings of the Society for Psychical Research* 41: 345–51.
26. ———. 1968. *Collected papers on the paranormal*. New York: Garrett Publications.
27. Birket-Smith, K. 1959. *The Eskimos*. Rev. ed. Translated by W. E. Calvert. London: Methuen.（First published in 1936.）
28. Björkhem, J. 1961. Hypnosis and personality change. In *Knut*

Lundmark and man's march into space: A memorial volume, edited by M. Johnson. Gothenburg: Värld och Vetande.

29. Bloxham, A. D. 1958. *Who was Ann Ockenden*? London: Neville Spearman.
30. Borzymowski, A. 1965. Experiments with Ossowiecki. *International Journal of Parapsychology* 7: 259–84.
31. Boswell, J. 1931. *The life of Samuel Johnson.* New York: Modern Library. (First published in 1791.)
32. ———. 1970. An account of my last interview with David Hume, Esq. In *Boswell in extremes: 1776–1778*, edited by C. M. Weis and F. A. Pottle. New York: McGraw-Hill.
33. Bozzano, E. 1906. Des apparitions des défunts au lit de mort. *Annales des Sciences Psychiques* 16: 144–82.
34. Broad, C. D. 1958. *Personal identity and survival.* London: Society for Psychical Research.
35. ———. 1962. *Lectures on psychical research.* London: Routledge & Kegan Paul.
36. Brougham, H. 1871. *The life and times of Henry, Lord Braugham, written by himself.* New York: Harper and Bros.
37. Brown, R., and Kulik, J. 1977. Flashbulb memories. *Cognition* 5: 73–99.
38. Brown, W. N. 1928. *The Indian and Christian miracles of walking on the water.* Chicago: Open Court Publishing.
39. Butler, S. 1961. *Life and habit.* London: A. C. Fifield. (First published in 1877.)
40. Caesar, Julius. 1917. *The Gallic war.* Translated by H. J. Edwards. London: William Heinemann.
41. Calderwood, D. 1844. *The history of the kirk of Scotland.* Edited by T. Thomson. Edinburgh: The Wodrow Society.
42. Carington, W. 1945. *Telepathy: An outline of its facts, theory, and implications.* London: Methuen.
43. Cass, L. K., and Thomas, C. B. 1979. *Childhood pathology and later adjustment: The question of prediction.* New York: John Wiley.

44. Cassou, B., Schiff, M., and Stewart, J. 1980. Génétique et schizophrénie: Réévaluation d'un consensus. *Psychiatrie de l'enfant* 23: 87–201.
45. Chadwick, J. 1967. *The decipherment of linear B.* Cambridge: Cambridge University Press.
46. Cicero. 1923. *De senectute.* Translated by W. A. Falconer. London: William Heinemann.
47. Clarke, A. D. B. 1968. Learning and human development. *British Journal of Psychiatry* 114: 1061–77.
48. Clarke, A. D. B., and Clarke, A. M. 1954. Cognitive changes in the feeble-minded. *British Journal of Psychology* 45: 173–79.
49. Clarke, A. M., and Clarke, A. D. B. 1976. *Early experience: Myth and evidence.* Shepton Mallet: Open Books Publishing.
50. Colegrove, F. W. 1899. Individual memories. *American Journal of Psychology* 10: 228–55.
51. Cook, E.W., Pasricha, S., Samararatne, G., Maung, W., and Stevenson, I. 1983a. A review and analysis of "unsolved" cases of the reincarnation type: Part I, Introduction and illustrative case reports. *Journal of the American Society for Psychical Research* 77: 45–62.
52. ———. 1983b. A review and analysis of "unsolved" cases of the reincarnation type: Part II, Comparison of features of solved and unsolved cases. *Journal of the American Society for Psychical Research* 77: 115–35.
53. Crewe, N. 1893. *Memoirs of Nathaniel, Lord Crewe.* London: Camden Society.
54. Daniélou, J. 1955. *Origen.* Translated by W. Mitchell. New York: Sheed and Ward.
55. Daniels, W. B. 1962. The Siamese twins: Some observations on their life, last illness, and autopsy. *Transactions of the American Clinical and Climatological Association* 73: 57–65.
56. Davidson, H. R. E. 1964. *Gods and myths of Northern Europe.* Harmondsworth, Middlesex: Penguin.
57. Davis, D. R. 1958. Clinical problems and experimental researches.

British Journal of Medical Psychology 31: 74–82.
58. De Laguna, F. 1972. *Under Mount St. Elias.* Smithsonian Contributions to Anthropology (monograph) 7: 779.
59. Delanne, G. 1924. *Documents pour servir à l'étude de la réincarnation.* Paris: Editions de la B. P. S.
60. Descartes, R. 1912. *Meditations on the first philosophy.* Translated by J. Veitch. London: J. M. Dent and Sons. (First published in 1641.)
61. ———. 1973. *Les principes de la philosophie.* In *Oeuvres philosophiques,* vol. 3. Paris: Editions Garnier Frères. (First published in 1644.)
62. Deschamps, H. 1970. *Les religions de l'Afrique noire.* Paris: Presses Universitaires de France.
63. Deutsch, O. E. 1955. *Handel: A documentary biography.* London: Adam and Charles Black.
64. Dickens, C. 1877. *Pictures from Italy.* New York: Harper and Bros.
65. Dickinson, G. L. 1911. A case of emergence of a latent memory under hypnosis. *Proceedings of the Society for Psychical Research* 25: 455–67.
66. Dostoevsky, F. 1914. *The idiot.* Translated by E. M. Martin. London: J. M. Dent and Sons.
67. Drane, A. T. 1880. *The history of St. Catherine of Siena and her companions.* London: Burns and Oates.
68. Dreyfus, H. L. 1979. *What computers can't do.* Rev. ed. New York: Harper and Row.
69. Driesch, H. 1908. *The science and philosophy of the organism.* London: A. and C. Black.
70. ———. 1914. *History and theory of vitalism.* London: Macmillan.
71. ———. 1930. Personne et suprapersonne. In *Transactions of the Fourth International Congress for Psychical Research,* edited by T. Besterman. London: The Society for Psychical Research.
72. ———. 1933. *Psychical research: The science of the super-normal.* Translated by T. Besterman. London: Bell and Sons. (First published in 1932 as *Parapsychologie: Die Wissenschaft von den*

"Okkulten" Erscheinungen. Munich: F. Bruckmann.)
73. Ducasse, C. J. 1951. *Nature, mind, and death.* LaSalle, Ill.: Open Court Publishing.
74. ———. 1960. How the case of *The search for Bridey Murphy* stands today. *Journal of the American Society for Psychical Research* 54: 3-22.
75. ———. 1961. *A critical examination of the belief in a life after death.* Springfield, Ill.: Charles C Thomas.
76. Dunnington, G. W. 1955. *Carl Friedrich Gauss: Titan of science.* New York: Exposition Press.
77. Dywan, J., and Bowers, K. 1983. The use of hypnosis to enhance recall. *Science* 222: 184-85.
78. Eddington, A. S. 1930. *Science and the unseen world.* New York: Macmillan.
79. Edelstein, S. J. 1986. *The sickled cell.* Cambridge, Mass.: Harvard University Press.
80. Efrón, D. 1944. Telepathic skin-writing (the Kahl case). *Journal of Parapsychology* 8: 272-86.
81. Efron, R. 1963. Temporal perception, aphasia, and déjà vu. *Brain* 86: 403-24.
82. Ellis, H. R. 1943. *The Road to Hel.* Cambridge: Cambridge University Press.
83. Ericsson, R. J., Langevin, C. N., and Nishino, M. 1973. Isolation of fractions rich in human Y sperm. *Nature* 246: 421-24.
84. Evans-Wentz, W. Y. 1911. *The fairy-faith in Celtic countries.* New York: Oxford University Press.
85. ———, ed. 1969. *The Tibetan book of the dead.* London: Oxford University Press. (First published in 1927.)
86. Farber, S. L. 1981. *Identical twins reared apart: A reanalysis.* New York: Basic Books.
87. Fielding Hall, H. 1898. *The soul of a people.* London: Macmillan.
88. Flower, N. 1923. *George Frideric Handel: His personality and his times.* London: Cassell.
89. Forman, M. B., ed. 1931. *The letters of John Keats.* Vol. 2. Oxford:

Oxford University Press.

90. Fraser, F. C. 1970. The genetics of cleft lip and cleft palate. *American Journal of Human Genetics* 22: 336–52.

91. Freud, S. 1938. Three contributions to the theory of sex. In *The basic writings of Sigmund Freud,* edited and translated by A. A. Brill. New York: Random House.

92. ———. 1950. Analysis of a phobia in a five-year-old boy. In *Collected papers,* vol. 3. London: Hogarth Press. (First published in 1909.)

93. Gallup Opinion Index. 1969. *Special report on religion.* Princeton, N.J.: American Institute of Public Opinion.

94. Gallup, G., Jr., with Proctor, W. 1982. *Adventures in immortality.* New York: McGraw-Hill.

95. Gardner, E. G. 1907. *Saint Catherine of Siena—A study in the religion, literature, and history of the fourteenth century in Italy.* London: J. M. Dent and Sons.

96. Gauld, A. 1982. *Mediumship and survival: A century of investigations.* London: William Heinemann.

97. Gauld, A., and Cornell, A. D. 1979. *Poltergeists.* London: Routledge and Kegan Paul.

98. Geddes, A. 1937. A voice from the grandstand. *Edinburgh Medical Journal* 44: 365–84.

99. Geley, G. 1927. *Clairvoyance and materialisation: A record of experiments.* Translated by S. de Brath. New York: George H. Doran. (First published in French as *L'ectoplasmie et la clairvoyance* [Paris: F. Alcan 1924].)

100. Gibbon, E. 1907. *Autobiography.* London: Oxford University Press.

101. Godbey, J. W., Jr. 1975. Central-state materialism and parapsychology. *Analysis* 36: 22–25. (Reprinted in *Philosophy and Parapsychology,* edited by J. Ludwig. Buffalo: Prometheus Books, 1978.)

102. Grant, J. 1937. *Winged pharaoh.* London: Arthur Barker.

103. Grattan-Guinness, I., ed. 1982. *Psychical research: A guide to its history, principles, and practices.* Wellingborough, England: Aquarian

Press.
104. Graves, R. P. 1979. *A. E. Housman: The scholar-poet.* London: Routledge and Kegan Paul.
105. Green, C. 1960. Analysis of spontaneous cases. *Proceedings of the Society for Psychical Research* 53: 97-161.
106. ———. 1968a. *Lucid dreams.* London: Hamish Hamilton.
107. ———. 1968b. *Out-of-the-body experiences.* London: Hamish Hamilton.
108. Green, R. 1974. *Sexual identity conflict in children and adults.* New York: Basic Books.
109. ———. 1979. Childhood cross-gender behavior and subsequent sexual preference. *American Journal of Psychiatry* 136: 106-8.
110. Greyson, B., and Stevenson, I. 1980. The phenomenology of near-death experiences. *American Journal of Psychiatry* 137: 1193-96.
111. Grof, S. 1976. *Realms of the human unconscious: Observation from LSD research.* New York: E. P. Dutton.
112. Gruber, E. R. 1978. Hans Driesch and the concept of spiritism. *Journal of the Society for Psychical Research* 49: 861-74.
113. Guemple, L. 1988. Teaching social relations to Inuit children. In *Hunters and gatherers: Property, power and ideology.* vol. 2, edited by T. Ingold, D. Riches and J. Woodburn. Oxford: Berg Publishers.
114. Guerrero, R. 1974. Association of the type and time of insemination within the menstrual cycle with the human sex ratio at birth. *The New England Journal of Medicine* 291: 1056-59.
115. Gupta, L. D., Sharma, N. R., and Mathur, T. C. 1936. *An inquiry into the case of Shanti Devi.* Delhi: International Aryan League.
116. Gurney, E., (completed by Myers, F. W. H.) 1889. On apparitions occurring soon after death. *Proceedings of the Society for Psychical Research* 5: 403-85.
117. Gurney, E., Myers, F. W. H., and Podmore, F. 1886. *Phantasms of the living.* 2 vols. London: Trübner.
118. Hardy, A. 1965. *The living stream: A restatement of evolution theory and its relation to the spirit of man.* London: Collins.

119. ——. 1966. *The divine flame: An essay towards a natural history of religion.* London: Collins.
120. Harlap, S. 1979. Gender of infants conceived on different days of the menstrual cycle. *The New England Journal of Medicine* 300: 1445–48.
121. Hart, H., and collaborators. 1956. Six theories about apparitions. *Proceedings of the Society for Psychical Research* 50: 153–239.
122. Hartleben, H. 1906. *Champollion, sein Leben und sein Werk.* 2 vols. Berlin: Weidmannsche Buchhandlung.
123. Hawkes, J. 1981. *A quest of love.* New York: George Braziller.
124. Hearn, L. 1897. *Gleanings in Buddha-fields.* Boston: Houghton Mifflin.
125. Heil, J. 1980. Cognition and representation. *Australasian Journal of Philosophy* 58: 158–68.
126. Heim, A. 1892. Notizen über den Tod durch Absturz ["Remarks on fatal falls."] *Jahrbuch des schweizer Alpenclub* 27: 327–37. (English translation by R. Noyes, Jr. and R. Kletti. *Omega* 3: 45–52, 1972.)
127. Heywood, R. 1971. *The sixth sense: An inquiry into extra-sensory perception.* London: Pan Books. (Also published as *Beyond the reach of sense.* New York: E. P. Dutton, 1974.)
128. Hippocrates. 1952. Vol. 2 of *Hippocrates.* Translated by W. H. S. Jones. The Loeb Classical Library. Cambridge, Mass.: Harvard University Press. (Also London: William Heinemann.)
129. Hodgson, R. 1897–98. A further record of observations of certain phenomena of trance. *Proceedings of the Society for Psychical Research* 13: 284–582.
130. Hoehne, K. A. 1980. Classification vs. typology: A difference of practical importance. *Journal of the American Medical Association* 244: 1099–1100.
131. Hughes, C. C., with Hughes, J. M. 1962. *An Eskimo village in the modern world.* Ithaca, N.Y.: Cornell University Press.
132. Hume, D. 1854. On the immortality of the soul. In *Philosophical works,* vol. 4. Boston: Little, Brown. (First published London, 1783.)
133. ——. 1911. *A treatise of human nature.* 2 vols. London: J. M. Dent

and Sons. (First published in 1739.)
134. Hume, R. E., trans. 1931. *The thirteen principal Upanishads.* 2nd ed., rev. London: Oxford University Press.
135. Iamblichus. 1965. *Life of Pythagoras.* Translated by Thomas Taylor. London: John M. Watkins.
136. Jackson, D. D. 1966. More on Siamese twins. (Letter to the editor.) *American Journal of Psychiatry* 123: 495.
137. James, W. 1904. Does "consciousness" exist? *The Journal of Philosophy, Psychology, and Scientific Methods* 1: 477-91.
138. Jongbloet, P. H., and Zwets, J. H. J. 1976. Preovulatory overripeness of the egg in the human subject. *International Journal of Gynaecology and Obstetrics* 14: 111-16.
139. Josephson, B., and Ramachandran, V. S., eds. 1980. *Consciousness and the physical world.* New York: Pergamon Press.
140. Kampman, R. 1973. Hypnotically induced multiple personality: An experimental study. *Acta Universitatis Ouluensis,* series D, Medica no. 6. Psychiatrica no. 3, pp. 7-116.
141. ———. 1975. The dynamic relation of the secondary personality induced by hypnosis to the present personality. *Psychiatria Fennica* (1975): 169-72.
142. Kampman, R., and Hirvenoja, R. 1978. Dynamic relation of the secondary personality induced by hypnosis to the present personality. In *Hypnosis at its bicentennial,* edited by F. H. Frankel and H. S. Zamansky. New York: Plenum Press.
143. Kant, I. 1976. *Träume eines Geistersehers, erläutert durch Träume der Metaphysik.* Stuttgart: Philipp Reclam Jun. (First published in 1766.)
144. Keith, A. B. 1925. The religion and philosophy of the Veda and Upanishads. 2 vols. Harvard Oriental Series, vols. 31-32. Cambridge, Mass.: Harvard University Press.
145. Ker, W. P. 1904. *The dark ages.* New York: Charles Scribner's Sons.
146. Kleinhauz, M., Horowitz, I., and Tobin, Y. 1977. The use of hypnosis in police investigation: A preliminary communication. *Journal of the Forensic Science Society* 17: 77-80.

147. Koestler, A. 1969. Abstract and picture-strip. In *The pathology of memory,* edited by G. A. Talland and N. C. Waugh. New York: Academic Press.
148. Korner, A. F. 1969. Neonatal startles, smiles, erections, and reflex sucks as related to state, sex, and individuality. *Child Development* 40: 1039-53.
149. ———. 1971. Individual differences at birth: Implications for early experience and later development. *American Journal of Orthopsychiatry* 41: 608-19.
150. Kupalov, P. S., and Gantt, W. H. 1927. The relationship between the strength of the conditioned stimulus and the size of the resulting conditioned reflex. *Brain* 50: 44-52.
151. Lenz, F. 1979. *Lifetimes: True accounts of reincarnation.* Indianapolis: Bobbs-Merrill.
152. LeRoy Ladurie, E. 1975. *Montaillou, village occitan de 1294 à 1324.* Paris: Editions Gallimard. (American edition: *Montaillou: The promised land of error.* Translated by Barbara Bray. New York: George Braziller, 1978.)
153. Lewis, G. K. [c. 1910.] *Elizabeth Fry.* London: Herdley Bros.
154. Lewis, H. D. 1973. *The self and immortality.* London: Macmillan.
155. ———. 1978. *Persons and life after death.* New York: Barnes and Noble.
156. Lewis, I. M. 1971. *Ecstatic religion: An anthropological study of spirit possession and shamanism.* Harmondsworth, Middlesex: Penguin.
157. Lidz, T., and Blatt, S. 1983. Critique of the Danish-American studies of the biological and adoptive relatives of adoptees who became schizophrenic. *American Journal of Psychiatry* 140: 426-35.
158. Lidz, T., Blatt, S., and Cook, B. 1981. Critique of the Danish-American studies of the adopted-away offspring of schizophrenic parents. *American Journal of Psychiatry* 138: 1063-68.
159. Locke, J. 1947. *An essay concerning human understanding.* London: J. M. Dent and Sons. (First published in 1690.)
160. Loftus, E. F. 1979. *Eyewitness testimony.* Cambridge, Mass., and

London: Harvard University Press.

161. Luckhardt, A. B. 1941. Report of the autopsy of the Siamese twins together with other interesting information concerning their life. *Surgery, Gynecology, and Obstetrics* 72: 116–25.

162. Luria, A. R. 1969. *The mind of a mnemonist.* Translated by Lynn Solotaroff. London: Jonathan Cape.

163. McClenon, J. 1982. A survey of elite scientists: Their attitudes toward ESP and parapsychology. *Journal of Parapsychology* 46: 127–52.

164. McDougall, W. 1926. *An outline of abnormal psychology.* London: Methuen.

165. MacKenzie, A. 1966. *The unexplained: Some strange cases in psychical research.* London: Arthur Barker.

166. ———. 1971. *Apparitions and ghosts: A modern study.* London: Arthur Barker.

167. ———. 1982. *Hauntings and apparitions.* London: William Heinemann.

168. McTaggart, J. M. E. 1906. *Some dogmas of religion.* London: Edward Arnold.

169. Madaule, J. 1961. *Le drame albigeois et le destin français.* Paris: Bernard Grasset.

170. Madell, G. 1981. *The identity of the self.* Edinburgh: Edinburgh University Press.

171. Makarem, S. 1974. *The Druze faith.* Delmar, N.Y.: Caravan Books.

172. Malcolm, N. 1970. Memory and representation. *Noûs* 4: 59–71.

173. ———. 1977. *Memory and mind.* Ithaca, N.Y.: Cornell University Press.

174. Malinowski, B. 1916. Baloma: The spirits of the dead in the Trobriand Islands. *Journal of the Royal Anthropological Institute of Great Britain and Ireland* 46: 353–430.

175. ———. 1927. *The father in primitive psychology.* New York: W. W. Norton.

176. Mann, T. C., and Greene, J. 1968. *Sudden and awful: American*

epitaphs and the finger of God. Brattleboro, Vt.: Stephen Greene Press.

177. Marks, I. 1978. Rehearsal relief of a nightmare. *British Journal of Psychiatry* 133: 461–65.
178. Marshall, J. 1969. *Law and psychology in conflict.* Garden City, N.Y.: Doubleday.
179. Martino, M. 1977. *Emergence: A transsexual autobiography.* New York: Crown Publishers.
180. Medawar, P. 1957. *The uniqueness of the individual.* New York: Basic Books.
181. Mi Mi Khaing. 1962. *Burmese family.* Bloomington, Ind.: Indiana University Press.
182. Mochulsky, K. 1967. *Dostoevsky: His life and work.* Translated by Michael A. Minihan. Princeton: Princeton University Press.
183. Monod, J. 1964. *Le hasard et la nécessité.* Paris: Editions du Seuil. (American edition: *Chance and necessity.* Translated by Austryn Wainhouse. New York: Alfred A. Knopf, 1971.)
184. Morris, J. 1974. *Conundrum.* London: Faber and Faber.
185. Munro, N. G. 1963. *Ainu: Creed and cult.* New York: Columbia University Press.
186. Murphy, G. 1945. Field theory and survival. *Journal of the American Society for Psychical Research* 39: 181–209.
187. Murphy, G., with Dale, L. A. 1961. *Challenge of psychical research: A primer of parapsychology.* New York: Harper and Bros.
188. Myers, F. W. H. 1889. On recognized apparitions occurring more than a year after death. *Proceedings of the Society for Psychical Research* 6: 13–65.
189. ———. 1903. *Human personality and its survival of bodily death.* 2 vols. London: Longmans, Green.
190. Nagel, T. 1979. What is it like to be a bat? In Nagel, T. *Mortal Questions.* Cambridge: Cambridge University Press. (Originally published in *Philosophical Review* 83: 435–50, 1974.)
191. Nash, C. B. 1984. Test of psychokinetic control of bacterial mutation.

Journal of the American Society for Psychical Research 78: 145–52.
192. Neidhart, G. 1956. *Werden wir wieder geboren?* Munich: Gemeinschaft für Religiöse and Geistige Erneuerung e. V.
193. Neisser, U., ed. 1982. *Memory observed: Remembering in natural contexts.* San Francisco: W. H. Freeman.
194. Nelli, R. 1972. *Les cathares.* Paris: Grasset.
195. Neppe, V. M. 1983. *The psychology of déjà vu: Have I been here before?* Jonannesburg: Witwatersrand University Press.
196. Newman, H. H. 1940. *Multiple human births.* New York: Doubleday, Doran.
197. Nicol, J. F. 1976. Review of *Cases of the reincarnation type:* Vol. 1, *Ten cases in India. Parapsychology Review* 7(5): 12–15.
198. Niel, F. 1955. *Albigeois et Cathares.* Paris: Presses Universitaires de France.
199. Noon, J. A. 1942. A preliminary examination of death concepts of the Ibo. *American Anthropologist* 44: 638–54.
200. Norbu, T., and Turnbull, C. 1969. *Tibet.* London: Chatto and Windus.
201. Noyes, R., Jr., and Kletti, R. 1976. Depersonalization in the face of life-threatening danger: A description. *Psychiatry* 39: 19–27.
202. ———. 1977. Panoramic memory: A response to the threat of death. *Omega* 8: 181–94.
203. Obeyesekere, G. 1968. Theodicy, sin, and salvation in a sociology of Buddhism. In *Dialectic in practical religion,* edited by E. R. Leach. Cambridge: Cambridge University Press.
204. ———. 1980. The rebirth eschatology and its transformations: A contribution to the sociology of early Buddhism. In *Karma and rebirth in classical Indian traditions,* edited by W. D. O'Flaherty. Berkeley: University of California Press.
205. O'Connell, D. N., Shor, R. E., and Orne, M. T. 1970. Hypnotic age regression. *Journal of Abnormal Psychology Monograph* 76: 1–32.
206. Okey, T., ed. and trans. 1910. *The little flowers of St. Francis.* London: J. M. Dent and Sons.
207. Orne, M. T. 1951. The mechanisms of hypnotic age regression: An

experimental study. *Journal of Abnormal and Social Psychology* 46: 213–25.
208. Osis, K., and Haraldsson, E. 1977. *At the hour of death.* New York: Avon Books.
209. Osty, E. 1923. *Supernormal faculties in man: An experimental study.* Translated by Stanley de Brath. London: Methuen.
210. ———. 1929. Ce que la médecine doit attendre de l'étude expérimentale des propriétés psychiques paranormales de l'homme. *Revue Métapsychique,* no. 2, pp. 79–148.
211. ———. 1932. Télépathie spontanée et transmission de pensée expérimentale. *Revue Métapsychique,* no. 4, pp. 233–56.
212. Owen, R. D. 1874. *The debatable land between this world and the next.* London: Trübner.
213. Palmer, J. 1979. A community mail survey of psychic experiences. *Journal of the American Society for Psychical Research* 73: 221–51.
214. Parrinder, G. 1956. Varieties of belief in reincarnation. *Hibbert Journal* 55: 260–67.
215. ———. 1970. *African traditional religion.* Westport, Conn.: Greenwood Press. (First published in 1954. London: Hutchinson's University Library.)
216. Parry, W. E. 1932. *The Lakhers.* London: Macmillan.
217. Pasricha, S. K. 1983. New information favoring a paranormal interpretation in the case of Rakesh Gaur. *European Journal of Parapsychology* 5: 77–85.
218. Pasricha, S. K., and Barker, D. R. 1981. A case of the reincarnation type in India: The case of Rakesh Gaur. *European Journal of Parapsychology* 3: 381–408.
219. Pasricha, S., and Stevenson, I. 1977. Three cases of the reincarnation type in India. *Indian Journal of Psychiatry* 19: 36–42.
220. Patanjali. 1953. *How to know God: The Yoga aphorisms.* Translated by Swami Prabhavananda, and Isherwood, C. New York: Harper and Bros.
221. Penelhum, T. 1970. *Survival and disembodied existence.* London:

Routledge and Kegan Paul.

222. Penfield, W. 1975. *The mystery of the mind.* Princeton: Princeton University Press.

223. Peris, M. 1963. Pythagoras, birth-rememberer. *University of Ceylon Review* 21: 186-212.

224. Perovsky-Petrovo-Solovovo, M. 1930. A phantasm of the dead conveying information unknown to the percipient. *Journal of the Society for Psychical Research* 26: 95-98.

225. Perry, J., ed. 1975. *Personal Identity.* Berkeley: University of California Press.

226. Philostratus. 1912. *The Life of Apollonius of Tyana.* Translated by F. C. Conybeare. London: William Heinemann.

227. Place, U. T. 1956. Is consciousness a brain process? *British Journal of Psychology* 47: 44-50.

228. Plato. 1935. *The republic.* Translated by A. D. Lindsay. London: J. M. Dent and Sons.

229. ———. 1936. *Five dialogues.* London: J. M. Dent and Sons.（本書には the *Meno* and the *Phaedo.* が収録されている）

230. Popper, K. R., and Eccles, J. C. 1977. *The self and its brain.* New York: Springer International.

231. Porter, R., and Collins, G. M., eds. 1982. *Temperamental differences in infants and young children.* Ciba Foundation Symposium 89. London: Pitman.

232. Poynton, J. C. 1983. Correspondence section. *Journal of Parapsychology* 47: 82-86.

233. Prabhavananda and Isherwood, C., trans. 1944. *The song of God: Bhagavad-Gita.* Hollywood, Calif.: Marcel Rodd.

234. Prasad, J., and Stevenson, I. 1968. A survey of spontaneous psychical experiences in school children of Uttar Pradesh, India. *International Journal of Parapsychology* 10: 241-61.

235. Prat, F. 1907. *Origène, le théologien et l'exégète.* Paris: Blond.

236. ———. 1911. Origen and Origenism. In *The Catholic Encyclopedia.* New York: Robert Appleton.

237. Price, H. H. 1940. Some philosophical questions about telepathy and clairvoyance. *Philosophy* 15: 363–85.

238. ———. 1953. Survival and the idea of "another world." *Proceedings of the Society for Psychical Research* 50: 1–25.

239. ———. 1972. *Essays in the philosophy of religion.* Oxford: Oxford University Press.

240. Prince, W. F. 1921. Analysis of the results of an old questionnaire. *Journal of the American Society for Psychical Research* 15: 169–84.

241. ———. 1922. Dreams seeming, or interpreted, to indicate death. *Journal of the American Society for Psychical Research* 16: 164–89.

242. ———. 1928. *Noted witnesses for psychic occurrences.* Boston: Boston Society for Psychic Research.

243. Putnam, W. H. 1979. Hypnosis and distortions in eyewitness memory. *International Journal of Clinical and Experimental Hypnosis* 27: 437–48.

244. Radhakrishnan, S. 1923. *Indian philosophy.* 2 vols. London: George Allen and Unwin.

245. Radin, P., ed. 1926. *Crashing thunder: The autobiography of an American Indian.* New York: D. Appleton.

246. Raymond of Capua. 1980. *The life of St. Catherine of Siena.* Translated by Conleth Kearns. Wilmington, Del.: Michael Glazier.

247. Rees, W. D. 1971. The hallucinations of widowhood. *British Medical Journal* 4: 37–41.

248. Reiff, R., and Scheerer, M. 1959. *Memory and hypnotic age regression.* New York: International Universities Press.

249. Rhine, L. E. 1961. *Hidden channels of the mind.* New York: Sloane.

250. ———. 1981. *The invisible picture: A study of psychic experiences.* Jefferson, N.C.: McFarland.

251. Richardson, A. 1969. *Mental imagery.* New York: Springer Publishing.

252. Richet, C. 1926. Des conditions de la certitude. *Proceedings of the Society for Psychical Research* 35: 422–44.

253. Ring, K. 1980. *Life at death: A scientific investigation of the near-*

death experience. New York: Coward, McCann and Geoghegan.

254. Roberts, A. M. 1978. The origins of fluctuations in the human secondary sex ratio. *Journal of Biosocial Science* 10: 169–82.

255. Roffwarg, H. P., Muzio, J. N., and Dement, W. C. 1966. Ontogenetic development of human sleep-dream cycle. *Science* 152: 604–19.

256. Rohde, W., Porstmann, T., and Dörner, G. 1973. Migration of Y-bearing human spermatozoa in cervical mucus. *Journal of Reproduction and Fertility* 33: 167–69.

257. Rollo, C. 1967. Thomas Bayes and the bundle of sticks. *Proceedings of the Society for Psychical Research* 55: 23–64.

258. Rorty, A. O., ed. 1976. *The identities of persons.* Berkeley: University of California Press.

259. Rose, R. 1956. *Living magic.* New York: Rand McNally.

260. Rose, S., Kamin, L. J., and Lewontin, R. C. 1984. *"Not in our genes."* Harmondsworth, Middlesex: Penguin.

261. Roughead, W. 1926. *The rebel earl and other studies.* New York: E. P. Dutton.

262. Ruben, W. 1939. Schamanismus in alten Indien. *Acta Orientalia* 17: 164–205.

263. Runciman, S. 1947. *The medieval Manichee.* Cambridge: Cambridge University Press.

264. Ryall, E. W. 1974. *Second time round*. Jersey: Neville Spearman. (American edition: *Born twice: Total recall of a seventeenth-century life.* New York: Harper and Row, 1974.)

265. Sabom, M. 1982. *Recollections of death.* New York: Harper and Row.

266. Sahay, K. K. N. c. 1927. *Reincarnation: Verified cases of re-birth after death.* Bareilly: N. L. Gupta.

267. Saltmarsh, H. F. 1934. Report on cases of apparent precognition. *Proceedings of the Society for Psychical Research* 42: 49–103.

268. Sandison, R. A., Spencer, A. M., and Whitelaw, J. D. A. 1954. The therapeutic value of lysergic acid diethylamide in mental illness. *Journal of Mental Science* 100: 491–507.

269. Sannwald, G. 1959a. Statistische Untersuchungen an Spontan-

phänomenen. *Zeitschrift für Parapsychologie und Grenzgebiete der Psychologie* 3: 59–71.

270. ———. 1959b. Zur Psychologie paranormaler Spontanphänomene: Motivation, Thematik und Bezugspersonen "okkulter" Erlebnisse. *Zeitschrift für Parapsychologie und Grenzgebiete der Psychologie* 3: 149–83.

271. Schliemann, H. 1881. *Ilios, the city and country of the Trojans, including an autobiography of the author.* New York: Harper and Bros.

272. Schmeidler, G. 1961a. Evidence for two kinds of telepathy. *International Journal of Parapsychology* 3(3): 5–48.

273. ———. 1961b. Are there two kinds of telepathy? *Journal of the American Society for Psychical Research* 55: 87–97.

274. Schopbach, R. R., Fried, P. H., and Rakoff, A. E. 1952. Pseudocyesis: A psychosomatic disorder. *Psychosomatic Medicine* 14: 129–34.

275. Schopenhauer, A. 1891. Parerga und Paralipomena. In *Arthur Schopenhauer's sämmtliche Werke.* Volume 2. Leipzig: F. U. Brockhaus.

276. ———. 1908. *Die welt als Wille und Vorstellung.* 2 vols. Leipzig: F. U. Brockhaus.

277. Schouten, S. A. 1979. Analysis of spontaneous cases as reported in "Phantasms of the living." *European Journal of Parapsychology* 2: 408–55.

278. Schrödinger, E. 1955. *What is life? The physical aspect of the living cell.* Cambridge: Cambridge University Press.

279. Schulsinger, F. 1985. The experience from the adoption method in genetic research. In *Medical Genetics: Past, Present, Future,* edited by K. Berg. New York: Alan R. Liss.

280. Sherrington, C. 1947. *The integrative action of the nervous system.* New Haven: Yale University Press. (First published in 1906.)

281. Shoemaker, S., and Swinburne, R. 1984. *Personal identity.* Oxford: Blackwell.

282. Sidgwick, [E. M.] Mrs. H. 1891–92. On the evidence for

clairvoyance. *Proceedings of the Society for Psychical Research* 7: 30–99.

283. ———. 1921. An examination of book-tests obtained in sittings with Mrs. Leonard. *Proceedings of the Society for Psychical Research* 31: 241–400.

284. Sidgwick, H., and Committee. 1894. Report on the census of hallucinations. *Proceedings of the Society for Psychical Research* 10: 25–422.

285. Sinclair, U. 1962. *Mental radio.* Springfield, Ill.: Charles C. Thomas. (First published in 1930.)

286. Slobodin, R. 1970. Kutchin concepts of reincarnation. *Western Canadian Journal of Anthropology* 2: 67–79.

287. Smart, N. 1964. *Doctrine and argument in Indian philosophy.* London: George Allen and Unwin.

288. Smith, B. M., Hain, J. D., and Stevenson, I. 1970. Controlled interviews using drugs. *Archives of General Psychiatry* 22: 2–10.

289. Smith, S. 1964. *The mediumship of Mrs. Leonard.* New Hyde Park, N.Y.: University Books.

290. Smythies, J. R. 1951. The extension of mind: A new theoretical basis for psi phenomena. *Journal of the Society for Psychical Research* 36: 477–502.

291. ———. 1956. *Analysis of perception.* London: Routledge and Kegan Paul.

292. ———. 1960. Three classical theories of mind. *Journal of the Society for Psychical Research* 40: 385–97.

293. ———. 1974. The mind-brain problem today: A viewpoint from the neurosciences. In *Parapsychology and the sciences,* edited by A. Angoff and B. Shapin. New York: Parapsychology Foundation.

294. Snellgrove, D., and Richardson, H. 1968. *A cultural history of Tibet.* New York: Frederick A. Praeger.

295. Southey, R. 1962. *Life of Nelson.* London: J. M. Dent and Sons. (First published in 1813.)

296. Spear, P. 1965. *History of India.* Vol. 2. Harmondsworth, Middlesex:

Penguin.
297. Spencer, B., and Gillen, F. J. 1968. *The native tribes of central Australia.* New York: Dover Publications. (First published in 1899. London: Macmillan.)
298. Spencer, R. F. 1959. *The north Alaskan Eskimo: A study in ecology and society.* Smithsonian Institution, Bureau of American Ethnology, Bulletin 171. Washington, D.C.: United States Government Printing Office.
299. Stalnaker, J. M., and Riddle, E. E. 1932. The effect of hypnosis on long-delayed recall. *Journal of General Psychology* 6: 429-40.
300. Stanley, H. M. 1909. *Autobiography.* Boston: Houghton Mifflin.
301. Stendhal. 1926. *Lucien Leuwen.* Paris: Librairie Ancienne Honoré Champion. (Originally published 1855.)
302. Stevenson, I. 1957. Is the human personality more plastic in infancy and childhood? *American Journal of Psychiatry* 114: 152-61.
303. ———. 1960. The evidence for survival from claimed memories of former incarnations. *Journal of the American Society for Psychical Research* 54: 51-71, 95-117.
304. ———. 1964. The blue orchid of Table Mountain. *Journal of the Society for Psychical Research* 42: 401-9.
305. ———. 1966. Cultural patterns in cases suggestive of reincarnation among the Tlingit Indians of southeastern Alaska. *Journal of the American Society for Psychical Research* 60: 229-43.
306. ———. 1969. The belief in reincarnation and related cases among the Eskimos of Alaska. *Proceedings of the Parapsychological Association* 6: 53-55.
307. ———. 1970a. Characteristics of cases of the reincarnation type in Turkey and their comparison with cases in two other cultures. *International Journal of Comparative Sociology* 11: 1-17.
308. ———. 1970b. Telepathic impressions. *Proceedings of the American Society for Psychical Research* 29: 1-198. (Also Charlottesville: University Press of Virginia.)
309. ———. 1970c. Precognition of disasters. *Journal of the American*

Society for Psychical Research 64: 187–210.

310. ———. 1971. The substantiality of spontaneous cases. *Proceedings of the Parapsychological Association* 5: 91–128.

311. ———. 1974a. Some questions related to cases of the reincarnation type. *Journal of the American Society for Psychical Research* 68: 395–416.

312. ———. 1974b. *Twenty cases suggestive of reincarnation.* 2nd rev. ed. Charlottesville: University Press of Virginia. (First published in 1966 as vol. 26 of the *Proceedings of the American Society for Psychical Research.*)

313. ———. 1974c. *Xenoglossy: A review and report of a case.* Charlottesville: University Press of Virginia.

314. ———. 1975a. *Cases of the reincarnation type.* Vol. 1, *Ten cases in India.* Charlottesville: University Press of Virginia.

315. ———. 1975b. The belief and cases related to reincarnation among the Haida. *Journal of Anthropological Research 31:* 364–75. (Reprinted with revisions in *Journal of the American Society for Psychical Research* 71: 177–89, 1977.)

316. ———. 1976. A preliminary report of a new case of responsive xenoglossy: The case of Gretchen. *Journal of the American Society for Psychical Research* 70: 65–77.

317. ———. 1977a. *Cases of the reincarnation type.* Vol. 2, *Ten cases in Sri Lanka.* Charlottesville: University Press of Virginia.

318. ———. 1977b. The explanatory value of the idea of reincarnation. *Journal of Nervous and Mental Disease* 164: 305–26.

319. ———. 1977c. Research into the evidence of man's survival after death: A historical and critical survey with a summary of recent developments. *Journal of Nervous and Mental Disease* 165: 152–70.

320. ———. 1977d. The Southeast Asian interpretation of gender dysphoria: An illustrative case report. *Journal of Nervous and Mental Disease* 165: 201–8.

321. ———. 1980. *Cases of the reincarnation type.* Vol. 3, *Twelve cases in Lebanon and Turkey.* Charlottesville: University Press of Virginia.

322. ———. 1981. Can we describe the mind? In *Research in parapsychology 1980,* edited by W. G. Roll and J. Beloff. Metuchen, N. J.: Scarecrow Press.
323. ———. 1982. The contribution of apparitions to the evidence for survival. *Journal of the American Society for Psychical Research* 76: 341-58.
324. ———. 1983a. *Cases of the reincarnation type.* Vol. 4, *Twelve cases in Thailand and Burma.* Charlottesville: University Press of Virginia.
325. ———. 1983b. Cryptomnesia and parapsychology. *Journal of the Society for Psychical Research* 52: 1-30.
326. ———. 1983c. Do we need a new word to supplement"hallucination"? *American Journal of Psychiatry* 140: 1609-11.
327. ———. 1983d. American children who claim to remember previous lives. *Journal of Nervous and Mental Disease* 171: 742-48.
328. ———. 1984. *Unlearned language: New studies in xenoglossy.* Charlottesville: University Press of Virginia.
329. ———. 1985. The belief in reincarnation among the Igbo of Nigeria. *Journal of Asian and African Studies* 20: 13-30.
330. ———. 1986. Characteristics of cases of the reincarnation type among the Igbo of Nigeria. *Journal of Asian and African Studies* 21: 204-16.
331. Stevenson, I., and Edelstein, S. J. 1982. The beliefe in reincarnation among the Igbo of southeastern Nigeria with particular reference to connections between the *ogbanje* ("repeater babies") and sickle cell anemia. In *Research in Parapsychology 1981,* edited by W. G. Roll, R. L. Morris, and R. A. White. Metuchen, N.J.: Scarecrow Press.
332. Stevenson, I., and Greyson, B. 1979. Near-death experiences: Relevance to the question of survival after death. *Journal of the American Medical Association* 242: 265-67.
333. Stevenson, I., and Pasricha, S. 1979. A case of secondary personality with xenoglossy. *American Journal of Psychiatry* 136: 1591-92.
334. ———. 1980. A preliminary report on an unusual case of the reincarnation type with xenoglossy. *Journal of the American Society*

for Psychical Research 74: 331–48.

335. Stone, L. J. 1954. A critique of studies on infant isolation. *Child Development* 25: 9–20.

336. Stratton, G. M. 1919. Retroactive hypermnesia and other emotional effects on memory. *Psychological Review* 26: 474–86.

337. Sunderlal, R. B. S. 1924. Cas apparents de réminiscences de vies antérieures. *Revue Métapsychique* no. 4, pp. 302–7.

338. Susukita, T. 1933–34. Untersuchung eines ausserordentlichen Gedächtnisses in Japan, pts. I, II. *Tohoku Psychologica Folia* 1: 111–134; 2: 15–42.

339. Swanton, J. R. 1908. Social condition, beliefs, and linguistic relationship of the Tlingit Indians. *Twenty-sixth Annual Report of the Bureau of American Ethnology (1904–05)*, pp. 391–485. Washington, D.C.: United States Government Printing Office.

340. Swedenborg, E. 1906. *Heaven and its wonders and Hell.* Boston: New-Church Union. (First published in Latin, 1758.)

341. Thakur, S. C., ed. 1976. *Philosophy and psychical research.* London: George Allen and Unwin.

342. Thalbourne, M. A. 1982. *A glossary of terms used in parapsychology.* London: William Heinemann.

343. Thomas, A. 1981. Current trends in developmental theory. *American Journal of Orthopsychiatry* 51: 580–609.

344. Thomas, A., and Chess, S. 1977. *Temperament and development.* New York: Brunner/Mazel.

345. Thomas, C. D. 1945. A discourse given through Mrs. Leonard and attributed to Sir Oliver Lodge. *Journal of the Society for Psychical Research* 33: 134–56.

346. Thomas, L.-V. 1968. *Cinq essais sur la mort africaine.* Dakar: Université de Dakar.

347. Thorndike, E. L. 1905. *The elements of psychology.* 2d ed. New York: A. G. Seiler.

348. Thouless, R. H. 1979. Theories about survival. *Journal of the Society for Psychical Research* 50: 1–8.

349. ———. 1984. Do we survive bodily death? *Proceedings of the Society for Psychical Research* 57: 1–52.
350. Thouless, R. H., and Wiesner, B. P. 1946–49. The psi processes in normal and "paranormal" psychology. *Proceedings of the Society for Psychical Research* 48: 177–96.
351. Toukholka, S. 1922. Expériences de clairvoyance avec Mme. Olga Kahl. *Revue Métapsychique* no. 6, pp. 429–33.
352. True, R. M. 1949. Experimental control in hypnotic age regression states. *Science* 110: 583–84.
353. Tulving, E. 1972. Episodic and semantic memory. In *Organization of memory,* edited by E. Tulving and W. Donaldson. New York: Academic Press.
354. Tyrrell, G. N. M. 1953. *Apparitions.* London: Duckworth.
355. Uchendu, V. C. 1965. *The Igbo of southeast Nigeria.* New York: Holt, Rinehart, and Winston.
356. Van Eeden, F. 1912–13. A study of dreams. *Proceedings of the Society for Psychical Research* 26: 431–61.
357. Vasiliev, L. L. 1966. *Studies in mental telepathy.* Washington, D.C.: U.S. Department of Commerce, Clearinghouse for Federal Scientific and Technical Information. (Originally published in 1962 as *Vnusheniye na rasstoyanii* [Zametki fiziologa]. Moscow: Gospolitizdat Publising House.)
358. Vesey, G. 1974. *Personal Identity.* London: Macmillan.
359. Voltaire. 1960. La princesse de Babylone. In *Romans et contes.* Paris: Editions Garnier Frères.
360. Waxler, N. 1979. Is outcome for schizophrenia better in nonindustrial societies? The case of Sri Lanka. *Journal of Nervous and Mental Disease* 167: 144–58.
361. West, D. J. 1948. A mass-observation questionnaire on hallucinations. *Journal of the Society for Psychical Research* 34: 187–96.
362. Whately, R. 1858. *Elements of rhetoric: Comprising an analysis of the laws of moral evidence and of persuasion.* Rev. ed. Boston: James

Munroe.

363. Wheatley, J. M. O. 1965. The question of survival: Some logical reflections. *Journal of the American Society for Psychical Research* 59: 202–10.

364. ———. 1979. Reincarnation, "astral bodies," and "psi-components." *Journal of the American Society for Psychical Research* 73: 109–22.

365. Wheatley, J. M. O., and Edge, H., eds. 1976. *Philosophical dimensions of parapsychology.* Springfield, Ill.: Charles C. Thomas.

366. Whitaker, L., Jr. 1961. The use of an extended draw-a-person test to identify homosexual and effeminate men. *Journal of Consulting Psychology* 25: 482–85.

367. White, R. A., and Dale, L. A. 1973. *Parapsychology: Sources of information.* Metuchen, N.J.: Scarecrow Press.

368. Whiteman, J. H. M. 1961. *The mystical life.* London: Faber and Faber.

369. ———. 1972. On the concept of repeatability in scientific experimentation. *Journal of the American Society for Psychical Research* 66: 227–29.

370. ———. 1973. Quantum theory and parapsychology. *Journal of the American Society for Psychical Research* 67: 341–60.

371. Whittaker, P. G., Taylor, A., and Lind, T. 1983. Unsuspected pregnancy loss in healthy women. *The Lancet* i: 1126–27.

372. Wolman, B. B., ed. 1977. *Handbook of parapsychology.* New York: Van Nostrand Reinhold.

373. Wolpe, J., and Rachman, S. 1960. Psychoanalytic "evidence": A critique based on Freud's case of Little Hans. *Journal of Nervous and Mental Disease* 130: 135–48.

374. Woodham-Smith, C. 1950. *Florence Nightingale, 1820–1910.* London: Constable.

375. Yuille, J. C., and Cutshall, J. L. 1986. A case study of eyewitness memory of a crime. *Journal of Applied Psychology* 71: 291–301.

376. Zaehner, R. C. 1957. *Mysticism: Sacred and profane.* Oxford: The Clarendon Press.

377. ———. 1962. *Hinduism.* London: Oxford University Press.

378. Zahan, D., ed. 1965. *Réincarnation et vie mystique en afrique noire.* Paris: Presses Universitaire de France.
379. Zeigarnik, B. 1927. Das Behalten erledigter und unerledigter Handlungen. *Psychologische Forschung* 9: 1-85.
380. Zelig, M., and Beidleman, W. B. 1981. The investigative use of hypnosis: A word of caution. *International Journal of Clinical and Experimental Hypnosis* 29: 401-12.
381. Zolik, E. S. 1958. An experimental investigation of the psychodynamic implications of the hypnotic "previous existence" fantasy. *Journal of Clinical Psychology* 14: 178-83. (Also unpublished case reports presented at the meeting of the American Psychological Association, 1958.)
382. ———. 1962. "Reincarnation" phenomena in hypnotic states. *International Journal of Parapsychology* 4(3): 66-78.
383. Zuger, B. 1970. The role of familial factors in persistent effeminate behavior in boys. *American Journal of Psychiatry* 126: 1167-70.

*　　　*　　　*

以上の参考文献中，邦訳のあることに気づいたものを，超心理学関係の文献に限って以下に掲げておく。

24. バーンスタイン，M.『第二の記憶』（万沢遼訳）光文社，1959.
94. ギャラップ，G.『死後の世界』（丹波哲郎訳）三笠書房，1985.
103. グラッタン＝ギネス，I.『心霊研究——その歴史・原理・実践』（笠原敏雄，和田芳久訳）技術出版，1995.
187. マーフィー，G.『超心理の科学』（中野久夫訳）時事通信社，1975.
208. オシス，K.，ハラルドソン，E.『人間が死ぬとき』（笠原敏雄訳）たま出版，1979.（第2版邦訳，『人は死ぬ時何を見るのか』1991年，日本教文社）
219. パスリチャ，S.，スティーヴンソン，I.「インドの生まれ変わり型三例の研究」笠原敏雄編『死後の生存の科学』（叢文社，1984）所収。
249. ライン，L.『超精神回路』（日暮雅通訳）国書刊行会，1986.
253. リング，K.『いまわのきわに見る死の世界』（中村定訳）講談社，

1981.
265. セイボム，M.『「あの世」からの帰還』（笠原敏雄訳）日本教文社，1986.
308. スティーヴンソン，I.『虫の知らせの科学』（笠原敏雄訳）叢文社，1981.
319. スティーヴンソン，I.「人間の死後生存の証拠に関する研究——最近の研究を踏まえた歴史的展望」『死後の生存の科学』所収。
320. スティーヴンソン，I.「性別異和症の東南アジア流解釈——その実証的事例報告」『死後の生存の科学』所収。
328. スティーヴンソン，I.『前世の言葉を話す人々』（笠原敏雄訳）春秋社，1995.
332. スティーヴンソン，I.，グレイソン，B.「臨死体験——死後生存問題との関連」『死後の生存の科学』所収。
333. スティーヴンソン，I.，パスリチャ，S.「真性異言を伴った第二人格の一例」『死後の生存の科学』所収。
348. タウレス，R. H.「死後生存の理論」『死後の生存の科学』所収。
357. ワシリエフ，L. L.『テレパシーの世界』（秋田義夫訳）白揚社，1973.

文献126のハイムの論文は，メスナー，R.『死の地帯』（尾崎鑾治訳，山と渓谷社，1983）に全文転載されており，勝五郎の事例に関するハーンの報告，「勝五郎の再生」（124）は，『仏の畑の落穂他』（恒文社）や『小泉八雲怪談奇談集』（河出文庫，1988）に収録されている。また，マックレノンの論文（163）とほぼ同じ内容の論文，マックレノン著『ESPおよび超心理学に対するエリート科学者の態度」は，笠原編『サイの戦場——超心理学論争全史』（平凡社，1987）に収録されている。

日本版序文

日本語に翻訳され出版される拙著は、これで三冊目になります。そのことを私は、心から喜んでおります。

本書（アメリカ版）の序文の中で強調しておきましたが、本書に登場する事例をお読みいただいただけでその信憑性《しんぴょうせい》が判断できるほど詳しい内容は、本書には盛り込まれておりません。第4章で紹介している一二例は、典型例を要約した以上のものではないのです。この一二例のうちのいくつかについては、他の数多くの事例とともに、別の著書や論文の中で、既に詳細な報告を行なっております。

本書の結論部では、こうした事例をさらに調査することの必要性を力説しておきました。このような調査は、おそらく日本でも行なわれることでしょう。日本でも調査を実施したらどうかというお勧めをいただいたこともこれまで何度かありましたが、私としては、長期にわたって調査を続けて来たおかげでなじみを深めているインドやスリランカ、ビルマ〔ミャンマー〕などの国に区域をしぼった方がよいと考えてまいりました。とは申しましても、日本の事例も少数ですが承知しておりますし、ある理由から、調査の日を待っている事例がもっとたくさんあるのではないかとも思っております。

本書の出版がひとつの契機となり、前世を記憶する子どもの事例に対する関心が日本の科学者の間に起こることを心より願うものです。それと同時に、この種の事例をご存知の方がおられたら、調査が可能になるように、ぜひ研究者にお知らせいただきたいと思います。そうすることによって、生まれ変わりに関する知識がさらに広がるものと信じております。前世を記憶している子どもたちの例をご存知の方は、当方にお知らせくださってもかまいません。その場合、日本語でお書きいただいてもけっこうです。

イアン・スティーヴンソン

ヴァージニア州シャーロッツヴィル

一九八九年五月九日

（連絡先）
University of Virginia Health System, Department of Psychiatry and Neurobiological Sciences, Division of Perceptual Studies, Box 800152, Charlottesville, VA 22908-0152, U.S.A.

目次

まえがき

本書は、生まれ変わりを思わせる事例についての私の研究を一般の方々にかみ砕いてお話しすることを目的に書かれたものである。生まれ変わりが実在することを裏づける証拠を詳しく説明する代わりに、本書では、これまで私がとって来た研究法や、そうした方法によって得られた成果、さらには、それに基づいた現段階での私なりの結論を簡単にまとめてお話ししようと思う。

生まれ変わりの実在を裏づける証拠のもとになるさまざまな事例をおわかりいただくために、一二例の典型例を第4章に要約して紹介しておいたが、その要約は、私がこれまで発表してきた詳細な事例報告からすると、単なる概略以上のものではない。これまで発表してきた報告では、対象にしている事例にまつわるあらゆる証拠をきちんと整理しようと努めている。（私はこれまで、詳細な事例報告を六五例発表しており、加えて、発表準備中のものも一〇〇例以上ある。）生まれ変わりに関してそれまで懐疑的な態度をとられていた（ないしはこうした現象を無視されていた）読者の方々が、本書を読まれただけで、生まれ変わりという現象が本当に存在すると確信するようになったとしても、それは私の本意とするところではない。生まれ変わりなどということをそれまで考えもしなかった方々に、そういう考え方も一理あると思っていただけたとしたら、それこそ私の望むところのものであるし、私の詳細な事例報告に盛り込まれた証拠に当たってみる価値がありそうだと一部の方々にお考えいただけたとすれば、望外の成果を挙げえたことになる。

本書では、生まれ変わりの裏づけとなる説得力のある証拠とない証拠とを、どちらにも偏ることなく公平に紹介するよう努めたが、証拠の解釈にまつわる検討は大幅に省略している。それによって読者の方々が、別著に当たり、この点に関する私の詳細な論考をご検討いただければ幸いである。

本書では、私の研究の概略や主な研究成果をかいつまんで紹介するが、本書はその他にもいくつかの目的をもっている。そのうちのひとつは、生まれ変わりについて遍《あまね》く見られる誤解を正すお手伝いを、本書を通じてしたいと考えていることである。西洋人の多くからすると、生まれ変わりという考え方は、ひどく現実離れした奇妙な着想のように映る。ヒンドゥー教や仏教、さらには、因果応報的なカルマ[*1]や動物として再生するというヒンドゥー教徒や仏教徒の考え方と結びつけられることが多いし、そうしたものとしか結びつけて考えようとしない人々も少なくない。私がこれまで調査してきた事例の中には、このような考え方を裏づける証拠はほとんどないが、その点についても簡単にふれておいた。また、生まれ変わりを信ずるヒンドゥー教徒や仏教徒以外のさまざまな民族の中には、因果応報という考え方や動物に再生するという考え方と生まれ変わりとを結びつけていない民族も少なくない。生まれ変わりは一定の形で起こらなければならないとする信仰は、生まれ変わりという考え方を完全に拒絶した場合と同じくらい、有意義な考察を妨げる可能性があるし、生まれ変わりが起こるしくみについて独善的な思い込みを抱いて私に手紙を書いて来る人たちは、生まれ変わりなどありえないと主張する者と同じくらい、既成概念を捨て去る必要があるように思われる。

本書には、もうひとつ副次的な目的がある。本書に触発されて新しい事例が集まって来るのを待つことである。特に西洋諸国では、生まれ変わり型の事例はまだ過少にしか報告されていないと私は考えている。私のもとに届く手紙の中に、息子[*2]が三歳の時に前世の話をしていたようだなどと知らせて来るものも時おりあるが、手紙を書いて来た時点では子どもはたいてい一〇歳や一五歳になっているし、さらに年長になってしまっていることも少なくない。その中には、もっと幼なかった頃には子どもの話を無視したり、笑いものにしたことすらあるとして、後悔の念に駆られる親もある。その後こうした子どもたちは、それまで記憶していたらしき事柄を忘れてしまう。もし私や私の後継者が、長年にわたって私たちがアジアを筆頭に世界各地で行なって来たのと同じように、現在進行中の事例を西洋でも研究できるとすれば、私たちの研究は長足の進歩を遂げるはずである。

新しい事例を知らせてほしいとお願いしておきながら矛盾するようであるが、本書では、薬物を使うにせよ瞑想《めいそう》や催眠を利用するにせよ、前世の記憶を意図的に探り出そうとすることにはあえて反対の立場をとりたいと思う。遺憾ながら催眠の専門家の中には、催眠を使えば誰でも前世の記憶を蘇《よみがえ》らせることができるし、それにより大きな治療効果が上がるはずだと主張するか、そう受けとれる発言をしている者もある。私としては、心得違いの催眠ブームを、あるいは、それに乗じて不届きにも金もうけの対象にしている者があるという現状を、特に前世の記憶を探り出す確実な方法だとして催眠が用いられている状況を、何とか終息させたいと考えている。

私からすると最も注目すべきように思える事例は、ほとんどが、西洋文化圏以外の地域で発見されている。そうした事例は、アジアや西アフリカに住む人々や、北アメリカ北西部で部族生活を営んでいる人々の間に多いのである。このように地理的な偏りが見られることにはいくつか理由がある。その理由はまだほとんどつかめていないが、私なりに推定できることを何点か述べておいた。ここでは、それに関連して、二点ほど指摘しておきたいと思う。第一点は、頻発する地域からしか事例が得られていないわけではなく、ヨーロッパや（部族以外の）北米の人々の間からもすばらしい事例がいくつか得られているという事実である。第二点は、西洋で一〇〇年以上にもわたって厳密に研究されて来た、霊姿やテレパシー的印象、テレパシー夢、自覚夢などのような現象と生まれ変わりを思わせる事例とは、主たる特徴が共通しているように思えることである。本書では、こうした共通点に対して繰り返し注目を促しておいた。それにより本書で扱っている事例が、それほどありそうにないわけでも、異国情緒豊かなものでもないことが明らかになり、つまりは信頼に足るものであることがおわかりいただける一助となれば幸いである。

註、参考文献、詳細な事例報告について

本書は、一般向きに書かれている。とはいえ、読者にも二通りのタイプがあると思う。忙しい生活を送っておられる方々は、註《ちゅう》や文献にはひとつも当たらずに読まれるであろうし、つまらない註などのために六分の一ほどの代金をむだ払いさせられたとうらめしく思われるかもしれない。しかし私としては、本書をお読みくださっただけでは、知識欲が満たされるどころかかえって刺激されるような方々にも関心をお寄せいただきたいと願っている。詳細な註や参考文献はこのような方々のお役に立つことを願って付されたものである。なお、註と参考文献は巻末にまとめておいた。

原典を突き止めるには

本文中に著者名が挙げられており、その著者に関する註や文献番号が付されていない場合には、巻末の参考文献をご覧いただければ、著者名のアルファベット順に文献が列挙されているので、探し求める原典が突き止められるはずである。

詳細な事例報告の掲載誌や掲載書を知るには

詳細な事例報告をお読みになりたい場合には、（その事例が既に発表されているものであれば）巻末の事例一覧表をご覧になればおわかりいただけるようになっている。この一覧表には、

前世を生きたという（あるいはごく一部には、人からそう言われている）人々の（苗字《みょうじ》ではなく）名前が、五十音順に列記されている。

謝　辞

大変な犠牲を払って私の研究にご協力くださった数多くの有能な方々に対しては、詳細な事例報告を行なっている拙著の中で既に謝意を表している。その方々の芳名をもう一度ご披露申しあげる代わりに、ここでは、最近の実地調査や本書の準備段階でご協力いただいた方々のお名前を掲げ、感謝申しあげたいと思う。

まず、最近の実地調査に当たり格別のご助力をいただいた、リタ・カストレン（フィンランド）、ドウ・ニン・アエ（ビルマ）、ニコラス・イベクウェ（ナイジェリア）、ティッサ・ジャワルデネ（スリランカ）、マディ・ムアカサ（レバノン）、サトワント・パスリチャ（インド）、ゴドウィン・サマララトネ（スリランカ）、ニサブ・シロラサ（タイ）、ウ・ウィン・マウン（ビルマ）の各氏に感謝したい。また、カン・ポラト氏（トルコ）には、同国の事例に関する情報をお寄せいただいた。

本書の一部ないし数章をお読みいただいたうえ、貴重なご助言をたまわった私の同僚や友人である、カルロス・アルバラード、ジョン・ベロフ、スチュワート・エデルスタイン、ブライアン・ゴッドウィン、ニコラス・マクリーン＝ライス、ジョージ・オーウェン、ジェイムズ・

ホイートリーの各氏にも深謝したい。以上の方々のおかげで、本書の誤りをかなり正すことができたが、それでもまだ誤りが残っているとすれば、少なくともその一部は、この方々のご指摘に私が全面的に従わなかったゆえである。

現在およびかつての研究助手の方々からも、大変貴重なご助言をいただいた。ここに、キャロリー・ワーナー、スーザン・アダムス、エミリー・ウィリアムズ・クックの各氏に感謝するものである。特にクック女史には、原稿を最初から最後まで二回もお読みいただいている。拙稿をきれいに――しかも何度も繰り返し――タイプしてくださったエリザベス・バードさんとパトリシア・エスツさんにも感謝申しあげたい。

エルシヴィア・サイエンス出版（生物医学課）には、発行誌からの、またアメリカ商務省技術情報局には、L・L・ワシリエフの論文からの引用許可をいただいた。

本書の草稿は大半が、安息休暇《サバテイカル》でケンブリッジ大学ダーウィン・カレッジに滞在している間に練りあげられたものである。その際、格別の便宜を図ってくださった同カレッジ理事長および理事各位にも深く感謝したい。

私が本書を書き上げるため、本来なら一緒に過ごせるはずの時をあきらめてくれた妻のマーガレットに、心を込めて本書を捧《ささ》げたいと思う。

最後に、私の研究を助成してくださったバーンスタイン兄弟超心理学健康財団に深甚なる謝意を表したい。

第1章　序論

本書が、生まれ変わりを直接扱ったものではないことを知ったら、がっかりされる方が一部におられるかもしれない。本書は、前世を記憶していると主張する子どもたちを対象にしている。このような子どもたちの体験を研究して行けば結局、生まれ変わりについて多少なりともわかるようになるかもしれないのである。しかし、そうであるとすればその前に、このような子どもたちがもっている記憶らしきものを最も適切に説明できるのは、生まれ変わりという考え方であることが確信できているはずである。

以下、こうした記憶について書く場合、「らしきもの」とか「とされるもの」などの修飾語を時おり省略するが、それは本書を読みやすいものにするためであり、こうした事例によって浮き彫りになる肝腎《かんじん》な論点を避けて通ろうとするためではない。しかし、そうした子どもの目から見れば、自分が身をもって味わっている前世の記憶は、現世で生まれてから後に起こった出来事に関する記憶と同じくらい現実的に（同じくらい本物の記憶のように）感じられるのである。このような子どもが前世について話し、それが事実と一致するのは、ある種の記憶に基づいているからである。[*1] こうした子どもを観察する者は、それが前世の記憶なのか、それとも他の方法で得られたものなのかを明らかにしなければならない。この点を念頭に置いていただければ、本書の表題が誤解を招くものではないことがおわかりいただけよう。

生まれ変わりそのものについて本書でほとんどふれない理由は、もうひとつある。私は、二〇〇〇例を超える事例から得たデータをもとに本書を執筆しているが[*2]、それは、これまで地球上で生活してきた何十億という数の人間と比べるとわずかなものにすぎない。これほど少数の事例から一般化を行なうことは、たとえこのような事例をすべて生まれ変わりの実例として解釈するのが最も妥当だと（実際にはそうではないが）確信しているとしても、軽率に過ぎるであろうし、各事例の間にはかなり類似性が見られるとはいえ、世間一般の人たちの生活をそのまま反映していると言うことはできない。事実、後ほど各例に頻発する特徴を紹介する中でおわかりいただけるはずであるが、この種の子どもたちが記憶に残している生涯は、平凡なものではない。それは、これまで事例を収集する際にやむをえず無計画な方法をとらざるをえなかったこととはあまり関係がない。前世の記憶は、ごく一部の人間にしか起こらない珍しい体験だということも（その理由は、せいぜいのところようやくわかり始めたところであるが）、これまで集めた事例が全人類の代表例とはならない理由である。

私は、生まれ変わりそのものについて書いているわけではないが、私の研究および本書の主題は、少なくとも時おりは生まれ変わりが起こるかどうか、という問題である。この問題は、結局、人間の人格（ないしその要素）が死後にも生存を続け、その後——おそらくは、何らかの非物質界にしばらく留《とど》まった後——別の肉体と結びつくかどうか、という問題に帰着する。生まれ変わりという形態は、人間の人格が死後にも生存を続けるとして考えられる唯一の様式ではない。これは、大半のキリスト教徒やイスラム教徒が考えているような様態ではないのである。また、生まれ変わりは、この可能性を科学的に検討する研究者がこれまで思い描いてきた死後生存の唯一の様式でもない[3]。

現在の科学者はほとんどが、人間の人格が死後に残るとも考えていなければ、残りうるとも考えていない[4]。死後の生命の存在を信じている科学者は、ほぼ全員が、特定の宗教の教えに由来する信仰に基づいてこうした存在を信じており、その大半は、人間の死後生存の問題が科学的に研究できる可能性に対して否定的な態度を示すであろう。ところが、今から一〇〇年少し前、イギリスの一部の科学者や学識経験者は、一般の科学で通常用いられている方法により、データを収集、分析することを通じて、死後生存を裏づける証拠が得られる可能性の検討を始めたのである。このような先駆者およびその後継者たちは、さまざまな方面からこの種のデータを手に入れている。本書で検討する事例は、死後生存問題を研究する者なら当然検討の対象とすべき情報群の一角をなしているにすぎないのである[5]。

先ほど、人間の人格ということを問題にしたが、『オクスフォード英語辞典』では、「人格」という言葉を次のように定義している。「事物とは異なる一個の人間としての特性、特質、ないしは、そうした人間であるという事実。……一個の人間としての個人的存在、現実の存在、こういう人間がいる、ないしはいたという事実、その人らしさ。……他人とは異なった当人らしさを生み出すそうした特性ないしその集合体」。この定義の冒頭の部分は、この問題の肝腎な点を突いている。人間は物体なのであろうか。それとも、それ以上のものなのであろうか。もし物体「以上のもの」があるとすれば、「それ以上のもの」は、それが何であれ、死後にも残りうるのであろうか。人間の意識の流れが死後にも存続するかどうかは、直接には当人にしかわからない。残された者は、故人が生存を続けていても、その間接的な証拠しか得ることはできない。特定の人物が死後にも生存を続けていると言うためには、どのような基準が必要なのであろうか。先ほどの定義の中の「その人らしさ」とはどういう意味なのであろうか。哲学者はこれまで、何がその人らしさのもとになっているかについて、かなりの議論を繰り返してきた。[*6] その結果、大半の哲学者は、各人の一生はそれぞれ独自なものなので、その記憶も独特なものであろうし、したがって、記憶が持続していることを裏づける証拠こそ、特定の人物が肉体の死後にも生存を続けていることを示す最も有力な――かつ、おそらくは唯一の――指標になるであろう、という点で意見の一致を見ているようである。

そのような理由から、誰かが死後にも生存を続けているのを示す証拠を探すということはふつう、その人物の記憶が持続している証拠の研究を意味していた。とはいえ、検討の対象となる情報は、過去の出来事の単なるイメージ記憶を超えたものでなければならない。この種の記憶はビデオテープに保存することが可能な種類のものであるが、ビデオテープやビデオデッキは人格とは言えないからである。人格の概念には、感情や目的が含まれていなければならないし、少なくともある程度は意識も含まれている必要がある。夜眠り翌朝目覚める時のように、死後に一時的な空白があるとしてもかまわないであろうが、死後に抱くことになる意識が、生存中に慣れ親しんだものとは大幅に異なるとしても、私たちが意識と呼ぶものが回復しない限り、死後に生存を続けていると考えるべきではないと思う。

前世を記憶する子どもたちから得られた、死後生存を裏づける証拠は、たとえば死者の霊姿から得られた証拠のような、他の形態の死後生存の証拠とは、ある重要な点で異なっている。霊姿の場合には、故人が何らかの形で生存を続けており、それが当人である証拠をこの世の人間に伝えることができる状態にあるらしいのに対して、前世を記憶しているとする子どもの場合には、生身の人間が過去世を生きたことを主張するのである。その子どもが前世の自分だとしている死者にまで遡《さかのぼ》って研究するよりも、死者から存命中の人物に下って研究する方が、いくつかの点で容易である。では次に、私がそう考える理由を説明することにしよう。

　これまでの証拠から考える限り、死者は（少なくとも、その霊的存在の証拠が得られる段階までは[*7]）、死自体による結果としてはそれほどの人格変化は起こさないのかもしれない。それに対して、死後の人格が新しい肉体と結びつく場合には、感覚器官もまだあまり発達していない、以前よりも小さく新しい肉体という枠の中に収められるので、かなりの順応を迫られる。さらに、この新しい肉体は、別の家族のもとに生まれるのかもしれず、そのため、その家族に対しても適応しなければならないので、必然的にさらなる軌道修正が必要となるであろう。子どもが、前世の記憶を人に伝えられるようになるまでには、本人の人格に内在する別の要素が多かれ少なかれ混じり合い、研究者がそれぞれを識別しにくい状態になってしまっていることであろう。そのため、このような子どもたちから得られる、死者が生存を続けていることを裏づける証拠は、たとえば、死者が臨終時の状態のまま霊姿《アパリション》として現われた場合に得られる証拠と比べると――少なくとも本当にその故人にまちがいないかどうかという点については――評価判定が難しい。霊姿の真偽の判断に際してはいくつかの解釈を考慮しなければならないが、少なくとも目撃される人物像は全身像であり、しかもはっきりと認められるものである場合が（必ずしもそうではないにせよ）少なくない[*8]。しかし、前世を記憶している子どもの場合はそれとは事情が異なっている。子どもたちが語る、断片的なものでしかないことも多い情報をもとに、研究者は、切れぎれの情報をつなぎ合わせたものから、他の誰でもない特定の人物がまちがいなく浮かび上がってくるかどうかを明確にしなければならないのである。特定の人物を同定する場合の基準という重要な問題については、後ほど説明することにしよう。

　私たちがこれまで入手している生まれ変わりの証拠からすると、生きている人間には――おそらくは人間以外の動物にも――心（ないし、そう呼びたければ魂）というものがあり、この世ではそのおかげで活動でき、死後にも生存を続けることができるということのようである。大半の生物学者は、こういった考え方に生気論[*9]という烙印《らくいん》を押し、そのような考え方は何十年も昔に信頼するに足りないとして却下されているではないか、と断言することであろう。しかしながら、新しい証拠からすると（また、無視されてきた昔の証拠の検討によってすら）、生気論が信頼に足るものであることがあらためてわかるかもしれないのである。これまで蓄積されてきた死後生存の証拠を、他の分野の科学者が先入観抜きに検討するとすれば、（人間は肉体以外の何ものでもないというような）憶説を除いて失うものはないと思う。少なくとも私が考える生まれ変わりは、進化論や遺伝学の知識を無にするものではない。とはいえ、生まれ変わりが事実であれば、進化には、（生物学的なものと個人的なものの）二通りの流れが存在し、この世に生を受けている間はそのふたつが相互に作用し合うことになろう。いかなる形で作用し合うのかについては、現段階ではあまり思い描くこともできないが、本書の後半で、そうした過程について若干の推定を試みるつもりである。

　生まれ変わりという考え方は、個々の人間がそれぞれ独自なものであることを理解する一助となる。遺伝学者は、ひとりの人間のもつ遺伝子群と本人が置かれている環境（という、大半の遺伝学者が現在認めている要素）の相互作用によって造り上げられた、この世に生を受けている人間を指して、表現型《フェノタイプ》という言葉を用いる。生物学者の大半は、一卵性双生児の場合ですら、それぞれの表現型が独自のものであることを認識している。そして、遺伝と環境の影響によって、こうした独自性が最終的に説明できると信じているのである。遺伝子の配列には、ほとんど無限とも言える組み合わせが考えられる。そこには、配偶子（受胎の際に結合する雄性および雌性細胞）の中の染色体のランダムな分布や、染色体間の遺伝子の組換え、時たま生ずる遺伝子の突然変異などが関係している。加えて、環境にも相当の違いがある。双生児の場合でも、多少なりとも環境が異なっており、この点についてある研究者は、かつて、接合型（シャム）双生児ですら、どちらかが先にドアを通らなければならないのだから、全く同じ環境に置かれているわけではない、と述べている。[*10]

　とはいえ、一般的には妥当に思える考え方でも、それにまつわる観察事実をあらゆる角度から検討すると、不十分であることがわかるかもしれない。現実には、遺伝子の変異と環境の影響というふたつの要素だけでは満足に説明できない独特の特徴を備えている人たちも一部にある。生まれ変わりという考え方は、第三の要因として考慮に入れるだけの価値があるということである。

人間が、遺伝子を混ぜ合わせることにより造り上げられた、ジャック・モノーの言葉を借りれば「偶然と必然」の産物であるなら、個々の人間は生まれながらにして均質ではないという問題に答えることはできないであろう。また、よく切り混ぜたトランプを配られたとしても、札は自分にとってよいようにも悪いようにも使えるではないか、と言ってみたところで、ほとんど抗弁にはならない。生まれながらにして盲目の者は、手札が何かを見ることもできないのである。生まれ変わりを信じても、先天的な全盲が即座に回復するわけではないが、本書で概説する研究をもとに考えれば、特定の人物がなぜ全盲状態で生まれてくるのかを、現在考えられている通常の解釈以上に明確に理解することができるかもしれない。ここで答えなければならない肝腎《かんじん》な疑問点は、誰かがなぜ全盲状態で生まれるのかということではなく、他の人間はそうではないのに、なぜ特定の人間が生まれながらにして全盲なのか、ということである。この疑問に答えるには、この世に生を受けている間、人間は肉体と結びついており、その人物（ないし人格）と肉体とは別物として区別できると考えなければならない。

また、もし生まれ変わりという現象が存在するとすれば、先天的に全盲の者も来世では視力が得られるという希望が十分もてることになる。生まれ変わりの証拠を批判する者は、これまで、この考え方にはいたずらに希望を抱かせる測面があることを指摘し、私たちが得ている証拠は、人間の願望充足的な考え方に由来するものにすぎないとして、こうした証拠を無視してきた。このような反対論は、人間が望むものはまちがっているはずだ、という誤った考え方を前提にしている。人間は、自分が信じたいものを信ずるように言われた時の方が、逆の場合よりも説得に乗りやすいかもしれない。そうであるとしてもやはり、私たちが信じたがるものは事実かもしれないのである。ある考え方が正しいかまちがっているかを厳密に検討する際には、その考え方が人間の願望を強めるか打ち砕くかとは無関係にその検討を行なわなければならない。

そのことを別にしても、私が研究してきた事例の中には、情報提供者が自らの信仰や願望とは正反対の証言を行なっているものもある。生まれ変わりという現象を信じていない家族や、特定の前世を記憶しているという子どもの主張をどちらかと言えば受け入れない家族のもとに生まれた子どもが、そのひとつの例である。この点についても、後ほど述べることにしたい。

次に、大半の方々にはなじみが薄いと思われるので、本書で用いる用語や私なりの用法について明確にしておきたいと思う。そのついでに、少々脱線するが、日常生活の中で起こるテレパシーの実例をいくつかお話ししておこう。この種の事例を多少なりともご存知の方なら、前世を記憶しているという子どもたちの事例をさらに的確に判断していただけるであろう。しかるのちに、本書の構成を簡単に説明するつもりである。

心霊研究で用いられる用語

本書で紹介するのは、心霊研究あるいは、場合によっては超心理学と呼ばれる科学分野で研究対象としている事例である。心霊研究という用語にしても超心理学という用語にしても、人間（および、おそらくは動物）の五感や筋肉活動に関する、現在の知識では説明できない現象の研究を指す言葉としては不十分である。十九世紀末に（ドイツで）初めて使われた超心理学という用語は特に不満足である。この領域で研究を行なっている大半の科学者が、物理学や生物学とのつながりを、心理学とのつながりと同じくらい重要と考えているのに対して、超心理学という表現では、この分野と心理学との結びつきのみが強調されてしまうからである。さらに、この言葉は、心理学者が研究対象としている現象に見られる（と心理学者が考えたがる）ような法則性は見られない現象であることを暗に意味している（あるいは、そうした現象を指し示すようになっている）からでもある。この分野で研究を行なっている科学者たちは、こうした現象にも法則性があるが、現代の物理学や生理学の中で観察されるものとは異なる法則に従っているのではないかと考えている。それぞれ別個に発生した事例の多くに共通する特徴が頻繁に見られることからしても、このような考え方は多少なりとも裏づけられる。

　超心理学という言葉には、不満足な点がもうひとつある。この言葉には、研究対象となる現象（および、そうした現象を研究している科学者）を、他の科学的研究から切り離してしまう傾向があるのである。歴史的には、いつの時代でもそうだったわけではない。現代の科学は、ごく最近に発生した偏狭な営みにすぎない。西暦一六〇〇年頃の西洋に興ったわけであるが、それまでヨーロッパでは（西洋以外の大半の文化圏では今日でもそうであるが）、現在超常的なものとされている現象が、疑問の余地なく受け入れられていた。とはいえ、変わった現象ではないとされていたわけではないし、こうした現象の個々の報告に疑念がもたれなかったわけでもない。ここで言おうとしているのは、西洋の科学者の間に、さらには西洋の教育を受けた多くの者の間にその後広まった、この種の現象に対する全般的な懐疑主義がこの時代には発揮されなかった、ということにすぎない。たとえばデカルトは、遠く離れたふたりの人間の間に起こる思念の伝達についてそれとなくふれているし、やはり現代科学の創立者であるベーコンも、本人言うところの「思念の束」の実験や、サイコロを投げて「想像力」が結果に及ぼす影響を見る実験を提案している。[11] 十九世紀末になるまで、現代風に言えば心霊研究に関心を抱いた科学者たちはまだ、心理学者と対等につきあい、同一の学会（当時の言葉では学術会議）に出席していた。こうした科学者やその後継者たちがどのような経緯で法を犯す者とされ、追放されるに至ったのかについては、来世紀に執筆される科学史の一章で扱われることになるかもしれない。ここでは、この分野で研究を行なっている大半の科学者は、自分たちの科学分野が最終的に他の科学と再結合することを願い、かつ期待している、という事実を述べるに留《とど》めよう。そうなった暁には、現在用いられている用語は廃語となることであろう。

しかしながら、当面の間、私たちは、未《いま》だほとんど解明されていないにしてもまちがいなく起こっている現象を指す言葉として先人たちが用いた用語を、できる限り的確に使わなければならない。ではここで、本書に頻出する若干の用語を定義しておこう。[12] 五感による作用でも筋力による作用でも説明できない場合、その体験や出来事は「超常的」という形容詞を冠して表現される。現在、超常的な感覚体験は超感覚的知覚と呼ばれているが、私個人としては、超常的認知とか、（もっと適切な呼び方としては）超常的気づきと呼びたいと思う。超常的感覚体験は、通常の伝達手段の対極にある。通常の伝達手段とは、外界からの情報が既知の感覚器官を介して、特に文字を読んだり、物を見たり、音声を聞いたりすることによって人間の心に到達するあらゆる伝達経路のことである。

　超感覚的知覚は、テレパシーや透視によって起こる。テレパシーという言葉は、心と心の間に起こる伝達を指して用いられ、読心術や思念伝達という昔の用語に代わって使われるようになった言葉である。透視という言葉は、他者の心を介することなく行なわれる（通常は物体に関する）超感覚的知覚を意味している。[*13]テレパシーと透視は、その時点で起こっている事象に関する情報を得ることであるが、超感覚的知覚には、他にもふたつの種類がある。未来に起こる、推定不能な出来事を知る予知（あるいは超常的予見）と過去の出来事を超常的に知る後知である。

　偶発的にであれ実験的にであれ、超感覚的知覚を体験する者は、受信者や体験者と呼ばれる。また、受信者が情報を得る相手は発信者と呼ばれるが、標的人物という言葉が当てられる場合もある。しかし発信者という言葉では十分ではない。この言葉には、本人が積極的に働きかけたという響きがある。そういう場合もないわけではないが、特に積極的な役割を演ずるでもなく、テレパシーが起こったことに気づかない場合もあるからである。

肉体のない状態でなお生存を続けるとされる故人の心から発せられたと思《おぼ》しき通信を受けることができる、という者も一部にある。こうした能力をもつ者は霊媒ないしは霊能者と呼ばれ、霊媒や霊能者を通じて交信してくるとされる死者は交信者と呼ばれる。本書では、こうした霊界通信について折々ふれるつもりである。

また、霊的ないし心霊的という用語も、超常的ないし超心理学的という用語の同義語に近いものとして随所で使うことになる。こうした用語は、特に、肉体のない人間が生者や胎児に影響を及ぼす可能性を検討する中で用いる予定である。

超常現象の研究法は二通りある。偶発的に起こる現象を観察するか、そうした現象を目撃した人物から証言を求める方法がひとつであり、もうひとつは、実験条件下で超常現象を誘発させようとする方法である。実験という方法により科学者は、実験条件を管理し、結果を解釈する際に、何らかの超常的作用があったとする以外の説明が確実に排除できるような方向に条件を変えて行くことができる。偶発例の研究では、ほとんどの場合、そのようなコントロールはできない。研究者が何らかの現象を、それが起こっている最中に自分の眼で観察できることもたまにはあるが、たいていの場合は、現場に到着する以前に起こった出来事を、できる限り正確に組み立てなければならない。このような状況は満足の行くものではないが、この領域で研究を行なう科学者は、もし偶発例の研究を見合わせるようなことをすれば、最も重要度の高い現象群を捨て去ることになり、貧弱な研究しかできなくなってしまう。偶発的超常体験は大半が、人の死のように人生の重大事に関係しており、実験室では絶対とも言えるほど起こらないものなのである。本書に登場する事例をご覧になれば、この点についておわかりいただけるであろうが、偶発例全般についても同じことがおわかりになるはずである。実験状況と同じくらい厳密な形で生まれ変わりを研究するのは意味があるであろうが、そのようなことはできないとして研究を放棄してしまうのはまちがいであろう。些《さ》細《さい》な点に正確であるよりは、重要な事象について確実なことを知ることの方が意味があると私は考える。

ここで読者の方々に申しあげておかなければならないことがある。人と人との間で五官を介することなく思考内容が伝達できる（さらには、他の事柄を知ることもできる）と思われるかどうかを、（まだはっきりさせておられなければ）はっきりさせる必要があるということである。それは、本書で扱われている事例を解釈するに当たって、テレパシーが（おそらくは透視と組み合わされて）、生まれ変わりに代わる重要な説明概念になるためである。後ほどふれるが、生まれ変わり型事例には五、六通りの解釈が考えられており、事例によってはいずれも最善の説明になるかもしれない。とはいえ、比較的有力な証拠が得られている事例の大半については、(1)証言に重大な欠陥がある、(2)前世の記憶があると主張する者は実はテレパシーや透視の能力をもっている、(3)生まれ変わりが実際に起こった、の三通りの解釈を考えればよい。超常的認知（テレパシーおよび透視）の存在を信じておられない方々には、選択肢が限定されてしまうことがおわかりいただけるであろう。

もし読者の方々が、テレパシーや透視のような能力の存在についてご自分の態度を決めかねており、しかも私と同じ性分をおもちになっておられるのであれば、身内や周囲、あるいは大学教授の言葉に従うのではなく、自分で証拠を検討してから態度をはっきりさせたいと思われるであろう。そのための資料なら十二分にある。この問題に関する信頼性の高い図書は、中程度の大きさの部屋の三面に並んだ本棚にぎっしり詰まるほど大量に出版されている。それに対して、信頼性に欠ける図書は、宮殿のような大邸宅の全室に設置された本棚を埋め尽くすほどの数にのぼるであろうが、二、三のしっかりした入門書や概説書をご覧いただければ、その種の図書で時間を浪費せずにすませることができる[*14]。

テレパシーや霊姿の実例

私見によれば、テレパシーの実在を裏づける最も重要な証拠は、日常生活の中で時おり起こる珍しい体験から得られるものなので、この種の出来事に対するご自分の姿勢を明確にしていただけるように、若干の事例を紹介しよう。

第一例は、一八六二年にシャイローの戦いで捕虜になった南軍の兵士の体験である。シカゴ郊外にあったダグラス収容所で捕虜生活を送っていたこの兵士は、ある幻を見て、後にそれについて次のように述べている。

> 次の日（四月一六日）……私は仲間たちがいる方へ行って、友人のウィルクス君の傍らに横になった。建物の半分が見渡せるような位置だった。向かいでトランプに興じている連中

のことをウィルクス君に話して聞かせていると、急に、首筋が何かに撫《な》でられるような感じがして、一瞬のうちに気を失った。次の瞬間、〔ウェールズの〕トレメアション村やヒラドッグの丘の、草が一面に生えた斜面がはっきり見えた。ブリンベラのミヤマガラスの森の上を漂っているみたいな感じだった。マリー伯母《おば》さんの寝室に向かってスーッと飛んで行った。伯母は床に就いており、今にも死にそうな病気のように見えた。私は寝台の傍らに立ち、頭を下に向けて自分の身体を眺めながら、伯母の別れの言葉を聞いた。その言葉は、悔やんでいるように聞こえた。本来の自分と比べると、あるいは自らの理想像と比べると、思いやりが足りなかったことで後悔の念に駆られているようだった。私はその青年がこう言うのを聞いた。「伯母さんのおっしゃることはその通りだと思います。でも、伯母さんが悪いわけでも、ぼくが悪いわけでもないんです。ぼくにはよくしていただきましたし、親切にもしていただきました。もっと親切にしてやりたいと思ってらっしゃったこともわかってました。でも、事情が事情でしたから、結局ああいう形にならざるをえなかったんです。ぼくも伯母さんのことを心から大切にしたいと思っていたんですけど、伯母さんに叱られるんじゃないかとか、傷つくようなことを言われるんじゃないかとか思って、口には出さなかったんです。そういう気持でお別れしたんだと思います。お悔やみになることはありません。伯母さんはぼくに対して必要なことはきちんとしてくださいましたよ。それに、お子さんのこともありましたでしょう。子どもさんたちの面倒を見なければいけなかったじゃないですか。そのあとぼくにあったことは、神のご意志で決まっていて、どうしようもなかったんです。さようなら、伯母さん」。

手を差し伸べると、死が迫っている伯母の細く長い手を握りしめたようだった。さようならと呟《つぶや》く声が聞こえると、すぐに私は目を覚ました。

私には、ほんの一瞬、目をつむっていただけのように思えた。私は、同じ姿勢で横になっていた。向かいの連中は相変わらずトランプをしているし、ウィルクス君も同じ位置にいた。

「いったい何があったんだ」と私は尋ねた。

ウィルクス君はそれに対して、「何も起こりようはないだろ。どうしてそんなこと聞くんだ。さっき俺と話をしたばかりじゃないか」と答えた。

「ええっ、俺はまたずいぶん長い間眠ってた気がするよ」。

翌一八六二年四月一七日、伯母のマリーは、ヒュノン・ベウノ〔ウェールズの本人宅〕で亡くなった。

ここで若干の補足をしておく必要がある。この中に登場する伯母は、兵士が昔、孤児になり住む家を失った時、養子として本人を引きとっている。自分の家族のことで既に手いっぱいだったにもかかわらず、責任感からそうしたのである。ところが意に反して、その子をあまりかわいがってやれなかったことで伯母は後悔しているのであり、そのために伯母の死に際してこの兵士がお別れを言いに行くという体験をしたように思われる。

次の事例では、一七九九年にスウェーデンを旅行していた若いスコットランド人が受信者になっている。イェーテボリーからノルウェイに向けて出発した青年の一行は、一日中行進して、一二月一九日午前一時頃になってようやく宿屋に到着した。一行はそこで一泊することにした。この若者は日記に次のように書いている。

一二月一九日……昨日の寒さで疲れたので、床に就く前に温かい風呂《ふろ》に入れたのはうれしかった。またここでは、非常に驚くべきことがわが身に起こった。あまりに驚くべきことなので、最初から全部ここに書き記しておかなければならないほどだ。高校を卒業してから私は、一番の親友のG君と一緒に、〔エジンバラ〕大学の講義に出席するようになった。神学の講義はなかったが、私たちはよく散歩しながら、霊魂の不滅やあの世のことをはじめ、重々しい問題についていろいろ論じ合ったり想像したりしていた。この問題およびその可能性は、（後で書くように、幽霊が徘徊《はいかい》することではなく、死人が生きている人間の眼前に姿を現わすことを言っているのだが）おおいに想像力をかき立てる対象となった。それから私たちは、どちらか一方が死んだ場合には残った方の前に姿を見せること、そうすれば私たちが抱いている「死後の生命」に対する疑問も氷解する、という趣旨のとり決めをふたりで血書することまでしている。大学を出てから、G君はインドへ行き、そこで官吏になった。G君はほとんど手紙をよこさなかったので、二、三年もするとG君のことはほとんど忘れてしまった。そのうえ、G君の家族はエジンバラとはほとんど関係がないので、G君の家族のことを見聞きするチャンスもほとんどなかったし、G君のことを家族から知らされることもなかった。そのため、学生時代の親近感もすっかり失《う》せてしまい、G君の存在もほとんど忘れてしまっていた。先ほど書いたように、私は温かい風呂に入り、湯舟につかっていた。つい今しがたまで凍えるような寒さの中にいたのに、今は、ぬくもりに浸りながらまわりを見回し、もうそろそろ風呂からあがるつもりだったので、脱いだ服を載せてある椅子の方に目をやった。すると、その椅子にG君が坐《すわ》っており、静かに私の方を見ていた。どんなふうに風呂からあがったのかわからないが、気がついてみると、床の上にペタンと坐り込んでいた。

G君によく似た幽霊は、あるいはそれが何であれ、もうどこかへ消え失せてしまっていた。その幻を見たショックがあまりに大きかったので、そのことを口にする気にも、スチュアート君〔同行者〕に話す気にもなれなかった。でも、その印象はあまりに生々しく、容易には拭《ぬぐ》い去れなかったし、心があまりに大きく揺り動かされたので、一二月一九日という日付とともに、その一部始終を、まだ鮮明なうちにここに書き留《とど》めておく。私が眠ったのはまちがいない。しかし、あれほどはっきりと目の前に出てきたものが夢とは、私には露ほども思えない。だが、G君とは何年も音信不通になっていたし、G君を想い出すようなきっかけも全くなかった。私たちがスウェーデンを旅行している間には、G君やインドに関係があることはもちろん、G君やご家族と間接的に関係ありそうなことも一切なかった。私はすぐに、昔G君と話し合った内容や取り交わした約束を思い出した。G君が死んだことはまちがいないし、G君が私の前に現われたのは、あの世が実在する証拠をG君が私に見せにきたという思いを心の中から追い払うこともできなかった。けれども、その間ずっと私は、全て夢だということで納得していた。それに、その感じがあまりに鮮明で、しかもその鮮明さが頭に焼きついて離れないため、そのことを人に話す気にもなれなかったし、間接的にほのめかすようなこともできなかった。身支度を整え、早く出発することで皆の意見が一致したため、朝六時までには支度が整った。それから、早目の朝食をとった。

後年、この受信者は、自らの体験談を活字にした際、次のような補足を行なっている。

エジンバラに戻ってまもなく、インドから手紙が届いた。G君の死を知らせる手紙であった。そしてそこには、一二月一九日に死亡したことが書かれていたのである。何という偶然の一致であろうか。だが、毎夜頭の中を通り過ぎる大変な数の夢を考えてみると、夢の内容と出来事とが一致する比率は、偶然で起こる確率から考えられるよりは低いであろうし、それほど高いものでもないであろう。

次の例は、子どもの頃、母親の目の前に霊姿として現われた男性（ロシア人）の事例であるが、ここでは本人の言葉をそのまま引用しよう。

当時、私は一二歳で、高校二年に進級したばかりだった。私はプスコフからあまり離れていない山小屋に出かけた。重い肝臓病をもつ母は、カルルスバート（現在のチェコ・ボヘミアのカルロヴィ・ヴァリ）まで父と湯治に出かけており、私は弟妹とともに叔母《おば》たちのもとに預けられていたのだった。私たち子どもは、ふだんよりも行動の自由が与えられ、その自由を満喫していた。ある日の夕方、木に登って洪水を逃れたというグラント将軍の息子たちをまねした冒険ごっこをやろうということになった。よじ登る木には、川の上にせり出した岸辺の大きな柳を選んだ。私がパガネルの役をすることになったが、役になり切ったあまり、パガネルと同じように木から川に落ちたのだが、泳げないため溺《おぼ》れ始めた。かろうじて枝をつかんだおかげで、切り立った岸にようやくの思いで辿《たど》りついた。弟と妹は、この出来事を木の上から凍りついた面持ちで眺めていた。叱られることはまちがいないので、そのことが私たちには特に心配の種だった。この冒険を叔母たちに隠し通すことはできなかった。私はずぶ濡《ぬ》れになっていたし、白いひさしのついた真新しい学帽が――誇りと愛着の対象が――川に流されてしまったからだ。家に戻ると、若い叔母たちは同情して、この件についてはカルルスバートに知らせないことにしてくれた。（叔母たちも、そのことを気にしていた。）叔母たちは、もう二度とそんなことをしないよう私たちに約束させた。ところが、母はやって来るなり、この出来事の一部始終を物語り、例の柳の木を指差したうえ、学帽が堰《せき》まで流されたことなどをことごとく言い当てた。その時の私たちの驚きや狼狽《ろうばい》ぶりはご想像いただけるであろう。母は、カルルスバートでことの一部始終を夢で見て、とり乱し、涙を流しながら目を覚まし、子どもたちの無事を問い合わせる電報をすぐに打ってほしいと父に頼んだ。父は、電報を打つ代わりに、病気の母を宥《なだ》めるため、滞在先のホテルの応接室で三〇分ほど昼寝をしてから部屋に戻り、母には電報を打って来たと嘘をついたのであった。

次の事例でも、直接に関係した人物の言葉をそのまま引用しよう。本人が遭遇した事故を、遠方にいる姉がどのように察知したかについて本人が書いた報告である。

> 一九歳の〔ドイツの〕学生の時、ヴュルツブルク付近で軍事教練中、大事故に遭い、九死に一生を得たことがあった。切り立った峡谷の縁を道路が走っており、そこを通過中に馬が棒立ちになってひっくり返り、そのため私は道に倒れ込んで砲架の車輪のほぼ真下に入ってしまった。その大砲は六頭の馬で引っ張っていたが、間一髪のところで止まってくれたので、恐ろしい思いをしたことを除けばかすり傷ひとつ負わず、車輪の下から這《は》い出すことができた。この事故が起こったのは、うららかな春の日の朝方であった。その日の夕方、私は、父から電報を受けとった。無事を問い合わせる電報であった。あとにも先にも私はこの時以外、そのような問い合わせをもらったことはなかった。常日頃、特に仲よくしていた長姉が電報を打たせたのだった。私が事故に遭ったのはまちがいない、といきなり父に向かって口走ったためだという。当時、私の家族はコーブルクに住んでいた。これは、偶発的テレパシーの一例である。私は思念を送り、特に仲のよかった姉がそれを受け止めてくれたのである。

机上の批判者は、以上のような報告に対しては、全く信頼の置けない、頭のおかしな連中の言うことだとして片づけることが少なくない。しかし、これらの実例に関係する人物については、そうした批判は当たらない。先ほど四人の名前を明かさなかったのは、名前を聞いただけで、以上の事例には信憑性《しんぴょうせい》があるとお考えいただきたくなかったからである。では次に、それぞれの報告者の名前を順に掲げることにしよう。イギリスのアフリカ探険家であり、リヴィングストンの〝発見者〟でもあるH・M・スタンリー、一八三〇年にホイッグ党が政権を握った時に大法官を務めた、イギリスの著名な雄弁家であり政治家であったブルーアム卿《きょう》、レニングラード大学で生理学教授を務めたL・L・ワシリエフ、脳波の発見者であるハンス・ベルガーの四人である。[*15]

ベルガーはこの体験に大きな影響を受け、天文学者になる夢をあきらめ、それに代わって、心と物質界との関係の研究に一生を捧《ささ》げる決意をした。そのおかげで私たちは大変な恩恵を蒙《こうむ》ることになったのである。他の三名の場合も、それぞれ内容は異なるが、先の体験によってやはり大きな影響を受けている。ワシリエフは、この体験を、（自ら大きな貢献をすることになった）超心理学に関する著書のひとつに引用しているが、少年時代のテレパシー体験が、後に本人を超心理学研究に向かわせる一因となっているように思われる。とはいえ、以上の体験をしたのは、この方面とは全く無関係の活動を通して世の尊敬を集めた人たちであるため、その言葉は真に傾聴に値することを、私としては特に強調しておきたいと思う。[*16]

懐疑論者はこれまで、当人が死亡した時刻にその霊姿が目撃されるのは偶然ではないかとする主張も行なってきた。初期の心霊研究者はこうした反論にかなりの注意を払い、死者の霊姿が死の時点で偶然に目撃される可能性を丹念に検討し、それを論駁《ろんばく》している。[17]

偶然の一致という論法は、たとえそれがまちがいではないとしても、本人が死亡した時点で夢や霊姿としてその姿が現われたものの、死の詳細な状況まではわからない、という事例にしか当てはまらないはずである。死亡した状況に関係した具体的な情報が（多くの例でそうなのであるが）実際に含まれており、それが受信者の通常の推理能力を超えるものである場合、私たちは、遠方で起こったふたつとない出来事を、同じくふたつとない知覚として受信したと考える。次に、実例を用いてこの点を具体的に説明しよう。この事例の受信者はアグネス・パケットという女性であるが、弟のエドマンド・ダンは一八八九年にシカゴ港で溺死《できし》しているのである。パケットは次のように述べている。

事故の朝、私は、いつもの時間に目を覚ましました。たぶん六時頃だったと思います。その晩はぐっすり眠っておりまして、夢も見ませんでしたし、とび起きるようなこともございませんでした。目が覚めた時は暗い、憂鬱《ゆううつ》な感じで、それを振り切ることはどうしてもできませんでした。朝食後、夫は仕事に出かけて、子どもたちも時間になると、支度をして学校に行きました。私はひとりポツンと家にとり残されたわけですが、そのすぐあと、お茶をいれて飲むことにしました。先ほど申しあげた憂鬱な気分が吹っ切れるんじゃないかと思ったからでした。台所に入って紅茶の缶を下ろしてうしろを振り向くと、目の前に弟のエドマンド（というか弟に瓜《うり》ふたつの幻）が立っていました。一メートルかそこらしか離れていませんでした。この幽霊は、私に背中を向けてと申しますか、一部背中を向けて立っておりまして、前方に倒れ込むところでした。二本のロープかロープの輪が弟の両足に引っかかったはずみで倒れたみたいでした。弟の姿は低い手すりというか舷墻《げんしょう》を越えて消えてしまい、この幻はほんの一瞬で終わりましたが、非常にはっきり見えました。私は持っていた紅茶を落とし、両手で顔を押さえて、「大変だわ、エドが溺れる」と大声をあげました。

　午前一〇時半頃、夫はシカゴから電報を受けとりました。弟の溺死を知らせる電報でした。帰宅した時、夫は、「エドがシカゴの病院に病気で入院してる。今その電報を受けとったところだ」と申しますので、私は、「エドは溺れたのよ、船から落ちるのが見えたのよ」と言いました。それから私は、朝見たことを詳しく話しました。私が見た時、弟は帽子をかぶっておらず、厚ぼったい青の水兵服は着ていましたが上着は羽織っていなかったことや、手すりというか舷墻越しに転落したことを話したわけです。ズボンの裾《すそ》をまくっていたので、白い裏地も目に入りました。また、弟が湖に落ちたあたりに浮かんでいた船がどんな形をしていたかも話しました。

　私は心配症ではありませんし、今お話しした内容にほんの少しでも似た経験をしたことは、あとにも先にも一度もありません。

　また弟は、めまいや失神を起こしやすいたちではありませんでした。

アグネスの夫であるピーター・パケットは、妻の体験および義弟の死について次のような証言を行なっている。

一八八九年一〇月二四日午前一〇時半頃、私はシカゴから電報を受けとった。義弟のエドマンド・ダンがその日未明三時に溺死したことを知らせる電報だった。私は自宅に直行し、その知らせを聞いて妻があまりショックを受けないようにという配慮から、「エドがシカゴの病院に病気で入院してる。今その電報を受けとったところだ」と告げると妻は、「エドは溺れたのよ、船から落ちるのが見えたのよ」と答えた。次いで妻は、先の証言で述べているように、弟がどのような格好をしておりどのような服を着ていたかを話してくれた。また、その船がどんな形をしていたかなどについても教えてくれた。

私はすぐシカゴに向けて発《た》った。現地に到着してみると、妻が話していた船のその部分は、妻はその船を見たことがないにもかかわらず、妻が言ったのと全く同じ形をしていることがわかった。また、その船の乗組員たちは、事故当時、義弟は帽子をかぶっていたと思うとは言ったが、それを除けば、弟の着衣などについて妻が語ったことは事実だと証言してくれた。乗組員の話では、事故が起こる二、三日前にダン君はズボンを買ったが、少し裾が長かったので、膝《ひざ》のあたりまでまくりあげて穿《は》いており、そのため、妻が見たような白い裏地が見えていたという。事故の時に乗り合わせたタグボートの船長は口が重かった。船長の考えでは、義弟はめまいを起こすか失神するかして向こう側に倒れたというが、ある船員（フランク・

イェモント氏）は私の友人に、曳行《えいこう》されている船の舳《へさき》に立っていて事故を目撃したことを話してくれた。それによると、義弟は、妻の言うように引き綱に足をとられて水中に投げ出されたのだという。思うにタグボートの船長は、機関助手（義弟）に引き綱を操作するよう命ずる権限がなかったので、責任を回避するような発言になったのではなかろうか。

義弟は、私の知る限り、めまいや失神を起こしたことはなかった。[*18]

言うまでもなく、人間は一生に一度しか死ぬことができない。したがって、人間が死ぬ時の具体的な状況には人それぞれ独特のものが必ずある。似たような状況で死ぬ者も一部にはあるし、特定の人物が死亡する時の状況がおおまかに予測できる場合もないわけではない。しかしながら、死の状況には一般に相異なる特徴があり、今紹介したエドマンド・ダンの場合にも、そうした特徴が見てとれるように思う。引き綱に足をとられて溺死したというダン氏のような死に方をする者は、いつの時代であれごく少数しかいないはずであるし、ダン氏自身には一度しか起こりえないのである。[*19]ダン氏の姉が、実際に弟が死亡した時間帯に、弟の死の状況と具体的な点で一致する幻を偶然によって見たとはとても考えられない。それよりも、弟の死の状況が（遠方にいる）姉にどういうわけかわかったと考える方が実際的である。姉になぜそれがわかったかは明確ではないが、それだけの理由で、わかったという事実を否定すべきではない。「稀《まれ》な事象や信じ難く思われる報告は、人間の記憶に残らないように抑制されたり否定されたりすべきではない」[*20]。

アグネス・パケットの体験談のようなものは、受信者がその出来事を通常の方法で知った後に、しかも多くの場合は、記憶が不完全なため細かい点がぼやけてしまい、不一致点が完全に忘れ去られてしまう可能性があるほど長い時間が経過した後に初めて記録されるのがふつうなので、こうした体験談は信頼できないのではないか、と指摘する批判者もある。これは、この種の事例（および、本書で主に扱っている子どもの事例）を検討するに当たって真剣に考えなければならない問題である。先のH・M・スタンリーが自らの体験を初めて文章化したのがいつなのかはわからないが、その体験があってから記録に付されるまでには大分時間が経っている可能性があるし、それが活字になったのは、私の知る限り、スタンリーの死亡後の一九〇九年になってからなのである。とはいえ、その出来事を通常の方法で知る前に、受信者（ないしはそれ以外の者）が、超常的な夢や幻らしきものを記録に残している事例はかなりの数にのぼる。ブルーアム卿《きょう》の事例は、友人がインドで死亡したことを知らされる前に、その友人の幻を日記に書き残しているので、この種のものとしては信頼性の高い実例である。

次に、この種の事例で私自身が調査したものを紹介しよう。この事例の受信者であるジョージナ・フィークス夫人は、第二次大戦中戦死した従兄《いとこ》オーウェン・ハウィソンの幻を見た。フィークス夫人は、その幻を見た時、従兄の死がわかった。事実、母親のベアトリス・ハウィソン（フィークス夫人の伯母《おば》）は夫人に、オーウェンの幻を見たかどうか尋ねていた。（家族の中ではフィークス夫人は、この種の体験が多いことで通っていた。）こうした背景があったため夫人は、いつか従兄の幻を見るだろうとは思っていたが、実際に見た幻は予測していたものとは違っていた。その幻の中で夫人は、従兄が自分のシャツの中から青い花をとり出しもう一度引っ込めるという場面を見た。従兄は、このような変わった行動を見せた後、姿を消したのである。フィークス夫人は、この、シャツの中から花をとり出してもう一度戻すという動作は意味があるようには思えなかったが、見えた内容を伯母に話したところ、伯母の話では、その幻はオーウェンの生前にあったある出来事とかなり一致するとのことであった。オーウェン一家はかつてケープタウンに住んでおり、近くのテーブル山に登った時、法律で採取が禁じられている青い花を一輪摘みとり、母親のところへ持って来たことがあった。オーウェンはその花を、シャツの中に隠して自宅に持ち帰ったのである。そしてオーウェンがその花を母親に見せようとした時、不意の来客がふたり、相次いでオーウェン宅を訪れ、ドアをノックした。そのたびにオーウェンは、すばやく花をシャツの下に隠したのであった。フィークス夫人は、この出来事については誰からも聞いていなかった。この幻は、オーウェン・ハウィソンが死後にも生存を続けている証拠として解釈すべきものかどうかははっきりしない。フィークス夫人がハウィソン夫人からテレパシーでこの一件を知った可能性が考えられるからである。（ここにとり上げなかった点も含めて考えると、テレパシーという可能性は私には考えにくい。）とはいえ、本例をここに紹介したのは、オーウェン・ハウィソンが死後にも生存を続けていることを裏づける証拠として解釈できると言いたいからではなく、自分の目撃した幻その他の出来事についてフィークス夫人がハウィソン夫人に宛てて書いた手紙の写しを、私が入手しているからである。その手紙を見ると、その幻と一致する出来事が存在することをハウィソン夫人から聞かされる以前に、フィークス夫人はハウィソン夫人にその体験を知らせる手紙を書いていることがわかる。ハウィソン夫人宛ての手紙には、後で私に話してくれたような細かい点が網羅されているわけではないが、幻として知覚された事柄が、記憶錯誤のため、現実の出来事と実際以上に一致しているかのように情報提供者が思い込んだとは考えられない実例として本例を扱っても差支えないことが、この手紙によって実証されるのである。[*21]

フィークス夫人の事例も含めて、完璧《かんぺき》な事例は存在しない。オーウェンが青い花をシャツの下に隠したという出来事をハウィソン夫人が何らかの形でフィークス夫人に話し、その後ふたりともそれを忘れてしまったのではないか、と考える者もあろうし、ハウィソン夫人の方が、フィークス夫人の幻と実際以上に一致するようにその出来事の記憶を変形してしまったのではないか、と推定する者もあろう。個々の偶発例は、懐疑的な者からいくらでも突っ込まれるという欠点をもっており、これこそ一部の心霊研究者が実験に心血を注ぐ理由である。実験に専念する研究者は、偶発例の研究者よりも批判を受けにくいと思っているのである。

これまで紹介してきた六例のような体験は、どの程度見られるものなのであろうか。本当のところはわからないが、イギリスや合衆国で行なわれた数件の調査によると、(一般人から抽出された)回答者の一〇―一七パーセントが、少なくとも一度は(必ずしも視覚的なものではないが)霊姿の存在を感知する体験をしたと信じている。[*22] それよりもはるかに多いのは、ふつうにはわかりようのない遠方で起こった変わった出来事がわかるなどの超常体験をしたという者である。こうした体験を実際に調べてみると、厳密な検討には耐えられないものが多いことがわかる。検討の結果、受信者の体験およびそれに対応するはずの出来事の一方ないし双方に関する観察や記憶に問題のあることが判明すると、その信憑性《しんぴょうせい》は低下する。[*23] 超常的交信を体験したと思っている者の場合にも、適切な評価が可能なほどには、詳細な情報が体験者から得られないことが多いし、そうした体験をしたいという強い願望などの通常の理由で説明できそうなものも少なくない。たとえば、配偶者に先立たれた者が、自分のそばに相手が来ている気配を感じたり、その姿を見たり、相手から何らかの交信を受けたように感じられたりしても、その体験の大半は、そういった願望や期待で十分説明できるかもしれないのである。[*24] この種の体験の中には、超常的交信の要素が含まれるものもあるのであろうが、その事実を裏づけるに足る証拠が見つかることは稀である。[*25]

以上のような問題点があるため、心霊研究者たちは、信憑性と超常性を区別する必要性を強調するようになる。信憑性とは、その種の体験をした者から（あるいは、そうした体験を調査した者から）得られる事例報告が、「それが本当に起こったとした場合」に想定される事柄に照らしてどこまで正確かということである。実際問題として、そこで起こった出来事を正確に知ることはほとんどできないが、報告の中に誤りや脱落、脚色などがあることがわかったり、それが推測できたりすることもある。そうなると、その事例の信憑性は低いと判断せざるをえなくなる。しかし、信憑性が高いとは言えても、超常的交信が起こったことを裏づける証拠にはならない事例もある。その典型例としては、同じ部屋の中で一緒に坐《すわ》っているふたりが、同じ人物のことや同じ話題についてたまたま同時に考えたような場合があげられる。その体験をふたりはきわめて正確に物語るかもしれないが、五感による接触が相互にあるため、五感の介在なくして交信が行なわれたことを証明することはできない。実際には超常的交信が行なわれていたのかもしれないが、それを実証することもできなければ、そのように考えるよう第三者に求めることもできないのである。

　したがって、超常的要素が含まれる証拠という観点から見ると、信憑性が高い事例の中にも意味のないものが多い。とはいえ、通常の説明が可能な事例を遠慮なく切り捨て、研究者に寄せられた事例の九五パーセントが失われてしまうとしても、本物の超常体験例は少数ながら残るであろう。また、さまざまなタイプの超常体験には著しい共通点もある。十八世紀の昔、心霊現象に強い関心を寄せていたイマヌエル・カントが次のように述べているように、こうした共通点はかなりよく知られていた。

> 同様の無知のため私は、種々の幽霊譚《たん》に真実が含まれることを全否定する気になれない。各々に対しては疑念を抱いても、全体として見る時にはある程度信ずる、という奇妙な条件が私の場合あるからである（143、五二ページ）。

「全体として見」た場合、この種の体験にはどのような共通点があるのであろうか。そこに見つかるのは、愛と死というふたつの主題である。体験する側もその対象となる側もほとんどの場合、愛情を抱き合っている。（同一家族に属していることも多いが、血縁関係ばかりではなく姻戚《いんせき》関係の場合もあるので、遺伝的要因が問題になるわけではない。）また、双方の間で交わされる交信は、死や何らかの死病ないしは傷害に関係しているのがふつうである。[*26]（先に紹介した六例は、両方の特徴の典型例である。）前世を記憶する子どもの事例も同様に、多くの共通点をもっている。愛と死という主題がこうした事例でも顕著に見られる事実を後ほど説明することにしよう。

以上、少々脱線したが、日常生活の中で起こるテレパシー体験について説明した。前世を記憶しているという子どもたちの事例の説明としてテレパシーが妥当かどうかを本書の後半で検討するつもりであるが、本節がその地ならしになれば幸いである。では、もう一度、用語解説に戻り、前世を記憶する子どもたちの事例を紹介、考察する中で用いられる若干の用語について解説することにしよう。

生まれ変わり型事例を説明する際に用いられる用語

私は前世の人格という言葉を、前世の記憶をもっている子どもの前世時代の人物と目される故人のいくつかの側面を指して用いる。そのうち、人格という言葉は不適切ではないかと考える方もおられるかもしれない。問題となる故人は単なる人格ではなく、肉体をもっていたからである。死によってその人間は終わったと考える者は多いであろうが、私が調査してきた事例からすると、人間のうちの何かが死後にも生き残り、新しい肉体と結びつくらしいことがわかる。死亡してから生まれ変わると思われるまでの間は、肉体は死んでいるので、生き残っている部分が何であれ、それを〝人物〟と呼ぶことはもはやできないが、そうした要素を〝人格〟ないしは〝肉体のない人格〟と呼ぶことはできるであろう。そこで私は、その子どもの前世の人物と目される故人および、死後に生存を続け、生まれ変わる際に新たな人間（および人格）を形成する一助となったであろうその人物のそうした側面の双方を指して、人格という言葉を用いてきたのである。

　死後にも生存を続け、その後に生まれ変わる人間の要素が存在するとして、それを魂という言葉で表現することに私は反対するものではない。しかしながら、この言葉は、多くの人々に宗教的な響きを感じさせるので、たいていの場合、私はこの言葉を避け、死後にも生存を続ける可能性のある要素を指して、人格という言葉を好んで用いている。心という言葉も使うが、それは特に、何であれ一個の人間がじかに体験する内的なものを指す時である。

　他にも、既決例と未決例という用語を定義しておかなければならない。その子どもが語った内容が他でもないある特定の故人を指していると共同研究者と私が納得した事例を既決例、そうした人物の見つからない事例を未決例としているのである。

　こうした事例では、通例、前世らしきものの記憶の形態が二種類ある。まず第一は、イメージ記憶である。つまり、現世で起こった出来事にまつわる通常の記憶が視覚的に思い浮かぶのと同じように、前世らしきものを記憶している子どもによく見られる記憶である。（例外はあるであろうが）ふつうにはイメージとして心に浮かぶことのない人物や場所の名前や、場合によっては日付や年齢も、イメージ記憶に含めている。こうした記憶は、もう一方の、行動的記憶と呼んでいるものとは異なっている。

私が行動的記憶と呼ぶものは、こうした事例やその解釈にとってきわめて重要なので、次にこの言葉の意味内容を少々詳しく説明することにしよう。心理学者は、たとえば癖や、特定の状況に対する一見不合理な反応など、それが生ずるに至った原因を当の本人が自覚していないにもかかわらず繰り返し起こる行動を研究してきた。行動とその原因の記憶とがこのように切り離されてしまっている現象を理解するうえで、後催眠暗示の研究は特に有効である。後催眠暗示とは、施術者が催眠状態にある被術者に対して、催眠状態から抜け出した後にある行動をとるよう命ずる暗示のことである。しかし、施術者がこうした暗示を行なう場合には、そうした暗示をかけられたことを忘れさせる暗示も同時に行なうことが多い。たとえば、施術者は、「あなたが催眠から覚めた後、私はハンカチを床に落とします。それを見るとすぐにあなたは自分の傘を広げます」という暗示を与えたうえで、ハンカチを見て傘を広げるよう言われたことは覚えていないように命ずる。次いで被術者を覚醒《かくせい》させ、適当に時間が経ったのを見計らい、何気なくハンカチを落とすと、被術者は少し驚き困惑した様子を見せるが、すぐに自分の傘をとり、部屋の中で広げるのである。施術者が、そのようなことをする理由を尋ねると被術者は、自分のとった行動を説明しようとする。その場合、この家の天井は雨が漏りそうだし、嵐が来るかもしれないので、雨漏りした時の用心に傘を開く必要があったのだとか、傘がきちんと開くかどうかを確認したかったのだなどという答が返って来るかもしれない。被術者は、室内で傘を広げるという自分の行動が、実は施術者から受けた暗示によって生じていることは完全に忘れている。このように被術者は、自分がいま行なっていることの原因を意識では知らないまま行動を起こすのである。[*27]

　人間の通常の行動は、もちろん後催眠暗示によるものではない。ここで後催眠暗示について述べたのは、その原因となった出来事を忘れているのに、何らかの行動パターンを発現させ、それが完全に自動的になってしまう場合がある、という事実を強調しておきたかったからである。私たちは歩くことができるが、最初によちよち歩きをした時のことを覚えている者はほとんどいない。経験豊かなピアニストであれば、人と話をしながらピアノを弾けるほどにひとつの曲に熟達することもできようが、以前その曲を練習した時の細かいことはほとんど、場合によっては完全に忘れてしまっているかもしれない。また、その原因となった出来事のイメージ記憶がなくとも、不愉快な行動的記憶をもっていることもある。たとえば、強い不安や恐怖症は、その原因となった恐ろしい出来事を忘れて大分経った後にも続くことが多い。心理学者や精神科医の大半は同意すると思うが、人間には、身につけるまでの過程は忘れてしまっても、子ども時代からもち越した行動的記憶が多いのである。[*28]同様に、行動的記憶を前世からもち越す可能性があることも、ここに指摘しておきたい。

　前世から来世へもち越す可能性のある（イメージ記憶および行動的記憶以外の）記憶としては、識閾下認知的記憶もある。行動的記憶という言葉は、習慣をはじめ、一個の人間に見られる多少なりとも自動的な行動を指しているが、それに対して識閾下認知的記憶とは、実際に保持していながら、身につけた覚えのない知識のことである。その実例として、幼少期やおそらくは前世で外国語を身につけているのに、どのようにして習ったのかを、あるいは一部の事例では、かつて習ったことすら覚えていない事例について考察するつもりである。

本章をしめくくるに当たって、本書の構成を簡単に説明しておこう。次章では、生まれ変わり信仰が世界中に見られる事実を明らかにしたうえで、人間がこうした信仰をもつに至った経緯を考察する。さらには、さまざまな民族が生まれ変わりを信じているが、その内容はそれぞれかなり異なる場合が少なくないという事実にもふれる。たとえば、誰がどのような状況のもとに生まれ変わるかという点で、考え方が相当に異っているのである。

次の（第3）章では、生まれ変わり信仰の裏づけとなる証拠にはどのようなものがあるかを考える。前世を記憶しているという幼児の事例を除けば、生まれ変わりの証拠とされるものは大半がほとんど無意味だと私は考えているが、この章ではその理由を説明するつもりである。また次の第4章では、前世を記憶している子どもたちの一二例の典型例を要約して紹介する。第5章では、生まれ変わり型事例に頻発する若干の特徴を検討する。

第6章および第7章では、生まれ変わり型事例を調査、分析する際に私が用いる方法を紹介している。第8章では、さまざまな文化圏の事例に見られる相違点という問題に戻り、そうした差異の実例をさらに紹介しながら、その理由として考えられる事柄について検討する。

最後の三章——特に第11章——は、それまでの章と比べて、より推論に基づきながら筆を進めている。まず第9章では、心理学、精神医学、医学の未《いま》だ解決されていないさまざまな問題点を考察する。生まれ変わりという考え方を通じて、その問題の解明に一石が投じられるかもしれないのである。生まれ変わりという考え方によってある程度の説明ができるように思われる実例を（そこでとりあげた各項目ごとに）掲げているが、それによってこうした推論が、さらにもっともらしいものになったのではないかと思う。第10章では、この種の事例に関連してとりあげられることの多い疑問に多少なりとも答えている。そして最後の第11章では、生まれ変わりという現象が実在するとすれば、どのような過程を経て起こるのかを私なりに推測している。この章では、生まれ変わりについて、（それまでの私の主張とは裏腹に）勇を奮って私見を述べておいた。しかし、私の発言は、（厳密な意味では、私が調査した事例のデータに基づくものではないにせよ）少なくともデータから言える枠内に留《とど》めるよう努めている。

第2章　生まれ変わり信仰

いわゆる現世に生まれる以前にもこの世に生を受けていたことがある、と信ずる者は少なくない。こうした信仰をもつ者からすれば、そう考えることは何ら異とするに足らないようである。生まれ変わりを信じている者は、「二度生まれることは、一度しか生まれないこと以上に驚くべきことでもない」[*1]というヴォルテールの言葉に頷《うなず》くであろうが、なじみのない者には生まれ変わりという考え方は不合理であり、ばかばかしいとすら感じられることも少なからずある。ところで、地球上に住む人間全体から見れば、生まれ変わりを信じない者の方が少数派に属するようで、こうした考え方を認めない者や耳にしたことすらない者よりも、生まれ変わりを信ずる者の方がおそらくは多いのである。

　西洋人の中には、東南アジアの民族の間でしか生まれ変わり信仰は見られないと誤解している者が多い。このような誤解が生じたのは、その地域に居住するヒンドゥー教徒や仏教徒が古代の聖典にそうした信仰を書き記しており、現代でも教義の中でそれを強調しているためであろう。そのような教義は、翻訳や伝道を通じて、あるいは必ずしも信頼が置けるわけではない通俗的な紹介によって西洋にも広まってきた。

　ところが、それ以外にも、生まれ変わりを信ずる人々は世界各地にいる。西アジアに住むイスラム教シーア派という大集団もこうした信仰をもっているし、イスラム教やキリスト教に完全には改宗していない西アフリカや東アフリカに住むいくつかの民族でも信じられている。ブラジルにも少数派ながら生まれ変わり信仰をもつ一団があるが、これは、アフリカ人がブラジルにもち込んだ信仰に由来するように思われる。そうした考え方が、十九世紀にフランスから移入された心霊主義《スピリチュアリズム》の概念と混じり合ったのである。

もうひとつ、生まれ変わりを信ずる民族で数が多いのは、北アメリカ北西部に居住する人々である。その地域の先住民族は、キリスト教の宣教師や教育者の力に押され、ある程度の侵食を受けたものの、(自らの伝統的宗教の一角を占める)生まれ変わり信仰を保持し続けた。キリスト教の宣教師や教育者がそれぞれ異なった立場から、地上には「ただ一度生を受くるのみ」という信仰を根気強く教え込んだにもかかわらずである。

他にも、生まれ変わりを信ずる民族はたくさんあるが、ここでは若干の例をつけ加えるに留めよう。二十世紀の文化人類学者の報告によれば、トロブリアンド諸島に住む人々やオーストラリア中央部の諸部族、北日本のアイヌ民族などの間にこうした信仰が見られるという[*2]。

生まれ変わり信仰があまりに広い範囲で見られるため、ショーペンハウエルは次のように述べている。「もしアジア人にヨーロッパの定義を聞かれる破目に陥ったら、私としてはこう答えざるをえまい。人間は生まれた時に始まり、無から造り出される、という途方もない妄想に完全に支配されている世界の一角である、と[*3]」。

ショーペンハウエルの時代以降、生まれ変わり信仰は西洋の文化圏にも広まった。二十世紀後半までには、ショーペンハウエルが嘆いた状態から抜け出すヨーロッパ人が増えてきたのである。ギャラップ・インターナショナルが一九六八年に行なった世論調査によれば、西欧八ヵ国に住む人たちの一八パーセントまでが、生まれ変わりを信じていることがわかった。その一年後に北アメリカで行なわれた同様の調査によると、対象となったアメリカ人の二〇パーセント、カナダ人の二六パーセントが生まれ変わりを信じていることがわかっている。その後、合衆国で行なわれた（一九八二年に発表された）調査では、回答者の二三パーセントが生まれ変わりを信じていると答えている[*4]。

キリスト教や正統派イスラム教の影響を蒙《こうむ》らなかった発展途上国の民族は、すべて生まれ変わりを信じているかというと、そうとも言い切れないようである。生まれ変わり信仰を含まない固有の宗教をそのままの形で踏襲した民族も少ないながら存在するからである。とはいえ、こうした例外は一部に存在するものの、正統派キリスト教やユダヤ教、イスラム教、さらには（多くの者にとって宗教にあらざる宗教となっている）科学の埒外《らちがい》にあるほとんど全員が、生まれ変わりを信じていると一般に考えてもよさそうである。このような状況に至った経過を次に考えてみよう。

生まれ変わり信仰は、インド＝ヨーロッパ語族の祖語が比較的狭い地域から広がったとされているように、ある一部の地域から発生し、それが世界各地に広まったのであろうか。そうであれば、かなり隔たってはいるが、有史以前ないし以後につながりのあった地域で生まれ変わり信仰が共通して見られる事実が説明できよう。たとえば、南アジアと西アジアは、少なくとも二〇〇〇年間、おそらくはもっと長い間にわたって、商人その他の旅行者によって結ばれていた。インドの生まれ変わり信仰は、紀元前一〇〇〇年頃に書かれた後期ヴェーダの時代にまで遡《さかのぼ》ることができる。[*5] インド学者ノーマン・ブラウンの指摘によれば、聖書に登場する、キリストが水の上を歩いたという逸話を執筆した者は、仏教の説話や伝説からそれを翻案、借用したのではないかという。もしそうなら、インド人は、生まれ変わり信仰を西アジアやヨーロッパに輸出した可能性もあることになる。テュアナ（現在は、トルコ南アナトリア領）で生まれたギリシャ人アポロニオスは、紀元一世紀にインドまで旅行し、そこで、イアルクスという賢者と哲学的な議論を行なった。現代のインド人なら、このふたりの対話の中に、生まれ変わりの話が時おり出て来ても驚きはしないであろう。[*6] アジア各地に住む人々の間に見られる生まれ変わり信仰は、共通の起源をもっているのかもしれない。[*7] 後ほど説明するつもりであるが、南アジアと（生まれ変わり信仰をもつ）西アジアの民族は、現在、生まれ変わりについて重要な点で異なる概念をもっている。とはいえ、中核的な信仰は共通の起源に基づいているのである。

しかしながら、生まれ変わり信仰をもつ他の民族もすべて、中央ないし南アジアからそうした考え方を移入したと考えると、重大な障害に直面する。アジアに共通の起源があるとした場合、イヌイットや北アメリカ北西部に住む諸部族に生まれ変わり信仰が存在するという事実はどう説明したらよいのであろうか。こうした民族の祖先は、何千年も前にアジアからアメリカ大陸に移住しており、それ以降（有史以前には）アジアとアメリカ大陸との間に大きな接触はなかった、と一般には考えられている。したがって、カナダ北部のイヌイットとガンジス渓谷に住む村人の生まれ変わり信仰が、共通の起源をもっているとはまず考えられない。[*8] また、生まれ変わり信仰が、アジアから西アフリカやオーストラリア中央部にまで伝わった可能性はさらに低い。

しかしながら、こうした信仰が、発祥の地から他の地域へと伝わったのではないとすれば、世界各地で、しかもまちがいなく別の時代に独自に生じたことになる。そうすると、こうした考え方が初めて生まれた時の経緯を考えてみる必要がある。

肉体の死後に人格が生存を続けるとする信仰は、肉親を失った者の悲しみや、死を待つ者の恐怖を和らげてくれる。とはいえ、生まれ変わりという考え方は、そうした慰めの手段としては不必要である。慰めを得るのが目的であれば、死後に暮らすことになるある種の楽園に長期間ないし永遠に留まっていると考えればすむからである。そうすると、死後に生存を続ける人間の一部が、新しい肉体に入り、この世での生活をもう一度始めることができるとする、より特殊な信仰が発生した原因を別に考えなければならない。

嘆き悲しんでいる遺族が、故人に生きて帰って来てほしいと願う気持は、自分の家族の中にその故人が生まれ変わったとする確信を強める力にはなるかもしれないが、故人とは全く無関係の家族のもとに生まれ変わったとされる場合には、この説明では全く不十分のように思われる。ところが、インドやタイ、トルコ、スリランカではほとんどの生まれ変わりがこのような形で起こるのである。他の家族から、かつて自分の家族の一員だった子どもがその家族のもとに生まれたことを聞かされた遺族は、その主張を受け入れれば、それによって多少の慰めは得られるかもしれない。しかし、こうした事例を見聞きして慰められるというだけでは、たとえば南アジアのヒンドゥー教徒や仏教徒が築き上げた生まれ変わり信仰の壮大な体系を説明することはできないであろう。

いかなる信仰であれ、最も身につきやすいのは、自分の両親から聞かされた内容を事実として受け入れる場合である。また、両親がある信仰を子どもに教え込もうとする時、ヒンドゥー教徒や仏教徒のように、教典という権威の裏打ちがあればさらに容易になる。（キリスト教徒の中には、生まれ変わりが存在しないことを教える目的で聖書という権威を利用する者もある。）南アジアの子どもたちのほとんどは、生まれ変わりをごく当然のことと信じて成長するので、外国人が生まれ変わりを信じていないのを知ると驚く者もある。

とはいえ、宗教的な伝承が明文化されている必要はない。アラスカのトリンギット族には口伝があっても聖典はないし、トルコ中南部に住むアレヴィス族も、生まれ変わり信仰の裏打ちとなる、明文化された権威をもってはいないようである。[*9] ナイジェリアのイボ族も、生まれ変わりを代々強く信じているが、聖典をもっているわけではない。[*10]

しかしながら、生まれ変わり信仰が（聖典や口伝により）次の世代、次の世代へと伝えられる過程がわかっても、最初に発生した時の状況が説明できるわけではない。最初に起こるまでの経緯は一様ではないのかもしれない。

哲学的な考察から生まれ変わりの存在を確信するに至った者もあるであろう。プラトンやショーペンハウエル[*11]、マクタガート、ブロード、デュカッス[*12]のような著名人をはじめ、かなりの数の哲学者は、生まれ変わりという考え方を真剣に受け止め、これを支持する論証を行なっている。自著『メノーン』の中でプラトンは、ある少年が、初めて見たと思われる幾何学の問題を解くことができた理由について、ソクラテスが行なった論証を紹介している。ソクラテスは、少年にその問題が解けた理由を、前世のイメージ記憶はもっていないにしても、前世で学んだ解答を少年が識閾《しきいき》下で記憶しているためだ、としているのである。

プラトンによればソクラテスは、人間が前世から来世へと知識をもち越すことについて独断的な主張を行なっている。次の通りである。「こういうふうに魂は不滅であって、これまで何度も生まれて来ているわけだから、この世のものも黄泉《よみ》の国のものもすべて見て来ているのだから、魂には知らないものはないのだよ。したがって、他のことはもちろん、徳についても、昔、身につけたことが思い出せるのは、何も不思議ではない。……何かを探究し、身につけるということは、すべて思い出すことなのだからね[*13]」

同様にマクタガートも、出会ったばかりでほとんど知らない相手に強く引きつけられるとか、家族の予測に反して変わった才能や関心を示すなどの一般によく見られる現象に対しては、生まれ変わりという考え方がその説明になるかもしれない（のみならず、他の概念では説明できないのではないか）と述べている。

第1章でも述べておいたが、当人らしさをどう定義すべきかという問題に関心を寄せた哲学者は他にもある。この問題にとり組む中で、特定の人物が死後にも生存を続け、生まれ変わったと考えるには、どのような基準が必要かという疑問に答えようとしたのである。

生まれ変わりの存在を裏づける証拠や生まれ変わり信仰に対して哲学者は、ごくわずかな貢献しか行なっていないと考えて差支えないようである。生まれ変わりを信じるべきかどうか迷っている者は、マクタガートやデュカッスが用いたような哲学的論証[14]によって生まれ変わりを信ずる方向へ傾くのかもしれないが、この種の論証だけではその裏づけとなる根拠がないので、こうした信仰を立証するには不十分であると思う。それでも、一部の哲学者は、多くの者に生まれ変わり信仰を不当なものと思い込ませる元凶となりそうな不当な憶説を排除するうえでは、ある程度の貢献をしているのである。

裏づけとなる証拠があるわけではないが、生まれ変わり信仰は、前世の記憶をもっていると称する者の話が下地になって発生することが時おり（おそらくはしばしば）あったのではないかと思う。このような人物がいるというニュースは、次から次へと広がり、その記憶の話は、数世代あるいはそれ以上にわたって語り継がれるかもしれない。とはいえ、こうした逸話が広まるにも、ある程度の限界がある。周知のように商人たちは、遠い世界の奇談を語るものであるが、聞いている者を喜ばせるのに、説得力ある証拠を出して見せなければならないわけではないし、変わった出来事の起こった場所が遠ければ遠いほど、その話を聞いた者は、現実に起こった出来事とは信じないようになる。橇《そり》で移動する者や猟師が、氷とツンドラに覆われた広大な地帯を横断し、集落から集落へと生まれ変わりの話をして歩いたと考えたのでは、グリーンランドからカナダ北部を経てアラスカに至る広い地域に居住するイヌイットの間に生まれ変わり信仰が存在するという事実はどうしても説明できないのである[15]。また、隣接するふたつの民族が生まれ変わり信仰をもっているとしても、必ずしも一方がもう一方を改宗させたことにはならない。（カナダ北西部とアラスカ中央部に住む）アタパスカ族とイヌイット族の祖先がアジアから北米大陸に移住した時期はそれぞれ異なるし、このふたつの民族は互いに全く通じない言葉を使っていたのである。かつては領土をめぐって争いを繰り広げたこともあったが、それを除けば、少なくとも人間の本性や死後の運命に関する考え方を披瀝《ひれき》し合うなどの接触は、ほとんどなかったようである。にもかかわらず、アタパスカとイヌイットは双方が生まれ変わり信仰をもっているのである。

したがって私としては、生まれ変わり信仰をもちながら明文化された教典の存在しない文化圏に住む人々がそうした信仰を抱くようになったのは、商取引のある圏内に居住する、前世を記憶しているという人物と接したり、その話を聞いたりしたためなのではないか、という結論に到達する。[16] このような人物は同じ村や近くの村に住んでいたかもしれないし、何世代か前に住んでおり、そのため、その人物の記憶が本人の死後にも語り伝えられていたのかもしれない。おそらくは、このような人物が多数出現し、それぞれが前世を記憶していると主張した結果、世界各地で生まれ変わり信仰が確立されたのであろう。

さまざまな民族の間に生まれ変わり信仰が発生したのは、前世を記憶しているとする主張がその引き金になっているのであろうが、ひとたびその信仰が確立されると、その裏づけとなる証拠が存在しなくても、こうした信仰は長い間続くのであろう。たとえば、ヒンドゥー教徒は数千年の昔から生まれ変わりを信じているが、十八世紀初頭に至るまでインドでは、最近の生まれ変わり型事例に匹敵する実例が存在した形跡は全くないのである。さらには、十八世紀初頭の事例の後にも、二十世紀初頭に至るまで生まれ変わり型事例は一例たりとも知られていない（私の知る限り皆無の）ようなのである。[17]

　とはいえ、二十世紀以前にもインドでは、記録が残されていないだけで実際には数多くの事例が存在した可能性があることは銘記すべきである。私が情報を得た二十世紀の事例は、実際に発生した事例のごく一部にすぎないことは確かであろうし、十九世紀以前には、現代のように、こうした事例にまつわる情報を報告し広く一般に知らしめるための利器はなかった。また、ヒンドゥー教の信仰のために、前世の記憶は陳腐なものであり、記録に留《とど》める必要もなければ、場合によっては注目する必要すらないものと見なされたのかもしれない。

　フランス南西部に住むカタリ派キリスト教徒も、事例という点ではほぼ皆無に等しいが、やはり強い生まれ変わり信仰をもっている。カタリ派は、十二、三世紀に発生した異端のキリスト教分派である[18]。この分派は、十三世紀半ばに、フランスのルイIX世やフランス北部の貴族たちの弾圧により事実上根絶された。カタリ派自体による記録も壊滅的打撃を蒙《こうむ》ったようであり、この会派について判明している事実は大半が、迫害者側である宗教裁判所の修道士たちが残した記録のおかげなのである。しかしながらこの場合も、知られている事例がほとんどないからと言って、実際にもなかったことにはならない。

　前世の記憶によって得られる証拠が存在しなくとも、生まれ変わり信仰が確立される場合もあるように思う。さもなければ、現代の西洋の、特に若い人々の間に生まれ変わり信仰が多々見られるという事実が説明しにくいように思われる。この種の人たちは、アジアの宗教や神智学について書かれた通俗書にある程度は接しているのかもしれないが、こうした書物は（大半が）根拠を欠いた主張を行なっているのであって、証拠を提示しているものではない。事例研究によって得られた証拠が一般に知れ渡るようになったのは、ごく最近のことなのである。このような人々はおそらく、何らかの直観や自分なりの哲学的考察を通じて生まれ変わり信仰を抱くに至ったのであろう。思慮の深い子どもは特にそうかもしれないが、新たに子どもが生まれるたびに神が新しく魂を造るとする伝統的なキリスト教の教義は、誰であれ信じられないのではなかろうか。また、魂という考え方を受け入れ、正統派キリスト教の教義を退けるとすれば、それぞれの魂は、現在の肉体と結びつく以前に何らかの形で存在しており、したがって、それ以前にも別の肉体と結びついていたのではないかとする推測が容易に可能となる。ショーペンハウエルは、「誕生がその人間の始まりだと思う者は誰であれ、死がその終わりだと考えるはずだ」と述べている。[19] 前章でふれておいたように、人間はそれぞれ異なった状態で生まれてくるという事実に思いを致す時、人間の一生は一回だけしかないとする教えは、多くの者の正義感とも抵触する。こうした教えに満足できなかったため、生まれ変わりという考え方に傾いたのかもしれないのである。

　生まれ変わりという現象があるとすれば、はっきりした前世の記憶はなくとも、その存在を暗示するものが見つかるかもしれない。[20] 二〇〇〇年ほど前、偉大なインドの賢者パタンジャリは、ほとんどの人間に見られる死に対する恐怖心を、ヒンドゥー教をはじめとする伝統的な発想に基づき、個々の魂が死に際して体験するような、自らの生涯を死後に回顧することに対する恐怖に由来するものと説明している。こうした体験の潜在的記憶は（多くの人間にとって不快なものにちがいないので）、もう一度死ぬことに対する恐怖心を生ぜしめるであろう。次に死ぬ時にも、自分のしてきた行ないをもう一度（おそらくは同様に不快な形で）振り返ることになるだろうからである。[*21・22]

　生まれ変わり信仰は、他の信仰と同じく、特定の国や文化圏の中でも受容度に変動が見られる。生まれ変わり信仰を長期的視点で眺めてみると、ある民族でこうした信仰が発生した明確な実例が一例と、長期にわたってこのような信仰を保持していた民族でその信仰が消滅してしまった実例がいくつか存在することがわかる。

　チベット人は、何もなかったところに生まれ変わり信仰（私見によれば特殊な形態の生まれ変わり信仰）を作り上げた実例である。仏教がチベットに伝来し広く信仰されるようになったのは、七世紀から十世紀にかけてである。チベットに移入された仏教は、生まれ変わり信仰を伴ってはいたが、インドから伝わって来た時点では、チベットの生まれ変わり信仰および生まれ変わり型事例の大半を他の民族とは異質なものにしている特徴は、まだ存在しなかった。いま言おうとしているのは、霊性の高い僧侶《そうりょ》（ラマ）になると、自らの来世を自在に変えられる能力をもつようになり、生まれ変わった後、前世の自分を明らかにする手がかりを提示できるとする考え方のことである。（このような人たちは、チベット人の間ではトゥルクと呼ばれる。）こうした概念がチベットに生まれたのは、十一世紀から十五世紀の間である。この概念は次第に体系化され、ある程度固定したものとなり、生まれ変わりを繰り返しながら全僧院の最高指導者としての地位を継承するという考え方へと発展した。チベットの生まれ変わりの概念はダライ・ラマに始まったわけではないが、ダライ・ラマや、ゲルク（「黄帽」）派というチベット仏教の一派がこの考え方をとり入れたのであった。それ以来、黄帽派は、新しいダライ・ラマを探し出すのに用いる儀式的手続きが、他の大ラマを見つけ出す際の範となるまでにこの概念を発展させたのである。[23]

生まれ変わり信仰をかつてもっていたのに、後に捨て去った民族としては、インドのイスラム教徒が最も印象深い実例として挙げられる。インドに住むイスラム教徒は何百万もの数にのぼるが、インドを四世紀にもわたって支配したムガール帝国を打ち建てるに至ったイスラム教徒の侵入者や侵略者の末裔《まつえい》は、そのうちのごく一部にすぎない。現在インドに居住しているイスラム教徒の大半は、イスラム教に改宗した元ヒンドゥー教徒の子孫なのである。[24]西アジアに始まり、アジアやアフリカ各地に拡散したシーア派の一分派であるイスマイル派は、一時生まれ変わりを信じていたが、西アジアに住む現在のイスマイル派はこの信仰をもっていない。[25]大英帝国のケルト人も、スカンジナビアやアイスランドのヴァイキング[26]と同じく、生まれ変わり信仰をもっていた。[27]ところが、その（ほとんどがキリスト教徒の）子孫たちの大半はこうした信仰をもってはいないのである。

また、南ヨーロッパに住んでいたキリスト教徒の少なくとも一部は、六世紀になるまで生まれ変わり信仰をもっていたことがわかっている。その当時この信仰は、公式に教義の一部になっていたわけではないが、教会の上層部はこれを、五五三年の第二コンスタンティノープル会議までは何とか受け入れられる考え方として黙認していたようである。[28]この会議全体の動きが、さらには、この会議には参加しなかったものの、つながりのある聖職者たちの動きが、生まれ変わりという教えを締めつける公告を発布せしめたのかどうかについては、議論の余地があるかもしれない。しかしながら、こうした考え方が、当時の正統派キリスト教徒の間で次第に受け入れられなくなり、その傾向がその後も続いたのは確かである。

私も、北アメリカ北西部に何度か調査行を行なう中で、生まれ変わり信仰が薄れてきている証拠を入手している。この地域で私は、先住民の間に見られる生まれ変わり型事例を長年にわたって研究してきた。ある時私は、生まれ変わりという考え方を知っているかどうか、また、そうした考え方を信じているかどうかについてイヌイットの人々を対象に、小規模の調査を非公式に行なった。この時の調査では、一〇八名のイヌイットに質問しているが、その結果、四〇歳以上の六六名中四七名（七一パーセント）までが、イヌイットの間に生まれ変わり信仰があるのを知っていたが、三九歳以下の四二名では、知っている者はわずか一三名（三一パーセント）にすぎなかった。生まれ変わり信仰について聞いたことのある四七名に対して、生まれ変わりは本当に起こると思うかどうかを尋ねたところ、二九名（六二パーセント）が、本当に起こると思うと答えている。この比率は、合衆国連邦四八州よりもはるかに高いので、若い世代の間に生まれ変わり信仰を耳にしたことのない者が多いとしても、こうした信仰はイヌイットの中にかなりしっかり根を下ろしていると言える。[*29] しかしながら、北アメリカ北西部に居住する先住民族の若者の中には、生まれ変わりに強い関心を抱いている者があり、現在三〇歳に満たない母親の中にも、この地域の事例について私のよき情報提供者になっている者があるという事実は、ここに明記しておかなければならない。

生まれ変わりに対する懐疑的態度を助長する過程は、生まれ変わり信仰を促進する過程と、方向は逆であるがよく似ている。インドで（たとえば十六世紀に）あるヒンドゥー教徒がイスラム教徒に改宗したとすると、その一家は一世代ないし数世代にわたり、生まれ変わりという考え方になつかしい思いを馳《は》せたことであろう。ところがその後は、まず縁遠いものに、最後には笑止千万なものになったのではなかろうか。このようにもの笑いの種になった頃に、改宗者の子どもが前世を記憶していると言い始めたとしたら、嘲笑《ちょうしょう》され、昔よりも厳しい基準で判断されるため、その子どもは意気消沈するかもしれない。また、生まれ変わり型事例と生まれ変わり信仰は相互に強化し合うと私は考えるが、もしそれが正しければ、抑えつけることにより事例は失われてしまうため、イスラム教徒に改宗した人々の間では、生まれ変わりという教義の実際的な裏づけがなくなってしまったことであろう。その結果イスラム教徒たちは、生まれ変わりという考え方を、信者がめでたく卒業した愚かな迷信として軽視することになったのではなかろうか。時間的に遠ざかることは、距離が遠くなった時と同じく、真実味をなくする働きをするのである。英雄ヘルギを主人公とする北欧の叙事詩の編者は、次のような実例を掲げている。「古代の伝承によれば……人間に再生すると信じられていた。だが、現在では、これは根も葉もない迷信だとされている。ヘルギとシグルンは再生したと言われる。その頃ヘルギは、『カルルヨート』の中で述べられているように、ヘルギ・ハディングヤースカティと呼ばれており、シグルンの方は、カラ・ハルフダナルドッティールと呼ばれていた。カラはバルキューレ〔オーディンに仕える侍女〕であった[*30]」。

信憑性《しんぴょうせい》がありそうな生まれ変わり型事例を知っている者は、けんか腰の懐疑的態度に接すると沈黙を守るであろうが、それまでの確信を完全に捨て去ることはないであろう。本当の信仰を隠しているので、実際にはそうではないのに、改宗したように見えるかもしれない。私は、この事実を裏づける証拠を、トリンギットとイヌイットで見つけている。その伝統的宗教は、現在、キリスト教や西洋科学の攻勢に対して守勢にまわっている。

北アメリカ北西部の先住民族やイヌイットを対象に（一九六〇年代初頭に）調査を開始してまもなく、私は、長い間イヌイットの中で医療に従事してきた看護師と出会った。私の研究について話したところ、その看護師は、生まれ変わり信仰などもうすっかり廃れてしまっていると答えた。私の来るのが二〇年遅すぎた、というのである。しかし、この看護師はまちがっていた。北アメリカ北西部に住むイヌイットをはじめとする先住民族の中で、私は、一七〇例の生まれ変わり型事例を見つけることができたからである。こうした事例は数多く存在していたが、好意的と見られる者にしか明かされることがなかったのである。

この看護師の他にも、地元の人たちからこうした事例の存在を教えてもらえなかった部外者は何人もいる。私はこれまで、短くて二、三ヵ月、長い場合には数年もトリンギットの間で暮らしながら調査研究を行なってきた六人の専門家と直接対面したり書簡を交わしたりしている。そのうちの四名は文化人類学者であった。あるトリンギットの一団は、そのうちの二名に自分たちの部族名を教えている。これは、このふたりのよそ者を仲間として受け入れたことを意味するものである。このことをここで引き合いに出したのは、西洋の人間がこれほど先住民族に接近しても、この人たちのもつ生まれ変わり信仰については、（ひとりを除いて）全く知らされなかったという事実を強調するためである。トリンギットが生まれ変わり信仰をもっていることを多少なりとも知っていたのは、六名中わずか一名にすぎなかったのである。この女性は、調査こそ行なわなかったが、生まれ変わり型事例についてもある程度の情報を得ていた。残る五名は、私に言われるまで、トリンギットの間に生まれ変わり信仰が存在することも、生まれ変わりに関係した事例があることも全く知らなかった。この人たちも、私と同じように尋ねさえしていれば、こうした問題について教えてもらえたのであろうが、トリンギットの友人たちは、笑われるのを覚悟してまで自分からこの話題をもち出すことなどするはずもなかったのである。

これまで、さまざまな民族の間に生まれ変わり信仰が見られることを述べてきたが、一次的（基本的）生まれ変わり信仰と私が呼んでいるものについてしか検討しなかった。一次的生まれ変わり信仰とは、人間の人格（魂ないし心）が、本人の死後、新しい肉体と結びつくとする信仰のことである。しかしながら、こうした一次的信仰に加え、誰がどのように生まれ変わるのか、前世に播《ま》いた種が来世にどのような影響を及ぼすのかという点については、実にさまざまな副次的信仰が見られるのである。生まれ変わりに関するこうした二次的信仰に対しては、一次的信仰と切り離して検討する方が意義が大きいと思うので、次に、そのうちのいくつかについて考えてみることにしよう[*31]。

　生まれ変わり信仰をもつのは東南アジアに住む民族だけではないか、と誤解している西洋人が他の民族にも見られることを初めて知った時、その人たちもヒンドゥー教徒や仏教徒と同じような考え方をとっているに違いないと想像しがちであるが、それはまちがっている。東南アジアの人々は、現世の行ないが来世の運命を決定すると信じている。これは、カルマという教理の基本である。ところが、生まれ変わり信仰をもちながら、カルマをはじめとする同類の考え方を全くとらない民族が実際には多いのである。生まれ変わり信仰をもっている民族が、ヒンドゥー教徒や仏教徒と同じくらい真剣に信じてきた、あるいは現在も信じ続けている概念が、他に少なくとも三通りある。

　生まれ変わり信仰をもつ西アジアのイスラム教シーア派の信者は、前世の行ないによって来世の運命が決するとは考えていない。魂は、次から次へと違った環境に生まれ変わり、それぞれの生涯で徳を積むべく最善を尽くさなければならない、と考えるのである。その生涯の成否は、来世には全く影響を及ぼさないが、結局は最後の審判の日に、本人の行状が記された帳簿が調べ上げられ、善行と悪行とが総決算されるが、それに従って神が各人について、永遠に天国行きか地獄行きかを決定するのである。[*32]

　西アフリカに住むある民族は、自らの倫理観とはほとんど無縁の生まれ変わり信仰をもっている。これは、西アフリカの人々の倫理観が未発達だということではない。それどころか、倫理規定や制裁規定は実に細かく定められている。にもかかわらず、西アフリカの生まれ変わりの概念は、こうした規定とはほとんど無関係なのである。この人たちは人生を、基本的に楽しく希望に満ちたものと考える。（これは、この世の生活を否定するヒンドゥー教徒や仏教徒の態度とは対照的である。）西アフリカの人々は、人間は死後、この世に生を受けるのを待つ霊魂の住むリンボ界へ行くと信じている。この人たちは、来世ではいま以上の生活状態や地位を望むが、現世で徳を積めばそうした希望が叶《かな》えられるとは考えていない。この人々が重視するのは、来世でいま以上の生活をしたいという願望を口にすることなのである。[*33]

アラスカ南東部に住むトリンギットも、これと似た信仰をもっている。トリンギットは、西アフリカの民族と同じく、現世の行ないが来世の運命を決するとも、わずかであれ来世に影響を及ぼすとも考えてはおらず、現世で表明した願望が次に生まれ変わる時の条件を決めると信じているのである。そのため、老い先の短いことを悟った年輩のトリンギットが、来世の両親になってほしいと願う夫婦を選んでいる場面を目撃することも少なくない。また、そのトリンギットは、来世でかくありたいと思うことを表明するかもしれない。たとえば、もっと強くなりたいとか、もっと高い教育を受けたいとか、もう偏平足には悩まされたくない、などと口に出して言うかもしれないのである。[*34]

前世と来世の関係にまつわる概念としては、第四のものが最も重要かもしれない。これは、それほどはっきりしたものではないが、ある程度の証拠が存在する唯一の概念である。いま言おうとしているのは、人間が（死ぬ前に、あるいは肉体のない状態にある間に）、次に生まれ出る家族を選び、それによって新しい人生の出発点となる条件を間接的に決定する、という考え方である。この考え方を裏づける証拠が存在すると言ったのは、どのような家族のもとに生まれ変わりたいかを表明して死亡し、後に、その意志が達成されたことを示す証拠を伴って生まれてくる事例が、トリンギットに数例、チベットのラマに二、三例ある他に、他の民族でも時おり見られるからである。[35] 予告夢があった事例もすべて、その夢に登場した肉体のない人格が、生まれ変わる先を選んでいるらしいことを示している。このことは、ビルマでよく見られる嘆願調の予告夢の場合に特に当てはまる。肉体のない人格が、特定の家族（通常はその夢を見る本人の家族）を選んだことを伝えたうえ（時には、夢を見ている本人がその人物の声をはっきりと聞き）、その家族のもとに生まれ変わるのを承諾してほしいと願うのである。

　生まれ変わる先が選択できるとする考え方は、ヨーロッパにも昔からある。古代ギリシャ人の中にもそう考えた者があったし、プラトンもそのことについて詳述している。『国家』の中でプラトンは、生まれ変わろうとしている魂は出生後の生活を選択していると述べている。[36] この信仰によれば、過去世で知識を身につけた者は、過去世をむだにして何も学ばなかった者よりもすばらしい来世を選ぶことができるという。とはいえ、プラトンは、来世を慎重に選ぶのに必要な英知が、そうしたものを身につけようとする前世の努力によって得られることはあるが、それを除けば、前世の行ないが来世に影響を及ぼすとは言っていない。

　生まれ変わりについてさまざまな民族がもっている考え方は、以上の他にもいくつかある。この問題については第8章でもう一度検討するつもりであるが、まず第一に、生まれ変わりという現象が本当に存在するのか、という問題に関連する証拠を紹介した方が、読者の方々に満足していただけるのではなかろうか。

第3章　生まれ変わりを裏づける証拠の種々相

少なからぬ数の人間が、さまざまな状況のもとで、前世の記憶らしきものを発現させている。そのうちのひとつ（幼児の偶発的記憶）を除けば、いずれについても超常的要素が含まれている証拠としては、ほとんど意味がないように思われる。その一方で、前世の記憶に由来する体験らしきものが、数は少ないながらさまざまな状況のもとで生ずるのである。本章では、意図的に掘り起こそうとした成人の事例よりも、偶発的に発生する幼児の事例を私が重視している理由を説明しながら、さまざまな状況のもとで発生した事例を考察することにしよう。

過去世リーディング

私見によれば、生まれ変わりの証拠として最も弱いのは、人の前世を言い当てる（〝見る〟）ことができると称する人物によるものである。他人の前世がわかるという主張は、証拠もないのにこの種の信仰が是認される例としてはまちがいなく格好の実例である。料金を支払って〝過去世リーディング〟を依頼する者は、そこで告げられた内容を鵜呑《うの》みにするのであろうが、私が見聞きした範囲では、そうした発言を信ずるに足る裏づけを得ることはできないのである。ほとんどの場合、多額の金銭を一様に要求するが、そういうことさえなければ、過去世リーディングは、悲しみの元ではなく笑いの種になるのかもしれない。そこで語られる〝前世〟は、必ずと言ってよいほど、歴史上の大事件の真只中《まっただなか》にある。十字軍の遠征やフランス革命、アメリカ南北戦争、さらにはイエス・キリストの磔刑《たっけい》などの出来事が、前世リーディングの中で繰り返し登場する。もし（過去世で）キリストの磔《はりつけ》を見ていたとされる者全員が本当にその場にいたとしたら、そこに立ち会っていたはずのローマ人兵士たちは、自分たちの居場所もないほどだったのではないかと愚考することがある。

過去世リーディングを一度受けた経験のある者は、大半が二度としていないらしいが、私にとってこの事実は驚きである。その人たちが、ある〝能力者《リーダー》〟の語った内容を別の〝能力者〟の言葉と対照させたとすれば、即座に料金を払い戻してほしいと思うことであろう。[*1] ただし、過去世リーディングについて少しでも肯定的な発言をすると、これに騙《だま》される者が増えるのではないかという懸念はあるが、ふたりの霊能者が連絡をとり合う機会がなかったにもかかわらず、ひとりの人物の前世について別個に、全く同じ（あるいはよく似た）内容を語ったという事例を私が二例知っているという事実は、ここに述べておかなければならない。また私は、ある人物がたまたま思い出していた記憶と符合する前世時代の生活をある霊能者が詳細に物語った事例を、その外に二例知っている。しかし、こうした事例は、必ずしも生まれ変わりを裏づける証拠にはならない。その霊能者が他人の前世時代に起こった出来事を本当に探り当てた可能性は否定すべきではないとしても、前世を占ってもらった客と霊能者との間にテレパシーが働いたことをうかがわせる証拠以上のものにはなりにくいのである。

催眠による遡行《そこう》

前世らしき時代にまで催眠によって遡《さかのぼ》る実験の場合には、過去世リーディングによるものよりも――一部の事例では――多少なりとも強力な証拠が得られる。とはいえ、私が受けとった手紙類や、こうした実験をもとにして書かれた大量の書物から判断すると、催眠によって記憶の障害が破られ、本当の前世の記憶が堰《せき》を切ったように迸《ほとばし》ることがあると信じて疑わない者が西洋には少なくない。このような人々は、催眠についてある程度の勉強すれば、それほどの確信はもてなくなるであろう。

特に、一部の専門家が催眠を特殊な意識状態ではないとしている今日、ここで性急に催眠の定義を試みるつもりはない。型通りの催眠誘導を用いずとも、被験者が指示に従い暗示に反応したいという気持になりさえすれば、少なくとも催眠現象の一部は起こりうることが実験によって証明されている。催眠状態になることが前提として必要だと従来考えられていた心理的身体的離れ業も、ふだんとは違うふるまいをしようとする動機づけがある程度高まった状態になりさえすれば、可能な場合がある。つまり、催眠の力によって被験者の達成能力は変化するのかもしれないが、催眠以外の心理的な働きかけによっても同じことができるのかもしれないのである。

とはいえ、その本態が何であれ、催眠状態にある被験者の注意は、驚くほど集中した状態になっており、外部の刺激や雑念が入らないような状況にあるという点では、催眠研究者の意見は一致しているように思う。こうした状況の中で被験者は、それ以外の条件ではほとんど考えられないほど鮮明かつ明瞭《めいりょう》に、過去の特定の場面に注意を集中することができる。その結果、たとえば一〇歳の誕生日の曜日とか、小学校時代の教師や同級生のことなど、ふだんは忘却のかなたにある少年時代の記憶を、微に入り細を穿《うが》って蘇《よみがえ》らせることもあるのである。[*2]

　ここまではともかくとして、こうした集中力をさらに高めて行く中で被術者は、思考の主導権を施術者に委《ゆだ》ねてしまうため、施術者の催眠暗示に抵抗できにくく（あるいは少なくとも抵抗する気が乏しく）なってくる。催眠暗示により施術者に何か思い出すよう命じられた被術者は、それほど正確に想起できない場合には、施術者を喜ばせる目的で不正確な発言を行なうことも少なくない。それでいながら大半の被術者は、自分が語っている内容に事実と虚偽が入り混じっていることに気づかないのである。[*3]

　催眠状態にある被術者は、前世まで遡るよう命じられた時、五歳以前の年齢にまで戻るよう命じられた時と同程度に、施術者の指示に従う傾向がある。[*4]「あなたは、これから、生まれる前の別の時代の別の場所まで戻ります」と施術者に言われると、被術者はその指示に従おうとする。施術者が、たとえば、「あなたは、この頭痛の原因が過去のどこかにあるのを思い出します」など、それほど明確ではない催眠暗示を与えた場合ですら、同じように従順にその指示に従うのである。催眠によって誘発される特殊な服従状態の中で被術者は、何らかの、過去にあった出来事らしきものを物語らずにはいられない衝動に駆られる（あるいは、そう仕向けられる）ため、現世の生活の中からそれらしきものが探し出せない場合には、前世らしき時代の記憶がそれまで全くなかった場合でも、それらしき話を作り上げるかもしれないのである。次いで、自分の記憶にある他の事柄をも利用しようとするため、義務教育しか受けていない者でも読書やラジオやテレビから拾い上げた歴史上の大事件に飛びつくのがふつうである。歴史の知識が全くなくとも、また、たとえあるとしても、施術者を落胆させないよう架空の話をして聞かせることになるかもしれない。

また、被術者は、催眠のもうひとつの特徴である演技力を利用することも多い。記憶の中に潜んでいるいろいろな情報をつなぎ合わせ、それをもとに〝前世の人格〟を作り上げてしまうのである。このようにして作られた前世の人格は、長年月にわたって繰り返し呼び出されても、それなりの感情や一貫した性格を示して見せることであろう。

通常は潜伏している心的内容を統合することや、それを多少なりとも筋の通った形に演ずることについて言えば、催眠は夢とかなり共通する要素をもっている。この点からすると、自分の夢に重きを置いていない者が、催眠中に体験する事柄は何であれ無批判に事実として受け入れてしまうことは少々驚きである。このように奇妙なことが起こるのは、催眠の施術者によって、また催眠状態を劇的な形に誘導することによって生ずる異常な興奮のためであろう。催眠術を見世物にしている者をはじめ、催眠に関係したきわもの的な主張を擁護する者たちは、催眠こそ記憶を蘇らせるための絶対確実な手段であるとする思い込みを助長してきたが、実際にはそれは、事実からほど遠いのである。

催眠により引き出された〝前世の人格〟が語る内容には、愚にもつかない時代錯誤が見られることもある。ある著書に載っていた例では、十字軍の時代のフランス王の飛脚をしていたという〝前世の人格〟は、ヴェルサイユ宮殿とボルドーの間を往復していたと語っている。ところが十字軍の時代（十一世紀から十三世紀）のヴェルサイユは、フランス政府とはあまりつながりがなかった。ヴェルサイユが重要な位置を占めるようになるのは、十七世紀以降なのである。[*5]

やはり催眠状態で年齢遡行を行なった別の被術者は、十七世紀のイギリスでジェイムズというレスター（本人の発言では〝レチェスター〟）伯として生涯を全うしたと述べている。この被術者は、〝クロムウェル卿《きょう》〟が自分たち一家を城から追い払った顚末《てんまつ》を語っている。ところが、この時代のレスター伯はロバート・シドニー（一五九五―一六七七年）であり、ジェイムズという名前ではなかった。また、ロバート卿は（ペンズハーストの）大邸宅を追われる身になったことは一度もなかったし、オリバー・クロムウェルは、護民官《ロード・プロテクター》ではあったが、一般には、クロムウェル卿とは呼ばれていなかったのである。

いま述べたような、時代錯誤をはじめとする誤りを見ると、平均的な高校生なら困惑することであろうが、これは、催眠のもうひとつの特徴である、通常の批判能力が消失したことの現われなのである。（註釈《ちゅうしゃく》も加えずにこのような不正確な発言をそのまま著書に引用している者は、執筆に際してはふつうの判断力を行使しているのであろうから、被術者に批判能力がなくなっていることを理由に自己弁護することはできないが、あまりに愚かしくて歴史小説に使えないようなものでも、〝前世〟としてまつり上げられてしまうこともあるようである。）また、いま挙げた二例から、（催眠により引き出された〝前世〟全般にもだいたい同じことが言えるが）自分たちが前世で歴史的に重要な役割を演じたことにしようとしたり、有名な人物や場所に関係づけようとしたりする傾向が被術者一般に見られることもわかる。

私たちとしては、このような事例に潜む数多くの誤りを見逃してもよいし、また、そうすべきなのかもしれない。しかしながら、その点を看過したところで、催眠により引き出された〝前世〟を額面通り受けとってよいことにはなるまい。その中で描き出される生活は、主として、政治的指導者や、たとえば偉大な芸術家や発明家などの著名人しか記録に登場しない古い時代のものである。十九世紀中葉以前に生を受けたほとんどの人間の生涯については、次のように言うことができる。もし、そうした一生について（事実確認に必要な）詳細な記録が存在するとすれば、被術者は、少なくとも理屈の上では、その気になればその記録を利用できたことになるし、逆に、もしその人物の生涯が不明瞭にしか描き出されていないとすれば、それが事実かどうかは、ほとんどあるいは全く確認できないであろう。[*6]

遡行《そこう》が前世にまで行なわれたらしく見える事例の中には、施術者がその後（同じセッションかその後のセッションで）、催眠状態にある被術者に、先に引き出された〝前世〟に登場する事柄がどこに由来するか尋ねているものがある。このように問い質《ただ》された被術者の中には、〝前世〟として語った内容の一部が図書その他の資料を基にしていることを想起し、それを名指した者もあったのである。[*7]

催眠は、正確な情報を引き出す手段として不当な名声を得ているが、それを別にしても、催眠によって解放される劇的な心の力のため被術者（および、時に立会人たち）は、説得力ある現実の記憶が本当に蘇ったかのように思い込んでしまう。私自身が催眠誘導を行なったふたりの被術者を見れば、空想を記憶として語る能力がはっきり見てとれる。

一方の被術者は、年齢遡行により、三通りの〝前世〟をあっさり〝想起〟した。そのうち、事実かどうか確認できる情報を含むものがひとつだけあった。十七世紀後半のフランスを背景に、当時の宗教論争に関係していた聖職者としての〝前世〟であった。たまたま被術者が、その聖職者の存在を書物や人の話から知っていたことが判明した。この女性の被術者は、別の〝前世〟では十六世紀イギリスの船乗りであったという。この船員が乗組んだ船は嵐に遭って座礁し、船員は水中に投げ出されて溺死《できし》した。その模様を演じる中で被術者は、恐怖を露《あら》わにし、呼吸困難に陥った。溺死するさまを再現しているらしき時、被術者の身体的状態があまりに切迫してきたため、別のもっと穏やかな場面を思い描くようすぐに暗示をかけざるをえなくなった。被術者はまもなく別の場面のイメージを描き、落着きをとり戻した。三通りの〝前世〟を思い出したかに見えるこの女性は、通常の手段で得た情報を利用して、空想にのめり込んだと私は考えるが、本人は、本当の前世を想起し、その時の出来事が蘇ったと思い込んだのである。その時の体験が現実的なものに思えたため、この女性は、他の可能性については考えようともしなかった。

私が催眠をかけたもうひとりの女性は、十九世紀のアムステルダムで送った〝前世〟を思い出した。この女性は時おり、オランダ語を話そうとする様子を見せたため、私は、オランダ語を話す同僚に同席を依頼した。ところがまもなくこの同僚は、この女性がオランダ語を全く話せないことに気づいたのである。（この女性は、旅行者が使う程度のドイツ語の単語をいくつか知っており、それをオランダ語に見せかけようとしていたのであった。）またこの女性は、アムステルダム市民なら熟知しているはずの市の中心部についても全く知らなかった。しかし、本節のテーマに関係しているのは、この被術者が催眠中に、オランダ女性の役柄を真剣に演じたという事実である。私は、その〝前世〟とされる時間帯の中で、この女性の年齢を容易に操作することができた。結婚式の当日に置かれると〝前世の人格〟は、花嫁になる喜びを全身に溢《あふ》れさせた。夫が死亡する日まで時間を進めると、涙を流し、その場に立会っていた者全員の心を揺り動かすほど強い悲嘆に暮れた。（その時、経験豊かな同僚がふたり同席していたが、被術者がその場面にふさわしい感情を繰り返し表出させたため、ふたりはそれに強い印象を受け、この女性は空想にのめり込んでいるだけだとする私の見解には容易に同意しようとしなかった。）

　とはいえ、公正を期すために述べておかなければならないが、この被術者は、通常の手段以外によって身につけた可能性のある、十九世紀のオランダに関する知識をわずかながら示している。たとえば、一八六六年にアムステルダム港に繋留《けいりゅう》されていた帆船を、正確に「ネーデルランド」号と呼んでいる。したがって、本例の前世はほとんどが創作だったのであろうが、中に若干の事実が含まれており、その一部はおそらく、超常的に得られたものなのであろう。

催眠を、前世の記憶を蘇《よみがえ》らせる手段と考えている者は、その種の催眠を何度かかけられた患者の症状が好転したという事実を引き合いに出す場合が多い。たとえば、〝前世〟で溺死した時の模様を語った後に、長期にわたって続いていた水恐怖症を患者が消失させたとすると、患者も施術者も、溺死した記憶を蘇らせたことで症状が改善されたと考えるかもしれない。しかし、これは、患者の症状の好転により、その技法やそれが拠《よ》って立つ理論の正当性が証明されるとする、心理療法家によく見られる誤信を裏書きする実例なのである。神経症的症状の好転や消失は、実にさまざまな治療者が実にさまざまな技法を用いても、同じように得られている。他の治療者が治療に失敗した後に成功を収めた治療者は賞賛に値はするが、その功績は治療者（および患者）自身に帰すべきものであり、その治療者が用いている技法や理論によるものではないのである。後ほど説明するつもりであるが、（事実と確認された具体的事象を含む）前世を記憶していると主張する子どもたちは、その前世で死亡した状況に沿った恐怖症を示すことが多い。とはいえ、こうした恐怖症は、子どもが前世の話を始め、その原因を説明するようになる前に出現することもあるし、子どもがその原因となった外傷体験を口にしている期間中続くこともある。また、子どもが前世のイメージ記憶を消失してもなおかつ続く例もある。こうした恐怖症を見ると、それに関係するらしい前世の記憶を回復することでその恐怖症が消失すると考えてよい根拠はない。このような問題はあるが、恐怖症の引き金になった外傷体験を思い出すことには治療効果があるという事実を全否定しているわけではない。（この問題は、第5章〔特に註15〕でもう一度とり上げる。）

私は、前世と思《おぼ》しき時代まで遡《さかのぼ》る大半の催眠実験の結果については懐疑的であるが、全てを無意味だとして切り捨てているわけではない。過去の特定の場所について漠然とした知識を口にする例が少数ながら存在するが、そうした事例では、私が調べた限り、通常の方法でそれを知った可能性はきわめて少ないように思われる。私は、バーンスタインの著書『ブライディ・マーフィーの探索』〔邦訳、『第二の記憶』光文社〕で述べられている事例は、この少数例に入ると考えている。[*8] また、私が調査した二例では、催眠状態で年齢遡行した被術者が、通常の方法では習ったことのない外国語を話す能力をもっていることが明らかになっている。この能力は、真性異言と呼ばれる。このふたりは、それぞれ外国語で会話することができた。つまり、同じ言葉を話す者と意味の通ずる会話ができたのである。[*9]

催眠により引き出された前世の人格の大半に、その価値を損なうような愚かしい点があるからといって、こうした事例から浮かび上がるひとつの正当な疑問を無視してよいことにはならない。このような実験の被術者たちは、自らの前世の背景としてどの時代や場所を選んでもかまわないのに、なぜ特定の時代や場所を選ぶのか、という疑問である。どの時代のどの場所に遡ってもよいと言われているのに、たとえば、十八世紀のフランスや十九世紀のドイツではなく、どうして十七世紀のスコットランドの生活を選ばなければならないのであろうか。その被術者が、本当に十七世紀のスコットランドで前世を送っていたとすれば、そのためにこそ、他でもないその時代のその場所で過ごした時代を再現したい気持に駆られたという可能性があるのである。次いで、こうした前世が構築される段になると、通常の方法で得られた情報の貯蔵庫から、凝縮された記憶が可能な限り引き出されるのであろう。その過程の中で、本当の前世に由来する記憶の断片が、磁石に引きつけられる鉄粉のように無理やり移動させられ、それ以外の点ではもっぱら架空の前世に引き寄せられる、という可能性があるということである。その結果として、ある種の歴史小説がつむぎ出されるのかもしれない。[10] アムステルダムで前世を過ごしたという先述の女性の例を見ると、その過程がおわかりいただけよう。このような現象は、夢の中で起こることも少なくない。一部の夢には、正確な記憶や（それよりもはるかに稀《まれ》ではあるが）超感覚的知覚によって得られた情報に混じって、明らかに非現実的な要素が含まれているのである。

　前世の記憶らしきものをはじめからある程度もっている者に催眠をかければ、細かい事実を他にも思い出すのではないか、と考える方もおられるかもしれない。私自身もそのように考えたため、自然に浮かび上がった前世の記憶らしきものをもつ数名の者に催眠をかけたことがある。この人たちのもつ記憶らしきものは前世に由来しているのかもしれないが、特に地名と人名については、事実かどうか確認できるほど明確な形では語られていなかった。催眠状態なら、人物や場所の名前を一部にせよ（あるいはそれ以上に）正しく思い起こしてくれるかもしれないし、そうすれば、この人々の記憶に残っているという前世の人格の存在が確認できるのではないかと考えたわけである。

　私は、このような実験を一三件、自ら行なったり指導したりしている。一部では私自身が施術を行なったが、それ以外の実験では他の術者に実験を依頼した。その結果はと言えば、ただの一件も成功しなかったのである。こうした実験が失敗に終わったのは、実験を行なった時点の被術者が（ひとりを除いて）すべて青年ないし成人に達していたためなのかもしれない。*11

この種の実験は、たとえば七、八歳くらいの児童を対象にしてもっと幅広く行なわれるべきである。この年齢の児童なら容易に催眠状態に導入できるし、本当の前世の記憶を残しているとすれば、年を経た時よりも意識の表層に近いところにあるかもしれない。また、前世の話に登場する内容を通常の方法で知ったとしても、その情報源に接した可能性については、若年の時の方がより明確にわかるのがふつうである。それに対して、成人では、前世にまつわる幻想の中で利用できそうなさまざまな情報源に、小さな子どもよりも長く、しかも頻繁に接触しているのである。

既視感という体験

初めての場所なのに、前に来たことがある気がするという体験をする者がある。心理学者はこれを「既視感《デジャ・ヴュ》」と呼んでいる。こうした体験をもつ者は、七六パーセントの高率にのぼっている。*12

一部の生まれ変わり型事例では、自分が前世を送ったという村に初めて行った時に既視感が起こる。本人の記憶に残っている時代と比べると、戸口や部屋や木立をはじめ、周辺の建物や空地などの状況が変わっていることにも気づくが、その村のすべてあるいはかなりの部分がなつかしく感じられるのである。[13] 既視感を経験しながら前世のイメージ記憶をもたない一般の人間は、いわば前世の先端部分だけ覚えていて、それ以上の記憶を意識化できないということなのかもしれない。

とはいえ、ほとんどの既視感についてはこのような解釈は不要であろう。既視感の多くについては、生まれ変わりという考え方よりも適切な解釈がいく通りかあるからである。[14] たとえば、一部の既視感は、私たちが予知と呼ぶ、推測によらず未来を知るという現象に基づくものかもしれない。予知は、時たま夢の中で起こる。ある人が、それまで一度も見たことのない場所の夢を見たとして、その時点ではわからないが、その後にそこへ行くことになるとしよう。その夢のことは忘れているが、その残渣《ざんさ》は意識の底に残っているかもしれない。記憶の実験から、「再認は想起にまさる」ことが明らかになっている。つまり、たとえばある人の名前を思い出そうとして出て来ない時でも、その名前が含まれている名簿を見ればわかる場合があるのである。先ほどの例では、夢を見た人は、その夢に現われた場所へ実際に行った時、理由は説明できないものの、そこがなじみの深い場所のように感じられるかもしれないし、場合によっては前に見たことがあると思うかもしれない。一部の既視感にはこの説明が当てはまるように思う。この場合、既視感を抱いた者は、なじみ深く感じられた場所が出て来た夢を、後で思い出したのである。

既視感の中には、それよりもはるかに単純な説明でこと足りるものもあるかもしれない。なじみ深く感じられる場面は、自分が過去に見た場面に似ているのに、その類似性に気づかないだけなのかもしれないのである。これは、知人とまちがえて見知らぬ他人に近寄って名前を呼ぶといった状況と似ている。その場合、誤って名前を呼ばれた相手は、私たちがそのまちがいに自分で気づかなければ、すぐにそのことを指摘してくれる。しかし、目の前に広がる風景や進行中の出来事は口が利けるわけでもなければ、私たちのまちがいを正してくれるわけでもないため、なじみがあるように感ずると、「昔ここに来たことがある」という誤解がそのまま続くことになるのかもしれない。

一部の既視感については、神経学的な説明が可能なのではないかとも言われてきた。もし大脳の両半球の機能の同期がわずかにずれているとすると、一方の半球を介して意識に到達する情報は、その半球では新しいものとして記録されるが、一〇〇〇分の一秒ほど遅れて到達するもう一方の半球では古い情報として記録されることであろう。そのような現象が実際に起こるという実験的証拠は知らないが、たとえそういう現象が起こるとしても、通常の手段ではわかりようのない場所を知っているという、稀に起こる既視感については説明できないであろう[*15]。

夢と悪夢

自分が今とは違う場所にいて、今とは違う時代の服装をしているような感じのする夢を見る者がある。この種の夢は繰り返されることが多く、不快な、悪夢的色彩をもつ場合もある。こうした夢を見る者の中には、子どもの頃に始まり、その後しばしば見るようになったと言う者もある。年長になるにつれてその夢を見る頻度が低くなり、しまいには全く見なくなる、という経過を辿《たど》ることもある。

この種の夢で（私見によれば）比較的重要なものの場合には、本人が夢の中の出来事を再体験しているかのように見える。この種の夢を見る者は、このような変わった夢とありきたりの夢との違いが言葉ではなかなか区別できないかもしれない。とはいえ、目覚めるまでは気づかないとしても、ふつうの夢は脈絡や首尾一貫性を欠き、全体として非現実的に感じられるとは言えるであろう。それに対して〝前世〟の夢では、その場面は完全に現実的で首尾一貫している。周囲は細部に至るまで、覚醒《かくせい》時と同様に鮮明かつ自然であり、ふつうの夢とは異なり、事物が奇異に感じられることはない。その夢が繰り返される場合には、内容が毎回全く同じであり、その夢の（危機状況に陥った時点が多いが）同じ場面で目覚めるのがふつうである。最後に、この型の夢は記憶に鮮明に刻み込まれ、大方の夢とは異なり、忘れ去られることがない。このように記憶に刻み込まれるという現象は、一度しか見ない夢でも起こる場合があるので、繰り返し見ることが記憶に刻み込まれるための必要条件ではない。

この種の夢を私に話してくれた人は少なくない。たとえば異常な恐怖心や特定の国に対する関心のように、当人の人格の一面と一致するものも若干あるが、ほとんどのものには、事実かどうか確認できるほどの具体性はない。

アリス・ロバートソン（仮名）というアメリカの少女は、（幼少期から）長年にわたって繰り返し悪夢に襲われたが、その鮮明な内容はいつも全く同じであった。この少女は、夢の中では踝《くるぶし》まで届く長い服を着た成人女性で、娘とわかる少女を連れて通りを静かに歩いていた。夕方で、太陽が地平線に近づいていた。すると突然、耳をつんざくばかりの轟音《ごうおん》がとどろき、大地が足元から崩れ落ちるような感じになった。そこでいつも少女は恐怖に脅え、金切り声を上げながら目を覚ましたのである。その結果、子どもを案ずる母親がいつも本人の枕元に走って来た。その子ども（当時のアリス）はいつも、悪夢の場面が現実にあったことを母親に説明しようとしたが、監督教会派の主教夫人であった母親は、そんなことはありえない、「ただ夢を見ていただけ」だと言っていつもアリスを宥《なだ》めようとした。結局アリスは、昔実際に起こった出来事を悪夢の中で再体験していることを母親にわからせるのは不可能だと悟り、説得をあきらめた。しかし、その後も、頻度こそ次第に低くなったものの、その悪夢は相変わらず続いていた。

アリスは、大きくなってから、夢の中で着ていた踝まで届く長い服はサリーであることに気がついた。この事実は、アリスがインドに強く引かれることと軌を一にしていた。アリスは娘時代に、（インド北部の）ダージリンの風景が登場する映画を見た時、強い既視感が起こった。その後、ダージリンについて書かれた本を初めて読んだが、その結果、一八九〇年から一九二〇年にかけて壊滅的な地滑りがダージリンで何回も発生しているという事実を知った。そこでアリスは、悪夢に出て来る前世の舞台はダージリンだと確信するに至った。しかし私には、それが事実かどうか確認することはできなかった。確認が可能なほど人名や地名を挙げることができなかったからである。本章の前半で、催眠を利用してさらに記憶を引き出そうとした事例が数例あることについて述べておいたが、アリスはそのうちのひとりである。しかしアリスは、悪夢にいつも登場する恐ろしい場面を催眠中に再体験したものの、新しい記憶はひとつも出て来なかった。

メアリ・マグルーダー（仮名）というアメリカの少女も、同じく不快な悪夢をやはり幼少期から見ていた。メアリはその夢の中では少女で、白人開拓者の集落が先住民の襲撃を受け、そのうちのひとりに追いかけられていた。アリスの夢と同じく、メアリの夢も鮮明で、内容も細部に至るまで毎回よく似ていた。しかし、この夢はいつも最後の場面まで続いたわけではなかった。先住民が何人かで本人を追いかけているだけの時もあったし、そのうちのひとりに捕まって、髪を摑《つか》まれている時もあった。ここでいつもメアリは、泣き叫びながら目を覚ますのであった。時おりメアリは、「お母さん、あいつらが私の髪を摑んでる」と口走った。特にメアリは、今の髪は金髪の直毛なのに、夢の中の髪は茶色の巻毛であるのに気づいていた。

悪夢の中で前世を再体験しているような気がしたもののメアリは、十八世紀に先祖が住んでいたヴァージニア州西部をたまたま訪れるまでは、そのことについてあまり深くは考えなかった。（メアリは中西部で育てられたので、成人に達して以降この地方を訪れるまでは、そのあたりのこともそこに住んでいた先祖のことも全く知らなかった。）その時メアリは、先住民の襲撃で焼け落ちた建物があったことから、先祖伝来の土地の一部が〝焼け小屋〟と言われている事実を知った。〝焼け小屋〟から四キロほど離れた道路脇に立っている史跡案内板には、ヴァージニア州最後の先住民による襲撃は一七六四年にその近くで行なわれていることが明記されている。焼け小屋一帯を現在所有しているメアリの遠戚《えんせき》にあたる男性は、先住民の襲撃に因《ちな》んでそう呼ばれるようになったとする言い伝えが事実であることを、私に証言してくれた。その男性によれば、その事件があったのは一七四五年から五〇年の間ではないかという。

メアリは、その悪夢に登場する前世の一場面らしきものについてそれ以上詳しいことはわからなかったし、その出来事が事実かどうかの確認もできなかった。とはいえ、その内容を見る限り、歴史的にはありそうなことである。[16]

私がこれまで調査してきた子どもたちがもっている記憶の大半は、通常の覚醒状態で意識に昇ってきたものである。しかし、記憶に残る前世の場面が夢や悪夢の中で現われた事例もいくつかある。[17] このような夢では、変形が起こることもあるが、超常的な要素が絡んでいる夢でも同様の場合が多いし、その点はふつうの夢も同じである。

その一例としては、アリフ・ハメッド（仮名）というレバノンの少年の事例が挙げられる。アリフは、バルコニーから大きな石材が剥《はが》れ落ち、本人を直撃するところで終わる前世を覚えていた。この男性はバルコニーの下で腰を下ろしていた時、その石に頭部を直撃されて即死したのである。アリフの記憶によれば、その人物が死亡する直前に、その家の周辺で山羊《やぎ》が何頭か草を食《は》んでいる場面が見えるという。アリフは、建築用の石材が積み上げられた上に山羊が登り、その一部をひっくり返す場面を何度となく夢に見た。前世の人格が死亡した時、その家の周辺に山羊が本当にいたかどうかはわからなかったが、アリフの記憶の一部については、事実であることを私が確認している。また私は、山羊がいたというのも本当だろうと思っている。

レバノンの山村部では、山羊は家畜としてふつうに飼われているからである。もしそれが正しければ、アリフが繰り返し見た夢にその場面の記憶がとり入れられ歪曲《わいきょく》されたことになる。この夢は、前世の人格が死亡した時点の状況に基づくもののように思われるのである。

したがって私は、繰り返し生ずる鮮明な夢の中には、前世の記憶に由来するものがあるのではないかと考えている。とはいえ、事実かどうか確認できない出来事が登場するこの種の夢について、もっとはっきりした判断ができるようにするにはどのような方法を用いたらよいのかもわからないし、どの点を基準に判断したらよいのかもわからない。その夢の鮮明度によって超常的なものかどうかを見極めればよいのかもしれないが、その判断が正しいことを保証してくれるものがあるわけではない。鮮明な夢は、そうではないものと比べ、超常的な要素が含まれている可能性が高いのかもしれないが、そのほとんどにそうした要素はないのである[*18]。また、事実と確認された点がいくつか含まれる夢の場合にも、通常の方法で得られた情報なのかどうかを検討しなければならない。

　私は、このように同じ夢を繰り返し見る人々に対して、軽率な解釈をしないよう特に注意してきた。こうした体験をもつ人々の中には、百科事典に飛びつき、夢に登場する場面や出来事と一致する生涯を送った人物にまつわる情報を探し出そうとする者もある。私のところに手紙を寄せてきたある女性は、十九世紀前半にヨーロッパで流行した洋服を優雅に着こなしている感じのする鮮明な夢を見たという。夢の中では、同じくみごとな着こなしをした貴族風の男性がその女性に言い寄っていた。私としては、その夢に登場することだけ調べて満足している方が賢明だったのではないかと思うのであるが、残念ながらこの女性はそれでは満足せず、自分の前世は、ババリアのルードヴィッヒI世に王位を捨てさせたほどの美貌《びぼう》のもち主であったローラ・モンテスという悪名高い舞踏家だったにちがいない、と速断したのである。（やはり私に手紙を書いてきた中に、別の理由から自分が昔ローラ・モンテスだったと思い込んでいる女性がいる。私としては、このふたりをそれぞれ相手に紹介すべきなのかもしれない。）

病気と薬物

ＬＳＤのような薬物の影響を受けている中で、前世の一端を蘇《よみがえ》らせたように感じられる体験をした者もある。ＬＳＤには、現世で起こった過去の出来事の記憶をきわめて明瞭《めいりょう》に蘇らせる力のあることが、一般のＬＳＤ体験から知られている。それゆえ私は、生まれ変わりが現実に起こるとすれば、ＬＳＤ（および同類の薬物）を用いると前世の記憶が蘇りやすくなる可能性があると思わないでもない。とはいえ私は、こうした薬物によって前世を、事実かどうか確認できるほど詳しく思い出した者をこれまでひとりも知らないのである。[*19] また、このような形で意識に上る記憶は、夢の場合と同様の変形を起こすかもしれない。

ＬＳＤには、不快な副作用ややっかいな問題が発生することがあるし、場合によっては、それが重大な問題に発展することすらある。ＬＳＤは、その効果がまだ明確には知られていないため、適切に利用されていない薬物だとは思うが、不適切な条件の下で用いられる時には、いつも危険が潜んでいる物質であると思う。ここで言う不適切な条件とは、主として、医師による適切な指示がない場合を指す。したがって、前世の記憶らしきものを引き出すための手段としてＬＳＤを用いることには、私としてはとうてい賛成できないのである。

前世の記憶のようなものが、（通常は発熱や譫妄《せんもう》状態を伴う）重病の際に意識に上って来た、という者も少数ながらある。たとえば、ギラン＝バレー症候群という神経疾患に罹《かか》った（私の共同研究者が面接している）ある女性は、（現世での）過去の出来事と、おそらくは十九世紀フランスで送った前世の中で起こったように思われる出来事のふたつを、鮮明なイメージとして体験した。後者は、現世の出来事の記憶と入り混じっていたが、本人にわかる限りでは、今回生まれて以降に体験した記憶のある出来事に由来するものではなかった。とはいえ、この患者は、重病であったことに加え、薬物による影響も受けていたので、変わったイメージを体験させた直接の物理的原因を特定するのは難しいであろう。

生まれ変わり型事例の中には、（ふつう発熱を伴う）病気に罹っている間に前世の記憶が発現しやすくなる者が若干おり、病気に罹っていた間に前世の話を初めてした者も少数ながら存在する。[*20]

瞑想《めいそう》

瞑想中に前世の記憶を蘇らせたように思われる者もある。シッディ（霊的超常的能力）は、ヒンドゥー教や仏教を中心に霊的に究めようとする者がたまたま身につけるものとされているが、これには、前世の記憶を蘇らせる能力も含まれる。私が知っているいくつかの例では、前世の記憶のようなものが、予測もしていなかったのに瞑想中に突然浮かび上がったとされるが、事実かどうか確認できる記憶をこのような形で蘇らせた者は、私の知る限りひとりしかいない。それは、（タイの尼僧である）プラトムワン・インタヌ師である。この尼僧は、瞑想中に、自分が生まれ育ったところからかなり離れた場所で送ったふたりの幼児の生涯をそれぞれ思い出し、それが事実であることが後で確認されたのである。

瞑想中、偶発的に生ずる前世の記憶らしきものは、事実かどうかの確認が行なわれず、したがって何の証拠にもならないが、当人にとっては意味があるかもしれない。（瞑想を行なっている人たちは、必ずしも証拠を探し求めているわけではない。）

しかしながら私としては、こうした記憶を意図的に蘇らせようと本人が企てた場合、瞑想中に呼び覚まされる前世の記憶らしきものを重視することのないよう警告を発しなければならない。このような目的で瞑想を行なう時には、前世の記憶と誤認しやすい幻想が生じる可能性が高まってしまう。瞑想中に前世の記憶を探し求める者は、催眠状態にある者と同じような状況に置かれている。両者とも、他に課題をもっているわけであるが、それを果たす手段として幻想を作り上げる可能性があるからである。

このように意図的に引き出そうとしない時でも、瞑想中には幻想が生じ、実際の記憶ととり違えられることがある。ここで念頭に置かなければならないのは、瞑想を行なっている西洋人の大半が、東洋に起源をもつ技法を採用しているという事実である。生まれ変わりが存在する可能性に無関心な者はほとんどおらず、瞑想をすれば前世の記憶が意識に上ってくるかもしれないと、ほとんどの者が思っている。そのため、瞑想中にたまたま生じたイメージをすべて前世の記憶だとして、無批判に受け入れやすいのである。

強烈な感情

私が知っている中に、深い悲しみのような強い感情に襲われた時に前世の記憶らしきものが蘇ったという成人がわずかながらいる。ゲオルク・ナイトハルトの事例は、この種の実例の最たるもののように思われる。ミュンヘンに住んでいるナイトハルトがまだ若かった頃、最初の妻と娘が短期間のうちに相次いで死亡した。そのため本人はうつ状態に陥り、それが数ヵ月続いた。そのような状態で迎えたある日、前世と思《おぼ》しき一連の場面が突然、心の中に蘇り始めたのである。各場面はひとりでに順序よく並んだので、ゲオルクはそのまま記録しておいた。その後ゲオルクは、具体的な事柄の一部が事実にまちがいないことを確認し、他の点についても、十二世紀のババリア（ミュンヘンの北東）で送った男性の生涯と一致するらしいことに気づいたのである。ゲオルク・ナイトハルトの事例ほどはっきりした証拠はないが、私が注目している同様の事例は他にもいくつかある。

覚醒《かくせい》時の成人による多種多様の体験

　成人の中にも、前世の記憶のようなものが、通常の覚醒状態の中で自然に「パッと浮かぶ」（あるいはもっと長く続く）という体験をする者がある。これまでの報告は、そうした現象の体験者が自ら提出したものがもとになっているので、こうした体験がどの程度の頻度で起こるのかはわからない。この種の偶発的な「ひらめき」を分析する場合、これまで紹介してきた他の種類の証拠を分析する時と同じ問題が発生する。事実であることが確認されなければほとんど無意味であるし、それが確認されたとしても、通常の情報源からその内容を知った可能性が棄却できなければ、やはりほとんど意味がないということである。[*21]

少年少女の偶発的体験

　幼時に端を発することの多い夢や悪夢を別にすれば、これまで考察してきたさまざまな証拠はすべて、成人から得られたものである。成人に達するまでに人間の心は、数多くの情報源から得られた種々さまざまな知識で満たされてしまう。こうした知識の多くは、心の奥底にひっそりと収められており、当の本人もその知識をもっていることを知らないことすらある。しかしながらそれは、前世の幻想が拠《よ》って立つ基盤となる。無意識の奥底に蓄えられた記憶は、前世の記憶を意図的に引き出そうとする時、このような形で特に利用されやすい。催眠による年齢遡《そ》行《こう》の場合や瞑想の中でこのようなことが起こる仕組みについては既に述べておいたが、幻覚剤が投与されている時にも、同じことが時たま起こるように思う。

以上の説明で、少年少女が自発的に前世について語った事柄を私が特段に高く評価している理由が、読者の方々にもある程度おわかりいただけたことであろう。ごくわずかな例外はあるが、このような子どもたちは、自分から進んで話すのであって、前世を思い出すよう求められているわけではない。また、前世の話を始めるのは幼児期がふつうであるが、それは、故人に関する情報が通常の経路からまだそれほど伝わってはいないはずの年齢なのである。そのうえ、そのような子どもたちが故人についていかなることを語るにしても、それを通常の手段で知った可能性を十分に検討できるのがふつうである。私は、これまで二五年間にわたって、このような子どもたちの事例に注目してきたので、次章以降はほとんどの紙幅を、こうした事例に充てることにしたい。次章では、一二例の典型例について紹介するが、全例が、幼児期に初めて前世の話をしているのである。

第4章　前世を記憶する子どもたちの一二の典型例

本章では、生まれ変わりの代表的事例を最大限に要約した形で紹介する。この一二例は、これまで私が調査研究を行なってきた八ヵ所の文化圏から選び出したものである。生まれ変わり型事例は仏教徒やヒンドゥー教徒の間でしか存在しないという、広く見られる誤解を正す一助とすべく、アラスカのトリンギット族およびレバノン、イギリス、フィンランドの各国から各一例、合衆国大陸部から四例を選び出している。(合衆国の五例については、すべて仮名を用いた。)

いずれの事例でも、前世を記憶しているとする人物は、幼児期のうちにその前世の話を始めているし、それぞれの事例で、その時期に子どもがそのような発言をした事実を、ひとりないし数名の成人が証言している。

そのうちの六例については、既に別著で報告しているが、残る六例についても、詳細な報告をいずれ発表するつもりである。[*1]

ゴーパール・グプタの事例

ゴーパール・グプタは、一九五六年八月二六日にインドのデリーで生まれた。両親は、ほとんど教育のない中流の下の階層に属している。ふたりとも、乳児期のゴーパールの発育に変わった点があったことには気づかなかった。

ゴーパールが（二歳から二歳半の間に）言葉を話すようになってまもなく、グプタ家に来客があった。父親がゴーパールに、客が使ったコップを片づけるよう命ずると、ゴーパールは、「そんなものは持たない。ぼくはシャルマだ」と答え、周囲を仰天させた。（シャルマとは、インドで最高のカーストであるバラモン階級に属する人々のことである。）それから癇癪《かんしゃく》を起こし、コップをいくつか割った。父親はゴーパールに、乱暴なふるまいをした理由と、仰天すべき発言を行なった理由とを尋ねたところ、ゴーパールは、マトゥラーという町で暮らしていた前世時代の記憶をつぶさに語った。マトゥラーとは、デリーの南方一六〇キロほどのところにある町である。

ゴーパールの話によると、当時本人は薬品関係の会社を経営しており、その社名はスク・シャンチャラクであったという。また、大邸宅に住み、召使いを大勢使っていたこと、妻とふたりの弟がいたこと、弟のひとりと口論し、その弟に撃たれたことなどについても語った。

前世でバラモンだったというゴーパールの主張からすると、そのコップにふれるのを拒否した理由は説明できた。バラモンであれば、自分より下の階層に属する者がさわった食器類には手をふれないのがふつうだからである。ゴーパール自身の家族は、バニャンという商人のカーストに属していた。

ゴーパールの両親はマトゥラーとは全く無関係であったし、ゴーパールから、その町で暮らしていたという話を聞いても、何も思い出せることはなかった。母親は、本人が覚えているという前世についてあえてゴーパールから聞き出そうとはしなかったし、当初は父親も、この問題には無関心であった。しかし父親は、ゴーパールが語った内容を時おり友人に話して聞かせていた。話を聞いた友人の中に、ゴーパールの話と符合する、マトゥラーで起こった殺人事件をおぼろげながら覚えている者がひとりいたが、父親は、本人が語った事柄が事実かどうか確かめるためマトゥラーまで出かける気にはならなかった。父親は、宗教的な祭典を見物する目的で（一九六四年に）マトゥラーまで出かけたが、そのおり、スク・シャンチャラク商会を見つけ、ゴーパールが語った内容が本当かどうかを販売の責任者に尋ねている。父親からその話を聞かされた責任者はそれに思い当たるところがあった。経営者のひとりが、何年か前、兄を射殺していたからである。撃たれた兄のシャクティパル・シャルマは、その二、三日後の一九四八年五月二七日に死亡している。

　販売責任者は、ゴーパールの父親が訪ねて来た時のことをシャルマ一家に話した。その後、何人かの家族がデリーにゴーパールを訪ねて言葉を交わし、マトゥラーに住む自分たち家族のもとへ遊びに来るよう誘った。その招待に応じたゴーパールは、マトゥラーに一家を訪ねた。両者がデリーとマトゥラーで対面した際、ゴーパールは、シャクティパル・シャルマが知っていたさまざまな人物や場所を見分け、シャルマについてかなり知っていることをうかがわせる発言を行なった。シャルマ一家は、シャクティパル・シャルマが妻に借金を申し入れた事実をゴーパールが語ったことに特に強い印象を受けた。シャルマは妻から借りた金をその弟に与えたかったのである。この弟は、共同経営者であったが、けんか好きで金遣いが荒かった。シャクティパル・シャルマは、もっと金を渡して、要求の多い弟を宥《なだ》めたかったのであるが、妻はこうした宥和《ゆうわ》策に賛成せず、夫の申し入れを拒んだ。そのため弟はますます怒り狂い、あげくはシャクティパルに向かって発砲したのであった。こうした内輪のいざこざは詳しくは公表されなかったので、家族内の関係者以外には、詳しい経過を知っている者はおそらくいなかったであろう。（殺人事件そのものは広く知られていた。）ゴーパールがこうした事柄を承知しており、それ以外にもいくつかの発言を行なったうえ、シャクティパルが知っていた人物を見分けたことから、シャルマ一家はゴーパールがシャクティパル・シャルマの生まれ変わりだと確信するに至った。

前世について語ったことに加え、ゴーパールは、裕福なバラモンならともかく、ゴーパール自身の家族にはふさわしくない行動を示している。ゴーパールは、家族の者に、自分はおまえたちよりも高いカーストに属しているという発言を平然と行なっているのである。いかなる家事もしたがらず、自分にはそのための召使いが何人もいると主張し、他の者が使ったコップではミルクを飲もうとしなかった。

インドの事例について、長年私と共同で研究を続けてきたジャムナ・プラサード博士は、本例の調査を一九六五年に開始した。私は、一九六九年に本例の調査に着手し、デリーおよびマトゥラーに住む双方の家族を対象に面接調査を行なった。私は、この事例の追跡調査を一九七四年まで続けている。

ゴーパールは、マトゥラーへ行きたいという願望を強く表明したことは一度もなかったし、一九六五年にマトゥラーを訪れた後に、もう一度行かせてほしいと懇願することもなかった。一九六五年以後の数年間、ゴーパールは、デリーに住む、シャクティパル・シャルマのふたりの姉妹を時おり訪ねているが、それ以降、両家の接触は完全に絶たれている。成長するに従ってゴーパールは、バラモン風の紳士気どりを徐々にやめ、自らの家族が置かれている質素な環境に次第に適応するようになった。シャクティパル・シャルマの生涯について話すことも少なくなって行ったが、一九七四年の段階でも父親は、依然としてゴーパールにはかなりの記憶が残されていると考えていた。

ゴーパールの事例は、シャクティパル・シャルマの生涯および死亡時の模様を通常の方法で知った可能性が低いという点で、証拠性が高いもののように思われる。シャクティパル・シャルマがマトゥラーの有力者一家の一員であったのは事実であるし、シャクティパルが殺害された事件が当時大きく報道されたのも事実である。しかしながら、シャルマ家とグプタ家は相当に離れた地域で生活していたことに加えて、カーストや経済的な階層も全く異なっているのである。双方の家族の生活圏がこのように全く違っているので、私としては、本例が表面化するまで相手の存在は互いに知らなかったとする双方の家族の言い分を、ためらうことなく受け入れたいと思う。

コーリス・チョトキン・ジュニアの事例

アラスカに住むトリンギットの老漁師ヴィクター・ヴィンセントが姪《めい》のコーリス・チョトキン・シニア夫人に向かって、自分が死んだらおまえの息子として生まれ変わるつもりだ、と語ったことが本例の発端になっている。ヴィクター・ヴィンセントは姪に小さな手術痕《あと》をふたつ見せた。ひとつは鼻柱の近くにあり、もうひとつは背中にあった。その痕を見せながら姪に、このふたつの痕跡《こんせき》と同じ場所にあざがあるから（来世では）すぐ見分けがつくはずだ、と語ったのである。

　ヴィクター・ヴィンセントは、一九四六年春に死亡した。その一年半ほど後（一九四七年一二月一五日に）、チョトキン夫人は男児を出産した。その子は、父親の名前を襲名し、コーリス・チョトキン・ジュニアと名づけられた。コーリス・チョトキン・ジュニアの体には母斑《ぼはん》がふたつあった。母親のチョトキン夫人によれば、その母斑は、かつて伯父《おじ》のヴィクター・ヴィンセントが見せてくれた手術痕と全く同じ部位にあったという。私がこの母斑を初めて見たのは一九六二年であったが、チョトキン夫人の話では、生まれた時にあった位置からはふたつとも既に離れてしまっているとのことであった。とはいえ、ふたつともまだかなり明瞭《めいりょう》であり、特に背中の母斑は印象的であった。長さ三センチ、幅五ミリほどの大きさで、周囲の皮膚に比べて黒ずんでおり、わずかに盛り上がっていた。手術痕が癒《い》えた時の状況とよく似ており、大きな母斑の両側の、手術で切開した皮膚を縫合する糸があるはずの位置に、小さな丸いあざが確かにいくつかついていたため、手術の痕に似ているという印象をますます深めたのである。

コーリスが一歳一ヵ月になったばかりの頃、母親が名前を復唱させようとしたところ、コーリスは腹立たしげに、「ぼくが誰か知ってるよね。カーコディだよ」と言った。これは、ヴィクター・ヴィンセントの部族名であった。コーリスが自分のことをカーコディだと言った話をチョトキン夫人がある伯母《おば》にしたところ、その伯母は、コーリスが生まれる直前、ヴィクター・ヴィンセントがチョトキン一家と暮らすようになる夢を見た話をしてくれた*2。チョトキン夫人によれば、ヴィクター・ヴィンセントが自分の息子に生まれ変わると予言していた話を、それまでその伯母に一度もしたことがなかったのはまちがいないという。

コーリスは二、三歳の時に、ヴィクター・ヴィンセントの妻を筆頭として、ヴィクターが生前に知っていた数名の人物を独力で見分けている。母親の話では、コーリスは、通常の手段で知ったとは考えにくい、ヴィクター・ヴィンセントの存命中に起こったふたつの出来事についても言い当てているという。また、コーリスは、ヴィクター・ヴィンセントとよく似た行動特徴もいくつか示している。たとえばコーリスは、髪の梳《と》かし方がヴィクター・ヴィンセントと瓜《うり》ふたつであったし、ふたりとも吃音《きつおん》があり、船や海の上にいることを非常に好み、きわめて宗教心が強く、しかも左利きだったのである。コーリスはまた、小さい頃から発動機に関心を示し、発動機を操作、修理する技術ももっていた。母親の話では、コーリスは船の発動機の操縦法を独学で修得したという。コーリスが父親からこの技術を受け継いだり学んだりした可能性はない。父親には発動機に対する関心も発動機を操作する技術もほとんどなかったからである。

九歳になった頃コーリスは、それまで記憶していたと思われる前世についてあまり話さなくなり、私が初めて対面した一九六二年には、もう何も覚えていないと語っている。私は、一九六〇年代初頭に三回と、一九七二年に一回の計四回コーリスと面接している。コーリスには吃音があったわけであるが、最後に面接した時にはその吃音は完全に消失していた。しかし、興奮すると吃音が出る傾向は残していた。宗教に対する関心は既に失われていたが、発動機に対する関心はまだ続いていた。ベトナム戦争の時コーリスは、砲兵として前線に出たが、近くで砲弾が炸裂《さくれつ》したため、聴覚に障害を受けた。一九七二年に私が最後に対面した時には、聴覚障害を除いては健康で、シトカの自宅近くのパルプ工場の仕事に意欲的に従事していた。

マ・ティン・アウン・ミョの事例

[*3]マ・ティン・アウン・ミョは、一九五三年一二月二六日にビルマ北部のナツル村で生まれた。両親は、ウ・アエ・マウンとドウ・アエ・ティンであった。マ・ティン・アウン・ミョを妊娠中に、ドウ・アエ・ティンは、上半身裸で半ズボン姿のずんぐりした日本兵が本人の後を追い回し、おまえたち夫婦のもとで暮らすつもりだと宣言する夢を見た。マ・ティン・アウン・ミョが、前世の記憶に由来するらしき行動を初めて示したのは三、四歳の時であった。飛行機が一機、ナツル村上空に飛来したのを見たマ・ティン・アウン・ミョは、ひどく怖がって泣き叫んだ。その後それは（最終的に）飛行機恐怖症にまで発展し、数年間続いた。やはり四歳頃、

めそめそしていたことがあったので、本人にその理由を尋ねたところ、日本に行きたいからだと答えた。その後次第に、第二次大戦中ナツル村に進駐していた日本兵だったという前世の話をするようになった。当時ビルマは日本軍に占領されていたのである。マ・ティン・アウン・ミョは、前世の自分は炊事兵であり、（連合軍の）飛行機が村に飛来し機銃掃射を加えた時、被弾して死亡したと語った。

マ・ティン・アウン・ミョはまた、自分が記憶しているとする前世について他にも何点か発言している。北日本の出身で、そこで結婚して子どもを儲《もう》けたことや、入隊するまで日本で小さな商店を経営していたような気がすること、日本軍がビルマから撤退している最中に戦死したことなどを話したのである（この点からすると、前世の人格は一九四五年に死亡したように思われる）。また、その飛行機から機銃掃射を浴びた時の着衣や行動についても、銃弾を避けようとした時にとった行動についても話してくれた。本人の話によれば、鼠《そ》蹊《けい》部に被弾し即死したという。

マ・ティン・アウン・ミョは、日本ということ以上に具体的な地名や人名はひとつも口にしなかった。その日本兵の名前も、出身地も覚えていなかったのである。そのため、本人の陳述と符合する日本人を探し出す作業には、着手することすらできなかった。しかしながら本人が語った内容は、日本軍がビルマ北部を撤退中にナツル村で起こった出来事とは一致していた。ドウ・アエ・ティンは、村に駐屯していた日本兵の中の炊事兵を知っていたばかりか、その男と親しくしていたことも思い出したが、その日本兵がそこで戦死したかどうかについては知らなかった。

マ・ティン・アウン・ミョは、一家から見ると変わった行動を示したが、日本兵の行動とは軌を一にしていた。ビルマ北部の暑さも香辛料のきいた食物も好きではなく、甘い食物を好み、魚を半生のまま食べたがった。ただし、日本人のように全くの生魚を口に入れようとしたわけではない。日本に帰りたいという願望をよく口にし、（本人の話では）ホームシックから膝《ひざ》を抱いてめそめそ泣くこともあった[*4]。また、自分の前で英米人の話が出ると、英米人に対する怒りを露《あら》わにした[*5]。

マ・ティン・アウン・ミョの行動で最も顕著なのは、際立って男性的な点であった。男児の服を着用し、男児のような髪型にしたいと言い張った。そのため、学校ではそれが一大事件に発展した。学校側が、女子生徒にふさわしい服装で登校するよう強く迫ったのに対して、それを拒否したのである。本人の態度が強硬だったため、一一歳頃、学校を中退せざるをえなくなった。教育がないことから、マ・ティン・アウン・ミョは仕事の選《よ》り好みがあまりできなかった。そのため、私が初めて会った時には、近くの駅で食物を売り歩いてわずかな収入を得るのみであった。

幼少期にマ・ティン・アウン・ミョは、戦争ごっこをして遊んでいた。父親がマンダレーに出かける時にはいつでも、おもちゃの鉄砲を買って来てほしいとねだった。三人の姉も弟も、子ども時代に戦争ごっこをして遊んだことはなかった。また本人は、本来男の子の遊びである蹴球《しゅうきゅう》や野球もした。

マ・ティン・アウン・ミョの両親には、本人が生まれる前に既に三女がいた。そのため、次に男の子が生まれてくることを望んではいたが、だからといって、マ・ティン・アウン・ミョを男児のようにしつけたわけではない。事実、（父親はそれほどではなかったようであるが）母親は、本人が男の子のような服装をすることに強く反対した。（父親は、私が本例の調査を開始する以前に死亡していたので、本人にどのような態度で接していたのかを直接聞くことはできなかった。）

さらに成長してもマ・ティン・アウン・ミョは、相も変わらず男性的な特徴を強く残していた。やはり男物の衣服を身にまとっており、男性との結婚には全く関心がなかった。それどころか逆に、女性を妻に迎えたいとすら語ったのである。明らかに本人は、自分を男性と考えており、女性に見られることを嫌っていた。ビルマ在住の共同研究者であるウ・ウィン・マウンが〝マ〟という女性の敬称をつけて呼ぶと、本人は、そんな呼び方はしてほしくないと言い、〝マウン〟（男児に対する敬称）をつけるか、敬称抜きで呼んでほしいと主張したという。ある時本人はウ・ウィン・マウンと私に、自分が男として生まれ変わることを保証してくれさえすれば、どんな方法で自分を殺してもかまわない、と言った。

マ・ティン・アウン・ミョの家族は、いま私が男っぽいのは前世で男だったためだ、という本人の説明を受け入れた。同様に、それ以外の変わった行動についても、その多くは日本兵だった前世時代からもち越されたものとして受け入れたのである。

本例は、生まれ変わり型の未決例としては格好の事例である。マ・ティン・アウン・ミョは、本人が記憶していると思われる前世の人格が特定できるほど詳しい事柄も語っていないし、事実かどうか確認できるような発言も行なってはいない。とはいえ、前世にまつわる本人の発言は、いずれも実際にありそうなことであり、前世で日本兵だったとする本人の主張と符合する変わった行動を示したのである。このような事例は、両親の影響というだけで説明できるものであろうか。それともマ・ティン・アウン・ミョ自身の内にある動機が表出したものと解釈してよいのであろうか。この問題については、後ほどもう一度とり上げることにする。

マ・ティン・アウン・ミョの事例は、〝性転換〟例とされる事例群に含まれるが、（私がこれまで多数の実例を研究してきた）この種の事例については、第5章および第6章で検討するつもりである。

私は、一九七五年の面接を最後に、それ以後マ・ティン・アウン・ミョには一度も会っていない。ただし、（一九七〇年以来ビルマで私の研究を手伝ってくれている）ウ・ウィン・マウンは、一九七七年と八一年の二回、本人と面接している。

シャムリニー・プレマの事例

シャムリニー・プレマは、一九六二年一〇月一六日にスリランカの首都コロンボで生まれた。両親は、コロンボの南方六〇キロほどのところにあるゴナゲラという町に住んでおり、シャムリニーはその町で育っている。

シャムリニーの両親は、娘には、口が利けるようになる前に水浴びに対する強い恐怖心があることに気づいていた。シャムリニーは、水につけられそうになると必ず金切り声をあげ、大暴れして抵抗した。やはり幼児の頃、本人は、バスに対するきわめて強い恐怖症も示し、両親がバスに乗せようとすると必ず泣き叫んだうえ、遠くからバスの姿が見えただけでも泣き出すほどであった。前世に恐ろしい出来事があったためにこのような恐怖症が起こっているのかもしれないとは思ったものの、両親にはこれらの恐怖症は不可解であった。

シャムリニーは、話せるようになると、自分が記憶しているという前世時代のことを、両親はじめ、興味をもって聞いてくれる者に次第に話して聞かせるようになった。その前世の舞台となったのは、ゴナゲラから二キロほどのところにある、ガルトゥダワという村であった。シャムリニーは、その町に住んでいた時代の両親の名前を挙げ、〝ガルトゥダワのお母さん〟のことをよく話した。また、姉妹のことやふたりの同級生のことも語っている。前世時代に住んでいた自宅についても詳しく述べているが、その家の所在地も特徴も、本人一家が現在住んでいる自宅とは全く異なっていた。前世で死んだ時の模様についてシャムリニーは次のように語っている。朝、登校前にパンを買いに出たところ、道路が水浸しになっていた。そこへバスが走って来て水をはねかけられ、冠水した田圃《たんぼ》に落ちた。両手を上げて、「お母さん」と呼んだが、そのあと眠ってしまった。

ガルトゥダワに住んでいたヘマセーリー・グネラトネという少女は、シャムリニーが語った通りの状況で、一九六一年五月八日に溺死《できし》していた。（この少女は、走って来るバスを避けようとして、誤って水田に転落したらしいのである。）ヘマセーリーは、当時一一歳の児童であった。シャムリニーの両親は、グネラトネ一家とは縁戚《えんせき》関係にあったが、ほとんど面識はなかったし、ヘマセーリーとは一度も会ったことはなかった。両親は、その当時ヘマセーリーが死亡したのを聞いて悲しんだことを思い出したが、その後はその出来事を完全に忘れてしまい、シャムリニーが前世で溺死した記憶をもっているという話をするようになっても、ヘマセーリーの溺死事件と結びつけて考えることはなかった。ところが、三歳の頃シャムリニーは、ゴナゲラの街角でたまたまヘマセーリーの従兄《いとこ》を見つけたのである。それから一年以上した時、やはりゴナゲラの市街で、ヘマセーリーの姉を見つけた。そうこうするうちシャムリニーは、ガルトゥダワに連れて行ってほしい、特に〝ガルトゥダワのお母さん〟のところへ行きたい、と執拗《しつよう》に要求するようになり、今の母親は、〝ガルトゥダワのお母さん〟に比べると落ちるとも言った[*6]。

　結局、シャムリニーの父親が本人を、ガルトゥダワのグネラトネ家に連れて行った。生まれ変わったとされる子どもが来ているという話を聞きつけた村人たちが、その家の回りにたくさん集まっていた。見ず知らずの人たちがいっぱいいたため、もっと落着いた雰囲気ならいろいろな人たちを見分けることができたのかもしれないが、この時は、期待されたほどには見分けられなかった。シャムリニーの父親の話では、本人はヘマセーリーの母親であるW・L・ポディ・ノーナがわかったというが、グネラトネの家族はその点に疑問を抱いていた。とはいえ、この時の訪問により、シャムリニーの発言が事実であることが確認された。その発言のほとんどが、ヘマセーリーの生涯に起こった出来事と符合していたのである。加えて、双方の家族がふたりの少女に関する情報を交換した結果、ヘマセーリーとシャムリニーには、特定の食物や服装の好みなどの共通点がいくつかあることが判明した。

私が本例の調査を開始したのは、一九六六年にシャムリニーが初めてガルトゥダワを訪れた二、三週間後のことであった。そのおかげで私は、シャムリニーが何を話しどういう行動をとったのかについても、情報提供者から記憶が新鮮なうちに聞き出すことができた。その後も私は両家を何回か訪れ、細かい点についてさらに詳しく聞き出し、情報提供者が提出した証拠に一貫性があるかどうかを確認したうえ、シャムリニーのその後の成長を見届けようとした。些《さ》細《さい》な点について若干の食い違いはあったものの、それを別にすれば、情報提供者相互の証言は一致していたし、前に聞いた証言と後で聞いた証言の間にも食い違いは見られなかった。

ガルトゥダワを初めて訪れてからシャムリニーは、グネラトネ家の人たちと何度か行き来したが、次第にそれも間遠になっていった。行き来が少なくなるのと並行して、シャムリニーの記憶も徐々に薄れてきた。五歳から七歳までの間にシャムリニーは、前世について自分からは話さなくなり、一九七三年に一一歳になった頃にはすっかり忘れてしまったように見えた。実際に忘れたのは、あるいはもっと前なのかもしれない。水に対する恐怖症も四歳までには消失し、バスに対する恐怖症も八歳までにはかなり薄れたが、まだわずかながら残っていた。そして、私が一九七三年に最後に会った時点では、その点を除いてシャムリニーはシンハラ族の少女として完全に正常な発達を遂げていた。

シャムリニーの事例でも、本人がヘマセーリーの生涯に関する知識を通常の方法で得た可能性は、少なくとも中程度はあるように思う。双方の家族がわずか二キロほどしか離れていないところに住んでおり、シャムリニーが前世の記憶らしきものを話し始める以前にも互いに相手の存在をわずかながら承知していたので、その点は確かに弱点と言える。しかしながら、私の考えでは、双方の家族がわずかに接触していただけでは、ヘマセーリーの生涯についてシャムリニーが詳しく知っていた事実も説明できなければ、本人の発言と対応する異常な行動も説明できないように思われるのである。

スレイマン・アンダリの事例

スレイマン・アンダリは、一九五四年三月四日にレバノンのファルーガに生まれた。一家は、イスラム教イスマイル派の分派であるドゥルーズ派に属していた。ところがこの宗派は、正統派イスラム教の教えからあまりにかけ離れてしまったため、現在では自ら、イスラム教とは別の宗教と考えている。ドゥルーズ派では、生まれ変わりが中心的な教義になっているのである。[*7]

幼少期のスレイマンは、前世時代の記憶をいくつか断片的にもっているように見えた。そのうちの一部は夢の中で想起されたものである。前世では子どもが何人かいたことを思い出し、一部については名前も覚えていた。また、ガリフェという土地の出身であり、搾油機を一台所有していたことも記憶していた。ところが、この種の大半の子どもとは異なり、かなり年長になるまでそれ以上のことは思い出さなかったのである。

本人が一一歳頃、ある出来事が刺激となって他にも記憶が蘇《よみがえ》って来た。本人は、当時、父方祖母と同居していた。そこに母方祖母が来て、ドゥルーズ派の宗教書を一冊貸してくれるよう頼んだ。それに対してスレイマンは、自分のうちにはないのかと、かなりぶっきらぼうに突っぱねたのである。（どうやら本人は、祖母がその本をもっていたらわざわざ借りに来るはずがないとは思わなかったようである。）母方祖母がぞんざいな応対を受けている様子を聞いていた父方祖母はスレイマンに、そのような態度をとった理由の説明を求めた。その時スレイマンは突然に、前世で宗教書をもっており、それを自宅からもち出させないようにしていたことを思い出した。自分の聖典を所有しているドゥルーズ派の信者は、崇《あが》め奉るかのような扱いをして自宅に注意深く保管するものなので、本人がとった態度は、少年の態度としては無作法であったが、年輩の信者がとるはずの態度とは一致していたのである。

この一件があってからスレイマンは、記憶しているとする前世について、新しい事実を多少なりとも意識的に想起しようとした。その結果、自分が昔、ガリフェの首長《ムクタール》だったことを思い出したのである。本人は、アブダラ・アブ・ハムダンというその首長の名前や、その生涯にまつわる具体的な事柄を他にもいくつか思い出した。ところが本人は、前世で首長だったなどと人に話したらばかにされるのではないか、と心配し始めた。家族や友人に、思い上がっていると非難されたり、嘲笑《ちょうしょう》の的になったりするのではないかと恐れ、その後二年ほどの間、その記憶を口外しないようにしていたのである。それから、最初は他の子どもたちに、次いでおとなたちに少しずつ話すようになった。

スレイマンの成人の親族の中には、本人が前世について話している内容が事実かどうか確認するため、本人をガリフェまで連れて行こうと言い出す者もあった。ガリフェは、ファルーガから三〇キロほどのところにあるが、同じレバノンでも行政区が異なっている。ふたつの村を結ぶ道路はあるが、私自身の経験では、行き来にはかなり骨が折れるうえ、特別の理由が必要なのである。スレイマンの家族は、ひとりを除けば、ガリフェとは全く関係がなかった。一時ガリフェで仕事をしていた家族がひとりあるが、その男性も、スレイマンがガリフェの前世時代について語った事柄を、自分の知識に照らして事実だと確認することはできなかった。その後この男性は、ガリフェであちこち尋ね歩いた末、ようやくスレイマンの発言を二、三確認することができた。それと並行して、本人の発言のいくつかが正しいことが、他の人たちによっても確かめられている。

アジアのこの種の事例では一般にそうであるが、前世に関するスレイマンの発言は他者の間でも知られるようになった。親戚《しんせき》の男性が、ガリフェの住人数名と（サウジアラビアで）会い、スレイマンが語った内容を話したところ、その人たちは、スレイマンの記憶がアブダラ・アブ・ハムダンという人物の生涯にまつわる出来事と符合することを証言してくれた。アブダラ・アブ・ハムダンは搾油機を一台所有しており、一九四二年に六五歳ほどで（おそらくは心臓病で）死亡するまで、長い間ガリフェの首長を務めていたのである。この事実を教えてくれたガリフェの住人は、遊びに来るようスレイマンを呼んでくれた。最初は嫌がっていたが、その後、本人は、一九六七年の晩夏と秋の二回にわたりガリフェを訪れている。スレイマンは、ガリフェでは恥ずかしがり、控え目な態度を示したようである。アブダラ・アブ・ハムダンの妻と子どもたちはその村でまだ健在であったが、スレイマンはそのいずれも見分けることができなかったし、写真に写っている家族が誰かもわからなかった。[*8] しかし、家族以外では三人を見分けることができたし、ガリフェの数ヵ所の場所もわかった。そのうち最も重要なのは、アブダラ・アブ・ハムダンが当時住んでいた家屋に通じてはいるが、一九六七年の時点ではもはや使われておらず、ほとんど跡形もなくなっている古い道を本人が指し示したことであろう。とはいえ、スレイマンの事例の重要性は、本人が前世に関係のある場所や人物をある程度にせよ見分けたという点にあるわけではない。前世にまつわる本人の発言や、本人が示した、前世に関連する若干の変わった行動にこそ、その重要性があるのである。

ガリフェに行く前、あるいは初めてガリフェを訪れた時、スレイマンは、自らの前世について一七項目の発言を行なった。その中には、アブダラ・アブ・ハムダンの大半の子どもたちの名前をはじめとして、その生涯にまつわる事柄がいくつか含まれていた。本人の発言は、二点を除いてすべて正確であった。本人は、アブダラ・アブ・ハムダンの息子の名前をサリムとしていたが、実際にはサリムはアブダラ・アブ・ハムダンの兄弟であったし、サリムは盲目だと語っていたが、盲目だったのはアブダラ・アブ・ハムダンのナセブという名前の息子であって、サリムではなかったのである。

私は本例の調査を一九六八年三月に開始し、一九七二年まで継続した。私は、ファルーガとガリフェで多数の情報提供者に面接調査を行なった。スレイマンはその後サウジアラビアに移住したため、一九七二年以降は一度も面接していない。

幼児の頃、スレイマンは、既に成人のような態度を示していた。子どもと一緒に遊ぶよりもおとなとの交わりを好んだし、おとなたちの集まりの中ですら、あたかも重要な人物であるかのように座の中心に坐《すわ》る傾向があった。誰かに咎《とが》められると抗議したし、このような時にはいつも、「私を叱ってはいけない。私はおとななのだ」といった発言をしていた。

前世では首長だったと言っていることを他人に知られたら笑われるのではないか、というスレイマンの恐れは確かに根拠のあることがわかった。家族や友人たちは、本人がそう言っているのをからかい、「村長《むらおさ》」という渾名《あだな》をつけたのである。それに対して本人はいつも腹を立てていたわけではなかった。特に、家族の何人かはこの渾名を、「信頼してますよ」とでも言っているかのように、好意的に使っていると感じられたからである。また、実際にも、アブダラ・アブ・ハムダンの生涯にまつわる本人の言葉が事実であることが証明されてからは、周囲から本当に信頼されるようになったのである。

スレイマンは、家族の者たちにも増して、宗教に強い関心を示した。これは、アブダラ・アブ・ハムダンが宗教に強い関心を抱いていた事実と符合する。アブダラ・アブ・ハムダンは、晩年にシャイフになった。シャイフになるということは、一般人よりもはるかに品行方正な生き方をするため修道生活に入るということである。

先ほど、スレイマンがガリフェに行きたがらなかったことや、最初に招かれた時には断わっていることを述べておいた。本人の家族は、アブダラ・アブ・ハムダンの生涯に起こった悲劇をガリフェに行って初めて知った時、本人の態度がそれまでよりもはっきりと理解できた。アブダラ・アブ・ハムダンは、子どもたちのことで気の休まる暇もなかった。先天性の形態異常をもった者が数名いたうえ、アメリカに移住した者がひとりと、父親との関係が険悪な者がひとりいたのである。加えて、晩年を暗澹《あんたん》たるものにする出来事がいくつかあった。ある友人を助けるためアブダラ・アブ・ハムダンは、村の長として作成すべき文書を愚かにも偽造したことがあったのである。その一件が発覚すると、首長の職を解かれた。さらに本人は、自らの資産を上回る資金を搾油機に投入した。その負債は、思った以上に重荷であるのがわかったため、妻の話によると、そのことで思い悩んだあげく、最終的に死因となる病気に罹《かか》ったのだという。そのため、アブダラ・アブ・ハムダンだったという記憶をもっている者がガリフェへ飛んで行かなかったとしても、誰も不思議には思わなかったのである。

　先ほど述べたように、アブダラ・アブ・ハムダンは、スレイマンが生まれる一二年前の一九四二年に死亡している。アブダラ・アブ・ハムダンがスレイマンとして生まれ変わったとすると、その間どこにいたのであろうか。この疑問に対してスレイマンは、その間もどこかで生きてはいたが記憶はないと答えている。前世の人格とされる人物が死んでから次に生まれ出るまでに（たとえ一日たりとも）間隔が空いている場合には、ドゥルーズ派の信者は決まってそう答えるのである。こうした中間的な前世があることを裏づける証拠がわずかながら見つかることもあるが、たいていは推測の域を出ない程度のものである。[*9]

しかしながら、アブダラ・アブ・ハムダンの記憶をスレイマンがもっている点について言えば、通常の伝達手段によって得られた情報に基づくものとは私は考えていない。スレイマンの村とアブダラ・アブ・ハムダンの村との間の距離（三〇キロ）は、ゴーパール・グプタの事例と比べるとかなり短いものの、シャムリニーの事例よりはかなり離れている。とはいえ、情報が容易に入手できるかどうかは、距離のみによって判断すべきではない。前世の人格について知っている事柄を通常の方法で知ったとすればどのような可能性が考えられるかを、あらゆる角度から検討しなければならないのである。このように考えると、私は、スレイマンの事例をシャムリニーの事例よりも上位に位置づけたい気がする。シャムリニーの事例では、本人の記憶が出現する前に、双方の家族が相手の存在をある程度にしても知っていたからである。この点については、ゴーパールの事例でも同じことが言えるかもしれない。ゴーパールの事例では、双方の家族の地理的、社会経済的な隔たりがスレイマンの事例よりも大きいが、ゴーパールが記憶していたのは、弟に殺されたことが広く世間に知れ渡った有名な人物の生涯であったのに対して、スレイマンは、本人の住んでいた村以外の者には、その生涯や死にざまがほとんど知られていない人物のことを思い出しているからである。

ボンクチ・プロムシンの事例

ボンクチ・プロムシンは、一九六二年二月一二日に、タイのナコーン・サクン省ドン・カ村で生まれた。父親のパモルン・プロムシンは、ドン・カ村近郊のある学校の校長を務めていたため、ささやかな収入しかなかったものの、それなりの教育は受けていた。

まとまった話ができるようになるとすぐに（あるいはおそらくはそれ以前から）、ボンクチは前世について話し始め、具体的な内容を徐々に家族に話して聞かせるようになった。それによるとボンクチは、（ドン・カ村から九キロほど離れた）ファ・タノンという村の出身だというのである。また、チャムラットという前世の人格の名前とともに、チャムラットの両親の名前を口にした。ナイフや自転車などかつて自分がもっていた物についても語り、家で二頭の牛を飼っていたことも話した。（ボンクチの家族は牛を飼っていなかった。）最終的に本人は、ファ・タノンで催された村祭りの日に、ふたりの男に殺された時の模様を語ったのである。犯人たちは本人に数ヵ所の刺傷を負わせたうえ、腕時計と首飾りを奪い、野原に遺体を投げ捨てて逃走したという。（以上の話をボンクチがしたのは二歳頃であった。）

ボンクチによれば、チャムラットが死んでから本人は、現場付近の樹上に七年ほど留《とど》まっていたという。そして、ある雨降りの日に、（現在の）父親の姿を見つけ、バスに乗って自宅に帰る父親について行ったというのである。ボンクチの父親がその後に思い出したところでは、妻が、ボンクチを妊娠してまもない頃、ファ・タノンまで出かけたことがあったという。そこで開かれた会合に出席したのであるが、その日は雨が降っていたというのである。

母親のサワイ・プロムシンは、ボンクチを妊娠する前に殺人現場周辺に筍狩《たけのこが》りに出かけたことがあったが、妊娠するどのくらい前だったかはわからなかった。母親の話では、ファ・タノン村の、チャムラット一家が住んでいる地区には一度も足を踏み入れたことはなかったという。[*10]
パモルン・プロムシンは、職業柄、ファ・タノン村の教師たちとある程度の面識があったが、ファ・タノン村には親戚《しんせき》はいなかったし、実際につきあいのある人物もいなかった。パモルン・プロムシンも妻も、チャムラットが殺された事件を耳にしたことは一度もなかった。チャムラットは、殺された時点ではまだ青年であった。ファ・タノンのような村で殺人事件が起こると、その知らせは、ドン・カ村をはじめとする近隣の村にも届いたことであろう。とはいえ、このあたりでは殺人事件が頻繁に発生するので、周辺で発生した殺人事件を住民が全て覚えているとは考えられないであろう。また、チャムラットは、ボンクチがそのことを話すようになる一〇年以上前に殺されているので、ボンクチの両親は、チャムラットが殺された事件は聞いていたのかもしれないが、ほとんど注意も払わず、すぐに忘れてしまった可能性が高いように思われる。

　ボンクチが語った内容については、チャムラットの家族にも伝わり、何人かの家族がボンクチに会うためドン・カ村までやって来た。（この頃、ボンクチは二歳半ほどであった。）その後、本人は、家族とともにファ・タノンの村に出かけた。このような行き来によって、ボンクチが前世について語った内容のほとんどが事実と確認されたのである。チャムラット殺害事件についてボンクチが語った中には、刺殺された時の模様など、私の情報提供者（および、後には私自身）にも確認できないものがあった。検死が行なわれていなかったからである。殺人犯のひとりは速やかに逃亡し、もうひとりは、逮捕され裁判にかけられたが、証拠不十分のため釈放された。とはいえ、私が面接した何人かの警官は、この殺人事件をかなりよく記憶しており、殺人犯と目される人物の名前など、ボンクチが語った内容の一部については事実であることを証言してくれた。

本例に関する記事が、一九六五年三月にタイで発行された各紙に掲載され、ある人がその切り抜きを私に郵送してくれた。ソフォン・ナクファイラジ博士（ナコーン・サワンにある国立病院の院長）は、一九六五年に本例に関する予備的調査を行なった。私が本例の調査を開始したのはその翌年の一九六六年である。私は、ドン・カ村とファ・タノン村に住む双方の家族に対して面接を行ない、その後も調査を続けた。私がボンクチとその両親に最後に会ったのは、一九八〇年三月であった。

ボンクチの変わった行動は、前世にまつわる本人の発言と同じくらい一家（および、その後に私）の注目を引いた。前世に関連した発言が最も多かった時期には、手を洗う時などに、家族の者からすると不潔な行動を示したし、両親には理解できない言葉をかなり使っていた。ボンクチはまた、家族があまり食べないものや、喜んでは食べないようなものを非常に好んだ。チャムラットの一家は（タイ人が、清潔という問題については自分たちよりも気を配らないと考えている）ラオス人であり、ボンクチが口にしていた聞き慣れない言葉はラオス語だったことがわかった。本例は、真性異言（習ったことのない言葉を話す能力）の有力な事例だと主張したいわけではないが、ボンクチの家族の中には、本人が口にした単語を使う者はいないので、私からすると、本人がそうした言葉を通常の方法で身につけた可能性は考えにくい。（ボンクチにラオス語を教えてくれるような相手は、ドン・カ村にはひとりもいなかった。）ボンクチが好んだ食べ物は、ラオス人が一般に好んで食べる粘り気の強い米飯であった。タイ人もこの種の米飯を食べないわけではないが、ボンクチの嗜好《しこう》は、タイの家族よりも、チャムラットのラオスの家族の方にはるかに近かった。

ボンクチは、チャムラットを殺害した犯人は許せないという態度を示し、機会があれば復《ふく》讐《しゅう》してやる、と何年か言い続けた。時おり、武器のつもりで短い棒を持ち、チャムラットの殺害犯に見立てた杭《くい》を実際に殴りつけることもあった。その際いつもボンクチは、ふたりの名前を口にしていた。

多くの事例と同じく、ボンクチも、おとなの自分が不当にも子どもの体に閉じ込められていると考えることが時おりあった。しばしばボンクチは、〝おとな発作〟とでも言うべきものを起こした。おとなのように歯を磨き（タイでは子どもはふつう歯磨きをしない）、近くの床屋で髭《ひげ》を剃《そ》ってほしいと言ったことも（少なくとも一度）あった。ボンクチは、同年輩の少女を無視したが、思春期を過ぎた若い女性には近づいた。それに対して女性たちはひどく驚き、警戒すらしたのである。プロムシン一家を訪れたある女性は、もっと長く滞在するつもりで来たのであったが、ボンクチに抱きしめられそうになったため、早々に退散した。とはいえ、ボンクチには少々好色なところがあったものの、そればかりではなかった。仏教の修道僧になりたいと言い出すこともあったし、手元にある生地で修道僧用の法衣を作ってほしいと求めることも少なからずあったのである。このように、少々対立するボンクチのふたつの衝動は、チャムラットの態度と符合するように思われる。チャムラットには、本人が死亡した時点で、将来を約束し合っている恋人があった。それと同時に、チャムラットは宗教にも強い関心を寄せ、修道僧になるつもりだと人に話していたのである。（このふたつは矛盾しない。タイでは、二、三ヵ月ないしはそれ以上仏門に入った後に還俗《げんぞく》し、妻帯する若者も少なくない。）

年長になるにつれ、ボンクチの前世記憶は次第に消失して行った。村では何人かの子どもに、「二回生まれた子」と呼ばれてからかわれていたため、実際以上に記憶がなくなっていることにしていたのかもしれない。いずれにせよ、前世の話を人にすることがなくなったため、一〇歳までにその大半を忘れてしまったのではないかと思われる。ボンクチの変わったふるまいも、イメージ記憶の消失とともに減少してきて、（私にわかる範囲では）次第に、どこから見ても正常な発達を遂げたようになった。私が最後に対面した一九八〇年には、一八歳の青年になっており、ナコン・サワンの学校で勉学に励んでいた。この時、ラオス人を思わせる行動のなごりとして見られたのは、粘り気の強い米飯を相変わらず好むことくらいのものであった。

ジリアン・ポロックとジェニファー・ポロックの事例

ジリアン・ポロックとジェニファー・ポロック（一卵性双生児）は、一九五八年一〇月四日、イングランド最北部のノーサンバーランド州ヘクサムに生まれた。ふたりは、二歳から四歳までの間に、ジョアンナとジャクリーンというふたりの姉の生涯を記憶していると見られる発言をいくつか行なった。一九五七年五月五日、精神障害を発症した女性がわざと歩道に車を乗り入れ、そこを歩いていたジョアンナとジャクリーン姉妹を一瞬のうちに轢《ひ》き殺した。その時ジョアンナは一一歳、ジャクリーンは六歳であった。

この悲惨な事故のため、両親のジョン・ポロックとフローレンス・ポロックは、悲嘆のあまり呆然《ぼうぜん》としてしまった。しかしポロック氏は、（妻はそうではなかったが）生まれ変わりを強く信じていたことから、妻が一九五八年初頭に妊娠した時、死んだふたりの娘が双子として生まれてくるはずだ、と自信をもって断言した。病院では否定されたにもかかわらず、妻は双子を生むはずだと言い続けた。そして実際に双生児が生まれたため、軽はずみとも思えたポロック氏の予言が、少なくとも双生児が生まれると言っていた点については正しかったことが立証された。氏の確信は、まもなくさらに裏づけられた。ジャクリーンの体にあったふたつの傷跡と大きさも部位も一致する母斑《ぼはん》が、妹のジェニファーの体にあることに夫妻が気づいたからである。ジェニファーの眉間《みけん》にある母斑は、ジャクリーンが昔倒れてつけた傷と一致していたし、ジェニファーの左腹部にある茶色の母斑は、ジャクリーンにあった同様の母斑と一致していたのである。

先述のように、二歳から四歳までの間に双生児の姉妹は、ふたりの死んだ姉の生涯についていくつかの事実を語っている。そればかりではなく、死んだ姉たちがもっていた、あるいはそれでよく遊んでいたおもちゃのような物品もいくつか見分けている。それに対して両親は、こうした物品をふたりが通常の方法によって知ったはずはない、と主張した。死んだふたりの姉のことを双生児と話し合ったことは一度もなかったし、双生児のふたりは、そうした物品を初めて見た時にわかったということであって、それまでそれを見ているはずがない、というのである。双生児の姉妹がまだ一歳になる前に、一家はヘクサムから引っ越し、四歳頃、両親に連れられて遊びに行くまで、ふたりは一度もヘクサムを訪れていない。ヘクサムに行った時ふたりは、まだ視界に入らないうちに、学校と、公園にあるブランコのことを自分たちから言い出した。ふたりは、（生後九ヵ月でヘクサムから転居するまでの）乳児期に乳母車でその公園へ連れて行ってもらったことはあるが、それによってその学校や公園のブランコの存在を知った可能性はない、と両親は考えている。

ジリアンとジェニファーは、死んだ姉たちと一致する行動も示した。ジャクリーンは姉のジョアンナにかなり頼っていたが、ちょうどそれと同じように、ジェニファーも（双生児の）姉のジリアンをかなり頼りにしていたのである。ふたりが字を習っている時、ジリアンは鉛筆を難なく持てたが、ジェニファーは手で握りしめていた。ジョアンナは、死亡するまでの数年間、鉛筆を正しく持って書くことができたが、（死亡した時点でわずか六歳だった）ジャクリーンは、筆記用具を握って持つ段階に留《とど》まっていたのである。

私は一九六四年に本例の調査を開始し、ポロック一家とは一九八五年まで接触を保っていた。ポロック氏が生まれ変わりを心から信じているという事情があるため、双生児の娘の前ではポロック夫妻（や家族の者）は死んだふたりのことを口にしなかったと言っても信じられない者があるであろう。そのような者からすれば、本例には証拠としての価値はそれほどないかもしれない。生まれ変わりの存在を確信していることで本例の価値が低下するか、場合によっては無になってしまうのではないかという指摘に対してポロック氏は賢明にも、その反論には一理あると思うが、私が生まれ変わりという考え方を受け入れているからこそ、たいていの西洋の親なら無視したり笑いとばしたりするような、ふたりの娘の発言や行動に注目し、記憶しておくことができたのだ、と答えている。

一九七八年に私は、ジェニファーとジリアンをはじめポロック一家の血液型およびその亜型を調べることにより、ふたりが一卵性か二卵性かを明らかにしようとした。その結果、ふたりは一卵性の双生児であることが判明した。つまり、遺伝形質は全く同一だということである。ジェニファーの体に見られるような母斑は遺伝的なものの場合もあるので、それが遺伝的な原因で生じているとすれば、ジリアンにも同じ母斑ができると考えられよう。ところがジリアンには母斑が全く見られないので、妊娠中に起こった何らかの生物学的異常からジェニファーの母斑が形成されたと思われるが、ジャクリーンの体にあった傷跡と部位も大きさもかなり一致する母斑がジェニファーにあることについては、この仮説では説明できないであろう。

ジリアンとジェニファーは、その後、正常な女性として成長を遂げた。そのはるか以前にふたりは、前世に関する記憶を完全に喪失していた。その後も私はふたりと何度か対面しているが、ふたりはかつて自分たちがもっていた記憶については少々懐疑的な態度を示している。つまり、その頃には既に前世の記憶は残っていなかったので、自分たちが生まれ変わりの存在を裏づける証拠になるとは言わなかったのである。とはいえ、幼少期に両親が自分たちを観察した結果として得られた証拠については否定しなかった。

サムエル・ヘランデルの事例

サムエル・ヘランデルは、一九七六年四月一五日にフィンランドのヘルシンキで生まれた。一歳から二歳にかけてサムエルは、ペルティ・ヘイキオという母方叔父《おじ》の生涯を記憶していることをうかがわせる発言を行なったうえ、何人かの人物を見分けている。その後サムエルは、自分の家族から見ると変わっているが、ペルティの行動とは符合する行動をいくつか示したのである。私は本例の調査を、一九七八年と八一年にヘルシンキで行なった。その時の情報提供者は、サムエルの母親と（ペルティの母親に当たる）母方祖母のふたりであった。

ペルティ・ヘイキオは、一九五七年六月八日、やはりヘルシンキで生まれ、一九七五年七月一〇日、重症の糖尿病のため市内で死亡している。一八歳になってまもなくのことであった。死亡するまでの数ヵ月間は、糖尿病放置患者の主症状のひとつである、水を大量に飲むという行動を示したが、昏睡《こんすい》状態に陥り死亡するまで、ペルティがそこまで重病だとは、その当時、誰にもわからなかった。ペルティの母親である（が、夫であるペルティの父親と離婚後、別の男性と再婚していた）アンネリ・ラゲルクイストと、姉である（と同時に、サムエルの母親でもある）マリヤ・ヘランデルのふたりは、ペルティの死を深く悲しんだ。マリヤは、サムエルを妊娠して一〇週目に、ペルティの夢を見た。その頃マリヤは、中絶を考えていたのであるが、夢の中でペルティが、「子どもはそのままにしておいて」と言うのを聞いた。

サムエルが、名前を聞かれて〝ペルティ Pelti〟だと言ったのは、わずか一歳半頃のことであった。(その当時はもちろん、その後しばらくの間も、本人は、〝ペルティ Pertti〟のｒが発音できなかった。)おまえの名前は〝サムエル〟だと教えようとしても、サムエルはほとんど従おうとしなかった。ぼくは〝ペルティ Pelti〟(後には〝ペルティ Pertti〟)だと言ってきかなかったのである。

前世の記憶らしきものについてサムエルが直接語ったのはわずかであり、しかもほとんどは、ペルティと親しかった(多くは写真に写っている)人たちや、ペルティがよく知っていた物品を見分けた時に発せられたものである。

一〇歳以前に撮影されたペルティの写真を見せると、サムエルは、それに刺激を受けていろいろと話すことも少なくなかったようであるが、それ以降の写真では、そういうことはなかった。ある写真を見た瞬間、サムエルは、犬に足を咬《か》まれたのを覚えていると言った。ペルティは三歳の時に犬に足を咬まれたことがあったが、サムエルは犬に咬みつかれたこともなければ、ペルティが咬まれたという話を聞いたこともなかった。また、その写真には、ペルティが犬に咬まれたことがわかるような手がかりは何ひとつ写っていなかった。

また、ある時サムエルは、歩行器を使って歩いているペルティの幼児期の写真に目を留めた。サムエルの話では、両足にギプスをはめて入院していた時の写真だという。本例をヘルシンキで調査していた時、私は、サムエルがそうした発言をするきっかけとなったというその写真を見せてもらった。ところがその写真には、ペルティが歩行器を使っている様子が写っているため両足に怪我をしていることは推測できるかもしれないが、両足にギプスが巻かれているのがわかる手がかりになりそうなものは写っていなかった。ギプスは、その写真を撮影する直前にとり外されていたからである。ペルティは、四歳頃に、事故で両足を骨折している。サムエルがその話をするようになったのは、やはり三、四歳の頃であった。

ペルティの写真を見てこれは自分だとサムエルは主張したが、同じことはいま述べた場面以外でも起こっている。一家は、時おり開いて眺めるアルバムに同様の写真を何枚か貼っているが、サムエルはペルティの写真を見るたびに「これはぼくだ」と言っていたのである。

ペルティの父親であるペンティ・ヘイキオの写真を見た時、サムエルは、「父さんだ」と言った。アンネリ・ラゲルクイストの二番目の夫は、ペンティ・ヘイキオに少々嫉妬《しっと》心を抱いていたため、ふだんこの写真は目につかないところに置かれていた。したがって、アンネリによれば、それを見てサムエルが「父さんだ」と言った時以前には、一度もその写真を見ていないのは確かだという。

サムエルはまた、ギターやコールテンの上着、古ぼけた腕時計など、ペルティの遺品をいくつか見分けている。針が二本とも飛んでしまっていたので、その時計は、がらくたの詰まった引き出しに放り込まれていたのであるが、その時計を見つけた時サムエルは、それに飛びついて、これはぼくのだと言い、自分の手元に置くと言い張った。サムエルは、その時計を枕の下に入れて寝ることもあったが、たいていは、ベッドの下にある引き出しにしまっていた。

サムエルは、ペルティの死について直接には一言も言わなかった。しかし、ペルティの死後に起こった出来事の記憶があることをうかがわせる発言は二回している。本人の話では、棺桶《かんおけ》がたくさん並んでいるところへ行ったことがあり、そのうちのいくつかは蓋《ふた》が開いていたというのである。（サムエルは、霊安室に行ったことは一度もなかったが、ペルティの遺体は、死後、霊安室に安置されていた。）サムエルはまた、ペルティの死後、母親（サムエルの祖母）がどれほど涙を流したかについても語ったが、この点については誰かから聞かされていたのかもしれないし、そう推定しただけなのかもしれない。

ペルティが埋葬されている墓地に連れて行かれた時サムエルは、ペルティの墓を見て、「ぼくのお墓だ」と言った。

サムエルの母親と祖母は、ペルティの行動と符合するサムエルの変わった行動をいくつか指摘している。幼少期にペルティは、浴槽につかっていて水を飲んだことがあった。その時ペルティは恐怖心を露《あら》わにしたが、それがきっかけで水恐怖症が起こることはなかった。その後、一五、六歳になった頃、ペルティは、薄氷を踏み割って埠頭《ふとう》に転落し、さらに海中に落ちた。しかし危ういところで溺死《できし》は免れた。その事故の後、ペルティは水に対する恐怖症を発現させ、泳ごうとはしなくなった。サムエルは、水に入ることに対して明らかな恐怖心を示した。特に入浴に抵抗したため、祖母は、あの子をお風呂《ふろ》に入れようとする時の大騒動といったら「悪夢」です、と言った。

サムエルが初めて言葉を話すようになった時、ペンティとマリアというふうに、両親を呼び捨てにした。また、母方祖母であるアンネリ・ラゲルクイストを、「お母ちゃん」とも呼んだ。この三人の位置づけは明確で、マリヤ・ヘランデルに向かっては、「ぼくの母さんじゃない」と言った。サムエルは、ラゲルクイスト夫人に対して強い愛着を示し、二歳頃には夫人の胸から乳を飲もうとした。（その頃サムエルは既に離乳していたが、ペルティはそうではなかった。）しかしサムエルは、五歳までには、ラゲルクイスト夫人を「お母ちゃん」とは呼ばなくなった。

ペルティには、クリスマス当日に、集まった人たちが一堂に会している部屋を歩き回り、ひとりひとりにキスするというほほえましい習慣があった。家族の他の者には見られない習慣だったらしく、一九七八年のクリスマスに全員が集合した時、わずか二歳半のサムエルが、ペルティと同じく、その部屋を歩き回り、その場にいる人たちにひとりずつキスするのを見て一同は仰天した。

またサムエルは、ペルティによく似たポーズもふたつ見せた。ふたりとも、立っている時には（しばしば腰に片手を当て）片方の足を前に出す癖があったし、時々両手を腰に当てて歩く癖もあった。しかし家族の中には同じような癖のある者はなかった。

ロバータ・モーガンの事例

私が本例を初めて知ったのは一九七一年二月のことで、シャーリー・モーガン夫人という本人の母親が、ミネソタ州の自宅からヴァージニア大学の私のもとへ電話で知らせてくれたのである。それによると、娘のロバータは、数年前、「別のパパとママ」がいると主張し始め、そのふたりにしきりに（というか、正気を失ったかのように）会いたがったという。ロバータの話では、（おそらくは、本人が記憶しているらしき前世時代に）〝別のパパとママ〟に、帰って来ると約束したので、その約束を守りたい、というのであった。

ロバータは、一九六一年八月二八日に生まれているので、一九七一年二月には九歳半になっていた。本人が前世の話を始めたのは、二歳から二歳半にかけてであった。（しかし、一九七一年の段階では、後述する理由から前世の話をしなくなって久しかった。）モーガン夫人の説明では、ロバータが前世の話を一番よくしていた頃には、生まれ変わりに関する知識が全くなかったので、でたらめを言っているとしか思っていなかったという。その後、本を読みいろいろ考えた結果、ロバータは本当に前世を覚えていたのかもしれないと思うようになったばかりか、ロバータに前世の話をさせないようにしたのでは自分の責任を果たしたことにならないのではないか、とも思うようになった。それからというもの夫人は、ほぼ完全に逆の極に走り、一九七一年には、いずれロバータが先方を訪問できるようにするため、どのようにすれば前世の家族が探し出せるかを日夜思い巡らすまでになった。そして、私に電話することにしたのである。

モーガン夫人から先述のような内容を聞いた私は、ロバータが記憶しているらしき前世について本人が語った内容をまとめて書き送ってほしいと依頼した。夫人はそれに応《こた》えてくれたうえ、その後の私信の中で、私のさまざまな質問にも答えてくれた。一九七二年七月に私は、ロバータと母親をミネソタ州の自宅に訪ねた。（この時の訪問では、ロバータの父親とは対面していない。）ロバータは私を暖かく迎えてくれたが、この時点では既に、前世の記憶は完全に消失していた。したがって、本例に関して私が得た情報はすべて、モーガン夫人の提供になるものである。面接や書簡を通じて夫人は、次のような情報を私に提示してくれた。

前世の話を最も頻繁にしていた頃ロバータは、「時おり、（前世の）両親や自宅の記憶を全面的に残している子どもが養女に来てでもいるみたいに」ふるまった。本人の話では、前世の家は、長い道を突き進んだところにあり、人里離れた丘の上の一軒家だという。さらに、自分が覚えているという自宅や敷地についても話したが、馬や犬がたくさんいる農場で暮らしていた、という点を除けば、夫人は、ロバータが語った事柄をほとんど覚えていなかった。四歳頃、ロバータは一度、馬の放牧場に連れて行ってもらったことがあった。誰かに「お馬さん恐くないの」と聞かれた時、ロバータは、「恐くないよ。馬にはたくさん乗ってたもの」と答えている。ロバータはまた、前世の父親が所有していた自動車の話もしている。（それが乗用車だったかトラックだったかについてははっきりしなかった。）ロバータは、時おり車を指差し、「パパが昔乗ってた車が（あるいはトラックが、あるいはパパの昔の車みたいのが）ある」と言った。

ロバータは、自分たち一家が当時暮らしていた町に、「別のパパやママ」がいる、と言った。（当時一家が住んでいたのは、私が訪ねたのとは違う町であった。）ある時ロバータは、母親と一緒に車に乗っていて、あそこに住んでるんだ、と言いながらある道を指差した。本人が指差したのは、幹線道路から脇に入って行く泥道であった。本人は、その道に車を乗り入れて前世の家族に会いに行きたがった。ところが母親は、そうしたくなかった。この時にはロバータが本当のことを言っているとは思えなかったからである。その後ロバータは、せっかく前世の家族に会えるところだったのに連れて行ってくれなかった、と母親を何日も責めた。[11]

　ロバータは、自分が昔もっていたのと似ているおもちゃを買ってほしい、と母親にねだった。どういうおもちゃかわからないと言われたロバータは、母親があまりに鈍いのにあきれてしまった。ロバータは、（本人の）前世を覚えていなければならないのに覚えていないとして、母親をよく叱っていた。（とはいえロバータは、母親が前世時代に関係があったと主張したことはなかった。）

　明らかにロバータは、前世の両親の容姿を視覚的なイメージとしてはっきり記憶していた。ある時ロバータは、前世の母親にふれ、「あの（前世の）ママみたいにしてよ。だけど、あのママはママと似てなかったよ」とモーガン夫人に言った。[12] ロバータは、食事の支度をはじめ、家事全般については前世の母親のやり方を好んだ。

　目新しい料理を（今の）母親が作った時、ロバータは、これは昔何回も食べたことがあると言ったことも、何度かあった。ある時母親は、家族を驚かせようとして、ホタテの貝殻を皿にしてトウモロコシを焼いて出した。それを食卓に載せるとロバータは、「こういうの何回も食べたよ。別のママがよく作ってくれたの覚えてないの」と言った。その時ロバータは、この料理をある名前で呼んでいたが、モーガン夫人はそれを忘れてしまった。夫人が、「別のお母さん」はどういうふうにしてその料理を作るのか尋ねたところ、ロバータは、「別のママ」の調理法について根気よく説明してくれた。ロバータはまた、母親が窓を水拭《みずぶ》きする時、前世の母親のようにもっと能率のよいやり方で拭かないのは愚かだ、とも考えていた。ロバータは、両親の話によく口を挟んだが、その時にロバータが口にした内容からすると、（母親が考えるに）通常の手段によっては知りえない話題や対象をロバータはよく承知していることがわかったという。

　ロバータの言葉からは、その前世がいつ頃のことなのかを突き止めるための手がかりはほとんど得られなかった。たとえばロバータの話を聞く限り、明らかに昔風の洋服を着ていたとは思えない。自動車を知っていたことからすると、ロバータの前世は、少なくともアメリカの農家に車が普及するようになって以降の時代のように思われる。ロバータは、前世の両親はまだ健在であり、両親がその気になりさえすれば探し出せるはずだと、言葉ではっきり言うことはなかったものの、それを当然のことと考えていた。

　ロバータは、男の子の服装をしたがる傾向が少々あった。とはいえ、前世で男の子だったと言ったわけではない。おもちゃをほしがったところからすれば、本人の記憶にあった人物は夭《よう》逝《せい》しているらしいことがわかるが、ロバータは、その人物がどのような形で死亡したのかについてもひと言も話さなかった。それどころか、死んだことを否定すらしたのである。ある時モーガン夫人がその点について尋ねた時、ロバータは、「あたしは死んでなんかいない。あのふたり〔別の両親〕からちょっと離れなきゃいけなかったの。それでふたりには、また来るからね、と言っといたの」と答えている。ロバータは、前世の両親が好きだとは一度も言わなかったし、事実モーガン夫人は、自分と前世の母親のふたりで人気コンテストをすれば、わずかながら自分の方が勝つだろうと思っていたという。前世の家族のもとへ帰りたいというロバータの内心の衝動は、愛情で結びついているためというよりは、また戻って来るという約束をしているために生じたもののようである。しかしながら、ロバータは、前世の自分や家族の名前を一度も口にしなかったので、（実際にはそうではなかったが）たとえ当時その気があったとしても、夫人には前世の家族を突き止める手立てはなかった。

　モーガン夫妻は、ふたりともキリスト教徒であった。夫人はペンテコステ派に、夫はローマカトリック教会に所属していた。いずれの宗派の教えにも、生まれ変わりという考え方は出て来なかった。モーガン夫人は、ロバータが前世の話を始めた頃には生まれ変わりについて全く知らなかった。そのような話に耳を傾ける気はなかったし、ましてや、〝別のママ〟のところに連れて行ってほしいというロバータの要求や、ロバータがいつもモーガン夫人を〝別のママ〟と比較して悪く言っていた事実を受け入れる態勢にはなっていなかった。どの親であれ、このような評価をされれば、がまんするにしても限度というものがある。モーガン夫人も例外ではなく、毎日ロバータに叩《たた》かれ続けたため、半年もすると堪忍袋の緒が切れて、ロバータが前世のことを口にするたびに罰を与えるようになった。そのためロバータは、（たとえば四歳の時に、昔、馬に乗っていたなどと、時おりうっかり口を滑らせてしまうことはあったが）次第に前世の話はしなくなり、ついには全く口にしなくなってしまったのである。

　ロバータが実際に前世の記憶を失ったのはいつなのか、私にはわからない。前世の話をすると母親に叱られるようになって以降も、まだしばらくは覚えていたのかもしれない。とはいえ、母親が本人の記憶を抑えつけるようになってからは、外から見る限り、母親が覚えている以上のことは記憶していないようであった。その問題は、初めは密《ひそ》やかに、後にははっきりとモーガン夫人を苦しめ続けた。そして最後には、先述のように、前世の家族を探し出して会わせてあげなければ、という思いに（夫人の表現を借りれば）〝取り憑《つ》かれる〟ようになった。また夫人は、前世の話を自由にさせてやらなかったとして自分を責め始めた。夫人によれば、当時のロバータなら、その記憶の事実性を裏づける人名や地名を挙げることができたはずだという。

夫人の態度が変わる時期は、残念ながら遅すぎた。この時ロバータは九歳半になっており、四歳の時に馬のことを口にして以来、前世の家族を特定する手がかりになりそうなものをそれ以上与えてはくれなかったし、それまで口にした場所や人物の名前を再び言うこともなかったのである。モーガン夫人は、以前住んでいたあたりで、馬を飼っている農場を探すことも考えたが、範囲がもう少し特定できるような手がかりがなければ、それも事実上不可能なように思われた。いずれにせよ、六年ほど前にロバータ自身が教えた農道に夫人がなぜ入ろうとしなかったのか、その理由は私にはわからない。

一九七二年の初夏にロバータと母親のもとを訪れてまもなく、母子からの音信が不通となり、転居先を調べることもできなくなって現在に至っている。そのため、ロバータのその後については全くわからない。

スーザン・イーストランドの事例

私が本例を初めて知ったのは、一九六八年のことであり、シャーロット・イーストランド夫人から手紙を受けとったのがそのきっかけであった。夫人は、ある雑誌で私の研究を紹介する記事を読み、娘のスーザンの発言や行動に関する情報を自発的に提供してくれたのである。それによると、スーザンは、ウィニーという夭逝した姉の生涯を、断片的にではあるが記憶しているようであった。私は、一九六八年から六九年初頭にかけて、イーストランド夫人と何回か書簡を交わした後、一九六九年夏に、アイダホ州の夫人宅を訪ねた。そのおり、前世を記憶しているというスーザンと、姉のシャロンのふたりにも対面しているが、シャロンとスーザンの義父に当たるロバート・イーストランド氏には会わなかった。夫人によるとイーストランド氏も、スーザンが前世の話をしている場面を何度か目撃しているという。

ウィニーは、六歳になった一九六一年に、車にはねられて死亡している。ウィニーの突然の死は、一家に大きな衝撃を与えた。母親であるイーストランド夫人は悲しみに打ちひしがれ、どのような形であってもかまわないからウィニーがもう一度自分たちのもとへ戻ってくることを強く希《ねが》った。この頃のイーストランド夫人は、生まれ変わりという考え方については漠然としか知らなかった。夫人が後で話してくれたところでは、インドでは人間が動物に生まれ変わることもあると（自分には考えられないが）信じられているという話を耳にしたことはあったが、人間として生まれ変わって来るという話は一度も聞いたことはなかったという。

にもかかわらず一家は、ウィニーが何らかの形で自分たちのもとへ帰って来るのではないかと考えていた。ウィニーの死後、半年ほど経った時、姉のシャロンは、ウィニーが家族のもとへ帰って来ようとしている夢を見た。また、その二ヵ月後イーストランド夫人は、自分の妊娠を知った時、ウィニーがまた家族と一緒にいる夢を見た。一九六四年、夫人が出産のため分娩《ぶんべん》室に入っている時、最初の夫（子ども全員の父親）は、「パパ、今うちに帰るからね」というウィニーの声をはっきり聞いたような気がしたという。このようにして、三年前に娘を失い、同じ子どもが自分たちのもとへ帰って来てほしいと希っている家族のもとに、スーザンが生まれたのである。ウィニーの生涯にまつわるスーザンの発言を検討するに際しては、以上の事実を念頭に置かなければならない。

二歳になった頃、スーザンは、ウィニーの生涯に関係するらしい発言をいくつか行なった。誰かに年齢を聞かれるとスーザンは、いつも、六歳と答えた。（六歳というのは、ウィニーが死亡した年齢である。）実際の年齢よりも年長だと思い込んでいる状態は、少なくとも五歳になるまで続いた。五歳の時にスーザンは、当時七歳だった兄のリチャードよりも年上だと言い張っているからである。ウィニーは、リチャードより三歳ほど年長だったので、ウィニーからすればスーザンの発言は正しいが、スーザン自身から見れば明らかにまちがっていた。

スーザンは、ウィニーが写っている二枚の写真に異常な興味を示し、「これはあたしだったの」と言った。イーストランド夫人は、これはウィニーの写真だと、スーザンにもしかすると話したことがあったかもしれないというが、おまえ（スーザン）はウィニーの生まれ変わりのような気がする、とスーザンに話したことはないという。スーザンはその写真を自分だと認めただけではなかった。その写真は自分がもっているとも言い張ったのである。スーザンは、一枚をベッドのそばの壁に貼り、もう一枚は何週間か持ち歩いた。そして時々、これは自分の写真だ、と主張していたという。

スーザンは、ウィニーと呼んでほしいとは言わなかったが、殴り書きが少しできるようになった頃、台所のドアにクレヨンで〝WINNI〟という文字を書いた。ただし、最後にあるべきEを落とし、Iも、縦に書かずに横に寝かせて書いたのであった。

同じ頃スーザンは、「私が学校に行った時」という言葉を頻繁に用いたうえ、学校のブランコで遊んだことを話した。ところがスーザンはまだ学校には行っていなかったし、自宅の裏庭にあるブランコに乗って遊んではいたが、学校のブランコで遊んだことはなかった。それに対してウィニーは、死亡する前に入学しており、学校のブランコでもよく遊んでいたのである。

ウィニーの生前、イーストランド夫人は、蓋《ふた》にネコのおもちゃのついた、クッキーの容器をもっていた。子どもがその中のクッキーをほしがった時には、いくつあげたらよいかそのネコに聞く、という遊びを夫人は子どもたちといつもしていた。それからネコを真似た声で、「ニャーン、ひとつ食べてよろしい」と答えるのである。(子どもの要求や空腹度を夫人が判断して、与えるクッキーの数を加減していたわけである。)ウィニーの死後、夫人は、その容器をどこかに片づけたまま忘れてしまっていた。そのため、その容器は、数年間しまい込まれたままになっていた。スーザンが四歳になった頃、イーストランド夫人は、その容器をとり出し、クッキーを詰めた。スーザンがクッキーをひとつほしいと言ったので、容器の蓋についているネコを使った遊びについてスーザンが知らないはずだということは特に意識せず、何気なく夫人は、「さあ、ネコちゃんが何と言うかなぁ」とスーザンに聞いた。するとスーザンは、「ニャーン、ひとつ食べてよろしい」と言って母親を仰天させた。イーストランド夫人は、その話を私にしている時に、スーザンのように頭のよい子なら、もしかするとそう推理して答えたのかもしれない、と語った。私としては、母親からのテレパシーを通じてそれを知ったという可能性もここに指摘しておきたい。とはいえ、スーザンが自分の意志で答えたという事実は、本人がウィニーの記憶を何らかの方法で身につけたとする解釈と符合するのである。

その後スーザンは、他にも、ウィニーが見聞きした出来事をいくつか口にしている。家族と連れ立って海辺に行き、そこでカニを捕まえた時のことを話したうえ、同行した家族の名前を挙げた。イーストランド夫人は、ウィニーが死亡する前年、ワシントン州の海岸へ一家で旅行したことを思い出した。浜辺で遊び、貝殻を拾ったり潮干狩りをしたことはあるが、カニを捕まえた記憶は夫人にはなかった。スーザンは、一緒に旅行に出かけた四人のうち三人の名前を言い当てたが、実際には行かなかった継父をその中に含めていた。しかし、その後に自分からその誤りを訂正し、ウィニーの（同時にスーザン自身の）父親が一緒だったと言った。

スーザンはまた、姉のシャロンと牧場で遊んだ話もした。馬を怖がらなかったことや、馬のお腹の下を潜《くぐ》ったことについても話した。いずれもウィニーのこととすれば当たっていた。ウィニーは、シャロンと一緒に牧場で遊んだし、馬を怖がらず、馬の下を一度通ったことがあったのである。

ある時イーストランド夫人はスーザンに、向かいに住んでいたグレゴリーという男の子を覚えているかどうか尋ねた。それに対してスーザンは、「うん、グレッギーのこと覚えてるよ。あの子とはよく遊んだもん」と答えたという。「グレッギー」というのはグレゴリーの愛称であったが、夫人は、スーザンがそう言うまでその愛称を口にしていなかったのである。

母親は、ジョージ伯父《おじ》さんを覚えているかどうかについても聞いてみた。その伯父は、自宅前の通りを少し行ったところに住んでいた。スーザンは、伯父の家がどんな形をしていたかは思い出せなかったが、伯父さんのことなら覚えていると言い、「あたしたち、登校する途中でいつも伯父さんのうちに寄って、ちょっと遊んだの」とも話したという。確かにウィニーはいつもそうしていた。ウィニーは、交通事故で死亡した当日にも、その伯父宅に寄って遊んでいたのであった。ここでつけ加えておかなければならないが、グレゴリーもジョージも、ウィニーが生前、家族とともに暮らしていた町の住人だったのである。スーザンは、アイダホ州にあるもっと小さな町に転居した後に生まれ、そこで育てられている。

読者の方々は、スーザンの母親が時おり、ウィニーの生前に起こった出来事を質問して本人の記憶を刺激しようとしているのに気づかれることであろう。このような会話をすると、子どもに何らかの情報を不用意に与えてしまうおそれがあるし、故人との同一視を促す一因にもなるかもしれない。とはいえ、イーストランド夫人のようにさまざまな点に注意が行き届く思慮深い人物によるものであれば、この種の質問によって、通常の伝達が行なわれる可能性を回避しつつ新たな記憶を引き出すことができるかもしれないのである。

実例をもう一例挙げておこう。ある時イーストランド夫人はスーザンに、あの子（ウィニー）は野原で新しい靴をなくしたことがあると話して聞かせた。それに対してスーザンは、笑いながら、あんな靴なくなったっていいもん、と答えた。また続けて「それでママは、町に行ってまた新しいのを買って来なきゃいけなかったよね」と言ったのである。ウィニーには、このような出来事が確かにあった。一足しかなかった靴を野原でなくしてしまったのである。

私は、一九六九年末までの時点で、本例については調査し尽くしたと考えた。しかしながら、いくつかの点を再確認し、スーザンのその後の発達について問い合わせるため、一九七七年、イーストランド夫人と手紙のやりとりをした際、スーザンが、ウィニーの生涯に起こった別の出来事を思い出したことを知った。イーストランド夫人に宛てた私の手紙を読んで聞かせたことが明らかにきっかけとなって、前世について新しいことを思い出したのであった。その時スーザンは、母親に連れられて（ウィニーが）ボウリング場に行った時のことを母親に話したという。母親がボウリングをしている間、ウィニーはその場を離れ、売店に行ったり母親のところに走って戻ったりしていた。たまたまそこに来ていた男の子も、ウィニーと一緒に走り回っていて、その男の子がウィニーにキスをしたという。イーストランド夫人はこの出来事をよく覚えていた。特に、その男の子がウィニーにキスしたことを聞いた夫が、ひどく怒ったからである。

スーザンは、「私はウィニーだった」とか「私はウィニーだ」といった直接的な表現は一度もしなかった。ウィニーの写真を見て自分の写真だと言った時が、表現としては一番それに近かった。スーザンは、母親の言葉を借りると〝昔〟の記憶のようなものをもっていた。ウィニーならしているが、本人（スーザン）はした経験がないことの記憶をもっていたからである。しかしながら、ウィニーの生涯に関するスーザンの記憶は、この種のほとんどの事例とは異なり、あまり筋の通ったものにはなっていなかった。換言すれば、スーザンは前世の記憶をもってはいたが、以前にもこの世に生を受けていたことがあるとはっきり思っていたわけではなかったらしい、ということである。

スーザンは、イーストランド夫人が私宛ての手紙の中で、「娘が何かを新しく学ぶ時、そんなことは前からわかっていて、ただ思い出せばいいだけだったような感じが時々いたします」と書いているように、急速に知識を増したのであった。

イーストランド夫人は、スーザンとウィニーには、似ていると思う性格特徴がふたつあることに気づいていた。夫人によれば、ふたりは、かなり積極的であると同時に、人格が円満でもあるという。こうした特徴は、姉のシャロンには見られなかった。夫人の話ではシャロンは、どちらかと言えば臆病《おくびょう》で、人格もあまり円満とは言えないという。

しかしスーザンは、身体的にはウィニーとあまり似ていなかった。ウィニーは、髪の毛が赤く、目は非常に黒っぽかったが、スーザンはブロンドで、目は青かったのである。スーザンもウィニーも、背中がかなり毛深かった。ふたりの父親もそうであったが、他の子どもたちは違っていた。またスーザンには、左臀部《でんぶ》に小さな母斑《ぼはん》があったが、それは、車にはねられた時に致命傷となった外傷と同じ部位にあった。（私は、その事故の後、ウィニーが運び込まれた病院から、ウィニーの医学的記録をとり寄せている。ウィニーはその病院で死亡したのであった。）家族の中には、同じような母斑をもつ者はいなかった。

本例は、どの点から見ても生まれ変わり信仰に好意的ではない宗教的背景の中で発生した、かなりの数にのぼるアメリカの事例のひとつである。イーストランド夫人は、生まれ変わりが起こる可能性を強く否定するあるキリスト教会に所属していた。私が訪れた時、夫人は、もし自分が生まれ変わりという考え方に関心を抱いたと見なされれば、教会から追放されるのではないかと思う、と話してくれた。夫人は生まれ変わりという考え方に実際に引かれたが、それ以外の教義については何とか教会に従い続けた。

一九六九年初夏に私が訪問する時点まで、スーザンがウィニーの生まれ変わりだと思っていることを子どもたちに話していないのはまちがいない、とイーストランド夫人は私に証言してくれた。しかし夫人は、その年の夏、私が訪問した理由に対して子どもたちが当然のことながら興味を示したので、たぶんその機会に子どもたちにそのことを話しているという。

マイクル・ライトの事例

ロバータ・モーガンの事例と同じく、本例の調査も、前世の記憶をもつという子どもの母親（キャサリン・ライト夫人）から受けた電話連絡をきっかけとして開始された。共同研究者と初めて話した時、母親は、息子の語った言葉に動転していることがわかった。その発言からすると、息子は、母親が今の夫と結婚する以前に交際していた恋人の生涯を記憶しているように感じられた（実際のところ、まちがいないと思っている）というのである。ウォルター・ミラーというその恋人は、自分の運転する車が道路を飛び出し、大破したことで死亡していた。

生まれ変わりという考え方に接しても、ライト夫人は動揺しなかった。それどころか、夫人は、こうした考え方を確信したのみならず、さまざまな超常現象をも信じていた。ここで夫人の心霊体験を詳述するつもりはないが、夫人のそのような態度や、それに関連して夫人が示した多少なりとも軽信的と思える傾向については、ここでふれておく必要がある。このような点からすれば、（一部の方々がお考えになるように）息子が前世について話したことを証言する証人としての信頼性は、もしかすると低くなるのかもしれない。しかしながら、私個人としてはそのような見方はしなかった。本例の証言はほとんどがライト夫人によるものなので、もしそう考えたとすれば、本例の報告などしないであろう。

とはいえ、心霊体験をすぐさま受け入れるような傾向がキャサリン・ライトにあったとすれば、一九七八年九月に、それほど切迫した状況で電話をヴァージニア大学に入れる必要がなぜあったのか、という疑問をおもちになるかもしれない。その疑問に対しては、テキサス州で本人に面接した同年一〇月までは、私にも答えられなかった。（本報告の元になっている情報はほとんどが、その時の面接および、一年後に同僚のエミリー・ウィリアムズ・クックが行なった面接を通じて明らかになったものである。）私が面接した時、ライト夫人は（地域社会の中で）自らの母親とただふたり生まれ変わりを信じているのがわかった。それと同時に、夫は夫人と同じ考えをもっているわけではないことも明らかになったのである。さらに夫人は、息子が妻の昔の恋人の生まれ変わりを自認しているのを聞いて、夫が喜ぶはずはないことも十分承知していた。ウォルター・ミラーが交通事故で死亡したからこそ自分が結婚できたという事実を、夫はすぐさま思い起こすであろうし、思い出してうれしい気持になるわけがないことは、夫人にも容易に想像できた。ウォルター・ミラーはその時、永久に死んだのではなく、今こうして自分の後《あと》がまにおさまった男の自宅に入り込んで来たということなのであろうか。

このようにライト夫人は、夫の反応を恐れていたが、結局は、それには根拠がほとんど、あるいは全くなかったことがわかる。一九七八年九月に私たちのところへ電話を入れた時点から、一〇月に私が夫人宅を訪れるまでの間に、夫人は、夫が激怒することが予測されるにもかかわらず、マイクルが口にした内容から自分なりに推測したことを夫に話して聞かせたという。ところが驚いたことに、マイクルがウォルター・ミラーの生まれ変わりだと妻は考えているのではないかと夫が思っていたことが、わかったのである。また、夫は、そのことを怒っていないようにも見えた。夫が意外にも夫人の考えを知っていたのは、ふたりの間にテレパシーが働いたためなのか、夫人の気づかないうちに通常の回路を通じてそのことが夫に漏れ伝わったためなのかについては、ふたりの関係がはっきりしなかったため、どちらとも判断することはできなかった。

キャサリン・ライトの恋人だったウォルター・ミラーに話を戻すと、一九六七年夏に死亡した時、ウォルターは一八歳弱であった。前途有望なアマチュア画家であり、人から好かれる高校生だったウォルターは、その秋に始まる三年の新学期を楽しみにしていた。ウォルターとキャサリンは、三年前に知り合い、正式なものではなかったが、ふたりとも婚約しているものとして交際していた。ある晩ウォルターは、ヘンリー・サリヴァンという友人とダンス・パーティーに出かけ、そこでおそらくは度を越して飲酒したのであろう。帰宅する途中、ウォルターは、運転席で眠り込んでしまい、道路から飛び出したらしい。友人は無事に救出されたが、ウォルターはほとんど即死の状態であった。

キャサリンは、恋人の死に強い衝撃を受けたが、時間が経つにつれ再び元気をとり戻した。そして、一年後の一九六八年、もうひとりの恋人であったフレデリック・ライトと結婚した。それまでフレデリックは、ウォルターの下の地位に甘んじていたのであった。ふたりの間には、初め女の子が誕生し、次いでマイクルが生まれた。しかし、それより先、ウォルターが事故死して一年と少し経った頃、ライト夫人は、ウォルターが生まれ変わって来るのがはっきりわかるような夢を見ている。それが事実なら、生まれ変わり型事例が頻発するほとんどの国で、妊娠中の母親はこの種の夢を見ると言える。事実、ライト夫人は、この夢を文字通りに解釈している。その夢の中でウォルターは、自分はみんなが考えるように死んではいない、もう一度生まれ変わるつもりだ、また君に絵を描いてあげたい、と言ったのである。その夢を見た後も、さらには一九七五年になってマイクルが生まれた後ですらライト夫人は、ウォルターは誰かの子どもとして生まれ変わって来るのだろう、と考えていた。夫人は、その夢を見た頃に妊娠中だったウォルターの妹のキャロル・ミラー・デイビスの子どもとして生まれて来るのではないかと思っていた。その夢のおかげでライト夫人は、ウォルターが生まれ変わって来ることを漠然とながら予測していたが、よもや自分の息子として生まれて来るとは考えもしなかったのである。

マイクルは、誕生時も正常であったし、幼少期の発育も順調であった。幼児期には、呼吸器系に少々の障害があったものの、それも後に消失した。三歳頃マイクルは、全く知らないはずの人たちや出来事を知っているらしい徴候を見せ始めた。そしてある日、「キャロル・ミラー」という名前を口にして、母親を驚かせたのである。キャサリン・ライトは、ウォルターが死亡した後も、妹のキャロル・ミラーとそれなりに親しくつき合っていたが、キャロルは一〇年ほど前に結婚していたので、それまで二回しかキャロルに会ったことのないマイクルには、キャロル・デイビスという結婚後の姓名しかわからないはずなのであった。

いま述べたようなことをマイクルが口にするようになっても、もっと詳しいことまで話すようになるとはライト夫人にも予測できなかった。その後マイクルは、ウォルター・ミラーが死亡した事故のことを詳しく語るようになったのである。母親によれば、マイクルは、最初はオートバイの話をしていたが、自分でその誤りを訂正し、「友だちと車に乗ってると、車は路肩を飛び出して、ゴロゴロと転がった。ドアが開いてぼくは外に放り出されて死んだ」と語ったという。最初に話した中にあったのか、その後に語ったのかははっきりしないが、マイクルはそれ以外の点についても語っている。たとえば、車のガラスが壊れたことや、（事故の後）自分が橋を渡って運ばれたことなども話しているし、友人と一緒に（道路際に）車を停め、トイレに行ったあとで事故に遭ったことについても話したのである。また、事故の直前に出席したダンス・パーティーがどの町で開催されたのかについても語っている。ライト夫人には、こうした発言のほとんどがウォルターの事故と完全に符合することがわかったし、私に見せてくれた（大破した車の写真が載っている）新聞記事からも、その事故について夫人が話してくれた内容が大筋では正しいことが確認された。衝突の衝撃でウォルターは車から投げ出され、首の骨を折って即死に近い状態で死亡した。その後、ウォルターを乗せた救急車は、事故現場付近にかかっている橋を通過した[*13]。ライト夫人には、ウォルターと友人が事故直前に車を停めてトイレに入ったかどうかはわからなかったし、生まれ変わり信仰のない社会の中で信じているのは自分くらいなのではないか、という気がしていたため、その点について確認できる唯一の人物にあえて話を切り出すこともできなかった。（その人物とは、その事故に遭いながら無事だったウォルターの友人ヘンリー・サリヴァンのことである。）また夫人は、私側からの確認も嫌がった。私にもその気はなかったが、たとえ本当の目的を隠したいと思ったにせよ、テキサスの小さな田舎町でそのようなことを調べれば、真の目的を隠し通すことはできないだろうと私たちには思われた。

　さらにマイクルは、母親のライト夫人にわかる限りでは、ウォルター以外には知らないはずのことについてもいくつか語っている。マイクルは、ウォルターの自宅やヘンリー・サリヴァンの自宅についてある程度知っていたうえ、ライト夫人に尋ねられてではあったが、ヘンリー・サリヴァンの苗字《みょうじ》を口にしたのである。またマイクルは、（わずかにまちがえたものの）ヘンリーの愛称も言い当てている。

ライト夫人の母親であるマーガレット・カーペンターも、ライト夫人との面接に同席し、マイクルが事故について語ったとして娘（ライト夫人）が話した内容は事実に相違ないと証言してくれた。夫人は母親の前で、あらためてその話をしたということである。残念ながら私たちは、マイクルが語った他の点に関する夫人の報告については、事実かどうかの確証をまだ得ていない。私の同僚のエミリー・ウィリアムズ・クックは、マイクルの家族のもとを訪れた際、父親のフレデリック・ライトと短時間面接しているが、その時には、マイクルが前世について話した内容をほとんど忘れてしまっていることがわかった。それが、マイクルの話した内容に注意を払わなかったためなのか、マイクルが前世の話をしている時に同席していなかったためなのかは、私にはわからない。

　本例について、十分満足できるほど把握できたとはとても言えないが、ここに紹介する価値があると考えたのは、アメリカの生まれ変わり型事例の多くに、また他の国の事例の一部にも見られる特徴が、よく現われているからである。本例の弱点は主に、マイクルの母親が息子の発言を少々熱心に聞きすぎた点および、先述の理由から、ウォルター・ミラーの家族や友人の証言とは別個に、マイクルの発言が事実であることを確認できなかったという点にある。事実かどうか確認可能な部分がある場合には、自分なりにその確認ができない限り、私としてはその事例報告の発表を見合わせるのがふつうである。しかし、本例の場合には、別の点から考えて、その原則を適用しないことにした。そう考えた私なりの根拠のひとつは、本例にはある意味での長所が存在するということである。本例は、生まれ変わりという考え方を忌み嫌っているとも言えそうな文化の中で発生したものである。また、ライト一家の中には、きびしい三角関係が家族内に存在することの裏づけとなる証拠の捏造《ねつぞう》を画策しようという動機をもった者はもちろん、そうした記憶を積極的に意識化させようとする者も容易には見つからないのである[*14]。思い通りに動機を設定してしまう精神科医の空想の世界でなら、ライト夫人は夫を苦しめるためにこのような話を考え出したのではないかとか、マイクルは両親を巧妙な方法で苦しめようとしてそのような作話をしたのではないか、と想像するのは容易であろう。そういうこともあったのかもしれないが、私にはそのようには思われない。その動機から起こした行動によって何らかの利得が得られることが明確にできない限り、他に証拠もないのにそのような動機をもち出すべきではない。マイクルが、母親の恋人の生涯について語ったことにより、誰かが得をしたとは私には思えない。また、夫人が私のところへ初めて電話して来た時のとり乱しぶりからすると、息子が語った内容を聞いて湧き上がった感情を（当時は）全く制御できなかったことがわかるのである。

エリン・ジャクソンの事例

私が本例を知ったのは、一九八〇年にエリン・ジャクソンの母親のマリリン・ジャクソン夫人が私宛ての手紙の中で知らせてくれたからである。それによると、エリンは、一九六九年にインディアナ州で生まれたが、三歳になった頃、記憶に残っているらしき前世について頻繁に話していたという。ジャクソン夫人と何度か書簡を交わした後、私は、ふたりの住むインディアナ州の町で、夫人とエリンに対面することにした。私は、一九八〇年夏にそこで長時間にわたる面接を行なった。その時には、エリンの父親は同席しなかった。ジャクソン夫人によれば、自分が覚えている以上のことは夫にもわからなかったであろうという。

ジャクソン夫人自身は、四歳頃にはエリンが前世の話をしなくなっていたため、何年か前の出来事を思い出すという形をとらざるをえなかった。エリンが前世について話したのはわずか一年ほどであったが、これは、前世を記憶しているように思われる大半の子どもの場合と比べると短い。

エリンは、前世の話をしていた頃、「男の子だった時」とか「ジョンと呼ばれていた時」という表現をしばしば使った。こうした表現は、「ジョンという名前だった時、みんなで湖に行って、大きな船を浮かべたの」とか、「男の子だった時、おうちに黒いイヌと白いネコがいたよ」などという表現として使われていた。エリンは、自分をかわいがりよく面倒を見てくれる継母と、ジェイムズという名前の兄弟がいる、と言った。本人の記憶によれば、ジェイムズは黒い服が非常に好きで、下着にも黒を着たがるほどだったという。

エリンは、前世で暮らした場所については話さなかったし、いつ頃のことだったかについても直接には語らなかった。しかし、広告の看板や電柱が立ち並び、車がひしめき合っている現代のアメリカの幹線道路が見苦しいことはしばしば口にしていた。田園地帯(および都会)の美しさが損なわれてしまったことについても、時おりひとり言のように呟《つぶや》いていたし、「馬がいた頃はずうっとよかった。車はひどいよ。何もかもめちゃくちゃにしただけじゃない」などという言葉も母親は聞いている。（アメリカの田園風景が損なわれるまでには、数十年の年月を要した。それが始まったのは、ヘンリー・フォードが自動車の量産方式を確立し、それにより近代的な幹線道路が建設されるようになった一九一〇年頃と言えよう。この見方が正しければ、エリンは、少なくとも一九三〇年以前の時代について語っていることになる。）

自分は昔、男の子だったという確信と軌を一にして、エリンは、男児のような服装をし、男児がするようなことをしたがった。男児と女児は違う服装をするものだということがわかる年齢になるとまもなく、男の子の服を着ると言い張ったのである。本人が水泳を習い始めた時、母親がセパレートの水着を買い与えたにもかかわらず、エリンはいつも下の方しか身に着けなかった。それをあらかじめ防止するため母親は、結局ワンピースの水着を本人に買い与えるようになったのである。エリンは、女物の服を着るよう母親に強く言われた時、屈辱を受けたと感じたようである。そして本人は、ジーパンやスラックスを非常に好んだ。私が対面した一〇歳の時点ですら、女物は年にわずか三回くらいしか着用していなかったし、その場合でも、レースや襞《ひだ》など、女物とはっきりわかるようなものがついていない服を要求した。また、髪の毛はいつも短くしておきたがり、長く伸ばすようになったのは、九歳頃になってからであった。

エリンは、人形には関心を示さなかったし、人形をもらっても、洋服をはぎとり、動物のぬいぐるみのようにしてしまっていた。家の中で好んで行なったのは、描画や読書やブロック遊びであった。戸外の遊びとしては、水泳や木登り、魚釣りなどを喜んでした。また、野球を習いたいという気持を強く表明したうえ、カブスカウトにも入りたがった。ところが、女の子にはカブスカウトに入る資格がないことを聞いて本人は激怒した。ジャクソン夫人の私信によると、エリンは時々、溜息《ためいき》を漏らしながら、「男の子だったらなぁ。どうして男の子になれなかったんだろう」と言っていたという。

エリンは高知能児であった。母親の話では、三歳の頃に、誰にも教わらずに字が読めたようだという。またエリンには、（本人の描いたスケッチを何枚か見た限り）その年代の子どもにしては異例の画才があったように思う。さらに、年輩の人間が書いたものとしてもすばらしいと思えるほどの詩も作っている。

一年ほどの間エリンは、前世についてかなり頻繁に（平均して一週間に一度くらい）話していた。四歳の頃から、次第に話す回数が減り、結局は全く口にしなくなった。私が面接した一歳弱の時点では、三、四歳頃、自分がどういうことを言っていたかはほとんど覚えていないようであった。とはいえ、私が母親と話している時にエリンは時おり口を挟み、記憶について説明を加えているので、その程度の痕跡《こんせき》は残していたと言える。記憶と並行して見られた男児的行動は、前世について自発的に話さなくなってからも四、五年は続いた。こうした行動の残《ざん》滓《し》は、私が面接した時点でもまだ認められたが、その頃は、ふつうの女の子として成長を遂げつつあった。

エリンの両親は、伝統的なプロテスタントであったため、本人が前世について話すようになった時点では、生まれ変わりという考え方を信じていなかった。ジャクソン夫人は、その当時、この方面に関する知識をほとんどもっていなかったようである。その後夫人は、この問題について書かれた何かの記事を読み、生まれ変わりを信ずるようになったが、夫は相変わらず信じなかった。夫人は、一九八〇年までに、生まれ変わりに関する通俗書を何冊か読んでいたが、だからと言って夫人が、生まれ変わりという考え方を世間に広めようとしていたと見ることはできないであろう。本例は、エリンの両親が本人に、前世にまつわる空想にのめり込ませようとした結果として生じたものと考えることはできないと思う。ジャクソン夫人によれば、エリンが前世について話した内容には真面目な興味を示し、本人が前世の話をする時にばかにすることなどは一度もなかったという。また、その当時の夫人には本人の話は単なる〝空想〟のように見えたわけであるが、夫人は、本人が話したがる以上のことを口にするよう勧めることもしていないという。この〝空想〟という言葉は、前世についてエリンが語っていた内容を最初はどう思っていたかを明らかにするために、ジャクソン夫人自身が用いたものである。

以上紹介してきた要約をお読みいただければ、前世の記憶をもっているとされる子どもたちが、通常の方法で得られたとは考えられない、特定の故人に関する情報をもっていることを裏づける証拠という点から考えて、こうした事例には長所があると同時に、弱点もあることがおわかりいただけよう。次に、こうした事例を調査するのに私が用いてきた方法および、それをどのようにして分析、解釈しているかについてお話ししようと思う。しかし、その前に、かなりの事例に頻発する特徴について、若干の私見を紹介しておきたい。

第5章　生まれ変わり型事例の典型例の特徴

前章で一二例の要約をお読みいただいたので、典型例がどのようなものか、おぼろげながらおわかりいただけたのではないかと思う。読者の方々は、たとえば、一二例中の少なくとも七例で、前世の人格が非業の死を遂げたとされているのに気づかれたかもしれない。（死因が判明していないものも二例ある。）本章では、その他に、典型例に頻発する特徴を紹介したうえで、典型例[*1]に見られる比較的重要な異型にご注目いただくつもりである。しかし、その前に、この種の事例が最も多く見つかる地域について述べ、双方の人物の社会的、経済的背景にも簡単にふれようと思う。

この種の事例はどこで見つかるか

前世を記憶していると主張する子どもたちは、特定の地域に行けば容易に見つけ出せる。それは、インド北部、スリランカ、ビルマ、タイ、トルコ中南部、レバノン、シリア、西アフリカ、北アメリカ北西部といった地域である。また私は、ヨーロッパや北アメリカで（北西部の諸部族以外にも）たくさんの事例を発見し、調査を行なっている。南アメリカでも見つけているが、いま述べた国や地域と比べると数ははるかに少ない。

現在インドに定住しているチベット難民の間に生まれ変わり型事例がかなり見られることからすると、チベットでも一時は、こうした事例が数多く存在していたにちがいない。私はこのようなチベット人の事例をいくつか調査しているが、家族その他、事例を直接に知っている情報提供者が離散してしまっているため、実際の調査はきわめて困難である。

私はある理由から、日本の一部やインドシナ東部（ラオス、カンボジア、ベトナム）でもこの種の事例が容易に探し出せるのではないかと考えている。私はこうした国の事例も数例知っているし、探そうとする者がいればたくさん見つかると思う、と手紙で知らせてくれた人たちもいる。しかし、これまでのところでは手つかずになっている。熱意がないわけではないが、時間がない私としては、少なくともある程度は徐々になじみを深めてきた文化圏に属する比較的少数の国に努力を傾注した方がよいと判断したためである。

先ほど挙げた国や地域の最も明らかな共通点は、事例が高率に報告されるとともに、生まれ変わり信仰が見られるという事実である。このような相関関係については、考えられる解釈を後ほどいくつか検討するつもりである。しかし、ここで私が強調しておきたいのは、ヨーロッパや北アメリカのような西洋諸国でも、こうした事例が存在するということ（しかも、平均的な西洋人が考えているよりもはるかに頻繁に生じているということ）である。また私たちは、アジアの、生まれ変わり信仰をもたない人たち（たとえば、レバノンのキリスト教徒やインドのイスラム教スンニー派）の間でもこうした事例を何例か見つけている。

私としては、この種の事例の真の発生率よりも、容易に事例が見つけ出せる地域についての方が、はるかに自信をもって語ることができる。私は、必然的に、誰かから知らせを受けて初めて事例の調査にとりかかれる、という立場に置かれている。ひとつの事例が表面化し、その知らせが私に届くまでの間には、かなりのフィルターが存在する。私に新しい事例の情報がすぐに届かない理由や、それらの存在が私に全く把握できない理由はいくつもあるのである。家族や、おそらくは少数の親しい友人などの、内輪の人間にしか知られていない事例がどの程度存在するのかはわからない。こうした事例は、同一家族内で生まれ変わったとされるものがふつうである。私はこの種の事例を、「内密例」と呼ぶこともある。研究を続け、さまざまな国で私の存在が知られるようになるにつれ、私に秘密を明かし、内密例について話してくれたり、時には、徹底的に調査させてくれる人たちも増えてきた。

また、本人の家庭の中ですら抑えつけられている事例も、どれくらいあるかわからない。こうした事例は、大半が生まれ変わり信仰をもたない、たとえば西洋諸国のような文化圏で特に発生しやすい。その場合、こうした子どもの両親は、自分の子どもが愚にもつかないことを口走っているとか、嘘をついているとかと思うかもしれないし、黙らせようとすることも少なくない。インドのイスラム教スンニー派および、レバノンやスリランカのキリスト教徒の間でこの種の事例が抑えつけられている理由も、同様の動機が働いているためとして説明できる。

とはいえ、生まれ変わり信仰を堅持している文化圏ですら、子どもに前世の話をさせたくないとして、それを止めようとする両親もいるかもしれない。このような記憶は子どもにとって有害であり、致命的なものになるかもしれない、と（インドやビルマに住む多くの人々のように）両親が考えると、子どもを抑えつけようとするかもしれないのである。また、子どもが話す事柄や、その言葉と符合する子どもの行動特徴を両親が嫌う場合も少なくない。そのため、子どもが、前世で起こしたあさましい動機による殺人事件について話したり、現在の家族よりもはるかに上流の（あるいは、はるかに下流の）階級に属する家庭で暮らしていたことを口にしたりすると、両親は、前世の話をさせないようにすることもある。

それでも私たちは、誰かが隊列を乱して情報を提供してくれたり、実際には記憶をもっていながら、前世についてはもう忘れてしまったかに装い、後に、家族の者よりも好意的に耳を傾けてくれる相手にその記憶を話したりする場合には、それによって、抑えつけられていた事例の存在が明らかになる。タイの修道僧であるチャオクン・ラジスタジャルンの事例は、その格好の実例である。幼少期にチャオクンは、母方伯父《おじ》の生涯をはっきりと記憶していた。家族はその発言を、本人がその伯父の生まれ変わりであることを示す証拠として全面的に受け入れた。ところが本人は、自分はおとなだと言い張り、たとえば母親に対して、まるで妹ででもあるかのように呼びかけたのである。そのため家族は、さまざまな策を弄《ろう》して、本人が伯父の生涯について話すのをやめさせようとした。[*2] そして、たとえば回転しているろくろに乗せてめまいを起こさせるなど、少々手荒な方法も用いたのであった。それ以上の荒療治を避けるため、本人は、実際にはそうではなかったが、前世のことは忘れてしまったふりをした。ところがその後成長した段階で、その記憶を何人かの他人に話すようになり、最終的にはその記憶を自伝風にまとめ、タイで出版したのである。

その事例が内密例ではなく、かつ抑えつけられてもいなければ、世界各地で（多くの場合、最初は通訳として）私を援助してくれたたくさんの共同研究者や助手の誰かを通じて、その情報が私のもとに届けられたかもしれない。インドやスリランカやタイでは、こうした事例が時おり新聞に掲載される。それに対して、ビルマやトルコやレバノンでは、新聞に載ることは稀《まれ》である。インドでは、たとえばゴーパール・グプタの事例のように、その地方の名士である実兄を射殺した人物について詳しいことがわかっており、しかも（新聞の読者の多くが喜びそうな）ある程度ドラマチックな要素があるものに限って、新聞報道が行なわれやすい。スリランカやタイの新聞は、あまり区別立てすることなく、話題性のあるものを筆頭に、ありきたりの実にさまざまな事件を掲載している。研究を始めて間もない頃は、新しい事例を探すのに新聞記事を頼みの綱にしていたが、最近ではそれもずっと少なくなった。それは、私の共同研究者や何人かの助手が、活字になっていない事件を探し出すのに熟達してきたおかげであるし、調査中の事例の情報提供者が、他の事例について教えてくれる場合が、現在では少なくないからでもある。それをもとに私たちは、できる限り速やかに調査の予定を組むようにしているのである。

実際に存在している事例は、報告されるものよりはるかに多いのはまちがいない、と私は見ている。[*3] その事実がわかったのは、特に、私の共同研究者や、私が副代理と呼んでいる方々の一部のお骨折りのおかげである。副代理とは、こうした研究に関心をもち、身のまわりで起こる事例を間近に見守ってきた人々のことである。私たちが存在を知っている事例を、ピンで地図の上に示してみると、このような賞賛すべき探偵が住む町の周辺にピンが集中しやすいのである[*4]。

一九七八年、デヴィッド・バーカーとサトワント・パスリチャというふたりの共同研究者は、インドのウッタル・プラデーシュ州アグラ地区の指定区域に居住する住民を対象に、組織的な調査を行なった。その結果、人口一〇〇〇人あたり二・二例の事例が見られることがわかった。他の国はもちろん、インドの別の地域でも同じような調査をする必要がある。

前世を記憶する子どもの社会的、経済的背景

アジアでは、私が調査した事例のほとんどが、経済的に貧しく、あまり教育も受けていない村人の間で発生している。しかしながら、それがアジアに住む大半の人々が置かれている状況なので、事例の背景として注目すべき点ではない。とはいえ、アジアの都市部に住む裕福で教育のある人たちの中にもこうした事例が見つかるという事実についても、ここで述べておかなければならない。手元のデータをもっと細かく分析すれば、双方の家族の社会的、経済的条件に、これまで知られていない要素のあることがわかるかもしれない。

本節では、合衆国の事例について、思い切って私なりの解釈を加えておこうと思う。（ここで引き合いに出すのは、アメリカ北西部に居住する部族以外の事例である。）こうした事例の情報提供者（ふつうは、前世を記憶するという子どもの母親）は小さな町や村に住んでいるこ

とが多く、大学教育を受けている者はほとんどいない。また、キリストの名のもとに設立された教会のさまざまな教義よりも、キリストの教えそのものに傾倒している傾向がある。さらに、超常体験や〝オカルト〟の記事が掲載されている通俗雑誌の少なくとも一種類を、時々ないしは定期的に購読している場合が多い。それにより、生まれ変わりという考え方や私の研究を知ったのかもしれない。以上の条件からすると、このような人々は本来の意味でのプロテスタント（抗議者）になる。この人たちは、宗教的信仰について直接に指導してもらう必要がない。したがって、こうした人々の大半は、驚きあわてることなく、子どもに前世の話をさせることができるのである。

生まれ変わり型事例に頻繁に見られるいくつかの特徴

完全型の事例には、大きな特徴が五つある。まず、ひとりの（ふつうは年輩の）人物が、（自分の死後に）もう一度この世に生まれ出るという予言をするところから始まる。その人物は、どの両親のもとに、あるいはどの場所に生まれたいとまで明言することも少なくない。その後、本人が死亡し、次いで誰かが——必ずしも遺族とは限らないが——ある家族のもとに本人が生まれ変わる夢を見る。その子どもが生まれると、故人の体についていた傷などの目印と一致する母《ぼ》斑《はん》（あるいは先天性欠損）がその子どもの体にあることがわかる。その子どもは、口を利くようになるとまもなく、その故人の生涯を（初めは断片的に、次第に詳細に）物語るようになる。またその子どもは、自分の家族の中では変わっているが、その故人が示した、ないしは示したと思われる行動とは（情報提供者によれば）符合する行動を見せる。

以上のように、完全型の事例には、もう一度生まれ変わるという予言が行なわれ、誰かがその夢を見て、生まれて来た子どもに母斑や先天性欠損があり、子どもが前世について物語り、それと並行して変わった行動を示す、という特徴がある。[*5] とはいえ、五つの特徴をすべてもった事例はほとんどない。生まれ変わりを明確に予言する例は稀であるし、その他の特徴が三、四点見られる場合でも、一部の要素が他のものと比べてはるかに目立つこともある。次に、以上五通りの特徴をひとつずつ検討することにしよう。

死ぬ前に生まれ変わりの予言をする

先述のように、生まれ変わる場所を明確に予言する例は、こうした事例が見られる大半の文化圏でも稀である。しかしながら、チベット人と北アメリカ北西部に居住するトリンギット族というふたつの民族では、この種の事例がかなりの頻度で見られる。トリンギット族では、前世の人格が生前に、来世の両親を特定している事例は、四六例中一〇例（二二パーセント）にのぼっている。

トリンギット族の中には、来世ではもっと健康になりたいとか、容姿をもっとよくしたいという願望を表明する者も多い。このような抱負は、予言というよりは希望という形をとることもあるが、前世で表明した願望が現世で実現されたように思われる事例も少数ながらある。またトリンギット族の中には、自分の（現在の）体にある瘢痕《はんこん》その他の傷跡と一致する母斑を、来世の肉体にそのままの形で出現させるという予言を行なう者も時おりある。そのような宣言をしておくことにより、自分が生まれ変わった時に確認してもらいやすいようにするのである。[*6]

　チベットのラマ僧も、来世にまつわる予言をすることが少なくない。[*7] ラマ僧の予言は、トリンギットと比べると不明瞭《ふめいりょう》な、間接的、暗示的傾向が強いが、どこに生まれ変わるつもりかを宣言したり、それとなくほのめかしたりすることもある。またそのうえに、体のどこに母斑が出ているはずだ、と明言することもある。とはいえ、来世で生まれる場所や状況についてラマ僧がほのめかす言葉は漠然としているため、その言葉をどう解釈すればそのラマ僧の生まれ変わりが見つかるのかはっきりせず、残された弟子たちが途方に暮れることもある。

　他の文化圏で生まれ変わりの予言が行なわれる場合には、年輩の人物が自分の家族内にもう一度生まれて来ると明言する例が多いようである。私は、トルコとインドでこの種の事例を多数調査している。トルコでもインドでも、同一家族内に生まれ変わったとされる例は珍しいのであるが、子どもが、先祖の誰かの生涯を記憶している場合には、その先祖は生前、その家族の中に生まれ変わって来ると予言していることが少なくないのである。

予告夢

　前世の記憶をもって生まれることになる子どもの関係者が、生まれ変わりたいという願望や意志を、自分の前に現われた故人が表明する夢を見る事例は少なくない。そういった夢を見るのはたいていが既婚女性であり、その後に生まれ変わって来る子どもの母親になる女性であるのがふつうである。時には、その女性の夫その他の親族や友人がこうした夢を見ることもある。私はこの種の夢を〝予告夢〟と呼んでいる。若干の例外はあるが、本人が生まれる前に、時にはその子どもを受胎するより前に起こるからである。[*8] 第4章で要約して紹介した一二例中五例で、このような夢が観察されている。

予告夢は、生まれ変わり型事例が見つかるすべての国で報告されてきた。とはいえ、ビルマ人やトルコのアレヴィス族や北アメリカ北西部の諸部族の間に比較的多く見られるのである。ビルマでは、こうした夢を見るのは、前世の記憶をもって生まれて来る子どもを身ごもる前が多いのに対して、北アメリカの北西部に住む諸部族の場合には、ほとんどが臨月に入った後であり、特に出産の二、三日前ないし二、三時間前から出産するまでの間が多い。

また、この種の夢はさまざまな形をとる。トリンギット族では、予告夢の中に現われる肉体のない人格が、生まれ変わりの意志を象徴的に伝える場合が多い。たとえば、夢の中でその人物がスーツケースをもって家の中に入って来て、それを寝室に置くとか、両親の寝室に入り、ふたりの間に寝るなどがある。それに対してビルマの夢では、肉体のない人格が、自分で選んだ家族の一員として生まれ変わらせてほしいと懇願するものが多い。この点から判断すると、夢を見ている者にはそうした願いをはねつける自由があるようである。

こうした夢に付随して、おもしろい現象が起こる場合がある。あるビルマ人女性は、夫が長旅で家を留守にしている時、今は亡き友人が本人の子どもとして生まれ変わらせてほしいと頼み込んでいるような夢を見た。この女性は、その申し出を快く思わず、(夢の中で)うちには来ないでほしいと拒絶した。旅先から帰った夫は、やはり今は亡き同じ友人の夢を見ていたが、(自分の夢の中で)その友人に、君がうちの一員として生まれ変わるなら喜んで迎えよう、と言っておいたことを話した。やがて子ども(マウン・アウン・タン)が生まれたが、その子どもは後に、母親には拒否されたが、父親には受け入れてもらえたということを匂わせる発言をしている。それでも、母親は、ビルマ人特有の陽気さでこの状況を受け止めた。

予告夢よりはるかに少ないのは、私が旅立ち夢と呼ぶ夢である。故人の遺族(おそらくは夫と死別した妻)が見るこの種の夢では、生まれ変わった自分はどこの家に行けば見つかるかを、当の故人が教えてくれるのである。

遺族が夢の中で故人から、赤ん坊として生まれ変わったと思われる後に、交信らしきものを受けたという事例もいくつかある。一例を紹介すると、ある女性は、今は亡き自分の息子が出て来て、「助けてよ。貧乏なうちに来ちゃったんだ。早く来て連れ戻してよ」と言う夢を見た。この女性は、夢の中で詳しい手がかりをつかみ、それによってその子どもを探し出すことができた。そしてその子どもが、この女性の息子の生涯を記憶していることが後にわかるのである。他の二例では、幼児の前世の人格が、(前世の家族のひとりが見た)夢の中で、自分の置かれている状況は不満だと訴えた。そのうちの一例では、前世の人格が、その子の父親は飲酒が過ぎると訴え、もう一例では、母親は子どもが飲みたがっているかどうかとは無関係に、自分の都合で哺乳《ほにゅう》していると主張した。そのためその乳児は、空腹を抱えていたのである。

予告夢では、夢を見ている者は、夢に現われ、もう一度生まれ変わりたいという意志を表明する人物が誰なのかわかる場合がほとんどである。とはいえ、夢の中に登場した人物が誰かわからなかったが、その子どもが生まれてから、その子が夢の中に出て来た人物とよく似ているのに気づく場合もある。たとえば、ネシプ・ユンリュタシキランの母親は、妊娠する前に、七ヵ所から血を流している見ず知らずの男性の夢を見た。ネシプが生まれた時、本人の体に大きな母斑がいくつかあったが、その後その母斑は、ネシプがその生涯を記憶している男性の致命傷となった傷と符合することがわかった。しかし母親は、この男性についても、その男性を殺害した犯人についても、夢を見た時点では全く知らなかったのである。

後になって関係があったことがわかる夢の中には、前世を記憶している子どもとのつながりが希薄なものもあるし、場合によっては、単なる象徴としか思えないものもある。スリランカの主要民族であるシンハラ族には、正体のはっきりした人物が登場する夢はほとんどない。ところがシンハラ族は、ヘビやゾウなどの動物が出て来る夢を、前世の記憶をもつ子どもが生まれてくる前兆と解釈するのである。私としては、この種の夢、特に、新たな展開があってから遡《さかのぼ》って意味づけが行なわれるような夢には重要性はほとんどないと考えている。

本人が生まれるより前、場合によっては妊娠前に見る、より一般的な予告夢では、その後に得られる証拠の価値を低下させることになる場合が多い。このような夢を見ると、その子どもの両親は、子どもに対して、その夢を見なかった時とは異なる接し方をするようになることがきわめて多いので、そのつもりはなくとも、その故人の行動特徴をその子どもに知らず知らずのうちに押しつけるようになるかもしれないのである。

母《ぼ》斑《はん》や先天性欠損

前世の記憶をもつとされる子どもの中には、情報提供者の証言をはじめとする証拠によれば、前世の人格の肉体についていた傷（その他の目印）と符合する母斑や先天性欠損をもって生まれて来る者が多い。また、一部には、本人のもっている疾患が、前世の人格がもっていたものと一致する場合もある。

既にこの世にいない人間の身体検査はできないので、このような事例では、故人の肉体についていた傷跡その他目印となるものの位置については、主として遺族や友人の記憶に頼らざるをえない。また、このような情報提供者は、たいてい、記憶をもつ子どもの体に見られる母斑の部位を承知しているため、前世の人格の体にあった傷跡の記憶を、子どもの母斑の部位や形状と一致させたいという誘惑が生ずるかもしれない。（そういうことはなかったと私が確信している場合でも、そのような歪曲《わいきょく》があったのではないかと批判する者が現われる可能性は残るであろう。）

私は、子どもの記憶と符合する故人の検死所見その他の、傷跡に関する医学的記録を入手することで、この難点を克服した事例を三〇例ほどもっている。この種の報告書は、前世の記憶をもつ子どもの体に見られる母斑のことは全く知らない状況のもとで、しかもその子どもが生まれる以前に書かれたものであることはまちがいない。また、この種の医学的記録によって、こうした事例の情報提供者から既に得ている、記憶に基づく証言の事実性が（若干の例外はあるものの）確証されているので、情報提供者から得た証言に対して私が一般に信頼を置いていることはまちがっていないと言える。

前世の人格に関係する母斑や先天性欠損は、生まれ変わりという考え方がこうした事例の最善の説明になることを裏づける最有力の証拠であるように私には思われる。この種の証拠は客観的に観察できる（私はこれまで、この種の数百例に及ぶ事例の写真を撮影している）ので、生まれ変わりという考え方以外でその大半に当てはまりそうな（私に考えられる）解釈としては、その赤ん坊の母親が、胎児の体に超常的な方法で影響を及ぼしたとするもの以外にない。しかしながら、生まれ変わりという考え方と同じくらい（平均的西洋人には）途方もないこの説明も、その子どもの両親が、後で突き止められることになる前世の人格について、本人が生まれるまで全く知らなかった一二例ほどでは、完全に棄却できるのである。

こうした事例に見られる母斑や先天性欠損は、超常的な力が人間の肉体の発育過程に影響を及ぼしうることをうかがわせてくれる、という意味でも重要である。母斑や先天性欠損には（生まれ変わりの証拠および超常的な力が人体に作用する証拠として）このように二重の重要性が存在することから私は、現在執筆中の著書の中で、こうした特徴をもつ多数の事例を報告したいと思うようになった。この著書はまだ出版されていないので、母斑や先天性欠損をもつ事例について本書の中でこれ以上ふれるのはあまり適当ではなかろう。[*9]

前世に関する子どもの発言

本節では、子どもが前世について話す年齢や話しぶり、さらには子どもの発言内容に共通して見られるテーマについて論ずるつもりである。また、前世の人格がよく承知していた人物や物品を子どもが見分けるとされることについても、簡単にふれる予定である。

前世について話す年齢および話し方　前世の記憶をもつ子どもが初めてその話をするのは、二歳から五歳までの間がほとんどである。一部の事例で言われるように、もっと幼ない子どもが前世のイメージ記憶をもっているとしても、ほとんどの場合、言いたいことを表現する言葉がまだ使えない。それでも一部には、心に内在するイメージを的確に伝える言語能力が発現する以前に、前世の話を始める子どももある。

それほどの早期に話し始める子どもの場合には、発音をまちがえたり、乏しい語彙《ごい》を身ぶりで補ったりすることが多い。困惑した両親の（子どもの側から見れば）乏しい理解力では、子どもの言っていることがわかるまでに一年以上かかるかもしれないが、子どもの言葉が次第に発達するおかげで、本人が描き出そうとする前世の全体像は次第に明確になってくる。いくつか実例を紹介すれば、どれほど早期に子どもたちが自らの記憶を周囲に伝え始めるものかがおわかりいただけよう。レバノンのイマド・エラワールは、自分の記憶に残っている前世時代に二連式の銃をもっていたことを話したがり、伸ばした二本の指で二本の銃身を表現しようとした。インドのクムクム・ヴェルマは、前世時代の息子の職業（鍛冶屋《かじや》）を家族に話したがり、金槌《かなづち》で鉄床《かなとこ》を叩《たた》く動作や鞴《ふいご》を使う動作を身ぶりでまねた。やはりインドのプシュパも、自分の夫が自転車の修理店を経営していたことを伝えたがり、あおむけになって、両脚で自転車のペダルを漕《こ》ぐまねをした。

共同研究者とともに私は、インドの二三五例を対象に分析を行なっているが、それによると、記憶に残っている前世について話し始める平均年齢は、三歳二ヵ月であることがわかった。前世について初めて話した平均年齢は、私たちが分析した他の五つの文化圏の事例と同じかそれに近かった。たとえば、アメリカの七九例でも、やはり三歳二ヵ月だったのである。[*10]

もっと年長になるまで前世の記憶が出現しないか、記憶があってももっと年長になるまで人に話さない子どもも若干ある。生まれ変わり信仰をもつ文化圏ですら、家族や友人にからかわれたり叱られたりするのを恐れ、記憶している事柄を口にしない子どももいる。（スレイマン・アンダリがその一例である。）

本人が少年期後期や成人に達した後、初めて前世を思い出したことがわかった場合には、何らかの超常的要素がそこに存在する証拠としては一般に意味がないと思う。とはいえ、成人に達した後、初めて筋の通った記憶が出て来たように見える者が一部にあるという事実は、私も承知している。こうした事例の大多数では（第3章で説明しておいたように）、ゲオルク・ナイトハルトの事例のように心理的ショックを受けた後か、プラトムワン・インタヌヤウッタラ・フダールの事例のように瞑想《めいそう》の最中やその後に、初めて記憶が出現しているのである。

本人のもっている記憶にどの程度の情報量が含まれるかは、事例によって相当の差がある。

記憶している内容がきわめて限られている者もあれば、厖大《ぼうだい》な記憶をもつ者もある。デリーに住むある少年は、前世記憶の最少記録保持者である。この少年によれば、自分はボンベイ（現在のムンバイ）の生まれで、煙がいっぱい立ち込めた場所で人々が嘆き悲しんでいるのを覚えているというが、それ以上の記憶はないのである。（煙が立ち込めて人々が涙を流しているという言葉は、火葬の場面を表わすものなのかもしれないが、本当にそうなのかどうかは確認されていない。）逆に、記憶量がきわめて多い事例としては、エドワード・ライアルやマルタ・ロレンツ、スワルンラタ・ミシュラのような事例が挙げられる。エドワード・ライアルは、非常に詳細な記述をふんだんに盛り込んだ本を一冊書き上げているのである。不正確な部分も若干あるし、事実かどうか確認されていない点もあるが、ほとんどは正確である。ライアルは、一部の記憶は少年期後期に発現させたが、大半はそれよりはるか後に出て来たものである。本人は自分の記憶に基づいていると主張するが、それほど多くのしかも正確な知識をいったいどこから得たのか、という疑問は残る。しかし、今ここで問題にしているのは、その情報量自体なのである。マルタ・ロレンツ（ブラジルの事例）の父親は、幼少期に娘が前世について語った一二〇項目の事柄を記録しておいた。ところが残念ながら、誰かがその記録を誤って捨ててしまったため、マルタが語った内容が正しく記録されているのは、結局全体の三分の一以下になってしまった。スワルンラタ・ミシュラ（インド）について言えば、本人は前世の生活をほとんど思い出しているという。これはおそらく誇張であろうし、本当かどうかも確認されていないが、大半の子どもたちよりもはるかに記憶量が多かったのは確かである。残念ながらこの事例では、私自身が未熟だったため、本人の記憶を的確に記録しえたのはごく一部にすぎなかった。

記憶量の多い事例は、現在考えられている以上に多いのかもしれない。残念なことに私たちは、前世の話をする最盛期に本人と対面できることはほとんどない。その後に初めて面会できた、という事例が多すぎるのであるが、その時には既に、細かい記憶がかなり失われてしまい、薄れつつある記憶の断片がかろうじて残っているか、場合によっては完全に消失してしまった後かもしれないのである。親たちの中にも、子どもが以前に語った内容をかなり忘れてしまっている者がある。とはいえ、私が調査した大半の事例の情報提供者は、その子どもが前世について語った事柄を四、五〇項目ほど記憶していた。

前世の話をしたがり、話す必要に迫られているかどうかについても、子どもによって相当の開きがある。マリカ・アロモウガムのように、何らかの物品や出来事がきっかけとなって記憶が蘇《よみがえ》った時にだけ前世の話をする者もある。逆に、前世のことにふれずにはいられず、飽くことなく話し続け、記憶の衰えない者もある。このような子どもたちは、時には数年にわたって前世の話を間断なく続けるので、家族は食事のたびに子どもから、前世の方がどれほど恵まれていたかを繰り返し聞かされるほどである。しかし、子どもの記憶量と前世の話をしたがる気持とは、あまり関係ないかもしれない。たとえばマヘス・デ・シルヴァは、前世については数点の記憶しかもっていなかったが、何らかの方法を用いて口封じをしなかったのが不思議に思えるほど前世の話を繰り返して両親（特に母親）を困らせていた。そこまで辛抱強い両親は、さすがに他にはいない。

前世の記憶がどの程度本人の心を揺り動かすか、という点についても、かなりの個人差がある。前世について語る時、現在形を用いる子どももいる。たとえば、「妻とふたりの子どもがいる」とか、「ぼくのうちはこれよりずっと大きい」などという表現を用いるのである。（現在形と過去形の正しい用法を教わり、その区別ができるようになってからすら、こうした言い方をすることもある。）それ以外の子どもたちは、人に話す時、前世と現世を必ず区別する。前世の話を始める時、「ぼくが大きかった頃……」などという言いまわしを用いるのである。

前世を記憶する子どもたちの中には、まるで成人の肉体からいきなり引き出され、頼りない幼児の体に押し込まれでもしたかのようにふるまう者もある。[11]たとえばセラル・カパン（トルコ）は、言葉を話すようになった時、ひと言目かふた言目には、「ぼくはここで何をしてるんだ。港にいたのに」と言ったという。言葉がもっと話せるようになった段階でセラルは、船に荷を積み込んでいる最中に船倉で眠り込んでしまった港湾労働者の生涯について詳細に語った。運が悪かったことに、クレーンを操作していた男が、その労働者がそこにいるのも知らず、油の入った重いドラム缶を落とし、本人を即死させたのであった。このような証拠から考えると、眠っていたこの男性は、二歳の幼児の体内で目を覚ました、とも言えよう。こうした事例を見ると、ブリッジの最中に脳卒中の発作を起こし、意識不明に陥った女性の事例を思い出す。この女性は、数日後に意識を回復した時、開口一番、「切り札は何なの」と言ったのである。

以上のことから、子どもたちは前世について話す時、さまざまな感情表現をすることがご理解いただけたかもしれない。まるで遠い昔のことででもあるかのように淡々と話す者も一部にはあるが、大多数は、記憶に残っている人物や出来事に強い執着を示し続ける。涙を流しながら前世の話をする者があるかと思えば、前世での生活に終止符を打たせた殺人犯を怒りに震えながら非難する者もある。兄弟やおとなが本人をからかって、前世の連れ合いなどの身内や親友が病気になったとか死んだとかの嘘を言ったところ、それだけで本人が泣き出してしまった、という例もいくつかある[*12]。

　前世の記憶に浸りきっていたかと思うと、次の瞬間には、ふつうの幼児の行動に戻るような者もある。たとえば、妻子の話を真面目にしていたかと思えば、次の瞬間には、走って行って幼ない兄弟たちと一緒に子どもらしい遊びにふけるかもしれないのである。

　前世の話をする時に、自分が現在置かれている状況から気持が離れてしまう子どもも一部にある。このような子どもは、前世にまつわる独り言を言うこともある。その場合、周囲の者には、ある程度トランス状態に陥っているように見えることもあるが、トランスという言葉では強すぎて当たらないかもしれない。自分の置かれている現実にすぐ戻ることができるからである。完全な人格変化らしきものを起こすウッタラ・フダールのような事例は、きわめて稀《まれ》なのである。

　大半の事例では、前世の記憶が出現するのは覚醒《かくせい》状態の時だけである。しかしながら、夢や悪夢の中で前世の記憶を明らかに（あるいは、おそらく）出現させた事例についても、私はこれまでいくつか調査している[*13]。また、これから眠ろうとしている時（および、おそらくは既に浅い睡眠に入っている時）や目を覚ました直後の方が前世の話をしやすいという子どもも若干あった。

前世の記憶を人に伝える場合、言葉のみを用いるか、それに身ぶりを加える程度の子どもがほとんどであったが、前世時代の人物や出来事を伝える目的で絵を描く者もあった。

大多数は、五歳から八歳までの間に前世の話をしなくなるが、もっと早い時期にやめる子どもあれば、もっと後まで続ける者もある。前世の記憶がすべて失われずに成人までもち越されたとされる例も若干あるが、その一方で、実際には記憶がまだかなり残っているらしいのに、すべて忘れてしまったふりをする者も一部にある。子どもが前世の話をしなくなったのは、忘れるのを〝助ける〟ためさまざまな手段を自分たちが講じたおかげだと主張する親も少なくない。ところが子どもたちは、両親に記憶を残すよう仕向けられたか、阻止されたかに関係なく、同じような年齢で前世の記憶を失ってしまうように見える[*14]。

前世の記憶が失われるのはふつう、家族という物理的、社会的環境から離れた行動が増加する年齢と一致するようである。学校に行く行かないにかかわらず、この年齢は子どもが、家族の者を相手にするだけではもはや生活して行けなくなり、家族ほど寛大ではない他人に順応しなければならない時期に当たる。このように適応することで新しい経験を積み、その記憶によって前世の記憶が覆われ、消えてしまったように見えるのではなかろうか。親たちはよく、子どもが前世時代の家族のもとへ初めて行くことも、記憶を失い始めるきっかけになると言う。それまでは前世の話が奔流のように流れ出ていたのに、先方を初めて訪れた後には、小川となり、まもなく消え去ってしまうこともあるのである。[15]

　前世の話をしている子どもにどの程度注目するかによっても、いつまでその話を続けるかが変わるようである。本人が前世の自分と見なす故人の身元が判明した事例では、突き止められなかった事例よりも後まで前世の話を続けることがわかっている。その理由として私が考えているのは、この注目度の違いである。前世の人格の身元が確認された子ども（既決例）は、前世の話を平均で七歳半弱まで続けるのに対して、確認されていない子ども（未決例）では、平均六歳弱で話すのをやめている。子どもの語った内容が事実と確認できない場合には、家族は子どもの発言に対する関心を失いがちになる。このように、周囲のおとなから刺激を受けないでいると、子どももまもなく話すのをやめるのかもしれない。逆に、その発言が事実と確認された場合には（特に、その頃に子どもが、相手方の家族からも注目されている場合には）、それが動機づけや刺激となって、前世の話を続けるのである。[16]

　社会的要因は、前世の記憶を喪失させる重要な要因のように思われるが、その子ども自身の心理的発達と比べると重要度は劣るのではなかろうか。前世の記憶を喪失するのは、言葉が急速に発達し、それに伴って視覚的イメージが失われる時期と一致する。前世の記憶は、まず第一に、視覚的イメージという形で（子どもの心の中に）発現するようである。[17]その後、言葉を使う能力が発達するにつれ、そのイメージを家族に伝えようとして次第に言葉に頼るようになる。しかしながら、言語が発達すると、たいていの人間では、そのために視覚的イメージが覆い隠されてしまい、ますますイメージが出現しにくくなる。幼児期を過ぎると大半の者では、視覚的イメージを保持する能力が大きく低下する。その年齢以降になると、ふつうの人間では大半が、夢の中や意図的に想起する時にしか視覚的イメージは浮かんで来ない。詩人や画家を別にすれば、視覚的イメージをふつうに用いて考える能力を保持している成人はほとんどいないのである。

若干の例外はあるが、前世の記憶をもつ子どもが、その記憶を三年以上にわたって語り続けるとはあまり思えない。実際にはそれ以下の場合が多い。二、三歳以前では、人に話したい事柄を表現するための語彙《ごい》や能力に欠けているし、五歳を過ぎると、言葉による情報のおかげで、主たる記憶らしきものの元になるイメージがすっぽり覆い隠されてしまうからである。そして前世の記憶の喪失が起こり、それ以上話すことがなくなってしまうのである。

前世の記憶の中心にあるテーマ　子どもの記憶は、前世で最後の日の近辺で起こった出来事の周辺に集中する傾向がある。[*18] 前世の自分の死にざまを覚えているという者が四分の三近くあり、しかも、自然死の時よりも横変死を遂げた時の方が、死の状況を記憶している比率が高い。前世の人格の死にざまや死の直前に起こった出来事の他にも、前世の人格がよく知っていたさまざまな人物や物品について思い出すこともある。その人物や物品と（死亡前の前世の人格と）の結びつきが新しいことは、結びつきの長さよりも重要な要因のように思われる。たとえばスクラ・グプタは、（前世の人格である）マナの結婚生活について細かい点を数多く記憶していたが、結婚前の年月の大半を一緒に過ごした実家の家族についてはほとんど覚えていなかった。

前世を記憶する子どもたちは、前世の人格の名前や、家族や友人や仇敵《きゅうてき》の一部の名前を覚えているのがふつうである。前世の人格が殺害されている場合には、犯人の名前を覚えている場合が多い。とはいえ、ここでもたくさんの異型がある。同じ文化圏内でも事例ごとに異なっているが、それぱかりではなく、文化圏ごとに見ても違いがあるのである。たとえば、インドやビルマやタイの事例では前世の人格の名前を覚えている者が多いが、スリランカや（北西部の諸部族を除く）北アメリカの事例の場合はそうではない。

名前をあまり記憶していない事例がスリランカに多いのは、シンハラ族が日常生活であまり本名を使いたがらないためではないかと思う。[19] シンハラ族は相手を呼ぶ際、肩書や自分との間柄を本名の代わりに用いたがる傾向がある。記憶は反復によって強化される性質があるので、前世の生活の中で本名を使わなかったために、現世で本名が思い出しにくいという結果になるのではなかろうか。

しかしながら、アメリカの子どもにも（本名を）記憶していないという問題が見られることについては、別の説明をする必要がある。アメリカ人の場合には、日常生活の中で相手を呼ぶのに抵抗なく名前を用いるからである。これまでのところでは、この点について満足のゆく説明はできていない。そこでまず、前世の記憶をもつアメリカの子どもは他の文化圏の子どもと比べて、どの方面にせよ記憶が乏しいのではないかと考えた。つまり、アメリカ人の子どもが名前をあまり覚えていないのは、記憶が全般に乏しいためなのではないか、ということである。

ところが、アメリカ人の子どもとインド人の子どもが前世について発言した項目の数を比較してみたところ、この推定は裏づけられなかった。とはいえ、事実であることが確認された項目に限ると、アメリカの子どもは、インドの子どもほど前世のことを話していないことが明らかになった。したがって、アメリカの子どもの発言には、記憶の空白を埋めるための空想が多いという可能性がある。これも、さらに検討を要する問題のひとつである。

前世で死亡してから現世で生まれるまでの間に起こった出来事については、ほとんどの子どもが語るべきものをもっていない。この種の子どもたちの記憶は、その間は全くの空白になっているのがふつうである。インドのパルモッド・シャルマは、この期間について、「お風呂《ふろ》の中で坐《すわ》ってたら足が小さくなった」という一言ですませている。(この言葉は、本人がその生涯を記憶している男性が、死亡する直前、自然療法の浴槽に入った時のことを指していたのである。)

とはいえ、前世の人格が死亡してから本人が生まれるまでの間に起こった出来事の記憶を残しているという者も一部にある。こうした記憶は大きくふたつに分けることができる。つまり(主として前世の人格の家族内で起こった)世俗の出来事と、肉体のない〝世界〟での体験である。

第一のタイプでは、前世の人格が死亡した後に遺族の間で起こった出来事が記憶に残っている。まるで前世の人格が、それまで生活して来て死亡した場所の周辺にどういうわけか留《とど》まり、肉体のない間、生者の行動を見守っていたかのようである。事実、そうしていたと主張する者も一部にある。第4章で述べておいたように、ボンクチ・プロムシンは、チャムラットを殺害した犯人が死体を野原に埋めたことや、本人（その時点では肉体のないチャムラット）が、ボンクチの父親の姿を見かけるまで、自分が殺された現場近くの竹やぶ周辺にいたのを記憶している。ディスナ・サマラシンへ（スリランカ）は、（前世の自分だという）ババノナの遺体が蟻塚の近くに埋葬されたのを覚えていた。埋葬の場所は、ババノナが死亡した後に決められたのであった。

やはりインドに住むヴェール・シンは、前世で死亡した後、前世の自宅の周辺に留まっていたという。その証拠として本人は、結婚式などの際にどれほどの飲食物が飲み食いされたかを語っている。結婚式に供された食事の話には、特に注目すべき点はなかった。内容は違うが、西洋の結婚式で供される型にはまった食事と同じく、予測できるものだからである。それよりも印象的だったのは、夜間に外出した家族と一緒にいたと本人が主張したことであった。これは、前世の人格（ソム・ドゥト）の母親が見た夢と符合していた。この母親は、肉体のないソム・ドゥトが、いま兄と一緒にいると語る夢を見ていたのである。ソム・ドゥトの兄は、夜、自宅をこっそり抜け出し、その地区で開催されていた祭りに出かけたのであった。（この兄は、聞かれるとすぐにそのことを認めたが、他の家族は、母親がその夢を見るまでこの事実を知らなかった。）ヴェール・シンはまた、ソム・ドゥトが死亡してから本人が生まれるまでの間に起こった、たとえば一家が訴訟に巻き込まれるという事件やラクダを一頭購入したこと、子どもが何人か生まれたことをはじめ、内輪の出来事も他にいくつか知っていた。

既に（両親が本人の記憶を抑えつけようとしてもうまくいかなかった例として）紹介しているチャオクン・ラジスタジャルンというタイの修道僧は、前世で死亡した後に、自分の葬式に参列したのを記憶しているという。本人の話では、その時、自分が軽くなった気がして、どこへでも簡単に移動できるように感じられたという。自らがその葬儀を司《つかさど》っており、弔問客を迎えていた気がするというが、自分の姿は参列している人たちには見えず、自分がその場にいることには全く気づかれないまま葬儀が進行していたという。

前世の記憶をもつ者の中には、肉体のない状態でいた時、ポルターガイスト現象を起こしたと主張する者が何人かいる。ヴェール・シンは、誰かが乗っているブランコの板を割ってしまったことがあるというし、ティン・セインは、後に（現世で）自分の父親となる男性に石を投げつけたことがあったという。

死亡してから生まれ変わるとされるまでの間の記憶としてもっと多いのは、前世で死亡してから現世に生まれ変わるまでの間（その期間についてはほとんどの場合不明であるが）逗留《とうりゅう》していたという別の世界の記憶である。ディスナ・サマラシンへは、前世の自分だとするババノナという老婦人の死後こうした世界に滞在していたことについて、かなり詳しく語っている。本人の話によれば、その世界の住人が身に着けている衣服は優雅であると同時に華やかなものであり、洗濯の必要はなかったという。望めばそれだけで食物が目の前に現れ、食べることもできたが、その必要はなかったともいう。そして、親切な〝支配者〟と出会い、結局その人物に、もう一度生まれ出るよう勧められたが、その場所は教えてもらえなかったというのである。

　肉体のない世界の記憶をもつビルマやタイの（あるいは、数は少ないながらそれ以外の国の）子どもたちの中には、自分たちの面倒を見てくれたうえ、後に、生まれ変わる先の家族のもとへ案内してくれた賢者のような人物とそこで出会ったという者もある。（子どもの頃）前世を記憶していたビルマの修道僧サヤドウ・ウ・ソバナ師は、こうした肉体のない指導者との出会いについて、私が知っている中では最も詳しい話をしている。その記憶によれば、賢者が本人を、前世時代に住んでいた村に連れ戻し、最初は自宅に連れて行ったが、結局その二、三軒先の家に案内し、そこに本人を置いて行ってしまったという。そこがサヤドウ・ウ・ソバナ師の両親が住む家であり、師はその家で生まれたのであった[*20]。

人物や物品を見分ける　前世の記憶をもつ子どもの中には、誰かが前世時代の村や町に連れて行ってくれさえすれば、前世時代に知っていた人物と再会することができるし、その人たち（や場所）を見分けることができると主張する者も少なくない。前世の人格がよく知っていた人物や場所や物品を本人が見分けたという証言は、多くの事例に見られる。このようなことは、その子どもの両親が前世の家族のもとへ本人を連れて行った時や、子どもの話を聞きつけた前世の家族が本人に会いに来た時に起こるのがふつうである。

　こうした事例の情報提供者は、子どもが人物や場所を見分けたことを、私よりもはるかに重視するが、そうした検分がある程度にせよ管理された条件の下で行なわれることはほとんどないのが実状なのである。子どもは、前世の家族と対面する際、必ずと言ってよいほど、新たにその家族の一員となった者から大群集に至るまで、大勢の人間にとり囲まれる。その人たちが子どもに、「この中に奥さんがいるかな」などという誘導的な質問をする場合が多いうえに、とり巻いている人々が期待に胸をふくらませながら前世の人格の妻を注視しているため、子どもはまちがえようがなくなってしまうかもしれないのである。

とはいえ、子どもが次の二通りの状況で見分けることに成功した場合には、信頼が置けるということも、ここで述べておかなければならない。まずひとつは、たとえば街を歩いている人など、たまたま出会った人物を自分から積極的に見分けた場合である。第4章で紹介したコーリス・チョトキン・ジュニアは、このようにして、（その生涯を記憶している）ヴィクター・ヴィンセントの義娘を見分けている。この女性がアラスカ州シトカの波止場にいた時、そこへコーリスがたまたま母親と一緒に来ていたのである。突然この女性に気づいたコーリスは、興奮しながら「うちのスージーがいる」と叫んだ。コーリスの母親は、スージーと知り合いであったが、コーリスの気づく方が早かったのである。このように本人が自発的に見分ける際に証拠としての価値が最も高いのは、一緒にいる者には全くわからない人物を本人が言い当てた場合である。アムパン・ペトチェラト（タイ）は、その生涯を記憶しているチュエイという少年の伯母《おば》（ジョイ・ルアン・グン）を、自分が住んでいる小さな町の通りで自分の方から見つけている。その時一緒にいたアムパンの母親は、ジョイ・ルアン・グンをそれまで全く知らなかった。トルコのイスマイル・アルティンキリヒも、自宅前の道を通ったアイスクリーム売りのふたり連れを自分の方から認めている。このふたりは、そのあたりにアイスクリームを売りに来ているので、イスマイルの家族もおそらくは顔を知っていたのであろうが、ふたりの名前は知らなかった。ところがイスマイルは、その名前を言い当てているのである。この種の出来事は数があまりに少ないが、いずれにせよ、子どもの家族がそのように仕向けたとする疑念は起こりえない[*21]。

もうひとつは、数はわずかであるが、信頼の置けるおとなが、うまく条件を整えて、子どもが知っている可能性のある人物を、人目のつかない静かな状況で本人と対面させ、「この人がわかるかい」という以上の聞き方をしていない場合である。スリランカのグナナティレカ・バデウィタナという少女は、(私の手によってではないが)初めて調査が行なわれた時、このような条件のもとで何人かの人物を見分けている。私はその場面を見てはいないが、その後グナナティレカがある人物を見分けた時など、同様に管理された条件下で見分けを行なった場面には数回立会っている。その時私は、グナナティレカの前世の人格だというティレケラトネという少年の友人を本人宅に連れて行く役割を受けもった。(本例も性転換が起こった事例である。)またその際に私は、ティレケラトネが知らなかった人物も同行させた。この人たちを知っているかどうか聞かれると、即座にグナナティレカは、(たとえば、″ローラ″と言うべきところを″ドーラ″と言ったという程度の些《さ》細《さい》なまちがいはあったが)、前世の人格の友人の名前を言い当てた。しかし、もうひとりについてはわからなかった。見分けることができた方の人物と知り合った場所を聞かれると、本人は、その町の名前(タラワケレ)を言った。その質問をされている時の状況から町名を推定した可能性もあるが、ティレケラトネの友人の名前についてはその可能性はないと思う。

またある時私は、あらかじめ知らせずに、マ・チョエ・ニン・テトというビルマの少女の自宅に、前世時代の親友を連れて行ったことがある。この人を知っているかと聞かれると、マ・チョエ・ニン・テトは、その少女の名前をはっきりと口にした。ところが、本人は、前世の人格を手術した心臓外科医と（別の時に同じような状況で）会ってもわからなかった。（この少女は、その手術中に死亡したのであった。）

人物を見分ける時によく見られる特徴について、もうひとつふれておいてもよさそうなことがある。誰かを見分けても、それ自体は（おそらくは誘導的な質問が行なわれたため）あまり意味がない場合でも、そのあとに、自分から意味のある発言を行なう者がある、ということである。たとえば、その人物の昔の愛称を言い当てるとか、「歯はどうしたの」など、ある意味で重要な個人的発言を行なう場合があるのである。

愛称を言い当てた実例としては、インドのジャスビール・シンの事例が挙げられる。ビルバル・シンという男性がジャスビールのいる部屋へ入って来ると、本人は自分の方から、「どうぞ、ガンジージ」と言った。そこにいた人が、「この方はビルバルさんだ」と言って本人の誤りを正そうとしたところ、ジャスビールは、「ぼくたちはこの人を『ガンジージ』と呼んでるよ」と答えた。ビルバル・シンは、確かに「ガンジージ」と呼ばれていた。耳が大きくて、風《ふう》貌《ぼう》がマハトマ・ガンジーにどこか似ていたからである。（接尾語の〝ジ〟はヒンディー語でふつうに用いられる敬称である。）

やはりインドのスワルンラタ・ミシュラも、ビヤ（本人がその生涯を記憶している女性）の友人を認め、その男性が眼鏡をかけていることを指摘した。この男性は、ビヤの生前には眼鏡をかけていなかったのである。やはり肉体のない世界について語ったディスナ・サマラシンへは、自宅前の道を歩いている少年を見分け、両親に、「あの子知ってるかい。私の青豆を盗《と》った子だよ」と言った。ディスナの両親はその後、問題の少年は（ディスナが前世の自分だという）ババノナの孫で、その子は幼少期に、ババノナが調理して入浴中そのままにしておいた豆を食べ散らかしたという出来事があったことを知った。

前世を記憶する子どもの中には、愛称を口にしたり、前世の人格の生涯に起こった、長い間忘れ去られていた小さな出来事を自分から言い出す者が多いが、このように自発的に語ることも、こうした事例の最も印象的な特徴のひとつであるように思われる。本人は、（相手と対面する前に）前世の人格について通常の方法で入手した情報を詰め込んでいただけなのではないか（あるいは両親から無理やり教え込まれていたのではないか）、という批判が時おりあるが、自発的に口にするという事実からすると、その批判は当たらない。

前世に関連する行動

前世を記憶する子どもは、自分の家族から見ると一風変わった二種類の行動の一方ないし双方を示すことが多い。

まず第一に、本人がもっているとされる記憶に沿った感情を、前世の家族に対して示す子どもが存在することである。もし前世が幸せな一生であり、不幸だった時間の方が短ければ、子どもは、まだ存命中の前世の家族のところへ連れて行ってほしい、と求めることもある。先方と対面すると本人は、喜びや懐旧の情や、あるいは逆に無関心や拒絶を示すかもしれない。このような反応はほとんどが、前世の人格と前世の家族との関係について判明した、あるいは推測できる事柄ときわめてよく一致する。

ラタナ・ウォンソムバト（タイ）の事例は、前世の人格の家族に対して、本人が各人を区別して応対する好例である。ラタナは、前世の自分だというキム・ランという老婦人の娘であるアナン・スタヴィルと対面した時には大変に喜んだが、キム・ランの夫に対しては無関心を装い、後には敵意すら示した。キム・ランは、不和の続いた晩年には、夫とほとんど口を利かなかったのであった。グナナティレカ・バデウィタナが、その生涯を記憶している少年（ティレケラトネ）の家族に対して示した行動を見ても、同じように相手を区別して行動しているのがわかる。グナナティレカは、ティレケラトネの姉妹やある教師と非常に仲がよかったが、兄に対してはきわめて冷たかった。ティレケラトネは、自分の姉妹とは仲よくしていたし、その教師を慕ってもいたが、兄は嫌っていた。兄は、ティレケラトネには不親切で、冷酷とも言えるほどの態度を示していたようである。*22

前世の家族に対して子どもがその後どのような態度や行動をとるかは、その家族が本人をどう受け止めるかによってある程度決まる。一部の事例では、子どもが前世の家族から完全に受け入れられる。こうした事例では、遊びに来るよう本人を誘ったり、贈り物をしたり、さらにはもっと実際的な援助を行なうのである。一方、前世の家族が子どもを拒絶する事例もある。こうした場合には、最初の訪問が最後となる。[23] 前世の家族が子どもの家族よりもはるかに裕福で、そのため子どもの家族が自分たちから金品を騙《だま》しとろうとしているのではないかと（私の経験では、そう考えてよい正当な理由もないのに）思い込んでいる場合、このような事態がよく発生する。[24]（たいていは、そのような時にしかこうした事態は発生しない。）その後の状況を観察できた事例では大半が、二、三年の間は双方の家族が親しく行き来し合うが、その後は、双方の生活形態が変わるに従って次第に交流が少なくなるのである。

もうひとつの変わった行動とは、家族の中では異質であるが、前世の人格がもっていたことがわかっている、あるいはもっていたと考えてまちがいない特徴とは一致する（恐怖症、嗜好《しこう》、関心、技能などの）行動特性のことである。こうした事例では、子どもの家族に同じような特徴を示す者がいないか、いてもはるかにその程度が小さいので、そのような特徴が子どもに出現した原因を、それまで子どもが経験して来た出来事の中に求めることはできない。

前世の人格の死因に関係する恐怖症は、私には特に印象深かった。しかも、このような事例は頻繁に観察される。前世の人格が横変死を遂げた二五二例中一二七例（五〇パーセント）に恐怖症のあることが判明しているのである。前世の人格が溺死《できし》している場合には、水に対する恐怖症を示しやすいし、射殺されている場合は、銃火器に対する恐怖症が起こりやすい。

恐怖症をもつ子どもは、原因となる刺激が般化されたような反応を示すことが少なくない。たとえば、理髪師に殺された記憶をもつラヴィ・シャンカール・グプタは、（本人の幼少期にはまだ近くに住んでいた）前世の人格の殺害犯である理髪師に対してばかりでなく、どの理髪師に対しても恐怖症を示したのである。ハサンという人物に殺された男性の生涯を記憶している（カン・ポラトが調査した）トルコの子どもは、（トルコにはかなり多い）ハサンという名前の人物全員に対して恐怖症を示した。

　言葉を覚える前、したがって前世での恐怖症の原因らしきものを説明できるようになる以前に恐怖症を示す子どももある。シャムリニー・プレマの事例を要約して紹介する中でふれておいたが、シャムリニーは、生後まもなくから、母親が入浴させようとすると、水につけられることに対して極度の恐怖を示した。シャムリニーは、口が利けるようになると、前世で溺死した時の模様を詳しく語った。ラル・ジャヤスーリアというスリランカの少年の事例でも、同様の現象が見られた。この少年は、言葉が話せるようになる前から、警官の姿を見ると明らかな反応を示し、可能な限り姿を隠そうとした。その後、自分は前世で反政府活動家だったと語ったのである。[*25]（スリランカで一九七一年に起こった反政府暴動は、警察当局の不必要な武力介入により鎮圧された。）

　特定の食物を好むこと（および、特定の食物を嫌うこと）も、こうした子どもたちが示す変わった行動のかなりの部分を占める。前に述べたように、ボンクチ・プロムシンは粘り気のある米飯を好んだ。（というか、非常に食べたがった。）このような米飯は、本人の家族は振り向きもしなかったが、ボンクチが前世の自分だとするチャムラットという青年の好物だったのである。

　個々に見れば、こうした行動には特別の意味をもつものはほとんどない。このような行動を示す者は子どもにもおとなにも大勢いるからである。しかしながら、全体として見れば、このような行動は印象的なものとなる。こうした子どもたちは、家族の中では異質であるが、前世の人格の特徴であった行動の症候群を示すことが少なくないからである。次に紹介する実例をお読みになれば、このような意味での変わった行動群が具体的におわかりいただけよう。マ・ティン・アウン・ミョは、男性的な行動特徴や飛行機恐怖症、数種の〝日本人的〟行動を示したうえ、戦争ごっこを好んだし、スジト・ラクマル・ジャヤラトネは、幼時に、酒や煙草を異常にほしがり、トラックや警官に対する恐怖症を見せた。また、シャムリニー・プレマは、特定の食物を異常とも思えるほど好んだことに加え、水につけられることやバスに対する恐怖症を示したし、エルカン・キリヒ（トルコ）は、飛行機恐怖症やアルコールに対する嗜好を示したうえ、ナイトクラブ経営ごっこという遊びも演じた。こうした行動群はすべて、それぞれの前世の人格の行動と符合していたのである。

　前世時代とは明らかに異なる社会的階層に置かれている子どもたちは、変わった行動を特にはっきり示す場合が多い。たとえば、現在は貧しい家庭に生まれているが、上流階級に属する裕福な家庭で暮らしていた記憶があるという子どもは、貧しいことや下層階級の生活習慣に従っていることについて両親を非難し叱りつけることもある。先述のように、ゴーパール・グプタは、以前には使用人にさせていたとして家事を忌避していた。やはりインドに住むビシェン・チャンド・カプールは、家族にあてがわれた安物の服を軽蔑《けいべつ》したような目つきで見ながら、ぼくならこんな服、召使いにもやらないよ、と言った。

　それに対して、現在より恵まれない家庭で前世を送った記憶をもつ子どもは、家族が不愉快に感ずるほど粗野なふるまいをする場合がある。バラモンの家庭に生まれたスワラン・ラタ（インド）という少女は、（最下層のカーストに属する）清掃人の生涯を記憶していた。スワラン・ラタは、愛すべき特徴もたくさんもっていたが、個人的な生活習慣は、（家族から見れば）嫌悪を催すほど不潔であったし、菜食主義の一家を、豚肉を食べたいと言って仰天させた。本人は、家族の者とは異なり、弟妹たちの排泄物《はいせつ》を喜んで（熱心とも言えるほどに）始末していた。現在よりも低い生活環境の中で過ごした前世を記憶している子どもの中には、現在置かれている状況を前世と比較して、喜びや感謝の念を表明する者もある。たとえば、アヌシャ・セネワルデナ（スリランカ）は、今の裕福な家庭ではあたりまえのマーマレードのような食物を喜んだりありがたがったりしていた。この少女は、昼食に小さなパンを、しかもそれすらふたりで分けあって食べなければならなかった貧しい村の学童の生涯を記憶していたのである。[*26]

　これまで本節で述べてきた変わった行動のほとんどは、第1章で行動的記憶としておいた記憶の格好の実例である。行動的記憶は、イメージ記憶よりも長期にわたって保持されることが少なくない。その場合、子どもは、同様の行動をしていた前世の人格の生涯の中で起こった事柄がもはや思い出せなくなった後でも、特定の食物を好むなどの行動を示し続けることもある。たとえば、ビシェン・チャンド・カプールは、肉食をしていた人物の生涯について以前もっていた記憶をほとんど失った後にも、（菜食主義の家族のもとから離れている時にはいつでも）

何年もの間、肉食を続けていることを私に話してくれた。ラヴィ・シャンカール・グプタ（インド）は、先述のように理髪師恐怖症をもっていたが、（人から聞かされた話から観念的には理解していたものの）恐怖症の原因が思い出せなくなった後も、（前世の自分だという）ムンナを殺害した犯人たちを相変わらず怖がっていた。

記憶の中では自分が成人であるため、それに呼応して、年長者から見れば同年輩の子どもよりもおとなびたところのある者が多い。こうした子どもたちは、一人前の成人としての態度を身につけており、時には、他の子どもたちに対して、あるいは一部のおとなたちに対してすら、ていねいな物腰で応対する。[27] つまるところ、たとえ本人がわずか四歳であるにせよ、妻子ある既婚男性であるとすれば、それこそ当然の態度と言えるのではなかろうか。とはいえ、こうした子どもたちの中には、それにふさわしい仕事をする者もある。たとえば、このような娘をもつ母親は、その娘が、他の娘たちよりもはるかに早い時期から責任をもって家事を切り盛りしてくれることがわかるかもしれないのである。

このような子どもたちが示す変わった行動のうちで、最も興味深く最も重要なもののひとつは、前世では逆の性別だったという子どもによく見られる行動である。（こうした子どもたちを私は、性転換型事例ないし性転換例と呼んでいる。）このような子どもの大半は、本人が記憶している前世時代の性別に相応する衣服を身に着け、そうした言葉遣いや遊びなどを（強弱はさまざまであるが）行なうのである。第4章で要約して紹介したマ・ティン・アウン・ミョやエリン・ジャクソンの事例がこの種の行動の好例である。[28]

前世の人格の死から本人が生まれるまでの間隔について

本章の末尾で簡単にふれるが、出生した日時が常識では説明できない事例をはじめとするごく一部の例外を除けば、前世の人格が死んでから本人が生まれるまでの間隔は、三年未満であるのがふつうである。中央値は文化圏によって異なり、レバノンの六ヵ月から、トリンギットの四八ヵ月までさまざまである。[*29]一〇ヵ所の文化圏から集めた六一六例の中央値は一五ヵ月であった。

横変死を遂げている場合には、自然死の場合よりも速やかに生まれ変わるという信仰が広く見られる。私たちが収集した事例もこの考え方を裏づける方向にある。北アメリカ北西部（という、合衆国の人口動態統計が最も信頼できる地域）で集められた事例では、非業の死を遂げている場合には、自然死の場合よりも死んでから生まれ変わるまでの間隔が（統計的な意味で）有意に短かった。インドの事例の分析でも、同様の結果が得られている。

成人の関係者の態度

子どもが前世について話すのを聞いた時、両親が最初にどのような反応をするかは、生まれ変わりを確信しているかどうかによって決まる。ふつうの西洋人の両親は、生まれ変わりを信じていないばかりか、その可能性を考えたことすらない。このような両親の中には、前世の記憶があるなどという子どもは、とてつもないうそつきでなければ、おかしな空想に浸りやすい子どもだと考える者もある。このような親たちは、もっぱら、自分たちがそのような異常児を生んだという話が隣近所に広まることを心配し、そういう悪いうわさをどうしたら最小限に食い止めることができるかを考える。私が注目するようになった西洋の事例は、両親がこうした態度をとらなかったか、一時はとってもそれを乗り越えた家族の中で発生しているのである。

アジアをはじめ、生まれ変わりという考え方を受け入れている地域では、初めから基盤がもっとしっかりしている。こうした地域では、前世の話をする子どもの両親は、子どもが正気を失ったとは考えない。自分たちのもとへ生まれて来る前にこの世で送った前世の記憶を本当にもっている可能性を認めているのである。とはいえ、（私の知る限り、同じ東南アジアでも他の国はそうではないが）ビルマやインドに住む人々は、前世を記憶していることは子どもにとって不健康な状態であり、場合によってはそれが致命的な影響を及ぼすことすらあると考える。そのため、両親が子どもの記憶を抑えつけることもある。それとは別に、両親は、子どもの発言内容によって、また子どもが前世について話し続け、しかも子どもの発言が世間に知られるようになった場合、自分たち家族にとってそれがどのような意味をもつかに従って、子どもの言葉や行動に対する態度を決める。

子どもが、別段変わった点があったようにも思われない前世の話をしている限り、両親はそれほど悩むことはないかもしれない。しかし、子どもが語る前世は、ありきたりのものではない場合が多いのである。たとえば、前世で殺されたという事例が多く、その時の殺人犯が現在どう思っているかを考慮に入れなければならないこともある。その時の犯人がまだ隣近所にいて、その子どもに悪く言われるのを嫌っているかもしれないからである。そのため、こうした子どもの両親は、子どもを黙らせた方が得策だと考えるかもしれない。

このような記憶をもつ子どもの中には、今の両親は〝本当の〟親ではないとして、両親を拒絶する者も少なくない。子どもたちによれば、本当の親はどこか別のところに住んでいるので、自分からこちらへ来るか、誰かが連れて来るべきだという。このような態度は、このうえなく愛情深い両親にとってすら重圧になる。自分の子どもに拒絶されたいと願う親はいないので、子どもに不快な比較をされて否定的反応をする結果として、子どもは家族の中でますます孤立することもある。幸い、こうした事例が最も多く見られる地域では、生まれ変わり信仰が親に対する子どもの拒絶の緩衝材になってきた。生まれ変わりを信じている両親は、何かより大きな力によって自分たち親子が新しい家族として形成されたのではないか、と(時には子どもともども)考える。そのような人々は、たとえ現在の状況が幸せなものではないにしても、最終的には何かよい目的をもっているのではないかと言うかもしれないのである。

華やかな上流階級の家庭で前世を送ったと主張するが、今は貧しい両親のもとに暮らしている子どもたちの場合には、問題点がもうひとつある。このような子どもの両親は、当初こそ子どもの主張を大目に見ておもしろがっているが、自分たちのあばら家を子どもが貶《けな》し続けると、それが次第に苛立《いらだ》ちに変わる場合もある。インドでは、前世の話をする子どもは若死にする運命にあるという迷信が広く見られるが、面倒な子どもを抑えつける適当な口実としてこの迷信が生み出されたのではないか、と時おり思うことがある。

それはともかく、多くの親たちは、結局、さまざまな策を弄《ろう》して子どもを抑えつけるようになる（本章の註2でその種の実例をいくつか紹介しておいた。）インドでは、何らかの理由から、どれほど多くの子どもが両親に抑えつけられているかを知れば、驚かれることであろう。インドの少数例を対象にした調査によると、前世の記憶をもつ子どもを（しばしば手荒な）手段を用いて抑えつけようとした母親は二七パーセント、父親は二三パーセントにものぼっているのである。[*30] この数字は、私たちの手元にある事例から得られたものである。完全に抑えつけられたため私たちの耳に届かない事例がどれほどの比率になっているかは、全くわからない。

親が子どもの発言を抑えつけるのはインドだけではない。他にも、さまざまな理由から、子どもが前世の話をするのを認めない国がある。アラスカ南東部に住むトリンギット族の間では、部族間の紛争に絡む殺人事件について子どもが話し始めると、昔の確執が呼び覚まされるのを嫌がる両親は、子どもの口を封じようとするかもしれない。ナイジェリアのイボ族の調査をしていた時、私は、子どもが非業の死を遂げた前世の話をするのはその子どものためにならない、と考える親がいるという話を何度か耳にした。

両親が子どもを抑えつけようとしたかどうかはともかく、子どもが話した内容は、うわさとなって周囲の人たちの間に漏れ広がるのがふつうである。そうなると近隣の人々は、その事例の長所短所を測り始める。時には、その子どもの親が子どもを利用して何かを企《たくら》んでいるのではないか、と悪口を言うことすらある。その場合、それに反発した両親は、子どもが正しいことを証明しようとするかもしれないが、その証明は、子どもが口にした内容を事実と確認することによって初めて可能となるのである。これは、子ども側の計画と合致する。いつも子どもは、前世の家族のもとへ連れて行ってほしいと両親に求めているからである。また、こうした動機があると、あるいは、子どもがしつこく要求するためか、親自身の好奇心のためかのいずれかである場合が多いが、たいていの両親は、子どもが常々口にしている家族を探し出そうとする。

子どもを除いた関係者に見られる動機のうち最も重要度の低いのは、他人に生まれ変わりを信じさせたい、という動機である。こうした事例の大半は純朴な田舎の人たちの間で起こるが、そうした人たちは、人が生まれ変わりの存在を確信しようがすまいが、そのことには全く頓着《とんちゃく》しない。かつては自分でもその事実性を疑っており、実例を目の当たりにしたことがその疑念の軽減に役立ったとしても、それによって他人を感化したいという狂信的な熱意が湧き上がるようには思われない。（生まれ変わりなど存在しないと信じている批判的な人間には、田舎に住むあまり教育のない人たちが、特定の人物の生まれ変わりだという子どもの主張の真偽を検討する際に懐疑的な態度を示すことの方が驚きであろう。）教育程度の高い人々の方が、自分たちの伝統的信仰と事例との関連性に、教育のない人々よりも強い関心を示すかもしれない。中には、かつておとなたちに教え込まれた事柄が事実であることが、特定の事例によって裏づけられたと思い、満足する者もある。とはいえ、（私の知っている）このような人たちの中には、宗教的宣伝を目的に、事例を発表しようとした者はひとりもいない。

前世を記憶する子どもたちのその後

先述のように、このような子どもたちは、五歳から八歳までの間に、その記憶を喪失する（あるいは少なくとも口にしなくなる）のがふつうである。ほとんどの子どもは、八歳になるまでに前世の記憶を完全に消失させてしまうが、もっと低い年齢で完全に忘れてしまう者も少なくない。イメージ記憶が薄れるにつれ行動的記憶も弱まりやすいが、前述のように後者は、イメージ記憶が完全に消失した後にもかなり長く続くことがある。

その子どもが前世のイメージ記憶を消失させ、行動的記憶も日々の新しい経験に屈して弱まると、その後の成長は、一般に全く正常となる。私は、初対面の時点で幼児だった子どもが成人に達するまで観察できた事例をたくさんもっている。既に結婚して、子どものいる人たちも若干ある。そのほとんどが、社会の中でそれなりの位置を占めており、同年輩の者と比べて明らかに異なった行動特徴を示すような者はほとんどない。この点は、幼時に逆の性別の特徴を示していた性転換例の子どもたちの行動にも当てはまる。このような子どもも、成長するにつれて自らの解剖学的性別をほとんど受け入れたのである。この点、マ・ティン・アウン・ミョは典型例ではなく、例外的な存在であった。

パウロ・ロレンツ（ブラジル）も、性転換例としては例外的である。パウロは、青年期に自殺した姉のエミリアの生涯を記憶していた。エミリアは、男性的な容姿をもち、結婚もせず、次は男に生まれ変わる、という予言を行なっていた。パウロ・ロレンツは、幼少期にはきわめて女性的であり、少年期や青年期にはそれよりは男性的になったものの、結婚はしなかった。パウロはまた、孤独で抑うつ的な人物であり、四〇代で自殺している。

ラニ・サクセナ（インド）も、中年になるまで一切妥協せず、男性的態度をとり続けた性転換例である。結婚して子どもを何人か生んだが、（私が本人を知った三〇代後半でもなお）男言葉を使っていた。ヒンディー語では、話し手の気性により一部の動詞が違ってくる。ラニが男性の使う動詞を用いていたのは、その生涯を記憶している男性の弁護士と自分を相も変わらず強く同一視している現われだったのである[31]。

性転換とは別の理由から、その後の成長に抵抗を示した子どもも若干ある。前世から抜け出し、現世の生活に飛び込むことができず苦しんでいるように思われる例もある。インドの（低いカーストに属する）ジャートの家族に生まれたジャスビール・シンは、（高いカーストである）バラモンの男性の生涯を記憶していた。ジャスビールは幼少期に、自分の家族に対してカーストの高い人間のようなふるまいをしたため、餓死寸前に陥ったことがあった。不潔だとして家族の食事を拒否したためである。そのことがきっかけとなって、ジャスビールは何度も兄に叩《たた》かれた。成長すると、ある種の優越感は消えたように見え、家族の食事は食べていたものの、依然として自分をバラモンと考えていた。たとえば、その生涯を記憶しているバラモンの男性の名前を、ジャートの家族の苗字《みょうじ》につけ加えている。青年期に入るとジャスビールは、自らの身分にふさわしいと思える仕事を見つけるのに非常に苦労した。結局、（私と一緒に本例の研究をしていた）インドの研究者が本人に仕事を探してやり、本人もいったんその仕事に就いたものの、その仕事が賤《いや》しいとしてやめてしまったという。バラモンの仕事には似つかわしくないと考えたためであった。

前世を記憶する子どもたちの中には、あまりに前世の記憶に浸りきり、そのために就学が遅れる者がある。インドのパルモッド・シャルマの事例がそうであった。パルモッドは幼児期に、ビスケットやソーダ水を売るお店屋さんごっこばかりしていた。（これは、本人がその生涯を記憶している男性の仕事だったのである。）母親が私に話してくれたところでは、この種の遊びに熱中していたあまり、本人は学校に行くのが一年遅れ、そのため、学校の勉強に完全にはついて行けなくなったという。後に入学した大学でも成績が悪く、最後に私が会った（本人が三〇代前半の）時には、地位の低い事務系の公務員であった。この仕事は、本人がもっている能力からすると痛ましいほどレベルの低いもののように私には思われた。

行動的記憶は、一部の者には長く続くのに対して、他の者には残らない。その理由はわからない。たとえば、ジャスビールは自分をバラモンだとして譲らなかったが、ジャグディシュ・チャンドラは現実に適応した生活を送るようになっている。カヤスト（中位のカースト）の家族のもとに生まれたジャグディシュ・チャンドラは、バラモンの子どもとして送った前世を記憶していた。幼少期には、バラモンの特徴を明確に保持していたが、（中年まで続いたものも一部あるとはいえ）成長するにつれ、その大半を消失させているのである。先ほど、逆の性別の特徴の一端を成人までもち越した性転換例を三例紹介したが、それとは逆に、やはり性転換例であるアムパン・ペトチェラトは、子ども時代には男性的な行動を示していたものの、一〇代後半から青年期になると、正常な女性として成長を遂げている。こうした事例の場合、その後に辿《たど》る道筋が異なるのは、前世の人格が死亡した年齢の違いによるのかもしれない。ジャグディシュ・チャンドラやアムパン・ペトチェラトは、バラモンとしての、あるいは男性としての行動があまり固定化しないと思われる幼時に死亡した前世を記憶していたのに対して、ジャスビール・シンやマ・ティン・アウン・ミョ、パウロ・ロレンツ、ラニ・サクセナなどの事例では、前世の人格が成人に達した後に死亡していることから、こうした態度が固定してしまっていたのかもしれない。

しかしながら、行動的記憶の消失ないし持続を決定する可能性のある要因を、その他に少なくともふたつ考える必要がある。まずひとつは、こうした子どもの両親が、変わった行動を許容するか阻止するかによって、持続する期間が左右されるかもしれないことである。ジャグディシュ・チャンドラの父親は、息子がバラモンのように尊大な態度をとった時には、笑いとばすという強力な戦術を用いている。ジャグディシュ・チャンドラがバラモン的態度をやめたのはそのせいかもしれない。それに対して、（前世の人格の死から生まれ変わるまでの間の記憶について述べた際に紹介しておいた、やはりインドの）ヴェール・シンの事例では、双方の家族が、両家のカーストの差にまつわる本人の葛藤《かっとう》を長引かせるような反応を起こしている。ヴェール・シンは、ジャスビール・シンと同じく、ジャートの家族のもとに生まれ、バラモンの前世を記憶していた。そのバラモンはソム・ドゥトという子どもであり、四歳頃に自然死を遂げていた。ヴェール・シンは、幼時にバラモン然とした行動を示したが、ソム・ドゥトはバラモン的態度があまり固定化されない年齢で死亡しているため、成長するにつれこうした特徴が薄れて行ったのではないかと思われるかもしれない。ところが、ヴェール・シンの家族は、ソム・ドゥトの家族と長時間一緒にいることを本人に許し、本人はその間、本来のバラモンとしての生活を送っていたのである。とはいえ、ソム・ドゥトの家族は完全には本人を受け入れなかったため、青年期になると本人は、半分はジャートで半分はバラモンという態度を示すようになった。

行動的特徴の強固さ、つまりはその持続性を決定するもうひとつの要因は、同様の状況ないし条件で生まれ変わりを繰り返した回数であろう。たとえば、女性として生まれ変わる前に六回続けて男性として生まれ変わっていた者は、それまで一回しか男性として生まれ変わった経験がない者よりも、女性として適応した生活を送るのが難しいかもしれない。この原則は、異常に持続性の強い多くの特徴全般にも当てはまるかもしれない。社会的、性的、宗教的、国家的レベルで見られるあらゆる種類の極端な偏倚《へんい》は、同じような肉体、状況、国家の中で生まれ変わりを繰り返すことにより、多少なりとも強化されるのかもしれないのである。

先ほど私は、外的な生活条件によって習慣が固定化されやすいことを述べた。（ここでは、人間の性別も、外的な生活条件に数えている。）しかしながら、前世から現世へともち越される行動特徴がどこまで持続するかを決定する最大の要因は、態度の非柔軟性（異なった環境に適応できないこと）ではないかと考えている。

若干の異型

本章をしめくくる前に、〝標準的〟な事例からかなり外れた二種類の異型について述べておきたい。

真性異言

第3章で私は、真性異言について簡単にふれておいた。真性異言とは、ごく一部の者が示す、通常の方法では習ったことのない外国語を話す能力のことである。信憑性《しんぴょうせい》のある真性異言の事例は、人間の死後生存を裏づける重要な証拠となる。[*32] しかしながら、真性異言は、前世で別の言葉を話していた記憶をもつ子どもでも、通常の生まれ変わり型事例の場合、顕著な形では出現しない。[*33] 情報提供者によれば、その言葉（たとえば、アジアの学校で教えられる英語）を兄弟たちよりも早く身につけた者が一部にあるというが、生まれ変わり型事例の中には、前世の人格が用いていた言葉を話せそうな者はほとんどいない。しかし、母語がなかなか、しかも不完全な形でしか身につかないように見える者は何人かいた。こうした状態を私は言葉恐怖症と呼んでいる。[*34]

死亡と出生の日付が逆転している事例

前世の人格が死亡するより前にその生涯を記憶する子どもが生まれている事例がいくつかある。（その間隔は、一、二日から数年に及んでいる。）この種の事例では、額面通り解釈すれば、本人の肉体が完成し、おそらくはある人格に支配されるようになった後、別の人格にとって代わられたかに見える。つまり、しばしば憑依《ひょうい》と呼ばれる、ある種の肉体泥棒ということになるのかもしれない。

　こうしたやっかいな事例を片づける最も手っとり早い方法は、日付に記録違いがあったと考えることである。一部の事例については、正確な日付がはっきりしないことから、この考え方が当てはまる。しかしながら、この種の事例のうち少なくとも一〇例では、正確な日付がわかっているので、この謎は依然として残ることを私は確信している。[*35]

　以上、生まれ変わり型事例の典型例を要約して一二例紹介し、大多数の事例に共通して見られる特徴について説明してきた。次の二章では、こうした事例を調査する際に用いている私なりの方法および、事例に関する私なりの分析や解釈についてお話しすることにしよう。

第6章　研究の方法

本章ではまず最初に、生まれ変わり型事例研究の歴史を手短に述べ、次いで、一九六〇年代初頭に私がこの種の事例の研究を開始した頃に判明した事実をいくつか紹介しよう。また私は、事例を研究するに当たって調査法を改良しているが、その際の主な改良点についても簡単に説明する。その後の、本章の中核となる節では、共同研究者とともに私が現時点で用いている調査法の概略を解説する。私たちは現在、私と共同研究者が同程度の比重でチームを組んで研究に当たることがふつうなので、（その節では）私というよりむしろ、私たちが行なっていることを詳しく紹介することになる。

一九六〇年以前の事例研究および事例報告

前世を記憶しているという話は、古代よりいくつか伝えられている。そのうち最も有名なのは、（第2章で紹介しておいた）ピタゴラス[*1]とアポロニオス[*2]の事例であるが、この二例については、信憑性のある記録はほとんど残されていない。私がこれまで研究してきた現代のものとある程度似た特徴をもつ事例で最も古いものは、ムガール帝国皇帝アウランジーブが十八世紀初頭に調査した（本書第2章でも述べている）インドの事例であろう[*3]。同様の事例としては、私の知る限り勝五郎の事例がそれに続く。勝五郎とは、農家の息子の生涯を記憶していた十九世紀初頭の日本の少年である。[4] 勝五郎の事例の後は、一八九八年にビルマの事例六例の要約が発表されるまで、再び長いブランクが続くのである。[5]

一九〇〇年から一九六〇年までの六〇年ほどの間に、(ほとんどはインドの)事例が、新聞や心霊主義関係の雑誌、フランスの心霊研究専門誌、何点かの書籍やパンフレットなどに多数報告された。[6] その大半は、一例報告として、あるいは二、三例をまとめただけで発表されたため、つまらない奇談として無視することも容易であったし、各例に共通して見られる特徴を見落としやすく、したがって、それを読んだ人たちは、同じような事例をもっと細かく検討してみたいという気にもならなかったのである。一九五〇年代に私は、それまで発表された、入手できる範囲の事例報告を集め、その比較検討を始めた。こうした事例をひとたび計画的に探し求めるようになると、かなり詳しい記録が残されていることに加えて信憑性があるように思われる事例を四四例見つけ出すことができた。(その後私は、この時期の事例を他にもいくつか見つけている。)一九六〇年に私は、そのうちの七例を簡単にまとめ、可能性のありそうな解釈をいくつか検討した論文を発表した。[7] その時の私の結論は(当時としてはかなり驚くべきもののように思われたが)、こうした事例によって得られる証拠を見ると(不完全なものではあるが)今後も発見される可能性のあるこの種の事例を丹念に調査する価値がありそうに思われる、というものであった。しかし私は、それほど待つ必要はなかった。一九六一年、インドに新しい事例が一例あることを知り、インドに調査行を行なうための研究助成をわずかながら得て、私の実地調査が開始されたからである。

一九六〇年代に行なわれた初期の調査

一九六一年に初めてインドに渡った時、これほどたくさんの事例が見つかるとは全く予想していなかった。最初の論文の中で分析した四四例中、インドの事例は一八例であるが、それは三五年ほどの間に集められたものであった。ところが最初の五週間のうちに私は、二五例もの事例を新たに見つけ出すことができたのである。そのことから私は、それまで障壁を突き破って人の口にのぼり、活字になった事例は、実際に存在する事例のごく一部にすぎなかったことを知った。一九六一年以降、共同研究者とともに私は、インドでは三〇〇例以上の事例を調査しているが、インドで現実に存在している事例全体からすると、私たちの集めた標本がどのような位置を占めるのかはまだわかっていない[*8]。

他にも、私の予想していなかった点がいくつかあった。私が検討した、既に活字になっている報告は、本人が前世について語った内容以外のことにはほとんどふれていなかった。発言内容に関連して、本人が何かを見分けたと述べているものはいくつかあったが、本人の家族からすれば異質に見えるものの、前世の人格についてわかった、あるいは推測できたこととは符合する行動を本人が示したことにふれているものは、ごくわずかであった。そのため私は、ジャスビール・シンの驚嘆すべき行動について（一九六一年に）情報提供者が話してくれた内容に対して、驚嘆するとともに強い印象を受けた。この事例は、私が調査した最初の事例のひとつである。第5章で私は、自分は本当はバラモンだからという理由で家族の食事を摂《と》ろうとしなかったことについて述べておいた。ジャスビールの家族は農民のカーストであるジャートなので、ジャスビールには一家の食事や調理法は受け入れられなかったのである。

　しかし、以上の事実をはじめ、変わった行動の存在を知って驚いたからと言って、すぐに的確な検討を行なったわけではなかった。こうした行動の重要性に気づくまでには、私自身としても考えられないほどの年月を要したのである。それからさらに時間が経過した現在、事例を厳密に検討する際、このような変わった行動が見られる場合には、少なくとも本人の言葉と同程度ないしはそれ以上に、その点に関する検討を加えなければならないと考えている。私がこのように考える理由については、後ほど説明するつもりである。

　私は、昔の報告を一九六〇年に検討した結果、その多くが、きわめて幼少期に前世の話を始めていることや、その子どもが成長するにつれて記憶らしきものが薄れる傾向があることなど、各例にほぼ共通して見られる特徴がいくつか観察されるという事実に注目するようになった。一九六〇年代に新しい事例を対象に行なった初期の実地調査でも、こうした特徴が頻繁に観察されることが確認されたが、そればかりではなく、子どもたちが記憶している前世の人格は非業の死を遂げていることなど、それ以外の特徴が存在することもまもなく明らかになった。

　事例があり余るほどの数にのぼるうえ、ある特徴が各例に高率に観察されたため、私は大きなジレンマに陥った。各例に最も当てはまりそうな解釈がそれぞれ検討できるように、少数例を選んで集中的に研究すべきなのであろうか。それとも、頻繁に観察される特徴の分析を目的として、（各例の信憑性《しんぴょうせい》をある程度まで確認するには十分であるが）*9広く浅く研究を進めるべきなのであろうか。第二の道を採った場合には（警戒を緩めることで、問題点のある事例が混入しすぎるということがなければ）、事例数が多いほど確実性の高い結論が得られるように思われる。結局私は、いずれの研究法をも捨て切れず、両方とも採用しようとした。その結果、徹底的に調査を行なった少数例についてはそれぞれからかなりのデータが得られたし、比較的浅い研究法を採った多数例についても若干のデータが得られたのである。

私はこれまで、（インドをはじめとする国々で）二五〇例ほどの事例の研究に力を注いできたことに加えて、それ以外にも一〇〇〇例ほどの事例を、不十分な形ではあるが（かなり共通して見られる特徴の分析に含めてもよいと思える程度には）研究してきた。ヴァージニア大学に記録が保管されているその他の事例は、私の協力者や助手が調査したものか、（若干の事例では）たいていの場合私と直接面識があり、私が信頼を置いている者が調査したもののいずれかである。また、こうした研究には見込みがありそうだという印象を最初に与えてくれた（今ではかなり少数になってしまった）事例も含まれている。

一九六〇年以降に見られた主な研究法の進歩

一九六〇年以前に報告された最有力の事例の中には、現在手元にある最高の事例に匹敵するものもいくつかある。しかし、大半の事例では、本人が通常の方法によって前世に関する知識を得た可能性を見極めるのに必要な情報が欠落している。要約しか残されていないものが多すぎ、その事例が進展する中で起こった出来事の時間的順序についても、子どもが正確にはどういう内容を誰に対して話したのかについてもよくわからないし、その発言が事実と一致することを誰が確認したのかについても、ほとんどあるいは全くわからないのである。こうした問題点を解消する目的で私が採用した方法は、次のような手順を中心にしたものである。複数の証人に面接調査を行なうこと、誰がいつ何を話したかを記録すること、情報提供者の信頼性を検討すること、報告内容に首尾一貫性があるかどうかを調べ、それまで見落としていた点を明らかにするため同一の情報提供者に繰り返し面接すること、前世の人格を知っているか、信頼の置ける情報をもっている情報提供者に、本人の発言が事実かどうかを別個に、可能な限り確認すること、重要な日時の記録や病院のカルテ、検死報告などの関係書類を全て探し出し、複写すること。

このような方法は別に目新しいものではない。弁護士や歴史学者は何百年も昔から同様の方法を使っているし、心霊研究者も、十九世紀末にその研究を開始して以来、同じ方法を用いて来たからである。現代に住む私たちは、昔の研究者には利用できなかったテープレコーダなどの武器をいくつかもっているが、超常的な要素が関係しているように思われる事例を研究する場合の基本的な考え方は、昔と全く同じなのである。

私がこのような方法を採用し、一部の協力者がそれに若干の補足を行なうようになるまでには、幾多の困難があった。生まれ変わりの事例に関係する家族の人口動態的特徴を記入したうえ、調べるべき点を教えてくれる備忘録的な役割も兼ね備えた適当な記録用紙を考案するのに、何年もの年月を要したのである。また、私が行なった初期の面接調査では、情報提供者が語った内容を逐語的ないしはそれに近い形で記録しておくことの重要性がわからなかったため、記録の中に大きな穴がいくつかあった。得られた答ばかりでなく、私たちが情報提供者に向けて発した質問もきちんと書き留めるようになったのは、一九七〇年頃からである。

では次に、私たちが現在用いている方法の主な特徴を紹介しよう。面接調査の方法が最も重要なのでそこから始めることにする。[*10]

現在用いられている研究法

面接調査の方法

面接調査の対象　最も重要な情報提供者は、面接できるとすれば、前世の記憶をもっているという子ども自身である。見ず知らずの他人と気やすく話せるかどうかは相当の個人差があるし、私とともに調査に従事して来た通訳についても、子どもたちを和ませ、その気があれば私たちと話させるようにする能力はそれぞれ異なっていた。

本人に次いで重要なのは、たいていの場合、両親である。そして、本人が私たちと話したがらなかったり、既に前世の記憶を失ってしまっている場合には、両親が最も重要な情報提供者になる。両親の次には、祖父母や兄弟姉妹、隣近所の人たちをはじめ、地域に住む関係者の証言に耳を傾けたい。私たちが面接する相手は全員が、自分の眼や耳で直接に情報を得ている者でなければならず[*11]、三番煎《せん》じの断片的情報を切り売りするような人物であってはならない。（残念ながら、アジアやアフリカでは、この種の人物が面接調査に時おり割り込んで来る。内密に話をする場所がなかなか見つからないためであるが、いずれにせよこのような人物には、おとなしくしていてもらう必要がある。）子どもが前世について話すのを聞いたことのある、村の長老や学校の教師などの（本人の家族以外の）知識人が重要な情報をもたらしてくれる場合も少なくない。このような人たちであれば、本人の両親よりも冷静な目で事例を観察しているので、本人の言葉にそれほど熱心に耳を傾けているわけでも、それほど気持を苛立《いらだ》たせながら聞いているわけでもない。また、こうした人々は、前世の記憶をもっているとされる子どもやその両親などの主たる情報提供者の信頼性を判断するに際しても、協力してくれることが多い。人が第三者に関する自らの意見を口にする場合、その相手のことよりも自分のことの方をいろいろと話す傾向があるが、その人物についても何か話してくれるので、ひとりの情報提供者の意見は、時に、私が他の情報提供者の信頼性を判断するうえで参考になることがあるように思う。

　前世の記憶をもっている子どもやその家族が私たちに話してくれた内容を（通常は文字で、時にはテープレコーダで）記録した後、私たちは、（それが突き止められた場合には）前世の人格の家族のもとへ出向き、その家族や地域の人たちにも同様の面接調査を行なう。

大半の事例では、本人やその家族が先方の家族と対面する以前に、私たちがその事例に接する機会はない。とはいえ、その家族がまだ突き止められていない時には、かなりの成功が見込まれる場合には必ず、成功する見込みはほとんどなくてもその価値がありそうな場合にも時おりは、私たち自身が突き止める努力をすることになる。このように、子どもが前世の家族についてそれほど語っていない場合でも、その発言と符合する家族を探し求めることもあるわけであるが、そのためにはどれほど時間を割いてもよいと考えている。なぜかと言えば、双方の家族がまだ対面していない時点で、本人が実際に何をどの程度話したのかについて、情報提供者が誤って記憶している可能性が確実に排除できた事例がまだ少ない現在、この場合には本人の語った内容が既に記録されているわけであるから、その家族を突き止めるのに成功すれば、それを、情報提供者の記憶が正しかったことの裏づけが得られた事例としてそこに加えることができるからである。後ほど説明するつもりであるが、このような事例の場合、生まれ変わり以外の考え方としては、今の私には情報提供者の記憶違いという可能性が最も高そうに思われるのである。

面接調査はどのように行なわれるか　(適当に自己紹介を行ない、私たちが何をしようとしているかを説明した後、)私たちは、たとえば、「最初はどんなふうに始まったのかお聞かせください」とか「最初にお気づきになったのはどういうことですか」とか「この例についてご存知のことを全部話してください」といったおおまかな質問を行なう。次いで、口を差し挟むことは一切せずに情報提供者が最初に話してくれた内容を（明らかに無関係な話を除いては）全て記録する。しかるのちに、その情報提供者が語った特定の事柄や出来事に戻り、もっと詳しく、あるいはもっとはっきり話してくれるよう求める。それから、重要と思われるのに本人が言い漏らしていそうな点について質問する。この時私たちは、先方をなじみのない土俵に引きずり込むことになるかもしれないわけであるが、もしそうであれば、先方にはその関連性がすぐにはわからないかもしれないので、そのような質問をする理由を労をいとわず説明する。

情報提供者の中には、引っ込み思案な傾向や思うことがはっきり表現できない傾向が強いあまり、自分から進んで話ができない者もある。このような場合には、細かい質問を（ことによると最初から）することで助け舟を出す。同じように、情報提供者の発言を確認する段階で、直接的な質問や、場合によっては相手の言いたいことを引き出すために誘導的な質問を行なう必要のある場合も少なくない。誘導的な質問を私は気嫌いするものではないが、何であれ質問した時には、その内容を記録しておく。

大半の情報提供者には、直接に見聞きした事柄に基づく証言と、うわさ話との違いの重要性が理解できないし、そのふたつが違うものであることすらわからない者も少なくない。そのため自分自身が見聞きしたことだけを話してほしい、という注文をつける（あるいは念を押す）ことも必要である。

私たちは、前世の記憶があるという者の発言や行動にまつわる情報についても前世の人格に関する情報についても、また聞きの証言を採用することは全く（あるいはほとんど）ない。先述のように、こうした証人は自分の考えを執拗《しつよう》に言い立てるので、たいていの場合私たちは、本当の証人とは区別して扱い、このような話には耳を傾けることすらしない。とはいえ、真の情報源を突き止めるための道案内として、またその重要性を判断する材料として、また聞きの情報提供者による情報も時として利用することがある。

どのようにして情報を記録するか　私たちは、テープに録音するよりもノートをとるという方法を好んで用いている。録音の場合、無関係のものが入りすぎるし、その場面の非言語的特徴の多くは記録されずに終わってしまう。（面接が進むにつれ、そうしたもののうちより重要度の高い特徴を記録することができるようになる。）また、遺漏や矛盾があるかどうかをすぐに知りたい時にも、文字で記録されていれば、録音された時よりも簡単に探し出すことができる。翌日の第二回面接で、前日聞き漏らした点について尋ねたり、矛盾点を質《ただ》したりができるように、こうした問題点をその地域を離れる前に把握しておかなければならない場合が時おりあるのである。とはいえ、本人自身が前世の記憶をもっているという場合には、その言葉をテープに録音しておいた方がよいと思う。また私たちは、情報提供者にあまり時間がない時や、私たち自身が予定より早くその場を切り上げなければならなくなった時にも、テープレコーダを利用することがある。（タクシーの運転手や牛車《ぎっしゃ》の御者は、こうした事例に私たちほど関心をもっていないので、その要求に応じて早々に切り上げなければならないことが往々にしてあるのである。）

可能な時にはいつでも、私たちの研究班のうちふたりが、面接中にノートをとる。私は、特に最近の何年かは、そのような形で調査できることが多かった。その場合には、ひとりの助手ないし共同研究者が（必要に応じて）主に通訳となり、もうひとりの助手が情報提供者の用いる言葉でノートをとり、同時にそれが正確かどうかを前者がチェックする。そして私が、情報提供者に向けて発した質問とそれに対する答を英語で（あるいは、時に応じてフランス語で）記録する。面接調査を行なった日の夜（ないしはその少し後）に、その日の調査で作成された二組のノートを比較検討することもよくあった。その際、私たちは、矛盾点や聞き漏らしに注意し、それに検討を加えたうえ、疑問点を解消するため再度の面接調査が必要だと考えることもある。また私は、自分でとったノートが正確かどうかを調べる目的で、時々テープ録音との対照を行なっている。

次章では、こうした事例に最もよく当てはまる解釈を見つけ出す場合の問題点について論ずるつもりであるが、ここで強調しておきたいのは、もし私の報告に不正確な部分があれば、それはすべて情報提供者の誤りに起因するものと考えられるように、情報提供者の発言内容を細心の注意を払って正確に記録してきた、という点である。

面接調査で私は通訳を使う必要がある場合が多い。そのため、通訳の能力という問題や、情報提供者が語った内容が通訳され記録に付される際、通訳の偏見によって歪《ゆが》められる可能性が出てくる。通訳上の誤りは（見つかったものについては）、詳しい事例報告の中で指摘しておいたが、もしかすると時々は発生していたのかもしれない。とはいっても、それほど数が多かったわけでも致命的なものだったわけでもないように思う。私は、数ヵ国で一〇年ないしそれ以上の年月にわたって同じ通訳と一緒に調査できるという幸運に恵まれた。したがって通訳たちは、私の調査法に慣れているので、そこで用いられる言葉の中で特に誤訳されやすい単語や言い回しもいくつか見つかっている。また、先方から得られた回答ばかりでなく、私たちが行なった質問も記録しておくことで、通訳が私の質問を伝えてくれているのか、自分なりの質問をしているのかを見極めることができる。通訳に習熟した者であればあるほど、私の質問よりも適切な言い回しを思いつくことが多いし、重要と思われる点を明らかにするためにはどのような質問をしたらよいか教えてくれることもある。このようなわけで、私の通訳を務めてくれている人たちは、面接調査の助手というよりは、共同研究者になっているのである。[*12]

前世を記憶する子どもの家族との面接調査で得られる情報　私たちが得たい情報は、主に次の五つのカテゴリーに分けられる。(1)その子どもが前世について語った内容、(2)その情報を子どもが通常の伝達手段により得たとした場合に考えられる可能性、(3)子どもが示す変わった行動の中で、前世に関係がありそうなものの観察報告、(4)母親がその子どもを妊娠していた時の、またその子どもの幼児期の発達に関する情報、(5)その子どもの出生順位や知的レベルの評価、一家の社会的、経済的状況、その事例に対する成人の関係者たちの態度、の以上五点である。

先ほど述べたように、本人がまだ何らかの記憶を残しており、それを私たちに話してくれるようであれば、その記憶に関する本人自身の発言を記録しておきたい。しかしながら、本人は、（少なくとも初めは）引っ込み思案のあまり私たちと自由に話せないことも少なくないし、子どもに話させるより両親が先に話したがることもある。このような時には、子どもが前世について語った内容を可能な限り話してくれるよう両親に求める。私は、子どもが初めて、しばしば舌足らずの言葉で話した内容に関する両親の記憶を特に重視している。私たちは、その子どもが質問に答える形で語ったと思《おぼ》しき内容よりも、自発的に語った内容を特に知りたいと考えている。また、双方の家族が既に対面している場合には、対面前と対面後の子どもの発言を分けて考える。その子どもが前世に関する情報を通常の手段によって得た可能性がないことを裏づける証拠の検討を行なう段になると、対面後に（あるいは、対面している最中に）語った内容は、どういうものであれ価値がかなり低下してしまう。とはいえ、対面前の発言同様、対面後の発言も記録に残している。

　両親の中には、子どもが実際に語った内容と単なる推定とをとり違えている者があるので、両親の推定という殻を打ち破らなければ、子どもの発言に辿《たど》り着かないこともある。イマド・エラワールの両親はたくさんの推定を行なったが、この事例は私が初めて調査したうちのひとつだったため、最初は、両親が単なる推定を話していることに気づかなかった。イマドが頻繁にその名前を口にしたため、族長の妻にちがいないと両親が考えた女性は、イマドの前世の人格の愛人だったことが判明した。両親は私に、（レバノンの）トリポリで判事をしていたアミンという親戚《しんせき》の男性のことをイマドが話したと言ったが、実際には、トリポリの裁判所で仕事をしていたとしか、イマドは言わなかったのである。それを聞いた両親は、たまたま裁判所の建物の中で仕事をしていた公務員にすぎないアミンを、判事に昇格させてしまったのである。

一九八六年に私は、両親による勝手な誤解の中で私が知る限り最も極端な例を（スリランカで）経験した。その事例で前世の記憶があるとされた子どもは、ウィマラワティ・サマラセケラという少女であった。（この少女は、ウィマラと呼ばれていた。）ウィマラの母親が私たちに話してくれたところでは、ウィマラの父親は前世ではウィジェセケラという医師であり、ウィマラはコロンボ三区（コロンボ市内のある地区）に住み、セント・トマス・カレッジに通っていたが、（前世の）母親が車を排水溝に落とすという事故を起こしたため、同乗していたウィマラが死亡したのだという。ウィマラが語った言葉を正確に教えてほしいと根気よく繰り返し求めたところ、ようやく私たちは、ウィマラが（身内に医師のいない一家としては珍しく）医学知識を小さい頃からもっているように思われたことと、ウィジェセケラという名前を口にしたことから、前世のウィマラの父親は、ウィジェセケラという名前の医者だったと母親が勝手に思い込んでしまったのであった。また、ウィマラは、コロンボに住んでいたと語り、三という数字を口にしたので、番地を言おうとしていたのかもしれないのに、コロンボ三区のことを言っていると母親は勝手に考えてしまった。ウィマラは、「キリスト赤ちゃん」と何度も口にしていたため、（仏教徒である）家族は、ウィマラの前世はキリスト教徒だと思い込んだ。その結果、前世の人格は、キリスト教系の大学であるセント・トマス・カレッジに通っていたのではないか、と推定したのであった。しかし、ウィマラ自身がそのようなことを言ったわけではなかったのである。また、ウィマラは、前世の母親が運転中の車を排水溝に落とした事故のことは口にしているものの、その事故で死亡したとは言っていない。ウィマラの家族は、ウィマラの言葉に当てはまる家族が簡単に探し出せると考えた。もしウィマラが、両親の推定した通りのことを本当に話していたとすれば、確かにそうかもしれない。ところが実際には、具体的なことはほとんど語っていないので、本例は現段階でも依然として未決例なのである。

双方の家族の間で通常の伝達が行なわれた可能性について聞き出すには、調査を行なう中で細かい点に最大限の注意を払う必要があるし、（情報提供者の側にも研究者の側にも）おそらくは最高度の忍耐が要求されよう。情報提供者はふつう、通常の情報伝達が行なわれる可能性がわずかにあったとしても、それに気づかないものである。そのため、それまでは相手の家族を知らなかったのはまちがいないのだから、この問題についてそれ以上詮索《せんさく》する必要がないことを、私たちに認めさせようとすることもある。ところが、細かく調べて行くと、その家族が見落としてきた、双方が接触している可能性が浮かび上がってきたことも何度かあった。

たとえば、（インドの）プシュパの事例では、双方の家族は一度も対面していなかったが、同じ市場で野菜を買っていた事実を私は探り当てている。この市場でプシュパの家族は、シク教徒の若妻を夫が無残にも殺害した事件を小耳に挟んでいたかもしれない。プシュパは、その事件について話していたのであった。そのようなことが実際にあったとは思わないが、その可能性は確かにあるのである。

スニタ・カンデルワルというやはりインドの子どもの事例では、本人の叔父《おじ》が（仕事を通じて）前世の人格の父親とわずかながら接触のあったことがわかった。双方の家族は、互いに二五〇キロほど離れた町に住んでいたので、相手の町には一度も行ったことはないし、まして相手の存在など聞いたこともない、という双方の主張は偽りではなかった。ところが、本人の叔父と前世の人格の父親が、前世の人格の住んでいた町で、仕事上の関係から対面したことがあったのである。（ふたりとも宝石商であったが、仕事を離れた関係はなかった。）

パルモッド・シャルマというインドの子どもの（既に二回引き合いに出している）事例でも、前世の人格がかつて所有しており、本例が表面化した時点でもその一家が引き続き経営していた、（パルモッドが住んでいたところから一二五キロほど離れた）モラダバードの商店で、本人の叔父が時々ビスケットを買っていた事実が判明している。

以上の三例で私は、前世を記憶する子どもたちの家族は、前世の細かい事柄を通常の方法で知ったわけではないと最終的には結論づけたが、双方の家族の間に通常の伝達があった可能性を詳細に検討して、その可能性が棄却できた段階で、その確信はさらに深まったのである。

本人の行動について得られた情報は、ふたつのカテゴリーに分けられる。第一に私たちは、前世についてその子どもがどんなふうに話しているかや、前世の記憶を語らしめる刺激となるように思われる状況はどのようなものかを、わかる限り全て調べる。前世の話をする時、強い感情を露《あら》わにするであろうか。現世の家族と前世の家族を比較しているであろうか。第二に、前世にまつわる発言と並行しているように見える変わった行動について、本人の家族が観察していることがあれば、それを全て調べるのである。第5章で述べたように、こうした行動には、奇妙な恐怖症や嗜好《しこう》、何らかの適性および技能、食物や衣服の好み、謙遜《けんそん》ないし尊大な態度などが含まれる。

次に、その子どもの行動がどの程度変わっているかが判断できるように、本人を両親や兄弟姉妹と比較する。また、たとえば火に対する恐怖症がある場合には、その原因となりそうな、火傷《やけど》などの特殊な体験をはじめ、その原型になるかもしれない事実を現世の環境の中で探す。

前世の人格の家族との面接調査を通じて得られる情報　相手の家族と対面する時、私たちは、その子どもが前世について口にした内容が正確かどうかをひとつひとつ判断してほしいとその家族に求める。たいていの場合、子どもの両親は、最も肝腎《かんじん》な点や、あるいはその全てを事実と確認しているというが、私は、それとは別個に自分の手で確認する作業がきわめて重要だと考えている。実際にはそうではないのに、子どもの話したことは正しいと両親が主張した例がかなりあるからである。（この点については、悪意はないのかもしれない。双方の家族が初めて対面する時には興奮が生ずるため、細かい点を見落としたり誤解したりしやすいからである。）また、前世の家族側の情報提供者は、子どもの家族が聞いたことも口にしたこともない、事実と符合する発言を子どもがしていたことを、私たちに話してくれる場合もある。

前世の人格の家族からは、その性格についても可能な限り聞き出す。その場合、死者の長所を過大に、短所を過小に報告するという一般に見られる傾向を念頭に置いたうえで調査しなければならないことも少なくない。（幸いなことに、こうした事例に関係する人物の多くには、道徳的な偏りはなく、それゆえ、そうした点については情報提供者が正直に話してくれると考えてよい。）故人の親族には、前世の記憶をもつ子どもの変わった行動を知っていると、故人の人格について話す時に、その知識に沿った話し方をすることになりやすいかもしれない。またその子どもの家族が、本人の行動を実際以上に前世の人格の行動に近づけようとするあまり、脚色を施してしまうかもしれない。とはいえ、この種の事例の主な情報提供者はみな熱心で、その結果としていつも誇大に報告しようとしている、と考えるのは誤りである。逆に、双方の家族が懸命に事例を擁護しようとしているのがわかることは稀《まれ》であり、一方の家族が（さまざまな理由から）否定的に考えたり無関心であったりする場合もあるし、双方とも同様の態度を示すこともある。とはいえ、双方の家族がその事例に信憑性《しんぴょうせい》があることを認めると、自分たちの観察の中で一致しない部分を無意識のうちにとり繕って私たちに報告している可能性はある。この場合にも、隣近所の人たちのように客観的な立場から観察している者の方が、前世を記憶する子どもや前世の人格と心理的に近い者よりも、私たちの力になってくれる場合が少なからずあるのである。

証拠となる書類

こうした事例の研究には、文字による記録が（残念ながら稀ではあるが）特に重要である。こうした記録は、記憶の不備を補ってくれるし、修正してくれることも少なくない。そのため私たちは、日記や（生年月日に対応する）ホロスコープ、病院のカルテ、出生および死亡届け、検死報告などをはじめ、その事例が発生する以前の事実を記録している、あるいは、単なる記憶以上に確実にその事実を裏づけてくれる書類や印刷された資料を調べようと（また、可能であれば複写しようと）努めるのである。一部の事例では、本人の両親その他の親族が、前世について子どもが最もよく話していた頃ないしはその直後に、子どもが口にした内容を自分なりに記録している。このような記録は、事例を研究するうえで特に貴重な証拠となる。

心理検査

これまで私は、生まれ変わり型事例を調査する中で心理検査はほとんど用いて来なかった。私としては、前世の記憶を有する子どもを組織的に検査するか、誰かにしてもらい、年齢や性別、社会経済的条件をそろえた対照群と比較してみたいと思っているが、現在のところまだ実現できていない。

性転換を起こした事例では、拡張版人物描画検査が、本人の性的同一性に関する有力な情報を提供してくれるかもしれないことに気がついた[*13]。自分で描く人物の性別を自由に決めさせた場合、その子どもはどちらを選ぶかということや、実際に描かれた人物が男性的に見えるか女性的に見えるかということが、この検査によって得られる主な情報である。

二回目以降の面接調査

私は、面接に夢中になる傾向があって、情報提供者（特に多忙な主婦）は他に用事をもっていることが多いという事実を忘れてしまうことがある。それでも私は、共同研究者たちに時おり背中を突《つっ》かれながら、情報提供者が疲れ切ったり困り果てたりする前に面接を終了させようとする。（相手を苛立《いらだ》たせるほど長い時間にわたる面接になることはあまりないようである。その後の面接調査で、私たちはほとんどいつも暖かく迎え入れてもらえるからである。）いずれにせよ、前世の人格側の情報提供者に面接し、それまで得られた情報を丹念に検討するまでは、前世の記憶をもつ子どもの家には行かないようにするのが望ましい。また、面接終了後に、あのことを聞いておくべきだったと私はいつも悔やむし、ずっと後になってから初めて気づくこともある。面接が終わった後に思いつくこうした疑問が重大と思える時には、私や共同研究者がさらに訪問調査を行なうのがふつうである。

情報提供者は、制止することなく話をさせると、言葉が奔流のごとく流れ出す場合が多いが、発表される事例報告は、それとは異なり、きちんと整理されたものでなければならない。面接調査で得られた情報をすべて選《よ》り分け、できる限り筋の通った形に整理し直さなければならないのである。事例報告の草稿を練る段階で、聞き漏らした質問項目が浮かび上がることも再三あって、そのためにもう一度面接することもある。

それまでの面接調査でつかんでおかなければならなかったのに失念していて果たせなかったという以外にも、再度面接を行なう理由はいくつかある。その後の面接によって、情報提供者の証言に矛盾がないかどうかを調べることもできるのである。とはいっても、矛盾があるのは絶対に悪いということではない。前回の面接終了後に、新しい事実を思い出したためかもしれないし、以前の証言の一部について、それまでとは違った考え方をするようになったためかも、二度目の質問の仕方が前回より的確だったことで、より信頼性の高い答が返って来たためかもしれないからである。二回目以降の訪問では、最初の訪問時に外出していて会えなかった情報提供者と面接できることもある。ひとつの事例にまつわる情報を集積して行く作業は、寄せ木細工を組立てる作業と似ているかもしれない。個別に見る限り意味のなさそうなものも少なくないが、にもかかわらず、たくさんの素材を組み上げて行くと、全体像が浮かび上がってくるからである。

調査票

こうした調査に従事している間、共同研究者とともに私は数種類の実用的な調査票を作成している。

そのうちのひとつは、誰に、いつ、どのように、どういう目的で生まれ変わりが起こると思うかなどの、生まれ変わりに関する情報提供者の考え方を詳細に聞き出すための調査票である[*14]。性転換が起こった事例の場合には、男性的、女性的行動について一連の質問を行なうための調査票を用いる。また、かなりの数の子どもが、前世にまつわる発言と関連して示す変わった行動についての質問項目をまとめた調査票もある。

追跡調査

私たちは最近、前世を記憶する子どもたちがその後、どのような発達を遂げるかを観察することに、ますます関心を寄せるようになった。そのためにも、再訪問を行なう必要がある。追跡調査の面接では、次のような点を明らかにすることを目指している。その子どもは前世について自分からは積極的に話さなくなっているか。もしそうなら、いつから話すのをやめたのか。前世の記憶を口にしなくなったきっかけとして考えられることは何か。記憶が消失してしまったのか、それとも、まだ残っているがそれを口にしなくなっただけなのか。前世のイメージ記憶が失われているように見えるとしても、前世に関連する変わった行動は依然として示しているか。前世を記憶していることで、家族や他人との関係にどの程度の影響が及んでいるか。前世の記憶は、現世への適応を促進したか、それとも妨げたか。

本章の冒頭で私は、このような事例の研究を開始した時、かなりの数の事例がすぐに見つかったことを述べておいた。また、それ以降も相変わらず数多くの事例が発見されている。とはいえ、新しい事例を見つけ出し調査することは、そうした事例に最も適合する解釈を探し出すのと比べるとはるかに簡単だということも、やはり研究を開始した当初に気づいている。次章では、生まれ変わり型事例について得られた情報を、私がどのように分析し解釈するかについて述べることにしよう。

第7章　事例の分析と解釈

前章で私の研究法を紹介する際に、個々の事例を少数選び出し徹底的に調査するという方法論と、より多くの事例を対象に広く浅く検討を行なうという方法論のいずれをとることも私にはできなかったことについて述べておいた。このようにどちらとも決めかねたことが賢明ではなかったとしても、そのおかげで少なくとも私たちは、事例を二通りに分析することができるようになった。私たちは一例一例を厳密に検討し、それぞれについて最も適切な解釈を探し求めることもできるし、多数の事例を対象に、頻発する特徴を見つけ出し、その意味を考えることもできるのである。次に、この二通りの分析法について順番に考察するが、その前に、私たちの手元にあるデータには分析する価値があると私が考えている理由を説明しておかなければならない。

証言の信頼性

先に説明しておいたように、前世の人格を特定するのに細心の注意を払い、翻訳上の誤りを極力減じ、情報提供者の証言を丹念に記録することによって、データが正確かどうかの責任を情報提供者の側に帰せしめるようにしてきた。私たちのデータのうち、書き記された資料から得られたものはごく一部にすぎないが、[1]それは、私たち自身ではあまり直接には観察できない種類のものである。[2]私たちは、少なくとも九割方のデータを、情報提供者の口頭による証言に耳を傾けることによって得ているのである。このようにして得たデータの価値は、情報提供者の発言が正確かどうかによって決まる。そのためにこそ私たちは、情報提供者の記憶の信頼性を厳密に検討し、何であれ記憶している内容を私たちに伝える際に、必然的に歪曲《わいきょく》が発生するとすれば、それはどのようなところかを判断する必要がある。本節では、情報提供者の記憶の正確さという問題について述べるつもりであるが、情報提供者が証言を歪《ゆが》めようとする動機については本章の後半で扱うことにする。

私や共同研究者に話す数日前、数週間前、数ヵ月前、あるいはもっと前に起こった出来事を正確に想起する能力が、情報提供者にどの程度備わっているかをまず明らかにしなければならない。この種の証言はどの程度信頼できるものなのであろうか。これまで行なわれたさまざまな実験から、観察眼のひどく欠けた人たちが一部に存在することが明らかになっている。このような人たちが現実に存在することを証明する実験は、たいてい、たとえば暴力的な場面を演じて見せ、しかる後に目撃者に、自らの記憶をもとにその報告書を作成するよう求めるというものである。こうした実験の被験者の中には、重要な点を観察、記憶することが全くできず、人を仰天させる者もある。しかしながら、同じ実験から、目撃者は、ある点についてはまちがっていても別の点については正しく、自分の眼で見た主な出来事は正確に報告することもあるという事実も明らかになっている。また、暴力場面のような大きな出来事が実際に眼の前で演じられるので、報告書の中で細部を混同したとしても、その出来事が起こったという事実を否定することはできない。弁護士は、事件の目撃者の証言の重要性を判断する際に、この事実を認めている。目撃者は、二台の車のどちらがきちんと右側を走っていたかは正確に覚えていないかもしれないが、二台ともスピードを出しすぎて衝突したという点についてはまちがえることがないのである。批判者はこの事実を看過し、目撃者が細かい点をいくつか混同すると、その出来事は起こらなかったのではないか、という結論にもって行こうとすることがある。[*3]

目撃者の証言に関するこの種の実験から、私がこれまでの調査で得たデータの信頼性は低下するのではないかという批判に対しては、もうひとつ反論できる理由がある。こうした実験ではいずれも、一度しか起こらず、しかも数分しか持続しない出来事について、具体的な点に注目し記憶するよう被験者に求める。確かに生まれ変わり型事例でも、短時間にしかも一回しか起こらないような出来事が生まれ変わりの証拠とされる場合がある。前世の記憶をもつ子どもが人物や物品や場所を見分けるとされる、その一瞬のうちに、しかも一度だけしか起こらない現象のことである。したがって、記憶をもっている子どもが、前世の人格の知り合いを見分けたとされる経緯について、その場に立会っていた者の間で意見がしばしば分かれるという事実は私にとって驚きではないし、その点についてはこれまでの報告の中でもしばしばふれておいた。先述のように、誘導的な質問などによりおとながさまざまな手がかりを与えてしまうと、本人が誰かを見分けたとしても、証拠としての価値は、ほとんどの場合、さらに低下する。

しかしながら、こうした事例でも、それ以外の点については、目撃者の証言に欠陥があるのが明らかになっている目撃実験の結果と同列に考えることはできない。たとえば、前世を記憶している子どもは、数年にわたって、前世にまつわる発言をほとんど途切れることなく繰り返し、しかもそれがあまりに頻繁なため、一家のもて余し者になってしまうことも少なくない。同様に、（豪華な食事や異性の衣服を要求するなど）それに関連する変わった行動も、何年にもわたって続くのがふつうであるし、言葉によるものよりはるかに長く続くことも少なくない。発言や行動がこのように持続的に繰り返されるため、見聞きする者の心にそうした記憶が焼きつきやすくなるのである。

不正確な証言が少なからずあることは否定できないし、現に私が発表している詳しい事例報告には、さまざまな情報提供者の証言に見られる食い違いに言及した註釈《ちゅうしゃく》が随所に施されている。こうした誤りを未然に防ぐのに私が主として用いている方法は、可能な時にはいつでも、同じ出来事について複数の情報提供者から証言をもらうことである。このような方法によって、情報提供者の証言にたくさんの食い違いが存在することがわかったわけであるが、それよりもっと重要なのは、情報提供者が一部の点をまちがえていた時でも、中心的な出来事については十分正確な証言が得られているという事実であろう。

アジアの農村部に住む人たちのように無学な人間の記憶は、高等教育を受けた者と比較すると劣るという偏見が西洋には広く見られるが、次に、情報提供者に関するこうした先入観を払《ふっ》拭《しょく》すべく、読者の方々への説得を試みたい。私は、こうした考え方がまちがっているのは確かだと思う。記憶が正確かどうかは数多くの要因によって決まるが、教育はそうした要因のひとつとはされていないからである。

以上の見解は序論的なものにすぎない。個々の事例についてさまざまな解釈を検討する中で、情報提供者の証言の信頼性をさらに考察するつもりである。

とはいえ、そうした解釈を検討する前に、前世の記憶をもつ子どもの発言に対応する故人をどのようにして特定するのか、という重要な問題を考えてみることにしよう。

前世の人格を正しく特定する

まず最初に解決すべき問題は、本人の発言内容が事実と確認されているかどうか、あるいはその作業がまだ行なわれていない場合には、確認される可能性があるかどうか、ということである。つまり、本人の発言（および行動）に符合する生活歴をもつ故人が既に見つかっているか、あるいは、それがまだであれば、見つかる可能性はあるか、ということである。こうした観点から見ると、生まれ変わり型事例は次の三群に分けられる。

まず第一は、本人が前世の人格について、特に人名や地名などの具体的情報をほとんど提供してくれないため、それに相当する人物が突き止められない事例である。自分に名前がないと、自分が何者かはっきりしなくなるが、他人からすれば、私たちが誰かを特定することができなくなるかもしれない。そのことは往々にして忘れられがちである。たとえば、「第一次世界大戦のイギリスの将軍ウィリアム・ロバートソン卿《きょう》」と「ロバートソンという兵隊」では、具体性という点でどれほど違うかを考えていただきたい。前者なら簡単に突き止められるであろうが、後者のロバートソンはそうはいかない。はたしてイギリス軍に所属していたのか、それともカナダ軍、オーストラリア軍、アメリカ軍、フランス外国人部隊のいずれに所属していたのかすらわからないし、いつ頃の人物なのかについてもわからないからである。さらに絞り込める手がかりが他にない限り、ロバートソンという名前の兵隊が洪水のように出てくるだけで、探し求める人物はその中にいるのかもしれないが、それ以上突き止めようとすることすらおぼつかないであろう。子どもが記憶しているらしき前世について、さらに絞り込むことができる情報が得られない事例は、結局、未決例に終始する以外にないのである。[*4]

しかしながら、前世を記憶しているとされる子どもが、前世時代に暮らした地域を正確に特定でき、加えてかなり具体的な事柄を二、三述べることができるとすれば、たとえ人名が全く登場しないとしても、前世の人格が突き止められ、その事例は既決例となるかもしれない。一九八六年に私は、こうした事例をスリランカで調査している。シダト・ウィジェラトネという少年は、個人名を一切言わなかったが、昔バラピティヤに住んでいて、そこで魚屋をしており、緑色のジープをもっていたと語った。バラピティヤとは、シダトの自宅から一〇〇キロほど離れたところにある海辺の小さな町である。バラピティヤで緑色のジープをもっていた者はひとりしかおらず、しかもその男性は魚屋であった。シダトが前世について他にいくつか語った内容も、この男性の生涯と正確に一致したため、私としては本例を既決例と見なしている。

ドロン・チャムパ・ミトラの事例も、前世の話を数多くしているにもかかわらず人名がやはりひとつも登場しないが、十分に既決例と考えることができると思う。ドロンは、かつて居住していたという、ブルドワンという都市の名前を挙げ、そこに暮らしていたある青年の生涯にまつわるたくさんの事柄を正確に物語ったうえ、最終的には、この男性一家が住んでいた家がどこにあるかを明らかにした。その家の中でドロンは、人物や物品をかなり見分け、しかもそのうちの一部については、私が申し分ないと考える条件の下でそれを行なっているのである。

　第二の群に入るのは、事実を語っていることは証明できるものの、探り当てられた前世の人格が本当にまちがいないかどうかについて若干の疑念が残る事例である。この群に属する事例では、本人の発言に相当する故人を突き止めることができる程度の情報は得ることができる。前世の記憶をもつ子どもが詳しい話をすればするほど、またたくさんの事柄を話せば話すほど、探し求める人物をまちがいなく突き止めたという確信は深まるが、何がしかの理由から、ある程度の疑念は残るかもしれない。

　インディカ・グネラトネの事例では、前世の人格を特定するのに、私は数年間も迷い続けた。ドロンと同じくインディカも、前世で暮らした町の名前（この事例では、スリランカのマタラ）を挙げたが、それ以外には、プレマダサという使用人の名前を口にするのみであった。幸いインディカは、裕福だったことや象を何頭か所有していたことも話してくれたため、捜索範囲がかなり狭められた。それでも、インディカが挙げた一七項目の事柄は、象をもっていたマタラ在住のふたりの資産家のいずれにもそのまま当てはまった。それ以外にインディカが語った事柄は、そのうちのひとりには当てはまらなかったが、もうひとりとは完全に符合した。決定打となったのは、その人物がプレマダサという使用人を置いていたことであった。それに対してもうひとりの候補者は、そういう名前の使用人は使っていなかったのである。このふたりの生涯を詳細に検討した結果、初めて私は、インディカの発言に対応する人物が突き止められたという確信がもてるようになった。つまり、この事例を既決例と見なしてよいと思えるようになったのである。

以上のように、インディカの語った事柄の多くが複数の人物に当てはまったという事実にふれたのは、軽率な両親（や研究者）が、子どもの発言に同じくらい（あるいは、ほとんど同じくらい）当てはまる人物は他にもたくさんいるのに、早まって、特定の人物にしか当てはまらないことにしてしまうと、どのような罠《わな》に陥ることになるかを示そうとしたためである。私見によれば、こうした事態は、自分の子どもの前世の人格は誰なのかを両親が早く決めたがっているような状況でしばしば発生する。

こうした態度は、レバノンのドゥルーズ派の信者に時おり見ることができる。インドでは、子どもが口にしている家族を探し出すのを急がないのがふつうである（相手の家族のもとへ連れて行ってほしい、という子どもの執拗《しつよう》な要求に耐え切れなくなるまで延ばすこともある）が、レバノンでは、自分の子どもが口にしている人物の家族を早く探し出したいという衝動に駆られることが少なくないようであり、その結果、誤りを犯すことがある。死んだ身内がどこで生まれ変わっているかを突き止めたいという、ドゥルーズ派の信者の多くが抱く強い願望も、同様の結果を招くことになるかもしれない。このような事情から、故人を正しく特定できたかどうかが疑わしい事例を識別することが大切なのである。

第三群に含まれるのは、本人が具体的な名前その他の細かい事柄を数多く口にしてくれたおかげで、その内容はひとりの故人にしか当てはまらず、他の故人には当てはまりえないと確信をもって言えるような事例である。ビルマの子どもたちの記憶は、前世の人格を確定するうえで特にすぐれているように思われる。その人物の名前とともに、兄弟姉妹や両親、さらには（自分が殺された場合には）殺人犯の名前まで明言する場合が少なくないからである。とはいえ、私が集めた事例の中で、名前を正確に語った記録の保持者は、ビルマの子どもではなく、レバノンのスザンネ・ガーネムである。私は、スザンネがもっていた前世に関する記憶を、（すべて網羅することはできていないのであろうが）五九項目記録している。その中には、前世の家族二三人の名前と、ふたりの知人の名前が入っている。また、本人は、そのうちのひとりを除く全員について、前世の人格と思《おぼ》しきサアダという女性との関係を正確に語っている。

個々の事例の分析

個々の事例を検討する際には、前世にまつわる情報を通常の方法で得た可能性はあるか、という疑問をいつも念頭に置かなければならない。その子どもが、言葉による表現に加えて、それに関係すると思われる変わった行動を示す場合には、家族の行動を真似たためなのか、それとも生まれてから後に身につけたものなのか、という疑問も検討の対象にしなければならない。

第一の疑問を考えるとすぐに明らかになるのは、子どもの発言に超常的な要素が含まれることを裏づける証拠にはほとんどなりえない事例が二種類あるという事実である。それは、本人の発言と符合する生涯を送った人物が見つからない事例（未決例）と、符合するとされる人物がその子どもの家族内ないしは近隣にいる事例（〝同一家族〟例ないし〝同一地区〟例）である。未決例では、子どもの発言が事実かどうか確認されていないため、それが通常の方法によっては得られない情報なのかどうかはっきりさせる段階にまで進むことはまずない[*5]し、同一家族例ないし同一地区例の場合にも、その情報に通常のレベルで接する機会がその子どもになかったことを裏づける説得力ある証拠が得られることはまずないからである。（重要な点であるが、この二種類の事例には、子どもが語った事柄以外にも、注目に値する特徴——たとえば、変わった行動や生まれつきの母斑《ぼはん》——が見られることもある。）

そこで本節では、双方の家族が別の地区に住んでおり、その事例が明らかになる以前には双方とも相手の存在を知らなかったという事例にしぼり、その評価について考察することにしよう。私たちはこのような事例を長距離例と呼んでいるが、こうした用語を用いるからといって、双方の家族を隔てる距離のみによって事例の重要度を判断しているわけではない。たとえばインドのような国では、近くの村に住む家族でも、カーストが異なれば、一〇〇キロも離れた村に住んでいる同じカーストに属する家族よりも、社会的には隔絶されているかもしれないのである。

とはいえ、双方の家族が異なった地域に住んでいる事例の場合には、双方の間で通常の連絡が行なわれた可能性がどの程度あるかを見極める必要がある。通常の方法によってその知識を得たとしても、遠方に住む家族のことを異常によく知っているように思われる事例にはいくつかのタイプがある。

　そうした知識を通常の方法で得た可能性として最も考えやすいのは、不正によるものである。事実、作話を基にした事例は時おり見られる。これまで私は、(前世の記憶をもっていると称する人物による)明らかな作話に基づいた事例を一例調べたことがあるし、それ以外にも、イスラエルとレバノンで同様の事例を一例ずつ耳にしている[*6]。

　もしかすると、いくつかの事例で私は、それと知らず騙《だま》されていたのかもしれない。そういう可能性は否定できないが、もしそうだとしても、そのようなことは稀《まれ》にしかなかったはずだと思う。この点に自信があるのは、こうした事例が頻繁に見られる民族の状況や心の動きをよく承知しているからである。アジアやアフリカの寒村に住む平均的な人たちには、そのようなたくらみを企て実行するだけの時間的余裕がない。私たちの面接調査の時間すら惜しむ人たちなのである。ましてや、捏造《ねつぞう》を行ない、加えてそれを隠蔽《いんぺい》するには、それよりもはるかに長い時間を要するであろう。そのようなことをしても金銭的には何の利益にもならないし、地元で名声を得ることもほとんど、ないしは全くないのがふつうである。また、いつも私は何重にも面接調査を行なうが、不正を働くためには、多数の証人の協力が必要なはずである。ところが、そのうちの誰かが、予行演習しておいた筋書を忘れてしまったり、共犯者を裏切るような行為をしたりするかもしれないことに加えて、記憶をもっているとされる子どもについても、厳しく訓練する必要がある。前世にまつわる発言とされるものを子どもは何度聞かれても同じように繰り返すという話を、私たちはたびたび耳にしてきたからである。私は、両親が子どもをそそのかすという話を何度か聞かされたが、その点については強く異を唱えるものである。そのような疑いをもたれる対象となる行為は実際には、子どもがいつも口にしている事柄を、見ず知らずの他人（共同研究者と私）の前でもその気になれば繰り返せることがわかっている場合に、他人の前で自分たちを失望させるような態度をとらせまいとして、おとなたちが懸命になって子どもに話させようとしている以上のものには、私には見えなかった。

不正が排除できれば、次に検討する必要があるのは、前世の記憶をもっているという子ども自身による完全な自己欺瞞《ぎまん》の可能性である。私は、隅から隅まで関係者の願望によって作り上げられたように思われる事例を二、三検討した経験をもっている。こうした事例では、たいていの場合、前世の人格は、その地域や国民の間で、あるいは世界的なレベルで有名な人物である。トルコ中南部でのレシャト・バイエルとともに調査に当たっていた私は、ジョン・F・ケネディの生まれ変わりとされるアレヴィス族の子どもが三人もいることを知った。そのうちのひとりの父親であるメーメト・アルカンは、（一九六五年一一月に）息子が生まれる二、三時間前、ケネディ大統領の夢を見たので、その息子に「ケネディ」と名づけた。一九六七年一一月、レシャト・バイエルとともに私は、二歳になったケネディと対面した。その時父親から聞いた話によれば、息子はケネディ大統領だったと言っている、というのである。メーメト・アルカンは、自分が息子に別人を押しつけているらしいことに気づいていなかったのは確かだと思うので、メーメト・アルカンや、(後には)ケネディがその村である程度もて囃《はや》されたとしても、意図的な作話ということにはならない。(ケネディ大統領は、外国では、フランクリン・D・ローズベルト以降、最も有名で最も尊敬を集めているアメリカの大統領である。)これには後日談がある。その時ケネディは二〇歳前後の青年になっていた。本人は、前世ではケネディ大統領だったと信じて疑わず、裕福だったことや結婚して子どもがふたりいたことなど、ケネディ大統領の生涯についていくつかの事実を覚えていると主張した。また本人は、カン・ポラトに、自分の胸にある母斑を見せたという。ところが、母斑がそこにあったのでは、ジョン・F・ケネディの生まれ変わりを主張する理由にならないわけである。私の経験では、この種の事例は比較的稀であり、誤りであることがかなり容易にわかるように思われる。

不正や自己欺瞞を排除することはほぼ全例で可能であろうが、それができたとしても、遠方に住んでいた人物について子どもが異常によく知っている、と周囲が誤って考えてしまう場合が、可能性ははるかに小さいとはいえ、他にもまだ二通りある。

そのうちのひとつは、前世の人格を知っていた人物を通じて、それとわからないうちにその情報が子どもに伝わってしまうという可能性である。たとえば、両親の留守中に、地方からその子どもの家に誰かが訪ねて来て、床で遊んでいる子どもの存在に気づかないまま、自宅近くで殺された男のことをその家の使用人に話して聞かせたところ、子どもはその話を覚えていて、その後、前世の空想の中にそれをとり入れる、という可能性があるのである。この種の可能性としては、さまざまなものを容易に考え出すことができる。子どもの両親が、その故人を直接知っていたが、その後その事実を忘れてしまい、そうこうするうちに子どもが、通常の方法やテレパシーを通じて両親からその故人について知っている事柄を引き出す、という場合もあるであろう。ある情報を通常の手段で入手し、そのことを後に忘れるという現象は、〝潜在記憶〟ないし〝情報源《ソース》健忘〟と言われる。私は、自分で調査したほぼ全例で潜在記憶が関係している可能性を念頭に置いて検討を行なっている。検討を進めた結果、驚かされることが時おりあった。細かく事例を検討して行くと、子どもが前世の話をするようになる前には相手の存在を知らなかったとしても、共通の友人が少なくともひとりいることがわかった例もあったし、間接的な伝達がそれまで考えられていた以上に行なわれていた可能性のある例もあったのである。前章で、双方の家族にわずかながら接触のあった三例（スニタ・カンデルワル、プシュパ、パルモッド・シャルマの事例）を簡単に紹介しておいた。前世の人格にまつわる情報が一方の家族からもう一方へ伝わったことを裏づける証拠はいずれの事例でも見つからなかったが、その可能性を完全に棄却することはできなかった。

　しかしながら私は、双方の家族がかなり離れたところに住んでいる事例の大半では、潜在記憶に基づく説明は当たっていないという確信をもっている。まず第一に、パルモッドやプシュパやスニタの事例と同じくらい丹念に検討した事例の多くでは、双方の家族の間にごくわずかの結びつきすら見つからなかったという事実が挙げられる。[*7]

　一方、こうした事例を潜在記憶で説明することに対しては、他にも何通りかの反論が可能である。私の考えでは、筋の通った前世の記憶を組み上げるのに必要な情報を、一回耳にした会話から幼児が吸収できるとは思われない。（こうした情報に子どもが接するとすれば、それは一回だけであろう。もしそうした機会が何度かあれば、両親がそれを承知しているはずだからである。）子どもが前世の話を始める段階では、心の中にもっていると思《おぼ》しきイメージ記憶を人に伝えるのに必要な語彙《ごい》が、まだ乏しい場合が少なくない。したがって、それほどの幼児が、たとえば人づてに聞いた殺人事件について平均的なおとなが話す時に用いる言葉を理解できるとは、ありえないことではないとしても考えにくいのである。

潜在記憶による（少なくとも一部の事例の）説明に対しては、前世の家族以外の者には知られていない（したがって、世間の耳目を集めた殺人事件の詳細が広く知れ渡るのとは異なり、家族以外の者には知りえなかったはずの）内密の事柄を、一部の子どもが知っているという事実によっても反論することができる。第4章で私は、こうした内輪の問題を子どもが知っていた事例を一例紹介しておいた。その中で私は、シャクティパル・シャルマが妻から借金しようとした事実をゴーパール・グプタが知っていたことについて述べている。スワルンラタ・ミシュラとエルカン・キリヒの事例も、その好例と言える。スワルンラタは、前世の人格がもうひとりの女性とともに、（本人が名前を挙げた）ある村へ結婚式に出席するため出かけた時の模様について話しているし、エルカン・キリヒも、前世の人格が友人に与えた時計に歯の痕《あと》がついていた事実を知っていたのである[*8]。

潜在記憶説に対するもうひとつの反論は、先述のものよりもはるかに強力であるように思われる。この種の事例には、言葉によって伝達される種類の情報よりもはるかに多くのものが含まれており、それをどう解釈するにせよ、前世にまつわる発言に関連して大半の子どもたちが示す変わった行動についても説明できなければならない。たとえばプシュパの事例では、前世の人格であるというシク教徒の少女が刺殺された事件を八百屋の店先で本人が聞いたとしよう。その話を聞いたことにより、その少女についてプシュパが知っているという事実は説明できるかもしれないが、本人がその少女と自分を強固に同一視している事実は説明できないであろうし、本人がシク教に並々ならぬ関心を（本人の家族はヒンドゥー教徒なのに）寄せていることや、ナイフに対する恐怖症をもっていること、殺された少女の家族に強い愛着を抱いていることなどについても説明することはできないであろう。こうした行動は役柄全体の一部であり、単なる言葉による知識を超えた人格の一側面なのである。もしプシュパが、前世で刺殺されたと思い込んでいるとしたら、ナイフに対する恐怖症も、その思い込みの一部として説明できるのではないか、と指摘する者もあるかもしれない。同様に、それ以外のプシュパの行動も、記憶に残っているという前世を本当に生きたとする強い思い込みの表われではないか、と解釈する者もあるかもしれない。しかしながらこの解釈では、プシュパが、刺殺された少女と自分とを同一視するに至った理由が依然として解明されないのである。

　私は、生まれ変わり型事例の説明としては潜在記憶仮説は当たっていないように思うが、〝記憶錯誤〟仮説については、同じように却下することはできない。記憶錯誤とは、情報提供者の記憶が歪《ゆが》んでいたり不正確であったりする現象を指して用いられる専門用語である。こうした事例の批判者に助言するとすれば、情報提供者の記憶に信頼性がないことを裏づける証拠を、何であれ集中的に探し出せばよいと教えることであろう。

記憶錯誤がいかにして起こるかを理解するには、あるいは少なくともそのひとつのパターンを理解するためには、その子どもが記憶していると思しき前世の話を初めてした時の言葉を、もう一度検討し直してみる必要がある。両親が、子どもの言葉をいくつか耳にして、本当はまとまりを欠いていたかもしれないのに、その言葉に一貫性があると考えたとしよう。その子どもはどのような人物の話をしているのかを推定し、次いで、それに当てはまりそうな人物を探し求め、子どもが口にした内容と一致しそうな生涯を送った人物の遺族を見つけ出したうえ、これまで子どもが前世について話した内容を先方に説明する。それに対して、説明を受けた家族は、その子が語った事柄は今は亡き身内の状況と一致するかもしれないと認める。双方の家族は、故人にまつわる詳しい話や、子どもが口にしてきた事柄について細かい点を話し合う。その際、双方ともそれに夢中になってしまったあまり、子どもは、双方が対面する以前にはごくわずかな内容しか、しかもおそらくは何ひとつ明確なことは話していないのに、うかつにも、当の故人について具体的な事実をかなり語っていたことにしてしまう場合がある。このようにして、その子どもが語った内容が神話となり、双方の家族に受け入れられるようになることがあるのである。では、この潜在記憶という解釈を用いると、どこまで説明することができるのであろうか。

この解釈が最もよく当てはまるように思われる事例が一部にあることは確かである。先述のように、ドゥルーズ派の信者の多くには、故人が誰に生まれ変わっているか、あるいは、目の前にいる人物の前世は誰なのかを探り当てたいという強い願望があるため、探し求める人物を早まって決めすぎるきらいがある。ドゥルーズ派の信者たちは、家族の誰かが死亡すると、ほとんどの場合、どこに生まれ変わっているかを知りたがるし、赤ん坊が生まれると、これまた家族は、その子どもが前世では誰だったのかを知りたがる。こうして、まだほとんど口も利けない乳幼児をもつ熱心な家族と、身内を失って未《いま》だ悲しみの渦中にある同じく熱心な遺族とが対面することがある。そのような状況では、実際にはそうではないのに、薄弱な証拠に基づいて、前世の人物が見つかったとして意見の一致を見ることが時おりにせよなかったとしたら、むしろ驚くべきことであろう。そのようにして双方の家族は、両家が対面する以前に、その子が前世について実際よりもはるかに多くのことを語ったかのように思い込んでしまうかもしれないのである。このようなことがあると、実際以上に有力な証拠が存在するかのように見えてしまうであろう。

ところが、ドゥルーズ派の一部の信者をはじめ数多くの事例でこの解釈を検討すると、それだけでは十分説明しきれないように思われる。まず第一に、子どもの発言内容が事実と確認されるより前に、しかも双方の家族が対面する以前に、子どもの語った事柄を誰かが言葉で記録していた事例には、この説明は当てはまらないからである。こうした事例では、双方の家族が対面する前に子どもが話したと家族が証言している内容を、まちがいなく子どもが口にしていたことがわかる。ただし、このような記録が残されている事例は、残されていない事例と比べると圧倒的に少ない（全例の一パーセント）のが、残念ながら現状なのである。[9]

とはいえ、共同研究者や私が、双方の家族が初対面してから数週間ないし数ヵ月以内に調査を開始している事例もある。[10] このような事例では、時間がそれほど経過していないため、情報提供者の記憶はまだ鮮明に残っていたように思われる。一般にはこうした対面は、子どもが前世の話を一年ないし数年続けた後に行なわれる。典型例の場合には、その間子どもは、前世に関する主な発言をかなり繰り返している。既に述べておいたが、このように繰り返し聞かされると、耳を傾けているおとなの心の中に、子どもが口にし続けた内容が定着しやすくなるであろうから、そうした記憶が、先方の家族と対面することで大幅に歪む可能性はなさそうに思われる。子どもが話した内容の記憶が、この種の事例のほとんどでひどく歪んでいるとすれば、情報提供者の記憶力に、実際の証拠から考えられる以上の欠陥がなければなるまい。そればかりか、そうした欠陥が複数の人間に存在しなければならないであろう。双方の家族が対面する以前にその子どもが語った内容について、（細かい点では若干の食い違いは見られるものの）数名の情報提供者がそれぞれの証言を相互に裏づけ合う形になる事例がほとんどだからである。

それでも、その事例を特定のパターンに当てはめようとする動機づけが強いため、記憶にそれだけの歪みが生ずるのではないか、と考える者もあろう。一部の事例にこうした動機が働いているのは確かである。両親は、前世に関する子どもの発言が事実であることを証明したがる場合が多いとはいえ、その内容が事実と一致していることが確認されれば、周囲の人間が疑念を表明したとしても、家族の正当性は証明されるであろう。また、先述のように、最愛の身内を失った遺族は、自分たちのもとにではないにせよ、少なくとも別の家族に本人が戻って来たと信じたい気持から、子どもの発言を評価するに際して誤った判断を下すかもしれない。

しかしながら、この種の事例と比べると、双方の家族のいずれかがその子どもの発言に無関心であったり、否定的な態度をとったりする事例の方がはるかに多いのである。先に指摘しておいたように、何らかの理由から、子どもの発言に違和感を覚える両親も多い。このような両親は、前世の記憶が残っていると子どもに害が及ぶと思い込んでいるのかもしれないし、子どもを先方の家族に渡すことになるのを恐れているのかもしれない。あるいはまた、現在の生活と比べて、きわめて貧しい、あるいは逆にきわめて裕福な環境の中で過ごした前世について子どもが語った内容が事実だということを他人に確認してほしくないのかもしれないし、好ましくないと思っている行動を子どもがとっている場合、本人の語った事柄が事実ということになるとその行動が強化される可能性があるので、それを嫌うためなのかもしれないのである。*11

前世の家族について言えば、生まれ変わりを信じているうえに身内を失って悲嘆に暮れているとしても、そのことからすぐさま推定されるほどには、その事例を事実と考える態勢になっていない場合もある。先述のように、こうした（特に裕福な）家族の中には、子どもの家族が自分たちから金品を巻き上げようとしているのではないか、と心配する人たちもある。また、一族の不名誉となる事実をその子どもに暴露されてしまうのではないかと考えて、戦々恐々としている家族もあれば、（矛盾しているようであるが）その子どもに対面すると、その身内を失ったことによる悲しみがまた呼び醒《さ》まされるのではないかと懸念する家族もある。*12

以上のようにさまざまな理由から、双方の家族のいずれかが、子どもの発言内容が事実かどうかを確認したがらない場合も少なくない。このような人たちは、子どもが事実を語っていることを、誇張どころか過小に評価しやすいであろう。要するに、時間が経つにつれて忘れやすくなったためなのか、記憶を変形しようとする意志が働いたためなのかはともかく、記憶錯誤によって一部の情報提供者の報告が不正確なものになる場合もあるし、その事例がすべて記憶錯誤によるものとして説明できる場合もあるが、大半の事例については、記憶錯誤が妥当な説明になるとは私には思われない。[*13]

詐偽的行為、潜在記憶、記憶錯誤という三通りの考え方は、西洋社会で超常現象とされている、たとえばテレパシーや死後生存のような現象の実在を想定せずにこの種の事例を説明するための主たる概念である。第1章で説明したように、超常的という言葉は、現在のところ、まだ西洋科学には採り入れられていない概念を指して用いられる言葉である。こうした超常的解釈について検討する前に、この種の事例を説明するための通常の概念をもうひとつだけ簡単に検討しておきたい。〝遺伝記憶〟ないし〝遺伝学的記憶〟と言われているものである。

前世の人格と思われる者が死亡し、その記憶をもった子どもが生まれてくるまでの間隔がかなり長い場合には、その子どもは、前世の人格の子孫となって生まれて来る可能性があり、理屈の上では、その生涯の記憶を遺伝的に受け継いでいるかもしれない。しかしながら、このような子どもたちが語る詳細なイメージは、遺伝に基づくとされる記憶をはるかに凌《しの》いでいる。遺伝記憶や本能という言葉を用いる時、ふつう私たちは、学習していないにもかかわらず網を張るクモや巣を掛ける鳥を考える。このような本能的行動という概念は、前世で張った網や掛けた巣のイメージを、クモや鳥が意識の上で抱いているとは仮定しないのがふつうである。このような行動は、むしろ、私が行動的記憶と呼ぶものに含まれる。とはいえ、鳥の囀《さえず》りのような動物の伝達音は、前世の記憶をもつ子どもたちが示す、過去の出来事のイメージ記憶にわずかながら類似している。もしそうなら、前世を記憶する子どもたちは、行動的記憶とともにイメージ記憶をも遺伝的に受け継いでいることになるであろう。

しかしながら、こうした事例のほとんどは、遺伝学的記憶という説明を当てはめようとすると、大きな難点に直面する。まず第一に、死から再生までの間隔はきわめて短いのがふつうであり、五年以上になることはほとんどないという事実が挙げられる。[14] 前世の人格の死後数ヵ月から数年して別の家族のもとに生まれた子どもが前世の人格の子孫になるとは、考えられないのではなかろうか。

また、遺伝的に継承される記憶には、前世の人格が未来の母親の胎内に宿った後に起こった出来事の記憶が含まれるはずはないのに、後に生まれた子どもがその間の出来事を記憶している場合もある。とすれば、特定の人物の死にざまの記憶が遺伝的に伝えられるはずはないのに、こうした子どもたちの大半は、（他のことはほとんど覚えていない場合ですら）前世の人格が死亡した時の模様を記憶しているのである。そのことは（第3章で要約して紹介しておいた）メアリ・マグルーダーの事例を考えると理解しやすいかもしれない。メアリ・マグルーダーは、頭皮を剝《は》がそうとして追いかけて来るアメリカ先住民の悪夢を繰り返し見たのであった。前述のように、この事例を遺伝記憶で説明することもできようが、そう解釈するためには必要不可欠な条件がひとつある。先住民に追いかけられている少女がその追跡を逃れ、その後子どもをもったとしたら、子どもたちは、母親の苦しかった体験の記憶を遺伝的に受け継ぎ、その記憶が代々継承され、最終的にメアリ・マグルーダーまで伝えられたということになるのかもしれないが、もしその先住民がこの少女を捕えて殺していたとすれば、この少女に既に子どもがいたとしても、そういった記憶がその子どもを通じて伝えられたという可能性はないであろう。[*15]

　では次に、何らかの超常的要素が関係しているとする解釈について考えてみよう。ここで検討の対象となる主な解釈としては、次の三点があると思う。超感覚的知覚と憑依《ひょうい》と生まれ変わりである。第3章で説明しておいたように、これまで私が調査検討してきた事例群を別にすると、それだけで生まれ変わりの存在を裏づける証拠はほとんどない。そのため私は、通常の説明にせよ超常的な説明にせよ、他のあらゆる解釈をできる限り排除したうえでなければ、いずれの事例についても生まれ変わりを最善の説明と考えることはしなかった。そこで、まず最初に超感覚的知覚と憑依について検討することにしよう。

　私は、生まれ変わり型事例の調査を開始した当初の何年間かは、こうした事例を説明する仮説として、超感覚的知覚を実際以上に重視していた。現在でも超感覚的知覚の可能性を重要視してはいるが、以前ほどには重きを置いていない。

　このように見方が変わった理由は主としてふたつある。ひとつは、前世の記憶をもつとされる子どもたちには、そうした記憶を除くと、超感覚的知覚の能力をもっていることを裏づける証拠が見当たることはほとんどないし、両親たちもそうした能力が子どもにあるとは考えていないことである。私はこれまで、自分の子どもにその種の能力があると思うかどうかを、何百名もの親たちに質問してきた。それに対してほとんどの両親は、前世の記憶をもつ子どもがそうした能力をもっていることを否定している。ある種の超感覚的知覚を子どもが時おり示したことがあると答えた親もわずかながらあったが、その裏づけとなる証拠は、たいていの場合ほとんどなかった。前世を記憶するこれほど多くの子どもたちが、他の方面では超能力を（頻繁には、あるいは少なくとも時々というほどには）示さないにもかかわらず、どうすればこれほどの量の情報が超感覚的知覚を用いただけで得られるのか私にはわからない。[*16]

また、再三述べているように、前世の記憶をもつ子どもは、ほとんどが、言葉を用いて前世を語るだけではない。このような子どもたちの大半は、一年から数年にわたって、場合によってはもっと長期にわたり、本人の家族からすれば変わっているが、前世の人格の行動について判明した、ないしはそれなりに推定できた事柄とは符合する行動を示すのである。

この種の子どもたちの中には、前世の人格に関係する刺激に対しては、強い感情を示しながらそれ相応の反応をする者が多い。たとえば、イスマイル・アルティンキリヒは、前世の人格とされる男性を殺害した犯人たちが、（きわめて長期にわたって続けられた裁判が結審した後）絞首刑に処せられたのを知った時、手を叩《たた》いて喜んだ。また、たとえば、前にも述べたが、イマド・エラワールやスクラ・グプタは、前世の人格が好意を抱いていた相手が苦境に立たされていると聞かされただけで泣き出してしまった。人間の感情は超感覚的知覚によっても伝えられるのではないか、と考える方もあろうし、事実そのような形の伝達が存在する証拠もあるが、今とりあげている行動面での反応ということについては、それよりもはるかに多くの問題が未解決のまま残されている。比較的進展した事例では、子どもたちは前世の人格の性格と生き写しの行動症候群を示すのである。（こうした症候群の実例は、第5章でいくつか紹介しておいた。）超常的認知の働きにより一個の人格をそっくりそのまま他人に移し換えることができる、と考えてよい根拠はない。実験超心理学も、そこで必要とされるような超感覚的知覚が存在することを裏づける証拠は提出していないし、それとは異質の偶発例の中にも、それに匹敵するものは稀《まれ》にしか見られない[*17]。

複雑な行動的反応群を超常的過程により伝達することはできないという側面を別にしても、このような子どもが他人をまねるには、それなりの強い動機づけがなければならない。しかしながら大半の事例では、こうした動機は見当たらないのである。先ほど述べたように、このような子どもの変わった行動は、自分の家族との対立を招くうえ、それによる利得が全くない場合が多い。また、こうした子どもの両親が、必要な情報を（五感を介してであれ、超感覚的知覚を介してであれ）何らかの方法で得たと仮定しても、自分の子どもに別の人格を押しつけたいとする理由が、大半の両親には見当たらない。

以上、必要にして十分な超感覚的知覚が、前世を記憶するという子どもと、前世の人格を知っている生者との間に生ずると想定して論を進めてきた。（存在があまり知られておらず、したがって容易にはふれることのできない資料に通じている子どもも時おりあるが、その場合は透視を補助的に利用すると考えなければなるまい。） 後知と呼ばれるある種の超常的認知を基にした説明では、情報源として生者の存在を仮定せず、あらゆる事象が刻み込まれている〝万能記憶〟からその情報を引き出すと考える。しかしながら、後知によって生まれ変わり型事例を説明しようとすると、他の超感覚的知覚の場合と同じ弱点が浮上してくる。たとえば、このような子どもが、前世を想起する時にだけ、なぜそれほど顕著な超常的能力を発揮するのかについては、後知で説明することはできないのである。

次に憑依について考えてみよう。肉体のない人格が生者を支配ないし生者に〝憑依〟することがあるとする考え方は、数世紀来、西洋知識人の間では前時代的な発想とされてきた。ところが、この考え方は時おり、生まれ変わりを思わせる事例の説明としても提起されてきたのである。[*18] 憑依は、第5章で簡単にふれた（死亡および出生の）日時が逆転している事例の説明としては、生まれ変わりに代わる有力な概念であるように思われる。また、前世の人格が死亡した時点が、その記憶をもつ子どもを数ヵ月後に出産する母親の妊娠二、三ヵ月に当たっていた、ラヴィ・シャンカール・グプタやスジト・ラクマル・ジャヤラトネのような事例もいくつかある。もし、受胎し胎児が発育するうえで、肉体をもたない心（ないし魂）と成長の途上にある肉体との結びつきが必要だとすれば、生まれ変わり型事例を憑依として扱うこともできるかもしれない。

しかしながら、私としては、生まれ変わりを思わせる典型的事例については、憑依という解釈を採ることには賛成しかねる。それにはいくつかの理由がある。まず第一に、憑依という概念では、四、五歳から七、八歳までの間に子どもたちがほとんどの記憶を消失させてしまうことが説明できない。なぜすべての憑依人格は、子どもたちが同じような年齢に達した時に子どもたちから離れなければならないのであろうか。第二に、前世の人格の家族やその住居の周辺を訪れることで子どもの記憶が刺激される場合が多いことは、憑依よりも連想の働きを考えた方が説明しやすいように思う。第三に、こうした子どもたちは、前世の人格が死亡した後に人物や建物に生じた変化については知らないのがふつうである。憑依している人格なら、全知ではないにしても、こうした変化については子どもたちよりもよく承知しているはずなのではなかろうか。第四に、憑依という解釈では、前世の人格に関係して発生するらしい母斑《ぼはん》や先天性欠損が説明できない、という点が挙げられる。その原因が何であれ、子どもが生まれる前に端を発していることは明らかなので、憑依が受胎時に、あるいは胎児の段階から始まるというのであれば、この概念と生まれ変わりという概念がどう違うのかわからなくなる。既に説明したように、本書では、母斑や先天性欠損を伴った事例にはあまりふれたくないので、憑依についてはここまでにしておきたい。その点については読者の方々のご寛容を請う次第である。次に、こうした事例の解釈として、生まれ変わりという考え方に何らかの利点があるかどうかについて検討することにしよう。

　先述のように、生まれ変わりという考え方は最後に受け入れるべき解釈なので、これに代わる説明がすべて棄却できた後に初めて採用すべきである。生まれ変わり以外の説明については、それぞれある程度の証拠がある。私が調査した事例にはいずれも少々弱点があるし、一部には、かなりの弱点をもつものもある。その弱点は多岐にわたっている。私がその子どものところへ出かけるのが遅すぎて、その時点では既に、肝腎《かんじん》な記憶が消えたり歪《ゆが》んだりしていた例もあるし、双方の家族の間に、それまで見過ごされていた結びつきがあったと考えられる例もある。また、おとながその子どもに何やら吹き込んでいるのが見つかったり、証言に重大な食い違いのあることがわかったため、その証言の信憑性《しんぴょうせい》が失われてしまった例もある。とはいえ、このような批判はどの程度妥当なのか、全例にどの程度当てはまるのか、と反問する向きもあろう。その場合、こうした批判に対してどのような判断を行なうかは、生まれ変わりという考え方に対して第一にどのような姿勢をとっているかという点にかなり左右されることがわかる。生まれ変わりを既に信じている者はおそらく、証拠に内在する弱点を看過するか過小に評価するのに対して、信じていない者は、そうした弱点を過大視したうえ、全例を却下してよいと考えるかもしれない。この状況は、壜《びん》に葡萄《ぶどう》酒が少し残っている時の見方が各人で異なるのと似ている。まだ半分も残っていると言う者もあれば、半分しかなくなってしまったと言う者もあるのである。[*19]

この状況は、解決の見込みがないわけではない。さらに調査すれば、正当な解釈がもっと明確にできるような証拠が見つかるかもしれないからである。たとえば、前世を記憶するとされる子どもの発言を、その事実性が確認される以前に誰かが文字で記録している事例がもっと見つかるかもしれない。私は、こうした事例を懸命に探し求めてきたが、現段階ではわずかな数しか見つかっていないため、このうえない失望感を味わっている。それでも、このような努力をもっと積み重ねて行く余地はあるであろう。[*20]

母斑や先天性欠損を伴った事例をさらに調査することによっても、また、たとえば性転換例や双生児例のような事例からも、もっと客観的なデータが得られることであろう。（こうしたタイプの事例については、第8、9章で詳しくふれるつもりである。）

ここで、私自身がこの種の事例をどう解釈したいと思っているかについて、述べておかなければなるまい。私は、全例を特定の概念で説明したいとも思わないし、どの事例にしても、一例だけでは生まれ変わりの存在を裏づける決定的証拠になるとも思っていない。とはいえ、一部の事例に対しては、生まれ変わりという考え方が最も妥当な説明になると思っているのである。ここで言おうとしているのは、生まれ変わりという考え方がこうした事例の唯一の解釈だということではなく、これまで述べてきた解釈の中では最も妥当に思える、ということ以上のものではない[*21]。

既に述べておいたように、本書は、生まれ変わりという現象が存在することを読者の方々全員に納得していただくためのものではない。本書を通じて一部の方々に、詳しい事例報告が載った拙書や拙論をお読みいただければありがたいとひそかに思っており、それこそが私のささやかな希《ねが》いなのである。もし読者の方々が、別著に関心をもってくださるのであれば、何よりも事例の細部にご注目いただきたいと思う。「より細かい点、より細かい点、独創性や真理は細部にのみ見出《みいだ》される」とスタンダールは登場人物のひとりに語らせている[*22]。細部には、事例を興味深くする以上のものがあるという点も含め、私はこの指摘に同意する。細部には、謎を解き明かしてくれる鍵《かぎ》が隠されているのである。

私の詳細な事例報告をお読みいただければ、私たちが説得力に欠けると考えている点が明らかになるのはまちがいなかろうが、それによって読者の方々が、生まれ変わりを裏づける証拠など存在しないと否定されるとは思われない。もしそのようなご意見をおもちの方があれば、その方に対しては、「どういう証拠があれば、生まれ変わりが事実だと納得されますか」とお尋ねしたいと思う。

多数例の分析

第1章では、多数の事例を対象に検討を進める意味にふれ、個々の事例だけでは疑念が湧くとしても、事例全体をまとめて考えるとその疑念が薄れるのがわかったというカントの言葉を、賛意を表しつつ引用した。では次に、前世を記憶する子どもの事例との関連で、この点をもっと細かく検討することにしよう。

今から一〇〇年以上昔、ウェイトリーは、同一の出来事を目撃したさまざまの証人から、共通した証言を探し求めることの意義について次のように述べている。

> 数名の目撃者の証言が（目撃者相互の間に協定のようなものが結ばれていた可能性がない場合）、肯定的なものであれ否定的なものであれ、互いに一致すれば……各証言を別個に考えた場合とは違う重みが全体に生ずることは明らかである。この場合、各証人が全く信用に

値しないと思われているとしても、同一の虚偽に全員が同意する可能性はほとんどないからである。

以上の文章の中でウェイトリーは、同じ出来事に関する、各人に共通した証言の重要性について述べている。しかしながら、ウェイトリーも指摘するように、この原則は、それぞれ独立してはいるが同じ種類の事象にまつわる個々の証言についても同様に当てはまる。

たとえ各証言にはほとんどあるいは全く説得力がなくとも、事実と異なるものにたまたま意見の一致が見られるという可能性はきわめて低いので、一致した証言には説得力がある、ということを以上述べたが……このことは、他方面の論証の多くにもそのまま当てはまる。……たとえば、一〇〇人のうちの誰かが石を投げてある物に当たるとした場合、その事実のみでは、その人物がその物体を目がけて投げていた可能性はわずかしかないが、一〇〇人全員が投げた石が同じ物に当たったとすれば、全員がその物体を狙って投げたことを疑う者はいないであろう。[*23]

もっと前の世代の研究者のことを書いている人たちは、一連の事例をまとめて扱った場合の強みを、別の比喩《ひゆ》を用いて表現している。何本かの棒を束にしたようなものだというのである。どの棒も単独では脆《もろ》いが、弱い部分がそれぞれ異なるので、一束にまとめ合わせると一本ずつの時よりも強くなる。[24]（この場合、目撃者の証言がそれに当たるであろうが、脆い環でできている鎖の方が、比喩として適切だと指摘する批判者もある。）

束の原理を生まれ変わり型事例に当てはめると、多数例に共通して見られる特徴を探し求めればよいことになる。このような共通点が見つかれば、その分だけ、事例を全体として見た場合の信頼性は高くなる。互いにかなり離れた場所にいる（相互にやりとりのない）情報提供者の証言が一致するということは、生まれ変わり型事例が、各例に共通点が存在する何らかの自然現象であることを裏づける証拠となるのである。したがって、標準的な事例ないしタイプの概略を描き出すことができる。[25]各事例は、そうした標準型から多少なりとも外れるかもしれないが、真正なものと判断された事例の範囲から逸脱しすぎているものは、いずれも信憑性がないと考えてよいであろう。

多数例を対象に検討を行なうことには、信憑性のない事例を見つけ出すのに役立つことと並んで、もうひとつ大きな意味がある。あるタイプの事例の事実性が立証できれば、それ以外の過程について既にわかっている事柄や他のタイプの事例を、その特徴に照らして検討することができるし、こうした比較によって、最終的には新たに確認されたタイプに内在する過程も把握できるようになるかもしれない。

ここで、もうひとつ注意しておかなければならないことがある。ある事例の情報が私たちの耳に届くのは偶然であるが、そのことからすると、私の調査した事例は、実際に発生している事例全体の代表例にはならないかもしれないという問題である。私たちが調査した事例が代表例になっていないとすると、肝腎要《かんじんかなめ》の点でそうなのかどうかということが焦点になるであろう。この問題については後ほどもう一度検討する。

既に（第5章で）述べておいたように、たとえば子どもが前世について話し始める平均年齢や、自分から話さなくなる年齢のように、事例全体に共通する特徴はいくつかある。次に、それ以外に共通して見られる特徴をいくつか紹介しよう。

まず第一は、「まえがき」で述べておいたように、前世を記憶する子ども全体を指す場合、なぜ男性名詞を用いるかの説明にもなるが、男性が過半数を占めるという特徴である。一〇九五例のうちの六二パーセントが男性で、女性は三八パーセントにすぎないのである。前世の人格についても、やはり男性の比率が高くなっている（六六対三四パーセント）。こうした性差は、唯一の例外を除いて、生まれ変わり型事例が見つかっているあらゆる文化圏で共通している[*26]。その理由として考えられる可能性については、第10章で検討するつもりである。

共通して見られる特徴のうち最も興味深く、おそらく最も重要だと思われるもののひとつに、前世の人格が横変死を遂げている事例がきわめて多いという特徴がある。六個の文化圏から集められた七二五例のうち、前世で非業の死を遂げた記憶をもつ事例は六一パーセントにものぼるのである[*27]。この比率は、対象となる事例を収集した六ヵ国の一般人口中の横変死の発生率をはるかに上回っている。しかし、各例を私たちに報告する際に生じた偏りが原因でそのような結果になった可能性についても考えておく必要がある。横変死は自然死よりも関心を引きやすいので、前世の人格が自然死を遂げている事例よりも横変死を遂げた事例の方が、情報提供者の記憶に長くしかも鮮明な形で残りやすかったのかもしれない。

横変死という条件が事例の報告率に影響を及ぼしているかどうかについては、収集の方法が異なるインドのふたつの事例群を比較することを通じて、間接的な形ではあるが検討することができた。第一群の事例は、二〇年ほどの間に特に系統立った方法を用いることなく収集したものである。この群に入るかどうかは、何らかの理由から共同研究者や私に事例の情報提供をしてくれた者が、誰かから求められたためではなく、たまたま自発的にその事例を記憶していたかどうかによって決められた。この群に属する事例は一九三例あった。それよりも規模のはるかに小さい第二群は、アグラ地区で行なわれた組織的調査の中で見つかった一九例から成っている。（この調査については第5章でふれておいた。）調査の対象となる者を無作為に選択したうえで、生まれ変わり型事例で記憶しているものがあるかどうか尋ねたのである。大きい方の、組織的方法を用いて収集したのではない群では、前世で非業の死を遂げた事例の比率が四九パーセントであったのに対して、小さい方の群では、三五パーセントにすぎなかった。この差からすると、私たちが集めた事例で横変死の比率が高いのは、ひとつには、自然死の事例よりも情報提供者の記憶に残りやすいためらしいことがわかる。とはいえ、横変死の発生率が三五パーセントでも、インドの一般人口中の発生率と比べるとはるかに高い。インドでの一般人口中の（当該期における）横変死の発生率は、七パーセント以下にすぎないからである。[*28]

したがって、こうした事例に横変死の比率が高いのは、報告時の歪《ゆが》みなどではなく、本質的な特徴であるように思われる。非業の死を遂げた場合には、自然死の場合よりも本人の記憶が残りやすくなるらしいということである。私たちが得たもうひとつの結果からも、このことが示唆される。前世で非業の死を遂げている既決例の中で、死ぬ時の模様を本人が語った事例は九四パーセントにものぼったが、自然死の場合には五二パーセントにすぎないことがわかったからである。

私が調査したすべての文化圏の事例で横変死の比率が際立って高いという事実は、最重要の特徴のひとつであるように思われる。この点については、一部の前世が他のものよりも記憶に残りやすい理由を第10章で検討する際に、もう一度考察するつもりである。次に、未決例との関連からこの問題をもう少し検討してみたい。これが本章で考察する最後の問題となる。

未決例は次の三点で既決例と異なっている。[*29] まず、未決例の子どもは、前世の人格の名前を、既決例の子どもほどは覚えていないという点である。これは、事例を解決できなかったことと無関係ではない。先に説明しておいたように、子どもの発言に対応する人物を探し出すためには、少なくとも何人かの名前が正確に出て来なければならないので、前世の人物の名前が出て来ない場合には、出て来た例よりもその事例の解決が難しくなるからである。

既決例と未決例のもうひとつの違いも、やはり簡単に説明できるように思う。未決例の子どもは、既決例の子どもと比べて、前世の話をしなくなる時期がかなり早いという事実である。未決例では、平均六歳未満で前世の話をしなくなるのに対して、既決例では平均七歳半弱まで話している。このような差が生ずるのは、既決例では周囲の者が、未決例の場合と比べて子どもに注目していることに加えて、前世の話をするよう促すためであることを第5章で述べておいた。それに対して、前世にまつわる発言の事実性が証明されていない子どもの両親は、子どもが話す内容に対して関心を急速に失ってしまう傾向があるため、子どもはその話をしないようになりやすいのである。また、既決例の子どもは、たいていの場合、先方の家族と行き来があり、そのおかげで、記憶が意識に残りやすく、そのために消えるのも遅くなりやすいのであろう。

　第三点は、未決例の子どもは既決例の子どもよりも、前世で非業の死を遂げた記憶をもっている比率がはるかに高いことである。既決例では、非業の死を遂げていることが事実と確認された事例は五一パーセントにすぎないが、未決例の子どもでは九一パーセントにものぼるのである。ここで、未決例の子どもは非業の死を遂げたという空想をもっているだけなのではないか、という疑問が浮上する。この子どもたちの発言は事実とは確認されていないわけであるから、単なる空想を口走っているにすぎないのかもしれないが、中には、本当の前世を漠然と記憶している者がいる可能性もある。そしてそれを潤色するために、非業の死という空想をもち出したのかもしれないのである。

　しかし、ことによると未決例の子どもたちの発言は、空想ではないのかもしれない。そうではなく、本当の前世を覚えているのであるが、既決例の子どもと比べ、事実と確認できる点が少ない（うえに、おそらくは誤りも多い）だけなのかもしれないのである。以上説明したように、未決例には既決例と異なる重要な特徴が三点あるが、既決例と共通する点も同じく三点ある。未決例の子どもは、既決例の子どもと同じ年齢で前世の話を始めることと、既決例と同程度の比率で前世での死にざまを語ることであり、死因に関係した恐怖症を示すことである。このような共通点が見られることからすると、未決例も既決例と同種か、さもなければ少なくとも同類に属するもののように思われる。

少々話を戻すと、未決例、既決例全体の七二パーセントの子どもが前世の人格の死にざまを記憶していたのであるが、その名前を覚えていたのは六三パーセントにすぎなかった。（死因が確認できた）既決例では、前世の人格が非業の死を遂げている場合には九四パーセントの子どもが死にざまを記憶していたのに対して、自然死の場合には五二パーセントにすぎなかった。また、既決例では、七六パーセントが前世の人格の名前を記憶していた。したがって、生まれ変わりという現象が実際に存在し、ある人物が非業の死を遂げた後、前世のわずかな記憶をもって生まれ変わって来たとすると、非業の死を遂げていることは、その人物の名前よりも記憶に残りやすいようである。多数の事例で同じような傾向が見られることからすれば、未決例ではこれが、既決例と比べて非業の死をかなり高率に記憶していることの説明に、ある程度はなるかもしれない。（とはいえ、その事実が、既決例と未決例の間に見られるこうした重要な相違点を生ぜしめる唯一の要因だと言おうとしているわけではない。）

以上で、多数例の分析について現段階で言えることはすべて述べたつもりである。既に上梓《じょうし》している拙著の中で私は、（これまで調査を行なってきた）すべての文化圏の事例で確認されている特徴を、〝普遍的〟という誤解を招きやすい少々誇大な言葉で表現したことが何度かある。このような言葉を使ったからと言って、こうした特徴が全例で見られるということではなく、私たちがこれまで調べて来たすべての文化圏の事例で高率に見られるということなのである。それ以外の特徴について言えば、文化圏による差は本章で述べたものよりもはるかに大きい。文化に関係している特徴については、次章でその一部を紹介するつもりである。

本章をしめくくるに当たって、以上考察してきた、多数例に共通して見られる特徴をどう説明すべきか、という問題を提起しておきたい。遠く離れた文化圏の事例に共通点が存在するのは、自分の住む文化圏以外の事例を情報提供者が知っているためだという可能性はありそうにない。アジアやアフリカの新聞雑誌に掲載される事例は、必ずと言ってよいほど自国の事例に限られている。たとえば私は、インドでスリランカの事例を読んだ記憶もなければ、スリランカでインドの事例を読んだ記憶もない。情報提供者の中には、当の事例の外に、自国の一、二の事例をある程度知っている者も一部にある。このような人たちは、その情報を、地域に住む人々から口伝えに聞いたか、新聞や雑誌に載っている事例を読んで知ったかのいずれかなのである。しかしながら、多数例に関するデータは、生まれ変わり型事例の情報を提供してくれた平均的アジア人の目にふれるような形ではこれまで発表されていない。したがって、私たちに情報を提供してくれた人たちは、他の事例に似せようとしても、その雛型《ひながた》とすべき事例を知らないし、自らの信仰と一致させるにしても、私が聞きたがっていそうなものに合わせるにしても、その手本となるものをもち合わせていないのである。[*30] したがって、情報提供者が他の事例に似せて証言しようとしているのでなければ、実際にあった出来事をありのままに報告していると考えてよいことになる。

第８章　さまざまな文化圏に見られる変異

本章では、文化圏によって、報告される事例の発生率が大きく異なることと、事例の特徴に差が見られることの二点について検討するつもりである。このふたつは完全に独立したものではないが、別個に考察する方が適切であるように思われる。

さまざまな文化圏で報告される事例の発生率に違いが見られること

報告される事例の発生率についてはわかっているものの、実際の発生率についてはほとんどわかっていない。その点については既に指摘しておいた通りである。とはいえ、報告された事例群の中ですら、文化圏によって大きな差が見られることがわかる。また、生まれ変わり信仰をもつ文化圏の方が、もたない文化圏よりもはるかに多くの事例が報告されているという事実についても先に述べておいた。この点に疑念をもたれる方は、レバノンのイスラム教ドゥルーズ派の信者の間には生まれ変わり型事例が多発するのに対して、近隣の村に住むやはりレバノンのキリスト教徒の間では稀《まれ》であるし、ドゥルーズ派の信者とキリスト教徒が隣り合って暮らしている村の中でもレバノン人キリスト教徒の間では稀である（私に言わせれば、ほとんどない）という事実を考えていただきたい。スリランカのキリスト教徒と仏教徒の間にも、インドのヒンドゥー教徒とイスラム教徒の間にも、報告される事例の発生率に同様の差が認められる。インドのイスラム教徒の間でも（レバノンやスリランカのキリスト教徒でも時おり見られるように）生まれ変わり型事例は発生するが、きわめて稀なのである。

このような差異が生ずる理由を最も端的に説明してくれるのは、文化圏によって生まれ変わり型事例の発現しやすさが異なるとする考え方である。私もこの考え方に与《くみ》するものである。生まれ変わりの可能性を両親が信じていれば、子どもが前世の話をしても、正気を失ったとは思わずに話させておくからである。しかしながら、文化的影響によって事例が発現しやすくなるとすれば、逆に同じくらい抑制される可能性もあるので、東南アジアや西アジアの一部や西アフリカでなぜこれほど多くの事例が発生するのか、という点を問題にするのであれば、同時に、ヨーロッパや北アメリカでそれほど少ないのはなぜか、という点も同じく問題にしなければならない。生まれ変わりを信じていない親は、信じている親と同じくらい自分の子どもに影響を与えるかもしれないのである。

しかしながら、世界の一部の地域に生まれ変わり型事例を発現しやすくさせる要因は、生まれ変わり信仰の有無以外にもあるはずである。そうした要因とはいかなるものであろうか。さしあたり、私たちの知るところとなった事例に対する影響力が世界各地での実際の発生率にほぼ比例していると仮定すると、生まれ変わり信仰の有無と事例の発生率との間に単純な相関があると考えたのでは、発生率に差が見られるという事実が説明できない。考慮すべき要因が他になかったとすると、平均的に言って人口の二〇パーセント以上が生まれ変わりを信じている西洋諸国では、現在よりもはるかに高い発生率が見込まれるはずである。アジアより西洋の方が、抑えつけられる事例が多いと私は見ているが、西洋では、アジアよりもはるかに発生率が低いという事実が、より抑制が強いとしただけで説明できるとは思われない。（インドでは二五パーセントほどの事例が抑えつけられていることがわかっているが、それでも数多くの事例が観察されるのである。）

したがって、こうした事例が多数見つかる国や文化圏には、事例の発現を促す重要な要因が他にもあると考えざるをえない。おそらくは次のような要因が関係しているのであろう。

生まれ変わり型事例が頻発する民族には（一般に）、以下のような特徴が（生まれ変わり信仰とは別に）存在している。

1　故人の思い出を、西洋の人間よりも深く心に留《とど》めている。故人は依然として活動を続けており、この世の出来事に介入することができるとされる。また、死者は生者の助けを、生者は死者の助けを必要とするとも考えられている。

2　また、生者に対する思いも、西洋の人間より強い。家族の絆《きずな》は、西洋人と比べて強固で拘束力も強い。家族の誰かが精神病になると、家族の者は、患者と一緒になってその病気に立ち向かう。それに対して西洋では、精神病患者の家族は患者を身内の輪から遠ざける傾向がある。驚くには当たらないが、たとえば統合失調症のような重度の精神病の回復率（および回復した状態でいる期間）は、工業先進国よりも発展途上国の方が際立って高いのである。[*1] 現代の西洋人が発展途上国を訪れてしばしば仰天する腐敗状態を家族的協力のひとつの表われと見なすこともできるかもしれない。腐敗から脱却し、たとえば地域社会や国家といったさらに大きな集団に従属するようになると、家族の絆は弱まるかもしれないのである。

3

こうした民族のもつ因果律の概念には、西洋の因果律よりもはるかに多くの内容が盛り込まれている。〝偶然〟や〝幸運〟や〝無作為性〟といった西洋の考え方に相当するものは存在しない。何か起こったとすれば、それは必ず、（悪人であれ善人であれ）誰かがその出来事を起こそうとしたか、そういうことが起こってもよいと考えたためなのである。このことは、特に病気に当てはまる。古来の伝統を汲《く》む治療師やシャーマンは、病気になったのは運が悪かったからだとか、偶然にすぎないなどと言ったとすれば、たちまち患者が来なくなってしまうであろう。このような治療師は必ず病気を、業が深いためであるとか、先祖の供養の仕方がまちがっているためであるとか、本人を妬《ねた》む者が悪霊を呼び出したためであるなど、人間が関係する理由をもち出し、偶然のためとは言わないのである。[*2]

4

遠く離れた者同士でも交信が可能だと信ずる度合は、西洋人よりも高い。たとえば、西洋の人間が超常的と考えるテレパシーなどの体験については、珍しいとはいえ通常の出来事の範疇《はんちゅう》に含まれる。また、夢を、事実を伝えるものと見ることが多く、生者は夢の中で時おり故人と再会できると信じている。このような国では、西洋的なプライバシーという概念はほとんど発達しなかった。それは、そのような選択をしたというよりは貧困や過密のためなのかもしれない。もしそうだとしても、日々の行動から他人が締め出せないとすれば、他者が五感を介することなく自分の心の中に侵入して来るテレパシー的交信を受けやすくなるであろう。

5　言葉の巧みさを、西洋人ほど重視していない。そのおかげで、西洋人よりもイメージを保持する能力が高い。

6　時間の流れが西洋とは異なる。西洋人からすると、アジア人やアフリカ人の〝時間の観念〟の欠如は腹立たしく見えるかもしれないが、逆にアジア人やアフリカ人の眼には、時計に縛りつけられている西洋人の几帳面《きちょうめん》さは哀れに映るかもしれないのである。

7　このような民族の間では、西洋と比較して、しなければならないことが少ないか、そこまでいかずとも四六時中何かしていなければならないという感覚は弱い。そのため、過去を振り返る時間が西洋よりも長くなり、現世はもちろん、記憶に残されている前世の生活も、意識に昇りやすくなるのであろう。

以上の要因は、私たち西洋に住む者が超常的と考える（前世の記憶ばかりでなく、テレパシー的印象やポルターガイスト、霊姿などを含む）さまざまな体験を起こしやすくするもののように思われる。私は、昔の純真さが失われてしまったことを嘆く者ではないが、このような相違点に思いを致す者は誰でも、西洋は技術文明を発達させる過程で、得るものがあった代わりに失うものもあったのではないか、と自問すべきである。

世界の一部の地域でこの種の事例が多発する事実の説明となる肝腎《かんじん》な要因を私は特定しなかったかもしれない。読者の中には、他にもそれらしき特徴を考えておられる方もあろう。報告される事例の発生率が各国で異なるという事実を、生まれ変わり信仰の有無だけで十分説明できるとしてあっさり片づけることはできないわけであるが、その点がおわかりいただけたとすれば、私としては十分である。このような差を生じさせる原因については、明らかにすべき点がもっとあるはずである。

しかしながら、私が重要だとして挙げた特徴が正しく説明できているとすれば、生まれ変わり信仰のみでは不十分なのと同様、こうした特徴も、前世の記憶をもつ子どもを多数出現させる要因としては不十分である。アジア、アフリカ、ラテン・アメリカの広大な地域では、そこに住む人たちのほとんどに先述のような信仰や態度が見られるにもかかわらず、生まれ変わり型事例がほとんど見つからないからである。とはいえ、そこに住む人たちは生まれ変わりを信じているわけではない。イスラム教スンニー派やキリスト教徒の間では正統な教義になっていないからである。要するに、こうした事例が多発するためには、生まれ変わり信仰とそれ以外の要因の両方が必要らしいということである。いずれにしても一方だけでは、多数の事例を発現させる条件としては不十分なのである。

この問題に関する考察を終える前に、関係のありそうな要因をもうふたつ紹介しておこう。まずひとつは、もし生まれ変わりが実際に起こるとすれば、生まれ変わり信仰そのものも現世から来世へと伝えられるかもしれないということである。第1章で論じたように、行動的記憶という概念は生まれ変わり型事例の説明に用いることができる。同章で私は、前世からもち越された認知的記憶が意識下にある可能性を指摘したうえ、特定の言葉の話し方を知っているという事例を挙げておいた。さらに第5章では、たとえば女性らしさやフランス人らしさ、イスラム教徒らしさなどの性向は、繰り返し同じ状況に生まれ変わることによって強化されるのではないか、とも述べておいた。ここでは、こうした事例の他に、生まれ変わり信仰自体をはじめ、さまざまな信仰の実例を紹介しておきたい。生まれ変わり信仰は、現世から来世へともち越され、この信仰に好意的な文化圏ではそのたびに強化される可能性がある。その場合、明確に記憶される必要はなく、直観的なものだけでよい。そうした直観は、心理的な構えないし状態として現世から来世へ移行することができるが、このような構えないし状態は、他のより明《めい》瞭《りょう》な記憶と結びつく可能性がある。もし子どもが、前世からもち越した生まれ変わり信仰をもって生まれるとすると、やはりたまたまもち合わせている前世のイメージ記憶がその概念体系にぴたりと収まることになる。それに対して、このような枠組をもっていない子どもは、自分がもっている前世のイメージ記憶をすべて拒絶し、事実上自分を抑えつけることになるかもしれない。

　前世の記憶らしきものを自ら抑えつけるような事態が時おり発生することは私も承知している。現在とは時間も場所も異なる状況で起こった出来事や場面の明確なイメージが幼少期に浮かんでいたが、その頃にはそうしたイメージがどのような意味をもっているのかわからなかった、と私に話してくれた者が西洋人の中に何人かいるからである。このような子どもたちは、こうしたイメージを無視していた（うえ、秘密にしていた）が、忘れてはいなかった。ところが、何年も後になって生まれ変わりの話を初めて本で読み、幼少期に浮かんでいた場面や出来事の不思議なイメージはもしかすると前世の記憶だったのかもしれない、と思うようになったのである[*3]。

もうひとつは、死んでから生まれ変わるまでの間隔が、報告される事例の発生率が高い国の方が低い国よりも短いかもしれないことである。西欧や北アメリカの事例では、アジアよりその間隔が長いらしいが、事実と確認された事例が西洋にはまだ少なすぎるため、その可能性をこれ以上強調してもあまり意味はない。

さまざまな文化圏の事例に見られる特徴の違い

前章で述べたように、私が調査したすべての文化圏の事例にはいくつかの特徴が共通して見られる。こうした特徴が出現する割合は、文化圏によって多少異なるが、全体としてはその差はわずかなものである。さもなければ、こうした特徴をあえて〝普遍的〟などと形容することはなかったであろう。一方、文化圏による相違がそれよりはるかに大きい特徴も若干ある。次に、そのいくつかを説明しよう。

ひとつは、前世を記憶する子どもと前世の人格とが同一家族に属する事例の発生率である。（既に述べたように、こうした事例を私は、同一家族例と呼んでいる。）この種の事例は、ビルマヤタイ、および合衆国の諸部族以外の事例、ナイジェリアのイボ族、アラスカのトリンギット族の全既決例の過半数を占めている。インドやレバノン、スリランカ、トルコでは、こうした事例はそれよりもはるかに少ない。

トリンギットの同一家族例には、ふたりの当事者の関係に一定の傾向が見られるという明確な特徴が存在することがわかっている。母系で結びついている事例が七五パーセントにものぼるのである。この事実は、トリンギットの社会が母系中心に成り立っていることと軌を一にしている。トリンギットは、父性系譜ではなく母性系譜をもとに自分がどちらの半族の一員であり、どのような位置を占めるかを判断するのである。[*4]

それに対して、ナイジェリアに住むイボ族の同一家族例では、前世を記憶する子どもと前世の人格との間に逆の関係が存在することがわかっている。ナイジェリアから私のもとに送られてくる予備的な家系図には、女性が全く含まれていない場合が少なくないが、その事実に象徴されるように、イボ族は父系社会なのである。それと並行して、イボ族の四三例の同一家族例のうち三二例（七四パーセント）で、双方の当事者が父系でつながっていることがわかっている。それに対して、母系でつながっていたのはわずか一一例（二六パーセント）にすぎなかったのである。[*5]

ビルマでは、女性の社会的地位は男性とほぼ同等であるが、ビルマの同一家族例では、ふたりの当事者が、母系でつながっている場合と父系でつながっている場合がほぼ同率であった。

予告夢も、文化圏によって発生率が相当に異なっている。トリンギットをはじめとする北アメリカ北西部の諸部族やビルマ、トルコではふつうにみられるが、イボ族やスリランカ、レバノンではほとんど見られないのである。予告夢は、夢に登場した人物が誰なのかわかった場合の方が記憶に残りやすい。同一家族例がほとんど見られないスリランカのような国では、正体不明の人物が出て来る予告夢を見ている者はあるのかもしれないが、もしそうだとしても、その人物が誰かわからなければ、その夢はまもなく忘れ去られるであろう。[*6] インドの事例を見ると、この解釈が裏づけられる。インドでは、私の記憶する限りひとつの例外もなく、予告夢は同一家族例にしか観察されていないのである。

レバノンに住むドゥルーズ族の事例に予告夢が見られないのは、死んだ直後に生まれ変わるという信仰をドゥルーズ族がもっているという事実と符合している。ドゥルーズ族の間では、魂ないし心は最後の審判の日が来るまで肉体のない状態では存在しえないと信じられているため、肉体を離れた魂が存在する可能性は考えられない。ドゥルーズ族の信仰からすれば、故人は既に幼児としてどこかに生まれ変わっているので、予告夢に登場するはずはないのである。[*7]

以上の話から浮かび上がってくるのは、前世で死亡してから生まれ変わるまでの間隔が文化圏によって異なるという問題である。これまで検討してきた事例では、その間隔は、（中央値は〔一〇ヵ所の文化圏から収集した六一六例で〕一五ヵ月であったが）わずか数時間から二〇年以上までさまざまであった。[*8] このようにばらつきが大きいことと符合して、大半の文化圏では、死んでから生まれ変わるまでの間隔は決まっていないと考えられる。

とはいえ、ドゥルーズ派や（インドの）ジャイナ教では、すべての人間でその間隔は厳密に決められていると信じられている。両者とも、肉体と結びつかない状態で魂は存在できないと主張しているが、死者が新しい肉体と結びつく時点については見解を異にしている。ジャイナ教徒の場合には、受精の瞬間に結びつきが生ずると信じているので、前世の人格が死亡してから新しい肉体をまとって生まれ変わるまでにほぼ九ヵ月かかると考える。私たちが収集した中には、ジャイナ教徒の事例があまりに少ないので、期待通りにいつも九ヵ月後に生まれ変わっているのかどうかについてははっきりしない。[*9]

それに対してドゥルーズ派の信者は、肉体が死ぬと、それまでその肉体と結びついていた魂は新しく生まれた肉体、つまり分娩《ぶんべん》直後の赤ん坊の体とすぐに結びつくと信じている。ドゥルーズ派の信者は、この原則に当てはまらないものは一切認めない。そして、前世の人格が死亡してからその子どもが生まれるまでに、たとえ一日であっても間隔があけば、本人にその記憶がなくとも、〝中間的前世〟がその間にあったと考えるのである。こうした中間的前世があるとすれば、生まれて間もなく死亡したためその間しか生き存《ながら》えなかったということなのであろう。前世を記憶するドゥルーズ派の子どもたちの中には、このような中間的前世の記憶をわずかながらもっている者が時たまあるが、ほとんどの子どもは何も覚えていない。

他の国にも、特にインドの子どもたちの中には、〝中間的前世〟を送ったという者が少ないながら見られる。このような子どもたちは、微に入り細を穿《うが》つが事実かどうか確認できないその間の記憶を語ることがある。スワルンラタ・ミシュラやゴーパール・グプタ、プシュパ、マンジュ・トリパティの事例がその実例である。こうした中間的前世については、いずれも事実とは確認されていない。

私としては、スワルンラタが本当の前世の記憶をもっていたと考えたい。本人の記憶に残る中間的前世に由来するらしき朗唱型真性異言を、スワルンラタは実際に示しているからである。それに対して、ゴーパール・グプタが（ロンドンで）送ったという中間的前世の少なくとも一部は、空想的なものであると私は思っている。これは、（本人の前世の人格である）シャクティパル・シャルマが死亡してから本人（ゴーパール）が生まれるまでの八年間は（本人が）どうなっていたのか、という質問に対する答として初めて出てきたものである。

インドのウッタル・プラデーシュ州カーンプルに住んでいたマンジュ・トリパティが語った中間的前世については、どのような解釈が妥当なのか未《いま》だにはっきりしない。この少女は、自分の前世は父方伯母《おば》であったという。本人の記憶には、事実と確認された内容がある程度含まれていたが、その伯母については誰かから聞くなどして知っていた可能性があるので、証拠としての価値はほとんどない。マンジュが生まれたのは、伯母の死後一二年ほどした時である。その間はカシミール州スリナガルで暮らしていたという。マンジュは、スリナガルで見られるような屋形船などが点在する風景について述べたうえ、この時代の前世についてかなり詳しく語ったため、私たちの調査班がスリナガルに二度も出向き前世の人格を探し出そうとしたが、二回とも失敗に終わっている。中間的前世に関するマンジュの記憶はすべて空想の産物だったのかもしれない。さもなければ、未決例の一部について私が考えているのと同じく、本当の前世の記憶と空想とが入り混じったものなのであろう。

プシュパは、（中心的な）前世で死亡してから今回生まれてくるまでのほぼ四年間、ある寺院の僧侶《そうりょ》の息子としてこの世に生を受けていたと主張しているが、この中間的前世については、事実かどうか確認できるような内容を一言も口にしていない。

以上のことから、異なった文化圏の事例で著しい変異が見られるもうひとつの特徴が浮かび上がってくる。前世で死亡してから今回生まれ変わるまでの、肉体のない状態でいた間に起こった出来事の記憶である。第3章で、こうした記憶は前世の人格の死後にこの世で起こった出来事と、肉体のない世界での体験のいずれかの記憶であることを述べたうえで、その種の記憶の実例をいくつか掲げておいた。

生まれ変わるまでの間に地上で起こった出来事を記憶している例は、いずれの文化圏でも時おりは見られる。その子どもが覚えているとする出来事は、前世の人格の葬儀や埋葬にまつわるものが多い[10]。母親が本人を受胎する直前に家族の中で起こった出来事も、こうした記憶として出てくることもある[11]。

肉体のない世界での経験を記憶していると主張する者も、すべての文化圏で散見されるが、特にビルマとタイに多い[12]。その理由は私にはわからない。かつて私はその理由を、ビルマやタイでは瞑想《めいそう》がかなり広く行なわれている事実に求めたことがある。仏教の瞑想は、心を浄化し、（それ自体を目指すものではないが）たまたま、肉体のない世界にいた時のことも含め、前世の記憶を意識に昇りやすくさせる力をもつと言われる。しかしながら、こうした記憶をもつ子どもの前世の人格は、全員が瞑想をしていたわけでも人格者だったわけでもない。

肉体のない世界での出来事を記憶しているという子どもの比率がタイやビルマで高いのは、必ずしも上座部（小乗）仏教と関係があるようにも思われない。上座部仏教は、ビルマやタイでは最も有力な宗教であるが、それと比べると幾分劣るものの、スリランカでも同様である。ところがスリランカでは、前世で死亡してから生まれ変わるまでの間のことを記憶していると主張する子どもはほとんどいないのである。

　文化圏による差はもうひとつある。動物として生まれ変わったとする主張である。南アジアの仏教徒やヒンドゥー教徒は、人間は畜生に生まれ変わり、その後にまた人間に生まれ変わることもあると信じている。私も、動物の前世時代を覚えているという話を時おり耳にしてきた。（この問題については、第10章で検討する予定である。）トルコで聞いた、伝聞に基づく一、二のあいまいな報告を別にすれば、私はこれまで、南アジア以外でこの種の事例を耳にしたことは一度もない[*13]。

　最後に、文化圏による事例の特徴の違いのうち、私見によれば最も重要なものを取り上げておくことにしよう。性転換例の発生率である。この種の事例が占める割合は、文化圏によって大きく異なっている。カナダ北西部に住むクチン族（アタパスカ語族）の五〇パーセントから、レバノンやトルコ、アラスカ南東部（トリンギット族）[*14]やブリティッシュ・コロンビア州の諸部族（ハイダ族、ツィムシアン族、ギトクサン族）の〇パーセントに至るまで、大きな開きがあるのである。それ以外の国の発生率はこの間に入る。たとえば、インドでは三パーセント、スリランカでは九パーセント、タイでは一三パーセント、（諸部族を除いた）合衆国では一五パーセント、ビルマでは二八パーセントとなっている。

性転換例が発生する文化圏の情報提供者に聞くと、生まれ変わる際に性転換は起こりうると答える。ところが、この種の事例が見られない文化圏の情報提供者に聞くと、そういうことはありえないと否定するのである。（このような質問をぶつけると、そんなことは聞かなくてもわかるはずだとでも言いたげに、無愛想な答が返ってくることもある。）しかしながら、性転換例が見られない地域の情報提供者の中にも、性転換が起こる可能性を強く否定する前に、一瞬ためらいを見せる者が時おりあったのである。その人たちをためらわせたものがあるとすれば何なのであろうか。それは私にはわからない。その人たちが性転換例を見た可能性も、さらには私と会うまでそのような話を耳にした可能性も、きわめて考えにくいからである。

性転換例が発生する文化圏では、一ヵ所を除くすべてで、前世は男性だったと主張する少女が（ここでも報告された事例を対象にしているのであるが）、女性だったという少年の三倍ほどにのぼっている。このようにかなり偏った比率がきわめて一貫して見られるので、性転換例が発生する文化圏に限ってではあるが、ほぼ〝普遍的〟な特徴と考えてよいかもしれない。[*15]

文化圏による特徴の違いを見つけ出すよりは、その説明を考えることの方が難しい。以下、可能性のありそうな解釈を二通り紹介するが、それ以外の説明はありえないなどと言うつもりはない。そのふたつを検討する際に、性転換例を実例として用いるが、それはひとつには、この種の事例が重要なためであり、もうひとつは、文化圏によって差異が見られる特徴の中では、他のものよりもはるかに多くのデータが手元にあるためである。その検討に入る前に、既に述べておいた基本的な点をもう一度振り返ってみよう。

文化は、その社会的、経済的活動のみならず、その文化圏に所属する者が共有している信仰によっても区分される。生まれ変わりを信じているか否かは、一部の文化圏を区分するうえでひとつの基準になる。生まれ変わり信仰をもつさまざまな集団は、こうした信仰が発生する過程および、生まれ変わりに関連して起こりうるものと起こりえないものについて、さまざまな副次的信仰を発展させてきた。（キリスト教徒であれば、イエス・キリストの教えに従おうとする者の中に無原罪の御宿りを信じている者といない者とがいることを思い起こせば、このことは何ら驚くには当たらないはずである。）一次的信仰とそれに付随する二次的信仰は、いつの世にもおとなから子どもへと受け継がれる文化遺産の一部になっている。宗教的信仰は子どもの頃から教え込まれるが、それは、少年期にもそれ以降にも続けられる。成人に達した後に（子どもの場合も同じであるが）、先人の宗教的信仰を拒絶し、別の信仰に飛び込む者もある。とはいえ大半は、子ども時代に教え込まれ、その後も引き続き教えられた信仰を無批判に受け入れてしまう。そして、ほとんどの場合、死を迎える頃までには、死に際して人間はどのようになりどのようにはならないかという考え方がかなり固定してしまい、自分たちが受け入れているものと異なる考え方に対しては、不合理であるとして、あるいは絶対的にまちがっているとして拒絶する傾向がある。人間は、自己の信念とは相容《あいい》れないように感じられるある種の体験や主張を、〝ありえない〟として攻撃することすらある。私は、生まれ変わりという考え方に対するこのような態度を、西洋人の間で何度も見せつけられてきたが、同じ態度が、生まれ変わりを信じ、どのように生まれ変わるかについて固定観念をもっている者の間にも見られる場合が少なくない。たとえば、母斑《ぼはん》をもった子どもの話を私から聞かされたジャイナ教徒は、それを笑止千万なことと考える。魂は死の瞬間に新しい肉体に入ると信じているジャイナ教徒には、新しい肉体についている母斑が、それに対応する部位にあった傷跡から生じたという考え方を受け入れることはできないのである。同様にドゥルーズ族なら、前世で今とは逆の性別だったという子どもを見れば嘲笑《ちょうしょう》するかもしれない。（これは架空の例である。これまで私は、前世では今とは逆の性別だったと主張するドゥルーズ族の子どもの話は一度も聞いていない。）このような子どもを抑えつけるには、強硬な手段をとる必要はない。子どもたちは、おとなと同じくらい、場合によってはおとなよりも敏感に察知することすらあるからである。キリスト教徒の子どもたちが、前世についておぼろげながら感じたことを抑えてしまうのとちょうど同じように、ドゥルーズ族の子どもは、逆の性別の人間として前世を送った記憶を隠蔽《いんぺい》し、その後完全に忘れ去ってしまうのかもしれない。このようにして、性転換型の事例は一部の文化圏には一例も出現しないのであろうし、そのためにその文化圏では、生まれ変わる時に性転換が起こるはずはない、つまり、ありえないという信仰が強化されやすいのであろう。

　以上のように考えると、ドゥルーズ族に性転換例が全く見られない理由がそれなりに説明できるかもしれない。ドゥルーズ族は、かなり小さな集団で生活している。（現在、地理的にはある程度広い地域に拡散している。）活字になった聖典を見ると、その信仰の精髄が具体的な形で表現されているのがわかる。とはいえ、性転換の可能性を信じていないトルコのアレヴィス族や北アメリカ北西部の諸部族については、同じように考えることはできない。そうした信仰を明文化した教典はアレヴィス族にはないであろうし、北アメリカ北西部の諸部族にないこともまちがいない。このような宗教は口伝によって後世に継承されるのである。また、北アメリカ北西部の諸部族は、現在、ブリティッシュ・コロンビア州とアラスカ州に跨《また》がる数千平方キロにも及ぶ広大な地域に拡散している。こうした部族には、全部族民が信奉すべき真理として特定の信仰を広める教祖的人物も、遍《あまね》く認められたシャーマンも存在しなかった。アラスカやブリティッシュ・コロンビア州の海峡や河川を往来して、生まれ変わる際に性転換することはありえないとする信仰を近隣の諸部族にふれまわった者は誰ひとりいないのである。

そうであれば、性転換はありえないとする信仰は生まれ変わりそのものによって広まったのではないか、という疑問が生ずる。既に指摘しておいたように、生まれ変わりが本当に起こるとすれば、人間が生まれ変わるという信仰は前世から来世へと伝えられるであろう。いま言おうとしているのは、生まれ変わりの起こり方や、前世から来世へ移行する際に起こる出来事にまつわる信仰も、前世から来世へと伝えられるかもしれないということである。

つまり、生前にかなり強く抱いていた信念は、次に生まれ出ることになる環境を含め、死んでから後の出来事に影響を与えるかもしれないのである。[*16]こうした信念は、後催眠暗示に似て、やはり強い衝撃に駆られて実行に移されるのかもしれない。次に生まれ変わる時に、反対の性別にはなれないとする思い込みをもったまま死んで行けば、生まれ変わることができたとしても、逆の性別にはならないのかもしれないのである。

また、たとえばトリンギット族のように、性転換などありえないという確たる信仰をもつ文化圏で、ある女性が死んで男性として生まれ変わってくるとした場合、そこから先の展開を推理することもできる。初めてトリンギットの男として生まれた時、前世では女性だったという記憶が意識下で保持されているかもしれず、そのため、たとえ前世のイメージ記憶がなかったとしても、この男性は、性転換の可能性を受け入れやすい状況にあることであろう。それに対して、繰り返し男性として生まれ変わった後には、女性だった頃の記憶は次第に薄れ、それにつれて、逆の性別に生まれ変わる可能性を次第に認めなくなって行くことであろう。そして結局は、他の点ではトリンギットの文化圏で支配的な信仰を多少なりとも疑問視する傾向を残すとしても、性転換はありえないと心底から強く思い込むようになるかもしれないのである。

信念ないし信仰が、死後および来世での経験を促したり抑えたりする役割をそれなりに演ずる可能性は、性転換例のみに留《とど》まらず、それよりもはるかに広い範囲に当てはまる。次章からは、そのうちのいくつかについて検討することにしたい。

第9章　生まれ変わりという考え方によってどのような現象が説明できるか

前世の人格が示したとされる、あるいはそう考えられそうな行動と符合するように思われる変わった行動を、前世を記憶すると主張する子どもたちのほとんどが示していることを初めて知った時の驚きについては、第6章で簡単に述べておいた。生まれ変わり型事例に超常的要素が関係しているか否かを判断するに際して、私は、このような変わった行動が重要な位置を占めることに少しずつ気づくようになった。このような行動には、生まれ変わりの証拠となる以外にもうひとつの意味があることがわかるまでには、さらに長い年月が必要であった。もうひとつの意味とは、もし生まれ変わりという現象が本当に存在するとしたら、現行の心理学や精神医学の知識では説明しにくい異常行動が説明できる可能性がある、ということである。さらに、生まれ変わりという考え方を使えば、現時点では謎とされているある種の生物学的現象や医学的現象が説明しやすくなるかもしれない。本章では、心理学、生物学、医学の領域にある未《いま》だ解明されていない問題を明らかにするうえで、生まれ変わりという考え方がどのような形で役立つ可能性があるかという点について私見を述べ、その検討を行なうつもりである。

生まれ変わりという考え方によって、どのような現象がこれまで以上に理解しやすくなる可能性があるかについて述べる前に、読者の方々にはもうひとつ仮定を設けていただかなければならない。（本章の性質上、生まれ変わりという現象が本当に起こることを既に先ほどから仮定していただいている。）つまり、前世の出来事のイメージ記憶をもつ者は一部にすぎないが、先述の行動を身につけるに至った過程や理由の説明になりそうなイメージ記憶はなくとも、前世に由来する行動的記憶を保持しているかもしれない者は多い、ということである。

前に二、三の例を紹介しているので、読者の方々はこのような仮定をしていただきやすくなっているかもしれない。いま言おうとしているのは、前世のイメージ記憶が消えた後にも、前世に関連した（特定の食べ物を好むなどの）行動を示し続ける事例のことである。読者の方々は、本章に掲げる実例を検討した後でこの仮定を受け入れてくださってもよい。以下に紹介する（ごく一部を除く）事例は、（事実と確認された）前世のイメージ記憶と、それに関連する変わった行動の両方を保持する子どもたちの中からとられている。読者の方々が、このような子どもの変わった行動を、イメージ記憶に伴う行動的記憶の一型と考えてよいと思われるとすれば、イメージ記憶はないのに行動的記憶をもった者が存在する可能性のあることも認めていただけるかもしれない。

子ども時代の変わった行動

以下に紹介する変わった行動の実例を検討するに当たり、問題となる行動はおおむね次のような条件を満たすことをおわかりいただかなければならない。（ここで〝おおむね〟という表現を使う必要があるのは、そうした行動をいつも満足の行くほど調査できたわけではないからである。）まず第一に、この種の行動は、本人の家族の中では変わったものであり、その中には、そうした行動を示す者はひとりもいないか、いたとしても本人と比べるとごくわずかなものにすぎない、という点が挙げられる。第二には、その行動の説明になりそうな経験を本人が（生後に）したという話は聞いていないし、その行動を身につけるに当たって手本となるような行動を示す者が家族や近所にいたという話も聞いていないことである。

乳幼児期の恐怖症

第4章および5章で、実例を挙げながら生まれ変わり型事例に見られる恐怖症について少々説明しておいた。また、一部の子どもは、言葉を覚えるより前に、したがってその恐怖症を（前世に由来するとして）両親に説明できるようになる以前にその症状を示すことについても述べておいた。また、このような子どもの中には、その恐怖症の説明になりそうな前世のイメージ記憶が消失した後にも恐怖症を示し続ける者もある。

こういった恐怖症は、通例、前世の人格の死因に関係している。恐怖症の出現率は、記憶の事実性が確認されている子どもと、されていない子どもでほとんど差はない。第4章で紹介したマ・ティン・アウン・ミョの事例は、その記憶が事実かどうか確認されていないにもかかわらず、強い恐怖症（この場合は飛行機恐怖症）を示した格好の実例である。恐怖症は、イメージ記憶の全くない子どもにすら起こることがある。このような場合、特定の故人が生まれ変わってきたことを裏づけるような特徴が、恐怖症の他に見られることもある。アラスカに住むトリンギット族のデレク・ピトノヴはその一例であろう。ピトノヴには、前世のイメージ記憶はないが、曾祖父《そうそふ》の叔父《おじ》に当たる男性の致命傷となった槍《やり》による刺創と一致する部位に母斑《ぼはん》があり、刀剣類に対する恐怖症を終生示したのである。

こうした事例に見られる恐怖症は、大半が、前世の人格の死因となったものに関係しているが、前世の終焉《しゅうえん》の地やそれとよく似た場所に対して恐怖症を示す子どももある。シュレイマン・ゼイツン（トルコ）は、メーメト・コシュマンという溺死《できし》した男性にまつわる記憶をもっていた。シュレイマンには、水全般に対する恐怖心が見られたが、（トルコ中南部を流れる）セイハン川の、メーメト・コシュマンが溺死したあたりを特に恐れていた。やはりトルコのネカティ・サイラクも、前世の自分が自動車事故で死亡した橋を渡るよう（幼少期に）言われた時、強い恐怖をあらわにした。同様にラヴィ・シャンカール・グプタも、前世の自分だという子どもが殺害された現場に対して恐怖症を示している[*1]。

前世で非業の死を遂げた記憶をもつ子どもは、全員がそれに沿った恐怖症を示すわけではない。前世で射殺された記憶をもっているゴーパール・グプタには銃器に対する恐怖症はなかったし、刺殺された記憶をもつボンクチ・プロムシンにも刀剣類に対する恐怖症はなかった。とはいえ、この世で起こった事故や負傷の後にも、同じように、恐怖症が起こる場合と起こらない場合とがある。自動車事故に遭い重傷を負った者の中にも、車に近寄りすらしない者があるかと思えば、事故に遭った後でも、機会がありさえすればためらうことなく車に乗る者もある。現世で受けた傷害その他に対する反応がこのように異なるのは、前世で重ねたさまざまな経験によるところもあるのかもしれない。もし前世で溺死している人物が現世で溺《おぼ》れそうになったとしたら、前世で溺死した経験のない者よりも、溺死しかかった後に恐怖症を発現させやすいのかもしれないのである。

死に際して、苦痛が並はずれて強い場合もあるように思われるが、死が迫り、死に至るまでの苦しみの大きさによって、恐怖症が起こるかどうかが決まるのかもしれない。しかしながら、さまざまな死因の事例で恐怖症が発生しているのも確かである。たとえば、前世の人格が溺死している四七例では水につかることに対する恐怖症が三〇例（六四パーセント）に、前世で蛇に咬《か》まれて死亡している二三例では蛇恐怖症が九例（三九パーセント）に見られたのである。

児童精神科医は、自分たちにも子どもの両親にも説明できない恐怖症を示す子どもが少なからずいることを知っている。このような恐怖症は、これまで知られている外傷体験に由来するものでもなければ、家族の者が示す同様の恐怖症をまねたものでもない。精神科医の中には、ふつうには説明できない恐怖症を、ある人物に対する恐怖心を他の人物や動物や物品などに象徴的に置き換えた結果と見る者もある。フロイトの報告による、馬恐怖症を示した少年ハンスの症例は、こうしたまわりくどい理屈づけが行なわれた一例である。フロイトは、ハンスが馬を怖がることにより父親の恐ろしい側面が覆い隠されたと考えたが、ハンスには、馬に関係して恐怖体験があり、本人の馬恐怖症は、他の理由をもち出さずとも十分説明できるのである。[*2]

恐怖症の引き金となる外傷体験を探し求める範囲を現世に限定すると、説明不能な恐怖症がもしかすると多いかもしれない。そこで、その原因を他に求める必要が生ずる。幼少期に発生する一部の恐怖症には象徴的な意味合いがあるのかもしれないが、それに関係した外傷体験が前世で起こっている可能性も考えてみなければならないのである[*3]。

幼児期に見られる変わった興味と遊び

子どもが何らかの変わった遊び（ないし、変わった興味を抱いていることを示す行為）をすると、心理学者や精神科医はそれを、年上の人間の真似をしているのではないかとか、言葉で表現できない感情や気持を別の形で表出する必要に迫られるためではないかと考えるのがふつうである。たとえば、戦争ごっこなら、攻撃衝動の吐け口として社会的に容認される方法と考えられるのであろうし、お医者さんごっこであれば、もし父親が医者なら父親と同一視できるからではないか、というわけである。子どもの多くは、成人した後に就く仕事に幼少期から興味を抱くものである。偉大な音楽家は一般に、幼時から音楽にまつわる関心や技能を示すが、その中には、両親の影響ということで説明のつく例がたくさんある。たとえば、バッハやモーツァルト、ベートーベン、ブラームス、エルガーの父親はすべて音楽家であった。ところが、ドボルザークの父親は食肉業者であったし、ディーリアスの父親は実業家、メンデルスゾーンの父親は（洗練された）銀行家、ヘンデルの父親は理髪外科医であった。ヘンデルの例は、特に示唆的であろう。父親の反対に遭ってもなおかつヘンデルは、幼少期から音楽に対する関心を示し続けたからである。母親は特別に息子の肩をもったわけではなかったので、叔母《おば》には励ましを受けたものの叔母の影響のみでは、父親の猛反対を押し切るには不十分だったように思われる。一家の先祖には、音楽に関心を抱いた者は全く知られていない。

矯正教育で有名なエリザベス・フライは、青年期に「下層階級の人々」に対して敬愛の念や気遣いを示し、後にそれが本人の一生の仕事となった。近代的な看護法を確立したフローレンス・ナイチンゲールは、後に天職となった仕事に対する関心を、幼少期に人形を繕うという形で示している。このふたりの女性はいずれも、家族のもつ伝統や傾向とは相反する関心を明確に発現させ、その追求を行なったのである。

後年、目ざましい成果を挙げた人物の中には、子どもの頃、おとなになったら何々をすると宣言している者もある。たとえばトロイを発掘したハインリッヒ・シュリーマンは、八歳にも満たない頃に、トロイを見つけると公言していたし、エジプト学の創始者であるジャン＝フランソワ・シャンポリオンも、子ども時代に、この方面に対する関心を表明していた。また、後年の回想によれば、エジプトの象形文字を解読しようと決めたのは、まだ一二歳にもならない頃であったという。ミケナイの線文字Bを解読したマイクル・ヴェントリスは、わずか七歳の時に、エジプトの象形文字に関するドイツ語の書物を買って勉強しているし、一四歳の時には、当時まだ解読されていなかったこの文字を解読するという誓いを立てている。

自分が一生を捧《ささ》げる仕事を幼少期から明らかにしている聖人のうちでも、シエーナの聖カタリーナは、（唯一無二ではないにせよ）異例の早熟ぶりを示した。聖カタリーナは幼少期に、出家ごっこをして遊んだり、食を断つなどの苦行を行なったりしていた。七歳の時には、自らの生涯をイエス・キリストに捧げている。父親はシエーナで染色業を営んでおり、母親ともども信心深く、娘が宗教的献身の生活に入ることに反対はしなかったが、一家の暮らしぶりを見ても、本人が聖女となったことを説明してくれそうな要因は見当たらないのである。[*4]

家族の中では異質の関心を早期に示すという現象は、後に名声を馳《は》せる人物にしか起こらないわけではない。ふつうの両親から生まれたふつうの子どもが、周囲の者が抱いているとは思えないような関心を示す例もあるのである。このような例は、私の耳にもいくつか届いている。そのうちの一例は、時計に魅了され、時計を修理する能力も示したが、それは家族の影響を考えただけでは全く説明できないという事例である。もう一例は、合衆国内陸部で育てられ、家族の中にはわずかにせよ関心をもつ者はいなかったにもかかわらず、海や船舶に魅せられた子どもの事例である。また、アメリカ先住民に異常に魅かれるアメリカの白人男児もいる。この少年は、先住民の民族衣裳《いしょう》を着たがり、先住民と白人の間で行なわれる論争では、必ず先住民側についたのである。家族の中には、アメリカ先住民にそれほど強い関心を抱く者はいなかったため、そのおかげで本人は、家族の中で少々孤立してしまった。しかしながらこの三名には、前世のイメージ記憶はなかった。

現行の人格理論では、以上の人々が、家族の無関心や反対にもかかわらず、後に天職とする仕事に幼少期から関心を示したという事実を適切に説明することはできない。この人たちの中には前世のイメージ記憶を残している者はなかったとはいえ、こうした関心が前世に端を発したとする可能性を考慮に入れることは、理に適《かな》っているように思われる。

この考え方の正当性を裏づけるため、私が調査した事例の中から、その種のイメージ記憶は残していないが、前世の記憶に由来するらしき変わった関心を幼時に示した子どもの事例を紹介することもできる。その一例として、コーリス・チョトキン・ジュニアの事例が挙げられる。コーリス・チョトキン・ジュニアが発動機に興味をもっていたことについては第4章で述べておいたが、明らかにそれは、遺伝的なものでもなければ、父親に倣ったものでもなかった。父親は、発動機には全くと言ってよいほど関心がなかったからである。

宗教に強い関心のあった人物が自分の前世だったという記憶をもつ子ども（たいていの場合女児）は、幼時から敬虔《けいけん》な態度を見せる。こうした態度は、ラタナ・ウォンソムバトの事例のように、信心深い家庭に見られることもあるが、ディスナ・サマラシンへの事例のように、家族が宗教に無関心だったり宗教を毛嫌いしていたりする場合もある[*5]。

一部の子どもたちの行動に、あまり感心できない傾向が見られることもある。前世が盗賊だった記憶をもつ子どもがスリなどの盗みを働いたという事例が二例あるのである。

前世の人格の職業が、遊びの中に現われる事例も少なくない。ウィジャナマ・キトシリは、放課後自宅に戻ると、毎日お店屋さんごっこをして遊んでいたし、パルモッド・シャルマの母親は、息子が駄菓子屋ごっこをして一年もの時間をむだにしたことを嘆いていた。このふたりは、商店を営む家庭で送った前世を記憶していたのである。（第4章で紹介した）マ・ティン・アウン・ミョとバジラン・B・サクセナは、幼時に戦争ごっこをして遊んでいる。このふたりは、兵士だった前世を記憶しているのである。前世を医師として過ごしたというヴィアス・ラジパルは、遊び仲間の子どもたちの熱を計ったり、聴診器を胸に当てる真似をよくしていた。前世は自動車整備工だったというダニエル・ジルディは、自宅のソファーの下に潜り込み、車の下で修理をしているつもりになっていた。学校の教師だったという記憶をもつラリタ・アベヤワルデナは、遊び友達を集合させ、架空の黒板を棒で指して遊んでいた。[*6]

清掃人の前世を幼少期に記憶していたインドのジュディト・クリシュナは、小枝を集め（清掃人が使うような）箒《ほうき》の形にして、自宅の敷地をいつも掃いていた。先述のように、前世が清掃人だったというインドの少女はもうひとりいる。スワラン・ラタというその少女は、きわめて不潔な習慣をもっていたが、弟妹たちの排泄物《はいせつ》については喜んで処理しているような態度を見せた。このふたりの少女は、清掃人の行動からは縁遠い中流階級のカーストの両親のもとに生まれ育っているのである。

このような子どもは、前世時代の嗜癖《しへき》も遊びの中でかいま見せることがある。たとえば私は、前世がアルコール依存症だったという子どもをふたり知っているが、ふたりとも、泥酔した人間が千鳥足で歩いたり倒れたりする様子を遊びの中でおもしろおかしく演じて見せた。そのうちのひとりは、スジト・ラクマル・ジャヤラトネといい、既に述べたように、トラックや警官に対する恐怖症をもっていた子どもである。

前世の人格が死亡した時の模様を遊びの中で再現した子どももある。（銃で）自殺した前世を記憶しているラメズ・シャムスは、銃で自殺する場面をよく演じていたというし、首を吊《つ》って自殺した記憶をもつマウン・ウィン・アウンも、本当に首を吊る時のように、首に縄を巻く遊びをいつもしていたという。また、前世で入水《じゅすい》自殺した記憶のある子どもも三人いるが、その三人ともが水に溺《おぼ》れる遊びをよくしていたのである。

前世時代の子どもの名前を人形や玩具《がんぐ》にそのままつけた子どももある。[7] 私は、子どもをもつ西洋人に、子どもたちは自分の人形に何をもとに名前をつけているかを時おり質問したことがある。その結果、それがはっきりわかった例も少なくなかったが、はっきりしない場合には、子どもが、潜在意識で記憶している前世時代に出会った人物の名前を人形につけたという可能性を考慮する価値があると思う。

幼少期に見られる異例の能力や誰にも教わることなく示す技能

この種の子どもたちの中には、習ってもいないのに何らかの技能を示したり、並々ならぬ能力を見せたりする者もある。前節で紹介したコーリス・チョトキン・ジュニアは、発動機に対して単なる関心以上のものをもっており、誰に教わったわけでもないのに、修理法まで知っていたらしいのである。また、スーザン・イーストランドの母親によれば、スーザンは、それまで経験したことのない事柄を、教わってもいないのに[8]、どうすればよいかを最初から知っているように見えることが時おりあったという。

とはいえ、このような能力や技能が、前世で積み重ねた訓練に由来していることを裏づける証拠は不十分なものでしかないという事実を、ここで述べておかなければならない。私の知る限り、生まれながらに何らかの技能をもっている子どもがその技能を前世からもち越したと主張した例は西洋にはないし、アジアにもほとんどない。しかし私は、(子ども時代には)習ったことのない聖典に出てくるかなりの長文を暗唱したと言われる女性の事例をインドで二例調査したことがあるが、このふたりは、その聖典を完全に暗記していた敬虔な宗教家の生涯を記憶していたのである。調査を開始した時点では、一方は青年期に、もう一方は中年期に入っていた。ふたりの年齢を考えると、幼少期に誰からも教わることなく暗唱したのはどの聖典のどの節なのかについても、それまでその聖典に接する機会があったとすればいかなる時であったのかについても、正確に突き止めることはできないように思われた。とはいえ、その子どもがまだ幼なければ、同様の事例を厳密に調査することにより、こういった天賦の才を示す子どもがその技能を前世で身につけたという考え方を裏づける証拠が得られるかもしれない。

嗜癖と渇望

前世を記憶する子どもの中には、酒類やタバコ、大麻誘導体などの麻酔剤をほしがって（あるいは要求すらして）おとなたちを仰天させた者もある。こうした子どもたちの話では、前世でこの種の嗜《し》好《こう》品によって慰めを得たのを覚えており、また飲むようになってはいけない理由がわからないというのである。このようなものを好む理由は、いずれの事例でも、両親の嗜好を真似たということでは説明できないように思われた。私が調べた限りでは、両親は、子どもがほしがったのと同じ薬物を飲んだことがないか、飲んでいたとしても幼児が飲むのを許してはいなかったからである。*9

気質

心理学者は、気質という言葉を、特定の刺激とは無関係に、一生を通じて多少なりとも一貫しても続ける人間の行動的特徴を指して用いる。音楽の方面で説明すれば、さまざまな旋律の根底に流れる基礎低音ということになろう。気《き》質《しつ》の一側面として、全般的な身体的活動水準がある。また、中断や妨害があってもひとつのことを追求し続けるという忍耐力も含まれる。もうひとつは、葛藤《かっとう》に直面した際、それに反応してすぐに怒り出す傾向、すなわち易《い》刺激性である。

気質の研究者は、生後数日目の乳児ですら、気質に著しい差が観察されることに気づいている。事実、活動水準のような、気質のひとつの表現形態は、既に胎児期に出現することもあるのである。気質に個人差が生ずる原因については、これまであまり研究されていないし、その原因を完全に解明したとする専門家もいない。気質になぜ違いが生ずるのかわからないとして、困惑の色を隠さない専門家もある。[*10]

私が調査を行なった数例では、前世を記憶する子どもと前世の人格との間に共通した（活動性や短気などの）気質が見られることを情報提供者が強調している。イマド・エラワールとディスナ・サマラシンへは、前世の人格と同じく短気だという。

早熟な性的衝動

前世を記憶する子どもたちの中には、早くも幼児期に、前世の人格の妻女や愛人や恋人に対して明白な性的関心を示す者がある。また、やはり幼少期に、前世の連れ合いに似た異性に言い寄った子どももある。私がこの種の行動に気づいたのは、前世の人格が、通例、性的活動性の最も高い年齢、つまり青少年期に死亡している場合のみであった。

この種の行動については、第4章で紹介したボンクチ・プロムシンの事例で詳しく述べた。[11]

性的同一性の混乱

現在とは逆の性別の人間として送った前世を記憶しているという子どもは、たいていの場合、前世の性別に沿った行動特徴を幼少期に示す。このような子どもたちは、現在の解剖学的性別を拒絶するか、拒絶しているようにふるまうことがある。たとえば、自分は男の子だと主張し、男児の服を着たり、男の子の遊びに興じたり、名前を男の子のように呼ばれたいと主張する少女がいるのである。[12]

私は、こうした子どもたちの何人かについては、一〇代後半ないし青年期以降まで追跡調査を行なっている。その結果、大半は次第に解剖学上の性別を受け入れるようになり、異性の服を着るのをやめ、あらゆる点で正常な発達を遂げることがわかった。ところが、それほどの適応を示さなかった例もいくつかあった。このような事例では、前世の性別に未練を残し、そのため不幸な生活を送るのがふつうであった。

マ・ティン・アウン・ミョの事例を要約して紹介する中で、(成人に達した後ですら)自分は男であって女ではない、と主張して譲らなかった本人の頑《かたく》なな態度にふれておいた。第5章では、インドのラニ・サクセナというもうひとりの性転換例について述べ、ヒンディー語を話す時、男言葉を頑なに使い続けたという事実を紹介しておいた。ここで、この事例に若干の補足を行なっておきたい。ラニ・サクセナは、バラナシの裕福な弁護士として過ごした前世を記憶していた。本人は、この弁護士一家とわずかながら関係のあるアラハバードの家族のもとに生まれた。しかし現在の家族は、その弁護士一家と比べると財産がはるかに乏しかった。ラニ・サクセナは、小さい頃から、バラナシで送ったこの弁護士の生涯を正確かつ詳細に覚えていた。（信頼の置ける情報提供者が私に話してくれたところによると、ラニ・サクセナが、ある時、本人は知らないがその弁護士ならよく知っていた人物を、姿を見る前に声を聞いただけで見分けた場面を目撃したという。その時ラニ・サクセナは、その人物が訪ねて来た家の一室におり、その姿が見えるより先に声を聞いていたのであった。）

男性的傾向を強く示したにもかかわらずラニは、インドの習慣に従って、結局、家族が選んだ相手と結婚した。ラニの変わった行動のため家族は、経済的に恵まれた男性を見つけることができず、結婚後ラニは、極貧の生活を強いられた。その後、子どもがふたり生まれたが、積極性は乏しかったものの、しっかりした母親としてふたりを育てた。前世時代のバラナシの弁護士は、女性を自分本位に利用していたため、ラニは、女性の生活を身をもって体験できるよう神が自分を女性として生まれ変わらせたと信じていた。とはいえラニは、自分が置かれている境遇に対して矛盾した態度を示した。一方では、自分を女性にしたうえに小さな土造の家での生活を余儀なくさせた神の裁きは正しいと思うと言いながら、もう一方では、自分を完全な男性と考え、未《いま》だ記憶に残しているバラナシでの裕福な生活に戻りたがったのである。

マ・ティン・アウン・ミョやラニ・サクセナのような事例は、西洋の精神科医が〝性同一性障害〟ないし〝性別異和症〟と呼ぶものとよく似ている。この種の症状の研究者の中には、（クラインフェルター症候群のような）生物学的要因をその原因と見なす者もあるが、それだけでは全例の説明はできない。[*13] 希望とは逆の性別の子どもが生まれてしまったので、両親が、望む性別の子どもとして育てようとした事例も若干あったが、これも、性別異和症全体の説明にはならない。[*14] このような症状をもった患者の中には、両親の育て方には関係がないことを自ら明らかにしている者もある。たとえば幼少期に、もの心がついてまもない頃から、自分は女のはずだと思っていたという男性患者がいるかもしれない。また、そのような患者は、女物の服を着るなど女性的な行動をとろうとすると両親に反対されたことをはっきり覚えているかもしれないのである。[*15]

私が調査した性転換例の子どもにある種の性的同一性の混乱が共通して観察されることから、私は、性的同一性の混乱（および同性愛）を示す者一般についても、前世で現在と逆の性別だったためにそのような結果を生じたのではないかと考えている。本章の冒頭で述べておいたように、こうした状態は、前世のイメージ記憶がない場合ですら起こることがあるのである。

一卵性双生児に見られる相違点

私がこれまで収集してきた事例の中には、三六組の一卵性双生児がいる。その一方ないし双方が前世の記憶をもっていたのである。双子の一方がもう一方よりも前世の記憶をたくさんもっていたのは、三六組全体の三分の二ほどであった。また、一方にしか前世の記憶がない場合もあった。そのような場合、記憶をもっている方の子どもが、前世ではもう一方の子どもと一緒だったと語った事例も何例かあった。

前世の人格がふたり揃って特定できたのは二六組であった。（残る一〇組については、一方ないし双方が未決例であった。）二六組の既決例中、前世の人格同士が同一家族内にいた（あるいは夫婦だった）事例は一九例であり、残る七例も、友人ないし知人同士であった。また、双方が全く知らない間柄だった事例は一例もなかった。

第4章で、ジリアン・ポロックとジェニファー・ポロックの事例を紹介した際、こうした関係について述べておいた。このふたりは、自分たちの姉に当たるジョアンナとジャクリーンの生涯を覚えていたのであった。同様に、ラムー・シャルマとラジュー・シャルマというインドの双生児も、別の村でやはり男の双生児として送った前世を記憶していた。また、ビルマのマ・キン・マ・ギーとマ・キン・マ・ネという女の双生児も、母方曾祖《そうそ》父母《ふぼ》の生涯を覚えていた。そのためマ・キン・マ・ギーは、前世では男性だったと主張し、（幼児期には）異性の服を着ていたうえ、曾祖父がもっていた特徴もいくつか示したのである。

シヴァンティ・ヘティアラトチとシェロミー・ヘティアラトチという双生児（女児）は、親友同士で同性愛の関係にあったふたりの青年の生涯を記憶していた。（この双生児はしたがって、ふたりとも性転換例ということになり、この種の大半の事例と同じく、ふたりとも、男性的な行動を強く示したのである。）

前世を記憶する双生児は、相互の関係の中で、前世時代と同様の態度を示す場合が多い。たとえば、ジリアン・ポロックは、ジェニファーに姉のような態度で接したし、ジェニファーもジリアンに依存する態度を示したのである。（ジリアンの前世の人格と目されるジョアンナは、ジャクリーンよりも五歳年長であった。）同様に、マ・キン・マ・ネは、ちょうど母方曾祖母が夫に対して見せたように、細々とした点に至るまでマ・キン・マ・ギーを支配したのである。マウン・アウン・チョ・ティンとマウン・アウン・コ・ティンというビルマの双生児（男児）は、精米所を営んでいた女性と、その精米所に自分の田圃《たんぼ》で収穫した米を納めていた米作農民の生涯を記憶していた。この（ほぼ確実に二卵性の）双生児の相互の行動や態度を見ると、裕福な精米所経営者の少々横柄な態度と米作農民の慇懃《いんぎん》な態度とがそのまま反映されていた。現在のふたりの関係はもちろん、前世の人格の立場や行動パターンも把握できている事例は一組あるが、その全例で、このような優越・従属関係のあることが明らかになっている。

一卵性双生児[*16]は、さまざまな個人差や異常や病気の原因を探り出すうえで、遺伝的要因と環境的要因が分離できる絶好の研究対象である。人間の行動や精神疾患の研究者は、生後まもなく引き離され、別々の環境で育てられた一卵性双生児に特段に注目して研究を進めて来た[*17]。端的に言えば、このような双生児に見られる行動上の違いは環境によって生じたものであり、相似する点は、遺伝素因が共通しているためだということになる。全般的に見れば、一緒に育てられた一卵性双生児を研究する場合にも、別々に育てられた一卵性双生児を研究する場合にも、両者の相違よりも共通点の方に主眼が置かれて来た。生まれ変わりという考え方は、その相違点と共通点の双方を解明するうえで利用価値があるかもしれない。

まず、別個に育てられた一卵性双生児に見られる共通点について考えてみよう。このように育てられた一卵性双生児では、一方が統合失調症を発症した場合、もう一方も発症する比率は、やはり別々に育てられた二卵性双生児よりも高いとされてきた。精神科医の中には、それを、こうした異常行動の根底に遺伝的要因が存在する証拠だと考える者が多い。とはいえ、そのような主張に対してはいつも異議が唱えられてきたし、この問題は依然として論争の的になっているのである。[*18] 別個に育てられた場合であれ一緒に育てられた場合であれ、一卵性双生児の行動が似ているのは、少なくとも一部は、前世時代を一緒に過ごしたことによるのではないか、その中で同じような習慣や態度を身につけ、生まれ変わった後にもそれが続いているということなのではないか、と私は考えるがどうであろうか。犯罪者だったふたりの男が同時に死んで一卵性双生児として生まれ変わってきたとすれば、そのふたりがまた罪を犯すようになったとしても格別に不思議なことではないであろう。

では次に、一緒に育てられた一卵性双生児に見られる相違点を考えてみよう。別々に育てられた一卵性双生児と同じく、その場合も遺伝的素因は同一である。ふたりの行動に見られる不一致点は、それぞれに対して両親が異なった態度で接するために生ずるのかもしれない。たとえば、一方の子どもがかなり小さく体も弱ければ、もう一方の子どもに対する時とは違って、気遣いなど特別の配慮がなされやすい。一緒に育てられた一卵性双生児の相違点についても研究者は、厳密に見れば子宮内環境が同一ではないために生ずるとしてきた。たとえば、一個の受精卵が二個に分割された後、一方の卵がもう一方よりも多量の血液供給を受けた（あるいはそれ以外の点で好条件に恵まれた）などとされるのである。こうした説明は、一方が正常なのにもう一方には先天性欠損があるような一卵性双生児にも用いられる。一例として、口蓋裂《こうがいれつ》を考えてみよう。これは、二〇〇〇回の出産に一回の割で生ずる先天性の障害である。一卵性双生児と二卵性双生児の間でこの障害の発生一致率に顕著な差が見られることは、この先天性障害に遺伝的要因が関係していることを裏づける有力な証拠である。二卵性双生児では、一方に口蓋裂のある双生児の八パーセントがもう一方にもある（一致例）が、一卵性双生児ではそれが三八パーセントにものぼるのである。しかしながら、一卵性双生児の三分の二近くは一致を見せないので、口蓋裂が一方にしかない場合には、遺伝的要因以外の何らかの要因が働いているはずである[*19]。こうした不一致例に対して一部の研究者は、母胎内で口唇が形成される時期に、双子の一方は血液の供給を不十分にしか受けなかったのではないか、あるいはその他の局所的異常があったのではないか、と説明している。

　しかしながら、ふたつの胎児が置かれている子宮内環境の違いだけでは、一卵性双生児に見られる不一致を完全に説明することはできないであろう。出生前の血液供給の差や、双子に対する両親の態度の違いの他にも、別の要因が関係しているのかもしれないのである。つまり、前世に由来する行動的記憶である。次に、この可能性について、私がスリランカで調査した一卵性双生児の事例を取り上げ、具体的に説明してみよう。

インディカ・イシュワラとカクシャッパ・イシュワラは、ある程度の類似が見られるものの、多くの一卵性双生児のように混同されるほど似ているわけではない。しかしながら、このふたりと家族から採取した血液をヴァージニア大学で（血液型とその亜型を）検査した結果からすると、ふたりが一卵性双生児であるのはまちがいない。この時採取した血液は、スリランカから帰国する際、私自身がもち帰ったものである。

インディカとカクシャッパは、以下に紹介するように、幼少期から大幅に相異なる行動を示していた。言葉が話せるようになるとインディカは、ふたりが生まれたところから五〇キロほど離れた町で送ったという前世のことを次第に詳しく話すようになった。インディカが覚えていたのは、無邪気で勉強好きの中学生の生涯であった。インディカは、たくさんの人名その他を口にしたが、そのおかげで、本人の言っている家族らしき人たちを突き止めることができた。その家族は、インディカが前世について語った内容のほとんどが夭折《ようせつ》した息子にそのまま当てはまることを認めた。その息子は、一三歳の時に重い（明らかに感染性の）病気に罹《かか》り、二、三日後に死亡していたのである。（この少年は入院先の病院で死亡しているが、その時のカルテは、私が調査を開始した時点では既に処分されてしまっていた。）

インディカが前世の話を始めた頃、家族はカクシャッパにも前世の記憶があるかどうか尋ねている。それに対してカクシャッパは、反政府活動をしていたと答えたのである。（第5章で私は、一九七一年春、スリランカで大きな反政府暴動が勃発《ぼっぱつ》し、相当の犠牲者を出した末、軍隊に鎮圧された事実があることを述べておいた。）家族の者は、反政府活動家だったというカクシャッパの話をおもしろがり、本人をからかった。それがもとでカクシャッパは、その話をしなくなってしまった。そのため家族の者は、カクシャッパの記憶に残る前世についてそれ以上知ることはできなかったのである。家族は知らず知らずのうちにカクシャッパの発言を抑えつけるようになったが、それまでに本人は、前世の人格が突き止められるほど詳しいことを口にしてはいなかった。しかしながら、その反政府活動家が前世時代に暮らした町の名前は挙げていた。この町は、反政府活動家の拠点としてよく知られていた場所であり、活動家の一部は実際この町で犠牲になっているのである。また、この町は、インディカが前世で暮らしていたという町から二、三キロほどしか離れていなかった。

　インディカは、礼儀正しい学者肌の少年であった。この少年は威厳に満ちており、現在の家族よりも、記憶に残る前世時代の生活環境にふさわしい敬意を、周囲が当然払ってくれるものと思い込んでいた。インディカの前世の家族は、現在の家族よりも裕福だったからである。それに対してカクシャッパは、〝たくましい〟とも言えるほどであった。カクシャッパの話題は、もっぱら銃や爆弾であり、書物の話題は出なかった。事実、本人は（小学校に入学した時）学校に行きたがらなかったのである。また本人は、常に恐怖心を抱いており、見ず知らずの他人を見ると逃げ出して物陰に身を潜めた。こうした行動は、スリランカの反政府活動家たちが一九七一年にストライキを打つ構えが整うまで、警察から身を隠そうとしていた頃の様子を彷彿《ほうふつ》させる。インディカとカクシャッパは、それぞれが全く異なった前世の話をするようになるとまもなく、ただでさえ対照的な性格が次第に浮き彫りにされてきていたことに加えて、家族からますますそう見られるようになった。そのおかげで、ふたりの行動やそれにまつわる情報提供者の報告がさらに対照的なものになったのかもしれない。そのような影響もある程度はあったのかもしれないが、ふたりの対極的な行動には、それぞれの記憶に残るそれぞれの前世に由来する行動的記憶を反映したものが含まれていると考えて差支えないように思われる。[20]インディカとカクシャッパが満一〇歳になった一九八二年に私は、再度ふたりと対面したが、その時には、ふたりの人格の違いが以前ほど目立たなくなっているのに気がついた。たとえば、カクシャッパは喜んで登校するようになっており、学業成績もインディカとほぼ同じであった。とはいえ、口論になるとカクシャッパは暴力に訴える傾向を示したのに対して、インディカにはそのような傾向は見られなかった。

　双生児の問題をしめくくるに当たって、接合型双生児（いわゆるシャム双生児）の事例があれば、こうした線に沿ってさらに研究を進めることができるという事実を指摘しておきたいと思う。初期の双生児研究の専門家であるニューマンは、ふつうの（分離型）一卵性双生児よりシャム双生児の方が、人格面にはるかに大きな違いが観察される傾向があることを指摘している。十九世紀中頃に生きたチャンとエンという最初のシャム双生児は、人格面で明瞭《めいりょう》な違いを示した。チャンは怒りっぽくいつもイライラしていたのに対して、エンは温厚な性格のもち主だったのである。また、チャンは酒を（特に晩年には）飲み過ぎることが多かったが、エンは一滴も口にしなかった。また、一方が食べたがるものを、もう一方は嫌った。[21]一般の一卵性双生児と同じくシャム双生児の場合も、遺伝的には全く同一であるし、分離型の一卵性双生児よりもはるかに似通った環境に置かれているので、接合型双生児は分離型一卵性双生児よりも似ている度合が大きいのではないかと一般には考えられるであろうが、実際にはそうではないのである。チャンもエンも、前世の記憶らしきものは全く口にしなかったが、ふたりの人格の間に見られた著しい相違は、前世に由来する（たとえば飲酒をするしないといった）行動的記憶の違いから生じたものではないか、と私は推測している。

親子関係

本書の前半で私は、実例を交えながら、こうした記憶をもつ子どもたちは、しばしば前世の家族のもとへ行きたがるという事実を述べておいた。そして、前世の連れ合いと再会したいとか、前世時代の子どもたちが幸せな生活を送っているかどうか心配だ、といった思いを起こさせるさまざまな動機について示唆しておいた。ここでは、こうした子どもが前世の家族と一緒にいたがるもうひとつの動機について検討してみよう。その動機とは、前世の両親は今の親よりもよかったという、一部の子どもが抱いている強力な思い込みである。このような子どもたちは、前世の両親を、「本当の親」などと呼び、現在一緒にいる不満足な親代わりと区別していることもある。こうした態度の実例は、シャムリニー・プレマとロバータ・モーガンの事例を紹介する中で述べておいた[*22]。その子どもの両親が、物質的にも心理的にも十分な接し方をしている場合ですら、「本当の親」のところへ行きたがることがある。このような事例では、前世の両親に会いたいという気持は、ふたりに対する愛着がまだ少し残っているためか、ふたりが幸せに暮らしているかどうかを気遣っているためかのいずれかであろう。

いかなる動機にせよ、子どもが別の両親の話を繰り返し、今の両親と頻繁に比較し、先方に行かせてほしいという希《ねが》いをしきりに表明すれば、その子どもは家族から孤立することになろう。どの程度孤立するかは、子どもが「本当の親」の話をどれほど続けるかにも、先方の両親に会わせてほしいという訴えをどれほど執拗《しつよう》に繰り返すかにもよるし、どれほどあからさまな比較を行なうかにも、（何よりも）こうした不愉快な行為に両親がどこまで耐えうるかにも、当然のことながらよるのである。

生まれ変わりが起こるとすれば、親子間の軋轢《あつれき》は、前世でふたりが今とは違う関係にあったことに端を発しているのかもしれない。つまり、子どもが、前世では今の親と同年輩ないしはそれより年長だった、と主張する例があるのである。[*23] その場合たとえば、昔は母親の祖父だったと言うかもしれないし、（もっと重要なのは）現在でもそうであるかのような態度をとるかもしれない。このような態度をとることによってどのような結末になるかは、（少なくとも一部は）その祖父が孫娘に対して、また孫娘が祖父に対してどの程度優しくしたか、あるいはどの程度利己的な態度を示したかによって決まるのであろう。

子どもが、前世で一方の親と特別な関係にあったという場合には、その子どももう一方の親との関係は、ぎくしゃくしたものになることもある。第4章で紹介したマイクル・ライトの事例は、この可能性を裏づける実例である。やはり第4章（註14）で、自分は前世で今の父親ないし母親の最初の連れ合いだった、と主張する子どもの事例を三例紹介しておいた。フィンランドのタルー・イェルヴィという少女の事例では、両親が何度もばつの悪い思いをさせられていた。タルー・イェルヴィは、前世で今の母親の最初の夫だったと主張し、本人も母親も「あんな人には用はない」として父親を締め出そうとしたのである。[*24]

前世で現在の一方の親と、愛情ある血縁関係ではなく、憎しみや、場合によっては恨みの念に溢《あふ》れた間柄にあった、と主張する子どもも若干ある。[*25] これまで、この種の事例について私が詳細な報告を行なったのは、レバノンのゾウハイル・チャールの事例だけである。ゾウハイルは、本人の母親と、灌漑《かんがい》用水の権利を巡って角突き合わせていた男性の生涯を記憶していた。ふたりとも、貴重な水を盗んだとして相手を非難していたのである。ゾウハイルの事例を見ている人たちは、それぞれにある程度は分があると考えた。ゾウハイルは、言葉を話せるようになるとまもなく、自分の水を盗んだと言って母親を非難し始めた。母親は、機転をきかせながら息子の攻撃をかわしているうち、本人の根深い恨みも二、三年後には大分薄れて来た。

この事例では、ゾウハイルが不満を抱いている理由を話したところ、母親は、自分に非があるとは認めなかったものの、灌漑用水を巡って争っていた事実を思い出すことができた。しかしながら、子どもが、特に理由を言わないまま、いわれのない恨みを親にぶつける例もあるであろう。こうした事例が、生まれ変わりという考え方に好意的な文化圏で発生すれば、親は、その子どもにまちがったことをしたためというより、その子どもの恨みは前世に由来するものと考え、前向きに対処することができる。それに対して、生まれ変わりという考え方をよく知らない西洋人は、傷つけたり虐待したりした覚えがないのに、子どもがいつも不機嫌だったり優しさに欠けていたりするのを見て途方に暮れ、傷つくかもしれない。このような場合、子どもの扱い方がまちがっているのに両親がそれに気づかないということもあるかもしれないが、それ以外の事例では、現在自分たちを困らせている子どもの態度の原因となった過去の出来事のイメージ記憶は親子とももっていないとしても、前世時代の態度が現在の親子関係にそのままもち越された可能性を検討してもよいかもしれない。

一部の精神科医は、長い間、統合失調症のような重症の精神病の原因を、幼児期に両親から虐待ないし拒絶されたことに求めていた。こうした精神科医は、このように精神病患者の両親を非難しながら、同じ親が他の子どもたちを適切に育てている理由は見落としてきた。そればかりか、後年発症する子どもが、生後まもなくから、他の子どもたちとは異なる行動をしていたという、患者の母親がしばしば観察している事実も無視してきた。それは、親に抱き上げられても喜んだり寄り添ったりしないなどの行動である。児童心理学者や児童精神科医は、現在では、両親に対する子どもの反応は誕生時ないしそれ以前から違っていることを認めているが、その原因については、遺伝的要因や胎内にいる間に起こった出来事を考えるのがふつうである。両親と子どもの関係に問題がある場合には（関係が良好な場合にも）、少なくともその一部についてはその原因をもっと遡《さかのぼ》って考えてみる必要があるように思う。

一見理不尽な攻撃性

生まれ変わりという考え方が、親子関係のある面を説明する一助となるかもしれないという指摘が正しければ、それは、家族以外の対人関係の中で見られる行動をさらに理解するうえでも役立つかもしれない。いま言おうとしているのは、他人に対して、あるいは集団全体に対して一部の人間が示す一見不合理な敵意のことである。生まれ変わり型事例では、前世の人格が横変死を遂げている例が高率に見られるわけであるが、そのおかげで、たとえば前世で殺害された者が犯人に対して抱きそうな、復讐《ふくしゅう》心に満ちた態度を前世から現世にそのままもち越しているらしき事例を研究できるという絶好の機会が与えられる。現世で経験した出来事に対して人間が示す反応から推定できるように、前世の自分を殺害した相手を許す子どももいれば、許さない子どももいる。こうした子どもたちの中には、大きくなったら、前世の殺人犯に自分の手で復讐してやりたい、と明言した者も何人かいる。第4章で、ボンクチ・プロムシンが、チャムラットを殺害した犯人たちの名前を大声で呼びながら、怒りに任せて杭《くい》を叩《たた》いた様子について述べておいた。このような子どもは、成長するにつれ復讐心を弱め、続いて、前世の人格の殺害犯に対して寛大な態度を示すようになるのがふつうである。

　前世を記憶する子どもが復讐心に満ちた態度を見せる場合、恨みの念が、前世の殺人犯が属している集団全体に向けられることがある。たとえば、警察官全体、ベドウィン全体、イスラム教徒全体に対して敵対心をむき出しにすることもあるのである。*26

　職業や部族や宗教の集団に対してまで敵対心が広がるとすれば、国家全体および人種全体に対して憎悪を抱くことも十分に考えられる。こうした態度は、ひとつの世代から次の世代へと伝わるものである。つまり、子どもは親の膝《ひざ》に抱かれながら、親の仇敵《きゅうてき》を自らの敵として行くのである。おそらくは、このような口伝えにより、南部人は北部人を、フランス人はドイツ人を、マクドナルド派はキャンベル派を憎むようになるのであろう。とはいえ、国家間および氏族間の敵対心は、子どもに話して聞かせただけでは伝わらないかもしれない。もし生まれ変わりという現象が起こるとすれば、外国人に殺された者がその国の国民全体に対して抱いた憎しみは、生まれ変わった後も続くかもしれない。いま考えている過程がそのままの形で浮き彫りにされたような事例では、事実の裏づけが得られているものは知らないにしても、事実であることが確認されていないビルマの事例の中には、この考え方をある程度にせよ裏づけてくれるものがある。前世では第二次大戦中ビルマで戦死した日本兵だったという記憶をもつ（現在二〇例に及ぶ）ビルマの事例である。（第4章で紹介しておいたマ・ティン・アウン・ミョがその一例である。）このような子どもの多くは、ビルマ人の家族の中では変わって見えるが、日本人、特に日本兵に特有の行動特徴をもっていた。[*27] その中には、子どもの頃、ビルマを時おり訪れた日本人に格別の関心を示す者もあった。また、自分の面前でイギリス人やアメリカ人の話が出ると怒り出す子どもも若干あったのである。

生まれ変わりという考え方で説明できそうなその他の異常

妊娠中に見られる異常な食欲

妊娠中に特定の食物を異常にほしがったり嫌ったりする女性は少なくない。また、感情や行動がいつもと違うことに気づく女性もわずかながらある。

妊娠中の女性は、生理的にも解剖学的にも大きな変化を起こすことに加え、まわりの人間、特に夫や（もしいれば）子どもとの関係も変化する。妊娠はきわめて大きな喜びや幸福感をもたらすこともあれば、不快感や不安感、場合によっては恐怖感すら生ぜしめることもある。順調な妊娠でも大きな生化学的、心理学的変化を伴うので、妊娠中の女性に起こる異常な食欲のほとんどはそれによって説明できるかもしれない。したがって、もし前世を記憶する子どもの母親が、後に子どもが示す嗜好《しこう》と一致する食物や、一部の事例では（情報提供者の報告によれば）前世の人格が示した嗜好に沿った食物をほしがったり嫌ったりする事例の存在を私が知らなかったなら、この問題を本章で論ずることはなかったわけである。

第4章で紹介したボンクチ・プロムシンの事例では、（ボンクチの前世の人格とされる）チャムラットの母親はチャムラットを妊娠中にある種の麺《めん》を食べたがったが、それは、その後チャムラットが食べたがったばかりかボンクチの母親がボンクチを妊娠中に食べたがり、後にボンクチ自身も食べたがったのと同じ種類の麺であった。[*28]

マウン・ミント・ティン（ウ・ウィン・マウンが調査したビルマの子ども）は、アルコール依存症だった前世を記憶しており、本人自身も小さい頃、酒類をしきりにほしがった。本節のテーマに関係しているのは、マウン・ミント・ティンを妊娠して四、五ヵ月の間、酒を飲みたいという欲求が抗しがたいほど強かった、という母親自身の報告である。妊娠後期には、その欲求を抑えるのに大変な努力を要したという。

前世を記憶する子どもを出産した母親の中には、妊娠中にいつもとは違う行動を自分がとっているのに気づいた者も若干あった。ディスナ・サマラシンヘの母親もそのひとりである。母親の話によると、ディスナを妊娠している間は異常に信心深くなり、修道僧の読経《どきょう》を聞きたい気持がふだんよりも強くなったという。ディスナは、早くも幼児期に敬神の念をはっきり示したうえ、瞑想《めいそう》の修行を相当に積んだ女性として送った前世の記憶を語ったのである。オルヌマ・スア・イン・ヨンの母親は、ふだんはトランプの賭《か》け事が好きだったのに、オルヌマの妊娠中にはそれができなかった。オルヌマは、幼少期にきわめて信心深い態度を示したが、そのひとつの表われとして、母親がトランプで賭け事をすることに強く反対し、トランプ仲間の間に割って入って邪魔したため、うるさがられたこともあった。

あるトリンギットの女性は私に、四人の子どもの妊娠中に、それぞれ違う体験をしていることを話してくれた。初めの三回の妊娠では、その最中に音楽に対して強い関心を抱いたが、生まれた子どもは三人とも音楽好きだったという。四回目の妊娠の時には、音楽には特に興味が湧かず、（私が思うに、いつもより）料理を作ったり縫い物をしたりしていたところ、その後生まれた子どもは音楽好きではなく、料理や縫い物が好きだったというのである。

夫（前世を記憶する子どもの父親）が、妊娠中の変わった行動にまつわる妻の話を事実だと証言してくれた事例も一部にあったが、こうした行動上の変化に関する報告はいずれも、その子どもが生まれた後に（しかも、子どもが前世の記憶を語るようになった後に）受けたものである。もうひとつはっきりさせておかなければならないのは、妊娠中の母親が特定の食物をほしがるなど、ふだんと違う行動をしたという報告は、ごく一部の事例にしか見られないという事実である。ほとんどの事例では、そのような質問に対して母親（ないしその他の情報提供者）は、前世を記憶している子どもの妊娠中、そういうことには気づかなかったと答えている。

私に情報を提供してくれた人たちは、子どものその後の行動に関する観察事実に合わせようとして、母親が変わった食物をほしがるなど、ふだんとは違う様子を見せたことにしてしまったのかもしれない。また、その子どもが母親から、妊娠中の変化に沿った行動をするよう仕向けられていた、と考えることもできよう。さらには、母親がふだんとは違うものを食べたがっていることが超常的に胎児に伝わり、そのため同じような嗜好が生後に見られるという可能性もある。次のような事例には、そういう見方も当てはまるかもしれない。つまり、母親が妊娠中に食べたがったものを、その後に生まれた子どもも好んだが、前世の人格が好んだのがわかっている食物とは違っていた、という事例である。

妊娠中の女性に起こるある種の行動上の変化については、現在のところ予備的な調査を行なっているにすぎない。しかしながら、その結果から考えると、さらに検討を進めて行くだけの理由は十分あると思う。その場合、当然のことながら、（妊娠中の女性に見られる）ふだんとは違う食物をほしがるなどの変わった行動と、その後に生まれた子どもが示す行動との関係を（過去に遡ってではなく）時間を追って調べて行く必要がある。それと並行して、生まれ変わろうとしている人格が妊娠中の女性に、自分の嗜好や態度を一部押しつける場合があるという可能性を念頭に置いて検討を続けることもできる。

左利き

一方の手を好んで使うという現象は、かなりの部分が社会的訓練によるもののように思われる。左手を使いたがる成人は、左手を使いたがる子どもよりもはるかに少ないからである。したがって、子ども時代のしつけによって右手を使いたがるようになるのであろうし、幼少期に左利きの傾向をもっていた者の多くは、右利き用に作られた器具や道具などに次第に適応して行くのである。

左利きの中には、生まれつきのように見える者もある。乳幼児期に左利きが見つかる例があるからである。こうした事実をはじめとする証拠からすれば、左利きの発現には遺伝的要因が関係しているらしいことがわかる。ところが、同一家族内にこの特徴が頻発する場合には、遺伝的要因の影響と、左利きの親を子どもがまねた可能性とを見分けるのは難しいかもしれない。おそらく一部の事例では、遺伝的要因と親を見倣った可能性の両方を考えなければならないのであろう。

利き手は習熟した行動パターンのひとつである。たとえば、針に糸を通すのもひとつの技能であるが、一方の手を使った方がもう一方よりうまくできるというのは、基本的な技能がさらに特殊化して発達したものである。右手であれ左手であれ、いずれかが利き手になることには利点がありそうに思える。片方が利き手になるおかげで、針に糸を通すなどの行動がより巧みにできるのであろう。一方の手をあまり使わないようにしながら、双方の手を同じように使って練習した時以上にもう一方の手で習熟するようにならない限り、針に糸を通すといった高度の技術はそれほど上達しないのではなかろうか。もしそうなら、人間の利き手が前世から現世へとそのままもち越されると考えてもよかろうし、その裏づけとなる証拠もわずかながら見つかっている。共同研究者とともに私は、前世を記憶する子どもが左利きであり、前世の人格も同じく左利きだったという事例を一〇例収集し、その点に関する情報を得ているのである。

ここで述べておかなければならないのは、一〇例中二例で、前世の人格が左利きだったかどうかについての証言が食い違っていることである。また、本人の発言が事実かどうか確認されておらず、したがって前世の人格が左利きであったとする裏づけが本人の発言以外にない事例も二例あった。さらに、前世を記憶する子どもと前世の人格とが（広い意味でも狭い意味でも）同一家族に属する事例が五例あったので、この場合、遺伝的要因を外して考えることはできない。（コーリス・チョトキン・ジュニアがその一例である。）

人間はなぜ全員が右利きではないのか、という疑問は正当な疑問であるように思われる。これは、どのようにして左利きになるのか、どうして左利きが持続するのか、という疑問の変形でもある。こうした疑問に対する包括的な解答をあえて試みようという気はさらさらないが、利き手の問題から、生まれ変わりに関連していくつかの推測はできる。まず第一に、右利きの人間が右手や右腕を失うと、その状況に適応し、左利きになるのがふつうである。イギリスの大提督であったネルソン卿《きょう》がその一例である。ネルソン提督は、一七九七年にサンタクルス・デ・テネリフェの海戦で負傷し、右腕を失った。その後ネルソンは、左手で文字がある程度上手に書けるようになったのである。[*29]

ネルソン提督のように、必要に迫られて左利きになった者なら、もし生まれ変わるとすれば、左利きになりやすい素因をもって生まれて来ることであろう。（この場合、死の時点での利き手が来世でも利き手になるのではないか、という前提で考えている。）この推測を直接裏づける事例を私は一例しか知らない。母方祖母の生まれ変わりとされるマ・キン・サンディというビルマ人女性の事例である。マ・キン・サンディは左利きであったが、祖母はそうではなかった。また、家族内には他に左利きの者はいなかった。ところが、祖母は脳卒中を起こし、死亡するまでの数ヵ月間は右手に麻痺《まひ》を残していたのである。そのため、右腕が役に立たなくなったという行動的記憶が残存しており、それによりマ・キン・サンディは左手を好んで使うようになったのではないかと私は推測している。

いかにして左利きになるか、という問題に関係しているビルマの事例は他にも三例ある。その三例はいずれも、両手の数本の指が先天的な形態異常であったり、根元から完全に欠けたりしている。本人や情報提供者の証言によれば、こうした先天性欠損は、前世の人格が殺害される直前に指に受けた刀傷と一致するという。たまたま三人とも、右手の形態異常がひどいため、物を持つ場合、右手が使いにくかった。そのためこの三人は、いずれも左利きであった。三人が私に話してくれたところでは、前世では三人とも右利きだったという。（前世について三人が語った内容は、事実であることがほぼ確認されたが、利き手についてだけは確められなかった。）もし将来、この三人が死んだ後に生まれた子どもが、いずれかの生涯を記憶しているとすれば、その子どもは左利きになるのではないかと私は推測している。

母《ぼ》斑《はん》および先天性欠損

第5章で、母斑や先天性欠損をもって生まれた子どもの事例の重要性について簡単に述べておいた。また、本書ではこの問題を詳しく扱わない理由についてもそこで説明しておいた。それでいながらここに加えたのは、母斑や先天性欠損が、生まれ変わりという考え方によって解明の糸口がつかめる可能性のある生物学的問題に含まれるからである。

個々の人間の独自性

個々の人間がそれぞれ独自なものであること[*30]は、永遠に私たちの関心と推測を誘う問題である。私たちは、家族や友人に見られる身体的、人格的特徴がどこに由来するかを思い巡らすことも少なくない。娘の青い眼は祖母から、強情な質《たち》は祖父から受け継いでいる、などと簡単に言うことがある。こうした言葉が飛び交う日常会話の中では、さまざまな身体的、行動的特徴は遺伝するという前提で話が進められている。家族にはない変わった特徴が誰かにあり、それを説明したい場合には、遠い先祖や、ことによると架空の人物からそれを受け継いだことにしなければならないかもしれない。

遺伝学者によれば、（誕生の時点で）個々の人間がそれぞれ独自の特徴をもっているのは、主として、父親の精子が母親の卵子に向かって進み始めるより前、両親の配偶子（精子と卵子）が形成される際に、染色体がランダムに配置されるためだという。それ以前に両親の染色体は、両親の両親の配偶子（生殖細胞）の中に、同じようにランダムに配置された結果として形成されているとされるのである。このような考え方に従えば、人間がそれぞれ独自の特徴をもっているのは、両親の染色体の中からランダムに選び出された染色体が私たちに分与されたためであり、両親の染色体はそのまた両親の染色体の中からランダムに選び出された染色体が両親に分与されたためである、とどこまでも遡《さかのぼ》ることになってしまう。結局、私たちに見られる独自の特徴群は、誰かがトランプを切り混ぜて配った時のように、偶然に生じたものということになるのである。

　仮に、生まれ変わりという現象が起こることをうかがわせる証拠が全くなかったとしたら、人間が生まれながらにしてもっている能力は遺伝子が偶然に混ぜ合わされた結果だとする考え方で満足しなければなるまい。ところが、ある程度の証拠が存在するため、個々の人間がそれぞれ独自の特徴を備えているのは、遺伝素因ばかりではなく、（少なくとも一部は）前世の人格が経験した事柄にもよるのではないか、という可能性が出てくるのである。ここで認めなければならないのは、生まれ変わりという考え方を擁護する者は、きわめて特殊な例を説明する際にいくつかの仮定を設ける必要があることである。とはいえ、ここで若干の実例についてふれておく価値はあろう。以下に紹介する事例が私たちの期待に沿ったものではないとしても、将来の研究で探し求めるべき目標の説明には少なくともなるはずである。

　私がこれまで調査してきた子どもたちの中には、本人の家族の中では変わっているが、ひとつの前世で経験した事柄に由来するとして理解できる特徴群を示す者がある。ディスナ・サマラシンへは、異常とも言える信心深さを示したばかりか、料理や草葺《くさぶき》屋根を作るなど家庭の細々とした仕事を小さい頃から知っていた。これは、本人が自分の前世だとするババノナという人物の特徴と一致していた。同様に、ラリタ・アベヤワルデナは、幼少期に先生ごっこをして遊び、ディスナと同じく、宗教的礼拝に異常な関心を示した。前世の自分だというニランティーという女性は、学校の教師だったばかりか、信心深いことで有名な女性だったのである。[*31]

ところで、一生の中で示すさまざまな特徴が、複数の前世に由来していると言えそうな事例はないものであろうか。残念ながら、複数の前世を記憶していると主張する子どもの信頼の置ける事例はほとんどないし、複数の前世が事実と確認できる証拠はそれよりもさらに少ない。実際に思い当たるのは、いま明らかにしようとしていることの説明になりそうな二例だけである。しかしそのいずれについても、もう一方の前世は事実かどうかが確認されていないのである。とはいえ、真偽のほどは不明であるが、一方は事実と確認され、もう一方は確認されていないふたつの前世を記憶しているという、ふたりの子どもに見られる特徴群について説明することにしよう。

前にも簡単にふれたスワルンラタ・ミシュラは、一九四八年に本人が生まれる九年前の一九三九年に死亡したビヤという女性の生涯について、事実と確認された発言を多数行なっている。ビヤは、その生前、結婚して子どもを何人かもうけている。スワルンラタは、人の面倒を親身に見る傾向を強くもっているが、それは、妻であり母親であったというビヤの経験に基づくものではないか、と考えてもよさそうに私には思われる。（とはいえ、現在の母親を見倣ってそうした行動をとっていた可能性を否定するものではない。）スワルンラタはまた、現在はバングラデシュ領になっているシルヘットで送ったとする短い〝中間的〟前世についても記憶しているという。そして、その前世時代に習ったベンガルの歌や踊りが今でも歌え踊れるというのである。私は、シルヘットでの前世については確認できなかったが、ヒンディー語が使用されているインド中央部で生活してきたビヤもスワルンラタも、ベンガルの歌や踊りを習ったはずがないのは確かである。したがって、スワルンラタがシルヘットで〝中間的〟前世を送ったとすれば、その時にベンガルの歌や踊りを習ったのではないかと考えても無理はないように思われる。（ベンガル語は、シルヘットの主要言語になっている。）

パルモッド・シャルマは二通りの前世を記憶していた。ひとつは、パルマナンドという功成り名遂げた実業家の生涯であり、これについては事実であることが確認されている。パルモッドは商売感覚が小さい頃から鋭かったが、それは、この前世に由来するものなのかもしれない。パルモッドは、聖者《サニヤーシ》だったというそれより昔の（確認されていない）前世についても覚えていた。パルモッドもパルマナンドも、家族と比べると特に宗教的な傾向が強かった。パルモッドのこうした傾向は、そもそもは、聖者として送った前世に由来し、パルマナンドの生涯の中で強められたのではないかと考えても無理はないように思われる。

遺伝と環境の限界

人間の人格を解明しようとする試みの中で、現在のところ優勢を誇っている遺伝および環境的影響というふたつの説明に欠陥があることを指摘し、生まれ変わりという考え方がさまざまな現象を説明するうえで役立つと言ったところで、こうした見方をより魅力的に見せることはできない。既に述べておいたように、私は生まれ変わりという考え方を、遺伝や環境の影響に関する研究から得られた既に確立されている知識に代わるものとしてではなく、そうした知識を補足するものとして考えているのである。とはいえ、遺伝および環境の影響という考え方を熱狂的に支持する者たちは、私が生まれ変わりについて行なっているよりはるかに奇矯な（自分たちのお気に入りの考え方を擁護する）主張を行なっている。また、拙著をお読みくださった方々ばかりでなく、こうした研究者の執筆になる著書を読まれた方々の中にも、この種の原因が実際以上に証明されていると思い込んでいる方がおられるかもしれない。

遺伝素因が統合失調症の一因になっているという主張は、その裏づけとされるデータとの間に大きなギャップが存在することを示す好例である。精神疾患の遺伝の研究者は、統合失調症に遺伝的要因が関係しているという主張をきわめて説得力豊かに行なってきたため、一部の精神医学の教科書には、それが確立された事実であるかのように書かれている。その中で引用される研究は、遺伝的に近縁の人々および、その人々が置かれている環境の類似点や相違点に注目しながら、さまざまな人間や集団における統合失調症の発生率を比較したものである。統合失調症の発症には遺伝的要因が絡んでいるという考え方を裏づけるデータとして最近主に提出されているのは、一緒に育てられた(一卵性および二卵性)双生児と別々に育てられた(同じく両型の)双生児を対象とした比較研究であり、統合失調症の両親から生まれた子どもが養子に出され(したがって両親の影響をおそらくは受けずに成長し)た場合と、統合失調症ではない両親から生まれた子どもがやはり養子に出された場合とでは、精神病の発症率が異なるとしている研究である。

この種の研究には、誤った結論を招きやすそうな要因がかなり潜んでいる。まず第一に、統合失調症は、たとえば血糖値の測定によって糖尿病の診断が下せるのとは違って、これまでのところ客観的な指標が全く知られていない疾患だという点が挙げられる。複数の精神科医がひとりの患者を同時に診察した時ですら、診断が多少なりとも異なることもあるのである。精神科医が患者を直接診察できず、別の人間が記録したカルテや病歴などを見ることしかできない場合には、診断の信頼性は著しく低下するであろう。(先ほど批判した研究の多くは、このような形の診断しかできていないのである。)それに加えて、統合失調症の正確な定義が存在しないため、診断基準があいまいになり、その結果、〝境界例〟ないしは〝統合失調症帯障害〟などと診断された人たちが列をなしているような状況にあるのである。

双生児の研究では、(血液型やその亜型を調べることでかなり減らせるとはいえ)一卵性か二卵性かを決める際に誤りが発生する場合がある。精神科的な診断を下す医師たちは、対象となる双生児が一卵性か二卵性かを必ずしも知らされていない(つまり、完全に〝盲検法的〟な条件が成立している)わけではないであろう。さらには、一緒にあるいは別々に育てられたと言われる双生児の環境を判定する際にも誤りが発生する可能性がある。別個に育てられたとされる双生児が、同一家族に属する別の人物に育てられていた事実が判明したなどということも時おりあるからである。このような場合には、本当に違った環境で育てられたと言えるかどうか疑わしいほど双方が会い続けるものである。また、養子縁組を仲介する人たちには（それが家族であった時にはなおさらであるが）、生物学上の両親と同じ社会的階層の中から養父母を選ぶ傾向があるが、それもまちがいを起こすもとになる。この場合、双子が別々に育てられても、似通った環境になりやすいからである。それとは逆方向のまちがいを招く原因になりやすいものもある。養子をもらい受けたいと思っている夫婦は、自分たちの子どもがいないとか、人の子の親になりたいという気持を異常に強くもっているなど、いくつかの点で変わっているはずである。家族から養子に出された子どもは、その点だけ考えても、生物学上の両親の庇護《ひご》のもとにある子どもとはかなり違った育てられ方をされるであろう。

以上のような誤った結論を招きかねない要因に注意を向けている批判者であれば、この種の研究の難点を過小に評価することはない。このような批判者は、活字になった研究報告を見る限りそうした問題点は解消されていないことを強調する。現段階では、統合失調症の原因に遺伝的要因が関与していることを裏づける証拠は得られていない。とはいえなにも私は、こうした要因は存在しないと言おうとしているわけではない。ただ、はっきり確認された要因はないと言っているだけなのである。この方面の遺伝研究者の前途にどれほどの仕事が待ち受けているかは、最近の双生児研究の結果を見ると一番よくわかる。こうした研究の大多数は、一卵性双生児では二卵性双生児と比べて統合失調症の発病一致率が高いことを明らかにしているが、その一方で（同一の遺伝素因をもつ）一卵性双生児でも高い不一致率が見られることもわかっている。事実、統合失調症と判定された一卵性双生児の一方は、何よりも正常と判定される確率が高いのである[*32]。

血縁のある者に（肥満であれ、統合失調症であれ犯罪傾向であれ）何らかの異常の発現する比率が他よりも高いという点で全員が意見の一致を見たとしても、遺伝的要因がその解釈として最も適当だとは私は考えない。本章で一卵性双生児の類似点を検討した際に指摘しておいたように、ことによると犯罪の常習犯が、生まれ変わるとすれば双生児になり、同じような犯罪的行動を繰り返す場合もあるかもしれない。同様に、同一家族内に肥満者が数名いる場合にも、太りやすい遺伝傾向のみがその原因ではないのかもしれない。前世に端を発する過食傾向が家族全体にあることもその一因になっているかもしれないのである。統合失調症の発病に関与するとされる遺伝的要因に対してすら（それが仮に実証されたとしても）他の解釈も可能である。統合失調症と呼ばれる精神病を発症させるストレスに対する反応は、状況の変化に柔軟に対応できないことに加え、自分の苦境を他人のせいにする傾向をもっているために生ずるものなのかもしれない。こうした態度は家族内に広まるし、そのような態度をとる家族が一緒に前世を送り、一緒に生まれ変わるとすれば、その人たちが同じような、あるいは似通った行動を示し、その結果、精神病を発病することも考えられるであろう。同一家族内に頻発する疾患すべてが、必ずしも遺伝性のものではないし、必ずしも環境によるものでもないのである。次に、環境的影響という解釈について考えてみよう。

人間の人格に個人差が見られるという事実の説明として遺伝をもち出す者の主張が行き過ぎであったとすれば、幼少期の環境の影響を重視する者も同じである。少なくともこの五、六〇年ほどの間、臨床心理学者も精神科医も、生後二、三年の経験は人間の人格形成にとってきわめて重要であり、したがって後年精神疾患を発症するか否かを決定するほどの影響力をもっているとする学説を唱えてきた。事実、この考え方は、精神分析学や行動主義よりもはるかに長い歴史をもっているが、精神分析と行動主義というふたつの学説の信奉者は、人間の人格にまつわるあらゆる点を説明しようとして、他の点ではきわめて異質な自分たちの主張に加えて、幼少期の経験を重視する考え方を、ともにとらざるをえなかった。ここで興味深いのは、精神分析と行動主義双方の信奉者が（本人たちにとってすら）異例なほど独断的に、唯一の共通概念である、生後二、三年間の経験はとり返しのつかない影響力をもつという考え方を受け入れたことである。

早くも一九五〇年代には、こうした推定に立って構築された理論および実践という大殿堂に亀裂が見え始めていた。それ以上のことは何ひとつ証明されなかったからである。幼時体験がきわめて重要であるとする主張にとって特に大きな打撃となったのは、幼少期に放置《ネグレクト》ないし虐待されたものの、その後に別の環境で正常な発達を遂げた何人かの子どもに関する報告が発表されたことである。厳密な観察を行なった結果、人格に対して不可逆的損傷が及ぶとするその学説の予言は実証できなかった。幼時体験を最重要と見る者にとってもうひとつ問題なのは、一緒に育てられた一卵性双生児でも、知能をはじめ、さまざまな人格的側面に明確な違いが観察されることである。ふたりの間に見られる相違の原因になりそうな環境の影響も、これまでのところでは確認されていない。その環境的要因があまりに微妙なため現段階ではまだ見つかっていないだけなのではないか、という推定のもとに研究者たちは、現在、微環境的影響と自ら楽観的に呼ぶものを探し求めている。微環境という言葉は、人格上の（説明すべき）巨視的差異と比較するとアンバランスであるように思われる。このような発想の裏には、自分が探し求めているものは自分の守備範囲内にあるはずだという固定観念が潜んでいるのがわかる。[*33]

発達心理学者も、次第に、出生後数日ないしは数週間という早い時期にまで遡《さかのぼ》るようになり、そこに研究の焦点を絞ってきた。そして現在では、胎内体験の影響を考慮に入れ始めてすらいる。こうした研究の結果も、必ずしも期待に沿ったものではなかった。たとえば、生まれる前に、あるいは生まれてからその行動を最初に発現させるまでの間にあった体験を考えたのでは簡単に説明できないような実にさまざまな行動を、嬰児《えいじ》は、出生直後とも言えるほどの時点で示す[*34]ことが明らかになっているからである。

遺伝学や環境の影響という考え方を信奉する者は、互いに相手が唯一の敵だと思い込んでいる点で共通している。まだわかっていない点を説明する第三の道を検討する必要があることには全く気づかないまま、両者ともさまざまな主張を繰り返し、相手の主張にさまざまな欠陥を見つけ出すということを繰り返しているのである。

第10章　前世を記憶する子どもにまつわるその他の問題

本章では、私が研究してきた事例についてよく出される疑問や、当然提出されるはずの疑問について考えてみることにしよう。前章までは、一般的で重要な疑問点を検討してきた。本章で扱うさまざまな問題点の中にも、これまで考察したものと同じくらい重要なものがある。

生まれ変わりと人口の爆発的増加

現在の世界人口は〔本書が出版された一九八七年当時〕ほぼ五〇億にのぼる。人口増加が始まった十八世紀末と比較すると、世界人口はおそらく当時の三倍にはなっているであろう。このように世界の人口が急増を続けているため、他の点では生まれ変わりに関心をもっている者の中にも、これから生まれてくる人間の肉体に十分見合うだけの数の心が用意されていないのではないか、と考える者もある。

このような疑問を呈する者は、これまで存在した、さらには存在しうる肉体の数と、それに生命を吹き込む人間の心の数が完全に一致するはずだという、根拠を欠く推定を行なっているように思われる。しかしながら、この点については、他にも推定できることがある。たとえば、人間の心は必要に応じて新しく創り出されると考えることもできるし、人間の心は複数に分裂ないし複製され、それぞれが別々の肉体に宿って生まれ変わると考えることもできる。イヌイットやナイジェリアのイボ族、チベット人、アラスカやブリティッシュ・コロンビア州のハイダ族、同じくブリティッシュ・コロンビア州のギトクサン族はいずれも、心が分裂ないし複製されて複数の人間として生まれ変わると信じている。[*1] もうひとつ考えられるのは、前世で動物として生を受けていた心が、現世では人間の体に宿っているとする仮説である。ヒンドゥー教徒や仏教徒はそうした、輪廻《りんね》転生と呼ばれる信仰をもっている。この信仰については次節で論ずることにしよう。

先に述べた（人間の心と肉体が数のうえで一致するという）仮定をしないにしても、この二〇〇年ほどの間に起こった人口の爆発的増加だけを理由に、生まれ変わりという考え方を却下する必要はない。原人が人間となったとされる時代以降に地球上に生まれた人間の数を少々内輪に見積もると、八〇〇億人ほどになる。[*2] そうすると、現在地球上で生活している五〇億の人間は、それぞれが、平均して一六回ほど生まれ変わりを繰り返している計算になる。この計算は、死亡してから生まれ変わるまでの間隔が一定であることを前提にしているが、その間隔にはばらつきがある可能性もある。ごく一部の心しか生まれ変わらず、それよりもはるかに多くの心が、この世に生まれ出るのを待っているか、逆に生まれ出るのを避けようとしている時代もあったかもしれないのである。

これまで調査された事例が人口全体の代表例と考えられるとすれば、生まれ変わる比率はそれほど高くはなりえないと思われる。第5章で説明しておいたように、死んでから生まれ変わったとされるまでの期間にはかなりばらつきがあるが、六一六例の中央値はわずか一五ヵ月にすぎなかった。しかしながら、私たちがこれまで調査してきた事例は、いくつかの理由から、代表例とは言えないかもしれない。その理由のひとつは、既に述べておいたように横変死が高率に見られることである。もうひとつの理由は、死亡してから生まれ変わったとされるまでの間隔が短いことが、前世の記憶を蘇《よみがえ》らせる一因になっているのかもしれないことである。私たちがこれまで行なった分析によれば、死んでから生まれ変わったとされるまでの間隔の長さと、その子どもの記憶量との間には相関が全くないことがわかっている。とはいえ、私たちが日常の中で経験するのと同じように、肉体のない世界でも時間の経過に従って記憶が薄れるとすれば、現在私たちが知っている事例での最大値（若干の例外はあるが、およそ二五年）よりもその間隔が長かった場合には、事実と確認できる記憶をもっている事例はほとんど見つからないことになろう。仮に生まれ変わるまでの時間がそれより長くかかるとすれば、記憶は相当に薄れるであろうし、私たちが行なっている疫学的研究によってこうした生まれ変わりを確認することはできないであろう。そうすると、現存する大半の心にとっては、死んでから生まれ変わるまでの間隔は、これまで私たちの注目を引いてきた事例よりも（おそらくははるかに）長い可能性が残る。つまり、肉体をもたない心の多くが生まれ変わる時を待っているのかもしれず、そのためにこそ、過去二〇〇〇年に見られたよりもはるかに大きな人口増加が起こっているのかもしれないということである。

　わずか二〇〇〇例からデータを得ているにすぎないので、跡形もなく消えてしまった何十億にものぼる人々についてまで本節で推論するのは面映《おもはゆ》い。ここでこのようにひと言弁解しておきたいのは、私と話す時に非常に多くの方が人口増加の問題をもち出されたからである。私がその点にある程度の注意を払ってきたことを、ここで明らかにしておくべきだと考えたわけである。

動物が生まれ変わる証拠はあるか

ヒンドゥー教徒や仏教徒は、動物も生まれ変わることを、さらには、過去の不行跡がそれに値する場合には人間が畜生として生まれ変わることもあると信じている。そして、動物に生まれ変わることによりその罪が償われた後には、また人間として生まれ変わることもあるという。このような考え方は、爆発的な人口増加から生ずる問題の中でまだ残されているものをすべて片づけてくれるように見えるかもしれない。おそらく人間の体として生まれ変わる用意ができているか、それを目指して着々と準備を整えている動物の心が、数多く存在することになるからである。とはいえ、仏教徒やヒンドゥー教徒は、動物の殺生はよくないことであり、そのようなことをすれば畜生に生まれ変わる罰を科せられる可能性があると信じているため、若干の問題は残るであろう。しかし、その信仰が正しいとすれば、人間と動物は数のうえでバランスが保たれていると考えてよいかもしれない。

第8章で私は、生まれ変わり信仰の存在と生まれ変わり型事例の発生との間には相互関係らしきものがあることについて述べておいた。つまり、生まれ変わり信仰があると生まれ変わり型事例が発生しやすく、そうした事例があると生まれ変わり信仰が強まる、という関係である。しかしながら、既に指摘しておいたように、生まれ変わり信仰だけでは、ある地域でこうした事例が特に多く見られることの説明にはならないので、前世の記憶をはじめとする超常的プロセスを強化してくれそうな他の要因も少々推定しておいた。本節で扱っている問題も、信仰のみでは事例発生の条件として不十分であることを裏づける証拠となる。信仰が唯一の条件であったとすれば、南アジアでは人間の場合と同じくらい動物の生まれ変わりの話があってもよいはずだからである。ところが実際には、動物に生まれ変わったという主張は、南アジアでもきわめて稀《まれ》であり、それ以外では皆無に近いのである。最初、私はこうした事例に対して偏見を抱いていたのであるが、それを乗り越えた後、そのような話を私にしてくれる人たちの証言をすべて忠実に記録したにもかかわらず、動物に生まれ変わったとする主張は総計で三〇例に満たなかった。そのうちの大半は、かつて動物に生まれ変わったことがあるという人たちの話であった。このような動物の時代が、人間としての前世と現世の間の〝中間的〟前世になっている例もあった。その一例として、第8章の註13に、マ・タン・タン・アエの事例を要約して紹介しておいた。[*3] その時点で生きている動物が、ある故人の生まれ変わりとされた例も若干ある。（その場合、たいていは、夢がその唯一の根拠になっている。）

　動物としてこの世を生きたという事例には、当然のことながら、人間の事例に見られるような証拠はほとんどないし、その大半には、自分は前世が動物だったとする（裏づけを欠いた）本人の主張を除けば、証拠が全くないのである。

全ての人間が前世の記憶をもっているわけではないのはなぜか

　本節の見出しには、こうした事例をある程度知っている人たちがよくとり上げる疑問をそのまま用いた。もう一度繰り返す必要はないと思うが、私たちはその疑問に答えられる状況にはない。記憶に残るような前世が全ての人間にあることを裏づける証拠は、これまでのところ存在しないのである。とはいえ、本節のテーマを考えるにあたっては、もしひとりの人間が生まれ変わるとすれば、大半の人間には前世の記憶が全くないにせよ、全ての人間が実際に生まれ変わるか、もしくはそうなる可能性があると推定してもよいであろう。それから、この疑問を逆転して、信憑性《しんぴょうせい》がありそうな記憶の発現を促進ないし抑制するように思われる条件についてわかっていることは何か、と問うことができる。そうすると、大半の子どもにはないのに、なぜ一部の子どもにだけ前世の記憶があるのかを明らかにするためのヒントになりそうな、共通した特徴を見つけ出すことができるのである。できるだけ繰り返しを避けながら、これまでの章から関連する情報や説明をまとめ、新しい解釈をいくつか紹介する。では、次のようなテーマについて順次検討することにしよう。どのような前世が一番記憶に残りやすいのか。生まれ変わりが本当に起こるとすると、どのようなタイプの人間が前世の記憶を最も残しやすいのか。記憶の出現を促進ないし抑制するように思われる条件には他にどのようなものがあるのか。

最も記憶に残りやすい前世

既に（第7章で）論じておいたように、このような子どもの前世の人格は、高率に非業の死を遂げている。六ヵ所の文化圏の七二五例中、前世の人格が非業の死を遂げている事例が六一パーセントにものぼることは、既に述べておいた通りである。また、非業の死が高率に見られるという事実は、前世の記憶が発現（および固定）するための真の要因の反映であり、事例を報告する際に発生した人為的産物ではないと私が考える理由についても説明しておいた。[*4]

非業の死に伴う状況は、一般に、残酷なことそのものと同じくらい注目に値する。非業の死は、被害者が頭部や頸部《けいぶ》の負傷により即意識を失う場合を除けば、極度の身体的苦痛を伴うのがふつうであるし、ほとんどが突然、予期しない時に訪れるものである。[*5] 戦争中、兵士たちは非業の死を遂げるが、戦死するかもしれないとは思っている。それに対して、殺人事件や暴動や自動車事故などに巻き込まれて死亡する者は、全く予測していない時に死が突然に訪れる。また、若者の方が年輩の者よりも非業の死を遂げる確率が高いという事実も念頭に置く必要がある。非業の死は、若年層で起こるのがふつうなのである。したがって、横変死を遂げた後、生まれ変わってその記憶を残していると思《おぼ》しき者にその出来事が与えた影響を考える場合、残酷性ばかりでなく、それに伴う身体的苦痛や、死が予期しない形で早い時期に起こりすぎたなどの要素も、すべて考慮に入れる必要がある。

こうした事例には非業の死が際立って多く見られるが、生まれ変わり型事例が発現するためには、殺人事件（ないしはそれ以外の横変死）以上のものが必要である。それは、事例報告が私の考えるよりもはるかに過小にしか私たちの耳に届いていないのでない限り、事例の発生数は、こうした事例が見つかる文化圏での横変死の発生数よりもはるかに小さいからである。つまり、横変死を遂げる者のうちでも、その後に生まれ変わった子どもが前世を記憶している例はごくわずかしかないということである。非業の死によって終止符が打たれる生涯を、それ以外のものよりもいわば記憶に残りやすくさせる要因は何か、という問題をここでもう一度検討することにするが、その前に、自然死を遂げた前世の人格の四〇パーセントほどが、いくつかの下位群に分けられることを指摘しておくことにしたい。

自然死を遂げた前世の人格を検討するに当たって、これをいくつかの群に分けることができる。各群が何例ずつになるかといった数量的分析はまだ行なっていないが、全体としては、自然死を遂げた前世の人格の大半が含まれるのではないかと思う。

自然死を遂げた故人のうちの一群は、かなり突然、つまり、前日には明らかに健康であったか近いうちに死ぬとは思われていなかったにもかかわらず死亡した者たちである。インドのスニル・ドゥット・サクセナは、六〇代前半で急死した男性の生涯を記憶していた。死亡当日の朝は、健康そうに見えたし、いつも通り仕事に出かけていた。昼近くに具合が悪くなり、その日の夕方には、おそらく心臓発作で死亡したのである[*6]。

自然死を遂げた者のうち、もうひとつのグループは、若くして死亡した者からなっている。この群は、一二歳以前に死亡した子どもたちである。ここで注意しなければならないことがある。生まれ変わり型事例が最も頻発するアジアの国々では、西洋諸国と比べると子どもの死亡率が高いことである。それでも、前世の人格全体の中で占める子どもの数は、私が調査を行なってきた国々で死亡する子どもの数と比べて（成人の場合よりも）多すぎるように思う。[*7]

もうひとつは、私が〝未完成の仕事〟と呼んでいる、志半ばで斃《たお》れた人々の一群である。[*8] その好例としては、まだ世話が必要な乳幼児を残して死んだ母親の事例が挙げられる。[*9] この群には、負債を抱えたまま（あるいは金銭を人に貸したまま）死んで行った者も入る。

また、前世の人格が〝継続中の仕事〟に従事していた一群も、ここに含めることができる。その典型例としては、自分の仕事やそれにより成した財を蓄え、使うことに余念がなかった裕福な実業家が挙げられよう。それ以上の財産を築こうとする意欲が既にない隠退した人々は、この群には入らないが、第一線で活躍していた実業家はここに入る。[*10]

自然死により、また横変死により突然に死亡した者、夭折《ようせつ》した者、志半ばにして斃れた者、継続中の仕事をもっていた者の以上五群を考えると、いずれも不完全な形で一生が終わっているのがわかる。死の時点では誰もが、さまざまな理由から、もっと長生きできると当然思っていたことであろうし、したがって、生まれ変わりたいという願望が強く湧き起こったことであろう。その結果、いわば人生を十分堪能《たんのう》して自然に死を迎えた者よりも早く生まれ変わることになったのかもしれない。[*11]

個々の事例を検討する場合、先述の要因が同時にふたつ以上見られることも少なくない。たとえば、非業の死を遂げた前世の人格の中には、夭折している者もあるし、横変死であれ自然死であれ、業半ばにして死亡した者の中には、突然死を遂げている例もあるのである。[*12]

生まれ変わりという現象があるとすれば、前世の記憶を最も残しやすいのはどのようなタイプの者か

前節では、子どもたちが記憶していることの多い、特に死の時点でふつうとは違う状況にあった前世にはどういうものがあるかについて説明しておいた。しかしながら、そこで述べたような前世を送って死んで行った人たちは、私たちが収集した事例よりも一般人口中にははるかに多いという事実を見てきた。したがって、前世の記憶に影響を及ぼす要因を他にも探し求めなければならないことになる。

死んだ後に生まれ変わるとすれば、どのような人たちが前世を一番思い出しやすいか、という質問が出るかもしれないが、残念ながらそれに答えることはできない。

前世を思い出しやすい者のうち一番はっきりしているのは、きわめて記憶力のよい者ということであろう。しかしながら、最も明白な問題というものは最も見過ごされやすいものであり、この点に私が着目したのもごく最近のことにすぎない。ここでは、それに関連する事例として、たまたま同時に調査することになったレバノンの二例を挙げることができる。一例は、スザンネ・ガーネムの事例である。この事例については、（前世での）関係者の名前を数多く思い出すことができた例として第7章で紹介しておいた。スザンネは、それぞれの人物について具体的な事柄を述べたが、その結果、前世について思い出した項目が最も多い部類に入っている。スザンネの前世の人格であるサアダの記憶力について尋ねたところ、身内の間では、特に人名の記憶力がきわめてよいとされていたことがわかった。サイド・ザールという子どもは、父親

によれば有名なドゥルーズ族の族長の生涯について話している。その族長の息子のひとりは、本例を知り、自らある程度の調査を行なった後、サイド・ザールと家族のもとへ私を案内してくれた。その族長は、有名な人物であり、非常に尊敬されていた。ドゥルーズ族の人たちはこの族長についていろいろ知っていたので、その族長が自分の家族として生まれ変わってきたと言えば、その家族の名声は高まることであろう。このふたつの理由から、族長の息子は、本例に対してきわめて慎重な態度をとり、直接の証拠はなかったが、その子どもの父親が本人にさまざまなことを教えたのではないかという疑いを払拭《ふっしょく》することはできなかった。本例を検討する中で私は、本人の発言項目が少ないことを述べたが、事実、本人は前世のことをきわめてわずかしか覚えていないように見えた。その点について族長の息子は、「それこそ、この例に信憑性があることを裏づける特徴かもしれませんよ。父は記憶力がものすごく悪かったですから」と答えたのである。この事例に信憑性があり、生まれ変わりという説明が最も妥当だと仮定すれば、その族長の記憶力がもっと悪かったとしたら、今回生まれ変わった時には何も覚えていなかったのではないか、と言えるかもしれない。

　とはいえ、現世で記憶力が優れているだけでは前世を思い出すための条件を十分に満たすわけではない。そうでなければ、優れた記憶力のもち主の中に前世を記憶している者がいなければならないことになるが、そういう実例が存在する徴候らしきものは全く見当たらないのである。[*13] そこで、前世の記憶を残しやすくさせる心理的特性をまた他に考えてみることにしよう。そうすると、精神的成長を遂げた時の安らかな状態に伴う清澄な心理状態がその要因になるのではないかという可能性が考えられる。

第3章で述べておいたように、仏教やヒンドゥー教には、瞑想《めいそう》を繰り返し徳を積むことで霊性を高めれば、心が浄化され、記憶力が向上するという信仰が昔からある。チベットのトゥルクは、霊性の高いラマ僧であった前世を記憶していると言われる。こうしたラマ僧は、たいてい、正規の修道生活を送っており、ほとんどの者が自然死を遂げている。このような生涯の中で起こった出来事は記憶に残りやすいものではなかったが、こうした生活を送った者は非凡であり、霊的修行を通じて身につけた清澄な心を、次に生まれ変わってからもそのまま保持し続けたのではないか、という者もあるかもしれない。

第5章で述べたように、チベットのラマ僧の事例については直接的な経験がほとんどないので、個々のトゥルクにまつわる主張を、私自身が直接に得た知識をもとに支持することはできない。ただし、きわめて敬虔《けいけん》かつ高潔であった人物の生涯を記憶している他の国の子どもたちの事例であれば、何例か調査したことがある。その中には、瞑想を行なっていた者もあれば、行なったことのない者もある。そして、全員が自然死を遂げているのである。こうした子どもたち自身も、幼少期から敬虔な態度や高潔な姿勢を示すことが多く、そのことから、前世の人格がもっていた霊性のイメージ記憶はもちろん、行動的記憶も保持していることがうかがわれる。先に他の脈絡の中で紹介しておいたディスナ・サマラシンへとラタナ・ウォンソムバトも、この小群に属する格好の実例である。[*14]

前世が敬虔な人格であった事例では、死んでから生まれ変わるまでの間隔が、平均すると、非業の死を遂げた事例や、先述のような早い時期に生まれ変わりやすい条件で自然死を遂げた事例と同様に短かった。したがって、敬虔な態度で前世を送った人物の生涯は、現在のところまだはっきりした理由はわからないが、死亡してから生まれ変わるまでの間隔が短いため、記憶に残りやすかったということなのかもしれない。

前世記憶の発現を容易ないしは困難にさせるように思われる他の条件

先に力説しておいたが、誰かが耳を傾けてくれさえすれば語り伝えたい記憶をもっている子どもに対して、両親は、そうした気持を強めたり弱めたりする力をもっている場合がある。また、生まれ変わり信仰自体が前世から現世へともち越される可能性についても既に述べておいた。生まれ変わり信仰をもって生まれた子どもにとっては、自分の中に前世の記憶があればそれが意味をもってくるであろうが、そうした信仰をもたずに生まれてきた子どもには意味はないであろう。

記憶を刺激ないし抑制する心理的ショックを特定できる事例もある。生まれ変わった男性が、現在、自分の体が女の子になっていることに気づき始めた時、本人にどのような反応が起こるかについては既に（第8章註15で）述べておいた。また、そのことに気づいてショックを受けた結果、それ以外の記憶も呼び醒《さま》される場合があるが、そのことから、前世が女性だったという男児と比べ、前世が男性だったという女児の方が多い理由が説明できるかもしれないという点も指摘しておいた。

インドの事例に見られる、数の上で偏りのあるもうひとつの現象もショックで説明できるかもしれない。インドには、現在の家族とは明らかに異なった社会経済的状況の中で送った前世を思い出す子どもがたくさんいる。（私たちはこうした事例を、それぞれ昇格例、降格例と呼んでいる。）このような子どもたちの三分の二は、物質的にはより恵まれていた前世を記憶しており、現在よりも恵まれなかった前世を記憶している者は三分の一にすぎない。[*15] インドの事情もほとんど知らず、この種の事例を月並みな心理学的理論で何とか片づけたいと考えている批判者は、恵まれないインドの子どもたちが、自分がみじめな状況に置かれていることを自ら慰めようとして、現在よりも恵まれた前世を送ったと空想しているのではないか、というかもしれない。しかしながら、いくつかの事実から、この解釈は当たっておらず、したがって、正しい解釈が別にあるらしいことがわかる。まず第一に、昇格例は、降格例より少ないにせよ実際に存在し、しかも実数としてはかなりの数にのぼるという事実が挙げられる。その中には、信憑性《しんぴょうせい》のある降格例と同程度の信憑性をもつものも見られるので、降格例と同じように説明が必要なのである。第二に、インドでは、現在より恵まれた前世を送ったことを子どもが記憶していても何の得にもならないし、それどころか、降格に値するような罪を（前世で）犯していると判断されてしまうかもしれないのである。第三に、昔は裕福だったという空想から何らかの慰めが得られるとしても、大半の降格例では、そのことを得意気に話したり、家族の食事を摂《と》らなかったり、貧しいことに不平を唱えたりなど、自分を家族から遊離させるような行動をとるため面倒な事態が生じ、そのおかげでかえってマイナス面が多くなってしまうのである。

第四に、仮にそのような動機があったとしても、こうした子どもたちの一部が家族の知らない人物についてどうして正確に知るようになったのかという問題の解決にはならないことである。降格例全体を願望充足的な空想によるものとして説明できないとすると、他の可能性を検討する余地が生まれる。思うに、現在よりも物質的に恵まれた状況で送った前世の記憶がわずかながらぼんやり浮かび上がると、そのショックで他の記憶も、その子どもの意識に上ってくるのではなかろうか。

軽いショックによって記憶が刺激されて出てくることがあるとすれば、もっと強いショックを受けた場合には、記憶の発現が妨げられる可能性がある。今はビルマ人に生まれている少年が、前世は日本人や欧米人だったと思うようになると、それが、記憶の発現を抑制するショックになるかもしれない。また、インドの子どもが、イギリスで前世を送ったと思ったり、トルコの子どもが、レバノンやリビアに住んでいたと思ったりした場合にもこうしたショックは起こるかもしれない。これまで、自分の母国以外の国で送った前世を思い出した子どもで、その発言の事実性が確認できるほど詳しい内容を語った者をひとりも知らない。外国で前世を送ったという子どもたちは、全体を漠然としか記憶しておらず、死亡した時の状況については具体的に覚えているものの、それ以上のことはわからないようなのである。

ここで重要な点は、国境を越えるということではなく、広く文化と言い習わされる生活環境が変わるということなのかもしれない。とはいえ、同一の政治区域内に内在する文化の違いは、ふたつの国の隣接地帯に見られる文化の違いよりも大きいこともあろう。たとえば、トルコの都市アダナやハタイに住む（まだほとんどがアラビア語を話す）アレヴィス族は、イスタンブールに住んでいるトルコ人よりも、シリアのアレヴィス族（やその他のアラブ人）との共通点を数多くもっている。こうした観点からすれば、イスタンブールで送った前世を記憶していたトルコ中南部の五人の子どもの中に、その発言が確認された者がひとりもいないのは驚くに当たらないことになる。

文化人類学者は、カルチャー・ショックと呼ばれる体験を多少なりとも承知している。これは、ある国から、風俗習慣の全く異なった国へ移住した者によく起こるストレス体験を指して用いられる言葉である。もし生まれ変わりという現象が実在するとすれば、ある国から別の国の生活へと環境が変わったためにカルチャー・ショックを起こす者もあるかもしれない。

以上行なった考察である程度明らかになったと思うが、子どもが前世の記憶を意識に昇らせ表明することには、数個ないしはそれ以上の要因が関係しているのである。しかしながら、前世の記憶が発現するための一定の公式のようなものがあるとすれば、それは次のような特徴をもっていると言える。つまり、前世を記憶する子どもの前世は、生まれ変わり信仰の強い国に住んでいた中流階級の男性であり、非業の死を遂げたか、さもなくば急死した人物ということである。そのような生涯を記憶している子どもは男児の場合もあれば女児の場合もあるが、前世の人格と同じ国や同じ文化圏に生まれており、その両親は貧しいが、叱りつけることなく子どもの言葉に耳を傾けることができるほど、自国の生まれ変わり信仰に染まっているはずである。

生まれ変わりは普遍的な体験か

　この問題については既にふれており、その中で弁解がましいことを申しあげておいた。これに対して私は、現段階はもちろん、近い将来にも全く答えることができないと考えている。二〇〇〇例のデータを一般化することで、数十億にものぼる人間について論じようというつもりはない。二〇〇〇例と言っても、全例で生まれ変わりが起こっていることを裏づける証拠が十分得られているわけではないという事実を、いつも念頭に置く必要がある。この点について私が最も強調したいのは、もし生まれ変わりという現象が実在するとすれば、全ての人間が生まれ変わるのかもしれないが、それは私たちには、わかりようがないということである。

　とはいえ、こうした事例から一般化された事柄の中には、まちがいが明らかなものがある。たとえば私は、横変死を遂げた者以外は生まれ変わらない、という話を聞いたことがあるが、これはまちがいである。自然死を遂げた者の中にも、私がこれまで調査した、非業の死を遂げているどの事例と比べても遜色《そんしょく》ないほど生まれ変わりの存在を裏づける証拠を示す例が、少ないながら見られるからである。

前世の記憶は役立つかそれとも邪魔になるか

　この問題を考えるには、「誰にとって」、さらには「人生のどの段階で役立ったり邪魔になったりするのか」という問いを発する必要がある。

前世を記憶している子どもの中には、本当の家族と思っている人たちから引き離されたと感じ、ひどい苦しみを味わっている者が多い。このような子どもたちは、相手からしっぺ返しを食らうような、人を傷つける言葉を吐くために、家族の中で孤立してしまう場合がある。そうすると、こうした子どもは本当にひとりぼっちになる可能性がある。〝本当の〟（前世の）家族からは物理的に引き離され、自分の（現在の）家族からは社会的に引き離されてしまうからである。このような子どもの両親はあまり恵まれた状況にはない。両親が望んでいた子どもは、自分たちからそっぽを向き、あなたがたは本当の両親ではなく、尊敬するに値しない代理にすぎない、と公言するからである。もし、このような子どもたちの大半が二歳から五歳の間に二組の両親のはざまで浮遊しているという点だけを考えるなら、前世を記憶していることはいずれの関係者に対しても利益をもたらすものではない。それを別にしても、記憶そのものは、楽しいものというよりは、不快な出来事にまつわるものであることが多い。殺人をはじめとする犯罪的行為が記憶の中心を占め、愛情や友情を伴う場面の記憶も一部にはあるかもしれないが、それが中心を占めることはないのである。

成長すると、前世を記憶していることによる利点の方が、マイナス面よりも大きくなる場合もある。子どもたちの中には、その記憶を現在の行ないを改めるための手段として用いる者がある。不合格になった試験の問題を研究して、次の試験に備えるのと似ているかもしれない。また、何らかの前世を記憶している者は、その内容がどうであれ、その経験から、個人の運命を遠い目で見て初めて可能になるような、世俗の不幸から超越した心境になれるかもしれない。[*16]
このような者の中には、死に対する恐怖心がなく、年上の者に向かって、死を恐れる必要のないことを説いて安心させようとする者もある。たとえば、マルタ・ロレンツの家に、肉親を亡くしてまもない人物が来て、「死人は蘇《よみがえ》りませんものね」と悲しそうに言ったところ、それに対してマルタは、「そんなこと言わないでよ。私も死んだけど、見てよ、また生き返ってるでしょ」と答えている。また、マ・タン・タン・アエも、父親が死の床にあった時、「よかった。これで父さんも楽になる。悲しい理由なんてないよ。死なんて全然不思議なことじゃないんだから。私たちだってみんな死ななきゃいけないんだ」と言ったのである。

女児よりも男児に前世を記憶している者が多いのはなぜか

第7章で述べておいたように、これまで分析した限りでは、（ほとんど）すべての文化圏で、前世の記憶をもつ者は男の子の方が女の子よりもはるかに多い。（ほぼ三対二の比率になっている。）このような性差が見られる理由はいくつかあると思う。

前世で横変死を遂げた事例と自然死を遂げた事例を比較したところ、自然死群よりも横変死群の方が男児の比率がはるかに高い（二対一以上）ことがわかった。これはおそらく、男性では、殺し合いその他により横変死を遂げる傾向が女性よりはるかに高いことによるのであろう。とはいえ、自然死群でも、インドやトルコ、アラスカ（トリンギット族）では男児の比率がかなり高い。タイ、スリランカ、レバノンの自然死群では、男女の比率はほとんど同じであることがわかっている。自然死群で女性が男性を数のうえで上回っているのはビルマだけであった。

男児の比率が高いのは、ひとつには、女子の事例を両親が抑えつけて包み隠し、その結果、私たちが調査できる標本ではその比率が低くなるためなのかもしれない。アジアの多くの国では、女の子は一般に、少なくとも結婚するまでは目立たないようにしていることが求められるため、前世の記憶をもっているなどという話が世間に知れ渡ると、満足な結婚をする機会が失われるのではないかと考えられることがある。このような理由から抑えつけられた事例を一例知っている私は、同様の事例が他にもあると見ている。

イボ族では男性の事例が女性のものよりもはるかに多いが、それは、イボ族の社会では男性が優位を占めていることの表われであると思う。イボ族は、男子が前世に誰だったのかを、女子の場合よりはるかに熱心に知りたがるのである。

先に、(第8章註15で)述べておいたが、男性の生涯には女性の場合よりも記憶に残りやすい出来事が多いであろうし、その分だけ男子の事例が多いのかもしれない。

しかしながら、以上の解釈だけでは(たとえそれらを組み合わせて考えたとしても)、女性よりも男性の事例が多いことが適切に説明できるとは思われない。この点については、生まれ変わり型事例の多くの特徴と同様、将来の検討が待たれるところである。

前世の記憶をもつ子どもたちは、なぜ複数の前世を記憶していないのか

この疑問に答えるには、まず、ふたつ以上の前世を記憶しているという子どもが少数ながら存在するという事実を述べておく必要がある。とはいえ、記憶に残されている第二の前世は、具体的な点がほとんど出て来ない中間的前世が大半であり、したがって事実かどうかは確認されていないのである[17]。（こうした事例を第8章で四例紹介しておいた。）これまで私は、両方とも事実と確認できるほど詳細にふたつの前世を記憶していた子どもをひとりしか見つけ出していない。前世の記憶が、ふつうの記憶と同じく時間の経過とともに薄れ行くものであれば、当然の結果であろう[18]。

私たちの集めた四例の事例を見ると、古い前世の記憶は、次に生まれ変わるまでの間に消失するらしいことがわかる。その四例では、それぞれの子どもは（家族内の情報提供者によれば）前世の記憶をもっていた人物の生涯を記憶していたが、その子ども自身は古い方の前世を全く覚えていなかったのである[19]。

記憶がふつうの方法では意識に上らない段階になっても、必ずしも消えてしまっているわけではない。ふだんと異なる状況のもとでは、再び意識に上ることもあるからである。サトワント・パスリチャとともに調査したインドの事例を見るとそのことがよくわかる。ラム・プラカーシュというその子どもについては、第8章（註9）で、死んでから生まれ変わるまでの間隔が決まっているというジャイナ教の教義について論ずる中でふれておいた。ラム・プラカーシュは、自分が生まれる少し前に死亡したシェヴ・ベハリ・ジャイナという男性の生涯について具体的に思い出し、それが事実と一致することが確認されている。ところが、私たちの集めた大半の事例とは異なり、ラム・プラカーシュは、シェヴ・ベハリ・ジャイナとして送った前世以前にも二回の前世を生きたことを覚えていると主張したのである。(ラム・プラカーシュは、その発言に該当する人物が見つかるほど詳しいことは、いずれの前世についても語らなかった。また、三回のうち最も古い前世は一〇〇年ほど前のものらしく、そうなると確認はきわめて難しくなるであろう。)シェヴ・ベハリ・ジャイナの家族から聞いたところでは、シェヴ・ベハリ・ジャイナとして生まれる以前に送ったとラム・プラカーシュが主張するふたつの前世について、シェヴ・ベハリ・ジャイナが語っているのを一度も耳にしたことがないというが、この点は大変興味深い。残念ながら私は、これをどう考えたらよいか教えてくれそうな例は他に一例も知らない。ひとつ考えられるのは、ラム・プラカーシュが、実際に記憶している、事実と確認された前世を潤色するために、ふたつの前世を空想して加えたのではないかという可能性である。とはいえ、ラム・プラカーシュには、そのようなことをする明確な動機はないようなのである。それどころか本人は、(おそらく)事実とは確認できないふたつの前世を覚えていると言ったことで、自分の家族やシェヴ・ベハリ・ジャイナの家族の信頼を大幅に低下させてしまったかもしれないのである。おそらくシェヴ・ベハリ・ジャイナは、幼少期にはこのふたつの前世を覚えていたのであろうが、前世を記憶する一般の子どもたちと同じく、成長した段階で忘れてしまったのであろう。そう考えれば、本人の妻や子どもたちがその話を聞いていないという事実が説明できよう。また、たとえシェヴ・ベハリ・ジャイナが記憶していなかったとしても、ラム・プラカーシュの家族には、三回の前世を本人に思い出しやすくさせるような特殊な条件が揃っていたのかもしれない。

自殺で終わった前世を記憶している子どもたち

二〇〇〇名ほどの子どものうち、自らの責任で死亡した人物の生涯を記憶していたのは二三名であった。そのうちの四名は、銃が暴発したために死亡していた。(そのうちのふたりは、弾が込めてある銃の銃身を持った瞬間に、残るふたりは、弾を込めたまま銃を掃除している最中に銃が暴発して死亡している。) また、警官や兵隊に追われている最中に自殺した者もふたりあった。残る一七名は、破産や失恋などにより生じた状況が死よりもつらいと思った時に自らの生命を絶っていた[*20]。

生まれ変わりという考え方がこうした事例にも当てはまるとすると、自殺した人間は何百年もの間、場合によっては永久に地獄に堕《お》ちるとする、一部の宗教で説かれている信仰がまちがっていることが立証されることになる。また、こうした事例は、自殺しても苦しみは終わらず、苦しみの生ずる場所が変わるにすぎないことを自殺願望をもつ者に気づかせてくれる。

自殺者群の中には、銃器や毒薬など自殺の手段として用いたものに対する恐怖症を示す者も一部にある。自殺の記憶は、自殺に向かいやすい性向を必ずしも断たなかった。たとえば、そのうちの三人は、子ども時代に欲求不満を起こした時、死んでやると言って両親を脅したことがあるという。また、中年になってから実際に自殺してしまった者もひとりいるし、耐え切れないと思う状況になったらたぶん自殺すると思う、と私に打ち明けてくれた者もひとりある。一方、事実かどうか確認されていない事例ではあるが、前世で自殺した記憶があるおかげで、自殺を思いとどまった、と話してくれた女性もある。

生まれ変わりの可能性を信ずることに対する障害

第2章で生まれ変わり信仰について述べておいたが、生まれ変わりを信じないことについては、特に一章を設けて論じるほどのことはないにしても、少なくとも一節を充てるだけの価値はある。本節では、読者の方々を生まれ変わりの信者に転向させようという意図は毛頭ないことをここに申しあげておく。私はただ、前世を記憶する子どもたちの事例を偏りのない態度で評価するのを妨げるように見える障害について、読者の方々の注意を喚起したいだけなのである。本節で検討しようと思う障害は以下の通りである。つまり、西洋では生まれ変わりという考え方になじみがないこと、人間の心（および記憶）は脳の中にあり、それ以外のところに存在する可能性はないとする思い込みや、死後の生命がどのようなものか人間には想像もつかないはずだとする思い込みがあること、生まれ変わりがあるとすれば、人間には自らの運命の責任は自らにあるらしいことになるが、そうした責任を受け入れたくない、とする者が多いらしいこと、といった点である。

生まれ変わりという考え方になじみがないこと

新概念恐怖症《ネオ・イデオ・フォビア》（〝新しい考え方に対する恐怖症〟という意味の私の新造語）は、世界中の人間を悩ませている。「人間にとって最大の苦しみのひとつは、新しい考え方に対する苦痛である」[21]。私たちには、なじみのないものを避け、その証拠も検討しないうちに、それを悪いものと決めてかかる傾向がある。「ある現象を心から信ずるようになるには、その現象になじまなければならない」[22]。

ここで、いかなる形であれ人間が死後にも生存を続けるという考え方は、西洋の教育を受けた大半の人間には（具体的な言葉で表現された場合には）なじまない、という事実について述べておく必要がある。（第1章でふれておいたように、生まれ変わりは、人間の死後生存の一型にすぎない。）五〇〇年ほど前には、ヨーロッパでも死後生存を信じない者はほとんどなかった（し、信じなければ、死刑になることすらあったようである）が、現在では死後生存信仰は奇異な考え方ということになってしまっている。死後生存信仰は、物質界の容易に統御可能な問題に焦点を絞った科学が成功するにつれ、次第に衰退して行った。こうした方面で科学者が行なった発言は、自分ではそれを経験できようのない者をも承服させる力をもっているが、現在、超常現象と呼ばれているものについて行なわれた発言にはそうした力はなかった。西洋では地震に遭った経験をもつ者はほとんどいないが、それでも、地震という現象の存在を疑う者はほとんどない。それに対して、たとえ地震の経験がある者よりも霊姿を目撃した体験のある者の方が数が多いとしても、高等教育を受けた者の大半は、霊姿の〝実在性〟を疑っているのである。地震は、全科学者がその信憑性《しんぴょうせい》を認めているが、霊姿の存在は未《いま》だに認められていない。したがって、死後生存という考え方がもっと受け入れられるようになるためには、より強力な証拠が得られそうな研究をこれまで以上に行なう必要がある。そして、科学者から過半数の票を勝ちとらなければならないが、これが、科学的方法を用いた、真理の唯一の判定基準なのである。

死後生存問題に関係するさまざまな種類の証拠のうち、生まれ変わりという現象の実在をうかがわせるものには、ふたつの弱点がある。ひとつは、こうした事例の発生する場所が、ほとんどの場合、西洋から地理的に遠く離れているという点である。このような問題に関心を寄せる何人かの研究者は私に、ヴァージニア州やヨークシャー州やパリ郊外で見つかった事例の方が、スリランカやビルマやレバノンの事例よりもはるかに信用できる、ということを再三指摘している。こうした反論については、ここに述べておくべきことが三点ある。まず第一に、私はこれまで、ヴァージニア州やヨークシャー州、パリ郊外の事例も何例か調査してきたし、この種の事例を探し出し、関係者に情報を提供してくれるよう説得する方法を知ってさえいれば、こうした地域ばかりでなく、西洋諸国全般でも生まれ変わり型事例の調査はできるだろうと思っている。第二に、〝未開発国〟の事例の信憑性を西洋の人間が疑うこと自体、この二、三〇〇年の間、西洋が政治的に世界の優位に立っていることによる傲慢《ごうまん》の表われである。南アジアの証人がヨーロッパや北アメリカの証人と比べて信用できないことを証明した者はいないのである。第三点は、生まれ変わり型事例が多発する国の信仰や状況には、その発現を促す重要な要因が、生まれ変わり信仰とは別に、おそらくはいくつか存在することである。第8章で私は、こうした要因に関する私なりの考え方を簡単に紹介したうえ、西洋の経済的発展が、心の動きや態度に、まだよくわかっていないにしても、プラス面ばかりではない大きな変化をもたらしたのではないか、と指摘しておいた。

西洋に住む人間が生まれ変わりという考え方を受け入れるうえでもうひとつ問題になるのは、ほとんどの西洋人がこうした考え方を知る過程である。生まれ変わりという考え方をとり入れたり、少なくともその厳密な検討を行なう価値があると考える西洋人は、そのほとんどが、神智学のさまざまな教義をはじめ、ヒンドゥー教や仏教について書かれた通俗書を通じて（直接、間接に）その知識を身につけているのである。第2章（および第8章）では、一次的な生まれ変わり信仰と、さまざまな文化圏に見られる、その上にちりばめられた二次的信仰との区別を試みている。

しかしながら、高等教育を受けた西洋人が生まれ変わりという考え方を受け入れるうえで最大の障害となっているのは、まちがいなく、人間は肉体以上のものではないとする確固たる信仰をほとんどの者がもっていることである。ある事柄を信じないという状況は、それ以外のことを固く信じているためであろうし、強い信念があると、自分で見聞きした事実をはじめ、さまざまな証拠が無視されてしまう場合すらある。ある時、友人たちに無理強いされて動物園に見物に入った教育のないアメリカ人農夫が、ラクダの囲いの前にやって来た。そのラクダを長いこと見つめていた農夫は、くるりとうしろを振り向いて歩きながら、「こんな動物いるわけないさ」と独り言を言ったという。このようにして、信仰が経験を打ち破ることがあるのである。

私は、顎《あご》のすぐ下にはっきりわかる母斑《ぼはん》をもつ純血のトリンギットと面接していた時に、もっと直接的な実例を観察した経験がある。このトリンギットの話によれば、その母斑などの証拠から母親は、本人が母方伯父《おじ》の生まれ変わりだと確信したという。その伯父は、その母斑と同じ部位を撃たれて死亡したというのである。また、そのトリンギットには、前世の記憶があることを裏づける有力な証拠をもった孫がふたりいた。ところが本人は、長老派教会の牧師としての教育を受けており、何を信ずべきか教えられているので生まれ変わりという考え方は認めない、と断固たる態度で私に語ったのである。福音書には生まれ変わりの教えは説かれていなかったため、それによって本人の考え方が規定されてしまったのである。

おそらく生まれ変わりという考え方の側面の多くは、西洋人にはなじみのないものとして映るし、したがってありそうにない現象と感じられるのかもしれないが、自分が若返るのを想像しにくいことの方が、生まれ変わりという考え方に伴う多くの側面より重要なのかもしれない。ほとんどの人間は両親が老い行く過程を見ているので、ある程度の努力をすれば不可能ではないにしても、自分が年をとるのを思い描くのはなかなか難しい。[*23] しかしながら、もし私たちが生まれ変わるとすれば必然的に起こる〝若返り〟は、それよりもはるかに奇妙なことと感じられるのである。[*24]

自分が若返るのを考えることが大半の人間にとって難しいのは、ひとつには、物理的な大きさを必要以上に重視しているためであろう。どんぐりがシイの木に成長するのは知っているが、大木に育つための要素がどんぐりの大きさに凝縮されていることについては、すぐには理解できないかもしれない。それが理解しにくいのは、死の時点で人間の人格がもっているさまざまな種類の情報をすべて収納するには大きな肉体でなければならない、と考えるためなのかもしれない。それほどの量の情報を、どうすれば幼児の体に、あるいは（それよりもはるかに驚くべきことであるが）小さな胚《はい》の中にすべて収納できるのであろうか。こうした考え方は、想像力が貧困な表われである。まず第一に、生まれ変わりが起こるとしても、前世で身につけた知識をすべて現世にもち越すと考えてよい根拠はない、という点が挙げられる。その点については次章で明らかにするつもりである。しかしながら、それよりもはるかに重要なのは、人間の心は、空間的な広がりをもっているが、脳の大きさ（および情報を格納する容量）に制限されてはいないらしいことである。

私が調べた子どもたちの中には、大半のおとなとは異なり、年齢や体の大きさの変化を思い描くのに抵抗のない者も少なくなかった。そのうちの何人かは、幼少期に、老人になって体力が衰え、病弱な体になった時の感覚を記憶していた。ディスナ・サマラシンへは、年老いて歯が全部抜け落ち、杖《つえ》がなければ歩けなかった当時のことを覚えていた。プラティマ・サクセナは、咳込《せきこ》みや発熱が続き、失禁まで起こした肺結核の末期状態を記憶していた。子どもたちの中には、（前世で死亡した後に）体の大きさが変わったことにふれた者もあったし、もう一度大きくなりたくてしかたがないという気持を表明した者もあった[*25]。

先述のように、ある現象を信ずるためには、それをよく知っている必要がある。しかし、生まれ変わりという考え方を単に知るだけでは、それを裏づける証拠を正しく評価するうえで十分ではない。その問題は、この研究について初めて聞かされた時、西洋の研究者の一部とアジア・アフリカ地域の研究者の一部がどのような意見を述べるかを紹介するといちばんはっきりする。その人たちは、明言するわけではないが、笑いながら、私が金銭を浪費していることを暗にほのめかすのである。とはいえ、同じような表現を用いても、両者の理由は正反対である。西洋の学者は生まれ変わりはありえないことをその理由にしているのに対して、アジアやアフリカの学者は、実証の必要もないほど明白な事実と考えているのである。[*26] このような判断を下す者のうち、具体的な実例を知っていて、それをもとに自らの意見を唱えた者はひとりもいなかった。本書に大きな目的があるとすれば、それは、前世を記憶しているという子どもたちがもたらす証拠を検討した後に初めて、生まれ変わりを信ずるか否かを読者の方々にご判断いただくことである。もう一度繰り返すが、その証拠は本書には提示されていないのである。

脳と心

現代の大半の科学者、およびまちがいなく神経科学者のほぼ全員は、人間の心は（したがって人間の記憶も）、脳の働きの現われ以外のものではない、と信じている。この仮説は、脳障害やそれよりも軽い機能障害によって人間の心的過程に影響が及ぶという事実から、かなりの裏づけが得られるように見える。印象的な場合が多いが、側頭葉に損傷を与えるような脳の外科手術や神経病理学の領域からその裏づけとなる証拠を引用するまでもなく、高熱を発したり、ウィスキーを少量飲んだりするだけでも、それに疑いを抱く者を納得させるに十分であろう。控え目な神経科学者であれば、脳の働きで心の働きを完全に説明できることが具体的にはまだわかり始めたばかりの段階であるのを認めはするが、それでも、自分たちや後継者の手で、自他ともに満足できるほどすべてが詳細に解明されるはずだ、と楽観的な見通しを立てている。このような人々は、脳と心の関係は他の理論では説明がつかないであろうから、それ以外の考え方は考慮に入れる価値はないと、信念に基づいて考えているのである。

しかし、私たちは、神経科学者のほとんどが受け入れている見解に全て従っているわけではない。ヒポクラテスは、「脳は意識への使者である」と述べているし、[*27] 現代ではおそらくベルクソンが、同じ考え方を表明した最初の哲学者であろう。[*28] この二〇年ほどの間に、一部の心理学者や哲学者、あるいはごく一部の神経科学者が、脳の働きで心（および記憶）を完全に説明できるかどうかを疑問視するようになっている。[*29] 科学者の中には、ピアノがピアニストの音楽表現の道具であるのと同じように、脳も心の道具なのではないかと考え始めている者もある。[*30]

この問題に関する、手に余るほど広範囲にわたる文献をここで検討することはできない。ここでは、私の言いたいことを単純化するため、私の考えている可能性をふたつだけ掲げよう。まず第一は、人間のあらゆる主観的体験を含む、私たちが心（ないしは心の働き）と呼ぶものは、脳の活動のひとつの表われ以上のものではない、とする考え方である。この考え方にはさまざまな亜型があるが、いずれにせよ一元論である。（この概念を、インドのヴェーダンタ哲学者がもっているような唯心論という正反対の概念からはっきり区別するため、物理的一元論とか物理主義と呼びたがる者もある。）二元論の対極にあるのは、心と脳は、生存中、相互に作用し合うが基本的には別ものだ、とする考え方である。これが二元論である。私たちはこの世にいる間、（ほとんどの状況で）自分の心を的確に表現するには脳を必要としている。その事実をここであらためて問題にはしないが、その代わりに、生きている脳は心の存在に必要不可欠か、という問題を考えてみたいと思う。精神現象は脳だけですべて説明できないことを示す証拠や論拠があれば、それは二元論を支持する方向にあることになろうし、誰かの心が肉体の死後にも生き続けることを裏づける証拠も同様である。本書が問題にしているのは、人間の心が死後にも生存を続けることを示す証拠である。次に、人間の心の死後生存を裏づける証拠から離れて、一元論（つまり物理主義）を受け入れる場合の五通りの問題点を手短に検討してみよう。

まず第一に、現在私たちがもっている脳に関する知識では、意識を説明することができない、という点が挙げられる。一元論者を自称する科学者や哲学者は、意識は人間の脳の働きの随伴現象にすぎないと主張する。しかし、この主張はまだ確証されたものではない。それよりも、意識自体がまず第一に存在するのを認めることの方が現実に即しているであろう。人は誰しもが意識をもっているし、人間の知識は全て意識の中にある。「心は、人間が経験する最初のものであり、かつ最も直接的なものである。それ以外は全て、心からかけ離れた推定である」[*31]。意識がなければ人間は、脳を観察することもできないし、意識は脳の働き以外によっては生じないとする、おそらくは誤った考え方をも含め、脳に関するいかなるイメージも描けないであろう。人間の脳を研究すれば、特定の波長の光が眼に入ると青い色を感ずる理由は明らかになるかもしれないが、青という意識をそれ以上に分割することはできない。意識が解明されれば脳も結局は説明できるであろうが、脳によって意識を説明することはできないであろう。また私は、脳以外のものによっても意識が説明できるとは思っていない[*32]。

以上述べた中で私は、意識の中で人間が経験する内容は脳の状態によって異なる、という事実を否定しようとしているわけではないし、人間の精神活動は全て意識的なものだと言っているわけでもない。それどころか私は、逆に、氷山の比喩《ひゆ》を使って意識と無意識を説明するのは陳腐なばかりか不合理だとも考えている。氷山の場合の九分の一どころか、通常の方法で意識に上ってくるのは、人間の心の一千分の一以下だと思わざるをえない。

第二点は、脳に関する現在の知識では、人間が心の中に描くイメージのもつ特徴が説明できないことである。脳内のニューロンをどう組み合わせても、私たちが丸い形を見ている時のような円形にはならない。円や四角形をはじめほとんどの図形を見る時に私たちが経験する知覚は、ニューロンの空間的配列とは対応していないのである。専門用語で言えば、人間の五感による知覚内容と脳内のニューロンの配列は同形ではない。（とはいえ、通常の意識がある間、脳は人間が形を認識するのに何の役割も演じていない、と言っているわけではない[*33]。）

第三に、現在の脳に関する知識では、記憶が十分に説明できないことが挙げられる。（ここで言う記憶とは、現世で起こった出来事の記憶のことであり、前世の記憶ではない。）神経生理学者は、何らかの経験をすることによって脳に変化が起こり、それが痕跡《こんせき》として残るが、その後に起こった出来事がその痕跡を刺激し、私たちが記憶と呼ぶ現象として、かつての出来事を思い起こさせるのではないか、と述べている。抽象的にはなるほどと思われるが、さまざまな種類の状況が限りなく存在する中で、どのようにしてその痕跡が賦活されるのかと考えると、その弱点が明らかになる[*34]。

第四点は、心的事象は、私たちが日常生活でなじんでいる空間とも、物理学者が記述する物理空間とも異なる空間の中で起こるということである。私たちが（生きた熊が目の前にいない時に）心の中で描いている熊のイメージは三次元の立体像であるし、私たちはその熊を、やはりイメージの中で描いた川から離れた場所に置き、その川で泳いでいる鮭に飛びかかる様を描くこともできる。しかし、イメージの中で描いた熊とその周囲の事物との距離についても、物理的空間の中で知覚する物体との距離についても、明確に表現することはできない[*35]。人間の肉体は物理的空間に、心は心理的空間にあるのである。

ふたりの人間の心は、肉体が（別の場所であっても）同じ物理的空間に置かれているのとは違って、同一の心理的空間に存在するのかどうかがはっきりしない。私が考えるように同じ空間に事実あるとしても、私たちはふだんそのことには気づかない。人間の心は、ふつう、心理的空間の自らの領分の中で、他者の思念の侵入から保護されているのである。ところが、稀《まれ》にその防壁が弱まり、テレパシーなどの超常的伝達が起こる。テレパシーを送ったり受けたりする人たちの心理的空間が何らかの形でつながっているということは、必ずしも同じ心理的空間の中にいることを意味するものではないが、私としてはそう考えたいと思っている。

第五点として、私たちが脳について理解している範囲では、テレパシーをはじめとする超常現象が説明できないことが挙げられる。脳内に未発見の器官があり、それが明らかになることでテレパシー交信がいつの日か容易になる、と考えることも不可能ではないが、それだけではそれ以上の説明はできない。テレパシーで交信を行なっているふたりの心の中にあるイメージがかなり一致する、という現象も説明できなければならないのである。それに対して、脳なくしてテレパシーの説明はできない、と言う者もあろう。そうは思うが、他の現象が説明できないからと言って、テレパシーの証拠を無視してよいことになるであろうか。

テレパシーやその近縁の現象は、現代のほとんどの科学者が人間の人格の本態について抱いている見解を打破するものではない、と考えている（さもなければ、そう装っている）人たちはまちがっていると思う。仮に（政治的な意味ではなく哲学的な意味での）唯物論が事実だとすれば、テレパシーは起こるはずがない。ところが現実には起こるわけであるから、唯物論がまちがっているのは確かなのである。[*36]

テレパシーが起こるという事実を一般の科学理論に適合させる理論が開発されるまで、この結論を受け入れるべきではないわけではない。そうではなく、テレパシーが起こるという事実との矛盾をなくすためには、唯物論という憶説の方を捨て去るべきなのである。私は、次に科学革命が起こった暁には、かつて西洋でも数百年の長きにわたって続き、西洋以外のほとんどの国では今なお続いている優位を二元論がとり戻すだろうと思っている。また私は、数十年前に先見の明のある心理学者が行なった次のような発言にも同意している。「テレパシーという現象は……死後生存に代わるものではなく、死後生存を事実上裏書きするものである」[*37]。

言うまでもなかろうが、本書で扱っているわずかな観察事実をはるかに凌《しの》ぐ、超常現象の大量の観察データからすると、心と体の関係にまつわる現在の考え方を根本的に変更する必要がある。一般の科学者の中にも、こうした見通しを立てている者は少なくないし、そのためにこそ、超常現象に関する証言の信頼性に異議を唱えるようになった者も若干あるのである。こういった防衛を行なう科学者は、有利な立場に置かれているように見える。管理条件下で超常現象を観察しようとしても、これまでのところでは、実際にそうした現象が起こったことの裏づけとして統計処理が必要なほどわずかな成果しか（ほとんどの場合）挙がっていないからである。そのうえ、この種の実験は、再現しようとしても腹立たしくなるほど再現性が低い[*38]。また、偶発例には超常的認知現象が数多く見られるのではないかと指摘する私のような科学者は、過去の出来事にまつわる人間の証言に自分たちと同じように信頼を置くよう、読者や聴衆に求めることもしなければならない。それでも私たちは、やはり自らの仮説を大切にしているし、私たちの大半は、一般の科学者を改宗させる、現在よりも強力な証拠が最終的に得られると相変わらず確信している。また、十分な数の科学者がまず自らの態度を変え、超常現象の裏づけとなる、これまで蓄積された大量の証拠を今より好意的に見るようになる、という可能性も（いずれそうなるはずだというより、そうなってほしいということだが）ある。

心は脳ではなく、脳を利用する側だとは言ったが、心が何でできているかについては述べていないし、私は、それについて何も言えないことも承知している。しかしながら、何らかの非物質的なものではないかという推定はできる。その本態がもっとよくわかるまで、これを「心《マイン》素《ド・スタッフ》」と呼ぶことにしよう。シュレディンガーのみごとな比喩を使えば、「単一のデータ（経験や記憶）の集まりよりほんのちょっとだけ多いもの、つまり、そういうデータが集められるカンバス」なのである。[*39]

死後の生命は考えられるか

本節でまず念頭に置いていただかなければならないのは、世界の大宗教のほとんどが（それほどの大宗教でなくともその多くが）、その教えやそれにまつわる神話の中に、死後の生命という考え方を含めていることである。こうした考え方には、平均的教育を受けた西洋人を引きつける魅力のない場合が多い。この種の考え方は、「永遠の至福」という概念のように漠然としたものか、さもなければ、現世で最高の状態がそのまま（おそらくはそれが改善され拡大された形で）持続してほしい、という希《ねが》い以外の何ものでもないものを表明しているように見える。ヴァイキングは、最高神オーディンの神殿ヴァルハラで饗宴《きょうえん》を楽しむと考えるが、それと同じように、トリンギットは、鮭の大酒宴を想像することになる。

死後の生命は自分には考えられないと教育ある西洋人が言う時、その人は、いま述べたような概念に対する失望や、私たちが慣れ親しんでいる肉体から離れた生命などあろうはずがないという信念を表明するのがふつうである。しかしながら、西洋の哲学者や心理学者の中にも、肉体を離れた死後の生命が存在するとすれば、それがもっていると思われる特徴はどのようなものかを述べている者が一部にいる。[40] このような推定は、既に確証されている知識の延長線上にはあるが、SF小説のようなものではない。推定の根拠となりうる情報がある程度にせよ存在するからである。まず第一に、前世を記憶していて、しかもそれが事実だと確認された子どもの中には、肉体のない世界にあった時、そこで起こった出来事の記憶ももっていると主張する者が少数ながらあることが挙げられる。[41]（この種の事例については既に第5章でふれ、いくつかの実例を紹介している。）こうした子どもたちが語った事柄の他にも、自覚夢[42]を見る人々や、死の瀬戸際まで行きながら蘇生《そせい》ないし脱出した人々[43]の証言を加えてもよいかもしれない。また、そうした憶測《おくそく》の中に、テレパシーが起こる状況やその過程について現在わかっている（まちがいなくわずかな）知識も含めてもよいと思う。[44] そうすると、死後の生命とはいかなるものかがある程度にしても推測できる。

肉体の感覚器官がないため、死後の知覚は、この世で慣れ親しんでいるものと違うのは確かであろうが、必ずしも知覚が停止してしまうわけではなかろう。死の間際まで行きながら回復した者は、たとえその肉体が意識不明に陥っているように見えたり、場合によっては（事実はそうではないが）本当に死亡したと思われたりしていても、知覚が（しかもその一部は通常とあまり変わらない知覚が）実際にあったと語る。本人の肉体が置かれている場所とは異なった空間の一点から見聞きしていたように感じられるその種の知覚体験は、通常の感覚器官によって生じたものではないのである。

死後の思念には、私たちになじみ深い覚醒《かくせい》時の世界よりも、はるかに多くのイメージが入り込んでいるかもしれない。言葉があまり介在しない（うえ、言葉による制約も少ない）だろうからである。その点、死後の思念は、幼児や夢を見ている人間の思考形態と似ているかもしれない。死後の世界は、プライスの言葉を借りれば〝形象的〟なものであろうが、架空のものではなく、夢を見ている者に夢が現実のものと感じられるのと同じくらい現実的なものであろう。[*45]

　夢の世界と同様、死後の世界でも、ある種の過去の出来事の記憶は、通常の状態にある時よりも浮かび上がりやすくなるかもしれない。死後に意識に上るかもしれない記憶は、深く思いを致したいものばかりとは限らないであろう。その中で自らの生涯や行ないを振り返るかもしれないが、既に（第2章の註22で）指摘しているように、自分の過去を振り返ることに対する無意識の恐怖を考えると、世界中の人間のほとんどが抱いている死の恐怖が説明できる、とパタンジャリは教えている。プラトンの著作に登場するソクラテスも、善人は死を恐れる必要はないと述べた時、死後の世界での審判や運命のことを考えていた。[*46] しかしながら現段階では、前世を記憶する子どもたちからは、こうした生涯の追想を行なったことを裏づける証拠はほとんど得られていない。この種の事柄を語った子どもはごくわずかな数にすぎないのである。[*47]〝走馬《そうま》燈《とう》的記憶〟と呼ばれることの多いこの種の追憶は、死の寸前まで行きながら回復したり、死を招くような危機状況から脱出したりした（西洋の）人たちの間で起こることが少なくない。ある共同研究者とともに調査したこの種の事例のうち、このような形で過去を追想した者は二七パーセントにものぼっている。[*48] こうした人たちの（全てではないにせよ）一部は、回復する前にはほとんどないしは完全に死亡したと思われていたので、実際に死んで行った人たちも、終止符が打たれたばかりの生涯で起こった出来事をざっと振り返るのではないか、と（断言できないのは確かであるが）推定してもよかろう。もしそうなら、パタンジャリが言うように、このような人々はその後、一生を振り返ったことを具体的には忘れてしまうのかもしれない。

そのようなわけで、私の考える死後の世界は、かなりの部分、その住人が死後に抱いた思念を基に形成されているようである。そこには、その人物が生きた文化や、その中で培った個人的経験、感情的傾向といったものが反映されることであろうし、当人がこの世で送った人生がどのようなものであるかによって、楽しいものにも、苦しいものにもなるのであろう。

こうした死後の世界では、肉体のない人格が互いに完全に孤立して存在していると考える必要はない。やはり肉体をもたない別の人格と出会うかもしれないし、生者間で起こるテレパシー類似のプロセスを介して相互に交信しているかもしれないのである。その業績については既に紹介しておいたが、生物学者であり哲学者でもあるハンス・ドリーシュは、この点について、「死者にとってふつうの伝達手段は、生者にとって〝超常的〟なのである」[*49]と簡潔に表現している。もしそうであれば、交信や交流は、主として生前に親しかった者同士の間で行なわれるのであろう。そうすると、一方が会いたがり、そのためもう一方もたまたま関心をもったという程度の間柄では、死後、接触できないことになると思う。生前の愛情関係や行状に従って、同じようなことをしてきた相手と死後に交流をもつということの方がありそうである。もし私たちが愛情の深い人間であったとすれば、やはり愛情深い人たち、特に自分がこよなく愛した人々に囲まれることになるであろう。逆に、もし私たちが唾棄《だき》すべき人生を歩んできたとすれば、それ相応の人たちに囲まれることになるのかもしれない。

　いま私が思い描いている世界に住む肉体のない人格は、私たちになじみ深いこの世で起こる出来事を見守っていたり、それよりもはるかに稀《まれ》ではあるが、生きている人間と交信したりしている可能性があるかもしれない。第5章で私は、前世の人格の死後に前世の家族内で起こった、しかも私の知る限りその子どもが通常の方法では知りえなかったはずの出来事について正確に語った子どもの実例をいくつか紹介しておいた。また、肉体のない状態に置かれている間、前世の家族や友人の前に姿を現わすことができたという記憶があり、その事実を第三者が裏書きしている例もある。たとえば、マウン・イン・マウンとチャオクン・ラジスタジャルンは、前世で死亡した後、霊姿となって出現したところを目撃された記憶をもっていたし、サヤドウ・ウ・ソバナ師は、肉体のない状態でいる間に体験した事柄を記憶していたが、それは、ふたりの生者が夢の中で体験した内容と一致していたのである。このふたりは、師の発言が事実であることを証言した。私が調べた事例の中には、私が予告夢と呼ぶものの中に肉体をもたない人格が姿を現わしたという事例が他にもたくさんある。とはいえ、サヤドウ・ウ・ソバナ師のように、肉体をもたないでいる間に生者の夢に登場したという記憶を残している者は稀である。

　ある種の霊姿の事例には、故人が遺族や友人と時おり交信を行なっていることを示すものがある。ここで言おうとしているのは、その人物が死亡して何ヵ月か、場合によっては何年かしてから目撃される霊姿のことである。この種の霊姿は、その目撃者が困難な目に遭っている時や危機状況に陥っている時に出現しやすいことからすると、死者は何らかの方法で自分の家族の内情に通じているらしいことがわかる。第1章で実例を紹介しておいたが、こうした死者の霊姿は、死の時点で出現する霊姿よりもはるかに少ないとはいえ、さらに研究を進める価値があると考えられるほど信憑性《しんぴょうせい》の高い事例が報告されている。[*50]

死が差し迫った人間は、自分があの世に旅立つのを迎えに来たように感じられる故人の幻を時おり見ることがある。こうした臨終時の幻の一部については、先に死亡している最愛の人物ともう一度結ばれたいという願望があるためだとして説明することができる。ところが、調査が行き届いている事例の中にも、霊姿として現われた人物が既に死亡していることを本人もその場にいる者も誰ひとり知らなかったという事例も、少ないながら存在するのである。[*51]

肉体のない世界にも法則があるのかもしれないが、この世のものとは違うであろう。時間の流れも異なるであろうし、空間も異質かもしれない。誰かのことを思うだけで、あたかも〝今〟が〝ここ〟と同義であるかのように、次の瞬間には相手の目の前にいることになるかもしれないのである。[*52]

こうした肉体のない世界はどこにあるのか、と問われれば私は、私たちが肉体と結びついている現世で、誰もがもっている心理的空間の中に存在すると答える。

ここでまとめると、いま私が言おうとしているのは、宇宙には物理的世界と心理的（ないし心霊的）世界の少なくともふたつが存在するのではないかということである。（とはいえ、その指摘をしたのは私が最初だなどと主張する気は毛頭ない。）このふたつの世界は相互に影響を及ぼし合う。私たちが現世にいる間は、肉体と結びついているため、肉体なくしては不可能な経験はさせてくれるであろうが、心の働きは制約を受ける。死んだ後には、肉体の制約から解き放たれるので、心理的世界のみで暮らすようになるのであろう。そして、その世界でしばらく生活した後、その人たちの一部、あるいはもしかするとその全員が、新しい肉体と結びつくのかもしれない。それを指して私たちは、生まれ変わったと称するのである。

以上おおまかに述べた内容が推測に基づくものであることを申し添えて、この問題に関する私見を締めくくろうと思う。私は、死後の生命の存在が考えられることを示したいだけであり、これまで詳述してきた個々の点を強調しようというつもりはない。とはいえ、こうした推測には、唯物論者が執着する宇宙の〝単一世界〟仮説を凌《しの》ぐ何ものにも代えがたい利点がある。こうした推論からすれば、テレパシーを裏づける証拠を無視しなくともよいということである。

個人の責任対運命の偶然

この問題を考えるに当たって、私は、説法を行なったり、場合によっては説教じみたことを言ったりすることになるのではないかと少々心配になるが、生まれ変わりを肯定する主張や、不完全ではあるがそれを裏づける証拠を丹念に検討した結果、生まれ変わりを信ずるうえで妨げとなる（合理的なものはもちろん）不合理な障害がはたして存在するかどうかという問題について考えざるをえなくなった。もし存在するとすれば、それは、生まれ変わりによって個人の運命に対する責任が生ずることによる重荷であろう。生まれ変わりという考え方は、いかにも希望をもたらしてくれる教義であるが、人間は現世で積み重ねた努力によって来世で何ものかを得る可能性があることを暗に示している。しかしながら、その希望は、個人の努力によってしか満たされないため、ほとんどの人間には受け入れがたいものであろう。私たち人間の中には、ものぐさな性向が潜んでいる。そのことは、生まれ変わりが存在する可能性を引き合いに出さずとも容易に理解できる。病症を抱える者の中には、食事量を減らし、飲酒を慎み、節煙することにより生き方を変えるよりも、医師に処方された薬を服用しながら死ぬまで治療を続ける道を選ぶ者が多い。社会に目を向ければ、他人の落ち度を正すための立法を求める者が一〇〇〇人いるとすると、ベートーベンが言ったように（私はそう理解しているが）、「神さま、私を正してください」と祈る者は一〇人しかいないであろうし、ましてや、ベートーベンのように自力で自分を正すよう努力する者はひとりくらいのものなのではなかろうか。もし一生の行ないの責任を受け入れることができなければその責任を二回以上の来世にわたって引き受けるよう求められたなら、それを喜びはしないであろう。とはいえ、ボードレールが書いているように、「個々人の内の、本人自身によるものを除けば、進歩――すなわち真の道徳的進歩は、ありえない」[*53]というのは、やはり真理である。

　平均的な西洋人は、自分の行ないや自分が置かれている状況に対する個人の責任を、さまざまな方法を用いて回避しようとする。キリスト教は、神が人の運命を定めるという考え方から、キリストが十字架に架けられて死んだことにより人間の罪はすべて贖《あがな》われたとする考え方に至るまで、さまざまな逃げ道を提供している。現代科学は、偶然という概念を用意しているが、この考え方は、賭博《とばく》師や保険業者から始まったものであり、科学者の創始になるものではない。既に十八世紀に、ギボンは、（私見によれば、ある程度は自己満足しつつ）次のような発言をすることができた。「人間が死ぬというあたりまえの運命をつらつら考えてみるに、私は人生という福引で当たりくじを引いたことを認めざるをえない。……文明の進んだ自由の国に、しかも裕福な由緒正しい家柄に生まれるという二重の好運は、一〇〇万分の一の幸運なのである」[54]。偶然という概念を表わすのに用いられる比喩《ひゆ》は時代によって異なっており、第9章で紹介しておいたように、現代風の表現を使えば、ひとりひとりの人間がそれぞれ特有の特徴をもっているのは、大半が、本人の両親の生殖細胞に染色体がランダムに振り分けられた結果だということになる。同じ概念について私たちは、これまで、不慮の出来事とか幸運とか宿命などという言葉を用いてきたし、今でも用いている。名称がどうであれ、その考え方のおかげで、我身に降りかかったことに対する責任を、その一端にせよ負わずにすむ。ほとんどの西洋人は、偶然という考え方に多少なりとも魅力を感ずると思うし、その分だけ、生まれ変わりという考え方に違和感を覚えるのかもしれない[55]。

一部の人たちは、自分たちの生活が偶然の力に支配されているという発想には魅力を感じないが、それでも、自らの生活に個人的な責任があるとは考えたくないのであろう。西洋の精神医学や心理学は、この二世代にわたって、あらゆる問題は両親の欠陥ないし、私たちが社会と呼ぶ、自分たちを除いた人間集団に起因するとして偶然信奉者たちに安らぎを与えてきた。

読者の方々は、南アジアをはじめとする国々に住む何千万という数の人々が生まれ変わりを信じていることからすると、この考え方が万人にとって不快なはずはない、と言われるかもしれない。私としてはそれに対して、ほとんどの南アジアの人たちは、その意味するところを全て（信奉してというのが言いすぎなら）十分理解したうえで生まれ変わりを信じているのではない、とお答えしたい。事実、この人たちは、カルマという教理を、責任を受け入れるのではなく、回避する手段として利用しており、現世の不幸をはるか昔の前世の人格のせいにすることにより、現在の行動を矯正しなければならない状況を回避することができるのである。また、ヒンドゥー教徒の中にも仏教徒の中にも、自らの宗教によって強いられる高潔な行ないだけしていれば、日常生活に必要なものがひとりでに手に入ると信じている者はほとんどいない。ヒンドゥー教徒は、人間の生活に干渉する神々に訴え、スリランカの仏教徒は、カタラガマ神のもとへ押しかけ、賄賂《わいろ》を使って、迫り来る災いから救い出してもらおうとする。ビルマの仏教徒は、ナットと呼ばれる精霊に救いを求めることが多いし、タイの仏教徒は、自宅のそばに守護霊を宿す小さな祠《ほこら》を造る。

ラーマクリシュナ・ミッションのスワミ・ムクリヤナンダという修道僧は、ある時私に、「私たちインド人は、生まれ変わりが起こることは知っていますが、だからといってどうということはありません。インドには、西洋と同じくらい大勢のならず者や悪人がいるのですから」と語ったことがある。おおまかにはこの言葉は正しいであろうが、生まれ変わり信仰に伴うすべてを受け入れる個人にもこの信仰が影響を及ぼすことはないという意味であれば、まちがっていると思う。[*56] とはいえ、それは、ラクダが針の目を通るのより難しいかもしれない。

第11章　生まれ変わりに関係する可能性のあるプロセスの考察

前章で（明言はしていないが）示唆しておいたように、生まれ変わりが普遍的現象であるとすれば、現在、手元にある事例によって生まれ変わりの本質を理解しようとすることは、すりガラスの窓を通して眺めるようなものである。これまでの章で、私の調査した事例の標本が世間一般の人たちの生活からいかにかけ離れたものであるかを十分強調してきたつもりである。したがって、生まれ変わりという現象が実在するとしても、こうした事例からは、ある種の偏りをもった一群の人々に見られる要因に関するわずかな事実しかわかりえないことになる。ほとんどの人間に起こるような生まれ変わりについては、何も言えないも同然なのである。とはいえ、ごく大雑把な輪郭でも描いておいた方が何もないよりはましなので、以下に私なりの推測を申し述べることにしたい。

本章で扱う問題は次の通りである。生まれ変わりがあるとすれば、何が生まれ変わるのか。なぜ他の家族でなく、特定の家族のもとに生まれ出るのか。生まれ変わろうとしている肉体のない人格は、生まれ変わった時に自分のものとなる肉体にどうすれば影響を与えることができるのか。前世の行ないは来世の状況に影響を及ぼすのか。

生きている人間の人格全体が何でできているかを知らなかったとしても、どの事例から得られた証拠をもとに考えても、人格全体が生まれ変わったと言うことはできないであろう。私たちは、前世に由来する可能性のある人格のいくつかの側面にしか注意を向けることができない。そのためにはまず、その子どもの言葉や行動をできる限り通常の理由を用いて（つまり、現代の遺伝学の知識や環境による影響ということで）説明すべく努める必要がある。そして、そのような理由では説明しきれない行動が残った時に初めて、それは、一回ないし複数の前世に由来するものかもしれないと考えてよいことになる。この線に沿って探究を行なえば、人格のどの側面が生まれ変わるらしいかがわかるはずである。既に見てきたように、完全型の事例では前世で起こった出来事のイメージ記憶や、前世時代の習慣や性向に対応する行動的記憶や経験の残渣《ざんさ》に加えて、前世の肉体にあった傷痕《きずあと》等のあざと一致する母斑《ぼはん》その他の異常が生まれ変わった肉体に観察される。

とはいえ、以上のようなさまざまの要素は物干し竿《ざお》に下がった洗濯物のようにそれぞれバラバラなわけではない。各要素は、私たちの体の各器官と同じように、全体的には統合されているのである。（その統一体の内部には――個々の器官が一個の肉体を構成しているように――連繋《れんけい》があるかもしれないが、統一性もあるのである。）実際の事例で観察されるいくつかの要素の間に結びつきがあることは容易に見てとれる。たとえば、別の村に妻子がいると主張する少年は、その村まで行って妻子に会いたがるし、医師の生涯を記憶している少年は医者の真似をして遊ぶのを好み、自分が射殺された時の模様を語る子どもは、その時の傷痕により生じたという母斑を指し示しながら、自分を殺害した犯人に復讐《ふくしゅう》したいという思いを表明する。要するに、録音済みのテープを収めた収納ケースのようにそれぞれバラバラな記憶が寄り集まったものではなく、全体がひとつの方向性をもっていることを裏づける証拠が見出《みいだ》されるのである。既に（第1章で）述べておいたように、誰かが死後にも生存を続けていることを明らかにするには、その人物の記憶のみならず、その目的が持続していることを裏づける証拠が必要なのである。そういった証拠は、生まれ変わり型事例に数多く見られる。

　生まれ変わったと推定される者では、先述のイメージ記憶、行動的記憶、身体的痕跡《こんせき》という三通りの要素が不思議にも結びついているので、前世と現世の間でもそれが一体になっていなかったとは、私には想像すらできない。このことからすると、この要素（ないしその表象）は、ある種の中間的媒体に従属しているらしいことがわかる。しかし、この中間的媒体がもっている他の要素については、おそらくまだ何もわかっていない。

　ある人格の心的要素を前世から来世へと運搬する媒体を、〝心搬体《サイコフオア》〟と呼ぶことにしたらどうかと思う[*1]。私は、心搬体を構成する要素がどのような配列になっているのかは全く知らないが、肉体のない人格がある種の経験を積み、活動を停止していないとすれば、心搬体は変化して行くのではないかと思う。また、生まれ変わりの過程の中でも多少は変化するのかもしれない。皺《しわ》だらけの老人の体は、その老人の生涯にまつわる記憶を語る幼児のみずみずしい小さな体とは大きく異なっている。老人はイメージ記憶をたくさんもっている。その幼児ももっているかもしれないが、そうだとしても、その子どもが言葉を覚え、その話を始めるまでには、イメージ記憶は次第に薄れ、わずかな残滓《ざんし》のみになってしまっているのがふつうである。[*2]行動的記憶も矮小《わいしょう》化され、前世で培った技能は、現世では（ごく一部の例外を除けば）単なる適性程度のものになり下がってしまうのかもしれない。その老人がたとえば斬殺《ざんさつ》されたとしても、その傷痕は既に癒《い》えている。生まれ変わった新しい肉体についている傷痕からは（ふつう）出血していないが、片手が切り落とされてから意識を失い死亡した場合には、その子どもは生まれつき片手がないかもしれない。したがって、老人の肉体の傷痕は変わらずにあるわけではなく、型紙のような働きをし、心搬体の一部として、次に生まれ変わる時に結びつく新しい肉体の形態に影響を及ぼすのである。

私は、前世の人格という言葉を、ある子どもがその生涯を記憶している人物に対して用いてきたが、ひとつの人格がそっくりそのまま生まれ変わりうるという言い方は避けてきた。そのような形での生まれ変わりが起こりうることを示唆する証拠は存在しないからである。実際に生まれ変わるかもしれないのは、直前の前世の人格および、それ以前に繰り返された過去世の人格に由来する個性なのである。[*3]人格《パーソナリティ》は、ひとりの人間がいずれの時点でももっている、外部から観察される心理的特性をすべて包含しているのに対して、個性《インディヴィジュアリティ》には、そのうえに、現世で積み重ねた経験とそれまでの過去世の残渣が加わる。したがって私たちの個性には、人格としては決して表出することのないものや、異常な状況以外では人間の意識に昇らないいものが数多く含まれているのである。

私が学んできた外国語の能力の消長を見ると、人格と個性の区別がはっきりする。私は、一九六二年にいくつかの事例を調査するためアルゼンチンを訪れた頃には、スペイン語で面接できるほどかなりスペイン語を話すことができた。その後の私は、スペイン語圏の人たちから時々もらう手紙を（辞書の助けを借りて）今でも読むことはできるが、スペイン語を話す能力を維持しようとする努力はしなかった。また私は、初歩的なスペイン語で返信くらいは何とか書けはするが、実用的な目的という点では、私のスペイン語はどこかへ消えてしまった。とはいえ、私の人格から消えてしまっただけであり、私の個性から消滅したわけではない。もう一度スペイン語を話そうとすれば、初めて習った時よりも容易に身につくことであろう。このようにスペイン語は忘れるがまま放置されていたのに対して、フランス語とドイツ語はまだかなり話すことができる。このふたつは、依然として私の人格――いわば私の活動している自己――の一部なのである。しかしながら、私が死んだ時には、フランス語とドイツ語を話す能力も私の個性の一部になるであろうし、私が生まれ変わるとすれば、現世で外国語を習った結果は、来世でその言葉が話せるということではなく、現世（あるいは過去世）で学んで話してきた言葉を習ううえでの適性として残るということであろう。また、知的なものであれ技術的なものであれ道徳的なものであれ、現在私がもっているような他のあらゆる技能についても、それと同じことが言えるのではないかと思う。さらには、そのように考えると私は、老年になっても、たとえばクラリネットの演奏のような新しい技術を身につけたい気持になる。[*4]

第9章で述べておいたように、神童の存在を生まれ変わりで説明できるだけの証拠はほとんどないし、西洋の神童が前世を記憶していると主張した例もひとつもない。とはいえ、この点についても（第5章で）述べておいたが、前世に由来すると思われる行動的記憶は、その行動を身につけた（前世での）状況にまつわるイメージ記憶が消失してから大分時間が経過した後にも、引き続き残されている場合がある。同様のことは、前世から現世へと移行する際にも起こるかもしれない。たとえば、ある人が前世で音楽や数学などの技術を修得していたとすると、その技術を身につけた前世のイメージ記憶は既にないにもかかわらず、現世ではそのことを裏づける証拠を示すかもしれないのである。

なぜ特定の家族のもとに生まれ出るのか

たとえばビルマ人やイボ族、北アメリカ北西部の諸部族をはじめとするいくつかの民族の事例では、双方の人格はほとんどが、同一家族ないしは拡大家族の中に含まれる。もし生まれ変わりが同一家族内で（あるいは互いに親しい二家族の間で）起こるとすれば、何らかの心霊的な力が肉体のない人格を、次に生まれ出る家族の方へ引き寄せることにより、そのような結果が生じたのではないかと考えることができる。

このようなことはどうして起こるのであろうか。私見によれば、こうしたことが起こるのは、共通の体験が私たちの中に心理的痕跡を残し、関係者の間に超常的な結びつきを成立させるからではないかと思う。また、ふたりの結びつきが続けば続くほど、また強ければ強いほど、その結びつきは強まるのではないかと思われる。[*5] 生命が脅かされる状況に置かれた時のようにその必要が生じ、しかも超常的な結びつきが十分強い場合には、地理的に遠く離れたふたりの間にテレパシーによる伝達が起こることがある。その場合、相手の身によからぬことが起こったという感覚や直観だけしか生じないことも多いが、遠方の人物が霊姿となって現われたのが見えるほど鮮明かつ詳細な知覚を生ずることもある。その実例については、第1章でいくつか紹介しておいた。この種の体験では、双方の人物は互いに波長が合っていると言えるが、ふたりの結びつきは、一方の弦を弾《はじ》くともう一方も振動するように調律された二本の弦の共鳴よりもはるかに複雑である。テレパシー的印象や霊姿体験は、相手の居所を突き止める力をもっている。死者や死を目前にした者は、何らかの方法で、超常的結びつきをもっている相手を探し出す。そしてその人物だけが（それよりも稀《まれ》な集団的霊姿体験の場合を除いて）その交信を受けるのである。[*6] 死者の人格も、同様の探査能力を用いて、来世で両親となる夫婦のもとへ辿《たど》り着くのではなかろうか。

第1章で述べておいたように、テレパシー的印象や霊姿の事例研究により、こうした体験は親子間でも夫婦間でも同程度の頻度で発生することがわかっている。同様に、同一家族内で発生する生まれ変わり型事例でも、双方の人物は、血縁関係のみならず姻戚《いんせき》関係によって結びついている場合もある。[*7] とはいえ、家族関係自体には、ふたりを本質的に結びつけるものはない。私たちがふつう、他人よりも自分の家族と強くしかもたくさんの超常的結びつきをもっているとすれば、それは、家族と一緒に過ごす時間が、特に、私見によれば弱い感情よりも引きつける力のある強い感情を共に体験する機会が多いからである。中には、自分の家族よりも友人との間に強い結びつきを示す者もある。そのため、血縁関係にはないが親友という間柄にあるふたりの間にテレパシー体験や霊姿体験が起こる例が多い。しかし、こうした体験が、見ず知らずの他人同士の間で起こることは稀である。[*8] 同様に、やはり血縁関係はないものの、前世の人格が、後に自分の両親となる夫婦に対して特に深い愛着を抱いていたことがわかった生まれ変わり型事例もある。[*9]

死ぬ前に、来世の両親となるべき夫婦を決めていた事例も一部にある。(トリンギット族とハイダ族には特にそのような傾向が見られる。)おそらく、こうした願望を公言することで愛情が強化されるのであろうが、その愛情は以前から存在していたはずであるし、心の中に秘められている愛情は、言葉を通じて表現されるものと同じくらい強い場合が多いのも確かである。

憎悪も人を結びつける力をもっているように思われる。既に述べておいたように、子どもが、自分の親と争っていた人物や、場合によっては自分の親に負傷させられたり殺害されたりした人物の生涯を記憶しているという事例もいくつかある。(第9章でゾウハイル・チャールの事例を簡単に紹介しておいた。この事例は、ゾウハイルの母親と激しく争っていた男性の生涯を記憶している子どもの例である。[*10])

罪業感や恩義も、引き合う力として働くように思われる。その中の少数例(すべてビルマの事例)では、子どもが自分の家族のひとりに前世で借金した記憶をもっていた。こうした少数例では、問題の負債はたいていの場合、私から見れば少額であるし、場合によっては微々たるものにすぎないこともあるが、何ごとに対してもいつかは代価を支払わなければならないと信じている敬虔《けいけん》な仏教徒は、債権者と自らとを結びつけ、その家族の中に生まれ変わるという責務を、自分の良心に負わせて死んで行くのかもしれない[*11]。

一部には、肉体のない人格が特定の家族に引きつけられたとしても、その理由が友情にあるのか他の動機にあるのか判別できない事例もある。第9章で妊娠願望について述べた中で紹介したマウン・ミント・ティンの母親は、息子の前世の人格と目される男性に地酒を飲ませて感謝されていた。マウン・ミント・ティンは、言葉が話せるようになる以前から、前世の人格が酒好きだったことをうかがわせる行動を示していた。そのため、前世の人格がこの女性の息子として生まれ変わったのは、前世の人格に酒をふんだんに飲ませてくれるので好都合だからとして十分説明できるように周囲の者には思われた。

これまで私は、前世の人格とその記憶をもつ子どもの家族との間に血縁関係や友人関係などがある場合、その家族の中に生まれ変わることに関係しそうな要因について検討してきた。それ以外の事例の場合には、なぜその子どもが他の家族ではなくその家族の中に生まれたのかという点についてあまり申しあげられることはない。事実、長距離例の大半では、前世を記憶する子どもがなぜその家族のもとに生まれたのかを解明する手がかりが、どのようなものにせよ全くつかめていないことをここで認めておかなければならない。また、そうした事例の情報提供者もその点は同様であり、その問題についてどう思っているかを尋ねると、たいていの場合、子どもがその家族の中に生まれた理由を（ヒンドゥー教徒や仏教徒の場合）カルマのためだとするか（キリスト教徒やイスラム教徒の場合には）神の思召《おぼしめし》によるとするのである。（前世を記憶する）子どもが生まれても、家族の者たちはその理由を、それほど頭を悩ませて考えることはない。この問題について情報提供者たちは、はっきりしたことは何も言えなかったが、この種の事例に関係するように思われる要因は三点認めることができる。

まず第一に、子どもが前世の記憶を口にするようになる以前に前世の人格を知っていたことを家族が否定した事例の中にも、双方の間にある程度の関係が存在した事実の判明したものが若干あることである。一部は商売上の関係であったが、仲もよかったことがわかっている。インドのこの種の事例に、ラム・ティラトの例がある。ラム・ティラトは、野菜を作っていた男性の生涯を記憶していた。その男性は、その子どもの家族が住んでいるあたりで野菜を売り歩いていたのである。ラム・ティラトは、（前世で）母親に野菜を売ったことを覚えていたうえ、その男性が死ぬ少し前、ラム・ティラトの母親の家に野菜の籠《かご》をうっかり置き忘れてしまったという。この男性はそこで野菜を売っていたのであった。

ジュギ・ラル・アガルワルというやはりインドの子どもは、前世の自分は現在の父親に穀物を引きとってもらっていた農民だったと主張した。父親は、その農夫の自宅から七〇キロほど離れたところにあるシルサガンジという大きな町で穀物の卸商を営んでいたのである。さらにジュギ・ラルは、父親がその農夫をいつも公平に扱ってくれたのを覚えていると語った。（インドの農民たちは、穀物を引きとる卸商はずる賢い取引をするものだと思っている。）またジュギ・ラルは、死んだ時、その穀物卸商の家族の中に生まれ変わりたいと思ったことも記憶していた。私は、ジュギ・ラルがその農夫の生涯について語った最も重要な点がまちがいなく事実であることを確認しているが、前世の人格と本人の父親の関係については確認できなかった。父親は、息子が前世の自分だと語っている農夫が大勢の顧客の中にいたことは思い出せないと率直に認めているし、その農夫の家族も、本人がココヤシの樹液から採ったジャッガリーという黒砂糖を売りにシルサガンジまで出かけていたのは知っていたが、どの卸商に売り捌《さば》いていたかまではわからなかった。以上のような難点はあったものの、前世に関するジュギ・ラルの主たる発言は事実と確認できたので、他でもない今の家族の中に生まれた理由に関するジュギ・ラルによる説明を、私はありうることだと考えている。

一部の長距離例に対する第二の説明は、記憶の中心を占める前世よりも古い別の前世で今の家族とある程度の関係があったとする、前世の記憶をもつ子ども自身が主張するものである。たとえば、(一方は事実と確認されているがもう一方は確認されていない)ふたつの前世を記憶しているスワルンラタ・ミシュラは、もうひとつの前世で姉妹のひとりと一緒だったと語った。スクラ・グプタも、記憶の大半を占める前世よりも前の前世で今の家族の一員だったと述べている。マンジュ・バルガヴァは、姉のウマーがいるため今の家族の中に生まれたと語ったが、本人によれば、ふたりは前世で一緒だったという。こうした事例では、過去世で一緒にいたという、その子どもの発言を裏づける記憶を家族が私に話してくれたことはごく稀にしかなかった。[*12]

前世を記憶する子どもが特定の家族を選んで生まれる場合に時おり関係しているように思わ

れる第三の要因を私は、地理的要因という言葉で表現してきた。それを裏づける証拠はふたつの事例群に見られる。

第一の群は、前世を記憶する子どもが、前世の人格の住居からは遠いが、死亡した場所ないしはその近くで生まれている事例である。前世が第二次大戦中にビルマで戦死した日本兵だったというビルマの子どもたちもこの中に入る。そのうち、マ・キン・サン・ティンとマ・キン・サン・インというふたりの少女は、日本軍の同一部隊に所属する（双子ではないが）兄弟だった記憶をもっており、（一九四五年四月、ピョブエ近郊にイギリス軍が進攻してきたため）ともに戦死した後、日本で生まれ変わろうとしたが果たせず、ビルマの戦没地に舞い戻って来たのだという。ふたりは、ピョブエ近郊の村の、戦死したとする地点から一〇〇メートルも離れていないところで生まれた。（かつてその場所には、日本軍の塹壕《ざんごう》が掘られていた。）この事例は、ビルマで戦死した日本兵だったというビルマの他の子どもたちの事例と同じく、依然として未決例に留《とど》まっている。

しかしながら、情報提供者の報告によれば、事実であることが確認されている事例でも、同様の結末になる場合がある。たとえば、ビルマ北部のタトコンに住んでいたある女性は、タトコンからマンダレーに向かう汽車の中で、突然、心臓発作のような症状を起こした。そのためこの女性は、タルンという町の近くで治療のため降ろされたが、まもなく死亡した。その後、この女性の生涯と死亡する時の模様を記憶しているマウン・ウィン・アエという男児がタルンで生まれた。本人の母親は、タルンで突然死亡した見知らぬ女性の遺体が横たわっているのを、大勢の人々と一緒に好奇の眼で眺めていたばかりか、その女性の葬送の準備まで手伝った。その後まもなく、母親は本人を身ごもった。本例は、マウン・ウィン・アエと母親との間に通常の情報伝達があった結果として生じたものと解釈できるかもしれない。また、マウン・ウィン・アエが胎内にいる間か出生した後のいずれかの時点で、ふたりの間にテレパシーによる交信があったとも考えられる。とはいえ、可能性はもうひとつ残されている。死亡した女性の人格が遺体の近辺に留まり、遺体を駅まで見物に来た未来の母親に引きつけられ、マウン・ウィン・アエとして生まれ変わったとする可能性である。[*13]

前世を記憶する子どもが、前世の人格の遺体が死後に運ばれた場所で生まれた事例もいくつかある。マウン・アエ・キャウというビルマの少年は、前世で射殺され、自分の遺体が小川に投げ込まれた時のことを覚えていた。マウン・アエ・キャウは、肉体のない状態にあった時、下流に流される遺体について行った記憶をもっていた。殺された場所から川下に何キロか下ったあたりで、川に浮かんでいる死体が、川岸に建っている家の近くにある小さな船着き場の杭《くい》に引っ掛かった。その家の女性が水中の死体に気づき、何人かの男性を呼んだ。男たちは、その死体を流れの中に押し戻し、イラワジ河の方へと流した。まもなくその女性はマウン・アエ・キャウを妊娠した。その後に生まれたマウン・アエ・キャウは、言葉が話せるようになった時、以上の出来事を物語ったのである。

母親が本人を妊娠する時の状況がマウン・アエ・キャウの場合と似ているのは、アウデシュ・ミシュラの事例である。アウデシュの家族は、カマルプールというところに住んでいた。

そこは、インドのウッタル・プラデシュ州シタプール区にある。アウデシュは、（二歳半頃に）前世の話を始めた時、自分は昔、ハンネ・ラルという者で、死後その遺体は川に流されたと語った。その後、肉体のない本人は、その川で沐浴《もくよく》中だった今の母親の姿を見つけ、母親について行った。アウデシュによれば、ハンネ・ラルは、カマルプールから一四〇キロほど離れたファイザバードの出身だという。それに対して母親は、ファイザバード近郊のアヨディヤという町を流れる川へ沐浴に行ったことがあった。アウデシュは、母親がアヨディヤへ出かけてからちょうど九ヵ月後に生まれた。アウデシュの父親は一緒にアヨディヤへは行かなかった。このことからすると、肉体をもたないハンネ・ラルが母親についてカマルプールまで来て、その後に母親がアウデシュの父親と性関係をもった時を利用したということのようである。アウデシュの発言が事実と確認されたのは、ハンネ・ラルという男性が昔ファイザバードに住んでおり、ペストで死亡していることがわかった時である。本人の家族が（おそらく感染を恐れて）遺体を遺棄したため、近所の人たちが近くの川に遺体を投げ込んでいたのであった。

トルコにもこれと似た事例がある。ユスフ・クセという少年が、ウダバシュイという村に生まれた。この村は、ハタイ地方アンタキヤの北側にあり、イスケンデルンとアンタキヤの中間に位置している。ユスフによれば、前世では、アンタキヤの南二〇キロほどのところにある村に住んでいたという。またユスフは、イスケンデルンからその村に帰る途中で、ウダバシュイの北（イスケンデルンの方向）一〇キロほどのところにある別の村で殺されたことを記憶していた。

なぜユスフは、前世の人格が住んでいた村でも、殺害された村でもなく、他でもないウダバシュイで生まれたのであろうか。この疑問に対する最も可能性の高そうな答が見つかったのは、殺された男の遺体がその後どのように扱われたかがわかった時であった。その男性を殺害した犯人は、遺体の首を切断していたのである。この事件はトルコでも特に無法の蔓《はびこ》った時代に起こったとはいえ、その殺人が行なわれた村の住人たちは、切断された頭部と胴体の処置に困り、警察から面倒な尋問を受けるもとになることを恐れた。そこで村人たちは、その首と胴を南に隣接した村へこっそり運び込み、そこに投げ捨てた。ところが、その村の住民たちも、やはり胴と首はありがたくないので、さらに南の村へと運んだ。そのようにして、その男の頭部と胴体は、結局ウダバシュイまで運ばれたのであった。その村に住む男性がその死体を見つけ、他村の住民の分別を欠いた身勝手な態度を嘆きながら、その遺体を埋葬する手配をした。頭部と胴体は元通りにつながれ、見苦しくないようにして埋葬された。その後まもなく、この敬虔《けいけん》な男性の妻がユスフを出産したのである。

　地理的要因が関係する事例をもう一例紹介しよう。ラリタ・アベヤワルデナという少女は、スリランカの首都コロンボの南東二〇キロほどに位置する小さな町で生まれた。前世の話を始めた時ラリタは、昔コロンボの北五〇キロほどのところに住んでいたと語った。本人の家族は、そのあたりとは全く関係がなかった。本例を調査した結果、ラリタがその生涯を記憶している女性は、コロンボの病院で死亡した後、それまで住んでいたコロンボの北方にある村に埋葬されていたことが判明した。ところが、死亡したその女性の兄弟のうちふたりが、ラリタの生まれた小さな町に住んでいることがわかったのである。そのうちのひとりは、その女性が大好きだった弟で、ラリタの自宅に面した道路沿いの、しかも二〇〇メートルしか離れていないところに住んでいた。また、その女性が死亡した頃を見てもその後の数年間を見ても、ふたりの兄弟の家族には出産適齢期の女性がひとりもいなかったことがわかった。もし生まれ変わりという考え方が本例の最も妥当な説明になるとすれば、ラリタがその生涯を記憶している女性は、死後、ふたりの兄弟のそばにいてその子どもとして生まれ変わりたかったのであろうが、それができなかったため、代わりに近所の家に生まれ変わった、ということのようである。

先述のように、ナイジェリアに住むイボ族の事例は大半が同一家族例であるが、イボ族は、〝宿敵〟例とでも呼ぶべき事例が存在することも認めている。この種の子どもは、かつて自分の村を襲撃して戦死した別の集落の男だった時代を記憶している。この男性は、自分の集落に戻って生まれ変わるべきなのに（イボ族に言わせると）不手際があったため、襲撃した村で生まれ変わったのである。

地理的要因が認められるように思われる事例群はもうひとつある。この群に属する事例では、後に父親や母親となる者が、前世の人格が死去した場所に行っている。ボンクチ・プロムシンの事例を見ればそのことがわかる。第4章で述べたように、ボンクチの父親は、母親が本人を妊娠する少し前に、前世の人格が殺害された現場周辺に行ったことがあった。ボンクチによれば、本人は（肉体をもたない状態で）、バスに乗って帰る父親について行ったというのである。[*14]

物理的距離がもっと遠い例を考えると、地理的要因が認められそうな事例は他にも少なくない。双方の家族が血縁もなく知り合いでもない事例の子どもは、ほとんどの場合、自宅から二五キロ以内のところで送った前世について語るが、双方の家族を隔てる距離がもっと遠い例も少ないながら見られることも確かである。たとえばジャグディシュ・チャンドラの事例では双方の距離は五〇〇キロであり、インディカ・グネラトネの例では一七五キロである。しかし、こうした事例は例外的なものである。ほとんどの子どもは、長距離例も含めて、前世の人格が暮らしていた地域にもっと近いところで生まれている。したがって、双方の家族は、地理的には同一と見なしうる地域に属していると言えるのである。

　ここでまとめると、私がこれまで調査してきた子どものほとんどは、次のいずれかの条件を満たしている。前世の人格が、その記憶をもつ子どもの家族の一員であったか、双方の家族が互いの存在を知って（おり、しばしば懇意にして）いた。前世の人格がその子どもの出生地の近辺で死亡しているか、前世の人格の家族がその子の生まれた地域社会と何らかのつながりをもっていた。その子どもの父親か母親のいずれかが、母親が本人を妊娠する直前（ないしは直後）に、前世の人格が暮らしていた地域や死亡した場所に行っていた。その子どもは、前世の人格の住まいから二五キロ以内のところに住んでいた。

　こうした事例からわかるのは、いかなる理由であれ、もし肉体のない人格が特定の両親の子どもとして生まれ変わるとすれば、物理的距離は全く障害にならないらしいということである。たとえば、ビルマで生まれたマ・ウィン・ミントという少女は、かつてビルマに住んでおり、最後はロンドンで死亡したイギリス人の生まれ変わりであることが確認された。トルコのアドナン・ケレヒという子どもの事例では、前世の人格は（朝鮮戦争中に）トルコ軍の派遣部隊の隊員として韓国で戦っている時に戦死したが、アドナンはトルコ南部のアダナという都市で生まれている。デリーで生まれたヴィニタ・ジャーという少女は、ロンドンで絞殺された少女の生涯を記憶していた。この事例は未決例であるが、ヴィニタは（幼少期に）ロンドンについて正確に物語り、きわめて〝英国風〟の行動を示した。スザンネ・ガーネムはレバノンのチョウエイファテで生まれたが、ヴァージニア州リッチモンドへ心臓手術のために出かけ、そこで死亡したサーダという女性の生涯を記憶していた。

ある人物が他でもない特定の家族のもとに生まれるのを決める要因について以上述べてきたが、関係者はそのプロセスに消極的な形で関与しているのではないか、という印象を、読者の方々は多くの点からもたれるかもしれない。そのことは、大半の事例ではまちがいなく事実である。私たちにわかる限りでは、肉体のない人格が特定の家族に引きつけられるのは、先述のような愛情（および、時としては憎しみ）という絆《きずな》によって知らず知らずのうちにそのような結果になっていたというふうに、ほとんど自動的なもののようである。

しかしながら、一部の事例では意志も関与しているように思われる。自分が死ぬ前に次に生まれ変わる家族を決めており、後に生まれた子どもがその人物の生涯を記憶している証拠を示すこうした事例では、意志もひとつの要因として考慮に入れなければならないであろう。

予告夢（特に嘆願調のもの）も、肉体のない人格が次に生まれ出るべき家族をあらかじめ選んでいることをうかがわせてくれる。若干の予告夢では、特定の家族の中に生まれ変わることを肉体のない人格が決定しているのがわかる。ハイダ族のある事例では、故人が後に母親となる女性の夢の中に現われ、生まれ出るのを待たされていることに対して不満を唱えている。サムエル・ヘランデルの母親は、（後にサムエルがその生涯の記憶を語ることになる）ペルティという亡兄が妊娠中絶をしないようしきりに説得する夢を見たが、その時の模様については既に第4章で説明しておいた。インドにも同様の事例（ラジャニ・スクラの事例）がある。ある家族のラジャニという娘が事故で死亡した。その後、母親は、ラジャニがもう一度お母さんの子どもとして生まれたいと言っている夢を見た。しかし母親は、もう子どもはほしくなかったので中絶してしまった。死んだ娘は再び夢に現われ、生まれ変わらせてくれないとして母親を非難した。結局、母親は同意し、ラジャニを生んだ。後にラジャニは、死んだ姉の生涯を記憶していることがわかったのである。

　ビルマの（ウ・ウィン・マウンが調査した）マウン・ティン・フーン・オーの事例でも、母親が予告夢を二回見ている。最初の夢では、今は亡き身内の女性が現われ、母親の枕の下に財布を入れた。二回目の夢では、夫と自分を乗せた馬にその女性も跨《またが》っているように見えた。母親はその夢を、死んだ身内が自分の赤ん坊として生まれ変わりたがっていることの表われと解釈した。それとほぼ時を同じくして、その身内の従弟《いとこ》も、本人の夢を見た。夢の中でその女性は、従弟の家族はやかましすぎるので一緒には暮らせない、と語ったという。

　以上述べた夢を、夢を見た者の願望や思い込みによるものとして説明することもできようが、次に生まれ変わる際に肉体をもたない人格の少なくとも一部には、特定の家族を自ら選ぶ場合があることをうかがわせてくれる実例ではないかと私は考えている。そのような夢には、生まれ変わりたいとする願望や切望すら見てとれるものがある。

肉体のない人格は次に生まれ変わる肉体にどのような形で影響を及ぼすか

生まれ変わりという考え方を雄弁に支持した哲学者マクタガートは、魂が、次に生まれ変わる時の肉体とどのような関係をもっているかについて検討している。マクタガートは、帽子とそれを被《かぶ》る者との類似性を指摘しているが、帽子では時代遅れと思われる方は、このアナロジーを衣服に置き換えていただいてもよい。次の通りである。

> ロンドンの街中を歩いていて、頭に被っている帽子が全く合わない男に出会うのはきわめて稀《まれ》だ。帽子というものは一般に、それぞれくじ引きで割り当てられたとしたよりも、はるかにぴったりと各人の頭に合っているものだ。とはいえ、頭の形と帽子の形の間には、何らかの因果的結びつきがあることはまずない。人間の頭は、帽子に合うようには造られていないし、たいていの場合、帽子も各人の頭に合うように作られているわけではない。そのようにぴったりと合うのは、各人が、特定の頭に特に合わせては作られていない帽子の山の中から、自分の頭に一番ぴったりした帽子を選び出すためなのだ。[*15]

ここで胎児を考えると、胎児はたくさん造られることにまず注目すべきである。そうすると、肉体をもたない人格は、自分に一番ぴったりした胎児を選び出したり（あるいは、造り出すことまでしたり）、他の胎児と結びつくのを避けたりすることができるものかどうか、という疑問が浮かび上がる。もうひとつは、自分が買った帽子に詰め物をしたりのばしたりして自分の頭に多少なりとも合うようにするのと同じく、肉体をもたない人格が自分の選んだ胎児に修正を加えることもできるのか、という疑問である。このうち、後者の可能性については、ここでいろいろお話しするのは時期尚早であるように思う。それに関する証拠のほとんどは、まだ発表していないからである。その証拠については、現在準備中の、母《ぼ》斑《はん》や先天性欠損を伴う事例を扱った著書の中で明らかにするつもりでいる。

選択可能な胎児の中から選び出すという可能性

これまで述べたように、双方の家族の間には、個人的、地理的な結びつきが見られる場合が多いが、そのことからすると、生まれ変わろうとしている肉体のない人格は、愛情や友情によってその家族と前世で結びつきがあったためか、先述のような地理的要因のため、特定の家族に（おそらくは強く）引きつけられるらしいことがわかる。肉体のない人格と両親となるべき夫婦との間に引き合う力があるとすれば、生まれ変わろうとする人格は、大半の場合、両親が提供する胎児は何であれ引き受けざるをえない立場に置かれているように思われる。この点、帽子とそれを被る者というマクタガートのアナロジーは役に立たないことがわかる。どの夫婦にしても、生まれ変わろうとしている者の求めに応じられる幅はわずかだからである。ほとんどの夫婦は、帽子屋が客に提供できるほど多様な胎児を用意することはできない。肉体のない人物が、医学用語を使えば、主としてあるいは全面的に疾病産生遺伝子によって起こるハンチントン舞踏病や鎌状赤血球貧血、血友病などの病気をもつ家族にいわば強く引きつけられるとすると、その人物は、そうした遺伝子をもつ肉体に賭《か》けてみなければならないことになろう。もし、たとえばある人物が、血友病の遺伝子をもっている女性の息子として生まれ変わるとすると、生まれて来た子どもが血友病をもっている確率は二分の一になる。（このような母親からでも、半数は血友病を発病する遺伝子をもたない子どもが生まれるのである。）

ひとたび両親となる夫婦を決めてしまうと、肉体の選択と言ってみても、生まれ変わりつつある平均的な人間にはどうすることもできないと思うが、ある種の選択過程の介在をうかがわせる事例も時おり見られる。こうした証拠は、性転換や双生児の事例に見出《みいだ》される。

性転換型の事例は、この問題を検討するうえで最良のデータを提供してくれる。ある人物が、次に生まれ変わる時には今とは違う性別になりたい、という願望を生前に表明したとしよう。[*16] 胚《はい》および、（胚が発育した）胎児の性別は、卵子を受精する精子の性染色体によって決定される。その精子がY染色体をもっている時には、胚の性別は男性となり、X染色体の時には女性となる。父親の精子は、半数がY染色体を、半数がX染色体をもっているので、どの胚にしても、男性および女性となる確率はそれぞれ五〇パーセントずつのはずである。このような状況の中で、肉体をもたない人格は、次のいずれかの方法により、希望する性別の胚と結びつくのであろう。つまり、肉体のない人格は、自分の望む性別にしてくれる精子を、受精を待つ卵子の方へと誘導する一方、逆の性染色体をもった精子が卵子に近づかないようにすることができるのかもしれないし、希望する性別の受精卵（および初期の胚）ができるまで、逆の性別の受精卵や胚を排出させるよう仕向けることもできるのかもしれない。

性交が排卵の一日ないし数日前に行なわれた場合には、排卵当日に行なわれる時よりも男児を妊娠しやすい。[17]（しかしながら、人工授精の場合には、その逆になる。[18]）Y染色体をもった精子はX染色体を伴った精子よりも活動性が高いが、[19]精子が進む体液の粘稠《ねんちゆう》度その他の特性によって、この利点が減じられたり、消失したりするのかもしれない。受精を迎える女性の体に生理学的な変化が起こると、二種類の精子の侵入力はそれによってそれぞれ異なった影響を受ける可能性がある。肉体のない人格は、自分の母親になるかもしれない女性に対して、テレパシーにより影響を与え、男性の受精卵になる確率を高めたり低めたりするような精神身体的変化を起こすのかもしれない。とはいえ、この方法は、次に結びつく肉体の性別を確実に決めるうえでは、当てにならない方法のように思われる。

次にありそうな可能性としては、受精卵の多くが次回の生理の際に排出されてしまうか、予定日の少し後に流産してしまうことが考えられる。この場合、当の女性は流産に全く気づかず、生理がいつもより遅れて量も多かったとしか思わないかもしれない。[20]肉体のない人格は、次に生まれ変わる時になりたい性別の胚ができるまで、このようにして早い時期に受精卵を排出させてしまうのかもしれない。そして、希望する性別の胚ができると、発育を続けさせるのではなかろうか。

平均すると、受精卵の（ほぼ）半数は男性、半数は女性なので、肉体をもたない人格は、性転換を起こす予定の時もそうではない時も、受精卵の性別を監視している必要があろう。性転換を起こす予定のない時も監視していなければならないという点は重要である。現在、手元に集まっている事例から判断できる限り、性転換は、発生率が比較的高い国ですら珍しい（たとえばビルマでも二八パーセントにすぎない）うえに、レバノンやトルコなどの国では全く発生しないからである。したがって、性転換を起こそうとする時よりも、回避しようとする時の方が監視が必要になるはずである。

特定の性別の受精卵を作り出すのに必要な精子を卵子と受精させることに失敗し、しかもその受精卵を流産させることもできなかったとしても、肉体のない人格は、第三の方法を用いて新しい肉体の性別を操作することができるのかもしれない。つまり、希望する性別の受精卵が母親の子宮内で発育するまで待ち、その胎児と結びつくという方法である。このようなことが起こる可能性をうかがわせてくれる事例も若干ある。それは、その子がもう一度自分たちのところへ戻って来てほしいと、死んだ子どもの両親が希《ねが》う事例である。その子どもがはっきりした母斑や傷痕《きずあと》をもっていれば、あるいは両親が（アフリカやアジアで一部行なわれているように）子どもの遺体に印をつけたり手足を切断したりしていれば、その後に生まれた子どもの体にそれと一致する母斑や先天性欠損があるかどうかを調べるであろう。そして、生まれて来た子どもにそういった身元証明になるものがあれば、死んだ子どもの生まれ変わりだと考えることであろう。[*21] 母斑や傷痕をもっていた子どもが死亡してから、その生まれ変わりとされる子どもが生まれるまでの間に、他にも子どもが生まれる場合もあるであろう。このような間に生まれた子どもたちは、死んだ子どもとその生まれ変わりと目される子どもとは（必ずしもそうとは限らないが）時おり性別が異なっている。このことからすると、生まれ変わろうとする人格は、性別に対する執着が強く、同じ性別の肉体が手に入るまで何とかして待ち続けているらしいことがわかる。とはいえ、この群に属する（性別という点ではどうやらもっと柔軟な考え方をとっているらしい）他の子どもたちは、それまでとは逆の性別の肉体で生まれ変わるのではないかと思われる。

双生児の事例の中には、以上の推測を裏づけてくれそうな実例がいくつかある。先述のように、私が調査した双生児の事例の大半で、ふたりがある程度親密な関係にあったという前世時代を、双生児の一方ないし双方が記憶していたのである。このような双生児たちは通例、同じ家族の一員であったり、親友同士であったりなど、互いに親密な間柄にあった。このような点からすると、この種の事例では肉体をもたない二個の人格が同時に生まれ変わりたいという強い願望をもっていたか、それ以外の何らかの理由があったらしいことがわかる。単生児として別々に生まれる代わりに双生児として同時に生まれたことには、先ほど述べた前世の結びつきが関係しているように思われる。

ふたりの人間が、生前、双生児として生まれ変わると公言し、その後、その予言が成就されたように思われる事例は、私たちの手元に一例もない。しかしながら、肉体のない人格が、村の友人と一緒に双生児として生まれ変わろうとしていたことを裏づける証拠が存在する事例は一例ある。このビルマの（ドゥ・ニン・アエが調査した）事例の中心人物はマウン・キャウ・ミント・ナインである。母親は双生児を妊娠中に、マウン・タン・アウンという今は亡き親族が、息子として生まれ出たい、ここに（夢の中ではその名前は出て来なかったが）仲間を連れてきている、と話しかける夢を見た。その夢を見てまもなく母親は、（胎盤がひとつしかなかったのでたぶん一卵性の）双生児を出産した。その後マウン・キャウ・ミント・ナインは前世の話をするようになった時、肉体のない世界にいる間、ウ・サインという人物を一緒に生まれ変わるべく誘った記憶について語った。それによると、ウ・サインは、かつて住んでいた村の自宅周辺に肉体のない状態のまま留《とど》まっていたという。双子のもう一方は、ウ・サインの記憶を全くもっていなかった。

双生児として誰かと親密な間柄で一生を送りたいと望む、肉体のない人格は、双子の胚が手に入るまでひたすら待ち続けるだけなのかもしれない。しかし、肉体をもたない人格自体が、母親の胎内に二体の胎児を成長させる可能性もある。もしそのようなことが起こるとすれば、受精卵（接合体）を、遺伝的には同一のまま二分する（一卵性双生児）か、二個の精子によってほぼ同時に受精が起こるような位置に卵子をふたつ移動させる（二卵性双生児）かの、いずれかの方法を用いるのであろう。[*22]

次に、生まれ変わろうとしている人格が、自分の体に特定の病気や障害を起こすようにある程度の操作を加えた可能性のある事例について考えてみることにしよう。ここでは、例として、明らかに遺伝性の鎌状赤血球貧血という疾患について検討してみよう。私がここでこの疾患をとり上げるのは、西アフリカに住む民族の中に、この疾患が特殊な生まれ変わりに関係していると考える者が多いからでもある。

　鎌状赤血球貧血の遺伝形式は完全に解明されている。ある夫婦がそれぞれ、この病気の特徴である異常な血色素を産み出す遺伝因子Sの保有者（ヘテロ接合体）である時、平均的にはその子どもの四分の一がホモ接合体となり、鎌状赤血球貧血に罹《かか》ることが予測できる。これは容易ならぬ疾患であり、子どもの多くはこの病気のため幼少期に死亡する。子どもがたくさんいる西アフリカの家族では、鎌状赤血球貧血による死亡数は他のさまざまな病気による死亡数とが同程度であるため、幼児の死亡率が高い。イボ族をはじめとする西アフリカの諸部族では、同一家族内で幼児が繰り返し死亡する場合、別の人格が死亡しているわけではないと考えられている。そうではなく、同じ人格が短期間の生まれ変わりを次々と繰り返し、生まれてから二、三ヵ月あるいは二、三年で死に、もう一度生まれてまた死に、また生まれ変わっているとされているのである。（こうした繰り返しが、ひとつの家族の中で数回発生することもある。）アフリカでは、このような子どもたちに特別な名前（イボ語でオバンジェ）がつけられているが、この概念は英語では、〝繰り返し《リピーター》の子ども〟という表現が一番ぴったりする。[*23]

　西アフリカでは乳幼児の死亡率が高いため、両親の悲しみは大きいが、その悲しみは、経済的な意味で大切な子どもたちを早期に失ってしまうことによる怒りという要素と入り混じっている。そのため、驚くには当たらないが、西アフリカに住む人たちは、〝繰り返しの子ども〟は生まれ変わって両親を苦しめるためにのみ夭折《ようせつ》することを心に誓った悪霊と結託している、とする信仰を生み出した。親たちは、体に病気のある子どもはもちろん、虚弱児ですら、〝繰り返しの子ども〟なのではないかと考え、死んでまた仲よくしようと誘惑する（肉体のない）一群の子どもの霊からその子を引き離すための策を講ずることもある。そして、オバンジェ呪《じゅ》医《い》を呼び、子どもの掌《てのひら》を傷つけてもらうなど、その子が死なないようにするための儀式を執り行なうのである。にもかかわらずその子どもが死亡すると、両親は遺体の手足を切断する。たとえば、ナイジェリアのイボ・ランドにあるアウグに住むイボ族の一団は、死んだ子どもの左小指の先を切り取ることが多い。その人たち（あるいは呪医）がそうした儀式を行なっている時、両親は、家族のもとに留まり一人前になるまで成長を続けようと思わない限り二度と戻って来ないよう、死んだ子どもの魂に言い聞かせる。それから、次の子どもが生まれるのを待ち、子どもが生まれた時、小指の先が欠けていると喜ぶ。それにより、その子どもが、夭逝《ようせい》した子どもの生まれ変わりと認めるからである。両親は、その子どもがまた生まれてきたことを歓迎し、〝繰り返しの子ども〟の同盟から脱退したか追放されたと見なし、成人に達するまで丈夫に育つことを期待する[*24]。

以上のことは、一見して感じられるほど本題から外れているわけではない。次に、最初は何らかの理由から鎌状赤血球貧血をもった子どもとして生まれ、いったん死亡した後、今度はその病気をもたずに同じ家族の中にもう一度生まれ変わることになるイボ族の架空の例を考えてみよう。こうした肉体のない人格が選択できる道は、どのようなものであろうか。鎌状赤血球遺伝子はX染色体にもY染色体にも載っていないので、前世の人格は、S遺伝子を運搬する精子による受精を阻止することはできないように思われる。あるいはそのような可能性もあるのかもしれないが、その物理的メカニズムについては全くわからない。もし生まれ変わろうとしている肉体のない人格が鎌状赤血球貧血をもった肉体と結びつくことになるとすれば、その人格は、未来の母親が四回受精するうち平均で一回生ずるホモ接合性胚子《はいし》を、何らかの方法で見分ける必要があることになろう。来世では鎌状赤血球貧血を起こさないことになっているため、その人格は、他の二種類の胚のいずれかと結びつくはずである。つまり、単なるS遺伝子保有者に留まる胚と、鎌状赤血球貧血の際に侵される血色素については正常な遺伝子をもっている胚の二種類である。後者と結びつく方が、前者よりも容易であろう。平均で四分の三の胚が、鎌状赤血球貧血の発病を免れるからである。

胚の選択に影響を与えるため、肉体をもたない人格は、いま受精しているのは（あるいは既に受精が終わったのは）どのような胚か――つまり、鎌状赤血球貧血を発病させるS遺伝子をもっているか否かを――何らかの方法で知る必要があろう。双生児について検討した中で推定されたように、肉体のない二個の人格は、ひとりの女性の二個の卵子をほとんど同時に受精が起こるよう操作するか、さもなければ、ひとつの接合体（受精卵）をある発達段階でふたつに等分するのかもしれない。

このような芸当ができると考えてよければ、肉体をもたない人格が、鎌状赤血球貧血をもった肉体へと成長を遂げる胚を選んだり避けたりすることが可能なのではないかと考えてもよいはずである。この時、超常的な手段によって知っておく必要のあることがあるが、その際に要求される能力は、特異能力をもつ一部の人間が示す以上のものではない。[25] ここで言おうとしているのは、たとえば性転換したうえで鎌状赤血球貧血のない状態で生まれ変わろうとしている肉体のない人格が、胚に関する情報を意識的に処理し、それによって合理的な決定を下している、ということではない。私が言おうとしているのは、単に、その人格がどのような問題に直面するかということであって、その問題の解決法を私が知っているということではないのである。何の前ぶれもなく死に直面した時、「妻のところへ行って、自分が死にかかっているのを知らせてやらなければ」と意識の上で思う者は、(いるとしても)ほとんどいないのではなかろうか。これまでわかっている限りでは、ほとんどの霊姿は無意識のうちに出現している。[26] 同様に、肉体のない人格は、来世の両親に引き寄せられ、次いで、その両親が提供してくれる特定の受精卵ないしは胚に引きつけられるのではないか、ということである。口から入った食物が胃の中で消化されるのを調節したり、通常の呼吸をコントロールしたり表皮の傷を跡形なく癒《いや》してしまうレベルよりもはるかに深いレベルにある精神活動は、こうしたプロセスを支配しているにちがいない。

　肉体のない人格が自分の母親になりそうな女性に影響を与えることができるかどうかという問題については、確固とした知識を出発点に論を進めることができる。少なくとも私たちは、心理的事象が女性の生殖器系の機能に大きな影響を与えることがあるという事実を承知している。ストレスを受けた結果、生理の時期が多少なりとも変動したという経験をしたことのない女性がいるものであろうか。そのような女性が存在するとは思われないが、心理的出来事によって、女性の生殖器官には、生理が遅れたり飛んだりすること以上にさまざまな変化が起こりうる。こうした影響が極端な形で現われるのは、偽妊娠すなわち想像妊娠の時である。現実はそうではないのに妊娠したと思い込むという状態に陥った女性は、そうした思い込みが続く間、長期にわたって生理が止まることもある。さらには、腹部や乳房が大きくなり、生殖に関係するホルモンに変化が生ずることすらあるのである。[*27] こうした身体的変化は、その女性が最終的に、自分は妊娠していないことを——何ヵ月もたった後の場合が多いが——気づかされると、そのとたんにすべて消失する。

受精能力をもつ女性でも、心理的要因によって妊娠が起こらなくなることを示す証拠もある程度存在する。不妊と思われている女性でも、養子を迎えると妊娠することが少なくない。このような事実からすると、その女性（およびその夫）は、本人（ないしはふたり）の受精能力に影響を及ぼしていた、子どもをもつことに対するある種の心理的抵抗を乗り越えたらしいことがわかる。トロブリアンド諸島に住む民族は、自由に婚前交渉を行なうが、婚前の妊娠は忌み嫌う。この民族は物理的な避妊法を全く用いないし、妊娠中絶も稀《まれ》ないしは皆無である。それでいながらトロブリアンド諸島の人たちの間では、結婚する前に妊娠する比率はきわめて低い。以上のような事実からすると、この地域に住む未婚女性の妊娠は、精神身体的プロセスによって抑制されているらしいことがわかる。[*28]

心理的要因が生殖機能に影響を及ぼすことを裏づけるもうひとつの証拠は、卵子が受精前に〝過熟〟するという現象の研究に基づいたものである。これが先天性欠損を引き起こす要因のひとつになっているのかもしれない。そして、心理的ストレスが、卵子の過熟を生じさせる原因のひとつになっているように思われる。[*29]

　これまで述べてきたような変化を起こすのに必要な程度まで、肉体のない人格が未来の母親ないし精子および接合体に直接影響を与えることがありうるかどうかについても、やはり考えてみなければならない。妊娠を切望したり忌避したりする時に起こる現象に関係した先述の証拠からすると（あまり強力な証拠ではないことは確かであるが）、肉体のない人格は母親の身体的状態に影響を与える可能性がある。心霊研究の歴史をひもといてみても、肉体のない人格が、自分の死ぬ時に体験した身体症状を霊媒を通して出現させた例がいくつかあることがわかる。[*30] もし肉体のない人格が、女性の体に、以上の例から示唆されるような影響を及ぼすことができるとすれば、女性の体内にある接合体や胚をそのまま成長させるように、あるいは逆に流し去るようにすることができるのではないか、と考えてもそれほど無理はないように思われる。

肉体のない人格は胚の発育にどのような形で影響を与えるのか

　前世の人格の傷痕《きずあと》やあざなどと一致する母斑《ぼはん》や先天性欠損をもつ事例からすると、肉体のない人格は、次の生まれ変わりで結びつく胚を選び出す以上の操作をしている可能性が示唆される。妊娠期間中に、胚の成長を加減することまでしているかもしれないのである。

　既に説明したように、本書では、母斑や先天性欠損をもつ事例についてこれ以上詳しい検討はしたくない。ここでは、別著ないし本書の改訂版の中でもう一度この問題を取り上げることをお約束するだけに留《とど》めておきたい。

前世の行ないが来世に及ぼす影響

　第2章で力説しておいたように、生まれ変わり信仰をもつ世界各地の民族の多くは、それぞれの倫理的規範と結びつけることなく生まれ変わりを信じている。生まれ変わり信仰を道徳的な側面と結びつけるのは、ヒンドゥー教や仏教に独特の考え方なのではないか、と言ってもまちがいではないかもしれない。しかし、ほとんどの西洋人は、ドゥルーズ族やアレヴィス族、トリンギット族、イボ族のような民族が保持している概念よりもヒンドゥー教や仏教の概念の方をはるかによく知っているので、生まれ変わりを信じている者の大半は、カルマというヒンドゥー教徒や仏教徒に共通の概念を頓着《とんちゃく》せず採り入れてきた。カルマという考え方によれば、善行や悪行を行なった直後の来世とは限らないが、過去世の行ないによって来世の運命が決まるのである。

　私が調査した事例では、前世の行ないが現世の外的状況に影響を及ぼしたことを裏づける証拠は見つかっていない。前世および現世の家族の社会経済的地位に大きな開きのある事例を検討しても、不品行によって社会経済的地位が下がり、徳行により上がることを示す徴候は見られない。裕福な環境の中で過ごした前世の記憶を残しながら、現世では貧しい物的状況の下に生まれた子どもたちの中には、あまりの落差をくよくよと思い悩み、格下げになったのは記憶に残っている前世で道徳上の罪や法的な罪を犯したせいだと考えていた。第9章で簡単に紹介しておいたラニ・サクセナや、やはりインドのビシェン・チャンド・カプールはそのグループに入る。ビシェン・チャンド・カプールの事例については既に随所でふれているが、最も明確な特徴についてはまだ述べていない。

ビシェン・チャンドは、貧しい両親のもとに生まれたが、裕福な青年の生涯を記憶していた。この、ラクシュミ・ナラインという青年は、愛人のアパートから出て来た男を見つけ、その男を射殺した。その後ラクシュミ・ナラインは、しばらく身を潜め、検察官を買収し、事件のもみ消しを図った。二、三年後、ナラインは自然死を遂げた。ビシェン・チャンドは幼少期に、この殺人の模様や、どのようにして刑罰を免れたかをよく自慢そうに話していた。本人の幼少期は、ラクシュミ・ナラインがかつてそうであったように、裕福な家庭のだだっ子そのものであった。ビシェン・チャンドは、自分の両親が貧しいことに不満を唱え、豪華な食事や衣服を要求したが、ふたりにその余裕はなかった。その後、本人は態度を改めた。ラクシュミ・ナラインが殺人を犯したために自分は貧しい両親の子どもとして生まれたのかもしれない、という思いが次第に起こるようになったからであった。（前世にまつわる他のイメージ記憶が消失した後も、殺人の記憶だけはしばらく残っていた。）ビシェン・チャンドはすっかり改心し、その後（私が本人を知った時には）、ラクシュミ・ナラインが殺人を犯した時に見せたような粗暴な態度はみじんも示さなくなっていた。

他の事例の中にも、前世の行ないは来世の運命を実際に左右するのではないかと考えたくなるような例がいくつかある。レバノンのゾウハイル・チャールの事例もそのひとつである。第9章で私は、ある子どもの前世の人格と思《おぼ》しき男性（ジャミル・アドナン・ザール）が本人（ゾウハイル）の母親と灌漑《かんがい》用水を巡って口論した模様について述べておいた。ゾウハイルはドゥルーズ族であった。先に説明しておいたが、ドゥルーズ族は、前世の行ないが来世の運命を決めるという信仰をもっているわけではない。にもかかわらず、ゾウハイルの事例を耳にした者は、その母親の息子として生まれてきたのは皮肉でありひとつの戒めであると考えた。この事例を前にした時、ドゥルーズ族の人々であれば、今の母親のもとに生まれてきたのは、ふたりのいずれかに何らかの不行跡があったためだとは言わないであろう。ゾウハイルの父親が私に話してくれたところでは、ジャミル・アドナン・ザールがゾウハイル・チャールとして生まれ変わる時に、ふたりの間にある強い憎悪の念がもう一度ふたりを結びつける要因として作用したのではないかとのことであった。

　以上の事例をはじめとする若干の事例の中に、因果応報のような過程が介在することをうかがわせる、私の気づいた唯一の徴候が見てとれる。とはいえ、このような事例であっても、この種の過程が実在することを裏づける証拠にはならない。前世と現世で自分の置かれている環境が異なっていることに対する本人（および世間一般の人々）の解釈は、結局のところ、その落差をもっともらしく説明している以上のものではないのであろう。それでも、因果応報という考え方に与《くみ》する人たちは、そのことを裏づける証拠がないにもかかわらず、二通りの説明を用いてこの考え方を正当化することであろう。自他ともに認める犯罪者であっても、たとえば自分の家族には献身的な愛情を注ぐなど、陰で大きな徳を積んでおり、そのおかげで物質的にはそれまでより恵まれた環境に格上げされたのであり、同様に、表では聖人君子のようなふるまいをしていた者でも、裏では悪行に耽《ふけ》っており、それによって次の生まれ変わりでは格下げになったのだ、と言うかもしれない。また、因果応報という概念の支持者は、このように考えたのでは全例がうまく説明できそうにない時には、不行跡の影響は何度も生まれ変わった後に初めて現われるのではないか、と主張するかもしれない。この種の説明は、反駁《はんばく》することもできないかわり、支持することもできない。こうした考え方を実証的レベルで検討する方法は、私には全くわからない。

　私が調査した事例からは、因果応報のような現象の存在を裏づける証拠は全く得られていないが、だからと言って、前世の行ないが来世の明暗を分けることはありえない、と言い切れるわけではない。前世の行状による影響が来世に及ぶとすればそれは、生まれ変わる際に物理的条件として外部に表われるのではなく、喜びや悲しみとして内部に生ずるものなのであろう。この点で（しかも、私見によればこの点でのみ）、生まれ変わり型事例は、生まれ変わりを繰り返す中で私たち自身が向上することに対する希望を与えてくれる。前世を記憶する子どもたちは、前世の人格と同じような関心や適性や態度を示すことが少なくない。こうした共通点は、職業という点のみならず、対人的行動すなわち、道徳的な意味での行ないという点にも見られる。ある子どもは、その生涯を記憶している物欲の強かった実業家のように、自分の手に握れる硬貨の枚数を数えるが、別の子どもは、前世の人格とされる信心深い女性と同じように、身銭を惜しげもなく物乞いに恵む。また、自分の前世だという盗賊がしたように、通りがかりの警官に向かって発砲でもするような形で棒を構える少年もいれば、前世の医者と同じように、遊び友達に対してしきりに診察や治療のまねをする少年もいる。

しかしながら、以上のような子どもたちは、全員が前世時代の態度を保持し続けていたわけではないし、一部の子どもに新しい習慣が芽ばえたという話を聞いたり、そのありさまを自分の眼で時おり見たりすることもできた。このような進歩には、新しい環境の影響が見てとれるかもしれないが、それと同時に、本人の自我自体の働きによって生じた心の成長も見逃せないと思う。アッシジの聖フランチェスコの側近であった聖アエギディウスの、「良きにつけ悪しきにつけ、人間が行なうことは全て、自らに対して行なっているのである」という言葉には深い真理がある。[*31] したがって、こうした事例の証拠を基に判断すれば、私たちの行ないを裁く主体は外部には存在しないし、私たちの功罪に従って次に生まれ変わる時に、私たちを昇格させたり降格させたりする存在もない。もしこの世が（キーツの言うように）「魂を造る世」[*32]であるなら、私たちは自分自身の魂を作っているのである。

徳性という点では天才である聖人たちは、他人に対して献身的な行ないをすると安らかな気持になると語っているし、それが事実であることも身をもって示している。ここで言う献身的な行ないとは、安らかな気持になれること以外、自分の得になるものを全く期待しない行動のことである。ピタゴラスが語ったとされる（とはいえ真偽のほどは疑わしい）言葉には、この教えが具体的に示されている。ピタゴラスは友人に次のような手紙を書いたと言われる。「君は不当に扱われていると嘆いておられますが、こう考えて慰めになさってください。本当の不幸は、不当なふるまいをすることにあるのだと」。

自らを向上させようとする場合、周囲の者が示してくれる以上の手本が必要だと思われるかもしれないし、犯罪者や道徳的に凡庸な人間の子どもとしてではなく、聖人の子どもとして生まれるという有利な立場を望まれるかもしれない。聖人の子どもに生まれれば、生まれ変わりに際して最高の昇格を果たしたことになるのであろう。そのようなことが起こりうる証拠は存在するものであろうか。その点については何とも言えないが、こうした事例に関係する、かくも多くの者をつなぐ家族や地域の絆《きずな》から逃れることが不可能なわけではない。大半の事例では、前世の記憶をもつ子どもと前世の人格との間に家族関係や地域的、宗教的な結びつきが存在することがわかっているが、一部には友情で結びついている例もある。こうした点からすれば、来世では古い家族関係を断ち切り、新しい関係を築くことも、現世と同じように可能らしいことがわかる。

前世の原因によって来世にその結果が生ずることを示す、私たちが現在もっている証拠について言えることは以上である。私は多くのことを言いすぎたかもしれない。本書を締めくくるにあたって、私たちはまだ何もわかっていないことを認めておかなければならないし、その点は強調しておかなければならないと思う。前世を記憶しているという子どもたちの研究を通じて私は、実際に生まれ変わった子どもが一部にいることを確信したが、それと同時に、生まれ変わりという現象についてはまだほとんどわかっていないことも思い知らされたのである。

付録

本書に引用された事例は、以下の一覧表に、前世を記憶するという子どもの（姓ではなく）名前の（五十音）順に並んでいる。本文中で（特にビルマの子どもやタイの修道僧に）時おり用いられている敬称は、この一覧表では外してある。

引用頻度の高い原典については、次のような略語を用いている。

『20例』→『生まれ変わりを思わせる二〇の事例』（文献312参照）

『生まれ1、2、3、4』→『生まれ変わり型の事例　第一―四巻』（文献314、317、321、324参照）

『母《ぼ》斑《はん》・欠損』→母斑や先天性欠損をもつ子どもの事例報告を扱った、現在執筆中の拙著

「未発表」となっている事例の中には、詳細な報告の発表が予定されているものもある。

＊　＊　＊

子どもの名前	詳細な事例報告が掲載されている文献
アウデシュ・ミシュラ（インド）	未発表
アウン・コ・テインとアウン・チョ・テイン（ビルマ）	未発表
アウン・タン（ビルマ）	『母斑・欠損』
アウン・ミント（ビルマ）	未発表

アエ・キャウ（ビルマ）　『母斑・欠損』
アシャ・ラニ（インド）　未発表
アドナン・ケレヒ（トルコ）　未発表
アヌシャ・セネワルデナ（スリランカ）　文献51
アムパン・ペトチェラト（タイ）　『生まれ4』（文献324）
アリス・ロバートソン（合衆国）　未発表
アリフ・ハメッド（レバノン）　未発表
アレクサンドリナ・サモナ（イタリア）　文献59、303
イシュワール・ゴドボレ（インド）　未発表
イスマイル・アルティンキリヒ（トルコ）　『生まれ3』（文献312）
イチティヤケ・アラムディン（レバノン）　未発表
イマド・エラワール（レバノン）　『20例』（文献321）
イン・マウン（ビルマ）　『生まれ4』（文献324）
インディカ・イシュワラとカクシャッパ・イシュワラ（スリランカ）　『母斑・欠損』
インディカ・グネラトネ（スリランカ）　『生まれ2』（文献317）
ヴィアス・ラジパル（インド）　未発表
ウィジャナマ・キトシリ（スリランカ）　『生まれ2』（文献317）
ウィジェラトネ（スリランカ）　『20例』（文献312）
ヴィニタ・ジャー（インド）　未発表
ウィマラワティ・サマラセケラ（スリランカ）　未発表

ウィリアム・ジョージ・ジュニア（合衆国・トリンギット）	『20例』（文献312）
ウィン・アウン（ビルマ）	未発表
ウィン・アエ（ビルマ）	未発表
ウィン・シュウェ（ビルマ）	未発表
ウィン・ミント（ビルマ）	未発表
ヴェール・シン（インド）	『生まれ1』（文献314）
ウッタラ・フダール（インド）	文献328
ウドー・ラム（インド）	未発表
エドワード・ライアル（イギリス）	文献264
エリン・ジャクソン（合衆国）	未発表
エルカン・キリヒ（トルコ）	『生まれ3』（文献321）
オム・プラカーシュ・マツール（インド）	『母斑・欠損』
オルヌマ・スア・イン・ヨン（タイ）	『生まれ4』（文献324）
ガミニ・ジャヤセナ（スリランカ）	『生まれ2』（文献317）
キャウ・ミント・ナイン（ビルマ）	未発表
キン・サン・ティンとキン・サン・イン（タイ）	未発表
キン・サンディ（ビルマ）	『母斑・欠損』
キン・マ・ギーとキン・マ・ネ（タイ）	文献318（ただし簡単な要約のみ）詳細な報告は『母斑・欠損』に収録予定。

グナナティレカ・バデウィタナ（スリランカ）　『20例』（文献312）
クムクム・ヴェルマ（インド）　『生まれ1』（文献314）
ゲオルク・ナイトハルト（ドイツ）　文献192
ケネディ・アルカン（トルコ）　未発表
ゴーパール・グプタ（インド）　『生まれ1』（文献314）
コーリス・チョトキン・ジュニア（合衆国・トリンギット）　『20例』（文献312）
サイド・ザール（レバノン）　未発表
サムエル・ヘランデル（フィンランド）　未発表
サムパト・プリヤサンタ（スリランカ）　『母斑・欠損』
サヤドウ・ウ・ソバナ→ソバナ（サヤドウ・ウ師）
サレム・アンダリ（レバノン）　『生まれ3』（文献321）
サンジヴ・シャルマ（インド）　『母斑・欠損』
シヴァンティ・ヘティアラトチとシェロミー・ヘティアラトチ（スリランカ）　『母斑・欠損』
シダト・ウィジェラトネ（スリランカ）　未発表
ジャグディシュ・チャンドラ（インド）　『生まれ1』（文献314）
ジャスビール・シン（インド）　『20例』（文献312）
シャムリニー・プレマ（スリランカ）　『生まれ2』（文献317）
シャンティ・デヴィ（インド）　文献115、303
ジュギ・ラル・アガルワル（インド）　『母斑・欠損』

ジュディト・クリシュナ（インド）　未発表
シュレイマン・ゼイツン（トルコ）　『生まれ3』（文献321）
ジリアン・ポロックとジェニファー・ポロック（イギリス）　『母斑・欠損』
スクラ・グプタ（インド）　『20例』（文献312）
スーザン・イーストランド（合衆国）　未発表
スザンネ・ガーネム（レバノン）　未発表
スジト・ラクマル・ジャヤラトネ（スリランカ）　『生まれ2』（文献317）
スニタ・カンデルワル（インド）　『母斑・欠損』
スニル・ドゥット・サクセナ（インド）　『生まれ1』（文献314）
スレイマン・アンダリ（レバノン）　『生まれ3』（文献321）
スレイマン・ボウハムジ（シリア）　『20例』（文献312）
スワラン・ラタ（インド）　文献219
スワルンラタ・ミシュラ（インド）　『20例』（文献312）
セヴリエ・バイリ（トルコ）　『生まれ3』（文献321）
セミ・ツツシュムシュ（トルコ）　『母斑・欠損』
セミル・ファリシ（トルコ）　『母斑・欠損』
セラル・カパン（トルコ）　『母斑・欠損』
ゾウハイル・チャール（レバノン）　『生まれ3』（文献321）
ソエ・ヤ（ビルマ）　文献51
ソバナ（サヤドウ・ウ師）（ビルマ）　『生まれ4』（文献324）

ソム・ピト（タイ）　『母斑・欠損』
ダニエル・ジルディ（レバノン）　未発表
タルー・イェルヴィ（フィンランド）　未発表
タン・タン・アエ（ビルマ）　未発表
チャオクン・ラジスタジャルン→ラジスタジャルン（チャオクン師）
チャールズ・ポーター（合衆国・トリンギット）　『20例』（文献312）
チョエ・ニン・テト（ビルマ）　『母斑・欠損』
ツサリ・ウィジャシンへ（スリランカ）　文献51
ティアン・サン・クラ（タイ）　『母斑・欠損』
ディスナ・サマラシンへ（スリランカ）　『生まれ2』（文献317）
ティン・アウン・ミヨ（ビルマ）　『生まれ4』（文献324）、文献320
ティン・セイン（ビルマ）　『母斑・欠損』
ティン・ティン・ミント（ビルマ）　『生まれ4』（文献324）
テイン・フーン・オー（ビルマ）　未発表
デレク・ピトノヴ（合衆国・トリンギット）　『20例』（文献312）
ドロン・チャムパ・ミトラ（インド）　『生まれ1』（文献314）
ナシル・トコセズ（トルコ）　『生まれ3』（文献321）
ナワル・ドウ（レバノン）　文献313
ニランカル・バトナガル（インド）　『母斑・欠損』
ネカティ・サイラク（トルコ）　『生まれ3』（文献21）

ネシブ・ユンリュタシキラン（トルコ）　『母斑・欠損』
ハイール・カム・カニヤ（タイ）　『生まれ4』（文献324）
パウロ・ロレンツ（ブラジル）　『20例』（文献312）
バジラン・B・サクセナ（インド）　『母斑・欠損』
パルモッド・シャルマ（インド）　『20例』（文献312）
ビシェン・チャンド・カプール（インド）　『生まれ1』（文献314）
ピタゴラス（ギリシャ）　文献135
ファルク・ファリス・アンダリ（レバノン）　『生まれ3』（文献321）
フサム・ハリビ（レバノン）　文献51
プシュパ（インド）　文献219
プティ・パトラ（インド）　『生まれ1』（文献314）
プラカーシュ・ヴァルシュナイ（インド）　『20例』（文献312）
プラティマ・サクセナ（インド）　『母斑・欠損』
プラトムワン・インタヌ（タイ）　『生まれ4』（文献324）
プラブー（インド）　文献303、336
ヘンリー・エルキン（合衆国・トリンギット）　『20例』（文献312）
ボンクチ・プロムシン（タイ）　『生まれ4』（文献324）
マイクル・ライト（合衆国）　未発表
マヘス・デ・シルヴァ（スリランカ）　『生まれ2』（文献317）
マリカ・アロモウガム（インド）　『20例』（文献312）

マルタ・ロレンツ（ブラジル）	『20例』（文献312）
マンジュ・トリパティ（インド）	未発表
マンジュ・バルガヴァ（インド）	未発表
ミント・テイン（ビルマ）	『母斑・欠損』
ミント・ティン（ビルマ）	『母斑・欠損』
ムー・ムー（ビルマ）	『母斑・欠損』
ムウェ・ロネ（ビルマ）	『母斑・欠損』
メアリ・マグルーダー（合衆国）	未発表
モウンゼル・ハイダル（レバノン）	『生まれ3』（文献321）
ユスフ・クセ（トルコ）	『母斑・欠損』
ラヴィ・シャンカール・グプタ（インド）	『20例』（文献312）
ラケシュ・ガウル（インド）	文献218
ラジスタジャルン（チャオクン師）（タイ）	『生まれ4』（文献324）
ラジャニ・スクラ（インド）	未発表
ラジュル・シャー（インド）	『生まれ1』（文献314）
ラタナ・ウォンゾムバト（タイ）	『生まれ4』（文献324）
ラニ・サクセナ（インド）	未発表
ラビ・エラワール（レバノン）	『生まれ3』（文献321）
ラムー・シャルマとラジュー・シャルマ（インド）	『生まれ1』（文献314）
ラム・ティラト（インド）	『母斑・欠損』

ラム・プラカーシュ（インド）　文献219
ラメズ・シャムス（レバノン）　未発表
ラメシュ・スクラ（インド）　未発表
ラリタ・アベヤワルデナ（スリランカ）　『生まれ2』（文献317）
ラル・ジャヤスーリア（スリランカ）　未発表
ランジト・マカランダ（スリランカ）　『20例』（文献312）
ルビ・クスマ・シルヴァ（スリランカ）　『生まれ2』（文献317）
ロナルド・マパツナゲ（スリランカ）　未発表
ロバータ・モーガン（合衆国）　未発表
ロール・レイノー（フランス）　文献59、303
ワルナシリ・アディカリ（スリランカ）　『生まれ2』（文献317）

原　註

（　）内の数字は参考文献番号

まえがき

1　カルマの意味

カルマ（業）とは、サンスクリット語で〝行為〟のことである。そのことからこの言葉は、行為の結果や、さらには善行や悪行の結果、特にその行ないをした直後の生まれ変わりの際に生ずる結果をも意味するようになった。ヒンドゥー教や仏教のカルマという教義には、さまざまな因果関係が含まれるが、原因となる行ないに見合った報復を受けるという意味で使われることが最も多い。たとえば、生まれつき盲目の人間は、前世で誰かの両眼を傷つけたのではないかとされる考え方である。

2　性別を表わす名詞

女性に対する不公平を解消する役にはほとんど立たないにもかかわらず、性別について中立的な表現を強迫的に用いても読者の方々にはご迷惑だろうと思うので、男性名詞をそのまま用いている。また、事例について述べる際にはいつも男性名詞を用いたが、それは、前世を記憶しているとする子どもの大多数がたまたま男性だからである。このような性差が見られる理由については、第10章で考察している。

第1章　序論

1　前世を記憶するという子どもの、事実と確認された発言

事実と確認される発言を行なう一方、こうした子どもたちは、不正確な発言をすることもある。また、事実かどうか確認できない発言しかしない子どもや、何も話さない子どももいる。こういったさまざまなタイプの事例については後ほど検討する予定である。

2　調査した事例の総数

ヴァージニア大学が収集した生まれ変わりを思わせる調査例は現在、二〇〇〇例強にのぼっ

ている。共同研究者や私が調査を継続しているため、その数は年々わずかながら増加している。それと同時に、既に収集されている事例でも、そのデータを再検討した結果、信憑性《しんぴょうせい》に疑わしい点が生じた場合には除外されることもある。

3　死後生存の様態として考えられるもの

デュカッス（73）とタウレス（349）は、人間の人格が肉体の死後にも生き残ると思われるさまざまな様態について述べている。

4　科学者が死後生存を信じないこと

ある調査によれば、死後の生命の存在を信じている比率は、一般の六七パーセントに対して、科学者ではわずか一六パーセントにすぎないことがわかっている（94）。

5　死後生存を裏づけるさまざまなタイプの証拠

死後の生命という問題にまつわる証拠としては、他に、霊姿、臨終時の幻、臨死体験、体脱体験、ある種の霊界通信などの研究によって得られるものがある。そうした証拠について私は短い概説論文を執筆している（319）。ゴールド（96）は、そのようなさまざまな証拠を整理した単行本をまとめているし、タウレスも概説論文を発表している（348）。

6　当人らしさの判断基準

少なくともジョン・ロック（159）の時代以降の哲学者は、各人の当人らしさの基準について考察してきた。この三〇年ほどの間に、この問題を扱った書物は急速にその数を増した。その一部を掲げると、エイヤー（4）、ルイス（154、155）、マデル（170）、ペネルハム（221）、ペリー（225）、ローティ（258）、シューメイカーら（281）、ヴェジー（357）らによるものがある。当人らしさという問題を（単なる引用を含めて）扱った現代の哲学者の執筆になる著書を、厚さにして四〇センチ近く読んでみたが、超常現象に関するデータに言及しているものはそのうち三点にすぎなかった。そのことからすると、私が本書で述べているような研究が疎外されている（あるいは、もしかすると現代の哲学者の方が孤立している）

ことが多少なりともうかがわれる。（超常現象に言及している哲学者については、本章の後半でふれる。）

しかしながら、現代の哲学者の中にも、調査研究に基づくデータとの関連で当人らしさの定義を検討している者が少数ながらある。デュカッス（73、75）は、この問題について説得力ある論文を執筆しているし、その点はブロード（34、35）も同じである。このふたりは、この問題を、生まれ変わりが存在する可能性との関連で考察しているのである。

ホイートリー（363）の論文や、哲学と超常現象との関係を扱った二冊のアンソロジー（340、364）所載の数編の論文もこの問題をテーマにしている。（この二書には、当人らしさや死後生存という問題には直接関係のない章もある。）

マーフィー（186）は、人間の死後生存の証拠に関する論文の中で、人間の人格が死後にも生存を続けることを信ずるに足る自分なりの基準を満たすには、記憶が持続していることを示す証拠だけでは不十分だと主張している。記憶以外にも、ある種の知的な目的が存在することを示す証拠が必要だと言うのである。

7　死後まもない時点では人格の変化は起こらないこと

このような表現をすると、人間は肉体の死後にも生存を続けるのかという問題から少々外れるように見えるかもしれない。人間が死後にも生存を続けるらしいことを示す証拠の中には、（本章の後半でふれる）霊姿や霊界通信の研究に基づくものもある。この種の現象を見ると、死後まもない人間が置かれる状況や環境はそれまでと比べて大きく変化するが、本人の性格（や人格）はあまり変わらないらしいことがわかる場合が少なくない。

8　霊姿とその解釈

霊姿体験を調べてみたいと思われる方は、ガーニーら（117）やマッケンジー（166）、ティレル（354）の著書を参照されたい。ゴールド（96）とマッケンジー（167）は、霊姿のさまざまな解釈の検討を行なっている。また、同様の拙論（323）もある。

9　生気論

生気論という考え方は、（現代では）ハンス・ドリーシュの見解や著作（69、70）に負うところが大きい。ドリーシュは、発生学者として出発したが、最終的には哲学者になっている。ドリーシュは、自ら行なった発生学の実験から、受精卵が生体まで発育するという現象は、当時はもちろん将来的にも化学や物理学の知識では適切に説明できないことを確信した。形態学のさまざまな問題を機械論的に説明するのに反対したドリーシュは、あらゆる生命体には統一、命令するある種の要素が含まれていると考えなければその問題は解決しないと主張した。そしてドリーシュは、その要素に対して、アリストテレスの生命力《エンテレキー》という言葉を充てたのである。

ドリーシュは、心霊研究に深い関心を寄せるようになり、一九二六―七年度の心霊研究協会会長に選出された。その小著『心霊研究』（72）は現在でも熟読する価値がある。グルーバー（112）は、生物学と心霊研究に関するドリーシュの考え方を好意的に概説した論文を発表している。ドリーシュ以外にも、生気論と呼ぶほどではないにせよ、同様の考え方を展開している研究者がいる（118、119）。

10　接合型双生児がドアを通ること

この表現は、ジャクソン（136）によるものである。

11　デカルト、ベーコンと心霊研究

デカルトは、『哲学の原理』（61、五〇一ページ）の中で、現在テレパシーと呼ばれている現象について論評を行なっている。実験を提案したベーコンの言葉は、死後に出版された『森また森』（5、一一〇ページ）に見られる。

12　超常現象を研究するに当たって用いられる用語

心霊研究で用いられる専門用語は、グラッタン＝ギネス（103）、タルボーン（342）、ホワイトら（367）、ウォルマン（372）の編著書にまとめて収録されている。

13 テレパシーと透視

本書では、テレパシーと透視の区別はあまりしないことにする。ある人物がもうひとりの人物の思考内容を知ったとしても、脳内の過程を透視したためかもしれないとして、テレパシーが起こることを証明するのは難しいとする研究者が一部にある。しかし、思考内容が読みとられる側も、その交信の中で読みとる側と同じくらい重要な役割を演じているのかもしれないわけであるが、そのことに思い至らせてくれる限りにおいて、テレパシーという用語は重要だと考える。両者とも重要な役割を演じていることを裏づける証拠は、実験（272、273）や偶発的体験（308）からも十分に得られている。

14 超常現象に関する入門書

この方面の入門書としては、かなり短いが網羅的なものとして、グラッタン＝ギネス（103）、ヘイウッド（127）、マーフィー（187）による著書を挙げることができる。また、ウォルマン（372）の編書も推薦できる。この書は、タイトル（『超心理学ハンドブック』）とは異なり、持ち運びが容易ではない。これは、先に挙げた三書と比べるとはるかに部厚く、より専門的な研究者向けの図書であるが、信頼性の高い情報が適切にまとめられている。

15 テレパシー体験を扱った四点の自伝的報告

この四名は、巻末の「参考文献」に収録されているそれぞれの著書の中でその体験を語っている。

16 超常的認知の実在性を証言する、信頼性の高い証人

他にも同じくらい信頼できるたくさんの人々が、ここに紹介したのとよく似た体験を記録に残している。たとえばスタンレーやブルーアムの伝記や自伝などに目を通すと、稀《まれ》ならずそうした体験談に出会う。プリンス（242）は、同様の体験記を数多く集め、貴重なアンソロジーを編んでいる。

他の分野で活躍した著名人で、超常現象の個

人的体験を支持する証言を行なった者は数多いが、こうした証言は重要な問題を提起している。つまり、その主張の解釈に従って次のいずれかの問題が発生するのである。もしその人たちが、自ら選んだ専門分野では優れて有能であったと（正当に）評価される一方で、超常的なものと思われる体験の報告については誤解を受けているとすれば、こうした方面では、本来の分野で達した合格点にはるかに及ばないのはなぜかを明らかにすべきであるし、逆に、こうした体験を報告する能力が本来の専門分野と同じくらいあると判断された場合には、一般の科学者が、承認された分野での見解に敬意を表する一方で、超常体験に関する意見については無視してきた理由を明確にすべきである。

　また、個人的体験は、超常的認知の実在を信じている科学者にとって、そうした信念に到達するうえで有力なきっかけになっているようである。マックレノン（163）が科学者を対象に行なった超感覚的知覚に関する態度調査によれば、そうした現象が起こりうると信じている者では、超心理学の専門書や雑誌に目を通したことをその理由に挙げた者はほとんどおらず、自身で説得力ある体験をした結果として信ずるようになった者の方が、それよりもはるかに多いことがわかったのである。

17　死亡時刻に出現する霊姿と偶然

　この分析の詳細については、シジウィックら（284）およびブロード（35）の論文を参照されたい。

18　アグネス・パケットの事例

　完全な報告はシジウィック（282）の論文に収録されている。

19　遠方の出来事と幻とが細かい点で一致すること

　ベルクソン（20）は、心霊研究協会の会長講演の中で同様の指摘を行なっている。そこでベルクソンが引用した事例は、夫が戦死した時刻に、その時のありさまが詳細に見えたという女性の例である。

サミュエル・ジョンソンは、一世紀半も昔にボズウェルと幽霊の話をしている時、いかにも本人らしい常識を示しつつ、同じく次のように指摘している。

　私は、人間が単に想像力が強いあまり、本当に見聞きした感じになるものと、想像力では作り出せないものとは、区別して考えているんです。ですからたとえば、私が人影を見て、「ジョンソン君、君はずいぶんと悪い男だな。悔い改めないと罰がくだるぞ」という声が聞こえたような気がしたとしましょうか。私の心には、自分の恥ずべき点があまりに深く刻み込まれておりますので、そのためにそういう声が聞こえて来たような感じがしたのかもしれません。ですから、自分の外から何者かが何か言って来たとは思いませんね。でもですよ、もしある人影が現われて、特定の人物が特定の場所で特定の時間に亡くなったという声が私に語りかけてきて、しかも私がそのことを危惧《きぐ》していたわけでもなければ、その事実を知る方法もなかったうえにですね、そのことがあとで、その時に見聞きした一切合切とまちがいなく同じだったことが証明されたとしますと、その時にはですよ、超自然界の知的存在が私にそのことを教えてくれたんだと納得するしかありませんね。(31、二四六ページ)

20　稀な出来事や信じがたい報告

ベーコン著『学問の進歩』(6、二九ページ)より引用。

21　南アフリカ、テーブル山の青い蘭の事例

　本例については詳細な報告がある(304)。マッケンジー(165)は、本例をさらに詳しく調査し、新しい情報をある程度加えた報告を公にしている。(問題の青い花は実際には蘭ではないが、本例を報告した時点で私はそう誤解していたのである。)

22　心霊体験の調査

　この種の調査の詳細については、パーマー

（213）、H・シジウィックら（284）、ウェスト（361）の報告を参照されたい。

23　偶発例にまつわる証言の弱点

偶発例の報告としては、これまで二種類が知られている。調査検討が行なわれている事例報告と、行なわれていない事例報告である。事例の調査には、（最低でも）手紙や（それよりも望ましいのは）面接により、その体験やそれに対応する出来事を情報提供者に詳しく質問するという作業が必要である。次に、その体験に対応する出来事については、研究者か、体験者の発言を鵜《う》呑みにするのではなく、他の何らかの情報源からその裏づけをとらなければならない。これまで発表されてきた未調査例は、たいてい、研究施設に届いた手紙を、調査もせず額面通り受けとったものにすぎないのである。

調査検討が加えられた事例は、未調査例と比較して有利な点がふたつある。まず第一に、面接（あるいはそれができない場合には繰り返し行なう書簡のやりとり）によって、信憑性《しんぴょうせい》のない事例や明らかに通常の説明で片づけられる事例を見つけ出し、それを除外できるという点が挙げられる。こうした事例は（未調査例としてはそのままの形で受け入れられるわけであるが）他の事例を計り知れないほど汚染するし、さらには、その事例群から引き出される結論の価値を低めることになるかもしれない。第二に、未調査例では、ひとつの事例が全体像としてとらえられることがほとんどないという点が挙げられる。情報提供者は、自身が体験者（受信者）であるのがふつうであり、発信者の身に起こったことを無視ないし軽視する場合がある。こうした不均衡から、ルイーザ・ライン（250）のように、超感覚的知覚では発信者は重要ではないなどという誤った結論が導き出される可能性があるのである。

ここで、未調査例のプラス面についても述べておかなければならない。未調査群の中にも、調査群で見つかる特徴が認められるものがいくつかあるが、その点からすれば、一部に信憑性のない事例が含まれており、個々の事例についてあらゆる側面を検討していない場合でも、必ずしも全体が損なわれるわけではないということである。

調査例の報告を検討する場合、読者の方々は一般に、一例ずつ、あるいは何例かまとめて発表されている心霊研究の専門誌に当たらなければならない。しかしながら、調査例の事例集は、公的な学会の刊行物とは別に何点か出版されている。その中には、ゴールドら（97。ポルターガイストの事例）、マッケンジー（166、167。霊姿と幽霊の事例）、ガーニーら（117。主として霊姿の事例）、スティーヴンソン（308。テレパシー的印象の事例）、ティレル（354。霊姿の事例）による著書がある。前世を記憶するという子どもたちを対象にした拙著は、すべて例外なく、調査研究を行なった事例をもとに執筆したものである。

未調査例の事例集としては、グリーン（105、107）、プラサードら（234）、ライン（249、250）、ザンヴァルト（269、270）による著書や論文が注目に値する。

24　夫と死別した女性が見る幻覚

リーズ（247）は、こうした体験に関する調査を報告している。

25　心霊体験と思われるものに対する通常の説明

この問題について私は、別の論文（326）で考察したうえ、関連文献を列挙している。

26　心霊体験における愛と死というテーマ

ガーニーら（117）は、（主として）霊姿体験を扱った著書の中でこうした特徴が存在することに注目している。その後に収集されたいくつかの事例群を通じて、受信者と発信者の愛情関係と死（ないしは重病や事故）のふたつが超常的伝達のテーマになっていることがきわめて多いという事実が確証された（105、234、267、308）。

27　後催眠暗示

十九世紀後半、ベルネーム（23）は、後催眠暗示の典型例を報告しているが、その業績は今なお研究に値する。後催眠暗示にかかっている被験者に圧力をかけ、いわば脅すと、自分が演じた奇妙な後催眠行動は、催眠中ベルネームに暗示をかけられたために起こったという事実を想起できる者が一部あることに、ベルネームは気づいたのである。

28　行動的記憶という概念

ベルクソン（22）やバトラー（39）は、行動的記憶の重要性を明らかにしている。ペンフィールド（222）は、脳の主たる動きは、一連の自動的行動のパターンを何通りも学習することではないかと示唆している。心が、脳を道具として使うことによって、自動的行動を思いのままに起こすのではないかというのである。

第2章　生まれ変わり信仰

1　ヴォルテール

ヴォルテールの著書（359、三六六ページ）より引用。

2　生まれ変わり信仰の見られる地域

さまざまな生まれ変わり信仰については、次の出典を参照されたい。

・西アジアのイスラム諸派――マカレム（171）、スティーヴンソン（312、321）。
・アフリカ（特に西アフリカ）の諸部族――ベスターマン（26）、デシャン（62）、ヌーン（199）、パリンダー（214、215）スティーヴンソン（329）、L＝V・トーマス（346）、ウチェンドゥ（355）、ザハン（378）。
・ブラジル――スティーヴンソン（312）。
・トロブリアンド諸島――マリノフスキ（174）。
・オーストラリア中央部――スペンサーら（297）。
・アイヌ――マンロー（185）。
・北アメリカ北西部――ド・ラグナ（58）、スロボディン（286）、スティーヴンソン（305、312、315）。

少々断片的ではあるが、これまで得られている証拠からすると、北アメリカ北西部を除くアメリカの先住民族も生まれ変わり信仰を一時もっており、その一部は現在でも信じているらしきふしがある。（たとえばラディン（245）は、二回の前世を記憶しているというウィネベーゴ族の男性が語った言葉を自著に収録している。）とはいえ、こうした民族は、北西部の諸部族とは異なり、生まれ変わり信仰をそれほど長期にわたって保持したわけでも、それほど強固にもち続けたわけでもなかった。なお、キリスト教の宣教師は、東南アジアに住む人々と比べると、北アメリカ北西部の部族民とそれほど長期にわたって接触していたわけではない。

3 ショーペンハウエル

この文章は、ショーペンハウエルの『余録と補遺』（275）、三九五ページより拙訳して引用した。

4 北アメリカにおける生まれ変わり信仰の調査

ギャラップ世論調査目録（93）およびギャラップの著書（94）に詳細なデータが掲載されている。

5 古代インドの聖典に見られる生まれ変わり信仰

詳細についてお知りになりたい方は、R・E・ヒューム（134）、ラダクリシュナン（244）、スマート（287）、ゼナー（376）の各書を参照されたい。

6 アポロニオスとイアルクスの会見

フィロストラトゥス（226）はその著『アポロニオスの生涯』の中でこの会見について述べている。

7 生まれ変わり信仰の起源はギリシャとインドで共通していること

古代ギリシャ人はさまざまな概念をインド人から、インド人は若干の概念をギリシャ人から借用した、と一般に信じられているが、キースは自著（144）の中で、その裏づけとなる証拠とされるものが実際には存在しないことを示す論拠を並べ上げている。双方に同様の概念が見られても、一方がもう一方からそれを借用したことを裏づける証拠にもならなければ、共通の起源があることを示す証拠にもならない。それでも、ギリシャとインドの生まれ変わりの概念が共通の起源をもっている可能性は残る。ルーベン（262）は、中央アジアの初期シャーマニズムの一形態がその起源なのではないかと指摘している。

8　アジア人と北アメリカの部族民の間の情報の伝播《でんぱ》

　原始時代にアジア人と北アメリカの部族民との間に接触があったことを裏づける（厖大《ぼうだい》でも有力でもない）証拠については別著で概説しておいた（312、二一七―二一九ページ）。仏教的な考え方は、アラスカに居住する人々には、十八世紀にヨーロッパ人が到来する以前に伝えられていたのかもしれない。とはいえ、そうした考え方が、北アメリカ北西部の部族民のもつ生まれ変わりの概念に大きな影響を及ぼした可能性はありそうにない。

9　トルコ中南部のアレヴィス族

「明文化された権威をもってはいないようである」と書かざるをえなかったのは、これまでそのようなものの存在を見聞きすることができなかったからである。私に情報を提供してくれたトルコ人たちは、その信仰の根拠となっているものについて聞いた時、知らなかったり、話をはぐらかしたりすることもあった。おそらくその人たちは、私のことを、自らの宗教書に書かれている知識を分け与えるだけの価値のない不信心者と考えたのであろう。もしそうであれば、その人たちは、出典は明かさなかったが、信仰は隠さなかったことになる。レバノンとシリアのドゥルーズ族もある程度似た態度を示す。その大半は、生まれ変わり信仰を包み隠さず話すが、部外者がその聖典を詳しく見ることは許さないのである。しかし私は、ドゥルーズ族がその種の書物をもっているのを知っている。ただし、アレヴィス族にもその種の聖典があるかどうかはわからない。

　コーランは、生まれ変わり信仰にわずかながら与《くみ》している聖典である。聖書と同じくコーランには、こうした考え方を支持しているとも解釈できる意味のあいまいな文章がいくつか並んでいる。私は別著に、コーラン中のこうした節を引用している(312、321)。また、トルコ中南部に住むアレヴィス族に見られる生まれ変わり信仰について述べた著書や論文もある(307、321)。

10 イボ族の生まれ変わり信仰

イボ族の間に見られる生まれ変わり信仰については別著で述べておいた(329)。

11 生まれ変わりに関するショーペンハウエルの確信

ショーペンハウエル(276)は、哲学的論証のみを通じて生まれ変わりの実在を確信するに至ったわけではないのかもしれない。ショーペンハウエルは、ヒンドゥー教や仏教の知識を当時としては幅広くもっていた。こうした教典はその頃ヨーロッパで翻訳され、研究されていたのである。

12 生まれ変わりという考え方を支持した哲学者

生まれ変わりを扱ったアンソロジーを編む者は、生まれ変わりを信じていたとして、あるいは少なくともこうした考え方に意味を認めていたとして、デヴィッド・ヒュームを引き合いに出すことが多い。そうした文脈でふつう引用されるのは、「魂の不死性について」というエッセイ中の文章である。その中でヒュームは次のように述べている。「輪廻《りんね》転生は、したがって、哲学が耳を傾けることのできるこの種の唯一の体系である」(132、五五三ページ)。直前の文章でヒュームは、(人間以外の)動物は多くの点で人間と似ているので、動物にも魂があることにしなければ、人間に魂があると言うことはできない、と指摘している。そのすぐあとに、輪廻転生に関する先ほどの文章が続くのである。(ヒュームは輪廻転生という言葉を、〔現在でも正しく用いられるべきであるが〕人間の魂であれいかなる動物の魂であれ、死後に他の動物の体として生まれ変わることを指して用いたように思われる。)ところが、ヒュームのエッセイ全体を読めば、誰であれ、ヒューム自身が人間（ないし動物）の魂の存在を、ましてやその肉体の死後の生存を信じてなどいなかったことがわかるはずである。ボズウェル（32）が明らかにしているように、ヒュームは自らの魂が死すべき運命にあることを固く信じて死んで行ったのである。

13　生まれ変わりに関するプラトンの発言

プラトンは、『メノーン』の中で行なっている論証以外にも、他の著作、特に『パイドーン』や『ティーマイオス』、『パイドゥロス』、『国家』などの中で生まれ変わりという考え方を詳述している。

『メノーン』からの引用文は、巻末の参考文献に掲げておいた版（229）の九一―九二ページからとったものである。

14　生まれ変わりに関するマクタガートとデュカッスの考え方

生まれ変わりという考え方に注目した現代の哲学者の中では、マクタガート（168）とデュカッス（73、75）のふたりが、私には最も明快かつ最も説得力に富む発言を行なっているように思われる。マクタガートは、前世の記憶については具体的にはふれておらず、どうやら、人間には前世の記憶は残りえないと考えていたようである。とはいえ、人間は、前世の認識的情報（私の言葉ではイメージ記憶）をもち越さないとしても、前世の経験から得た教訓は来世にもち越すことができると考えていた。一世代遅れて登場したデュカッスは、具体例の調査を奨励したうえ、事例報告にもかなりの注目を払っている。

15　イヌイットの生まれ変わり信仰

イヌイットの生まれ変わり信仰については、バーキット＝スミス（27）、グウェンブル（113）、ヒューズ（131）、スワントン（339）の著書や論文を参照されたい。

グリーンランドのイヌイット語が話せる者なら、アラスカのイヌイット語を理解するのもそれほど困難ではない。この事実からすると、現在のイヌイットの祖先が北部ツンドラ地帯に広がった後、イヌイット語はほとんど変化していないらしいことがわかる。おそらく、(グリーンランドとアラスカのイヌイットはもちろん、その中間地帯に居住するイヌイットの間に見られる)生まれ変わり信仰も、ひとつの中心から伝わったものなのであろう。また、先述のように、その信仰は、現在のイヌイットの祖先とともに、アジアから渡来したものなのかもしれない。

16 前世の記憶とされるものから生じた生まれ変わり信仰

　ペリス(223)は、ピタゴラスに関するエッセイの中で、生まれ変わり信仰および、少なくとも一部の人間には前世を想起することができるとする主張は、同じくらい古い時代から存在しているのではないか、と指摘している。ピタゴラスは、生まれ変わりという考え方を人に教え広めたばかりか、自らの前世もいくつか記憶していると主張していた。そのためピタゴラスは、前世の記憶から生まれ変わり信仰を発展させたことを示す格好の実例になっている。同様に、紀元前二〇〇年から紀元二〇〇年までの間に書き上げられた(『マハーバーラタ』中の)バガヴァッド・ギーターも、生まれ変わり信仰と前世を記憶しているとする主張とを関係づけている(233)。その中でクリシュナは、アルジュナに次のように語りかける。

　アルジュナよ、君と私とは、
何度もの前世を生きてきた。
私は全部覚えているが、
君はひとつも覚えていない。

　もうひとつの実例は仏教に見られる。本生経《ほんじょうきょう》という説話集には、仏陀《ぶつだ》が記憶していた前世が記されているとされる。ペリス(223)が指摘しているように、この種の例はいずれも、神ないし偉大な賢人が前世を記憶しているとする主張に関するものであり、平凡な人間が前世を記憶しているという考え方からは大幅にかけ離れている。とはいえ、以上の例には、前世の記憶は霊的な修行を重ねて霊的な高みに到達して初めて出現する、という考え方の萌芽《ほうが》が見てとれる。生まれ変わりという概念を事前にもっていない場合、その人物はどのように前世の記憶を位置づけるのか、という疑問も当然のことながら出るであろう。その点については、前世の記憶をもっていても、それを位置づけるべき枠組みとなる概念を前世からもち越していない場合には、その記憶を受け入れないことがあるという事実を、後ほど述べるつもりである。したがって、生まれ変わり信仰が確立されるためには、自分自身、ないしは自分が信頼を置いている人物のいずれかが前世のイメージ記憶をもっていることと、生まれ変わりが起こるという信念（ないし直観）をもっていることの、ふたつの条件が必要なのであろう。

17　**インドの初期の生まれ変わり型事例**

十六世紀に『ラーマーヤナ』を翻訳したトゥルシ・ダースは、前世の記憶をもっていたというが、その主張についてはほとんどわからないため、ここで実例としてとり上げることはできない。十八世紀ムガル帝国皇帝アウランジーブは、生まれ変わり信仰をもたない熱烈なイスラム教徒だったにもかかわらず、自らの信仰と矛盾する事柄をも喜んで検討しようとする態度を示している。アウランジーブは、ある事例の証人を何人か自分のもとに呼び寄せ、現代の研究者が用いているのと同じ方法で証人たちに質問している（312、一五―六ページ）。私が知っているインドの第二例は、二十世紀初頭のものである。この事例については、スンデルラル（337）が報告を発表している。

18　**カタリ派**

カタリ派の間に見られる生まれ変わり信仰については、ルロワ＝ラドュリ（152）、マドール（169）、ネリ（194）、ニール（198）、ランシマン（263）による著書を参照されたい。ルロワ＝ラドュリは、カタリ派のある信者による、前世（もっと正確に言えば、動物だったという二回を含む三回の前世）を記憶しているという主張に関する報告を行なっている。

19 「人間の誕生が人生の始まりだと誰であれ信じている者……」

ショーペンハウエル（276、第二巻、五五八ページ）より引用。

20 生まれ変わりを暗示するもの

暗示という言葉を意図的に用いたのは、私がここで言おうとしている内容が、ワーズワースの『霊魂不滅の頌——幼年時代の追憶より不死の暗示』に具体的に描き出されていると考えるからである。

21 死後に自らの人生を回顧すること

死の瀬戸際まで行きながら回復した者の中には、心の中に、それまで生きてきた人生のさまざまな場面が流れるように見えたという者がある。一部の研究者はこのような体験を、そうした記憶が一度に展開されるように感じる者があることから、〝走馬燈的《パノラミック》記憶〟と呼んでいる。この種の体験についてお知りになりたい方は、グレイソンら（110）、ハイム（126）、ノイエスら（201）、スティーヴンソンら（332）の各論文を参照されたい。

ここで注目すべき点が他にふたつある。まず第一点は、（臨死体験中の）走馬燈的記憶に関する最近の報告を見ると、その体験が不快なものとしては描かれていないことである。第二には、前世を記憶しているという子どもたちの中には、前世で死んだ後、その一生を一瞬のうちに回顧するという体験があったのを覚えている者がほとんどいないという事実が挙げられる。シャンティ・デヴィやナシル・トコセズ、イシュワール・ゴドボレの事例はその例外であり、前世の最後に、一生を一瞬のうちに振り返るという体験があったという。

生まれ変わりが起こるとすれば、イメージ記憶がなくても、私たちは前世の記憶を潜在的にたくさんもっているのかもしれない。その一部については、行動的記憶として述べておいたが、先述したように、私たちは、前世に由来する認識的記憶も潜在的に残している可能性がある。プラトンの（先述の）著書『メノーン』は、そのことを実証しようとする試みであった。『メノーン』に登場する少年幾何学者は、イメージ記憶こそないものの、幾何学の問題を解く基盤となる認識的記憶を潜在的にもっていたと考えることができよう。これは、明らかに、プラトン描くところのソクラテスの発想である。

22 死を恐れる理由

人間は死ぬと何もなくなってしまうと信じている者は、病のため悲惨な生活を強いられており、他人の眼には「生きている甲斐《かい》がない」と映る場合ですら、死を恐れ、何とかして死を回避しようとすることが少なくない。パタンジャリ（220）による死に対する恐怖の説明は、このような場合にも当てはまるであろうが、他の説明も可能かもしれない。私たちは、この世に生を受けている間、〝私〟という意識の流れに強く結びつけられている。それが永遠に終止符を打たれるのはとても嫌なことであり、何とかして避けるべきもののように感じられる。自分の〝私〟が死後にも何らかの形で存続すると信じている者は、肉体がもはやあまり役立たなくなった時には、信じていない者よりもたやすくあきらめることができる。

とはいえ、死に対する恐怖心がいつも身勝手な理由から生じていると言い切ってしまってはならない。残される者が死に行く者に対する時と同じように、死んで行こうとしている者が残される者を心から心配することも少なくないのである（1）。また、第10章で詳述する予定の、〝仕事をやり残した〟前世を記憶している子どもたちを見ると、人に援助の手を差し伸べ続けるためにもっと長生きしたいと望んでいる者が一部にあることがわかる。

23 チベットの生まれ変わりのパターン

ベル（16）およびスネルグローヴら（294）は、トゥルク制度の発展を詳しく説明している。トゥルクとは、高位のラマとして生まれ変わりを繰り返した経歴のもち主とされる。

24　インドのヒンドゥー教徒のイスラム教徒への改宗

スピア（296）は、ヒンドゥー教徒（や仏教徒）をイスラム教に改宗させた要因をいくつか挙げている。まず、強制的に改宗させられた者が一部にあるほか、ムガル人による支配の中で政治的利得を求めて改宗した者もある。スーフィー（イスラム教神秘主義者）の説教を聞き、その生き証人に接した者の多くは、イスラム教は優れた宗教だと考えた。また、カーストの低い、あるいはカーストから外されているヒンドゥー教徒（および仏教徒）の少なからずは、バラモンの圧制から逃れてイスラム教に改宗した。

25　イスラム教イスマイル派の生まれ変わり信仰の喪失

この出典は別稿（321）に掲げておいた。イスマイル派の生まれ変わり信仰の変遷については、もう少し検討を加えておいてもよかろう。西アフリカに住む近代的イスマイル派は生まれ変わり信仰をもっていると聞く。もしそれが事実であれば、（大部分が）西インドに住んでいたその祖先は、ヒンドゥー教の影響を受けていたらしいことがわかる。そのおかげで、西アジアのイスマイル派信者が生まれ変わり信仰を捨てても、なおかつそれを保持し続けることができたのであろう。

26　ヴァイキングの生まれ変わり信仰

デヴィッドソン（56）とカー（145）の著書による。

27　ケルト族の生まれ変わり信仰

エヴァンス＝ウェンツ（84）は、今世紀初頭のスコットランド、ウェールズ、アイルランドに居住していたケルト人が生まれ変わり信仰をもっていたことを裏づける証拠を見《み》出《いだ》している。

ユリウス・カエサルは、自ら調査したガリア人の間に生まれ変わり信仰が見られたことについて述べている。ドルイドと呼ばれるケルト族の僧について、カエサルは次のように書いている。「僧たちが広めようとしている主たる教義は、魂は死なず、死後に、あるもの〔肉体〕から別のものへと移行するというものである。そして、そのおかげで死の恐怖が退けられるゆえ、僧たちはこの信仰を、豪胆になるための最大の誘発剤と考えている」（40、三三九ページ）。

28　**五五三年の第二コンスタンティノープル会議と生まれ変わりという教義の否認**

生まれ変わりに関する神学者オリゲネスの教えおよび、その後に受けた非難については、プラットの論文（235、236）を参照されたい。ダニエルー（54）の著書も参照のこと。

29　**イヌイットに見られる生まれ変わり信仰の衰退**

この問題については、イヌイットの間に見られる生まれ変わり信仰やその事例に関する私の短報（306）の中で簡単に報告している。

30　**「古代の伝承によれば……」**

エリス（82、一三九ページ）より引用。

31　**生まれ変わり信仰の亜型**

事例報告を扱っている拙著（312、314、317、321、324）の中で私は、生まれ変わりを思わせる事例の調査を自分で行なったさまざまな国に見られる生まれ変わり信仰のさまざまな様態について、一章を設けたり、序論部で述べるなどしてきた。この問題については、別稿（305、315、329）やパリンダーの論文（214）をご覧になれば詳しくおわかりいただけよう。

32　**イスラム教シーア派の生まれ変わり信仰**

レバノンやシリアに住むドゥルーズ族および、トルコのアレヴィス族は、本文で述べているような信仰をもっている（321）。

オベイエセケレ（203、204）は、生まれ変わり信仰を、〝素朴なもの〟と〝倫理性を賦与されたもの〟とに分けた。それによれば、素朴な形の生まれ変わり信仰をもっている者は、自らの倫理的価値観と生まれ変わりのプロセスを結びつけることがないのに対して、倫理性が賦与された生まれ変わり信仰をもつ者は、そのふたつを結びつけて考えるという。オベイェセケレは、トロブリアンド諸島に住む民族とアフリカのイボ族を、素朴なタイプの信仰をもつ民族の実例として挙げている。それに対して、ヒンドゥー教徒や仏教徒は、倫理性を伴った生まれ変わり信仰をもつ好例である。しかしながら、生まれ変わり信仰に倫理性を賦与した結果、ヒンドゥー教や仏教のカルマのような教義ができあがったにちがいないというオベイエセケレの主張は正しくない。ドゥルーズ族は、生まれ変わりに関する自らの考え方と倫理的価値観とを結びつけているが、カルマのような概念を作り上げるには至らなかったからである。

33 西アフリカの民族に見られる生まれ変わり信仰

この問題について詳しくお知りになりたい方は、パリンダー（214）、スティーヴンソン（329）、ウチェンドゥ（355）の各論文を参照されたい。ナイジェリアのイボ族に見られる生まれ変わり信仰に関する拙論には、この問題に関する考察を行なっている文献を掲げている。

34 トリンギット族に見られる生まれ変わり信仰

生まれ変わりに関するトリンギット族の概念は、別著に要約してある。スティーヴンソン（305、312）参照。

35 来世に対する選択

前世で選んでおいた両親のもとに生まれ変わったと思《おぼ》しきトリンギットの事例としては、コーリス・チョトキン・ジュニア、ウィリアム・ジョージ・ジュニアの例が挙げられる。

36 プラトンの『国家』で述べられている生まれ変わりの概念

この問題に関係しているのは、第一〇巻（228）で語られているエルの体験である。プラトンは、他の著書（『パイドゥロス』と『ティーマイオス』）では、生まれ変わりのプロセスについて多少異なった書き方をしており、前世の行ないは、その報いとして来世の状況を左右する可能性があることを示唆している。

第3章　生まれ変わりを裏づける証拠の種々相

1　〝過去世リーディング〟

私はこれまで、自分の前世を八人の人たちに別々に見てもらっている。ところが、どれをとっても他のものとは全く一致しなかったのである。もしかするとそれぞれ別の前世について語っているので矛盾はないのではないか、と考える方がおられるかもしれないが、そうとは考えられないことをはっきりさせるため、そのうちのいくつかでは、同じ時期に私がそれぞれ別の国にいたことになっているという事実を明記しておきたい。このようなリーディングを私にしてくれたのは、さまざまな経歴や職業をもっている人たちである。インドのスーワミーもいたし、アメリカの霊能者も、オーストリアの主婦もいたのである。私にわかる限りでは、この八人に共通点は全くなかったが、人の過去世が読めるという主張についてはいずれも確固たる自信をもっていたことに加えて、誠実な人たちだったのである。

一部には、他人の前世が超常的にわかる能力を本当にもっている者もいたのかもしれない。第2章でイアルクスについてふれておいたが、この人物は、テュアナのアポロニオスがもっていた記憶らしきものと一致する、アポロニオスの前世について語っている。

他人の前世を本当に読みとることができる人間が稀《まれ》にいるということを、ありえないとして否定するものではない。そうではなく、そのようなことができると称する者はほとんどが、そうした能力をもっておらず、他者のみならず自らをも欺いていた、ということを指摘しているのである。

2　催眠による年齢遡《そ》行《こう》中には記憶の精度が高まること

トゥルー（352）は、通常の〝覚醒《かくせい》〟状態での想起と比較して、催眠中には幼少期の詳細な出来事が正確に想起されやすいことを立証している。ライフら（248）は、トゥルーの実験の追試が完全にはできなかったが、トゥルーとは別の質問を用いて、催眠中には想起が起こりやすいという事実を確認している。しかし、オコンネルら（205）はライフらの実験の完全な追試には成功していない。

バーバー（12）は、催眠による年齢遡行中に記憶が表出しやすくなることを確認する実験を手際よくまとめて紹介したうえ、それに対する批判を行なっている。

3 催眠中の想起の誤り

オーン（207）は、想起するよう求められている幼少期の出来事が想い出せない場合、年齢退行していると思しき被験者はしばしば作話を行なうことを明らかにしている。正確な記憶と不正確な記憶とが混在し、自分がまちがったことをしているという自覚をもたないまま被験者は、それを口にするのである。また被験者は、幼児期後期に（あるいはさらに成長した後に）起こった出来事の記憶を〝借用〟し、それを、退行した年齢と思しき時期に起こったことにしてしまう場合もある。

パトナム（243）および、その後に登場したゼリグら（380）は、催眠状態にある（が年齢遡行を行なっていない）被験者に自分が目撃した出来事について誘導的な質問をすると、通常の覚醒状態の時よりも誤りが多くなることを明らかにしている。

数十年前にスタルネイカーら（299）は、催眠状態にある者は通常の状態にある時より数多くの事柄を想い出せるが、催眠誘導されている時には、想起する内容が通常の状態と比べて不正確になる、という観察をしている。ダイワンら（77）も、同様の観察を行なったことを報告している。

4 前世の空想を誘発させる際の暗示による影響

ベイカー（10）は、催眠をかけた者が肯定的ないし否定的暗示を被験者に与えることによって、前世の空想が発生するか否かに顕著な差が見られることを明らかにしている。

5 十字軍の時代のヴェルサイユ

ブロクサム（29）が、催眠による年齢退行で〝前世〟まで遡《さかのぼ》った本例の報告を行なっている。

6　出生、死亡、婚姻の記録

婚姻や埋葬などの出来事や、土地の保有、ある種の租税などの記録は、一部ヨーロッパ諸国では何世紀にもわたって教会に保存されてきた。しかし、記録に残されていない出来事も少なくない。また、火災や湿気、戦争、過失などにより、古い教区記録が数多く失われている。出生や死亡、結婚の行政側による記録が始まったのは、イングランドとウェールズでは一八三〇年代、ドイツでは一八七〇年代に入ってからである。合衆国の行政側による信頼のおける記録が残されるようになったのも、十九世紀半ばになってからであるし、一部の州ではもっと遅い。その当時に残された記録が見つからないからといって、一八五〇年以前には誰々は存在していない、などと言おうとしているわけではないが、そうした記録がなければ、その人物が存在したことは証明できないであろう。

7　催眠により誘発された〝前世の人格〟における通常の情報源

ディキンソン（65）は、被験者の意識には記憶として残っていなかったのに、通常の手段によって何年も前に得た知識が意識に昇る場合があることを示す事例を、徹底的に検討したうえで発表している。その〝ブランシュ・ポイニングズ〟の事例は、自動書記による通信例であるが、通常の方法で得た情報を組み立てて、どこから見ても矛盾のない人格を造り上げてしまうという驚くべき能力が人間の心に潜在していることをみごとに浮き彫りにしている。この事例の被験者が、〝ブランシュ・ポイニングズ〟として組み上げられた人格の構成要素となった数多くの具体的事象のほとんどが登場する小説を、少年時代に読んでいるのはほぼ確実であった。〝ブランシュ・ポイニングズ〟が交信してきた後に行なわれたセッションの中でディキンソンは、〝ブランシュ・ポイニングズ〟の情報をどこから得たのかについて質《ただ》したところ、その女性は、『モード伯爵夫人』という歴史小説を見た（そしておそらくは読んだ）のを思い出した。その小説には、〝ブランシュ・ポイニングズ〟からの通信の内容がそっくりそのまま出ていたのであった。

一部の心理学者は、被験者の意識にその記憶がなくとも、本や雑誌などから（場合によっては何年も前に）通常の方法によって得た知識が、催眠により誘発された〝前世〟の材料になっていることを突き止めた。こうした実例については、ビヨルケム（28）、カンプマン（140、141）、カンプマンら（142）、ゾリク（381、382）らの報告を参照されたい。

ある人が何らかの情報を得て、そのことを忘れてしまったにもかかわらず、その後そのことを知っていることがわかったとすると、この現象は、潜在記憶ないし情報源健忘と言われる。私は、別稿でこの問題の検討を行なっている（325）。本書第9章でも検討するつもりである。

8 『ブライディ・マーフィーの探索』の事例

「嘘は、真実が出発する前に、地球を半周する」。そのため、事実を知らない者の中には、〝ブライディ・マーフィー〟の事例は潜在記憶で説明できることが既に明らかになっている、と誤解する者が多い。しかし、これまでのところそのようなことが明らかにされているわけではないのである。その記憶をもっていた女性が十九世紀アイルランドの生活について示した知識はすべて、本人が少女時代に知っていたとされる近所のアイルランド出身者から得ることができたと主張する者も一部にあった。デュカッス（75）は、こうした主張と、それがいわれのないものであることを示す証拠とを厳密に検討している。この女性は、そのアイルランド出身者の子どもたちと知り合いだったことは覚えていたが、アイルランド出身者自身と口を利いた記憶はなかった。そのアイルランド出身者は、少なくとも〝ブライディ・マーフィー〟が語った十九世紀初頭のアイルランドに関する、ほとんど知られていない詳細な事柄をすべてこの女性に伝えることはできなかったはずなのである。超心理学の批判者の中には、そもそもの出典を参照することなく、その事例の虚偽性が既に暴露されているという話を、相互に借用し合いつつ引用している者がある。ところが、暴露されたという主張が実は誤りであることが逆に暴露されていることを知らない者もあるのである。そのような批判者は、デュカッスの論文や、バーンスタインの事例報告の改訂版（24）を熟読すべきである。

　しかしながら、ブライディ・マーフィーの事例は、潜在記憶で説明できることが証明されているわけではないが、ブライディ・マーフィーの発言に対応する人物がこれまで見つかっているわけではないので、生まれ変わりの存在を裏づける有力な証拠にはならないのである。

9　催眠状態で起こる応答型真性異言

　私はこれまで、信憑性《しんぴょうせい》があるように思われる、催眠中の応答型真性異言の事例を二例、論文や著書の中で発表している（313、316、328）。

10　催眠退行中に綴《つづ》り出される歴史小説

　同様に私は、精神疾患患者のある種の妄想は、おぼろげに記憶している前世の記憶に由来する可能性があるのではないかと推測している。たとえば自分を王妃ジョゼフィーヌだと妄想的に思い込んでいる女性は、十九世紀初頭のフランスで前世を送り、その時代に、ジョゼフィーヌに心酔し、自分と強く同一視していた、という可能性が考えられるのではなかろうか。昔、ヴァージニア大学病院に、自分を、『風と共に去りぬ』のヒロインであるスカーレット・オハラと思い込んでいる患者がいた。この女性はもしかすると、南北戦争前に南部で送った前世の記憶を無意識の中でもっていたのかもしれない。宗教的な妄想をもっていた別の患者は、自分がスペインの修道女、聖テレサの生まれ変わりだと思い込んでいた。この患者の場合、精神疾患の経過の中で、修道女として送った前世の記憶が漠然とした形で残っていて、それが聖テレサだったという妄想に発展した可能性がある。

11　幼年期後期の健忘

催眠中に前世の記憶を引き出すことがごく一部の事例を除いてできない原因は、自然に出現していた前世の記憶が、幼年期後期に入ると消失してしまう原因と同じである。この重要な問題については、第5章で考察する予定である。

12　既視感の発生率

ここに掲げた数字（七六パーセント）は、典型的なアメリカの町（ヴァージニア州シャーロッツヴィル）の住民と大学生を無作為抽出して行なった調査に基づいてパーマー（213）が発表したデータを組み合わせて算出したものである。他の標本では、発生率が異なるかもしれない。調査によって差が見られるのは、ひとつには、体験に関する質問の仕方がさまざまであり、その質問に対する解釈が回答者によって異なるためである。心理学者もそうであるが、回答者の中にも、特定の会話などの出来事が以前にもあった気がするという体験まで既視感に含める者がある一方、それまで行ったことのない場所に親近感を覚えるという意味に限定している者もある。パーマーの調査票では、場所と出来事の両方が既視感に含まれている。

既視感という体験は、精神障害の徴候と見なすべきものではない。頭の冴《さ》えた人たちにも、こうした体験をしたことのある者は多いのである。その中には、小説家のチャールズ・ディケンズ（64、三七ページ）や詩人のA・E・ハウスマン（104、一六六ページ）もいる。ネッペ（195）は、既視感体験を徹底的に検討している。

13　建造物の変化に関する子どもの発言

パルモッド・シャルマ、プラカーシュ・ヴァルシュナイ、ラビ・エラワール、スワルンラタ・ミシュラらがそうした発言を行なっている。（こうした事例の詳細な報告については、対応する参考文献を付録の中で明示しておいた。そこでは、事例の苗字《みょうじ》ではなく名前を〔五十音〕順に並べてある。）

14　既視感と前世の記憶

既視感体験が前世の記憶に基づく場合が多いとすれば、こうした体験をもつ者の中には、イメージ記憶をも同時に発現させる者がもっと多いはずである。事実であることが確認されている私たちの事例の中にも、既視感体験が見られるものがある。このような場合、かつて暮らしていたという町や村に到着すると、なつかしく感じられる風景を目のあたりにすることによって、新たな記憶が表出することもある。既視感を経験したことのある成人の中には、その体験があった場所について、その時ないしはその少し後に、予想すらつかないはずのことがわかったという者もある。たとえば、本人が立っている場所からはまだ見えていないのに、次の角を曲がると鍛冶屋《かじや》があるなどということがわかり、実際それが当たっている場合があるのである。この種の事例を私は何例か聞いているが、本人が、誰かと一緒にその場に行く前に、たとえば鍛冶屋があるということを本当に本人が口にしたかどうかについて、他の証人から確証が得られた事例はこれまでのところ一例もない。一部の事例では、本人が気後れしたために思ったことを言わなかったのであろうが、それ以外の事例でも、証人が死亡ないし離散してしまっており、証言が得られなかったのである。しかし、既視感が、前世の記憶を含む超常的認知に由来する場合が多いとすれば、この種の事例の中に、事実が確証された事例があることを耳にしているはずだと思う。本註が刺激となり、将来的にはこうした体験がもっと適切に記録されるようになってほしいものである。

15　既視感体験の神経学的解釈

エフロン（81）がこの解釈を提唱している。

16　繰り返される悪夢と遺伝的記憶

メアリ・マグルーダーの何人かの先祖が、本人の悪夢と同じような先住民の襲撃に遭っていることはほぼ確実であるため、一部には、本例を遺伝的記憶の一例と解釈する者もあろう。遺伝的記憶という問題については、第7章でもう一度検討するつもりである。

17 覚醒《かくせい》時に記憶を有するうえで、それに関連した夢を見る子どもたち

前世の記憶らしきものを覚醒時のみならず、夢の中でも発現させる子どもたちとしては、プラカーシュ・ヴァルシュナイ、サレム・アンダリ、スレイマン・アンダリらがいる。

18 夢の迫真性と超常的要素

私が分析した一二五件の予知夢のうち五六件（四五パーセント）で〝真に迫っていた〟という報告が得られている（309）。プリンス（240、241）は、その時点では健康状態がよかったはずの相手が登場した四四九件の〝真に迫った〟夢を分析した。その結果、そのうちの二五件（八パーセントほど）で、夢とその人物の死が時間的に一致しているのがわかったという。こうした夢を見た者の大半は、迫真性のない夢と比べて真に迫った夢は稀《まれ》にしか起こらないと述べている。迫真性のある夢のほとんどには超常的要素は含まれていないようであるが、迫真性のない夢よりもそうした要素が含まれている可能性は高いように思われる。

私は、超常的要素がその夢に混入している指標として、夢の迫真性の重要性を強調したいと思っているわけではない。超常的要素らしきものが存在するためであろうが、迫真性以外の何らかの理由から特定の夢を記憶している者は、後にその夢を真に迫っていたと表現するかもしれない。したがって私たちは、次の三通りの可能性を考慮しなければならない。迫真性のある夢は、ない夢よりも記憶されやすいのかもしれないこと、他の夢よりも超常的要素が混入している可能性が高いのかもしれないこと、こうした要素が含まれている夢は、振り返って考えた時、真に迫っていたと見られやすいのかもしれないことである。その夢がどのように感じられるかということと夢の内容との関係については、さらに検討を重ねる必要がある。

19 幻覚誘発剤と前世記憶

グロフ（111）は、幻覚誘発剤により陶酔状態にある時、前世の記憶を発現させる者が一部に

ある可能性を論じている。サンディソンら（268）が述べているLSDによる陶酔状態での体験の一部は、前世の記憶らしきもののように私には思われる。しかしながら、サンディソンらは、それを、抑圧されていた記憶がLSDによって解放された証拠と解釈しようとしているが、抑圧された記憶とされるものの中に登場する明確な具体的事象がどこに由来するか、という問題にはふれていない。

20　病気中に初めて出現する、あるいは病気の時の方がそれ以外の時よりも出現しやすい前世の記憶

その実例は、マ・ムー・ムー、ヴィニタ・ジャーの事例に見られる。

21　前世記憶の一端を反映しているのかもしれない偶発的〝閃《ひらめ》き〟

レンツ（151）は、こうした体験を集めて発表しているが、それを額面通りに受け入れ、精神病理学的なものであれ超常的なものであれ、他の種類の体験との関連づけは行なっていない。

これまで、本物の前世記憶を基に執筆したと称する人たちによって書かれた歴史小説がたくさん出版されている。そうした著作を必ずしも生まれ変わりの証拠として本気で受け止めるつもりはないが、そのうちの一部（102、123）については、誠実に書かれていると認めることができる。

第4章　前世を記憶する子どもたちの一二の典型例

1　詳細な事例報告

先述のように、こうした報告が掲載されている原典については、付録の中でまとめて紹介しておいた。（前世の記憶をもつ子どもの名前を〔五十音順に〕リストアップしている。）本書で紹介されている事例の要約は、原報告をかなり圧縮したものであることを念頭に置いていただきたい。事例報告では、簡潔であることと詳細であることとは必ずしも両立するわけではない。

2　来るべき出産に関係した予告夢

これは、生まれ変わり型事例によく見られる夢の一例である。故人が夢の中に現われ、特定の家族のもとに生まれ変わりたいという願望ないし意向を表明する。そうした夢を見るのは、夢の中に登場する故人の生涯を後に思い出す子どもの母親となる女性の場合がふつうである。しかし、コーリスの事例のように、親戚《しんせき》や友人がその夢を見ることもある。私はこうした夢を〝予告夢〟と呼んでいる。予告夢については次章で詳しく述べるつもりである。本章で紹介している事例でも、予告夢の見られた事例が他に四例ある。

3　ビルマで用いられる敬称

ビルマでは、マは少女に対する敬称である。年を経て成人になり、（結婚しているかどうかは別にして）地域社会の中で認められた地位に就くと、ドウという敬称がつけられる。同様に若い男性と年長の男性の敬称はマウンとウである。ビルマでは、敬称はきわめて重要なものであるため、名前からほとんど切り離せなくなっている。したがって、本書に登場するビルマ人に対してはすべて敬称を付している。

4　前世の家庭や家族のもとに戻りたいとする子どもたちの願望

こうした子どもたちの中には、前世の家族のもとに戻りたいという強い願望を表明する者があまりに多いため、これを、生まれ変わり型事例に頻発する特徴と考える者があるかもしれない。しかし、こうした行動を示さない子どもも若干ある。本人の主張が事実と確認された事例では、前世の家族に会いたい、あるいは会いたくないという子どもの気持は、たいてい、対応する前世の人格とその家族との関係について知りえた、あるいは推定しえた内容と一致することがわかっている。本章のスレイマン・アンダリの事例は、前世時代、不幸な生活を送っていた場所に行きたがらなかった子どものひとつの実例である。

その子どもと現在の家族の関係も、こうした態度に影響を及ぼす。しかしながら私は、現在の家族から、前世の人格がその家族から受けた以上の愛情を受けているように（私の見る限りでは）見える場合ですら、前世の家族のもとに行きたいという強い願望を表明した事例を何例か見つけている。そうした事例では、他のいくつかの要因のうち少なくともひとつが、その子どもに影響を与えているのかもしれない。まず第一に、その子どもは、前世の家族に対してよりも、前世の生活様式にあこがれているのかもしれない。気心の合わない妻が住んでいるとしても、使用人たちのいる豪邸の方が魅力的に感じられるのではなかろうか。（インディカ・グネラトネの事例がこのタイプの実例である。）第二に、その子どもは、私の言う〝やり残した仕事〟があることをわきまえているのかもしれない。この種の例としては、対応する前世の人格が死亡した時点では、まだ世話が必要な乳幼児がいたという事例が挙げられよう。（スクラ・グプタ、ラリタ・アベヤワルデナの事例がその格好の実例である。）第三に、昔の習慣を前世からもち越しているうえ、新たに出会った人々や生き方に適応することに苦痛を覚えるため、現在の生活状態より劣っているように第三者の眼に映る場合ですら、よりなじみの深い状況にある種の郷愁を覚えるのかもしれない。ケレンシアというスペイン語は、慣れ親しんだ場所をこのようになつかしむことを、どの英単語よりも的確に表現している。（プラカーシュ・ヴァルシュナイは、本人の記憶にある前世の家族のもとへ行きたい理由として、こうした動機以外にはないことを明らかにした子どもである。）

5　マ・ティン・アウン・ミヨの英米人に対する敵対心

この点は、本例の調査の後半になってから直接に質問して初めてわかった。マ・ティン・アウン・ミョの母親は、私との面接の中で自分からその点にふれることはなかった。したがってこの点は、本例の詳細な報告の中では述べられていない。

6　本当の母親と〝別の母親〟との、子どもたちによる比較

このような子どもたちは、自分の両親と、記憶の中にあるという前世の両親とを比較することがかなり多いが、必ずしも実の〔生物学上の〕両親をよく言うわけではない。こうした行動の実例としては他にも、（本章で紹介している）ロバータ・モーガンや、ヴェール・シン、ラビ・エラワールの事例がある。

7　イスラム教ドゥルーズ派の信仰

ドゥルーズ派の信仰、特に、その中に見られる生まれ変わり信仰については、別著で述べておいた（312、321）。ドゥルーズ派について詳しいことをお知りになりたい方は、マカレムの著書（171）を参照されたい。

8　変貌《へんぼう》を遂げた人物や場所が子どもたちにわからないこと

アブダラ・アブ・ハムダンが死亡してからスレイマンがガリフェを訪れるまで、二五年もの歳月が流れている。本人にわかったはずの人物や場所は、その間にかなり変わってしまっていた。後ほど説明するが、再認ができても、こうした事例の証拠としてはきわめて薄弱なものにしかならないにもかかわらず、生まれ変わったとする主張を裏づける目的で再認を求められる子どもが時おり大変な目に遭わせられることについては、ある程度考えてあげなければならない。（とはいえ、外見が変わるという問題は、写真には当てはまらない。）

9　ドゥルーズ族の事例の〝中間的〟前世

〝中間的〟前世の説明になりそうな事例やその存在を裏づける証拠については別稿で考察している（321）。

10　前世の人格と現在の家族とを結びつける地理的要因

双方の家族がそれまで相手の存在を全く知らなかった事例の中には、現在の家族の誰かが、母親が本人を妊娠する少し前に、前世の人格が住んでいた場所や死亡した場所を訪れている例も若干ある。それ以外の事例では、前世の家族の誰かが、母親が本人を妊娠する直前に、現在の家族が住んでいる地域を訪れたり、そこに転入したりしている。第11章で、こうした地理的要因を詳細に検討したうえ、適当な実例をいくつか挙げている。

11　帰りたいという願望

本章註4参照。

12　母親同士の比較

本章註6参照。

13　死後に起こった出来事を知っていること

その橋を渡って運ばれたというマイクルの言葉からすると、ウォルター・ミラーが死亡した後に起こった出来事の記憶が残っているらしいことがわかる。この種の記憶は、大半の文化圏の事例ではきわめて稀《まれ》であるが、ビルマやタイの事例ではしばしば見られる。ボンクチ・プロムシンの事例がその一例である。

14　両親と本人の間に三角関係が見られる事例

記憶をもっている子どもが、前世で自分は父親の先妻だったと主張した事例については、インドのアシャ・ラニとビルマのマ・ティン・ティン・ミントのふたりを調査している。フィンランドのタルー・イェルヴィの事例では、タルーは（記憶している前世で）母親の先夫だったと述べている。（この事例は、したがって〝性転換〟例でもある。）

第5章　生まれ変わり型事例の典型例の特徴

1　事例の定義

読者の方々の中には、私がどのように〝事例〟を定義しているかを知りたい方がおられるかもしれないので、ここで私なりに、この言葉の意味するところを述べておきたい。生まれ変わり型事例という言葉を使う時、私が言おうとしているのは、ある人物（その事例の当事者）が、特定の死者の生まれ変わりと認められる事例ということである。

大半の事例では、前世の記憶らしきものをもっている子どもは、その故人の生涯の記憶と自ら考える事柄を口にすることにより、自らがその人物と同一であることの証明を行なう。また、このような子どもたちは、この種の事例に共通するそれ以外の特徴も同時に示すのがふつうである。そうした特徴についても本章で述べるつもりである。

しかしながら私は、前世のイメージ記憶をもっているのがわかるような発言を行なわない子どもの事例も、少数ながら調査しており、私たちが収集した事例群に含めている。こうした事例では、周囲の人たちが、次のような点を根拠にその子どもを特定の故人の生まれ変わりとしている。もう一度生まれ変わって来るというその故人の予言、予告夢（後ほど詳述）、母斑《ぼはん》や先天性欠損、その子どもが示すある種の変わった行動、以上の特徴がふたつ以上見られる場合、などである。（もしその子どもが前世について何も口にしない場合には、これらの特徴のうち少なくともふたつなければ、私たちの事例群には含めていない。）

2 事例の発現を抑えつけるのに用いられる手段

アジアでは、自分の子どもの前世記憶を抑えつける手段として、さまざまな方法が用いられる。よく使われるのは、ろくろのようなものに子どもを乗せ、目が回るまで回転させる方法である。（それによって子どもを混乱させ、そうした記憶を心の中から追い払おうとしているようである。）それ以外にも、子どもの口を泥水で漱《すす》ぐ、少々噛《か》みくだいた食物を子どもの口に押し込む、一週間に二回ずつ、子どもの頭の上に箒《ほうき》を載せる。靴底で子どもの頭を軽く叩《たた》く、お守りを身につけさせる、などの方法がある。ビルマでは、子どもにアヒルの卵を食べさせるという方法がかなり信頼性が高いとされている。体罰は最後の手段であるが、実際にも時々行なわれる。私が知っているインドの子どものうち、ジャスビール・シン、プラカーシュ・ヴァルシュナイ、ラヴィ・シャンカール・グプタの三人に対しては、前世の話をしないようにするため体罰が加えられていた。

ロバータ・モーガンの事例に見られるように、西洋でも前世の記憶をもつ子どもに両親が体罰を加えることがある。

3　事例の発生率

事例報告に関する最初の著書（312）の中で、事例が数多く見つかったいくつかの地域について事例の発生率をおおまかに推定しておいた。

4　事例を探し求めた成果

タイとビルマは、たくさんの共通点をもった隣国同士であり、両国とも国民のほとんどは再生を信ずる上座部仏教徒である。したがって、事例の実際の発生率はほぼ同じなのではないかと思われるかもしれないが、報告されている事例数は相当に違っている。一九六六年以来私どもが調査を行なっているタイではわずか四五例しか見つかっていないのに対して、一九七〇年末になってから調査を開始したビルマでは、タイの二〇倍ほどに当たる五〇〇例以上に関する情報が集まっているのである。

タイとビルマの報告例の数がこのように異なるのは、ひとつには、両国の経済的な発達段階が異なるためかもしれない。タイは、依然として発展途上国と見られているが、経済的にはビルマよりもはるかに発達した国である。西洋で超常現象と呼ばれているものに関する概念が、経済的発展により必然的に大きく変化する可能性については第8章で論じている。

とはいえ、タイとビルマの報告例数の違いは、ほとんどが、ビルマの共同研究者であるウ・ウィン・マウンという個人の根気強い調査活動のたまものと私は考えている。ウ・ウィン・マウンは、厖大《ぼうだい》な量の手紙をやりとりしたり、ビルマの村々に数えきれないほど出かけたりすることにより、時間をかけて（しかも、それより重要なことであるが）たゆみなく勤勉に事例の調査を続けてくれたのである。タイでは、こうした研究に関心を持つ有能な人たち数名が、私自身が訪問できた時にともに事例の調査を行なってきたが、ウ・ウィン・マウンと同じ（というより、おそらく他の人間にはまねのできない）方法で時間をかけ、根気強く事例を探し求めようとした者はひとりもいなかった。

ウ・ウィン・マウンがなし遂げたことは、広大という点では他に例を見ないものであるが、決して目新しいものではない。他の共同研究者や協力者たちも、アジアでは事例を探す気になればどれほど容易に見つけることができるかを明らかにしてくれた。有能な協力者としては、もうひとり、故ラム・シンの名前を挙げることができる。ラム・シンは、以前インドのラージャスターン州ジャラワールのマハラジャのもとに勤めていたが、私の研究に関心を抱き、退職後に地元で私のために事例を探し求めてくれた人物である。一九六〇年代末から一九八一年に亡くなるまで、氏は私のためにたくさんの事例を探し出してくれた。新聞を通じて知った事例も一部あったが、それ以外は、地元の人たちの間に作りあげた連絡網を通じて情報を収集していた。氏の真剣な努力のおかげで、氏が暮らしていた小さな地域から、それ以外のラージャスターン地方全域で得られたのと同じくらいの数の事例を見つけることができた。氏の〝縄張り〟は、ラージャスターン地方全体の二〇分の一ほどにすぎなかったが、私が初めて一七例の事例を知ったのは氏のおかげなのである。ちなみに、ラージャスターン地方の他の情報提供者全員が（一九八四年までに）集めてくれたのは、わずか一六例にすぎない。

5 〝完全型〟は完璧《かんぺき》という意味ではないこと

各特徴が〝完全に発現〟している完全型の事例でも、その証拠的価値がどの程度あるかは、それだけではわからない。現象的には豊富な事例でも、証拠としては貧弱かもしれないのである。何が証拠として価値があるかという問題については、第6章と7章で検討している。

6 トリンギット族の間で行なわれる生まれ変わりの予言

コーリス・チョトキン・ジュニアの事例（第4章で要約して紹介）は、次に生まれ変わる時に自分の両親となる夫婦を選択できることと、生まれ変わる者が宿った新しい肉体に母斑が出現するのが予言できることを例証する実例である。ウィリアム・ジョージ・ジュニアの事例も、この二点を裏づける実例と言える。

7　チベット族の間に見られる生まれ変わりの予言

ノルブら（200）は、チベットのラマ僧による再生の予言について若干の記述を行なっている。

私が知っているチベットの事例はほとんどが、子どもの頃、別のラマ僧として送った前世について語ったラマ僧の例である。トゥルクと呼ばれるこの種の事例については、第2章で簡単にふれておいた。こうした人々は、チベット人全体の中ではほんの一握りにすぎない。このような人たちは、霊的に進化しているため、次に生まれ変わる場所や状況を少なくともある程度は自由に決定できる力をもっているとされる。年輩のラマ僧が死ぬ前に行なう予言を見ると、こうした能力を確信しているのがわかる。（チベットの一般人の間にも前世の記憶をもつ子どもがいると言われるが、私が知っているのは一例のみである。）

インドに流入したチベット難民の事例を調査する中で私は、情報を提供してくれそうな人々が離散してしまっている（一部はチベットに残留している）ため調査の条件としては不適当であることに気がついた。一個の事例の情報提供者は一、二の地域に固まっている国がふつうであるが、私が調査したチベットの事例では、それと比べると弱い証拠しか得られていないのである。

8　予告夢

次の事例で予告夢が報告されている。ウィリアム・ジョージ・ジュニア、イスマイル・アルティンキリヒ、セヴリエ・バイリ、ナシル・トコセズ、コーリス・チョトキン・ジュニア、スーザン・イーストランド、マ・ティン・アウン・ミョ、サヤドウ・ウ・ソバナ師、マウン・イン・マウン、エルカン・キリヒ、マ・ティン・ティン・ミント、マイクル・ライト、サムエル・ヘランデル、オルヌマ・スア・イン・ヨン。

トリンギット族の予告夢については、トリンギットの事例を報告している一九六六年の拙論(305)である程度詳しく述べておいた。

9　母斑と先天性欠損

私はこれまで、母斑や先天性欠損をもつ事例については詳細な報告を二、三件しか行なっていない。もっと重要な事例としては、次のようなものがある。デレク・ピトノヴ、チャールズ・ポーター、ヘンリー・エルキン、ウィリアム・ジョージ・ジュニア、コーリス・チョトキン・ジュニア、ラヴィ・シャンカール・グプタ、ウィジェラトネの各例である。第4章で、コーリス・チョトキン・ジュニアのふたつの母斑の一方と、ジェニファー・ポロックのふたつの母斑について述べているが、こうした事例については、ある論文(318)の中でも少し詳しく述べている。

10　前世の話を始める年齢

六ヵ所の文化圏の六九三例では、初めて前世の話をした平均年齢は三歳一ヵ月であった。子どもが前世について話し始める年齢の正確なデータについては、クックら(52)およびスティーヴンソン(327)の論文を参照されたい。

11　体の大きさが変わったことを訴える子ども

前世時代と比べて体の大きさが変わったことにふれた子どもとしては、マルタ・ロレンツ、マイクル・ライト、スクラ・グプタ、パルモッド・シャルマ、ヴィアス・ラジパル、ラムー・シャルマ、ラジュー・シャルマ、ラリタ・アベヤワルデナ、ルビ・クスマ・シルヴァ、ボンクチ・プロムシン、ラビ・エラワール、チャオクン・ラジスタジャルンらがいる。

12　子どもをからかって泣かせること

このように少々残酷な目に遭った経験をもつのは、スクラ・グプタとイマド・エラワールである。ディスナ・サマラシンへは幼少期に、からかうような調子で〝ババノナ〟と呼ばれると泣き出すことがあった。(ババノナとは、ディスナがその生涯を記憶していた老婦人である。)私は、自らこのようにからかうことにより、一度ディスナに涙を流させた経験がある。

13　夢や悪夢の中に出現する前世の記憶

ウィジャナマ・キトシリ、プラカーシュ・ヴァルシュナイ、スレイマン・アンダリ、サレム・アンダリの事例がその実例である。

14　記憶の消失

本人がどう話しているかはともかく、前世の記憶を既に消失してしまっているのかまだもち続けているのかを判断する際に考慮すべき要因については、別稿（312）で詳しく論じている。女児の場合は、一〇代後半になって記憶が残っているとしても、それを隠す傾向があるように思われる。三歳の幼女が自分の夫について話し、会いたいと言うのと、一五歳の少女が同じ発言をするのとは、全く別の問題なのである。インドのスクラ・グプタは、幼少期には、耳を傾けてくれる人なら誰に対しても気軽に話していたが、思春期に入ってからは、夫がいるなどと言うと人聞きが悪いので〝地下に潜った〟ひとりである。

子どもたちの中には、実際には既にほとんど消失してしまっているにしても、自分が当初もっていた記憶と、幼少期に話していたと人から聞かされているものの記憶とを、明確に区別している者もある。

15　前世の家族との対面後、子どもの緊張が弱まること

前世の家族と初めて対面した後、子どもの緊張が急速とも言えるほどに弱まるという現象は、恐怖症のような強い神経症症状をもつ患者が、その原因となった外傷体験を想起するとその苦しみから解放されることがあるのとある程度類似している。忘れていた出来事が意識に上ると患者は、その出来事とその後の体験とを結びつけることができる。それにより、その出来事が及ぼす悪影響が中和されるのである。こうした解離（心の中でさまざまな記憶が孤立している状態）が打ち破られる時、強い感情が出現するが、この感情は、消されていた記憶が回復する際の副産物であって、それ自体が治癒を促す要因になるわけではない（57、164、177）。スミスら（288）は、この重要な問題に関する文献をさらに渉猟し、考察を行なっている。子どもが前世の人格の家族と対面することで解離が破れ、前世の記憶と、その子どもの人格の残余の部分とが統合されるのかもしれない。実際にもよくあることだが、対面によって刺激されることで新しい記憶が出て来るとすれば、そのおかげで統合作用に拍車がかかるのかもしれない。

16 幼少期に前世の記憶を消失させる要因

既決例と未決例で記憶が消失する年齢が異なることを示すデータについては、クックら（52）の論文を参照されたい。

単に時間の経過だけが、記憶が消える原因ではない。前世の記憶は、その後に経験を積み重ねることによる干渉効果によって意識から消え去ってしまうのである。記憶の消失に関係するいくつかの要因について詳しくお知りになりたい方は、この問題について別稿（314、二五—二九ページ）で行なっている考察や関連研究の紹介を参照されたい。

17 イメージ記憶の消失と言葉の発達

認識的記憶には二種類あるとされる。ケストラー（147）は、〝抽象的な〟記憶に対して、「〝鮮明な断片的〟記憶ないし、〝映写フィルム的〟記憶」があることを述べている。抽象的な記憶には言葉が必要である。タルヴィング（353）は、この二種類の記憶を、〝意味論〟的記憶と〝挿話的〟記憶と呼んでいる。（ベルクソン〔22〕も同じ区別をそれより前に行なっている。）この二種類の記憶については、第1章で述べておいた。〝行動的記憶〟と区別するため、この種の記憶は私の言う〝イメージ記憶〟に含めている。

リチャードソン（251）は、心像に関する著書の中で、「私たちは、現代の工業化社会の中で成人するため、経験を符号化するのに言葉を用いることが、幼少期の、イメージを使った方法に優先すると推測される」（一三七ページ）と述べている。もっとゆっくりしたものであろうが、非工業化社会でもやはり同じような現象が起こる。

18　死やその直前に起こった出来事にまつわる記憶が集中的に見られること

前世の人格が死亡する何年も前に起こった出来事を記憶している子どもが時たまある。検討の結果、この種の記憶はふつう、結婚記念日の贈り物や負傷などの強い感情を引き起こす出来事にまつわるものであることがわかっている。その実例については、クムクム・ヴェルマとラリタ・アベヤワルデナの事例報告の中で紹介しておいた。

19　スリランカの固有名詞

この問題については、スリランカの事例を扱った拙著(317)の序論で詳しく論じている。

20　死亡してから生まれ変わるとされるまでの間に起こる賢者との出会い

一部の子どもが、肉体のない世界で出会ったとする賢者については、タイとビルマの事例を報告している拙著(324)の中で詳しく述べておいた。

21　偶発的に誰かを見分けること

実例としては、他にも、ラタナ・ウォンソムバト、セヴリエ・バイリ、ナシル・トコセズ、ジャスビール・シン、イマド・エラワール、モウンゼル・ハイダル、ラビ・エラワールの各例がある。

22　前世の家族のそれぞれに対して子どもの反応が異なること

前世の人格が前世の家族に対してとっていたのと一致する態度をそれぞれに対してとった実例としては、他にも、ラリタ・アベヤワルデナ、ディスナ・サマラシンへ、プシュパ、ガミニ・ジャヤセナの事例がある。

23　前世の人格の家族に前世の記憶をもつ子どもが受け入れられること

子どもを完全に受け入れ、援助を行なった前世の人格の家族は、他にも、スワルンラタ・ミシュラ、ラビ・エラワール、ラム・プラカーシュの各例に見られる。

24　前世の人格の家族が記憶をもつ子どもを拒絶すること

ドロン・チャムパ・ミトラ、スニル・ドゥット・サクセナの事例にその実例が見られる。この二例では、前世の家族が裕福なため、その子どもの家族から援助を期待されたり要求されたりするのを恐れたのかもしれない。

25　言葉が発達する前に出現する恐怖症

スジト・ラクマル・ジャヤラトネ（スリランカ）の事例にもそれが見られる。この子どもも、前世の話をするようになる前から、警官恐怖症とトラック恐怖症とを示した。この事例の前世の人格は、密造酒を造っており、警察との間で何回も嫌な目に遭っていた。またこの男性は、高速で走行するトラックにはねられて死亡していた。

26　双方の家族の社会経済的階層が著しく異なる事例

自分の家族よりも社会経済的階層が高い家族の中で送った前世を記憶しており、それに相応する高飛車な態度を示した例については、ジャスビール・シン、ヴェール・シン、インディカ・グネラトネ、ジャグディシュ・チャンドラの事例報告の中でも詳しく述べられている。

現在の家族よりも社会経済的に低い階層に属する家族の中で送った前世を記憶していた子どもとしては、他に、ディスナ・サマラシンへがいる。

27　成人のような態度

成人のような態度を示した子どもとしては、スレイマン・アンダリ、クムクム・ヴェルマ、ハイール・カム・カニヤ、ボンクチ・プロムシンらがいる。

28　性転換型の事例

現在とは逆の性別の人間として前世を送った子どもには、他にも、グナナティレカ・バデウィタナ、パウロ・ロレンツ、ルビ・クスマ・シルヴァ、アムパン・ペトチェラトがいる。

29　前世の人格が死亡してからその記憶をもつ子どもが生まれるまでの間隔

こうしたデータの一部については、既に別稿（324）で報告している。

30　**前世の記憶をもつ子どもの記憶を抑えつけるためインドで用いられる方法**

この数字は、サトワント・パスリチャの博士論文（インド、バンガロール州、国立精神衛生・神経科学研究所、一九七八年）からとられたものである。

31　**逆の性別に相応した行動を続けること**

前世の記憶はないが、幼少期に逆の性別にふさわしい行動を示すアメリカの子どもたちは、年長になるにつれ、性的にも異なった成長を遂げる。R・グリーン（109）は、こうした子どもたちの追跡調査を行ない、一部は青少年期および成人後に同性愛を発展させるのに対して、大半の子どもたちは異性との愛情関係を発達させるようになることを明らかにしている。

32　**真性異言**

信憑性《しんぴょうせい》があり重要であると私が考える少数の真性異言の事例は、スワルンラタ・ミシュラ、イェンセン（313）、グレートヒェン（316、328）、ウッタラ・フダールの各例である。

33　**前世の母語の記憶が残せないこと**

第一次大戦で戦死したアーサーというイギリス人の記憶をもっているとするインドの子どもが、英語の話し方までは記憶していないという話を聞くと、最初は驚くべきことのように思われる。（これは、これまで未発表のバジラン・B・サクセナの事例である。）口から発せられる言葉と、非業の死を遂げるなどの出来事に対応するイメージが異なるという点が、その説明になるかもしれない。心の中に椅子のイメージがあるとすれば、その時に椅子という言葉を考える必要はないし、ましてやそれを口に出して発音する必要もない。仮に私が死後に生まれ変わり、椅子を目にしたとすると、なじみ深いものと感じられようし、その意味ではそれを椅子と認めるであろうが、だからといって、私が見ているものを、椅子という言葉で呼ぶとは必ずしも限らないであろう。もし私がドイツに生まれ変わり、そこで椅子に見覚えがある感じがしたとしても、ドイツ人の両親は、私が注目している物体をシュトゥールと教えるであろうし、そのため、それを椅子と呼びたい気持を現世からもち越しているとしても、それが抑えつけられやすいかもしれないのである。

しかしながら、ほとんどの子どもは、前世からもち越した言葉をいくつか記憶している。前世の人格を突き止めるには、その人格を明確にしてくれる人物や場所の名前を（ほとんどの場合）子どもが記憶していなければならない。わずかな名前しか覚えていない子どももある一方で、数多く記憶している子どももいる。

34　言葉恐怖症

ビルマとタイの事例を報告している拙著（324）の中で私は、第二次大戦中にビルマで戦死した日本兵だった前世を記憶しているビルマの数名の子どもが、ビルマ語を覚えるのに抵抗があったという事実について論じておいた。言葉恐怖症の実例としては、他にも、レバノンのナワル・ドウの事例がある。

35　前世の人格の死亡年月日とその子どもが生まれた年月日とが逆になっている事例

この種の事例としてはこれまで、ジャスビール・シンとチャオクン・ラジスタジャルンの例を報告している。他の事例についても、続刊の事例報告書の中で発表していきたいと思う。

第6章　研究の方法

1　ピタゴラス

出典はイアンブリコス（135）。

2　アポロニオス

出典はフィロストラトゥス（226）。

3　アウランジーブが調査した事例

私は、この事例報告の（十八世紀に出版されたウルドゥー語の原文をコピーしたものと、その部分の英語訳とをもっているが、この報告が掲載されている原著全体を検討したことはない。この原著は、ムンシ・スバン・ライの執筆になる『クラサト・ウト・タワリク』である。

4　勝五郎の事例

ラフカディオ・ハーン（124）は、一八二〇年代に発生したこの事例の日本文の原資料から翻訳した作品を公刊している。私は、この事例の要約（303）を発表している。

5　十九世紀末のビルマの事例

こうした事例は、フィールディング＝ホール（87）によって報告されている。

6　一九〇〇年から一九六〇年までの間に発表された事例報告

そのうち最も注目すべきは、スンデルラル（337）とサハイ（266）による報告である。このふたりは、それぞれ数例ずつの事例を発表しており、スンデルラルは四例、サハイは七例である。また、ふたりとも、証言を丹念に記録することの重要性をきちんとわきまえていた。対象となった子どもが前世について語った内容が、その発言が事実かどうか確認する作業の開始される以前に文字で記録されている事例を、スンデルラルは一例（プラブーの事例）、サハイは二例（ジャグディシュ・チャンドラとビシェン・チャンド・カプールの事例）を報告している。グプタら（115）は、シャンティ・デヴィの事例に関して注目すべき報告を行なっている。マトゥラーという前世時代の町に本人を連れて行く前に、前世に関するシャンティ・デヴィの発言を記録しているわけではないが、グプタらは、この事例を研究するために（双方の家族とは無関係の）委員会を自ら組織し、その後まもなく、かなり詳しい報告を発表しているのである。

生まれ変わりを思わせる事例の研究史に欠かせないのは、ドランヌ（59）の注目すべき編著である。ドランヌはこの書に、『生まれ変わり研究に供すべき参考資料』という控え目なタイトルをつけている。同書は、主として、ドランヌがさまざまな出典から収集した事例報告のアンソロジーである。そのため、同書に収録されている報告は玉石混交といった感がある。一般雑誌や新聞から抜粋したものの中にはほとんど無価値のものもあるが、その一方でドランヌは、アレキサンドリナ・サモナやロール・レイノーのような若干の事例については、比較的長文の詳細な報告を収録している。またドランヌの業績は、単なる雑文集をはるかに超えるものであり、各事例についての著者なりの洞察力あるコメントを付している。同書は英語には一度も翻訳されていないし、私の知る限り、私以外の英語圏の研究者には全く関心をもたれていないが、私としては、この著書に負うところが大きかった。

7 一九六〇年に分析された四四例

私は、別稿(303)でその事例を要約、分析している。

8 インドにおける事例の発生率

バーカーら(13)が行なった調査を通じて、少なくともインド北部の一地方での事例の発生率はある程度わかっている。バーカーらは、人口一〇〇〇人中二例の発生率を認めているのである。この数字は厳密には、発見された事例の人口比であって、調査された標本中の事例の発生率ではない。

9 事例の信憑性

信憑性と超常性の区別の重要性について第1章で述べたことを思い起こしていただきたい。ある事例に信憑性があると言う場合、情報提供者の報告をはじめ、私たちが入手した証拠が、実際に起こった出来事をかなり正確に描き出している、ということを意味している。しかしながら、信憑性はあっても、超常的要素が含まれていることを裏づける証拠が存在しない場合もある。前世の記憶をもつ子どもと前世の人格とが同一の家族に属する事例では、そのような状況になることが多い。情報提供者は完全に信頼できるかもしれないし、その子どもも、通常の方法で知ったわけではない、前世の人格の生涯に関する具体的発言を行なっているのかもしれないが、その子どもが前世の人格の家族のもとに生まれているため、家族の者からその故人についていろいろと聞かされる機会があった可能性が否定できないのである。

10　研究の方法

私の研究法の詳細については、拙著（314）に述べておいた。

11　直接情報提供者の定義

直接情報提供者とは、自ら見聞きした事柄を語る情報提供者、つまり目撃者のことである。他人から聞いたことしか言わない者は、法律用語で言えば間接証人である。この場合、話に尾ひれがつくとさらに状況が悪くなる。

12　通訳の利用

通訳の介在によって証言が大きく歪《ゆが》むとは思われないが、通訳により、情報の重大な逸失が起こることがあるとは思う。また、この逸失は、情報提供者から伝達される言語的情報にしか起こらないわけではない。最も経験豊かな面接者ですら、また、その文化圏で用いられる言葉が話せる場合ですら、自分の属する文化圏以外の文化を完全には理解しえないという点でも、情報の逸失が起こるのである。

13　拡張版人物描画検査

私は、ホイッティカー（366）が発表したこの検査の修正版を用いている。

14　生まれ変わり信仰調査票（ＢＲＱ）

Ｌ＝Ｖ・トーマス（346）は、この調査票の原型となったものを作成し、セネガルで実際に使っている。何回か修正を繰り返し、トルコで（レシャト・バイエルと私が）この調査票を試験的に用いた後、サトワント・パスリチャが、さらに改良を加え、インドで用いた。また、タイでも使われている。

第７章　事例の分析と解釈

1　文章という形で残されている情報が正確であること

第６章で、探し当てて使いたいと思うような、文章として残された情報の例をいくつか挙げておいた。この種の証拠書類は、大半が、対象となる出来事が起こった直後に作成され、（用紙とインクが保《も》つ限り）不変の証拠として固定されるので、口頭による証言よりも一般に正確である。とはいえ、文字による記録は、情報を提供する人物および、記録を残す人物がそれを正確に行なうかどうかにかかっている。文字として残された記録はそのまま鵜《う》呑《の》みにすべきではなく、少なくとも数回は、他の証拠と照合してみなければならない。かつて私は、前世の人格の没年が墓石に誤って刻み込まれているのを見つけたことがある。

2 研究者による直接の観察

私たちは、時として、前世の記憶をもつ子どもから直接に話を聞くことがある。また、両親が報告する何らかの変わった行動を子どもがとっている場面を観察できることもたまにある。さらに、きわめて稀《まれ》ではあるが、私たちは適切な管理が行き届いた条件の下で、子どもが誰かを見分ける場面を目撃したこともあった。（グナナティレカ・バデウィタナとマ・チョエ・ニン・テトが関係者を見分ける場面を私自身が目撃したことについては、第5章で述べておいた。また私は、完全とは言えない条件の下ではあったが、イマド・エラワールが何人かの関係者を見分ける場面にも立会っている。）

3 目撃者の証言

十九世紀後半に活躍した初期の心霊研究者たちは、目撃者の証言の限界に気づくようになり、心理学者や法律研究者よりも何年か前にその弱点を考慮に入れ始めている。

私は、一九六八年までに行なわれた、目撃者の証言の精度を対象にした実験のほとんどを検討したことがある（310）。弁護士のマーシャルは、目撃者の証言に関係した厳密な実験を行ない、その結果を公正な立場から分析した論文を発表している（178）。ロロ（257）は、細部に関する目撃者の思い違いが信頼性の判断とどのように関係するかを分析している。

目撃者の証言に関する代表的実験の被験者は学生であり、スライドや映画に登場する場面を記憶させる形で行なわれる実験の多くでは、細部についてはもちろん、いかなる点についても記憶しようとする動機がほとんど見当たらないことも確かである。現実に起こった出来事（強盗と被害者間に起こった銃撃戦）を目撃した通行人の証言を検討したユイルら（375）の報告は、こうした出来事の記憶は数ヵ月後ですらきわめて正確に保たれる可能性があることを明らかにしている。

4　未決例

共同研究者とともに私は、七例の未決例を要約して報告しているが、その中で、子どもの発言に対応する故人を探し出そうとしたものの成功しなかったという事実にもふれておいた（51、52）。ランジト・マカランダ、ウィジャナマ・キトシリ（以上スリランカ）、オルヌマ・スア・イン・ヨン（タイ）、マ・ティン・アウン・ミョ（ビルマ）の各例もやはり未決例であるが、この四例については、既に詳細な報告を発表している。

未決例のうち特に不可解なのは、記憶をもっている子どもがかなりの数の実名を（しばしば確信をもって）挙げているのに、それでもその発言に対応する人物が見つけ出せない事例である。フサム・ハリビとマウン・ソエ・ヤがその実例である。

5　未決例における超常的要素

未決例の子どもたちの中には、通常の方法で知ったとは思われない出来事や（住んでいたという）場所について詳細に語る者がある。実例としては、かつて暮らしていたというバナドゥラという町で「神さまが焼かれた」と語ったスリランカのツサリ・ウィジャシンへの事例がある。この言葉は、一九五八年に起こった暴動で、あるヒンドゥー寺院とそこに安置されていた神像が焼け落ちた事件を指しているように思われる。ツサリが生まれたのはそれから一〇年以上たった一九六九年であり、しかも、パナドゥラの北二五キロほどのところにあるコロンボの市内であった。パナドゥラのヒンドゥー寺院焼失事件についてこの少女が通常の方法で知った可能性は、非常に低い。

6　不正による事例

ふたりの共同研究者とともに私は、まちがいなく不正によると思われる事例をこれまで三例調査している。この三例については、(他人の不正によるものではなく)自己欺瞞《ぎまん》という解釈が妥当と思われる事例とまとめて報告する予定である。

ノルブら(200、二三五―二三六ページ)も、チベットのこうした事例を一例報告している。

7 潜在記憶

このような事例をはじめ、超常的要素が関係していることを示す事例を批判する者は、潜在記憶によるものにちがいないと高らかに宣言する場合が多い。不信が根底にあり、潜在記憶の話を聞きかじったこの種の批判者は、個々の事例で潜在記憶が関係していることを実証しないまま、観念的にこの概念を当てはめてしまうのである。潜在記憶の実例で十分に検討が加えられたものは、これまでほとんど報告されていない。この問題を扱った私の総説では、これまで発表された実例をほとんど網羅している(325)。それ以上の事例が存在するのはまちがいなかろうが、潜在記憶という説明をとりたがる者には、その実例をこれまで以上に報告する責務が多少なりともあるのである。

潜在記憶の可能性を排除できると私が完全に確信している事例が一例ある。シュレイマン・ゼイツンの事例である。この少年は、すぐ隣で大砲が発射されても聞こえなかったと言われるほどの先天性聾唖《ろうあ》者であった。本人が幼時にある男性の生涯と死にざまを知っていたのは、通常の方法でその知識を得たためではないか、と真剣に主張できる者があるであろうか。

8 前世の記憶をもつ子どもが家族内で起こった内輪の出来事を知っていること

家族以外の者には知られていない内輪の出来事を前世を記憶する子どもが知っていた例としては、他にも、イスマイル・アルティンキリヒ、マウン・イン・マウン、イマド・エラワール、ラビ・エラワール、ラタナ・ウォンソムバトの事例がある。(以上の事例は、長距離例に限定して選び出したものではない。このうちの何人かは、前世の人格と同じ地域に住んでいたのである。）

9　双方の家族が対面する前に発言が記録されている事例

一九七五年に私は、このタイプの事例を若干（一二例）リストアップしている（314）。このリストの件数はその後、徐々に増え、現在は二〇例ほどになっている。

10　主な出来事とそれが文字で記録されるまでの間隔

主な出来事とは、ここでは、双方の家族が初めて対面した時のことを指している。共同研究者か私がそれを初めて記録したのがふつうであり、子どもの両親その他が記録している例は稀であった。私は、インドとスリランカの一四例について、双方の家族が初めて対面してから最初に記録されるまでの間隔を一覧表にまとめている（314、二七ページ）。この一四例では、その間隔の中央値は三・五ヵ月であった。その後、私たちは、少なくともインドとスリランカの事例については、この間隔をさらに短縮したと思っているが、これは単なる印象にすぎず、数字で裏づけることはできなかった。

11　子どもの家族がその事例に対して否定的な態度を示すこと

実例としては、プラカーシュ・ヴァルシュナイ、バジラン・B・サクセナ、ラヴィ・シャンカール・グプタ、プティ・パトラ、ジャスビール・シンの各例がある。

前世を記憶する子どもの家族は、その事例に対してさまざまな態度を示す可能性がある。事例を公表したがる者もいれば、子どもを抑えつけたがる者もいるかもしれないのである。たとえば、ゴーパール・グプタの父親は、ゴーパールの事例を（最終的には）真剣に考えるようになったが、母親は、それによって家族生活が崩壊することには賛成しなかった。

12　前世の人格の家族がその事例に対して否定的な態度を示すこと

実例としては、スニル・ドゥット・サクセナ、ラビ・エラワール、ドロン・チャムパ・ミトラ、プティ・パトラ、ラリタ・アベヤワルデナ、イスマイル・アルティンキリヒ、セヴリエ・バイリ、シュレイマン・ゼイツン（当初のみ）、エルカン・キリヒの各例がある。

13　記憶錯誤

バーカー（218）は、ラケシュ・ガウルの事例を記憶錯誤例と解釈したが、パスリチャは同意しなかったので、この事例は記憶錯誤例としては適当なものではない。この事例を記憶錯誤例と解釈する場合の長所、短所についての考察は、パスリチャらの報告（218）および、本例に関するパスリチャのその後の報告（217）を参照されたい。

14　前世の人格が死亡してからその記憶をもつ子どもが生まれるまでの間隔

七ヵ所の文化圏の事例を対象に各文化圏ごとに算出した、前世の人格が死亡してからその子どもが生まれるまでの間隔の中央値については、別稿（324）に発表しておいた。その間隔は、短い場合で六ヵ月、長い場合は四八ヵ月であった。

15　他人の死の遺伝的記憶

ある共同研究者は、片方の親が死亡する前に生まれた子どもはその時の模様を詳しく知っており、それがもとになって、片方の親の死に関する情報が遺伝を通じて子孫に伝えられる可能性があるのではないか、という指摘を行なっている。その検討を行なうに当たり、いかなるイメージ記憶も遺伝的に伝えられることを前提として認めるため、その可能性を排除することはできない。とはいえ、この考え方は、前世を記憶する子どもが前世の人格の死の模様を語る時に必ずと言ってよいほど付随する強い感情をあまり考慮に入れていない。人間は、人の死を、自分のもののように感ずることができないのではなかろうか。また、子どもが伝えようとしているのはおそらく、まさに自分の死という個人的体験であり、他人の死ではないのである。

16　前世を記憶する子どもの超感覚的知覚

超感覚的知覚をもっている証拠をわずかながら示した子どもには、グナナティレカ・バデウィタナ、シャムリニー・プレマ、ラタナ・ウォンソムバトがいる。

17　子どもが示す行動特徴の症候群

ここに要約して示した事柄は、別稿でさらに詳しく論じている（321）。ホジソン（129）は、G・Pという交信者が霊媒のリアノラ・パイパー夫人と会席者の間に生じたテレパシーによって作り上げられた架空の存在ではありえないと考える理由を明らかにする際に、これと同様の論法を用いている。

18　生まれ変わりを思わせる事例の説明概念としての憑依《ひょうい》

前世の記憶らしきものを憑依で説明することは、少なくともスウェーデンボルグ（340）の時代から行なわれており、それ以降その解釈に従った者は少なくない。

19　あらゆる事例の欠陥

これまで記録された中で最も有力なもののひとつと私が考える事例でも、他の点では多少なりとも好意的な研究者からすら攻撃されてきた（197）。今言おうとしているのは、ジャグディシュ・チャンドラの事例である。その父親であるK・K・N・サハイ（弁護士）は、ジャグディシュ・チャンドラが記憶に残している前世について語った主な内容を、他の、客観的な立場からこの事例を眺めることのできる人たちに事実かどうか確認してもらう前に記録しているのである。ジャグディシュ・チャンドラの家族はバレイリに住んでいたのに対して、前世の人格の家族はバナーラス（現バラナシ）に住んでいた。両市は、同じ州の端と端に位置し、両市の間の距離は、五〇〇キロほどあるが、これは、大半の事例と比較してはるかに大きいのである。そのうえ、双方の家族は、カーストの違いによっても隔絶されていた。この事例が発生した一九二〇年には、カーストはまだインド人の生活にとってきわめて重要な要素であった。

ジャグディシュ・チャンドラの父親は、その事例報告の中で、「バナーラスには友人も親戚《しんせき》もいない」と述べている（266）。ところが同じ報告の後半で、父親は、息子の発言が事実かどうかを最終的に確認するため現地に赴いた時、従姉《いとこ》の家に滞在したと述べているのである。ニコルはこの食い違いから本例を虚言によるものと見なし、K・K・N・サハイが、この従姉を通じてバナーラスの家族について得た情報をもとに、自分の息子にそうした発言をするよう指図した可能性があると考えた。私見によれば、この判断は不当であると思う。ジャグディシュ・チャンドラの語った事柄が事実かどうか確認する目的で（本人と一緒に）K・K・N・サハイがバナーラスに赴いた時には、当地に住んでいた従姉は既に死亡していたため、ふたりは、当時まだ存命中の従姉の夫のもとに滞在したのである。K・K・N・サハイは、従姉の夫を〝親戚〟とも〝友人〟とも考えなかったのであろう。サハイは、従姉一家を通じてバナーラスの住人とつながりがあったかどうかについては、それ以上のことを述べているわけではない。その点は残念であるが、その部分が欠落していることが本例の致命的な欠陥になるとは、私には思われない。K・K・N・サハイは、私が初めてインドを訪れる前に死亡しているため会ったことはないが、この一家と懇意になった私としては、K・K・N・サハイがデータを捏造《ねつぞう》し、自ら調査したとする六例の事例とともにその報告を行なったとはとうてい考えられない。情報提供者が誠実で信頼に足るという印象を個人的に抱いたところで、一部の批判者には問題にもされないことは私も承知しているが、情報提供者の個人的名声が高ければ、事例を評価する際、かなりの説得力をもってくるはずである。

20 双方の家族がまだ対面していない事例をこれまで以上に探し出せる態勢を整えること

　これまでよりも規模の大きい研究班を組織し、これまで以上の人材を投入することができれば、発生したばかりで双方の家族が対面する前の事例を、今まで以上に見つけ出すことができるであろう。こうした事例に関心を抱いたジャーナリストや地元の人たちが最初に現地に赴いて、前世を記憶する子どもが口にしていた事柄を文章で記録することもしないまま、先方の家族のもとへ子どもを連れて行った長距離例が、スリランカとインドに数例存在するのを私は知っている。このようなジャーナリストは、おかげでおもしろい新聞記事をものにしたが、本研究にとって大きかったはずのそうした事例の潜在的価値は、そのおかげで失われてしまったのである。

スリランカで私たちは、一部のジャーナリストの協力を得て、事例を詳細かつ丹念に記録する価値について（一般のジャーナリストのみならず）両親の教育を行なおうと、若干の努力を重ねたことがあった。しかし、事例の優先権は、子どもの両親にあるのである。既に述べたように、両親がその事例を完全に伏せておきたいと思っている場合を除けば、子どもの要求や自らの好奇心に従って、子どもの発言に対応する家族を探し出そうとするのが人情というものである。昔、私が事例調査のためインドの小さな町に滞在していた時のことであった。まさにその町を離れようとしていた（し、実際にそうしなければならなかった）時、こうした（双方の家族がまだ対面していないという）事例の情報が飛び込んできた。その時、私は若干の記録を行ない、私が再訪できる時まで、その子が昔住んでいたという町へその子どもを連れて行かないよう父親に誓約させるのがせいいっぱいのところであった。幸い、子どもの父親はそれに同意してくれた。ところが、残念ながらこの家族は、インドの、外部の人間には少々入りにくい地域に住んでいたため、私がその町をもう一度訪れるまでに二年もの年月を要してしまった。ようやく再訪がかなった時には、父親は私がもう来ないものと思い込んで、子どもを先方の町に連れて行き、そこで前世の家族と対面させた後だったのである。

21　**生まれ変わりが最も適切な解釈と考えられる事例**

この種の事例としては、イマド・エラワール、スワルンラタ・ミシュラ、ジャグディシュ・チャンドラ、ビシェン・チャンド・カプール、スクラ・グプタ、プラカーシュ・ヴァルシュナイ、ドロン・チャムパ・ミトラ、シャムリニー・プレマ、グナナティレカ・バデウィタナ、ガミニ・ジャヤセナ、ルビ・クスマ・シルヴァ、クムクム・ヴェルマ、スレイマン・アンダリ、ラジュル・シャー、パルモッド・シャルマ、スニル・ドゥット・サクセナ、ボンクチ・プロムシン、ラタナ・ウォンソムバトの事例がある。

以上の事例は、すべて長距離例である。いずれの事例でも、その子どもの発言の事実性が確認される以前ないし、確認されてから二、三ヵ月以内に、子どもの発言内容を誰かが文章で記録している。情報提供者の証言には、大きな食い違いや不備はなかった。（ただし、ジャグディシュ・チャンドラの事例に対するF・ニコルの批判にふれた本章註19を参照のこと。）

22 〝もっと細部を〟

スタンダール（301、第四巻、一六九ページ）より引用。

23 さまざまな証人による一致した証言

ウェイトリー（362）の著書の八八および九六—九七ページより引用。

24 多数例の強みを、束ねた棒の比喩《ひゆ》を用いて表現すること

ウェイトリーの原理を、心霊研究における多数の調査例に当てはめたのは私が最初ではない。ガーニーら（117）は、この分野の科学的研究の初期の時代にこの原理を応用している。ハートら（121）は、多数例（ハートの研究としては霊姿の事例）に比較的共通して見られる特徴を研究する方法に、特に重要な貢献をしている。

25 タイプという概念

医学が大きく進歩したのは、病気のタイプないし症候群を特定したおかげであった。症候群とは、ひとりの患者に同時に発生し、共通した病因をもつさまざまな症状や徴候の集合体である（130）。

26 前世を記憶する子どもと前世の人格の性比

小さな事例群から得られた数値は発表しているが、前世を記憶する子ども全体のデータは未発表の分析からとっている。前世の人格の性別に関する若干のデータは拙著（321）に発表しておいた。

本文に述べた唯一の例外とは、スリランカの子どもの性比である。この国では、男女の事例がほぼ同数だったのである。

27　前世を記憶する子どもの事例における横変死の発生率

このデータは、クックら（52）および（それよりも少し小さな系列については）スティーヴンソン（321）の論文に発表されている。

28　横変死――報告の偏りか現実の現象か

インドのもっと大きな標本に関するデータは、クックら（52）の論文に、それより規模の小さい調査によって得られたデータは、バーカーら（13）の論文に発表されている。

インドの一般人口中で横変死が占める割合は、マハーラーシュトラ州とラジャスターン州の二州のみのデータに基づいて算出されたものである。しかしながら、インド全体の数値が、この二州の場合の約七パーセントから大きく隔たっているとは考えにくい。

調査の対象となった者は、いついかなる時に耳にしたいかなる事例であれ思い出すよう求められたため、自然死の事例よりも横変死の事例の方が想起しやすかったのかもしれない。もしそうなら、こうした事例を報告する際にもある程度の歪《ゆが》みが生じた可能性はある。とはいえ、こうした歪みはふたつの要因によって減じられるであろう。ひとつは、調査対象者が、思い出せるいかなる事例の記憶をも探り出すよう求められたことである。このように〝強制的想起〟をさせると、たまたま思い出した事例をなにげなく報告する時よりも、広い範囲で発生した事例を思い出しているはずである。もうひとつは、調査区域が地理的に限定されており、故人が、死亡した時点でその区域内にある村に住んでいなければならなかったことである。そのため、横変死のように耳目を引きやすい特徴があるおかげで伝わってきた遠方の事例は除外される。

共同研究者とともに私は、『生者の幻影』(117)に掲載されている霊姿の事例報告をこうした観点から分析している。霊姿の出現からその報告が行なわれるまでの間隔を、出現した人物が非業の死を遂げている事例といない事例で比較したところ、報告されるまでに五年以上経過している事例では、非業の死を遂げた事例は自然死を遂げた事例よりも報告される率が高いが、五年以内に報告された事例では、両群間に差のないことがわかった。こうした結果(未発表)を見ると、非業の死のように耳目を引きやすい要素を伴った霊姿の事例は、自然死を遂げた事例よりも記憶に残りやすい(し、おそらくは口から口へと伝えられやすい)ように思われる。しかしながら、この差は、事例発生後五年以内にその存在を知った研究者には気づかれないであろうし、発生後五年以上経ってから報告された事例にこのような差が見られるからといって、非業の死を遂げた事例の発生率が高い理由がすべて説明できるわけでもない。

以上紹介した霊姿の事例の分析結果を、生まれ変わり型事例の分析にどの程度まで当てはめることができるかについては、私にはわからない。双方の事例で非業の死が占める割合がなぜここまで高いのかについては、さらに検討を重ねる必要がある。本註(および対応する本文)に掲げた証拠は間接的なものであり、決定的なものではない。しかし、非業の死は多くの事例に共通して見られる真の特徴であり、現行の事例収集法に起因する副産物ではないらしいことがわかる。もしそうなら、この特徴は重要なので、私としては、もっと説得力に富む証拠が得られるまで待つよりも、不完全なものであるにせよ現在手元にある証拠を提出することの方が理に適《かな》っているように思う。

29　未決例のデータ

本節のデータはクックらの論文(51、52)に発表されている。

30　標準的事例の特徴が情報提供者に伝わる可能性はないこと

例外として、非業の死はこうした事例に際立って見られる特徴だという広く見られる信仰がある。多くの国にこの信仰が存在するが、ここまで広い範囲にわたってこの信仰が見られる理由は、私にはわからない。しかし、非業の死は全例のほぼ三分の二ほどに見られるので、一般化を急ぐ人たちは、二、三例しか知らないのに、そのことから、非業の死に伴う残酷性が多くの、ないしはすべての事例で重要な役割を演じている、とあっさり結論づけてしまうかもしれない。

第8章　さまざまな文化圏に見られる変異

1　発展途上国では統合失調症の予後が良好なこと

ワクスラー（360）が、この発言を裏づける関連データをまとめている。

2　偶然以外の病気の原因

I・M・ルイスの恍惚《こうこつ》的宗教に関する著書（156）は、病気の原因に関する考え方を扱った最初のものではないが、本文で述べた個人的原因をいくつか論じている。

3　前世の記憶を説明する概念の枠組が必要であること

生まれ変わり信仰はおそらく、誰かが別の人物の生涯のイメージ記憶をもっていたことにより、さまざまな時代にさまざまな場所で発生したものではないかということを、第2章で示唆しておいた。そうしたイメージ記憶をもった者は、それを、生まれ変わりという考え方を基盤として解釈したのである。ここで言おうとしているのは、自分がたまたまもっていた前世の記憶に意味をもたせるには、時により、生まれ変わりという考え方が必要な場合があるかもしれない、ということである。このような指摘が矛盾しているとは私には思われない。前世から直観という形でもち越された生まれ変わり信仰は、やはり前世からもち越されたイメージ記憶をより理解しやすくさせるのではなかろうか。とはいえ、人によっては、生まれ変わり信仰をあらかじめもたずとも、イメージ記憶を生まれ変わりの裏づけと考えるかもしれない。西洋の事例の中に、子どもの頃、自分では理解できない前世のイメージ記憶らしきものをもっていた子どもが一部にある。家族がもっている信仰には、その子どもが自分の記憶らしきものの枠組とすべき生まれ変わりという概念はなかった。にもかかわらず、生まれ変わりについて書かれた本や雑誌を読む前に、そうした子どもは、自分は昔にも生きていたにちがいないと考えたのであった。（第3章で詳述しているアリス・ロバートソンの事例は、このような経過を辿《たど》った実例である。）私は、このような子どもたちが到達した結論が必ずしも正しいと言っているわけではないし、その一部が誤りであることはほぼまちがいないと思っている。いま言おうとしているのは、前世の記憶らしきものが、ひとりの人間のもつ、世界や自己の本性に関する概念といかに作用し合うかということ以上のものではない。

4　トリンギット族の同一家族例における母系の関係

この問題については、トリンギットの事例に関する拙論（305）の中で詳しく述べておいた。しかし、これまで調査されたトリンギットの事例の実数は、その論文で分析を行なって以降かなり増加している。

5　イボ族の同一家族例における父系の関係

詳しくお知りになりたい方は、拙著（329、330）を参照されたい。

6　スリランカでは予告夢が忘れ去られること

夢の中に登場する人物の正体が夢を見ている者にわからないからといって、スリランカに予告夢が稀《まれ》であるという事実が完全に説明できるわけではない。あらゆる国の予告夢は、迫真性があるとされるのがふつうであり、何かを伝えようとしているらしき故人が、夢を見ている者の知らない人物である場合ですら、予告夢はきわめて記憶に残りやすいのである。それゆえ、夢に現われる死者が見ず知らずの他人であるのがふつうであるとしても、私の考えている以上に予告夢がスリランカで発生しているとすれば、スリランカの予告夢の報告はもっと多いはずなのである。

7　ドゥルーズ族の予告夢

ドゥルーズ族の予告夢については別稿で若干例を紹介している（321）が、そのうちの二例には予知的な色彩が見られる。つまり、まだ存命中の（しかも健康状態が良好と思われる）男性が、妊娠中の女性の息子として生まれて来る、という夢だったのである。その後、その男性は突然死亡し、それと時を同じくしてその女性に子どもが生まれた。こうしてその夢は、死後すぐに生まれ変わるとするドゥルーズ族の信仰と一致したのである。

8　前世の人格が死亡してからその記憶をもつ子どもが生まれ変わるまでの間隔

第5章一一七ページ、および第7章註14参照。

9　死亡してから生まれ変わるまでの間隔を九ヵ月とするジャイナ教徒の信仰

ジャイナ教徒の考え方と一致するのは、ラジュル・シャーの事例である。また、この事例の前世の人格は、ラジュルの家族が確信をもってジャイナ教徒の公式を採用したおかげで突き止められたのであった。ラジュルは、ギータという前世の人格の名前と、その頃に住んでいたジュナガドゥという町の名前を挙げた。そこでラジュルの家族は、代表をひとりジュナガドゥに送った。その家族は、その町で、ラジュルが生まれる九ヵ月前の住民死亡台帳を調べた。するとその月に、ギータという名前の人物が載っており、さらにその他の資料から、このギータという人物の父親の名前を見つけ、その父親を探し当てた。ラジュルの家族はこうして、前世についてラジュルが語った他の事柄も事実であることを確認したのである。

ラム・プラカーシュは、クシャトリヤというカーストに属するヒンドゥー教徒であったが、前世の人格はジャイナ教徒であった。この事例でも、死亡してから生まれ変わったとされるまでの間隔はちょうど九ヵ月と言われていたが、私は、ラム・プラカーシュの生年月日についてはラジュルの場合ほど確信がもてないでいる。

10　前世の人格の葬儀ないし埋葬の記憶

ディスナ・サマラシンへ、チャオクン・ラジスタジャルン、エルカン・キリヒの事例でこうした記憶が見られる。

11　母親の胎内に宿る直前に起こった出来事の記憶

ボンクチ・プロムシンの事例がその実例である。

12　肉体のない世界の記憶

ディスナ・サマラシンへ、サヤドウ・ウ・ソバナ、チャオクン・ラジスタジャルン、ナシル・トコセズの事例でこうした記憶が見られる。ディスナ・サマラシンへは、スリランカの事例としては例外的に、こうした体験を語っている。

13　人間が動物として生まれ変わること

トリンギット族（や他のいくつかの民族）は、王子がカエルに変えられたという西洋の伝説のように、人物が動物に変身し、おそらくはまた人間に戻るという可能性が時としてあると信じているが、この信仰を、人間が動物に生まれ変わるという信仰と混同してはならない。

前世が動物だったという子どもの事例を私はいくつか耳にしているが、いずれの事例でも、生まれ変わりが事実であることを確認するための手がかりは（当然のことながら）ほとんどなかった。ビルマのある少女（マ・タン・タン・アエ）は、自分が生まれる何年か前に死亡した仏教の尼僧の生涯をかなり詳しく想い出した。この生涯の記憶には、事実と確認された事柄が含まれていたし、本人は子どもの頃から、記憶に残っている生涯と軌を一にする、並みはずれて敬虔《けいけん》な態度を示していた。この少女はまた、その尼僧が死亡してから自分が生まれるまでの間、牡牛《おうし》として中間的前世を送っていたとも述べている。その牛は、第二次大戦中ビルマが日本軍に占領されている時、爆弾が落ちて死んだという。牡牛として送ったという前世については全く確認することができなかった。

14　トリンギット族の間に見られる性転換例

生まれ変わる際に性転換してはならない、という禁止命令や性転換例そのものが実際に存在しないことについて私が述べたことは、アラスカ州南東部（突出部）に住むトリンギット族に当てはまる。極北の地ヤクタートのトリンギット族は、性転換はありうると考えているし、事実、デ・ラグナ（58）は、そこに住むトリンギットの間に性転換例が見られると述べている。さらに北方に住む他の部族（たとえばアタパスカ族やイヌイット）は、性転換の可能性があると信じているし、性転換例も実際に存在する。しかし、（北アメリカ北西部の）極南部沿岸地帯に住む部族はいずれも、性転換の可能性を信じておらず、実際に性転換例もない。その境界線は、北緯六〇度付近にある。私にわかる限りでは、性転換の可能性を信じているか否かの境界線は、インドネシアのバリ島とロンボク島の間を走る線（ウォーレス線）のように明確に両者を区分している。（ウォーレス線とは、東洋区とオーストラリア区の動物相を分ける境界線のことである。）

デ・ラグナ（58）が示唆しているところによれば、沿海地帯に住むヤクタート・トリンギットは、性転換が起こる可能性があるという信仰を、内陸部に住むアタパスカ族から受け継いでいるという。その事実からすると、生まれ変わる際に性転換することがあると信ずるアタパスカ族は、ヤクタート・トリンギットにこの考え方を伝えたということのようである。その後しばらくして、実際に起こった性転換例の話が、その信仰を譲り受けたトリンギット族の間に出現したのであろう。

15　**女性から男性への性転換例よりも、男性から女性への性転換の方が多いこと**

その例外となっている民族は、ナイジェリアのイボ族である。

現在ビルマには、他の国とは異なり、こうした性差の説明となる理由の見当がとりあえずつけられるほどたくさんの性転換例が存在する。私は別稿で、ビルマの性転換例七五例の分析結果とその検討を行なっている(324)。

ビルマの少年たちはおそらく、少女が男性として送った前世を口にするよりも、女性として送った前世を口にするのに抵抗があることであろう。その点からすると、このふたつのタイプの事例の比率に偏りがあるのは、少なくとも一部は、私たちが現在用いている調査法による副産物ということになろう。しかし、他の解釈も考えられる。大半の文化圏と同じく、ビルマでも、男に生まれる方が女に生まれるよりよいと考えられているうえ、ビルマの人々は、（前世で男性だった場合）女性に生まれ変わることを大幅な格下げと見なしている。生まれ変わりが起こるとすれば、死亡して少女の体に生まれ変わった男性は、わが身にそのようなことが起こったのを知ったとたんにショックを起こすかもしれない。そしてこのショックにより、前世の記憶がさらに発現する可能性もあるのである。

また、男性は、女性よりも変化に富む冒険的な生涯を送るため、男性の生涯の方が女性の生涯よりも記憶に残りやすいという可能性もあるかもしれない。私はこの推論を、共同研究者の女性にぶつけたところ、その女性はこれを即座に否定した。女性も、記憶に残りやすい経験を男性と同じくらいするし、出産のように男性にはできない経験もいくつかあると言うのである。しかしながら、性転換例の場合でも非転換例の場合でも、前世の人格が男性であった事例が女性であった事例の二倍近くにのぼっているのも事実なのである。この問題については第10章であらためて検討するつもりである。

16　生前の信仰が死後の状況を作る

これは私の独創ではない。このことは『チベットの死者の書』(85)にはっきりと述べられている。

第9章　生まれ変わりという考え方によってどのような現象が説明できるか

1　乳幼児期の恐怖症

スレイマン・ボウハムジ、イマド・エラワール、スジト・ラクマル・ジャヤラトネ（以上、車恐怖症）、シャムリニー・プレマ、ルビ・クスマ・シルヴァ（水恐怖症）、ソム・ピト（刀剣恐怖症）、エルカン・キリヒ（飛行機恐怖症）、パルモッド・シャルマ（凝《ぎょう》乳ないしヨーグルト恐怖症）にも、乳幼児期に事実と確認された記憶と恐怖症とが見られた。イマド・エラワールを除く全員は、それぞれの前世の人格の死因に関係したものを、特に恐怖症の対象としていた。

2　小ハンスの症例

ウォルピら（373）は、小ハンスが馬に関係した外傷体験をもっていることに着目し、この少年の恐怖症をフロイト（92）が必要以上に象徴的に解釈したことを強く批判している。

小ハンスの症例は単純に説明できるので、生まれ変わりとは関係ない。にもかかわらず、この症例について述べたのは、恐怖症の象徴的意味を探ろうとすると、前世で起こったと思われるものも含めて、直接の原因となった外傷体験の存在を裏づける証拠からどれほど離れてしまうかを、具体的に説明しようとしたためである。

3　乳幼児期の恐怖症に関する他の解釈

子どもの恐怖症の原因を詳細に調べるには、その子どもを妊娠中に母親が、その恐怖症の説明になりそうな驚愕《きょうがく》体験をした証拠があるかどうかについても探る必要がある。スコットランド王ジェイムズⅥ世（イングランド王ジェイムズⅠ世）には、刀剣類に対する恐怖症があった（41）。ジェイムズの妊娠中に、母親であるスコットランド女王メアリーの秘書官リッチオがメアリーの目の前で刺殺されるという事件がその恐怖症の原因ではないか、と考える者があるかもしれない。しかし、これまでのところ、私は、母親の驚愕体験が子どもの恐怖症を最も適切に説明するように思われる生まれ変わり型事例を一例も知らない。

4　幼児期に見られる天職意識

本文に引用した実例について詳しくお知りになりたい方は、次の原典を参照されたい。

・ジョージ・フレデリック・ヘンデル

フラウワー（88）
ドイッチュ（63）
・エリザベス・フライ
ルイス（153）
・フローレンス・ナイチンゲール
ウッドハム＝スミス（374）
・ハインリッヒ・シュリーマン
シュリーマン（271）
・ジャン＝フランソワ・シャンポリオン
ハルトレーベン（122）
・マイクル・ヴェントリス
チャドウィック（45）
・シエーナの聖カタリーナ
レイモンド・オブ・カプア（246）
ガードナー（95）
ドレイン（67）

5　早期小児期に見られる異常な関心

家族の者から見ると異質の関心を早期小児期に示した子どもは他にも何人かいる。グナナティレカ・バデウィタナ、ハイール・カム・カニヤ（宗教に対する関心）、ダニエル・ジルディ、ラメシュ・スクラ（自動車に対する関心）、クムクム・ヴェルマ（ヘビに対する関心）などである。

6　幼少期に前世の人格の職業を遊びの中で再現すること

イチティヤケ・アラムディンやスクラ・グプタの事例でも同様の行動が見られる。このふたりは、乳幼児の世話ごっこをして遊んだが、ふたりとも、乳幼児を残して死亡した女性の生涯を記憶していたのである。ナイトクラブ経営者の生涯を記憶していたエルカン・キリヒは、幼児期にナイトクラブ経営ごっこをして遊んだ。エルカンは、架空のラキ（トルコの蒸留酒）を注ぎ、遊び友だちの幼女に、マイクに見立てた棒を持たせ、歌手役を演じさせた。仏教の尼僧の生涯を記憶していたビルマのマ・タン・タン・アエは、尼僧のように布施を集める遊びをしていた。

7　遊びの中に登場する、前世の人格の子どもの実名

スクラ・グプタとスレイマン・ボウハムジの事例にその実例が見られる。

8　変わった能力や教わったことのない技能

幼少期に変わった能力や教わったことのない技能を示した子どもは他にも、パウロ・ロレンツ（ミシンをかける技術）、ビシェン・チャンド・カプール（インドの打楽器タブラを演奏する技能）、ディスナ・サマラシンへ（料理と、屋根を葺《ふ》く材料を編み上げる技術）、スワルンラタ・ミシュラ（ベンガルの歌と踊りの能力）がある。

9　嗜癖

幼少期に、嗜癖《しへき》を生じさせる薬物や陶酔作用をもつ薬物に対する嗜好《しこう》を示した子どもには、ビシェン・チャンド・カプール、マウン・ミント・ティン、ラメシュ・スクラ、ロナルド・マパツナゲ、スジト・ラクマル・ジャヤラトネ（アルコール）、サンジヴ・シャルマ、スニル・ドゥット・サクセナ（タバコ）、ジャグディシュ・チャンドラ、オム・プラカーシュ・マツール（カンナビスの抽出物）がいる。

10　気質

ポーターら（231）は、この問題に関する研究の総説をまとめている。トーマスら（344）と、トーマス（343）の論文も参照のこと。

11　早期に見られる性欲

早期に性欲が観察された事例としては、他にも、イマド・エラワール、ネシプ・ユンリュタシキランの事例がある。ビシェン・チャンド・カプールも、少年期に、前世の人格が愛人のシャルマと共に味わった快楽にまた浸りたいと望んでいた。

フロイト（91）が言う性欲の〝潜伏期〟が始まるとされる年齢は、私が調査した子どもたちが前世の記憶を消失させる平均年齢とたまたま一致する。おそらくフロイトは、〝潜伏期〟という概念の中に、もっと大きな真理を垣間《かいま》見ていたのであろう。全体が見える前に一部が見えることはよくあるのである。

12　性的同一性の混乱

性的同一性の混乱がある程度見られた性転換

例には、パウロ・ロレンツ、グナナティレカ・バデウィタナ、アムバン・ペトチェラト、ドロン・チャムパ・ミトラ、ルビ・クスマ・シルヴァ、マ・ティン・アウン・ミョ、エリン・ジャクソン、ラニ・サクセナ、マ・キン・マ・ギーの事例がある。

13　性別異和症の生物学的解釈

ベイカーら（8）は、（クラインフェルター症候群のような）生物学的要因は一部の事例には存在するかもしれないが、存在しない事例の方が多いことを明らかにしている。

14　両親の影響が性別異和症の原因であることを裏づける証拠は存在しないこと

ズーガー（383）は、両親の影響で全例を説明することはできないとしている。

15　性別異和症は両親の責任ではないこと

マルティノ（179）とモリス（184）による、性倒錯を描いた自伝的文章の中にその実例が見られる。こうした子どもの母親は、ある雑誌の記事（3）にその証言を寄せている。

16　一卵性双生児

双生児が一卵性か二卵性かを判断する場合、いつも私は、容姿、特に顔の特徴が共通しているかどうかに依《よ》らなければならなかった。出産時に胎盤がひとつだったかふたつあったかを情報提供者が知っていることもたまにはあったし、その双子が生まれた時、一卵性か二卵性かを医師から聞いていた例も時たまあった。六組の双生児については、血液型を調べることにより一卵性か二卵性かを決定した。

17　別個に育てられた一卵性双生児

別個に育てられた一卵性双生児の研究については（一緒に育てられた一卵性双生児と比較して）大量の文献が存在する。ファーバー（86）は、こうした研究の総説をまとめている。

18　別個に育てられた一卵性双生児の研究に対する批判

こうした研究については、ローズら（260）およびカッスーら（44）が強く批判している。

この問題については、本章の最終節で詳しく論じておいた。

19　一卵性および二卵性双生児の口蓋裂の不一致

この問題については、フレイザー（90）が総説を行なっている。

20　一卵性双生児の行動の不一致

グリーン（108）は、八歳の時、非常に異なる性的方向を示した（アメリカの）一卵性双生児の事例を報告している。兄は男児として正常に発達したのに対して、弟の方は、明らかに女性的な行動を示したのである。つまり、男の子よりも女の子と一緒にいたがり、女の子の服装をして人形ごっこをし、男の子たちの乱暴な遊びを嫌がったのであった。この双生児は一卵性だったためグリーンは、ふたりの行動の違いを説明してくれそうな要因が生育環境の中にあるかどうか調べ、それを探し当てたと考えた。男性的な双子（兄）の方は父親の名前をもらっていた。ふたり（の双生児）とも、兄の方が父親の名前をもらったのは父親にかわいがられているからだと思い込んでいると、母親は見ていた。一方、女性的な子ども（弟）の方は、三歳時に（回復まで二年半も要した）重病にかかり、（病院での面会があるたび）母親と一緒に過ごしていたのに対して、兄の方は父親と過ごす時間が多かった。また、母親は、妊娠中に娘が生まれるのを望んでいたという。

この双生児と両親との関係がそれぞれ異なっていたことや、それに付随して両親の態度も異なっていたということで、ふたりの行動の性的方向の差がもしかすると説明できるのかもしれない。しかしながら、グリーンの報告を見ると、ふたりがまだ乳幼児で環境による影響がそれほど大きくない時点でも、ふたりの間に明瞭《めいりょう》な差異が観察されていたことがわかる。たとえば、後に女性的行動を示すようになる子どもは、乳幼児期に、もう一方よりも抱っこしやすかったし、容貌《ようぼう》から女児と見誤られることが多かったのである。三歳から五歳半までの二年半、弟の方が母親と親密に接触していたという事実だけで、人形ごっこをしたり女児の服を着たりなどの顕著な女性的行動が十分説明できるとも思われない。女手ひとつで育てられた男の子の多くは、そうした女性的行動を示すことはない。グリーンの事例は、残念ながら、生まれ変わりという要因が関与している可能性を念頭に置いて行なわれたものではない。わずかふたつの要因（この場合は、遺伝と生後の環境による影響）にだけ注目しながら研究を行なうと、環境的要因を示唆する証拠が実際以上に重視されてしまうかもしれない。現在の西洋精神医学の体系では、障害をもった児童やその家族を観察している研究者は、他の説明を全く念頭に置いていないため、両親の影響があったことを裏づけるわずかな証拠を過大に評価しているのかもしれない。インドやビルマのような国では、マ・キン・マ・ギーとマ・キン・マ・ネの事例に見られるように、グリーンが研究した双生児の事例も違った形で解釈する。（とはいえ、マ・キン・マ・ギー姉妹は二卵性双生児なので、ふたりの行動の性的方向が異なる理由としては、生後の環境的影響と前世という要因ばかりでなく、遺伝的要因をも考慮する必要がある。）

21　シャム（接合型）双生児

シャム（現在のタイ）に住んでいた頃〝発見〟されはしたが、チャンとエンはシャム人ではなかったし、初めて厳密に研究された接合型双生児でもなかった。とはいえ、ふたりはそれでも最も有名なので、ふたりの人格についてはおそらく他のどの接合型双生児よりもよく知られているであろう。ダニエルズ（55）、ルックハルト（161）、ニューマン（196）の各論文は、チャンとエンの人格の違いについて述べている。

22　親子関係

自分の両親を拒絶し、〝本当の両親〟を探したがった子どもの実例としては、他にも、プラカーシュ・ヴァルシュナイ、ラヴィ・シャンカール・グプタ、ヴェール・シン、ガミニ・ジャヤセナ、ワルナシリ・アディカリ、ウィジャナマ・キトシリ、ラビ・エラワールの事例がある。

23　**両親と同等か両親よりも目上だと子どもが主張すること**

ハイール・カム・カニヤ、チャオクン・ラジスタジャルン、ティアン・サン・クラ、マウン・イン・マウンの事例がその実例である。

24　**一方の親の最初の配偶者だった前世を記憶している子ども**

他にも、マ・ティン・ティン・ミント、アシャ・ラニの事例が挙げられる。

25　**前世からもち越された、両親に対する怨念《おんねん》**

父親が殺害した男性の生涯を子どもが記憶していたとされる例について、レバノンから二例の情報を間接的に得ている。そのうちの一例では、子どもが父親を、罪を犯したと非難して苦しめ続けたと言う。もう一方の子どもは、別の戦略を用いた。その子どもは、成人に達するまで沈黙を守り、それから銃と旅券ならびに査証を手に入れた。そうしておいてから、父親に昔の罪状を突きつけ、発砲し、レバノンから逃亡したというのである。当然のことかもしれないが、この二例とも私自身で調査することはできなかった。

26　**一見すると不合理に見える敵意**

前世の人格を殺害した犯人に対して復讐《ふくしゅう》心を見せた子どもには、他にも、ラヴィ・シャンカール・グプタやセミ・ツッシュムシュがいる。

前世の人格の殺人犯に対する怨念を、その殺人犯が所属する宗派やもっている職業が共通しているという理由で、その集団全体にまで広げた子どもとしては、ニランカル・バトナガル（イスラム教徒）、ラヴィ・シャンカール・グプタ（理髪師）、サレム・アンダリ（ベドウィン族）、セミル・ファリシ（警官）がいる。

27　**一部のビルマの子どもが示す〝日本人的〟性格特徴**

こうした特徴については別稿(324)に詳述しておいた。マ・ティン・アウン・ミョ（第4章）はそのうちの一部を示している。

28　**妊娠中の異常な食欲**

この種の現象は他にも、ガミニ・ジャヤセナ、スジト・ラクマル・ジャヤラトネ、オルヌマ・スア・イン・ヨンの事例に見られる。

29 右腕を失った状態に対するネルソン提督の適応

私が子ども時代に読んだ記憶のあるサウジー著『ネルソンの生涯』という本には、ネルソンが右腕を失う前後の筆蹟《ひっせき》の写しが掲載されていた。ネルソンが右腕を失ったのは、一八〇五年に死亡する八年前のことである(295)。

30 個人の独自性

本節の見出しはメダウォア(180)の著書のタイトルから意識的に拝借した。人間の独自性は肉体の発育を支配する遺伝情報にのみ由来する、という考え方に異議を唱えたいためである。

31 前世に関連する変わった行動の症候群

第5章で、マ・ティン・アウン・ミョ、スジト・ラクマル・ジャヤラトネ、シャムリニー・プレマ、エルカン・キリヒの事例に見られる変わった行動の症候群の実例を他にもいくつか紹介しておいた。

32 統合失調症における遺伝的要因の研究に対する批判

シャルシンガー(279)は、(肥満症や統合失調症を含め)さまざまな障害について、養子になった者を対象にした研究を簡潔にまとめ、詳しい報告をリストアップしている。ただし、シャルシンガーは、こうした研究法に対する批判をすべてとり上げているわけではない。こうした批判については、ローズら(260)がまとめている。詳しいことをお知りになりたい方は、カッスーら(44)やリッツら(157、158)の論文を参照されたい。いずれの論文にも、批判の対象となった研究の原著論文がリストアップされている。

33 その後の人格の発達に対して、幼少期の体験が決定的重要性をもつという神話

ストーン(335)は、その後の人格の発達に対してこうした体験が決定的重要性をもつとされる乳幼児期の孤立状態の研究に関する批判を最初に行なった研究者のひとりである。同じ年にクラークら（48）は、早期小児期に観察された行動上の欠陥が一生持続するという主張を疑問視させるデータを発表している。一九五七年に私は、人間の人格の発達に（その後の体験と比較して）幼少期の体験が大きな影響を及ぼすという考え方に疑義を呈する拙論を発表している（302）。その論文の中では、幼少期に特別の重要性があるとする憶測を裏づけるたしかな観察事実は存在しないという事実を明らかにしているにすぎない。その後、私は、この問題に関する検討を行なわないまま、まもなく、本書で扱っているような研究に移ってしまった。

その後に発表された報告や総説としては、キャスら（43）、クラーク（47）、クラークら（49）（関連論文のアンソロジー）、トーマス（343）らの論文がある。

ここで強調しておかなければならないのは、強い社会的ストレスが悪影響を及ぼすという考え方自体を問題にしているのではなく、幼少期に受けたストレスの方がその後に受けるものよりも影響力が大きい、とする考え方に疑問を唱えているにすぎないということである。

34　新生児に見られる個人差

コーナー（148、149）は、新生児に見られる個人差に関する報告を行なっている。

第10章　前世を記憶する子どもにまつわるその他の問題

1　生まれ変わりに際して魂が複数に分裂するという考え方

R・F・スペンサー（298、二八七―二八八ページ）は、イヌイットの間でこの考え方が見られることを述べているし、ノルブら（200）はチベット人の間に、ド・ラグナ（58）は、シベリア北東部に住むヤクート族の間にこの概念が見られることを報告している。私自身も、カナダに住むハイダ族の間にこうした考え方が存在することを報告している（315）。

一個の魂がふたりないしそれ以上に分かれて生まれ変わるというイボ族の考え方については、

イボ族の生まれ変わり信仰を扱った拙論に紹介されている(329)。

特にイボ族の事例の情報提供者は、一個の魂が分裂するという考え方を支持する注目すべき事例について話してくれたことがある。たとえば、その人たちは私に、数人の子どもを見せてくれたことが何度かあったが、その子どもたちはいずれも、同じ故人の生まれ変わりだと言われていた。イボ族の間では、こうした多重型事例の前世の人格とされる故人は、ふつう、位の高い人物のように思われるが、そのため遺族や親類縁者は、それぞれ自分の家族のもとに生まれ変わってほしいと願うのであろう。この種の願望は、ひとりの故人が数人の子どもに生まれ変わったとする考え方を生む一因なのかもしれない。こうした事例を私自身でいくつか検討してみるに、ある故人の前世を記憶している証拠は、その故人の生まれ変わりとされる子どもたちの中でも、特定の子どもにより明確に見られるらしいことがわかる。イボ族は、他の大半の文化圏の情報提供者がそう判断するのに必要な証拠よりもはるかに弱い根拠に基づいて、ひとりの子どもを特定の人物の生まれ変わりと認めるようである。イボ族の事例の中には、第7章で述べておいた、ジョン・F・ケネディ大統領の生まれ変わりとされるトルコの数名の子どもたちのように、自己欺瞞《ぎまん》によるものもあるのかもしれない。

特定の故人の生まれ変わりとして複数の候補が出現しても、心や魂が実際に複数に分裂したり、同じものが発生したりすることがあるのか、という問題に対する解答にはならない。(このふたつは同一の概念ではないのである。)

2　これまで地球上にどのくらいの人が生活して来たか

地球上でこれまで暮らして来た人数の推計と、その推計が載っている出典については、既に別の論文(311)で紹介しておいた。しかし、その論文の中では、ヒト科が初めて出現してから六〇——一六〇万年が経過しているという推定を採用しているが、それは、現在受け入れられているよりもはるかに短い。最近では、人類の起源は、四〇〇—五〇〇万年前、ないしはそれ以前にまで遡《さかのぼ》ると推定されている。

3　動物としての前世

次に掲げる子どもたちも、中間的前世として動物の時代があったとしている。ワルナシリ・アディカリ（野ウサギ）、プラトムワン・インタヌ（漠然とした記憶であるが、サル）。

4　記憶を固着させる要因としての非業の死

心理学者が行なった数多くの実験から、刺激の強さとそれによって生ずる反応の大きさとの間には関係のあることがわかっている。クパロフら（150）は、条件反射の実験によって得られた、この主張を裏づける数多くの証拠について検討している。嫌悪感を催させる刺激を用いた実験では、火傷《やけど》をした子どもは火を怖がるという諺《ことわざ》が事実であることが証明されている。

E・L・ソーンダイクは、この関係について次のようにきわめて明確な発言を行なっている。「いかなる心理的状態や活動であれ、それがいかなる状況に対してもその反応として起こる可能性は、その状況ないしその一部が、さらにはその状況を感ずる心の状態全体がその状況と結びつく頻度や時間的な近接度、強度、およびその結果として生ずる満足感と比例する」（347、二〇七ページ）。

ソーンダイクが「強度およびその結果として生ずる満足感」について述べたことは、その状況が、身体的不快感や苦痛をはじめとする「強度および不満感」をもたらした場合にも同様に当てはまるであろう。

大事故に巻き込まれるとか大地震に遭うとかの強烈な体験をすると、その出来事自体のみならず、その出来事が発生するまでの数時間の間に起こったことも、それらの体験自体は変わったことも特に記憶に残りやすいものとも考えられなかったとしても、異常に詳しく記憶される（過剰記憶）場合があることに、心理学者は注目している（37、50、336）。強い感情を引き起こす出来事の細部が、その出来事が起こった時点ではなくその後に、その出来事を振り返って、それが起こった時点ではしなかったような意味づけをすることで、記憶として固定される可能性がある。自らの死はそのような出来事なのであろうし、死の意味は、死の時点よりもその後になってからの方が大きく見えるのかもしれない。そのことは、死に付随する状況にも同じく当てはまるであろう。

現世での証拠が昔からたくさんあることからわかるように、非業の死を遂げると、自然死の時よりもはるかに大きな印象が記憶に刻み込まれるものである。ここで思い起こすのは、ドッドの死刑執行について述べたサミュエル・ジョンソンの次のような言葉である。「自分が二週間以内に絞首刑に処せられるのがわかると、その人の心は驚くほど集中するようになる」（31、七二五ページ）。この点については、死刑の宣告を受けた犯罪者の証言もある。その囚人は、刑場に引かれて行く時、「このことは私にとって大きな戒めになるでしょう」と語ったというのである。ドストエフスキは、射殺されそうになった時に感じたことについて、人の心を打つ物語を書いている（182）。銃で撃たれそうになった経験のおかげで、『白痴』に、死刑を宣告されたある犯罪者の最後の思いを鮮やかに描き出すことができたのは確かである（66、六一ページ）。その中でドストエフスキは、死を目前にして、男の心の働きが昂進《こうしん》した様子を詳しく描写している。

こういう時に罪人があまり気絶しないのは不思議なことですな。それどころか頭はものすごく回転していて、フル回転してる発動機みたいにひっきりなしに、たぶんものすごい勢いで働くのだね。私が思うに、いろいろな考えがどんどんすごい勢いで湧いてきて頭の中を駆け巡るにちがいない。どれも尻切《しりき》れトンボで、その場にそぐわないおかしな考えがどんどん湧き出してくるんだと思うね。たとえば、「あの男、俺の方を見てるな。あいつ、おでこに疣《いぼ》があるじゃねえか。それに、この首切り役人のボタンはひとつはち切れてて、一番下のは錆《さび》だらけだぜ」なんて思いがね。それでいながら何もかもわかってて、何もかも覚えているんだよ。

前世を記憶する子どもたちは、死の、特に突然死ないし横変死の直前の時間帯に知覚が強まることを鋭く見抜いたドストエフスキの正しさを裏づけているように思われる。死の数時間前、場合によっては数分前までの間に起こった出来事がそうした子どもたちの記憶の中でひときわ際立っていることが多いのである。

インドのウドー・ラムという子どもは、壁が崩れ、前世の人格が圧死する直前に、その壁のあった建物から蛇が一匹這《は》い出したのを覚えていた。

ビルマのマ・ミント・テインという少女は、前世の自分が殺された時に身につけていた指輪や金のブレスレットや腕時計のことを覚えていた。この男性は刃物で切りつけられて指を落としたのであるが、その一撃を避けようとして両手を挙げた時、それらが目に入ったのであった。男性は、その直後に斬殺《ざんさつ》された。

レバノンのゾウハイル・チャールは、前世で死ぬ直前に、枕元で泣いていた前世の人格の叔《お》母《ば》がハンカチを顔に当てた場面を記憶していた。

5　横変死は突然に起こること

西洋医学が進歩し、広く採用されるようになったおかげで、治療法が変わり、それまでなら即死していた重傷者の多くが救われるようになった。そのため現在、西洋では、横変死を招く原因で死亡する場合でも、急死という形はとらないかもしれない。しかし、本書で検討している事例の大半が見つかっているアジア諸国では、農村部はもちろん都市部の多くでも近代的な医療施設や医療技術の恩恵には現在でも与《あずか》れないので、こうした地域では横変死は同時に突然死でもあるのがふつうである。

6　超常的要因が関与する他のタイプの事例における突然死

自然死ではあっても突然に起こる死が、他のタイプの事例でも高率に観察されてきた。十九世紀に初めて研究された一連の霊姿の事例を共同研究者とともに分析した結果、霊姿として出現した人物が自然死を遂げている場合、私の述べた定義により突然死と判断されたのはそのうちの五〇パーセントであった(323)。

この地上に住む人間はいずれも、徐々に死ぬよりも突然に死ぬのを嫌がるようである。トルコには、「三日のうちに神のもとに召されますように」という表現がある。これは、一瞬のうちに死ぬこと(〝頓死《とんし》〟)と、長患いした後に死ぬことの両方を避けたいという気持の表われである。キリスト教徒には、霊的に死に備えるだけの時間的余裕がないことから、突然死を恐れる者が多い。機械に巻き込まれて(十九世紀半ばに)死んだニュー・イングランドのある男性の墓石は、通りがかりの人たちに、「この人の死は突然かつ凄惨《せいさん》なものだった」ことを知らせている。実際に、墓石に刻まれた同様の碑文を集めた書籍には『突然に凄惨な』(176)というタイトルが付されている。突然死はまた、遺《のこ》される者たちに別れを告げる機会をも奪ってしまう。(アルドリッチ(1)は、死を目前にした患者の悲しみについて詳述している。)自然死を遂げた者が霊姿となって現われる事例では突然死が高率に見られるが、それは、愛する者に何か伝えたいという強い願望があるためなのではなかろうか。

7　幼時に自然死を遂げた前世の人格

実例としては、グナナティレカ・バデウィタナ、ジャグディシュ・チャンドラ、ラジュル・シャー、ガミニ・ジャヤセナ、ヴェール・シン、プラカーシュ・ヴァルシュナイ、プラトムワン・インタヌの事例がある。

8　〝仕事をやり残した〟まま自然死を遂げた前世の人格

〝仕事をやり残した〟事例は、ゼイガルニーク効果に含めることができるかもしれない。ゼイガルニーク(379)は、仕事が完了している場合よりも未完成の場合の方が詳しい内容をよく覚えている、という人間一般に見られる記憶傾向を最初に研究した心理学者である。非公式なものではあるが、この効果が最初に観察されたのは、ドイツのあるレストランのウェイターであった。この男性は、自分が給仕した客全員が食べたものを、代金を受けとるまでは正確に覚えていることができたが、客が支払いを済ませたとたん、客の注文をすっかり忘れてしまったのである。

9　幼児を遺して自然死を遂げた前世の人格

実例としては、スクラ・グプタ、ラリタ・アベヤワルデナ、シャンティ・デヴィ、スワルンラタ・ミシュラの事例がある。ビヤ（スワルンラタ・ミシュラの前世の人格）の子どもたちは、前世の人格が死亡した時点では、他の事例の子どもたちよりも少々年長であった。

10　〝仕事をやりかけている時〟に自然死を遂げた前世の人格

実例としては、パルモッド・シャルマ、スレイマン・アンダリ、スニル・ドゥット・サクセナ、エルカン・キリヒ、インディカ・グネラトネの各例がある。スレイマン・アンダリを除く全員の前世の人格は、裕福か、場合によってはかなりの資産家であり、ふつうに生活するには十分すぎるほどの財産をもっていた。その人たちにとっての〝やりかけの仕事〟は、それまで以上に財産を蓄えたいという願望であった。

11　すぐに生まれ変わりたいという願望

釈迦《しゃか》は、再生の原因は地上に化肉した際に得られる快楽を強く望むことだと教えている。仏教の聖典ないし口伝には、私の知る限り、再生の望みが強い時の方が弱い時よりも速やかに生まれ変わるという話は出て来ないが、こうした信仰は、それを望むことで再生が起こるという基本的信仰の必然的帰結と言えよう。

12　複数の条件を満たす前世の人格

実例としては、プティ・パトラ、セヴリエ・バイリ（幼児を遺して横変死）、ゴーパール・グプタ、エルカン・キリヒ（精力的に仕事を続けている最中に横変死）、アムパン・ペトチェラト、シャムリニー・プレマ、スーザン・イーストランド、ジリアン・ポロックとジェニファー・ポロック、ルビ・クスマ・シルヴァ（幼時に横変死）、ファルク・ファリス・アンダリ、ラビ・エラワール、マイクル・ライト、サレム・アンダリ（二〇歳未満で横変死）の各例がある。

13　前世の記憶をもたない、記憶力の優れた者

記憶力の優れた人物の報告については、ルリア（162）、ナイサー（193）、薄田《すすきた》（338）の各論文を参照されたい。

14　自然死を遂げた、きわめて信心深く博愛的であった前世の人格

実例としては、他にもマ・タン・タン・アエ、クムクム・ヴェルマ、シャンティ・デヴィ、ハイール・カム・カニャ、チャオクン・ラジスタジャルン、サヤドウ・ウ・ソバナ師の事例がある。

15　インドでは〝降格〟例および〝昇格〟例の発生率が高いこと

ゴーパール・グプタ、ビシェン・チャンド・カプール、スニル・ドゥット・サクセナの各例は社会経済的な格下げの、スワラン・ラタ、クムクム・ヴェルマ、ジュディト・クリシュナ、ラジュル・シャーの各例は格上げの実例である。以上はいずれもインドの事例である。

私たちは昇格例や降格例を主にインドで調査してきた。それはひとつには、未《いま》だ残されているカースト制のため社会経済的階層の差が際立っているインドでは、生まれ変わり型事例が多発する他の文化圏よりも貧富の差が著しいからであり、もうひとつは、私たちの手元にインドの事例が多いという事情があるからである。

とはいえ、昇格例や降格例は他の文化圏でも見られないわけではない。たとえばスリランカでは、ディスナ・サマラシンへとアヌシャ・セネワルデナが昇格例、インディカ・グネラトネ、ウィジャナマ・キトシリ、ワルナシリ・アディカリが降格例となっている。

16　前世の記憶から学ぶ

ビシェン・チャンド・カプールによれば、ある男を殺した金もちの道楽息子であった前世の人格の生涯を回顧することによって、前世時代よりも優れた人間になれたという。パルモッド・シャルマは、前世の記憶が残っているおかげで視野が広まり、そのため、日常的な問題が容易に処理できることに加えて、禍福がつかの間のものにすぎないことがわかったという。

17　〝中間的前世〟を思い出した子どもたち

実例としては、プシュパ、スワルンラタ・ミシュラ、ワルナシリ・アディカリ、ゴーパール・グプタ、マンジュ・トリパティ、イマド・エラワールの事例がある。

18　肉体のない状態にある時、記憶が消失すること

どの交信者と比較しても遜色《そんしょく》のないほど、真の霊的存在であることが証明されている交信者〝G・P〟は、時がたつにつれ記憶が薄れ行くのを嘆いていた（129、三二四ページ）。プラトムワン・インタヌという例外的な事例があるとはいえ、それが、記憶の消失に時間の経過が重要な役割を果たすという事実の反証になるわけではない。この少女が記憶していた二回の前世は、いずれも幼児のものであり、しかも、プラトムワンが生まれて二、三年以内にその記憶が出現しているからである。

19　過去世を記憶していた前世の人格

実例としては、ビシェン・チャンド・カプール、マ・ウィン・シュウェ、マウン・アウン・ミント、モウンゼル・ハイダルの事例がある。

20　自殺した前世を記憶している子どもたち

実例としては、マルタ・ロレンツ、ラメズ・シャムス、マウン・ウィン・アウン、パウロ・ロレンツ、ファルク・ファリス・アンダリの各例がある。

21　新しい概念による苦痛

バジョット（7、一六三ページ）より引用。

22　信ずるためにはよくなじむ必要があること

〝Pour croire complètement à un phénomène il faut y être habitué〟（252、四四一ページ）。本文

中の文章はこの原文からの拙訳。

23 自分がいずれ年をとることが想像しにくいこと

チャールズⅡ世が一六六七年にクラレンドン卿《きょう》を大法官の職から退けると、(チャールズⅡ世のまだ若い愛人であるキャスルメインをはじめとする)クラレンドンの敵対者の一部は、その失脚を聞いて狂喜した。クラレンドンは、王宮を去る時、開け放たれた窓からその声を聞きつけて振り返り、「ああ、奥方さまでしたか。お元気でいらっしゃれば、お歳を召されることをどうかお忘れなきよう」と言った(53)。クラレンドンは正しかった。キャスルメインは一七〇九年に六八歳で死亡したのである。

私を楽しませてくれた偉大な小説のうち、幼少期から老年期を経て死に至るまでの人間の一生を描こうとした者はふたりしかいない。『老女物語』を書いたベネットと、『女の一生』を書いたモーパッサンである。

伝記作家は、主人公の誕生から死までの全生涯を描き出そうとすることが多いが、心理学者は、ひとりの人間の生涯全体の研究に対しては小説家よりもはるかに関心が低い。心理学者や精神科医が行なった最も長い追跡研究でも、例外はあるが、一〇―二〇年を越えるものは稀《まれ》なのである。

24 〝若返り〟のプロセスを想像すること

トロブリアンド諸島に住む民族は、生まれ変わる前に魂(バロマ)が若返るプロセスを経ると信じている(174)。マリノフスキは、そのプロセスを、ヘビが脱皮する過程とよく似ているとしているが、この少々不適切なアナロジーがマリノフスキによるものなのか、トロブリアンド諸島に住む民族が考えたものなのかはわからない。

25 体の大きさの変化を口にする子どもたち

第5章の註11で、体の大きさの変化に気づいたことを(直接間接に)口にした一二人の子どもたちの名前を挙げておいた。こうした子どもたちはいずれも、幼少期に、成人の体でいた時の感覚を記憶していた。プラトムワン・インタヌは、これとは違う種類の体験をしている。幼児であった前世の記憶を残していた少年期に、幼児のように自分の体が小さくなった感覚を実際に味わったのである。

26 アジアおよびアフリカに住む教育程度の高い人たちの、生まれ変わり型事例に関する意見

本文では、一般的な姿勢について述べたが、西洋とアジア、アフリカの教育ある人々は、こうした事例に対する態度や事例に関する知識を、しばしば異にしている。次の実例をお読みになれば、それがおわかりいただけよう。タイでは、（西洋である程度の教育を受けた）国家公務員が私の事例調査に長年、辛抱強く協力してくれたが、（やはり西洋である程度の教育を受けた）別の（元）国家公務員は、仏教は疑問の余地のない真理であると信じていた（うえ、仏教の宣伝活動のような講演を時おり行なっていた）にもかかわらず、実際の事例については愚かしいこととして、自分の手で事例の検討をしようとは一度もしなかった。ビルマでは、やはり西洋でかなりの教育を受けた元公務員が長年、私の事例調査に協力してくれたが、その一方で、私の研究を知って以降、私に対して節度あるふるまいがほとんどできなくなった、西洋の大学で博士号を取得しているある心理学教授に出会ったのも、同じビルマであった。自分の研究室から数キロのところにある自宅周辺で、たまたま事例が数多く見つかっていたにもかかわらず、そのようなありさまだったのである。この教授は、その地区で事例が見つかることについて特に意見はもっていなかったし、机を離れて事例の調査を一例でもしてみようという気にも全くならなかった。

27 脳は意識への使者

ヒポクラテスのエッセイ「聖なる病」（128、一七九ページ）より引用。同じページの少し後でヒポクラテスは、「脳は意識の通訳である」と述べている。

28 脳と記憶に関するベルクソンの見解

ベルクソン（20）は、脳の疾患に起因する記憶障害は単に、記憶を蓄え他者とコミュニケーションを行なうのには健康な脳が必要だということを示しているにすぎないのではないか、という指摘を、かなり以前に行なっている。記憶障害は、記憶は脳内にしか存在しえないことを裏づける証拠にはならないのである。

29　脳と心が同一のものであることに疑念を抱いている神経科学者

脳の働きで心を説明しようとする考え方に疑念を表明している神経科学者は、ペンフィールド（222）とエックルズ（230）のふたりである。もうひとりは、晩年に、「人間はふたつの基本的要素からなるという考え方は、ひとつの要素のみからなるとする考え方より本来的にありそうもないとは思わない」と述べたシェリントン（280、XXIVページ）である。

30　心の道具としての脳

超常現象に関する最重要の理論的論文のひとつの中で、タウレスら（350）は、人間の心の、脳に対する通常の作用と、テレパシーが生ずる時のように、時おり起こる人の心に対する超常的作用は、両者とも、同じ法則のもとに統合されるのではないか、と指摘している。

31　人間の経験の中で最も直接的なものとしての心

エディントン（78、三七ページ）より引用。この中でエディントンは、明らかに意識について語っている。

32　他のものに還元不能な意識

ここでは、意識という言葉がどのようなことを意味するかという問題を、あまりにあっさりと片づけているように見えるかもしれない。この問題は、何世紀にもわたって哲学者を悩ませてきた。ウィリアム・ジェイムズ（137）は、意識という言葉では意味がないのではないかと考えた。しかしながらジェイムズは、その発言の真意を次のように説明している。「私はこの言葉が何らかの実体を意味するという考え方を否定しているだけであって、何らかの機能を指していることについては、全く正当だと考えているのである。……思念によって発動され、そのおかげでこれ〔意識〕の特性が引き出されるような機能が経験の中に存在している。その機能とは、ものごとを知ることである」（四七八ページ）。

意識的経験が他のものに還元できないことについて、論文を一編しか読めない程度の時間しかない場合には、ナジェル(190)の論文をお薦めしたい。一元論の立場をとっている論文としては、プレイス(227)のものがある。プレイスは、意識は脳の働きだとしているのである。ジョゼフソンら(139)は、意識の研究に役だつ入門書を編纂している。

私には、意識は変化せず、変化するのはイメージや感情が意識に表出する際の形態のみであるように思われる。最近刊行された著書や論文では、〝意識の状態〟特に〝変容〟状態が注目されているが、こうした見方は見当はずれかもしれない。これまで、変わった心的経験を、幻覚誘発剤や催眠、瞑想《めいそう》のような外部からの、しかも場合によっては耳目を引きやすい誘導法と結びつける傾向があった。幻覚誘発剤を用いても、意識自体が変化するというより、同じ意識の中にいつもと違うイメージや感情が出現するだけなのかもしれない。これは、メスカリンやLSD-25を用いた時の自らの高揚体験を振り返って考えた時に私自身が抱く、偽らざる感想である。そのような時、私の意識は変化せず、いつもとは非常に違ったイメージや感情が出現するに留《とど》まったのである。つまらないこじつけのような区別をしているだけなのではないかと思われるかもしれないが、私にはそうとは思われない。

テレパシーが日常生活の中で起こったり、霊姿が目撃されたり、子どもたちに前世の記憶が見られたりなどのさまざまな心霊体験が、ふつうの状態にあるふつうの人たちに起こることに、私としてはもっと注目したい。そのような体験があった時、体験者の意識には新しい事柄が入って来るが、〝意識の状態〟は必ずしもいつもと変わるわけではない。このような体験をする人たちは、しない人たちと比べてどこか違っているのかもしれないが、どのような点で違うのかについては、まだほとんどわかっていない。

33 知覚的経験とニューロンのパターンとが同型にならないこと

スミジーズ(291、292)やマルカム(173)は、この問題をさらに掘り下げて検討を加えている。

34 現行の記憶の神経生理学的説明は不適当であること

ベロフ(17、18)やゴールド(96)、マルカム(172、173)らがこの問題について論じている。L・R・ベイカー(9)やドレイファス(68)、ハイル(125)らは、脳のコンピュータ・モデルを(したがって心のコンピュータ・モデルも)批判している。

35 心理的空間と物理的空間

デュカッス(73)とプライス(238)以外にも、スミジーズ(290、292、293)、ホワイトマン(370)、ポイントン(232)らが心理的空間という概念について論じている。この問題に関する私なりの考え方については、別稿(322)で詳しく述べておいた。

デカルト(60、一三九ページ)は、心は肉体とは異なり、空間という属性をもっていないと述べているが、これは重大な誤りであると思う。ヒューム(133、第一巻、二二八ページ)が修正を加え、他の哲学者も同様の論評を行なっているにもかかわらず、デカルトの誤謬《ごびゅう》のおかげで、肉体ばかりではなく心にも空間的広がりがあるとする考え方が受け入れられない状態が今なお続いているのである。

36 テレパシーと唯物論は相容れないこと

この問題について検討した科学者のほとんどが、こうした考え方をとっている。しかし、ゴッドベイ(101)は、テレパシー(およびその他の超常現象)は唯物論と相《あい》容れないわけではないとしている。

数名の物理学者をはじめとする一部の科学者は、物理学がさらに進展すれば超常現象の説明ができると考えている。私はそのような考え方には与《くみ》しないし、私たちが目標にしている超常現象理解のためには、物理学の概念が描き出す世界を越えた現実的世界を仮定する必要があるように考えている。

37　死後生存が事実であることの裏づけとしてのテレパシー

この文章はキャリントン（42、一四三ページ）より引用した。

38　超常的認知の実験

私は、多くの実験によりテレパシーや透視の実在を裏づける証拠が得られているという事実を過小に評価するつもりはない。要求通り実験が反復できないことは、心理学者が行なう多くの実験と共通している。心理学実験の多くもやはり、時おり不安定を示すのである。他の科学者も、隕石《いんせき》や火山、地震など、思い通りには起こらない現象を釈明することなく研究している。

超常現象を研究するに際して、物理学や化学の実験で知られているような再現性を超常現象が示すと考えると、重大な誤りを犯すことになる。ほとんどの超常現象は、二通りの状況のいずれかでしか起こらない。先述のように、生命が危険に晒《さら》されている状況で起こるか、ごく一部の非凡な人間にしか発揮しえない特殊な技術によって生ずる（269）かのいずれかなのである。すべての人間が絶対音感をもっているわけではないのと同じように、すべての人間が超感覚的知覚の能力をもち合わせているわけではない。

生まれつき能力をもっているきわめて稀《まれ》な超能力者を運よく被験者にできた研究者は、集団を対象にした実験によって得られるよりはるかに優れたテレパシーや透視の証拠を報告している。いま言おうとしているのは、ステファン・オソヴィエキ（25、30、80、99）、オルガ・カール（210、211、351）、クレイグ・シンクレア（285）のような能力者のことである。

39　記憶が集積されるカンバスとしての心の成分

シュレディンガー（278、九一―九二ページ）

より引用。

40　肉体のない世界のさまざまな概念

デュカッス（73）とプライス（238、239）がこの問題について論じている。キャリントン（42）も、死後の生命の本態についていくつかの示唆を行なっている。

ヒンドゥー教や仏教の聖典や注解書には、霊魂の世界に関する描写がある。エヴァンズ＝ウエンツ（85）は、そうした物語のうち最も身近なものについて紹介している。

41　肉体をもたない人間として存在した記憶

ディスナ・サマラシンへ、プラティマ・サクセナ、チャオクン・ラジスタジャルン、サヤドウ・ウ・ソバナ師、ソム・ピトの各例にそうした記憶が見られる。記憶内容が乏しいものとしては、ナシル・トコセズの事例がある。

42　自覚夢

自覚夢については、C・グリーン（106）、ヴァン・イーデン（356）、ホワイトマン（368）の各論文を参照されたい。

43　死を目前にしながら死を免れた者の体験

このような（現在では臨死体験と呼ばれることの多い）体験の実例とその分析については、グレイソンら（110）、ノイエスら（201、202）、リング（253）、セイボム（265）、スティーヴンソンら（332）の各論文や著書を参照されたい。

44　死後の生命がいかなるものかについて推測をめぐらせてよい根拠となる情報

霊媒を仲立ちとする交信者の多くが暮らしているという世界について語られた、おびただしい量の情報については本文ではふれなかった。そのほとんどは、一顧だにする価値のないものである。たとえば、通常の方法によっては知りえない故人に関する詳細な事実を開示することを通じて超常的能力をもっていることを裏づける証拠を提示した経験のない霊媒が語ったものだからである。加えて、霊媒を通じて交信してきた存在が霊界での生活について語る内容はほとんどが、必ずしも意識の上にあるものではないにしても、霊媒自身の心が明らかに反映されたものである。とはいえ、超常的能力を示す霊媒を通じて交信を送ってくる、注目に値する交信者が、死後の生命とはいかなるものかについて語った事柄をも無意味だと考えているわけではない。たとえばエマニュエル・スウェーデンボルグは、カント（143）を満足せしめたほど強力な超能力の証拠を示したうえ、死後の生活をつぶさに語っている（340）。この種の能力者の詳細については、バルフォア（11）、ホジソン（129）、C・D・トーマス（345）らの論文や著書を参照されたい。

45　肉体のない世界ではイメージが中心になること

プライス（238）は、来世は〝形象的な〟世界ではないかと述べている。

肉体のない人格の思考は世の成人たちと比べてイメージが豊富なのではないかと思うが、言葉が使われていないと言おうとしているわけではない。生まれ変わり型事例では、名前を正しく記憶している場合も少なくないし、前世の人格が使っていたもののその子どもの家族は誰も使っていない言葉の単語をいくつか覚えていることもある。このような単語が前世に由来するものだとすれば、前世で死亡してから生まれ変わるまでの間にもその単語を記憶していたのではないかと推定することが可能なのではなかろうか。

46　善人は死を恐れる必要がない

プラトンがソクラテスによるとしたこの信念については、『パイドーン』（229）に詳述されている。

47　前世を記憶しているという子どもが語る走《そう》馬《ま》燈《とう》的体験

こうした子どもは何人かあるが、そのうちのひとりは、ナシル・トコセズである。

48　臨死体験者による走馬燈的体験の記憶

グレイソンら（110）の論文をご覧いただければ詳細にご検討いただけよう。同様のデータは、リング（253）やノイエスら（202）の研究でも得られている。

49　肉体をもたない人間同士では、テレパシーがふつうの交信手段であること

ドリーシュ（71、二六ページ）より拙訳して引用。

50　死後に出現する霊姿

実例は、マイヤーズ（188、二九―三〇ページ）や、ペロヴスキ＝ペトロヴォ＝ソロヴォヴォ（224）、ガーニー（116、四二三―四二六ページ）の各論文を参照されたい。

51　臨終時の幻

実例については、ボッツァーノ（33）、バレット（14）、オシスら（208）の各書を参照のこと。

52　〝今〟イコール〝ここ〟

臨死状態にある時や死亡した後に、ある人物や場所のことを考えると次の瞬間にはもうその人物の近くやその場所にいた、という体験をしている者が若干ある。チャオクン・ラジスタジャルンもこうした体験を記憶している。ゲデス（98）とラディン（245）もこの種の実例を報告している。

53　ボードレールと個人の進歩

ボードレールの著書（15）一三六二ページより拙訳して引用。

54　ギボンと出生の偶然

ギボン（100、二一七ページ）より引用。

55　偶然という考え方が西洋で受け入れられていること

とはいえ西洋人、特にアメリカ人の多くは、偶然に対してアンビヴァレントな態度を示している。生命保険会社の収益が増加していることや、医療ミスが発生した場合、たまたま起こったミスと医療過誤の境界を不明瞭《ふめいりょう》にしていることからすると、危険すなわち偶然の出来事から解放された生活を国民は強く望んでいることがわかる。五体満足な赤ん坊が生まれなかったとして産婦人科医を告訴することは、本書のテーマのひとつと密接な関係がある。先天性欠損の原因は誰に、あるいはどこにあるのであろうか。私たちは、他人の不幸については原因を偶然に求めがちであるが、いざ自分たちのことになると、偶然であるはずはない、と考えがちなのである。

56　不行跡に対する歯止めとしての、死後に処罰を受けるのではないかという恐怖

　自分が犯した罪の報いを死後に受けるとする信仰を強くもっていても、中世ヨーロッパでは犯罪や不道徳なふるまいを防ぐ手立てにはならなかった。中世ヨーロッパでは、こうした信仰が支配的だったのである。しかし、当時の人々が死後の生命（および、自らの行ないの報いが死後に返ってくること）を信じていた結果として、清廉潔白な行ないをするようになった者もある一方で、罪を犯す方向に走るようになった者もあるのである。

　中世以後、キリスト教は、科学の進歩に恐れおののいて、自らの教義を退縮させてきた。西洋の教育ある人々は、キリスト教の代表者の一部が誠実な生活を送っていることや苦しんでいる者に援助の手を差しのべていることを見て賞《しょう》讃《さん》はしても、こうした首唱者が死後の世界やその中で起こる出来事について話したところで、それを信ずる者は（教育ある者の中には）ほとんどいない。圧倒的多数の西洋人にとって、死後の世界は考えられないことであり、（死そのものとともに）話題にするのもタブーになってしまっている。生まれ変わりという考え方は（今回はある程度その裏づけになる証拠とともに提出されているが）、知的な西洋人のほとんどはむしろ考えないような、「死んだら自分はどうなるのか」という問題をあらためて提起しているのである。

第11章　生まれ変わりに関係する可能性のあるプロセスの考察

1　心搬体《サイコフォア》

　この言葉は、「魂を運ぶもの」を意味するギリシャ語をもとに造ったものである。（心搬体という言葉にご賛同くださり、正確な語源をご教示くださった、ヴァージニア大学古典文学科のデヴィッド・コヴァクス教授に感謝するものである。）心搬体は、シュレディンガー（278、九一―九二ページ）言うところの、経験が集積されるカンバスに相当する。

私は、前世と来世のはざまで心の媒体の役割を演ずるとされる非物質的な身体について書かれたヒンドゥー教や仏教の相当数の文献にかなり精通している。しかし、こうした文献は宗教的伝統の中から生まれているうえ、観察事実が根拠になっているとしても、賢者が自ら洞察し、弟子たちに伝えた主観的なものでしかない。私はこうした証拠を過小に評価したりはしないが、私自身が調査した事例のように事実であることが公に確認されるデータとは異なっている。またこうした事例は、心搬体のようなものの存在を裏づける直接の証拠にはなりえないことを認めなければならないが、このような事例には、前世を記憶する子どもたちが語った、超常的要素が関係しているうえに、事実であることが確認できる情報がある程度にせよ含まれているので、一般的には聖典の権威がいかに尊ばれようとも、そうした権威に対して抱くよりも強い確信をもって、このような事例をもとに推測を進めることができるのである。

　このような中間的媒体に関する南アジアの人々の考え方は一部、西洋の体脱体験を扱った通俗書に（神智学や、それから派生した信仰体系を通じて）とり入れられたが、幽体《アストラル》といった言葉は、避けるべき意味合いをもっているように思う。そのような理由から、宗教的ないしオカルト的教えとは関係なさそうな新しい言葉を造る方が賢明であるように思われたわけである。

　肉体をもたない存在では頭に思い描きにくいため、人間の死後生存という問題に関心のある哲学者や心理学者の中には、死後の存在を具象化して検討している者もある。そのため、こうした哲学者や心理学者は、死後の媒体ないし、生まれ変わりが起こるとすれば生まれ変わるまで使われる中間的媒体という問題を考えるようになったのである（34、364）。

2　幼児期に見られる前世のイメージ記憶

チャオクン・ラジスタジャルンは、自らの記憶する前世の中で起こった出来事や事象を幼児期にはすべて想い出すことができたという。

　また、乳幼児期に自分の置かれている状況が完全にわかっていたが、言葉がまだわからなかったため、そのことを周囲の者に伝えることができなかったと私に話してくれた者も何人かあった。その中には、ベビーベッドに寝かされた自分を見おろしているおとなたちの愚かしい言葉を記憶しており、それに対してなすすべなく喉《のど》を鳴らすことしかできなかったのを覚えている者もいた。チャオクン・ラジスタジャルンをはじめ、この種の主張については、いずれも事実かどうか確認されていない。

　しかしながら、乳幼児期に、場合によってはまだ母親の胎内にいる間に起こった（事実であることが確認された）出来事を記憶しているという者もある。こうした事例の中でも比較的信頼できるものには、記憶に残る出来事に関する情報を本人が通常の手段によって得たわけではないことを裏づける証拠が存在する。これまで報告されている実例については別著（324、一四〇ページ）に掲げておいた。

　新生児は、日中の三分の一と睡眠時間の半分ほどを、年長の子どもや成人が夢見の状態としているのと同じような状態で過ごしていることが、生理学的測定により明らかにされている(255)。この事実を報告する論文を執筆した研究者たちは次のように述べている。「ＲＥＭ〔夢を見ていることを示す急速眼球運動〕期に新生児は、当惑や軽蔑《けいべつ》、疑念、軽い喜びなどをはじめとする感情や思念を表わす複雑な表情を浮かべる。これまでのところわれわれは、同じ新生児でも覚醒《かくせい》状態にある時には、そのような感じの表情は観察していない」（六〇九ページ）。同じ論文の中でこの研究者たちは、次のような発言もしている。「急速眼球運動の観察される新生児の睡眠段階……が成人のＲＥＭ睡眠と関係していることはほとんど疑いえない。したがって、ＲＥＭ期は、経験により生ずるものではなく、生得的な神経生理学的過程に起源を有するものにちがいない」（六一一ページ）。なぜそう考えなければならないのであろうか。それは、胎児は受精前には何の経験もしていないはずだ、という仮定のうえに立って考えを進めているためにほかならない。もし生まれ変わりが起こるとすれば、成人の夢見に対応する状態にある乳幼児は、前世の場面を再体験しているのかもしれない。もしそうなら、こうした状態にある乳幼児の顔にさまざまな表情が浮かぶことの説明もできるであろう。そのような表情は、過去の経験の記憶によって呼びさまされるさまざまな感情の反映なのかもしれないのである。

3　人格と個性

デュカッス（73）は、このふたつの言葉を、人間の死後生存と生まれ変わりの可能性を考える中で用いている。

生まれ変わるのは死んだものと同じか同じでないか（あるいは、同一であるとともに同一ではないか）という問題は、釈迦《しゃか》自身は無益と考えた論争に仏教の釈義学者を巻き込んできた。前世を記憶する子どもたちから得られる証拠は、ひとつの事例に関係するふたつの人格の間に連続性が存在することをうかがわせてくれる。とはいえ、このことは、ふたつの人格が同一のものであることを意味するわけではない。あらゆるものは――とりわけ人間の心は――絶えず変転しているのである。

4　老年期に新たな技能を身につけること

大カトーは、真偽のほどは疑わしいにしても、老年になってからギリシャ語の勉強を始めたと言われる（46）。偉大な数学者であるカール・フリードリヒ・ガウスも、やはり年老いてからロシア語の勉強を始めている（76）。生まれ変わりが起こるとすれば、このふたりが老境に入ってから重ねた努力は時間のむだにはなっていない。

5　共有体験と心霊的絆《きずな》

どのようなものであれ交流があれば心霊的絆が多少なりとも形成されるし、交流が長ければその分だけ、その絆も強固なものとなる。感情的要素の強い共通体験をすると、こうした結びつきは非常に強くなる。外洋船で同じテーブルに着いた者同士は、親しい間柄になるのがふつうであり、その関係は、船旅が終わってもしばらく続く場合がある。ところが、その船が沈没し、救命ボートで一週間ほど一緒に漂流したあげく救助されたとすれば、その友情はさらに長く続くのである。同様に、艱難辛苦《かんなんしんく》をともにし、戦友として生き抜いてきた記憶は、戦友会を持続させる原動力となる。

先に引用したソーンダイク（347）や、その少し前にバトラー（39）が指摘しているように、強烈な体験も記憶を強化する。バトラーも船旅の例を挙げ、次のように述べている。「初めてアメリカに旅行する時に氷山に出会う……などのように、非常に珍しい……体験であれば、利害を全く蒙《こうむ》らない場合でも、強い印象を受けるであろう。しかし、もしその氷山に衝突し、船が転覆ないしそれに近い状態になったとすれば、それよりもはるかに強い印象を受けるはずであるし、単に氷山を目撃した時よりはるかに氷山のことが頭にこびりつき、はるかに多くのことが記憶に残るはずである」。

6　愛情を抱き合っている者同士の間で起こるテレパシー的印象体験と霊姿との交信

このような関係は、霊姿に関してはガーニーら（117）、テレパシー的印象体験に関してはスティーヴンソン（308）の著書で明らかにされている。後者には、他の事例集に掲載されている同種のデータも紹介されている。

発信者と受信者の間に親密な個人的関係が存在するという一般原則から外れているものとしては、集団的霊姿体験の他にも、稀《まれ》にしか見られない〝傍観者例〟がある。これは、発信者が知っている人物とたまたま同席していた者は霊姿を目撃しているのに、霊姿が何かを伝えようとしている肝腎《かんじん》の相手にはその霊姿が見えない、という事例である。したがって、この場合の目撃者はいわば傍観者であるが、目撃者となるべき人物より感受性が高かったのである。具体的な事例報告については別稿（323）を参照されたい。

7　家族の者同士は心霊的絆がきわめて強いこと

家族内の心霊的絆が強いのは、一回の生涯で感情的経験を共有することだけがその原因ではないのかもしれない。同一家族例の子どもは、要するに、前世の自分だという人物の生前、現在の家族とさまざまな経験を共にしているという。そのためこうした子どもは、自分の家族と強い絆で結ばれたうえで新しい人生を始めるが、その絆は、家族関係の持続に従って強まるのであろう。先に指摘しておいたように、同一集団内に繰り返し生まれ変わることにより、家族内の絆が強まることはもちろん、さらに大きな同族や国家に対する忠誠が生まれるのかもしれない。

以上のような推論の大海原に乗り出すと、あらゆる大陸や島々が海面下でつながっているように、あらゆる人間をつなぐ共通の魂ないし〝宇宙の魂〟のような概念に向かって漂って行くことになるかもしれない（237、239）。人間はすべて結ばれているが、その絆は一部の者に対してより強い、という考え方に私としても魅力を感じないわけではない。さらに検討を重ねることにより、何世紀にもわたって神秘家たちに語り継がれてきた、「あらゆる宗教は、神は本来的に複数の役割を兼任するものであるという認識を余儀なくされている」（376、一六七ページ）という言葉が、いつの日か客観的に確証されるかもしれない。

8　他人同士の間では、テレパシー的体験や霊姿体験は稀であること

家族の中や親友同士の間で起こった超常的体験らしきものが事実かどうかを確認するのは比較的容易なので、他人同士の間で起こる事例が稀なのは、もしかするとこの種の事例を調査、報告することが少ないためなのかもしれない。しかしながら、スハウテン（277）は、『生者の幻影』（117）に掲載されている事例を分析する中で、〝他人の事例〟が少ないのは報告の際の偏りによるためではないことはほぼ確実であり、したが

って、超常的交信のひとつの特徴であることを明らかにしている。

9　生まれ変わり型事例で、友情が心霊的絆として働くこと

実例としては、マウン・イン・マウン、マルタ・ロレンツ、マウン・アウン・タン、ヘティアラトチ姉妹の各例がある。第二次大戦中に戦死した日本兵だったという記憶をもつビルマの子どものうちのふたりの両親は（日本軍がビルマを占領していた当時、ビルマ人としては珍しく）日本兵と親しくしていたのを覚えていた。そのうちの一例が、マ・ティン・アウン・ミョの事例である。

10　生まれ変わり型事例で、憎悪が心霊的絆として働くこと

もうひとつの実例（と思われるもの）としては、サムパト・プリヤサンタの事例が挙げられる。

11　負債に対する自責の念がふたりを結びつける力として働くこと

負債や盗みに対する自責の念は、霊姿の事例の一部では、霊姿出現の動機らしきものになっている（189、第二巻、三四八ページ。212、二二六―二二九ページ）。

12　現在の家族の一員を前世で知っていたという子どもの主張

同様の発言を行なった子どもとしては、他に、ラタナ・ウォンソムバト、バジラン・B・サクセナがいる。

現在の家族を前世で知っていたとするスクラ・グプタの発言については、本人の詳細な事例報告の中ではふれていない。

双生児の事例では、その一方もしくは双方が、相手と前世で密接な関係をもっていたのを記憶している場合が多い。実例としては、ヘティアラトチ姉妹、マ・キン・マ・ギー姉妹、ポロック姉妹、シャルマ兄弟の事例が挙げられる。以上の事例はいずれも、双方が前世の記憶をもっていた。

13　特定の場所が、妊娠の可能性を高めるとす

る信仰
　他の事例の情報提供者も、同様の出来事を語っている。後に前世の記憶を口にする子どもを妊娠する直前に、母親（ないし、場合によってはその夫）が、その子どもの前世の人格の遺体を見に行っているのである。同じくビルマのマ・ムウェ・ロネの事例もそのひとつである。
　ローズ（259）は、死後の霊魂は特定の石の周囲に寄り集まるとする、オーストラリアに住むアルンタ族の間に見られる信仰について述べている。妊娠を望む女性は、夫と共にその場所に行くが、その一方で望まない女性が、その石の近くに行かなければならない場合には、なるべく人目につかないように通り過ぎる、という習慣があったのである。スペンサーら（297）も、やはりオーストラリア中央部に住む先住民族について書いている中で、霊魂が寄り集まり、女性が妊娠する危険性が特に高い場所について詳述している。

14　前世の人格が死亡した場所の周辺に、前世の記憶をもつ子どもの未来の親が行くこと
　同様の例としては、他に、プティ・パトラの事例がある。

15　生まれ変わりのアナロジーとしての衣服と肉体
　マクタガート（168、一二五ページ）より引用。このアナロジーを考えたのはマクタガートが最初ではない。生まれ変わりを意味する（ドゥルーズ族が広く用いている）アラビア語はタカモスであるが、これは文字通り「自分のシャツを着替える」という意味だからである。カモスは、明らかに、キャミソールやシュミーズのような言葉と同じ語源をもっている。

16　来世で性転換したいと生前に望むこと
　グナナティレカ・バデウィタナとパウロ・ロレンツの事例がその実例である。パウロ・ロレンツの事例は同一家族例であるが、グナナティレカの事例の双方の家族は、その事例が発生する以前には全くの他人同士であった。とはいえ、ティレケラトネ（グナナティレカの前世の人格と思《おぼ》しき少年）は、性転換したいという願望を間接的に表明していたにすぎないが、明確な言葉を使わない範囲でできる限りはっきり表明していたという事実をここに付言しておきたい。

17　排卵直前に性交が行なわれた場合、受精卵が男性になる可能性が高いこと

詳細については、ゲレロ（114）やハーラップ（120）の論文を参照されたい。

18　性交の時期と、自然受精および人工授精の場合の性比

詳細についてはゲレロ（114）の論文を参照されたい。

19　Y染色体をもった精子の方が運動性が高いこと

詳細については、ロードら（256）、エリクソンら（83）、ロバーツ（254）の各論文を参照されたい。

20　健康な女性に起こる全く気づかれない妊娠

ホイッタカーら（371）の推定によれば、人間の妊娠の八パーセントは「本人が妊娠を気づかないほど初期の段階で解消してしまう」（一一二六ページ）という。

21　生まれ変わってくる者を突き止めるため、遺体に印をつけること

生まれ変わりを期待して子どもの遺体に印をつけるという風習についてお知りになりたい方は、フィールディング＝ホール（87）、ミ・ミ・カイン（181）、ヌーン（199）、パリー（216）、ウチェンドゥ（355）、スティーヴンソン（329）の著書や論文を参照されたい。この型の事例としては、既にアムパン・ペトチェラトの事例を発表している。残念ながらこの事例では、アムパンの前世の人格と見られる少年の遺体に印をつけた人物は、遺体のどちら側につけたかを忘れてしまっていた。しかし、その印は、アムパンの母《ぼ》斑《はん》と同じく胸の上部につけられたのは確かだという。

この事例については、母斑と先天性欠損をテーマにした、現在準備中の拙著で詳しく述べるつもりである。

22 ひとりの女性の卵子を肉体のないふたつの人格が操作すること

双子の母親になる女性がその前世の人格をふたりとも知っている時、しかも、それに関連する予告夢を見ている場合には、その女性は双生児を生むことを期待し、卵子や接合体に影響を与えるような精神身体的変化を自分の体内で起こしたという可能性も考えられる。しかし、そのような考え方は、その女性が（無意識の中であれ）特定の妊娠の際に双生児を出産する決意を固めた理由は何かという問題を考慮に入れていない。また、母親が、前世の人格をふたりとも（生前にも、その後に見た夢の中でも）全く知らない事例もある。

ポロック姉妹の事例では、ふたりの姉の前世をそれぞれが記憶していた。ところが姉妹の母親は、再び妊娠した時、双子が生まれるという夫の予言を全く信じようとしなかった。したがって、双生児が生まれるようにしたのは母親だとしても、意識の上でしたわけではない。

一個の接合体が二個に分かれるところを考える時、丸いケーキを包丁で半分に切るように、肉体のないふたつの人格が接合体をふたつに分割するイメージを描いても意味はない。それよりも、（砂鉄が放射線状に並んだ）磁場がふたつ、一部重なり合った状態にあるところを描いた方が実際に近いであろう。次いでその磁場が分離し、砂鉄を半分ずつ受けもったふたつの磁場が形成されるのである。

23 鎌状赤血球貧血と繰り返しの子どもたち

エデルスタインと共に私は、ナイジェリアのアウグに居住するイボ族の社会で、鎌状赤血球貧血と乳幼児の死亡率との関係を（予備的に）調査している（331）。それによると、私たちが調査した子どもたちの家族では、鎌状赤血球貧血は乳幼児の高い死亡率と何の関係もないことがわかった。そのような結果にはなったが、遺伝的要因と超常的要因の相互作用を探究するためのモデルとして考える限りにおいては、生まれ変わりと鎌状赤血球貧血の間の関係を検討する余地はあると思う。

24　イボ族の間に見られるオバンジェ（繰り返しの子ども）という概念

この報告は、繰り返しの子どもたちに関する報告書、私が面接調査したナイジェリアの情報提供者による証言、私自身が行なった事例調査などをもとにまとめている。これまで私は、繰り返しの子どもたちの事例を、生まれてから死亡し、もう一度生まれ変わるという、いわば全周期とでも言うべき期間にわたって調査したことはない。とはいえ、繰り返しの子どもの遺体の手足を切断したため生じるとされる先天性欠損をもった子どもたちをはじめ、その周期の各部分は自分の目で見ている。

オバンジェにまつわるイボ族の儀式の効力に関する研究は、これまでのところ一件も行なわれていない。前世でオバンジェに目印をつけたり手足を切断したりするため生ずると考えられている先天性欠損や母斑をもって生まれてきた子どもは、改心したものと受け止められ、したがって、乳幼児期を無事に過ごすはずだと考えられている。しかしながら私は、にもかかわらず乳児期に死亡している子どもを二名知っている。

この問題についてさらに詳しくお知りになりたい方は、エデルスタイン（79）やスティーヴンソン（329、330）の著書や論文を参照されたい。

25　驚くべき透視の実例

これまでに最高かつ、最も信頼性の高い研究の対象となった霊媒のひとりであるグラディス・オズボーン・レナードは、一度も行ったことのない家の中にある閉じた本に書かれた文章を何らかの方法で読み、その文章が何ページに出ているか（場合によっては、そのページのどのあたりにあるか）ということや、その書物が本棚のどのあたりに置かれているかということを正確に言い当てる能力をもっていた。E・M・シジウィックは、レナード夫人の書籍実験に関する厳密な分析を行なった論文を発表している（283）。スミス（289）とゴールド（96）は、この書籍実験の要点を要約して紹介している。

オルガ・カール（210、211、351）やステファン・オソヴィエキ（25、30、80、99）も透視やテレパシーを用いて同じくらい正確に言い当てている。

ナッシュ（191）は、バクテリアを用いた実験を行ない、遺伝子の突然変異率が念力によって変化することを明らかにしている。つまり、微細な〝ターゲット〟を突き止め、それに影響を与えることが可能だということである。

26 自分の意志で姿を現わす霊姿

心霊研究の歴史をひもとくと、ある人物が遠方にいる相手の前にいわば自ら望んで姿を現わし、その相手に目撃されたという事例の報告が少数ながら存在することがわかる。ボルジモフスキ（30）やガーニーら（117、第一巻、一〇三—一一〇ページ。第二巻、六七五—六七六ページ）の著書や論文にその実例が紹介されている。

27 想像妊娠に伴う生化学的変化

詳細については、ショップバッハら（274）の論文を参照されたい。

28 トリブリアンド諸島に居住する民族に見られる、妊娠に対する精神身体的抑制

この知見はマリノフスキー（175）の著書から得た。トロブリアンド諸島に住む民族の習慣について述べる際、現在形を用いたが、マリノフスキが調査を行なって以来、おそらく状況が変わっていることであろう。

29 卵子の過熟

この部分は、ヨンクブロエトら（138）の研究に基づいている。

30 死を目前にした人間が体験した身体症状を再現する霊媒

実例については、バルフォア（11）やオスティ（209）の論文や著書を参照されたい。

31 人にすることを自分にもすること

聖アエギディウスの言葉は、オーケイの著書（206、一六〇ページ）より引用した。

32 魂を作る世

キーツはこの言葉を、弟夫婦に宛てた手紙の中で用いている（89、三六二ページ）。

文庫版解説

笠《かさ》原《はら》 敏《とし》雄《お》（訳者）

著者の人物像

不世出の科学者であったイアン・スティーヴンソン（一九一八―二〇〇七年、以下、著者）は、前世の記憶をもつ子どもたちの実地調査を、科学的な角度から世界各地で初めて組織的に行なった研究者として、わが国でもよく知られていますが、他の分野での功績はあまり知られていないようです。著者は、三九歳の若さで名門大学の精神科主任教授に就任したほどの俊才であり、したがってそれまでの経歴もたいへんに華々しいものでした。のみならず、本書第10章の後半などからもうかがわれるように、きわめて高潔な人物だったのです（著者の人となりについては、東長人《あずまながと》〔東、二〇〇七年〕およびレックス・スタンフォード〔Stanford, 2008〕の回想録も参照されたい）。

著者は、「理論の奴隷」（今西、一九七三年、三五三ページ）になることを極度に嫌い、さまざまな圧力に屈することなく、先端的な研究をアカデミズムの代表たる大学の中でたゆむことなく続けてきました（死別する最初の妻からも反対されたそうです）。その結果として、人間の本質を解明するうえで最重要とも言うべき研究分野を独力で切り拓《ひら》くことができたばかりか、著者亡き後も大学の中で研究を続けることが可能な体制を整えることができたのです。それはひとえに、科学的研究と生きかたとが不即不離の関係にあったためなのではないかと思います。

昭和初期の詩人であった中原中也《なかはらちゅうや》や、稀代《きたい》の生物学者であった今西錦司《いまにしきんじ》もそうですが、時代を画する仕事をしながらも、生前に正当な評価を受けることのなかった人たちは、その生涯がむだのない一巻の絵巻物のようになっているものです。そのため、私たちは、それらの人々が紡ぎ出した作品ばかりでなく、その作者自身にも強く引きつけられることになるわけです。日記が読まれ多くの伝記が書かれるのも、そのひとつの現われなのでしょう。二十世紀のガリレオと呼ばれる（Lief, 1977, p. 171）著者も、その点では同じ位置づけにあるように思います。

一九一八年一〇月三一日にカナダのモントリオールの裕福な家庭に生まれた著者は、幼時から気管支炎をくり返し、病臥《びょうが》を余儀なくされる時間が長かったこともあって、母親の書棚に並んでいたさまざまな領域の本を、関心に任せて読破したそうです。一九八〇年三月に私が、飯《いい》田橋《だばし》のホテルグランドパレスの部屋で、南アジアでの調査から帰ってきたばかりの著者と初めて対面した時にも、T・S・エリオットの著書が、使い古されたジュラルミン製のスーツケースからのぞいていました。ふたりの息子に、就学前からモンテッソーリやドルトン方式（同じ頃、吉田秀和《よしだひでかず》や井尻正二《いじりしょうじ》も旧制小樽《おたる》市立中学校で受けていた個別学習を中心とした教育法）の教育を施していたという教育熱心な母親の蔵書の中には、超常的現象や神智学や東洋の宗教の本がたくさんありました。著者の超常現象研究は、ここに胚胎《はいたい》していたのです。

「異常に記憶力のよかった」（Stevenson, 2006, p. 13）著者は、一六歳で高校を卒業するとスコットランドの大学に入学し、それまで魅了され続けていた歴史を正規に学びます。帰国後も歴史の勉学を続けたそうですが、二〇歳の時に進路を変え、地元のマギル大学で医学を修めるのです。歴史の研究は、自分の進むべき道ではないことがはっきりしたためでした。その点では、尊敬する父親（オクスフォード大学出身でタイムズ紙のオタワ主席特派員）の仕事であるジャーナリストも同じでした。いずれも人間の幸福にはあまりつながらないように思えたのです。

　しかしながら、歴史に対する関心はその後も消え去ったわけではありません。その正確な知識は、医学的研究や超常現象研究に、さらには本書で扱われる生まれ変わり型事例（「憑依《ひょうい》型事例」に対する用語）の調査研究に生かされることになるのです。歴史の勉強からは、物質的なものの〝はかなさ〟と、その対極にある人間の向上心の永続性（二歳年長である実兄の表現を借りると「果てしなき苦悩」〔White, 2008, p. 16〕）とを学んでいました。事物の本質にまつわるほとんどの着想は、一世を風靡《ふうび》したところで露と消えるという現実を思い知らされたことから、当代の医学的常識に挑戦し続ける決意を固めたのです。

　現行の科学知識体系は、どの時代であれ、おおいに疑問を差し挟む余地があるにもかかわらず、多くの科学者は、科学という方法論と、それによって導き出される科学知識とを、そうでなければ科学の進歩などありえないはずなのに、なぜか混同しているのです（Stevenson, 1989, p. 1）。ここで重要なのは、科学者が特殊な人たちというわけではないことです。誰であれ科学者という立場に置かれれば、ほとんどが定説という権威に忠誠を誓うようになってしまうのです。

研究分野の遍歴

肺炎を三回も起こしていた著者は、一九四三年に医学部を卒業し、地元の病院に籍を置きますが、このままでは生命が危ぶまれるという医師の警告に従って、寒冷なカナダの地を離れ、温暖なアメリカ南部に移ります（同じ理由から、小学校時代にも母親と兄の三人で二年ほどをハリウッドで過ごしたことがありました）。勤務先は、ルイジアナ州ニューオーリンズにある大学でした。そのおかげで、長年の宿痾《しゅくあ》から半ば解放された著者は、後に著名な生化学者となる同僚とともに、ネズミの肝臓を対象にした生化学的実験を行ないます。そして、その努力が実り、ドイツの大家が唱えた定説を覆す念願のデータが得られたのですが、ことは順調には運びませんでした。その快挙を聞きつけたドイツ人研究者から、それをドイツで発表することはできない、論文を投稿しても、圧力がかかって不採用にされてしまうと言われたからです。一般の科学者は、そこで不平を鳴らしたりめげたりするのでしょうが、人間の本質に熱烈な関心を寄せる著者は、全く違う受けとめかたをします。「独創的な研究を行ない、その成果を発表しようとする際に立ちはだかるあらゆる障害に対して、この時から強い関心を抱くようになった」からです（*ibid.*, p. 2）。著者の場合、ふつうの科学者の姿勢とは根本から異なっていて、関心がより根源的な方向へと向かうのです。その後は、罪もないネズミをたくさん殺さなければできないたぐいの実験に対して強い嫌悪感を覚えるようになったこともあって、部分ではなく、人間全体に肉薄できそうな研究に従事したいと考えるようになります。

ところで、著者の母親は、自らの考えかたが体の健康を左右するという強い信念をもっていました。著者は、黎明期《れいめいき》にあった心身医学に大きな関心を抱くようになるのですが、ことの始まりは母親のこの確信にあったのだそうです。ふり返ってみれば医学研修生の時代にも、感情の変化に伴って身体的変化が起こるという現象に強い関心を寄せていました。初めて担当した患者の中に、狭心症をもつ男性がいたのですが、ある日、病棟に入ると、その患者が看護師に向って激しい怒りをあらわにする場面に遭遇します。するとその患者は、直後に狭心症の発作を起こして胸をつかんだのでした（*ibid.*, p. 3）。

そうした経験も手伝って、従来の身体的原因論を放棄した著者は、一九四七年からコーネル大学ニューヨーク病院のハロルド・G・ウォルフという著名な研究者のもとで、ストレスと心臓疾患の関係を研究することになります。心が体に及ぼす影響自体は、既に旧約聖書（箴言《しんげん》第一七章二二節）の時代から気づかれていたとはいえ、ウォルフは、心身医学研究の創始者のひとりと目される、わが国でもよく知られた研究者です。ちなみに、この時代（二十代後半）に書かれたある博物学者の評伝（Stevenson, 1947）を見ると、著者は、本来の専門分野にあらざる動植物の分類学やその歴史にも驚嘆するほど詳しかったことがわかります。

研究を進めるうちに、心身医学で器官選択と呼ばれる問題に直面します。それは、著者のもつ呼吸器系の慢性疾患とも関係してくるのでしょうが、同じストレスを受けても、喘息《ぜんそく》発作を起こす者もあれば、血圧が高くなる者もいるし、胃潰瘍《いかいよう》を起こす者もあるわけです。共同研究者の中には、その選択を、象徴的、目的論的に意味づけようとする者があったのですが、著者は、そうした解釈を受け入れることができませんでした。そして、発症する器官はどのようにして選択されるのかが、著者の終生の「ライトモチーフ」（Stevenson, 1989, p. 6）になり、後には、性格の形成や、精神病を含めた疾患の成立には遺伝と環境というふたつの要因以外に、前世に由来する第三の要因があるのではないかと考えるようになります。また、性格形成という問題については、本書でも詳述されている、ビルマ人として生まれ変わったとされる元日本兵の事例が大きな意味をもってくるのです（本書三一六ページ。スティーヴンソン、一九八四年、Stevenson & Keil, 2005）。

その頃、怒りや驚愕《きょうがく》の時だけでなく、大きな幸福の状態に置かれた時にも同じように身体症状が起こることがわかってきます。この時も、医学以外の資料にも幅広く目を通すという習慣がおおいに役立ちました。特に劇的だったのは、スペインの画家ゴヤとベートーベンの事例です。いずれも病床にあったのですが、ゴヤの場合には、すぐに見舞いに行くという知らせを息子から受けた直後に、ベートーベンの場合には、生活上の窮状を解消してくれるはずの一〇〇ポンドがロンドンから舞い込んだ直後に死亡しているのでした（Stevenson,1970, pp. 93-94）。

それどころか、ナチの強制収容所から解放されるという最大級の好事のまさに直前に死亡した人々もいたのです。その人々は、「赤十字の白いバスがコンクリートの広場に連なって入ってくるのを目の当たりにし、それに乗ってここから抜け出せることを知った時、筆舌に尽くせないほどの喜びと希望にあふれ、眼を輝かせた。〔中略〕そして、その場で倒れ、死んでしまったのである──文字通り喜びのために」（Nansen, 1949, pp. 468-69）。

この報告は、この収容所に監禁されていて、後にユニセフの創設にかかわるオッド・ナンセン（ノルウェーの探検家、フリッチョフ・ナンセンの次男）によるものです。死亡したのは、もちろん一部に違いありませんが、それにしても目的論的解釈で太刀打ちできないのは明らかでした。著者は、それらの事例をまとめて報告しようとしますが、ここでも、かつて定説に抗《あらが》う所見を発表しようとした時に立ちはだかった障壁と全く同じものに直面するのです。

ハロルド・ウォルフは、他に並ぶ者がないほど厳密な姿勢で研究を続けてきた医学者で、共同研究者にも同じ姿勢を求めていたそうですが、その一方で、心身症の症状には自らを守ろうとする目的があるはずだという考えかたに固執していました。そのため、著者の得た所見に対して冷ややかな態度を示したのです。著者がその論文（Stevenson, 1950, 1970）を発表できたのは、二年を過ごしたニューヨーク病院を離れた後のことでした（Stevenson, 1989, p. 5）。

ニューヨークの気候に不安を感じていた著者は、一九四九年に再び南部に移ります。そして赴任したルイジアナ州立大学でも生化学的な実験に従事するのですが、今度の対象は動物ではなく人間でした。幻覚剤を体験していたことで知られるオルダス・ハクスリーと対面して影響を受け（White, 2008, p. 18）、

ルイジアナ州立大学の頃の著者。
（Stevenson & Matthews, 1952, p. 13）

そこでは、メスカリンやLSDという薬物を使った実験を行ないます。それらの薬物が、精神病の治療に使えるかどうかを検討するためでした（Stevenson, 1955）。自分でも何度か試してみた結果、幼児期の記憶が鮮明に蘇《よみがえ》ったのみならず、それまで鈍かった視聴覚が鋭くなり、なきに等しかった審美眼もかなり表出してきたのです。LSDの場合には、「完全な安らぎ」が使用後三日ほど続きました（Stevenson, 1989, p. 10）。この体験は、「本当に言葉で表現できない」ほどのものでした。それでも著者は、そうした状態に薬物なしで達成することのほうを旨とするのです。では、その中で別人になったのかというと、そうではありませんでした。「薬物が脳内に引き起こした変化により解き放たれた、尋常ならざるイメージや感情が意識に侵入してきた」にすぎず、自分という自覚自体に変化はなかったからです（*ibid*., p. 10. 本書五二ページ）。

著者は、絵画や音楽、詩歌をはじめとする文学など、知識を得る手段は科学的方法以外にもたくさんあることを強調しますが、のみならず、人間は十全なる森羅万象の一部だという、あらゆるものの中で最も重要な真理に、神秘体験を通じてじかにふれることができるとも考えているそうです（*ibid*., p. 7）。そうであるとしても著者は、神秘的体験を言葉で伝えることはできないので、言葉で伝達可能な科学的方法のほうを重視するのです（Shroder, 1999, p. 99）。

その後も著者は、心が体に及ぼす影響に依然として強い関心を寄せていました。ところが、当初の予測と違って、心身医学の将来性に疑念がもたれるようになってきたのです。この領域に従事していた科学者たちは、内科や精神科に移って行きました。著者は、そうした関心から精神科を選択しますが、それまで精神科の訓練を受けたことがあまりなかったため、当時のアメリカ精神医学界で主流であった精神分析の研修所に入ります。ところが、そこの雰囲気は、事実を重んずる自らの折衷主義とは正反対のものでした。フロイトの理論をひたすら信奉するという、宗教的信仰と同質の姿勢は、著者の性に根本から合わなかったということです。

初期の時代のフロイトは、神経学者のジャン＝マルタン・シャルコーを師とし、その後はヨーゼフ・ブロイアーと共同で研究を進めていたわけですが、それ以降は、自分に忠言してくれる仲間たちから隔絶してしまったのでした。精神分析家の集まりは開かれたものにして、仲間内だけで動くことはしないほうがよいという忠告を、オイゲン・ブロイラー（「精神分裂病」概念を唱えたことで今なお有名なスイスの精神医学者）から受けていたそうですが、それも無視していたのです（Stevenson, 1989, p. 7）。

ちなみに、超常現象研究の国際学会である超心理学協会（Parapsychological Association）から距離を置くようになっていた著者は、同じ志をもつ天体物理学者、ピーター・スタロックに誘われる形で科学的探検学会（Society for Scientific Exploration）を、ロンドンの心霊研究協会（SPR）創立百年に当たる一九八二年に創設しますが、それは、ある意味でブロイラーの忠言に従ったためなのでしょう。

話を戻すと、精神分析の理論のうちでも、性格傾向はほとんどが幼児期の経験で決まるという断定的主張には特に納得できませんでした。これは、精神分析だけでなく、ほとんどの人格理論や心理療法理論の屋台骨に当たる常識的な考えかたでもあるわけですが、運命論を押しつけられている感じを受けたからです。そこで、その理論に疑問を呈する論文を、一九五六年のアメリカ精神医学協会の年次大会で発表します。この論文（Stevenson, 1957）は、翌一九五七年、著者がヴァージニア大学精神科に着任した年に、同協会の機関誌である『アメリカ精神医学雑誌』に掲載されるのですが、この論文を見た一部の精神科医が激怒したのです（Stevenson, 2006, p. 13）。実際に、ロンドンの精神医学研究所の教授からは、「丸腰で街を歩いてもだいじょうぶなのか」とまで心配されたそうです（Stevenson, 1989, p. 8）。今はむしろ正反対の状態になっていますが、当時のアメリカ精神医学は、フロイトの独断論としての精神分析にここまで席巻《せっけん》され、その戒律で自らを縛りあげた理論の奴隷状態と化していたということです（その点については、残念ながら現在の精神医学も同じでしょう）。ここに、揺るぎなき著者の信念を、さらには覚悟をみることができるはずです。著者の超常現象研究は、単なる思いつきで始めたことではなく、さまざまな経験に裏打ちされた、ある意味で必然的な結果なのです。

超常現象研究へ――唯物論（物理的一元論）への挑戦が始まる

著者は、通常科学の枠内での多大な業績が評価されて、一九五七年に、三九歳の若さで名門ヴァージニア大学の第二代精神科主任教授に就任するわけですが、超常現象に対する関心は、それと相前後して再び高まります。そのため、教授にまで昇格していたルイジアナ州立大学の時代から、超常現象関係の資料に幅広く眼を通すようになっていました。のみならず、医学教育を受けたおかげで身につけることのできた科学的方法を使って、それまで本で読んできた事例の裏づけを得ることを考えるようになるのです。そして、敬愛するＳＰＲの創設者、フレデリック・マイヤーズやエドマンド・ガーニーの著作を中心に、心霊研究関係の文献をそれまでよりも組織的に読み進めるようになりました。

最初は超常現象関係の本の書評を書いていたのですが、書くことで理解が深まることを知ったため一九四九年から医学関係の評論を寄稿していた『ハーパーズ・マガジン』という老舗《しにせ》の一般向け月刊誌に、「超感覚的知覚にまつわる心地よからぬ諸事実」という論考を発表します。一九五九年七月のことでした。その論考が、超常現象（ＥＳＰおよび念力）の統計的な実験的研究をデューク大学で行なっていたジョゼフ・Ｂ・ラインの目にとまり、その縁で著者は、まもなくライン研究所を訪れます。ライン夫妻らと超常現象に関する雑談をしていると、寄せられた報告をもとに偶発的超常体験例の統計的研究をしていた妻のルイーザが、著者を別室に呼び、個々の事例は科学的には全く無意味なものであることを教え諭そうとしたのです。しかし時は既に遅しで、著者は、ひとつひとつの事例の信憑性《しんぴょうせい》を体験者やそれに関係した証人たちに丹念に確認し、それを公平な立場から記述、検証するという古典的方法の重要性を、ＳＰＲの創設者たちから十二分に学んだ後だったのです（Stevenson, 2006, p. 14）。この時、双方の旗幟《きし》の違いがより鮮明になったと言えるでしょう（本書四三三ページ）。

その後、著者は、偶発例の研究を幅広く行なうようになります。さまざまな文献や資料から渉猟した、タイタニック号沈没にまつわる予知体験（Stevenson, 1960c, 1965）を収集して発表する一方で、超常現象関係の文献に通じている編集者らの協力を得て、英米の心霊研究協会

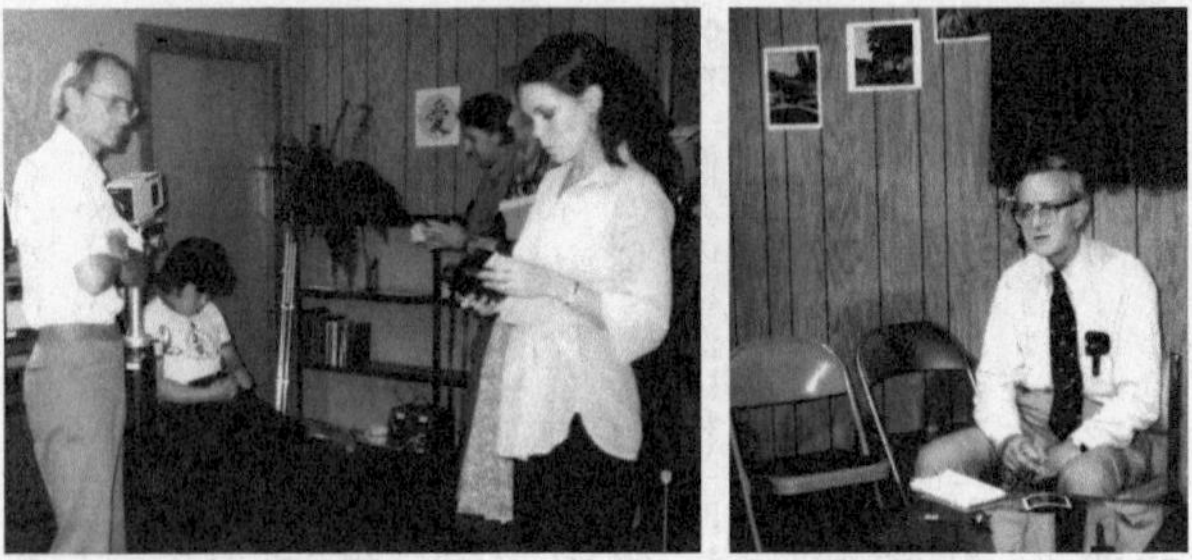

清田益章を対象にした実験での休憩時（1980 年９月。右写真が著者、左写真は、手前左からマイクル・デニス、当時の助手のウィリアムズ＝クック〔現、ウィリアムズ＝ケリー〕、奥の左が清田益章、右がユルゲン・カイル。奥の壁に「愛」と書かれた色紙が貼られている。この頃の人格研究室は、民家を改造した建物で、その向かいにプレハブのこの実験室があった）

の刊行物などから集めた古典的事例とともに、自ら調査した、〝虫の知らせ〟に代表される三五例のテレパシー的印象体験を詳細に検討したうえで、一九七〇年に *Telepathic Impressions* という著作（邦訳、『虫の知らせの科学』一九八一年、叢文社）を発表するのです。

人間の人格の一側面という点から念力にも関心があって、明治・大正期のわが国の心理学者、福《ふく》来《らい》友吉《ともきち》が創始した念写（福来、一九一三年、Fukurai, 1931）の追認実験も、ゲイザー・プラット（ラインの研究所にいた心理学者）とともに、テッド・シリアスという念写能力者を対象にして行なっています（Stevenson & Pratt, 1968, 1969）し、清田《きよた》益章《ますあき》を対象にした念写や金属変形の実験も、コロラド大学の精神科医、ジュール・アイゼンバッド、ワシントン大学の物理学者、ピーター・フィリップスらとともに、一大プロジェクトとして実現させています（Eisenbud,1982;

Keil, *et al.*, 1982, Shafer & Phillips, 1982）。

福来については、当時としては信じがたいほど厳密な実験法を採用していたことや、迫害をものともせずに研究を続けた揺るぎのない姿勢に対して、深く尊敬していると私に話してくれたことがあります。福来の姿勢が、著者のものと同質だからなのでしょう。そして、読んだことがないのならぜひ読むようにと言って、福来の英文の著書（*Clairvoyance & Thoughtography*. London: Rider, 1931）の全文（B５版、二四七ページ）をコピーして私に送ってくれることまでしているのです。

死後生存研究とは何か

順序からすると、ここで本書の主題である生まれ変わり型事例の研究の解説に入ることになるわけですが、それは、一部の例外を除いて本書に譲ることにして、ここでは、死後生存（死後存続）研究の目的や概略を簡単に説明することにします。

人間には心ないし魂があるという古来の考えかたに対しては、現行の科学知識を奉ずる主流科学者から相手にされていない状態（実際には、頑強な心理的拒絶）が続いています。そもそも、心や魂などというものが存在することは「科学的に証明されていない」というのがその理屈なのですが、残念ながらそれは、ふたつの理由で正しくありません。ひとつは、実際にはその証明が未《いま》だにできていない（正確に言えば、その検証を忌避している）ことです。その裏づけになりそうな現象は昔からたくさん報告されているわけですから、そうした現象は心や魂の実在の証拠にならないと言いたいのであれば、科学的方法を使ってそのことを証明しなければなりません。すべては脳の活動の結果なので、心や魂は実在しえないというよくある論法は、実際には同語反復にすぎず、反証にはならないのです。この問題についてはアンリ・ベルクソンも、「意識が死後は消滅すると考えるただひとつの理由は、身体の解体が見られるということ」なので、「その立証の責任は、この考えかたを肯定するひとたちよりも、否定するひとたちのものになるでしょう」（ベルクソン、一九九二年、七四―七五ページ）と明言しています。もうひとつは、心や魂が実在するかどうかを科学的方法を使って検証しようとするのが死後生存研究なのですから、それによって蓄積された証拠群をすべて否定しない限り、心や魂の実在を否定するのは不可能であることです。唯物論の無謬性《むびゅうせい》を無条件に信奉しない限りできないわけですが、そうした行為は、科学の作法を旨とすべき科学者の立場を自ら放棄するに等しいことになるでしょう。死後生存研究は、現行の科学知識体系の基盤になっている唯物論に対する最強の挑戦になっているのです。

　心が脳とは別個に存在することになると、現行の科学知識体系は、根底から崩れ去ってしまいます（本書三六七ページ。笠原、二〇二〇年、第5章も参照）。科学という営みにとって最も重要なこの問題について、著者は次のように述べています。「生物学者は生気論という烙印《らくいん》を押し、そうした考え方は何十年も前に却下されていると断定するが、新たな証拠からすると、生気論が信頼に足るものであることがわかる。これまで蓄積されてきた死後生存の証拠を他の分野の科学者が先入観抜きに検討すれば、人間は肉体以外の何ものでもないという憶説を除いては失うものはない」（本書一九ページ）。唯物論は哲学者の創始になる、ひとつの仮説にすぎないのです。

死後生存研究は、心が脳とは独立して存在するものかどうかを、他の超常現象（ＥＳＰと念力）よりも直接に検討することができる研究分野です。その点を考えると、死後生存研究こそが、超常現象研究の中でも最も重要な分野になるわけですが、本当は、多くの科学者にとっても同じことが言えるはずなのです。

死後生存研究は、それぞれの現象に従って、いくつかの領域に分かれます。それを、いわば現世から来世まで時間を追って列挙すると、次のようになります。著者は、これらの領域のほとんどについて厳密な実験や観察を行なっています（拙編書『死後の生存の科学』〔叢文社〕にそれらの一部が収録されています）。

1 **肉体離脱体験**（ＯＢＥ）――生きている人間の意識が、自分の肉体を、偶発的に、あるいは意図的に抜け出し、また戻ってくるという体験（『霊魂離脱の科学』〔叢文社〕参照）

2 **臨終時体験**――肉体が死ぬ前の、意識が清明な時に起こる、内容的には臨死体験とほぼ同じ体験（『人は死ぬ時何を見るのか』〔日本教文社〕参照）

3 **臨死体験**（ＮＤＥ）――いったん〝死亡〟し、蘇生《そせい》した後に物語る、その間に起こった体験（『「あの世」からの帰還』〔日本教文社〕、『臨死体験』〔春秋社〕他参照）

4 **死者との交信**――霊媒と呼ばれる能力者を介して故人から受ける通信（『死後の生存の

科学』第三部参照）

5 **霊姿**——くり返し目撃される幽霊に対して、単発的に目撃される幻影（『死後の生存の科学』第五、六章、『死後生存の証拠』〔技術出版〕第一部第一章参照）

6 **ある種のポルターガイスト**——生者の中心人物が見つからない、くり返し起こる物理的現象（『死後の生存の科学』第七章参照）

7 **憑依**《ひょうい》——ほとんどの場合は短時間だけ、本来の人格とは別の人格に肉体が乗っとられる状態（『死後の生存の科学』第一二章参照）

8 **真性異言**——生後に習ったはずのない母語以外の言葉を話す現象（『前世の言葉を話す人々』〔春秋社〕。Ohkado & Okamoto, 2014 参照）

9 **出生前記憶**——生まれる前の、母親の胎内にいる前後からの記憶（『転生した子どもたち』〔日本教文社〕第8章。Ohkado & Ikegawa, 2014 参照）

10 **生まれ変わり**——前世の人格が別の肉体に宿って生まれてくること

ここで興味深いのは、それぞれの領域の研究者の数に大きなばらつきが見られることです。臨死体験の研究者は数多いのですが、SPRの創設者たちが最も重視した、それ以降の領域では非常に少ないのです。臨死体験の研究者が多いのは、対象となる体験の数がそれなりに多いためでしょうが、他の領域と比べて〝うさんくささ〟が少ないことも大きな理由になっているのではないかと思います（本当の因果関係はその逆でしょうが）。臨死体験以降の分野には、著者のグループを除けば、研究者がほとんど参入していないのが実情なのです。

ところで、世間で関心をもたれている分野に〝過去世リーディング〟や〝前世療法〟と呼ばれるものがあります。これらは、〝霊能者〟の〝リーディング〟によって、あるいは催眠状態を通じて前世を知ろうとする方法ですが、稀《まれ》な例外を除けば、信頼性がほとんどないようです(Stevenson, 1994)。著者は、「まえがき」で次のように述べています。「私としては、心得違いの催眠ブームを、あるいは、それに乗じて不届きにも金もうけの対象にしている者があるという現状を、特に前世の記憶を探り出す確実な方法だとして催眠が用いられている状況を、何とか終息させたいと考えている」(九―一〇ページ)。第3章の冒頭にそのための一節が設けられていることからもわかるように、このことも本書の大きな目的になっているのですが、初版が出てから既に三十年以上が経過しているにもかかわらず、著者の思惑通りにはなっていないようです。

生まれ変わり型事例の調査研究の始まり

著者がヴァージニア大学に着任した翌年の一九五八年に、アメリカ心霊研究協会が、創設者のひとりであるウィリアム・ジェームズを記念して、「超常的心理現象および、そうした現象と人間の死後生存問題との関係」についての論文を募集します。著者は、ヴァージニア大学での選考面接の際に、超常現象に関心をもっていることに加えて、「生まれ変わりという考えかたに引かれていて、これまで読んできた中でも、前世を記憶しているという人たちの報告に出会っています」と率直に語ったそうです（Tucker, 2008, p. 36）が、その言葉に違《たが》わず、このコンテストに応募して首尾よく優勝するのです。もちまえの読書癖のおかげで集めることのできた四四例（多い順に、インド、ビルマ、イタリア、アメリカ、英国、ベルギー、ギリシャ、キューバ、モーリシャス、フランス、シリア、カナダ、日本）の古典的事例を分析したものでした。その中で、七例の実例を簡単に紹介していますが、その第一例は、江戸時代後期に平田《ひらた》篤胤《あつたね》が調査し、ラフカディオ・ハーンが英文で紹介した勝五《かつご》郎《ろう》の事例（小泉、一九八六年）なのです（Stevenson, 1960a, p. 65）。本書についても同じことが言えますが、二部に分かれたこの論考（Stevenson, 1960a,b）に目を通すと、著者の博覧強記ぶりを思い知らされるはずです。

この論文を書いた時点では、そうした事例を自分で調査することは考えていませんでした。本業が忙しすぎて、時間がとれなかったためです。そこに恩人となるふたりの人物が登場します。ひとりは、ニューヨークに超心理学財団を設立していた、精神霊媒（交霊会で念力現象を起こす物理霊媒に対して、死後の存在と交信するとされる霊媒）としても著名なアイリーン・ギャレットであり、もうひとりは、乾式複写（ゼロックス）の発明者である物理学者、チェスター・カールソンでした。ふたりとも、著者のこの論考に注目したのです。

インドに新しい事例が見つかったという知らせを受けていたギャレットは、一九五七年頃に著者から生まれ変わりに関心のあることを聞いていたためもあって、その調査行の費用の負担を申し出ました。もう一方のカールソンは、その調査研究のために高額の寄付をしようとしたそうですが、著者はそれを謝絶し、テープレコーダの購入費だけを負担してもらいました。こ

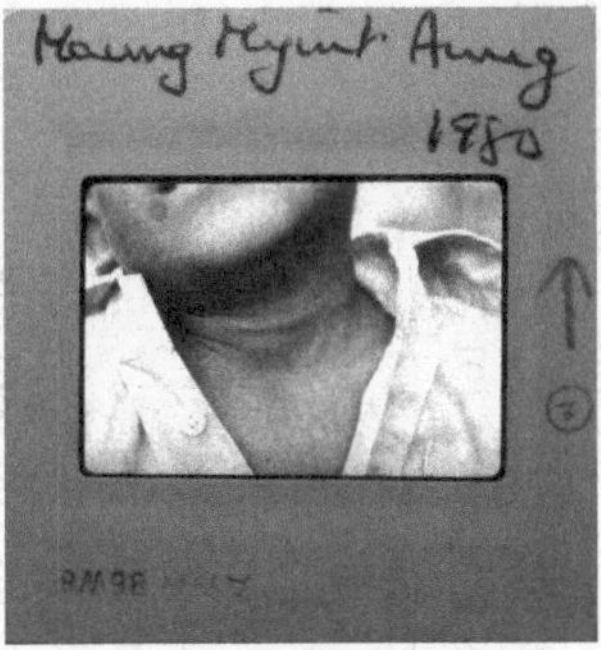

講演の際に使うようにと、著者より訳者に送られたスライド８枚のうちの１枚（原版はカラー。著者自身が子どもの名前と撮影年を書いている。後に遠藤周作の求めにより、日本キリスト教芸術センターで講演した際に使用した。写真の男児は、喉をかき切って自決したという日本兵の前世を記憶していた〔『生まれ変わりの刻印』（邦訳、1998 年、春秋社）、口絵図３および 56、57 ページ参照〕）

の調査を単発的なものとしか考えていなかったためです。ところが、いざ夏休みを利用して現地に行ってみると、四週間ほど滞在したインドでは新たに二〇例ほどが、一週間ほど滞在したセイロンでも五例が見つかったのでした。さらには、文献的研究からは知りえなかったこともわかりました。子どもたちは、前世の記憶をもっているだけではなかったのです。

子どもたちは、その家族の中では変わっているとしても、その記憶とは符合する行動を示していたのです。そのような事情から、調査を重ねる必要が出てきたわけです（Steveson, 2006, pp. 16-17)。また、前世で死因となった傷痕とよく似た母斑や先天性欠損（上図参照）をもつ子どもが少なからずいたことも後にわかります。著者は本書でくり返し約束していますが、後者に関する調査研究は、後（一九九七年）に大きな二巻の学術書（二二六八ページ）として結実するのです。

著者は、前世の記憶をもつ双生児の事例も、前世で双方が親密な関係にあり、無縁の例は事実上なかったことから特段に重視しています（三〇四—三二一ページ。Stevenson, 1997. vol. 2, pp. 1931-2062; 1999, pp. 1359-60）。著者が双生児に着目したのは、八歳下の弟妹が双生児であることと無関係ではないのかもしれません。

カールソンは、二番目の妻のドリスがESP能力をもっていたことから、超常現象の研究への支援を真剣に考えるようになっていました。そのため、その後の調査研究が可能になるようにとり計らってくれたのですが、他の支援者と違って、匿名にすることを求めたうえ、著者の研究を詳細に知ろうとしたのです。現に、著者の聞きとり調査を見学したいと言って、アラスカのトリンギット族の調査に同行し、時おり対象者に向って控え目に質問することまでしたのでした（*ibid.*, p. 16）。なお、著者の調査の実際については、インドとレバノンでの調査に同行取材したワシントン・ポスト紙の編集者、トム・シュローダーの著書 *Old Souls*（邦訳、『前世を覚えている子どもたち』）が参考になります。特に発展途上国で調査が行なわれた場合、どれほど過酷で忍耐を要するものかがよくわかるはずです（この本は、著者の紹介で私が邦訳することになり出版社から原著が届いていたのですが、当のシュローダーも知らないうちにある出版社に翻訳権を先取されたという経緯があります）。

著者は、一九六三年のサバティカル休暇を使って、前世を記憶する子どもたちに関する最初

の論文 *Twenty Cases Suggestive of Reincarnation* を執筆します（Tucker, 2008, p. 37）。アメリカ心霊研究協会は、その長文の論文を紀要として出版する準備を進めたのですが、インド調査で二、三例の通訳を務めた人物が、著者とは無関係の（ライン研究所での）実験で不正を働いたことが疑われたのです。そのため、別の通訳を使って再調査する必要に迫られたわけですが、この時の費用もカールソンが負担してくれました。その結果、正しく通訳されていたことが確認され、その論文は新事実を加えて（三六二ページ）刊行されました（Stevenson, 2006, pp. 16-17）。

この論文は後に増補改訂され、一九七四年にヴァージニア大学出版局から第二版として刊行されたのですが、『前世を記憶する20人の子供』というタイトルで出版された邦訳版で問題が発生します。訳者が全体をかってに〝小説化〟してしまっていたのです。訳者に質《ただ》したところ、日本の読者には難しすぎるので読みやすくしたとのことでした。著者に事情を伝えた結果、この〝翻訳版〟は絶版となりました。あらためて翻訳して出版するのは難しいでしょうから、わが国の読者にとってはかえすがえすも残念なことでした。

その後の展開

チェスター・カールソンは、一九六一年から著者の研究を資金面で支えてきました。そのため、カールソンが亡くなればその時点で援助は途絶えてしまうので、その場合には通常の精神医学や心身医学の研究に戻るしかないと考えていました。ところが、前向きな人には自然と協力態勢が敷かれるもので、六八年にカールソンが急死すると、誰もが驚いたことに、カールソンからヴァージニア大学へ百万ドルと、それよりも少し多い額が著者の超常現象研究のためとして、遺贈されていたのです（Shroder, 1999, p.107）。理事会内には反対意見もあったそうですが、学長は、そうした反対を押し切ってその寄付を受理します。アメリカ建国の父であり第三代大統領でもある同大学の創設者、トマス・ジェファーソンが一八二〇年に発した建学の理念を尊重した結果でした。そのおかげで著者は、資金面の心配をせずにすむようになったのです。

その前年の一九六七年に、著者は精神科主任教授の席を降り、かねてからの念願であった超常現象研究に専念できる態勢を整えていました（Stevenson, 2006, p. 17）。そして、精神科の中に小さな部門（最初の名称は、著者の意に反して超心理学研究室、一九八七年に人格研究室、二〇〇四年に知覚研究室）を設けたのです。そこでは、生まれ変わり型事例の調査研究のみならず、他の領域の死後生存研究も行なわれるようになりました。

一九六〇年代と七〇年代の途中までは、著者ひとりで研究を続けていましたが、カールソンのおかげで資金面の心配がなくなったため、研究助手や秘書を、さらには先述のゲイザー・プラットやレックス・スタンフォード、ジョン・パーマーといった研究者を在籍させる余裕も生まれました。この三人は、既に大成していた、あるいは後に大成することになる優れた研究者です。ドリス・カールソンからそれまで続けられていた支援が一九七三年に停止されると資金難に陥りましたが、幸いにも再び余裕が生まれるようになりました。

その後は、次第に共同研究者も増え、そのためもあって、生まれ変わり型事例を含めた死後生存領域の研究を、著者とは独立に行なう科学者が何人か誕生するまでになるのです。著者はそれを、「後継者たちは私の考えに縛られていない」と素直に喜んでいます（*ibid.*, p. 19）。オリジナリティのある研究であれば、自らの考えと違っていても尊重したいということであり、これが、真の意味での科学者のあるべき姿です。著者は「もしこの世が（キーツの言うように）『魂を造る世』であるなら、私たちは自分自身の魂を作っているのである」（四一五ページ）と述べています。これこそが、生きることと探究することが密接につながった、自らの成長をたゆみなく続けようとする著者が絶えず直面してきたテーマなのでした。

著者の研究に対する評価

著者は、超常現象関係の論文をその方面の専門誌に発表してきましたが、医学や心理学などの正統的専門誌からは掲載を拒絶されていました。最初に突破口を開いたのは、ヴァージニア大学出版局の創設者、ウォーカー・コーウェンでした。一九七〇年六月に著者が *Telepathic Impressions* という長文の論文を『アメリカ心霊研究協会紀要』に発表すると、著者の本は「未来のため」のものだと考えるコーウェンは、それを一九八ページの書籍として同時刊行してくれたのです（その邦訳が、先述の『虫の知らせの科学』です）。以後、コーウェンが死去する一九八七年まで、著者は同出版局から著書を出すことができました（Stevenson, 2006, pp. 18-19）。それは、先にふれた『20人の子供』、生まれ変わり型事例を扱った四点の事例集、真性異言の事例を扱った二点、そして、著者が初めて一般読者向けに書いた本書です。

そのうち一九七四年に出版された『20人の子供』については、肯定的な書評が主流専門誌を含めていくつか出たのですが、一般の科学者からはほとんど無視されました。ところが、翌七五年に出版された事例集の第一巻（インドの一〇例）に対して、アメリカ医学協会機関誌（*JAMA*）の元編集主幹が書いた好意的書評（King, 1975, p. 978）がまもなく同誌に掲載されると、それに感銘を受けた（Tucker, 2008, p. 38）、老舗《しにせ》の精神医学・神経学専門誌である *Journal of Nervous and Mental Disease* の編集長、ユージン・ブローディ（メリーランド大学精神科主任教授）が、生まれ変わりに関する著者の理論的論文を同誌に掲載してくれました。すると、その別刷りを求める手紙が、世界中の千人を超える科学者から届いたのです（Stevenson, 1989, p. 17）。

ブローディは、その年の同誌一一月号（第一六五巻三号）を Ian Stevenson on Reincarnation と銘打った、著者の生まれ変わり研究の特集号として発行し、巻頭に自らの見解を明記しました。執筆者が科学的にも個人的にも信頼に足る人物であり、正統な研究法をとっていて合理的な思考をしている限りにおいて、「人間の行動に関する知識の増進をめざす雑誌が、このようなテーマの論文を自動的に不採用にすべきではないし、そうしてはならない責務がある」（Brody, 1977, p. 151）というのです。ここに科学の国に住む科学者の度量の大きさを見ることができます（わが国は、科学技術の国ではあっても科学の国とは残念ながら言えません〔今西、一九八六年、二二一ページ。岡田、一九九四年、一三四ページ参照〕）。著者がそれまで通常科学の領域で培ってきた信頼が、ここで大きな役割を果たしたわけです。

同誌はその後も、著者のものを含めた超常現象関係の論文を何編か掲載していますし、二〇一〇年に死去したブローディの跡を継いだジョン・タルボット（メリーランド大学精神科教授、元アメリカ精神医学協会会長）も、生まれ変わりを含む超常現象研究の論文をやはり何編か掲載しています。著者や共同研究者による超常現象関係の論文が掲載された医学雑誌や心理学雑誌は、他にも、*American Journal of Psychiatry, Archives of General Psychiatry, British Journal of Psychiatry, JAMA, Lancet, Medical Hypotheses, Psychiatric Annals, Psychological Reports* などいくつもあるのです。また、行動療法の創始者である英国の著名な心理学者、ハンス・アイゼンクも、著者の生まれ変わり研究について、「真の意味できわめて重要なことがわれわれの前に明らかにされつつあるという見解からむりやり目を逸らせることは、誠実であろうとする限りできない」（Eysenck & Sargent, 1993, p. 173）と率直に述べています。

では、こうした研究が正統派科学者から受け入れられる日が近づいたのかというと、十九世紀後半に死後生存研究が始まって以後一四〇年ほどの経過を俯瞰《ふかん》する限り、そのようなことは考えられません。関心がいつも個人のレベルで止まってしまっていて、広がりを見せないからです。そこには重大な理由があるはずです（笠原、一九九五／二〇二〇年、序章、第5章参照）。

行きつけらしい街中の古色豊かなレストランの前で（左から著者、清田益章、訳者。1980年9月）

著者が遺したもの

著者は、一九八三年に前世を記憶するアメリカの子どもたちの七九例を分析する論文（Stevenson, 1983）を発表しています。二〇〇三年には、*European Cases of the Reincarnation Type*（邦訳、『前世を記憶する子どもたち2　ヨーロッパの事例から』二〇〇五年、日本教文社）を出版しました。このような子どもたちは、発展途上国とされる東南アジアやアフリカばかりでなく、欧米にもいることを示すためでした。そして、ヨーロッパの事例集に続いてアメリカの事例集を出す予定にしていたそうです（Tucker, 2008, p. 39）が、残念ながらまにあいませんでした。

しかし、著者は私たちにたくさんのものを遺《のこ》してくれました。ふつうの意味で最も大きいのは、言うまでもなく、人間の心ないし魂の実在を裏づける、まさしく未来のために残された大量の著作や膨大な原資料です。誰であれ、それをもとに人間の最も重要な問題について自分なりの判断が下せるわけです。

後継者である児童精神科医、ジム・タッカーによれば、著者は、ある時、笑いながら語っていたそうです。生まれ変わりの可能性を主流科学が真剣に考えるようになることが今生の目標なんだが、それが達成されなければ、私の人生は失敗だったことになるね（*ibid.*, p. 41）と。いつかはそうなるはずですが、著者が生きている間にはそのようなことはもちろん起こりませんでした。それどころか、私たちが生きている間にも、そのようなことにはならないでしょう。アーサー・ケストラーは、唯物論という「要塞の柱は、既に何本かの亀裂が入っており、中空の状態をさらしている」ことを既に五十年以上前に指摘しています（Koestler, 1967, p. 4）。にもかかわらず、この要塞《ようさい》は、少なくとも表向きは今なお微動だにしていないのです。

ただ、著者が遺してくれたのは、信頼性の高い膨大な資料や著作ばかりではありません。終生、人間の本質の探究から目をそらすことのなかった、生きざまがむだのないみごとな作品のようになっている巨峰のような人物が現実に存在することを示す確たる証拠も、同時に遺してくれたのです。ウィリアム・ジェームズと並んで著者の敬慕したアンリ・ベルクソンは、この点について次のように述べています。

> 最高位の創造者である人間性の探究者は、当人の行動自体が真剣なものであるばかりか、他者の行動も増大させることができ、寛容であるのみならず、寛容という炉床を燃え立たせることができる人たちです。〔中略〕そのような人たちは進化の頂点に立っていますが、それと同時に、進化の源泉に最も近いところにもいて、深みから浮かび上がる衝動を私たちに感じさせてくれるのです。私たちが直観の働きによって、生命の原理そのものに深く入り込むことができるとすれば、それは、このような偉大な人たちの生きざまを学び、こ

れらの人たちが体感することを共鳴的に体感しようと努める以外にありません。深みの謎へ入り込むためには、時として、高みに注目する必要があります。地球に隠された火は、火山の山頂に現われるのです。(Bergson, 1920, p. 32)

〔付　記〕

本書は、第二版が二〇〇〇年に別の出版社から出ている（しかも、邦訳するようにと著者から送っていただいていた）のですが、他のことにかまけて時間的な余裕がなかったこともあって、やむなく初版からの三〇年前の翻訳を、最低限の修正を施したうえで再刊することにしました。なお、単行本では「精神分裂病（schizophrenia）」と訳していましたが、現在用いられている病名の「統合失調症」としました。読者の寛容を乞《こ》う次第です。

このたびの文庫化は、KADOKAWAジュエル文庫編集長、松下正孝《まつしたまさたか》氏の熱意と、それを快く受けてくださった学芸ノンフィクション編集部、林由香《はやしゆか》さん・廣瀬《ひろせ》暁春《あきはる》さんのお力添えによるものです。ここにお三方に深く感謝したいと思います。

〈文庫版解説参考文献〉

東長人（二〇〇七年）「回想　イアン・スティーブンソン博士のこと」『超心理学研究』第一二巻一・二合併号、三―一二ページ

今西錦司（一九七三年）『今西錦司座談録』河出書房新社

今西錦司（一九八六年）『自然学の提唱』講談社学術文庫
岡田節人（一九九四年）『生命体の科学——テクノロジーと文化』人文書院
笠原敏雄（一九九五年）『隠された心の力——唯物論という幻想』春秋社（第二版、二〇一〇年、アマゾン・オンデマンド）
小泉八雲（一九八六年）「勝五郎再生記」『仏の畑の落穂他』恒文社
I・スティーヴンソン（一九八四年）「性別異和症の東南アジア流解釈——その実証的事例報告」笠原敏雄編『死後の生存の科学』（叢文社）所収
福来友吉（一九一三年）『透視と念写』東京宝文館（福来出版より復刊）
H・ベルクソン（一九九二年）『精神のエネルギー』レグルス文庫
Bergson, H. (1920). *Mind-Energy: Lectures and Essays*. New York: Henry Holt and Company.
Brody, E.B. (1977). Research in reincarnation and editorial responsibility: An editorial. *Journal of Nervous and Mental Disease. 165*, 151.
Eisenbud, J. (1982). Some investigations of claims of PK effects on metal and film by Masuaki Kiyota: I. The Denver experiments. *Journal of the American Society for Psychical Research, 76*, 218-33.
Eysenck, H.J., and Sargent, C. (1993). *Explaining the Unexplained: Mysteries of the Paranormal*. Garden City Park, NY: Prion.
Fukurai, T. (1931). *Clairvoyance & Thoughtography*. London: Rider.

Keil, H.H.J., Cook, E.W., Dennis, M., Werner, C.A., and Stevenson, I. (1982). Some investigations of claims of PK effects on metal and film by Masuaki Kiyota: III. The Charlottesville experiments. *Journal of the American Society for Psychical Research, 76*, 236-50.

King, L.S. (1975). Reincarnation. *JAMA, 234*, 978.

Koestler, A. (1967). *The Ghost in the Machine*. London: Hutchinson.（邦訳『機械の中の幽霊』ぺりかん社)

Lief, H.I. (1977). Commentary on Dr. Ian Stevenson's "The evidence of man's survival after death." *Journal of Nervous and Mental Disease, 165*, 171-73.

Nansen, O. (1949). *From Day to Day*. New York: G.P. Putnam's Sons.

Ohkado, M., and Ikegawa, A. (2014). Children with life-between-life memories. *Journal of Scientific Exploration, 28*, 477-90.

Ohkado, M., and Okamoto, S. (2014). A case of xenoglossy under hypnosis. *EdgeScience*, No. 17, 7-12.

Shafer, M., and Phillips, P.R. (1982). Some investigations of claims of PK effects on metal and film by Masuaki Kiyota: II. The St. Louis experiments. *Journal of the American Society for Psychical Research, 76*, 233-36.

Shroder, T. (1999). *Old Souls: The Scientific Evidence for Past Lives*. New York: Simon &

Schuster.（邦訳『前世を覚えている子どもたち』ヴォイス）

Stanford, R.G. (2008). *Ian Stevenson: A man from whom we should learn*. Journal of Scientific Exploration, 22, 120-24.

Stevenson, I.P. (1947). John Ray and his contributions to plant and animal classification. *Journal of the History of Medicine and Allied Sciences, 2*, 250-61.

Stevenson, I. (1950). Physical symptoms during pleasurable emotional states. *Psychosomatic Medicine, 12*, 98-102.

Stevenson, I. (1955). Psychiatry. *Annual Review of Medicine. 6*, 201-10.

Stevenson, I. (1957). Is the human personality more plastic in infancy and childhood? *American Journal of Psychiatry, 114*, 152-61.

Stevenson, I. (1960a). The evidence for survival from claimed memories of former incarnations. Part I. Review of the data. *Journal of the American Society for Psychical Research. 54*. 51-71.

Stevenson, I. (1960b). The evidence for survival from claimed memories of former incarnations. Part II. Analysis of the data and suggestions for further investigations. *Journal of the American Society for Psychical Research. 54*. 95-117.

Stevenson, I. (1960c). A review and analysis of paranormal experiences connected with the sinking of the Titanic. *Journal of the American Society for Psychical Research, 54*, 153-71.

Stevenson, I. (1965). Seven more paranormal experiences associated with the sinking of the Titanic. *Journal of the American Society for Psychical Research, 59*, 211-25.

Stevenson, I. (1970). Physical symptoms occurring with pleasurable emotional states. *American Journal of Psychiatry, 127*, 175-79.

Stevenson, I. (1977). The explanatory value of the idea of reincarnation. *Journal of Nervous and Mental Disease, 164*, 305-26.

Stevenson, I. (1983). American children who claim to remember previous lives. *Journal of Nervous and Mental Disease. 171*, 742-48.

Stevenson, I. (1989). *Some of My Journeys in Medicine*. Lafayette, LA: University of Southwestern Louisiana.

Stevenson, I. (1994). *A case of the psychotherapist's fallacy: Hypnotic regression to "previous lives." American Journal of Clinical Hypnosis*, 36, 188-93.

Stevenson, I. (1997). *Reincarnation and Biology*, 2vols. Westport, CT: Praeger Publishers.

Stevenson, I. (1999). Past lives of twins. *Lancet, 353*, 1359-60.

Stevenson, I. (2003). *European Cases of the Reincarnation Type*. Jefferson, NC: McFarland. （邦訳『前世を記憶する子どもたち　2　ヨーロッパの事例から』日本教文社）

Stevenson, I. (2006). Half a career with the paranormal. *Journal of Scientific Exploration, 20*, 13-21.

Stevenson, I., and Keil, J. (2005). Children of Myanmar who behave like Japanese soldiers: A possible third element in personality. *Journal of Scientific Exploration, 19*, 171-83.

Stevenson, I., and Matthews, R.A. (1952). Detection of the dangerous paranoid patient. *Postgraduate Medicine, 11*, 12-16.

Stevenson, I., and Pratt, J.G. (1968). Exploratory investigations of the psychic photography of Ted Serios. *Journal of the American Society for Psychical Research, 62*, 103-29.

Stevenson, I., and Pratt, J.G. (1969). Further investigations of the psychic photography of Ted Serios. *Journal of the American Society for Psychical Research, 63*, 352-64.

Tucker, J. B. (2008). Ian Stevenson and cases of the reincarnation type. *Journal of Scientific Exploration, 22*, 36-43,

White, K.L. (2008). Ian Stevenson: Recollections. *Journal of Scientific Exploration, 22*, 11-17.